2013년도
대한민국학술원 선정
우수학술도서
이 도서는 교육부의 지원으로
대한민국학술원에서 선정한
"2013년도 우수학술도서"임

근대한국외교문서 편찬위원회 편

近代韓國外交文書

제1권

제너럴 셔먼호 사건·병인양요

동북아역사재단

近代韓國外交文書

근대한국외교문서 편찬위원회 편

제1권

제너럴 셔먼호 사건 · 병인양요

동북아역사재단

간행사

대외관계사 자료집인 『近代韓國外交文書』는 1864년 고종 원년으로부터 1910년 국권 상실에 이르기까지 조선과 대한제국이 수행하였던 외교적 행위 및 당시 주요 열강들의 대한반도 정책과 관련된 중요 외교문서를 발굴, 수록하는 것입니다.

주지하듯, 외교문서는 정부 간 상호작용과 외교적 관습의 기록물임과 동시에 한 민족의 대외 인식의 정신적 구조를 포괄적으로 반영하는 역사 자료의 총괄적 성격을 띠고 있습니다. 따라서 미국이나 중국, 일본 등 주요 열강들은 국가사업의 일환으로 공식 외교 자료집을 줄곧 발간해 오고 있습니다. 그러나 우리나라는 여러 사정상 공식적 권위를 갖는 외교 문서집을 아직껏 출간치 못하고 있었습니다. 외교 문서의 부재는 외교사 연구에 막대한 지장을 초래함은 물론 외교정책 수행에서도 중대한 실수를 초래할 수 있기 때문에 좀 과장하여 말하면 국가 안위와 직결되는 것입니다.

현재 서양 중심의 국제정치학 전통이 절대적으로 학문적 권위를 가진 한국의 정치학 풍토에서는 외교사라고 하면 의례히 서구 열강이 주체가 된 국제 관계사를 의미합니다. 그리하여 한국 외교사를 연구하려는 외국 학자들은 타국에서 발간된 외교 문서에 의거해서 연구를 수행하고 있는 형편입니다. 이러한 편향된 연구가 한국의 국제 관계사에 대해 많은 오해와 왜곡을 낳고 있음은 두말할 나위가 없습니다.

이러한 오해 및 편견을 극복하기 위해서는 한국의 외교문서에 대한 기초적 수집과 철저한 분석 작업이 급선무라고 판단하여 저희 동북아역사재단은 근대한국외교문서(대외관계사 자료집) 편찬을 위해 적극 지원하고 있습니다. 그 1차년도 지원의 결실로서, 한국 근대 외교사 연구의 대표적 전문가들로 구성된 편찬위원회가 이번에 '제너럴 셔먼호 사건', '병인양요', '오페르트 사건', '신미양요' 등 1860년대의 중요한 외교적 사건과 관계된 외교문서를 발간하게 되었습니다.

사실 그간 『舊韓國條約彙纂』(국회도서관, 1964~1965), 『한국관계 영 · 미 · 중 외교자료집』(박일근 편, 1984), 『舊韓國外交關係附屬文書』(고려대학교 아세아문제연구소 편, 1972~1974) 등이 발간된 바 있습니다. 그러나 이들은 주요 조약문을 모았거나 극히 제한된 사료들만을 편찬한 것으로, 외교 사료를 총괄적, 연계적으로 이용하는데 불편한 점이 적지 않았습니다. 이번에 발간된 『近代韓國外交文書』 1권과 2권이 근대 한국 외교사 및 관계사 연구의 초석이 되고 또 국내외의 관련 연구자들에게 기본 사료를 제공하는 계기가 되었으면 하는 바람입니다.

2009년 11월

동북아역사재단 이사장 정 재 정

서문

조선은 19세기 중엽 이후 이질문명권의 행위자들과 만나게 된다. 그러나 19세기 서양 세력이 동북아 지역의 행위자들과 조우하는 팽창의 본질은 18세기의 만남과는 역사적 성격이 달랐다. 16세기로부터 시작된 서양과 동북아의 접촉은 근본적으로 서로 상대방의 존재를 인정하는 만남encounter이었다. 이런 의미에서 16, 17, 18세기는 동시대적이다.

19세기의 접촉은 단순한 만남이 아니라 충돌clash이었다. 폭력적인 충돌이었다. 폭력은 단순한 물리적인 강압만을 의미하지 않는다. 자신의 사고방식과 이익에 상대방을 종속시키려는 접촉이다. 이런 충돌은 현재까지 국제정치의 본질을 이루고 있다. 19, 20, 21세기는 동시대적이다.

그러나 한반도는 이러한 국제정치의 일반적인 특징과 더불어 세계정치의 주변성에서 비롯된 특징을 함께 지니고 있다. 변경(邊境) 또는 오지(奧地)의 사고방식이 배양되기 시작했다는 역사적 한계는 병인양요와 신미양요로부터 노출되기 시작하였다.

이러한 오지에는, 아프리카의 경우에서 또렷하듯이, 서양의 공권력이 처음부터 전면에 나서서 침투하지는 않았다. 신부, 깡패, 그리고 해적들의 행위를 거쳐서 이루어졌다. 이러한 일은 19세기의 전 세계적인 현상이었다. 그러나 조선은 이와 같은 현상이 세계적으로 확산되는 최후의 단계에서 이들 공권력의 대리자들과 만나게 되었다. 병인양요는 신부들의 행위로 인한 프랑스의 침략이었고 신미양요는 제너럴 셔먼호라는 해적선의 난입으로 야기된 미국의 노략질이었다.

『近代韓國外交文書』 제 1, 2권은 이들 두 침략사건에 관한 국내외 대외관계 자료들을 수록하였다. 조선과 이질문명권의 행위자들과의 불행한 무력적인 충돌은 조선의 서양 인식과 더불어 서양 세력의 조선 인식의 틀을 형성하기 시작하였다. 대외관계의 역사적 질병을 형성한 이런 정신구조가 오늘날 어떠한 의미를 지니는지 이 문서집들은 밝혀주리라 믿는다.

2009년 11월

『近代韓國外交文書』 편찬위원장 김 용 구

편집방침

1. 본 문서집은 한반도의 역사적 현주소를 밝히는 데 중요하다고 판단한 좁은 의미와 넓은 의미의 국내외 외교문서를 망라해 수록하였다. 좁은 의미의 외교문서는 정부의 토의 문서와 훈령, 외무 담당자들의 교섭과정 문서*documents préparatoires*, 그들의 왕복 문서, 본국정부에 발송한 보고문, 그리고 국제조약을 가리킨다. 그리고 넓은 의미의 외교문서는 이 밖에 교섭 담당자들의 회고록이나 문집을 비롯한 개인 문서를 포함한다.

2. 본 문서집의 편집은 주요 열강의 외교문서집 편찬 방식에 따랐다. 주요 국가들은 외교문서를 보관하는 특별 기관을 보유하고 있어서 이 기관의 문서들 중 대외관계에 중요하다고 판단되는 문서들을 기사본말체로 편집하고 있다.

3. '중요하다고 판단'하는 편집자들의 '인식'이 외교문서집 발간의 국제정치적 성격을 나타내 주고 있다. 대외관계 문서집의 효시인 19세기 각국의 칼라 북스Color Books, 미국의 *Foreign Relations of the United States*를 비롯하여 제1차 세계대전 이후에 발간되기 시작한 독일의 *Grosse Politik der europäischen Kabinette 1871-1914*, 소련의 *Vneshnaya politika Rossii: XIX i nachala XX beka*, 그리고 *Dokumenty vneshnei politiki SSSR*, 영국의 *British Documents on the Origins of the War, 1898-1914* (G. P. Gooch & H. Temperley eds.), *Documents on British Foreign Policy, 1919-1939*(R. Butler & E. L. Woodward eds.), *British Documents on Foreign Affairs*(K. Bourne & D. C. Watt, eds.), 프랑스의 *Documents diplomatiques français 1871~1914*, 일본의『日本外交文書』들이 모두 이런 방식을 취하고 있다.

4. 이들 외교문서집은 자국의 문서보관소의 문서들을 선별하여 편집하고 있다. 이들 선별된 문서들과 이를 채록한 원문서와의 관계를 검증하는 작업은 특수 분야를 연구하는 전문 연구자들이 담당하고 있다. 외교문서 편집과는 차원이 다른 연구 분야이다. 그러나 본 문서집은 '한국'의 '문서'집이기에 조선 문서인 경우, 채록 문서와의 관계를 가능한 한 규명토록 노력하였다.

범례

1. 조선에서 사대질서의 '外交' 개념과 전혀 다른 diplomacy의 번역어로 '외교'란 낱말이 사용되기 시작한 것은 1880년 이후의 일이다. 따라서 1866년 병인양요와 1871년 신미양요의 대외문서를 '외교문서'라고 지칭하는 데에는 비역사적인 측면이 있다. 그러나 본 문서집은 1910년까지의 문서를 편집하는 사업으로 1880년 이전의 자료를 편의상 외교문서라고 분류하였다.

2. 조선은 1895년에, 중국은 1912년에, 그리고 일본은 1872년에 양력을 채택하였으나 본 문서집에서는 그 이전의 음력을 모두 양력으로 환산해 적었다. 1917년 소련혁명 이전의 제정 러시아력(曆)도 양력으로 환산하였다. 19세기 제정 러시아력은 양력보다 12일이 앞서 있다. 이들 날짜를 모두 양력으로 환산시킨 것은 특히 아편전쟁 이후 한반도 문제를 포함한 세계의 모든 문제들이 세계외교사의 흐름과 연결되어 있기 때문이다. 다만 독자들이 동양 자료를 검색하는 데 도움을 주기 위해 중요한 날짜인 경우 음력을 병기하되 한자로 표기함으로써 양력 날짜와 구분하였다.

3. 중국과 일본의 인명, 지명은 모두 원음으로 표기하였다. 러시아어의 영문 알파벳 전자(轉字)는 *The Current Digest of Post-Soviet Press* 방법에 의거하였다. 한글 표기는 한국 교육인적자원부 편수자료를 따랐다.

4. 본 문서집은 연구자들에게 검색상의 편의를 제공하기 위해 문건 별로 문서의 내용에 관하여 간략한 정보를 표시하였다.

예

95①

② ③ ④ ⑤
朴承輝(1866. 8. 21/高宗三年七月十二日) → 議政府(1866. 8. 24/高宗三年七月十五日)

제너럴 셔먼호 문정(問情) 보고 ⑥

① 본 문서집이 부여한 고유의 문서번호이다.

② 문서의 발신인(기관)을 가리킨다. 문서의 수/발신인(기관)은 직함 등을 생략하고 인명만을 원어로 적는 것을 원칙으로 하였다. 한편, 일본과 같이 일부 동일인물의 성명 및 동일부서의 명칭이 시기별로 달라지는 경우에는 아래와 같은 원칙에 따라 표기하였다.

• 대마번(對馬藩)의 경우 폐번치현(廢藩置縣)과 관련하여 공식적인 명칭이 수차례 변경되었다. 관례적인 의미로 '對馬藩'으로 통일해 표기하였다.

• 宗義達과 같이 인명이 변경되었을 경우, 고친 이름[改名]을 기준으로 표기하되 기존의 이름을 괄호 내에 병기하였다.

예) 宗重正(宗義達)

• 동일한 부서가 여러 가지 다른 이름으로 원문에 나타나는 경우 독자의 혼란을 피하기 위해서 단일한 명칭으로 통일하였다.

예) 朝鮮事務辨理中, 朝鮮事務辨理御中, 朝鮮事務 → 朝鮮事務掛

③ 문서의 발신일을 가리킨다.

④ 문서의 수신인(기관)을 가리킨다.

⑤ 문서의 수신일을 가리킨다.

⑥ 본 문서집이 작성한 문서의 제목이다.

5. 문서의 수/발신일을 특정하기 어려운 교섭 담당자들의 회고록, 수기, 메모, 일기와 같은 사문서의 경우는 다음과 같이 작성일자나 회담일자 등을 중심으로 표시하였다.

예

190

板倉勝靜, L. Roches (1867. 3. 13/慶應三年二月八日)

조불(朝佛) 분쟁 중재에 관한 대화

6. 문건의 배열은 발신일을 기준으로 하였으나, 발신일을 확인할 수 없는 문건의 경우는 수신일에 의거하여 배열하였다. 어떤 문건의 발신일과 또 다른 문건의 수신일이 동일한 날짜에 겹치는 경우는 수신된 문서를 먼저 배열하였다. 문서에 발/수신일이 나타나지 않고 월(月)만이 표시된 경우는 그 내용을 분석한 후, 문맥상 다른 외교문서와의 전후 관계를 고려하여 발송되었다고 추정되는 날짜에 의거하여 배열하였다. 내용으로 선후관계를 추정하기 어려운 문서는 해당 월의 말미에 배열하였다.

7. 중요한 외교문서의 경우, 각 국가의 외교관들이 이를 자국 언어로 번역해서 본국에 보고하는 것이 일반적인 관례이다. 이와 같이 특정한 문서에 대해 여러 언어로 작성된 번역문이 존재할 경우, 본서에서는 이를 [英譯文], [漢譯文], [日譯文], [佛譯文] 이라고 표시하여 해당 문서 다음에 첨부하였다. 특정한 외교 교섭에 관해 참

석자들이 서로 다른 언어로 기록한 문건 역시 번역문의 범주에 포함된다. 번역은 단순히 문자 기호 사이의 등가적 교환이 아니고 번역자의 특정한 정치적 의도나 작위가 개재되는 실천적 행위이다. 특히 외교문서와 같이 정치적 성격을 띠는 문서에 있어서는 번역 과정에서의 특정한 언어의 선택, 미묘한 어감의 차이, 오역의 발생 여부 등을 더욱 면밀하게 살펴볼 필요가 있다. 본서에서는 원문서와 번역문을 병행 수록함으로써 연구자들로 하여금 사건의 시말을 보다 다각적으로 파악하는데 도움을 주고자 하였다.

8. 독립된 외교문서로 간주하기에는 형식적, 내용적 측면에서 부족한 면이 있으나 특정한 외교문서의 작성과정이나 사후처리 과정을 이해하는데 도움이 되는 문서는 [관련문서]라고 표기하여 해당 외교문서의 뒤에 첨부하였다. 또한 회고록이나 수기, 대화기록, 광범위한 보고서 등 넓은 의미의 외교문서도 중요한 사료적 가치를 가지는 자료들은 [관계자료]라고 표기하여 각 장의 말미에 별도로 수록하였다.

9. 동일한 외교문서인 경우에도 이를 기록하고, 전달하고, 재수록하는 과정에서 일부 자형이 변경되거나 오탈자가 발생하는 경우가 있다. 이 경우 본 문서집에서는 각 국가의 공식 외교문서집에 수록된 문서를 기준으로 수록하였으며, 오탈자가 있다고 의심되는 경우에는 (*Sic*)라고 표시하였다. 아울러 각 국가의 공식 외교문서집에 수록되지 않은 미간문서 가운데는 문서 자체의 훼손이 심하여 특정 글자나 단어를 판독하기 어려운 문서들이 존재한다. 이와 같은 미식별 문자에 있어서 로마자는 [______], 한자와 일본어는 ○의 기호로 표시하였다.

약어표

* 한글로 표기된 것은 한국 자료, 한자는 중국과 일본 자료, 로마자는 구미(歐美) 자료를 의미함.
* 자료의 나열은 한글 음 차례에 따름.

綱要: 『維新史料綱要』, 10冊(東京: 東京大學史料編纂所, 1937~)

江戶: 『江戶』, 7冊, 大久保利謙 編(東京: 立体社, 1980~1982)

동문: 『同文彙考』, 4책(서울: 국사편찬위원회, 1970)

동진기: 『東津禦侮輯要(東津禦侮日記)』, 서울대학교 규장각 소장[청구기호: 古4252.4-2]

동진략: 『東津鎭創建事略』, 서울대학교 규장각 소장[청구기호: 古4252.4-3]

秘書: 『秘書類纂 朝鮮交涉資料』, 3冊, 伊藤博文 編(東京: 原書房, 1970)

事務: 『朝鮮事務書』, 9冊(東京: 日本 外交史料館)

실록: 『高宗實錄』, 3책(서울: 探究堂, 1970)

양박등서: 『洋舶事甘結及文報謄書成冊』, 서울대학교 규장각 소장[청구기호: 古951.541 Y17]

양요록: 『洋擾記錄』, 국립중앙도서관 소장[청구기호: 위창古2159-15]

양요초: 『洋擾史草』, 국립중앙도서관 소장[청구기호: 古2159-6]

어양: 『御洋隨錄』, 서울대학교 규장각 소장[청구기호: 想白古359.6 Eo95 00]

外事務: 『朝鮮外交事務書』, 9冊, 韓國日本問題研究會 編(서울: 成進文化社, 1974)

용호: 『龍湖閒錄』(서울: 국사편찬위원회, 1979)

遺稿: 『匏庵遺稿』, 2冊, 栗本鋤雲(東京: 東京大學出版會, 1975)

履歷: 『中山忠能履歷資料』, 10冊(東京: 東京大學出版會, 1973~1975)

夷務始末: 『籌辦夷務始末』, 7冊(臺北: 國風出版社, 1965)

李文: 『李文忠公全集』, 7冊, 吳汝綸 編(臺北: 文海出版社, 1962)

李鴻章: 『李鴻章全集』, 39冊, 顧廷龍 • 戴逸 主編(合肥: 安徽教育出版社, 2007)

일기: 『承政院日記』, 15책(서울: 국사편찬위원회, 1967~1968)

일록: 『日省錄』, 65~84책, 서울대학교 규장각 편(서울: 서울대학교도서관, 1995~1996)

日外: 『日本外交文書』(明治年間), 73冊 (東京: 日本 外務省, 1933~1963)

日韓資料: 『日韓外交資料集成』, 10冊, 金正明 編(東京: 巖南堂書店, 1966)

全覽:『續通信全覽』, 54冊, 日本外務省 [原]編纂, 通信全覽編輯委員會 編(東京: 雄松堂出版, 1983~1988)

中美:『中美關係史料』, 3冊, 中央硏究院 近代史硏究所 編(臺北: 中央硏究院近代史硏究所, 1968)

中日韓:『淸季中日韓關係史料』, 12冊, 中央硏究院 近代史硏究所 編(臺北: 中央硏究院近代史硏究所, 1972)

中朝續編:『淸代中朝關係檔案續編』, 中國第一歷史檔案館 編(北京: 中國檔案出版社, 1998)

평안계:『平安監營啓錄』, 서울대학교 규장각 소장[청구기호: 奎 15110]

한불:「韓佛關係資料」,『교회사 연구』2집(서울: 한국교회사연구소, 1979)

황해계:『黃海監營啓錄』, 서울대학교 규장각 소장[청구기호: 奎 15107]

AADM: *Anglo-American Diplomatic Materials Relating to Korea, 1866~1886*, Park Il-Keun ed., (Seoul: Shinmundang, 1982)

ADPP: *American Diplomatic and Public Papers; The United States and China, Series II, The United States, China, and Imperial Rivalries, 1861~1893*, Vol. 9~11, Jules Davids ed. 3 vols. (Wilmington, DE: Scholary Resources, 1979)

BDFA: *British Documents of Foreign Affairs*, Kenneth Bourne & D. C. Watt, eds. Part I Series E Vol. 2; *Korea, Ryukyu Island, and North-East Asia, 1875~1888* (Frederick, MD: University Publication of America, 1989)

Documents: *Documents relatifs à l'histoire des relations franco-coréenne*, Choi Seok-Woo(崔奭祐) compilés par: (Seoul, 1986)

FRUS: *Foreign Relations of the United States*, 1866~1882.

NARA I & II: National Archive Records Administration Micro Films

Roze I: BB4 1511-4, 5, 6, 국사편찬위원회 소장 로즈제독 문서

Roze II: BB4 1511-7, 프랑스 해군성 소장 문서

TNA: The National Archive (舊 PRO: Public Record Office)

편찬위원회 명단

편찬위원장 : 김용구 (한림대학교 한림과학원장)

편찬위원 :

김홍수 (공군사관학교 인문학부 교수)

신욱희 (서울대학교 외교학과 교수)

우철구 (영남대학교 정치외교학과 명예교수)

이근욱 (서강대학교 정치외교학과 교수)

이상찬 (서울대학교 국사학과 교수)

장인성 (서울대학교 외교학과 교수)

최희재 (단국대학교 사학과 교수)

연구원 :

강혜윤 (서울대학교 외교학과 박사과정 수료)
김종학 (서울대학교 외교학과 박사과정 수료)
민회수 (서울대학교 국사학과 박사과정 수료)
박준형 (일본 와세다대학교 문학연구과 박사과정)
배민재 (서울대학교 국사학과 박사과정)
안종철 (인하대학교 HK연구교수)
이경미 (서울대학교 외교학과 박사과정 수료)
이지영 (서울대학교 동양사학과 박사과정 수료)
정진숙 (서울대학교 국사학과 박사과정)

연구조교 :

김보경 (서울대학교 외교학과 석사과정 수료)
김양규 (서울대학교 외교학과 석사과정)
문용일 (서울대학교 외교학과 석사)
정민경 (서강대학교 정치외교학과 석사과정)
정신혁 (연세대학교 사학과 석사과정 수료)
정　연 (서울대학교 외교학과 석사과정 수료)
조덕현 (서울대학교 외교학과 석사과정)
하주형 (서울대학교 동양사학과 석사과정 수료)

차례

제1부 제너럴 셔먼호 사건

제2부 병인양요

〔關係資料〕

제1부
제너럴 셔먼호 사건

1

朴承輝(1866. 8. 21/高宗三年七月十二日) ➞ 議政府(1866. 8. 24/高宗三年七月十五日)

제너럴 셔먼호 문정(問情) 보고

黃海監司朴承輝以黃州異樣船問情馳啓

狀啓以爲黃州牧三田坊外松山里前洋異樣船来泊形止纔已馳啓而卽接黃州牧使 丁大植今月初九日申時成貼馳報內今初七日戌時量與虞候 申永翰譯學李容肅營軍官池命臣眼同發行初八日寅時量卽到異樣船所泊處使刑吏李耆魯營吏辛夢辰等先通地方官問情之由則答以来見云故舟泊於彼船近處彼人數十名各持銃刀排立船頭始許登船彼四人或倚坐或坐捎頭仍請同坐後書問何國人緣何到此則書答我等乃是西洋三國之人而上座崔蘭軒何噶特竝居英吉利普来屯居美利堅巴使居但國云擧皆深目高鼻碧眼黃髮的是西洋人無疑而崔蘭軒一人非但善爲華語稍解我國言或可辨或不可辨至於擧談盡委於李八行然船中事渠皆主張所謂李八行趙半良係是上國人被英聘爲幕云其餘二十四人或暹羅及廣東土海縣人爲鄕導爲雇傭爲水手均是從人云而欲問其姓名則係我舟中之事無關君等問但國所在則答在西洋距兩國一千五百里而三國人同爲行商今七月初一日自山東離發歷白翎 椒島串席島轉向平壤而我舟貌似兵船實欲通商貴地紙米金蔘貂皮等物換我洋布器皿別無相害之心換貨早畢直自平壤回舟不然雖往王京通商後歸云故問旣云往平壤通商則有我國人相應交易者乎答沒有又以来泊外洋容或無怪而越入內洋我國原有邦禁不可前進爲言則答誰敢攔我一直要往若値西風隨卽發往問儞船有同来與否則答此事我等不能細述亦非我事乃國事耳更無所答船制則內塗灰外塗墨加油如漆上有白粉四方板屋兩處一住官人一住從人而面面牕孔皆嵌玻瓈兩桅俱是松木精治塗油上竪白洋木方旗帆葉以白色洋大綾爲之兩傍各設大砲一坐下架木輪上安鐵筩而上狹下廣三次示放聲若轟雷驚人耳目又有巡更長銃三柄穴端揷鎗刃可一尺許鳥銃則小佩大掛難以枚數環刀則西洋四人各持一柄擧皆明晃閃爍屋內書冊畵張琴鍾膏藥等雜貨歷觀一遍無以盡記欲見從人所居則謂以禮不必往觀防遮不見下繫小艇如我國小漁舟樣其色碧裝載則云有洋木等通商之貨而船底則不使之見未能明知積置虛實數爻而酬酢之際忽地書示請君遣价賜我大米牛肉鷄子蔬菜柴木等物以洋布答謝云云而若値上國人與各國人漂到者則例致館廩而洋人之越入內洋事出意外且有難自下擅便故答以此等僻村猝難辦備且候風直發尤難施行云則崔蘭

軒顯加辭色曰撒謊撒謊諸君如有欲賜之意我舟雖行亦近君地沿江而走亦非難事何拘此地彼地乎自撕問情紙摺入懷中連加催行故不得已以行船在卽歸當備送爲答則回嗔作善出給問情紙更說送必答謝云故以不必答謝爲言大米一石牛肉三十斤鷄子六十箇菁菜二十束柴木二十丹入給計料而彼船離發之前有難經歸姑留津頭近處以觀動靜而同洋人姓名年歲居住服着及船隻長廣器械什物竝修成冊上送矣登船問情之際自多遲滯以致修報之經日不勝惶悚而一時到付臣營虞候 申永翰所報及譯學李容肅手本內辭緣與牧使所報一辭同然而鱗次黃州牧使丁大植初九日申時牒報內問情之由纔已牒報彼人所請米肉等物辦備之際少爲遲滯矣當日申時彼船發向平壤所去水路故使首吏米肉等物載船隨往於止泊處給之之意飭送雖緣伺察動靜之意自邑擅便極涉未安而大抵該牧本非沿海之邑也猝當罕見之事生疏做錯容或無怪而彼船旣云發向平安道地方則畢竟回路由黃州等地故沿海各邑瞭望防守之節各別擧行之意發關嚴飭而彼人姓名年歲容貌服着居住及船隻長廣器械什物一依該兵使所報開錄于後竝以馳啓○崔蘭軒年三十六長七尺五寸面鐵頭髮黃圈鬚黑服色則灰色氈帽黑白班絨單衫參黑皮靴子腰有革帶佩小洋銃及環刀文職四品英吉利人也何噶特年三十七長七尺面鐵髮黃鬚鬔服色則白洋布裹帽黃藺單衫袴跣足藤鞋革帶佩小洋銃及環刀武職一品英吉利人也普来屯年四十八長七尺五寸面鐵髮黃圈鬚白髥服色則黑氈帽白洋木單衫黃藺單袴色絲交織鞋革帶佩小洋銃及環刀武職一品美利堅人也巴使年四十五長七尺五寸面鐵鬚髮黃圈服色則黑緞裹帽紫絨單衫白木單袴黑皮鞋革帶佩小洋銃時表及環刀但國人也李八行年三十趙半良年二十八皆長七尺面鐵髮辮鬚無服色則白木單衫袴鴉青三升鞋竝大淸人也二十四人姓名年記問之則崔蘭軒泛稱下人不容詳問未能的知而容貌服色頭鬚均是大淸人樣也船樣長十八丈廣五丈高三丈兩桅一個高十五丈一個高十三丈大三圍二大帆色白桅繩又係二小帆亦色白熟麻乭桅帆左右各十二條其餘船用雜物一體問情彼不錄示故未得詳錄而什物器械各人所持外藏在船底者居多不使開見又不詳答實難照數而從船長三把廣二把綠漆無桅帆云云

2

朴珪壽(1866. 8. 22/高宗三年七月十三日) ➞ 議政府

제너럴 셔먼호 문정(問情) 보고

平壤保山鎮境来泊舡是白在異㨾舡問情次臣營中軍李玄益帯率軍官方益鏞平壤庶尹申泰鼎眼同馳送之由已為馳啟為白有在果即接臣營中軍李玄益平壤庶尹申泰鼎本月十二日亥時成貼牒呈内今初十日亥時量中軍庶尹與營官方益鏞同為離發十一日戌時量到彼異舡所泊處則已為移泊於本府草里坊一里新場浦口是乎所時已夜深故翌日是在十二日辰時量使中營吏金樂洙府刑吏趙元國等先通地方官問情之由則彼答以来見云故乘舟抵泊于彼舡之傍彼人或持銃鎗排立舡頭始許登舡而其中四人或坐椅或坐梢頭仍請同坐後以紙筆書問何國人緣何到此則其中一人稍觧我國言語自言姓崔名蘭軒英吉利國人這位姓趙名凌奉北京人這位姓趙名邦用盛京穆溪縣人這位姓李名八行即舡主但國人仍曰我們是西洋國之人行商次今七月初自山東離發歴黄海這諸島轉向黄州界留住数日欲翫平壤兼見省城大人今方到此是如為乭只又問爾們欲見省城大人有甚麽事情乎答云不是別的吾舟中畧載回錦洋布斜文布斜文絨玻璃器千里鏡自鳴鍾八音盒等物件欲換貨貴地土産大米沙金紅蔘紙属虎皮豹皮等物是如是乭遣仍以手劃頸曰我邦七人怎麽事故而如是乎如是乎吾舡雖似兵舡今往平壤與彼處無寃耳現有客人在舟欲往平壤通商貿易云是乎所答以爾國人被刑與否非千里外外州守臣所知而交易一欵此是皇朝法禁亦非藩邦之所敢擅許者也云則崔蘭軒又曰聞王都城中有一白塔何意云故答以未知剏立何年而果有一白塔云爾則又曰貴地因何趕逐天主教人今我耶蘇聖教躰天道正人心以化邪俗仁義忠考皆備皆使天下人民可従良善非同天主教云故答以此两教俱是我國法禁故人民不敢擅云爾則又曰法國大舡已往王京比吾舟不同耳因怒之甚恐有搶奪吾舟乃貿易為換賣也云故答以爾國大舡互往王京云者誠未知甚意而爾們雖為換賣而来其所交易非敢擅許則當於何時歸去乎云則黙頭不答而屈指幾次従近當發云是乎所問爾們四人外舡中同来者為幾許人是旀西洋人外又有他國人否答云吾們同来者為二十人而洋人五人清人十三人烏鬼子二人是如如是酬酢之際忽然書示曰吾舟中只有黄州所得糧饌而僅為数日之資吾所用者大米牛肉鷄卵柴木矣吾二人必須同汝舟而往願為借助則當以洋布等物為謝云云是乎所答以物種則當依所請而同舟下陸事係未安云則彼答以吾念爾國律嚴不為深其若我之規則當

如是乎若如此吾等不往矣當求速辦云是如乎此非上國人與各國漂到人則物種擅給極為未安是乎矣其在柔遠之義亦不可不然大米一石牛肉五十斤鷄二十五首鷄卵五十介柴木二十束入給則喜色滿面稱謝不已而彼舡離發之前有難徑歸仍留浦口近處以觀動靜是乎旀四人姓名年歲居住服着雖為開錄舡隻十六人初不言姓名故不得擧論為乎旀長廣器械什物并為開錄于後而今此草里坊浦口距邑治已為不近而又越三津適値驟雨之暴霔問情自爾遲滯極為悚悶是如為白乎所盖此異舡四隻已為發去而惟大舡一隻獨入內地者誠極訝恠是白乎矣既云從近還發且無糧饌等資云而地方官所給不免零星稟覆之際自致曠日是白㢤除良亦自臣營大米二石見其遑汲之狀有不可膠守法例故牛肉五十斤生猪一首生鷄二十首鷄卵五十介柴木二十束使之贈給而事係擅便不勝惶恐是白乎旀同四人姓名年歲居住着服及舡隻長廣器械什物一依地方官所報開錄于左為白乎旀彼舡去留防守之節另加察飭這即馳報之意更為題飭於臣營中軍李玄益平壤庶尹申泰鼎處是白遣嗣後形止鱗次登聞計料緣由并以馳啟為白臥乎事

後

崔蘭軒年三十六英吉利國人面鉄頭髮黃鬚髯黑服色段灰色氊帽黑白斑絨單衫袴黑皮靴子腰有革带佩小祥銃及環刀是白齊

趙凌奉不言年紀但稱北京人面鉄髮黑服色段黑色氊帽白斑絨單衫黃繭單袴佩所祥銃及環刀是白齊

趙邦用年二十八盛京穆溪縣人面鉄髮辮髯無服色段白木單衫袴是白齊

李八行年三十但國人面鉄髮辮髯無服色段白木單衫袴鴉青三升鞋是白齊

十六名姓名謂以雇傭梢工不為指名亦不欲相見容貌服色及姓名居住不得開錄是白齊

舡摠段長可十八文許廣可五文許高可三丈許两桅帆一箇高可十五文許一箇高可十三丈許大三圍許二大帆色白桅繩又係二小帆亦色白熟麻㺚桅帆左右各十二條其餘雜物彼不錄示故不得詳軸懸錄是白齊

什物器械各人所持外不使開見又不詳答無由照数故不得懸錄是白齊

從舡段長可三把許廣可二把許綠漆無桅帆是白齊

3

高宗(1866. 8. 23/高宗三年七月十四日)

서양 선박과의 접촉을 엄금하는 교서

傳曰 近日異舶之出沒於海洋者 未知何故 而聞我國人 多有和應入處云 棄其父母之邦 冒入他國之船者 揆以常情 必無是理 而抑又思之 則挽近之爲牧伯守宰者 多行酷厲之政 全昧懷綏之方 失志亡命之徒 遂欲偸活 以至此境 是豈獨渠輩之罪乎 然而此皆出於邊禁蕩然之致 興言及此 誠極寒心 另加探察 如有蹤跡殊常之類 往来逗遛於沿海諸處 這這跟捉 一竝梟警 以示朝家嚴邦禁屛異俗之意 自廟堂措辭行會

李容象 ➞ 議政府(1866. 8. 24/高宗三年七月十五日)

제너럴 셔먼호 문정(問情) 보고

平安兵使　李容象以龍岡縣　異樣船問情馳啓

狀啓以爲龍岡縣多美面上七里珠英浦異樣船六隻来泛之由已爲馳啓而卽接龍岡縣令　兪初煥本月初八日酉時馳報內登時離發前進則該浦民之言內初七日巳時三隻中船下流於三和地一隻大船轉向急水門云故次次沿陸到于東津該津越邊則黃州地界也厥船艤泊於黃州界此地水闊相距果近十里旣非本縣界則問情一款似難擧論而事雖重大勢難越境親審故登高遠望募伶俐慣水將吏使之探来船則洋船而洋人輩招招上船把水助登擧袖相揖其中洋魁能解我國言先通姓名而糢糊難記仍勸酒一盃曰此是北京之酒勿慮而飮云味果冽香矣飮畢觀其貌樣則形狀奇恠身體壯大頭着抹額身穿紅衣在傍二人貌似塗漆眼如惡獸黑白其衣手執鎗釰其言曰吾儕皆是西洋人彼立者卽是北京人也而暫泊此處欲往平壤而平壤山川何如汝之所居之地有甚寶物有何城郭耶云爾故答以爲有城甚固然本無寶物云則又言曰我邦七人以何事見死於汝國兩班耶我邦船隻多數送泛於汝國三南江中而吾儕期往平壤云問答不過如斯而披示帖冊一本首篇我國一統地圖次篇各邑地圖山川則黑畵而皆女人繡繪其文若篆□不可識辨仍勸入船閣中左右擺列衣纓之物而其中有一體四穴或六穴之銃長近五六寸示之曰鳥銃也百發百中矣又勸彈自鳴琴餘音淸亮云而將吏回告若是分明異船果入急水門內則明再明間似到於浿江故多發伶俐解事將吏沿江探望隨機馳告而今此異樣船隻旣入平壤急水門內云其所探察不容毫忽到泊去留形止詳探馳報之意發關嚴飭於平壤府　庶尹　申泰鼎　處而亦自臣營帶率軍官前郞廳朴麟煥爲先定送使之偵探而該縣令所報中三隻中船旣下流於三和境則宜有該府使形止之報而尙此寂然事甚訝惑今方關問於該府使鄭志鉉而程道與船樣依該縣令所報開錄于後馳啓○多美面上七里珠英浦自海口歷三和八龍岡初境距官門六十里越邊卽安岳地界自珠英浦至急水門相距二十五里越邊黃州地界也船樣則有兩棹四帆其大有難周回看之而大低大於京江之雙帆稅穀船其樣異於我國之船未知何以裁制而國名只說西洋不言其國姓名若以文字相話則可以解得而其能我國言者以言相譸糢糊不辨人數則皆在船中未見其形多少未能詳知云云

5

朴珪壽(1866. 8. 24/高宗三年七月十五日) ➜ 議政府

제너럴 셔먼호 문정(問情) 보고

平壤府草里坊一里新場浦口来泊異様大舡一隻問情之由已為馳啟為白有在果即接臣營中軍李玄益平壤庶尹申泰鼎本月十四日卯時成貼馳報内異様舡昨日寅時量自新場浦掛帆溯流申時量止泊於萬景臺下頭老島前浦口乙仍于酉時量中軍庶尹齊登異舡爾們之終不回棹又為上来委折另加盤問是乎則答以土產換貿然後可以回舡是如故外國之交易乃是我國之法禁自我朝廷奏請皇朝然後或可許施而爾舡若有艱乏之物當有優給至於交易宲不敢擅行是如委曲言之則洋人崔蘭軒清人趙凌奉等頗有聽従底意様而惟舡主財主两漢一向堅執期欲換貿為説是乎旀見今江漲水勢甚急彼舡自不得溯流移泊近岸姑無進退之動静是如為白有卧乎所交易二字非敢擬議而一直阻搪回耐黠胡終不回舡逗留遷就宲為可悶是白如乎嗣後形止另加詳探陸續馳報之意措辞題飭為白乎旀縁由馳啟為白卧乎事

朴珪壽(1866. 8. 24/高宗三年七月十五日) ➜ 議政府

제너럴 셔먼호 동태 보고

平壤府萬景臺下頭老島前浦口異様大舡一隻止泊之由已為馳啓為白有在果即接臣營中軍李玄益平壤庶尹申泰鼎本月十五日辰時成貼狀啓馳報内當日卯時量彼崔蘭軒等七人同乘小青舡越津登陸是乎如可四人則乘舟還歸三人則仍陟萬景臺四面眺望後謂見城池前往数里許玉峴地之際中軍為庶尹之力挽回到萬景臺下柳岸而蘭軒忽放一銃則先歸四人聞其聲搖小舟而来載歸三人于原泊處是乎加尼忽然自原泊處稍移於三帿許上流至今停泊終不退去是如為白有卧乎所今此異舡之逗留数日終不返棹者已極乖當是白㐘除良萬景臺距城内不滿二十里地而謂以交易期欲入城不退據法而開諭乃有下陸之擅行其心所在極為叵測防守偵探之節更加嚴飭為白乎㫆緣由馳啓為白卧乎事

7

朴珪壽(1866. 8. 26/高宗三年七月十七日) ➞ 議政府

제너럴 셔먼호 동태 보고

平壤府萬景臺下止泊異樣大舡一隻移泊於三帿許上流之由已為馳啟為白有在果即接臣營中軍李玄益平壤庶尹申泰鼎本月十七日申時成貼狀啟馳報內昨日未時量異樣舡自前泊處又為泝向上流三帿許滄灘止泊是乎如可今日巳時量又自滄灘離發未時量泝上三里許閑灘仍為止泊是乎遣彼崔蘭軒等八人乘小青舡来泊閑似亭前磯蘭軒等四人登亭四人留在舡中是乎只問其何不還歸又何上来是乎則答以交易後還歸云云是乎乃細探其動静則似有欲去之心而微露其更望助給之色是乎旀申時量還歸大舡是乎所嗣後形止連探馳報計料是如為白有臥乎所今此異舡之入此境已為八日之久而非但不有回棹之意漸益泝上至于近城十許里地而昨日三帿今日三里寸寸前進是何意思是白乎喩始終開諭一直倔强究其情狀萬萬痛惋藉以交易露其妄想反覆無常無以測度是白如乎嚴加防守更為飭諭之意措辭題飭於臣營中軍及平壤庶尹處為白乎旀嗣後形止陸續登聞計料緣由并以馳啟為白臥乎事

李容象 ➞ 議政府(1866. 8. 27/高宗三年七月十八日)

제너럴 셔먼호 문정(問情) 보고

平安兵使 李容象以異樣船問情馳啓

狀啓以爲異樣船一隻到泊于平壤境草里防二里場沙浦口之由昨已馳啓而卽接平壤庶尹 申泰鼎本月十三日午時馳報內中軍庶尹與營軍官方益鏞同爲離發十一日戌時量到彼船所泊處則已爲移泊於本府新場浦口時已夜深故十二日辰時使中營吏金樂洙等先通問情之由則彼答以来見云故乘舟抵泊於彼船之傍彼人或持銃鎗排立許登書問何國人緣何到此則其中一人稍解我國言語自言姓崔名蘭軒英吉利人這位趙凌奉北京人趙邦用盛京穆溪縣人李八行卽船主但國人仍曰我們是西洋國之人行商次今七月初自山東離發歷黃海道諸島轉向黃州界留住數日欲翫平壤兼見省城大人今方到此問爾們欲見省城大人有甚麼事情乎答云不是別的吾舟中略載回錦洋布斜文布斜文絨玻璃器 千里鏡自鳴鍾八音盒等物欲換貴地土産大米沙金紅蔘紙屬虎豹皮物而仍以手劃頸曰我邦七人怎麼事故而如是乎吾船雖似兵船今往平壤與彼處無冤耳現有客人在舟欲往平壤通商交易云此問爾國人被刑與否非千里外外州守臣所知而交易一款此是皇朝法禁亦非藩邦之擅許者也崔蘭軒曰王都城中有一白塔何意云故答以未知創立何年而果有白塔云則貴地因何趕逐天主敎人今我耶蘇聖敎體天道正人心以化邪俗仁義忠孝皆備皆使天下人民可從良善非同天主敎云故答以此兩敎俱是我邦法禁故人民不敢擅習云則又曰法國大船已往王京比吾舟不同耳因怒之甚恐有搶奪吾舟乃交易爲換賣也云故答以爾國大船之往王京云者誠未知其意而爾們雖爲換賣而来其所交易非敢擅許則當於何時歸去云則點頭不答而屈指幾次從近當發云而又問爾們四人外船中同来者爲幾許人而西洋人外又有他國人否答吾們同来者爲二十人而洋人五人淸人十三人烏鬼子二人酬酢之際忽然書示曰吾舟中只有黃州所得糧饌而僅爲數日之資所用者大米牛肉鷄鷄卵柴木矣吾二人必須同汝舟而往願爲借助則當以洋布等物爲謝云云答以物種則當依所請而同舟下陸事係未安云矣其在柔遠之義亦不可恝然大米一石牛肉五十斤鷄二十五首鷄卵五十箇柴木二十束八給則喜色滿面稱謝不已而續接庶尹本月十三日馳報內十二日酉時彼人六名乘小靑船以探水深次溯往上流犯昏還歸矣十三日寅時離船抵本府萬景臺下豆老島前仍爲止泊而聞彼人之言則以換貨事期云城下云彼行去留形止連探馳報之意措辭題飭緣由馳啓

9

朴珪壽(1866. 8. 28/高宗三年七月十九日) ➜ 議政府

중군(中軍) 이현익(李玄益) 구출 경위 보고

平壤府閑灘止泊異樣大舡一隻溯向閑似亭上流停泊之由已為馳啟為白有在果即接平壤庶尹申泰鼎本月十九日戌時成貼馳報内昨日酉時量彼人六名自閑似亭上流停泊處乘小青舡漸漸溯上故巡營中軍瞭望次乘小舟随後矣彼舡等瞥然来到曳去中軍所乘之舡執留中軍於渠舡中是乎所庶尹委到彼舡之傍經夜曉諭終不還送是乎加尼當日巳時量彼舡又為離發溯向上流乱放大碗口及鳥銃而到黄江亭前仍為止泊後彼人五名乘小青舡探搜次溯上烏灘之際滿城人民聚會江邊高聲還我中軍而彼答以入城當有分曉云則不勝共憤乱投石塊而城下防守校卒輩亦不得手袖傍觀或弓或銃多般施威則彼人等棄小青舡直走羊角島上端逃還乘其大舡仍為退泊於羊角島下端故同小青舡奪取以置於上流是乎旀申時量營下退校朴春權與中營所属挺身乘舟突入于彼舡之頭救下中軍而還歸是乎乃所佩印信落水見失而中軍被執時随去之傔人俞淳遠通引朴致永自彼舡中投下江水姑未還来其所死生未及的知是乎所防守之節各別謹嚴嗣後形止連探馳報計料為白有卧乎所狡彼黠胡肆入内江旬日之間已迫近城專無忌憚殊極駭痛而以其柔遠之義備盡開諭之道是白乎矣謂以交易期欲入城其心所在極為叵測是白沙除良拘執中軍經夜不還事事憤惋莫此為甚中流淺欄之舟不難殄滅無遺是白乎乃不敢擅自措處姑觀其順退與否是白乎旀中軍李玄益段被拘異舶雖出不意印信見失亦係可駭溺職貽羞更無可論為先罷黜為白去乎其罪狀令攸司稟處教是白遣其代彼舡令該曺各別擇差不日下送是白乎旀防守偵掠之節另飭舉行之意措辞題給於平壤庶尹處為白乎旀緣由馳啟為白卧乎事

朴珪壽(1866. 8. 30/高宗三年七月二十一日) ➞ 議政府

내응자 단속 및 경계 강화 보고

節到付議政府関内節啟下教今七月十四日傳曰近日異舶之出没於西南海洋者未知何故而聞我國人多有和應入處云棄其父母之邦冒入他國之舡者揆以常情必無是理而抑又思之則挽近之為牧伯守宰者多行酷厲之政全昧懷綏之方失志亡命之徒遂欲偸活以至此境是豈獨渠輩之罪乎然而此皆出於邉禁蕩然之致興言及此誠極寒心另加探察如有蹤跡殊常之類往来逗留於沿海諸處這這跟捉一並梟警以示朝家嚴邦禁屛異俗之意自庙堂措辞行會事傳教教是置傳教内辞意奉審為有矣才以邉禁申飭事草記行會而國綱之觧弛如此海防之踈虞又如此此輩之潜相誑誘通其嘘噏軽其父母之邦冒越他人之國是可忍也孰不可忍也毋或苛政所迫苟活不得騷騷然失其良性行此兇圖者乎今下聖教嚴正諄複為司牧之任寧不怵焉知警乎譏訶之節倍當嚴密另飭沿海邑鎮如有容貌蹤跡殊常閃忽而逗留候望者探察拘覈先斬後啟是矣一或放過入於糾摘責関孤負自速威罰除尋常惕念舉行関到形止先即馳聞宜當向事関是白置有亦海防譏訶之節各別嚴密如有容貌蹤跡殊常之類這即跟捉鉤覈并施梟警之意措辞関飭於沿海各邑鎮為白乎旀縁由馳啟為白卧乎事

朴珪壽(1866. 8. 31/高宗三年七月二十二日) ➜ 議政府(1866. 9. 3/高宗三年七月二十五日)

제너럴 셔먼호와의 교전 경과 보고

平壤府防水城前磯移泊異樣大舡一隻停留之由已為馳啟為白有在果即接臣營兼中軍鉄山府使白樂淵平壤庶尹申泰鼎本月二十二日午時成貼馳報内異舡少無退去之意或掠奪商舡之糧八饌物銃放所及我人被殺至為七人被傷亦為五人之多以今爻象萬無順還之望究其情狀去益痛惋是乎所防水之節各別團束嗣後動静連續馳報計料是如為白有臥乎所夷舡之闖入内地多日逗留前所未有而敢以交易之計輒發恐嚇之説究厥情節不勝駭惋為其遠人之故必欲善辞退送諭以法禁非不屡矣賙以糧資非不厚矣終不退去益肆猖狂至有拘執中軍之舉而奪還以後一向㪅砲放銃被殺被傷至為十二人之多到今事勢不可不剿滅乃已乙仍于臣於是出坐江邊董飭臣營兼中軍及平壤庶尹或以砲擊或以大攻期即殄殲是白加尼自被舡巧設縄綱罥拒火舡未得延燒是白乎乃銃乎金奉調射殪彼漢一名是白遣終日相戰之際彼舡之藥丸今幾向盡况又舡擱浅灘進退不得雖不過数十名黠謀利器亦自俱存似難容易擒獲是白乎矣以此軍民憤激之心随機應變量宜調度亦有其策是白乎旀今方激勵士氣剋日奏功嗣後形止陸續登聞計料縁由并以馳啟為白臥乎事

朴珪壽(1866. 9. 1/高宗三年七月二十三日) ➞ 議政府

제너럴 셔먼호와의 교전 경과 보고

平壤府防水城前磯移泊異樣大舡一隻終不退去益肆猖狂之由已為馳啟為白有在果即接臣營兼中軍鉄山府使白樂淵平壤庶尹申泰鼎本月二十三日戌時成貼馳報内異樣舡連為停留於原泊處或放大碗口或放鳥銃故嚴飭校卒輩以砲以射出力攻擊而彼舡制度極其堅固只以銃搶猝難打破終日相持日暮停止是乎旀彼舡酉時量退泊於下流二帳許是乎所防守瞭望之節另加嚴密嗣後形止連續馳報計料是如為白有卧乎所蓋此異舡高為三丈無異攻城奏功此遲不勝悚悶制勝之策今方爛商講究為白乎旀縁由馳啟為白卧乎事

13

朴珪壽(1866. 9. 2/高宗三年七月二十四日) ➞ 議政府(1866. 9. 5/高宗三年七月二十七日)

제너럴 셔먼호와의 교전 경과 보고

平壤府防水城前磯移泊異樣大舡一隻益肆猖狂期即殄殲計料之由已為馳啟為白有在果彼舡制度甚是堅固既難以銃搶打破則制勝之策莫先於火攻乙仍于與臣營兼中軍及平壤庶尹爛商講究劃定方畧為白有如乎即接臣營兼中軍鉄山府使白樂淵平壤庶尹申泰鼎本月二十四日戌時成貼馳報内當日寅時量異樣舡自原泊處稍稍流下止泊於三帿許浅灘故多發銃手及射手遮攔水下諸處是乭加尼午時量自彼舡裏砲放銃我人一名至於被殺則滿城人民及防水校卒輩齊聲發喊盡力攻擊是乎旀仍令積柴舡隻一齊放火及至延燒則彼人崔蘭軒趙凌奉两漢跳出舡頭始請救生故即為擒捉縛致於岸上矣許多軍民不勝憤忿齊會打殺是乭遣彼舡延燒之際彼人之或出舡頭或投江中者軍卒等這即追捉以射以銃一場斷殺後計其屍首則被銃所斃者為十三名被火爛死者為四名而并計日前射殪之一名則合為二十名無遺殲滅是乎所舡隻段并與器械什物没数燒燼向前奪置之小青舡一躰燒火是如為白有卧乎所噫彼夷舡泝江深入猖蹶稔惡視同無人其所恃者舡機之堅利也謀計之詭黠也當此不可不剿滅之際屹然若堅城硬敵本營武備之恬嬉頹惰寔為寒心而今幸燒破厥舡殲戮無遺全省之騷擾渙散始可以鎮定幀息是白乎旀臣營兼中軍鉄山府使白樂淵段倉卒兼任整頓紀律親冒銃砲擒拿凶醜是白遣平壤庶尹申泰鼎段明審敵情堅確不撓臨機辦應心力俱殫畢竟剿滅可歸令功並只施以褒賞之典恐未知何如是白乎旀其餘軍校争先勇赴出義奮發之類自臣營分等施賞是白遣當初異舡之肆然入境既不能防捍泝流直上逼近城底而又不能趕逐以致恐嚇之説恣其胸臆拘執之辱及於副將終不能斷殺乃已有違聖朝柔遠好生之德意自顧職臣不勝惶恐待罪縁由并以馳啟為白卧乎事

高宗, 時原任大臣(1866. 9. 3/高宗三年七月二十五日)

시원임대신 등을 불러 서양선박 출몰에 대해 논의

召見時原任大臣以下于熙政堂 領敦寧 金左根 判府事 趙斗淳 判敦寧 李景在 左議政 金炳學 奉朝賀 尹致羲 永平君昱 完平君昪 東寧尉金賢根判宗正卿 李敦榮 李圭徹 知宗正卿 李景夏 李周喆 李東鉉 李鳳周 宗正卿 李寅奭 李南軾 李世輔 李鍾淳 李承駿 李章濂 李重榮 原任提學 金炳冀 檢校提學 金炳國 提學 金學性 原任提學 金輔根 鄭基世 原任直提學 金大根 金炳淅 曺錫雨 金炳德 申錫禧 李承輔 檢校直提學 金炳地 原任直提學 金炳弼 金輔鉉 原任直閣 金德根 鄭健朝 檢校直閣 李淳翼 原任直閣 李喬翼 李承五 檢校直閣 閔升鎬 原任待教 洪淳穆 趙鳳夏 尹滋德 趙秉協 檢校待教 徐相翊 鄭範朝 趙寧夏 趙慶鎬 檢校 副提學 李載元 金炳始 副提學 李載冕 原任副提學 徐戴淳 趙龜夏 檢校 典翰 李明應 李冕光 李根秀原任典翰 趙康夏 金昌熙 典翰 金奎弘 副應教 洪遠植 校理 韓鎭棨 洪大鍾 副校理 李裕承 兪貞煥 修撰 李彙秉 李應金 副修撰 金亮淵 任冕鎬 議政府右參贊 任百秀 上護軍 金炳喬 洪鍾應 申觀浩 趙然昌 知中樞府事 徐衡淳 大護軍 李根友 洪祐吉 沈敬澤 李源命 金應均 金世均 金益文 李興敏 朴齊韶 韓啓源 尹正求 李明迪 李豊翼 宋廷和 李顯稷 禮曹參判 兪致崇 戶曹參判 權永秀 漢城府左尹 金元植 同知中樞府事 金敬鎭 行護軍 林肯洙 趙啓昇 沈承澤 鄭海尙 李裕膺 金炳奎 金在顯 朴来萬 閔致庠 徐相鼎 趙熙哲 洪鍾雲 洪淳大 嚴錫鼎 尹堉 韓應國 尹定善 金鼎鎬 金炳準 南鍾順 金尙鉉 黃鍾顯 姜蘭馨 洪秉壽 申命淳 李元熙 吳吉善 李熙昇 申命溫 李熙永 蔡東健李 敏庠李兼熙 李容熙 韓仁植 鄭圭應 權溶 任弘模 都承旨 曺錫元 左承旨 鄭顯德 右承旨 李源珪 左副承旨 朴履道 右副承旨 李沇應 同副承旨 鄭雲龜 記事官 李承洙 假注書 金秉鍵 記事官 權命菊 趙墉別兼春秋 南一愚

金左根奏曰江華異舶問情後雖已歸去要與有公文相訂之事則其不復来未可遙度而至若近迫箕城之船狡彼情態動靖極爲叵測實不勝憤惋矣趙斗淳曰自古國有憂虞則內修然後外攘自强爲內修先務此外無他道理矣李景在曰洋舶之出沒外洋曾或有之今番之深入內洋情狀誠叵測矣江華所泊雖已退去平壤則尙此逗

遛極爲憤惋而憂虞亦不些矣金炳學曰中國咨文以後今始登筵矣異舶之出沒內洋京外騷訛莫之鎭定而臣冒忝見任未有一言一事之裨補者下情萬萬悚悶矣予曰異船前或入外洋云而今始入內洋矣炳學曰前所未有矣予曰我國之人似有和應而然也斗淳曰果然矣予曰行會於八道四都凡踪跡殊常之類各別詗捉可也炳學曰更爲嚴關申飭矣斗淳曰先爲內修則外攘自擧矣炳學曰內修外攘別無他術國之元氣在乎正學必以正學爲急先務則邪妖自辟譬如人之元氣充實則百邪不入矣如彼邪譎之道敢干於聲明文物之邦乎若其正學之要亦在乎勤講學此之謂萬化之原也伏願深留聖念焉斗淳曰聖學爲萬化之原而左相之言甚切當矣炳學曰見今殿閣之微涼已生從近開講勉進聖學是臣區區之望矣予曰留念矣

15

高宗(1866. 9. 11/高宗三年八月三日)

사교(邪教) 척퇴(斥退)를 명하는 교서

教中外大小民人等書　王若曰　咨爾中外臣僚庶民　咸聽予一人誥　惟我國家聖神相承　崇儒重道　禮俗彬蔚　君子習仁賢之化　婦人著貞信之譽　齊道漸磨罔不以明正學敍彝倫　爲修紀立極之本　故聲明峻茂之教　媲侔中華　遂稱天下文明之國　不幸七八十年之間　有所謂西洋學者　濫觴於辛亥　滋蔓於辛酉　民興胥漸　罔克胥匡　以生我正廟純·廟兩聖朝　廓揮乾斷　大行天討　舊染汚俗亦幾乎　咸與維新　而梟獍遺育　狼軀易種　己亥之獄　多由於辛酉餘黨　今春之變　尤憯於己亥凶徒　近日捕廳諸囚之自速典刑　又何頑不知戢　詈不畏法也蓋其傳習　悖書潛相告諭　招引異類　奉若神明　糾結年久　誑誘今廣　浸潤薰染思以其道　易一國　燎原滔天之禍　凜凜乎　若在朝夕　未知有何近理亂眞之說蠱惑其心志　繆迷其作爲至此極也　其曰天主學者　非以天爲主之學也　故其言曰　天不能自成其爲天　如萬有之不能自成其爲萬有　必有造之者而後成　天主爲萬有之初有　又曰造天堂　以福事天主者之靈魂　造地獄　以苦不事天主者之靈魂　人有罪　應入地獄者　哀悔於耶蘇之前　竝祈耶蘇之母　以轉達於天主　卽赦其人之罪　靈魂亦得升於天堂　噫　堂獄之說　卽佛家不經之說　而已經先儒勘破　今無容更辨　彼所謂造天之天主　果何物也　在易之傳　以形體　謂之天以主宰　謂之帝　曰天曰帝之異其稱者　譬如橫看豎看之成嶺成峯　而非天外更有帝也　彼反引儒者之言曰　昭受上帝　天其申命用休　曰文王在上　於昭于天　曰獲罪于天　無所逃也　曰郊祀之禮所以事上帝　曰樂天畏天事天　莫非天學之微言法意　中國之教　無不先天學者　噫嘻　甚矣　吾儒所謂天與帝　豈彼謂造天之帝乎　惟仁與義　卽吾人秉彝之性　而學而兼者　至有墨氏之兼愛　曷嘗有無父無君之心而誤認之禍　不自知其入於斁倫敗常　夷狄而禽獸而有人將相食之憂　何況彼所謂天主之教　本不知天與帝之名位　何如　而分而二之　陽托尊天敬天之名　陰濟慢天褻天之行　違經悖理　不待智者而可辨　往往有篤信其說　迷不知返者　此豈非聰明者之過歟　予是以劈破原頭　重言復言　尙或有凜然驚瞿　幡然改圖者乎　至若匹庶蠱蠢之類　目不識丁　都不曉天與帝之爲何樣名目　而尙且甘心於堅振領洗等種種作法　如醒如狂　如魔壘之兵　如迷藏之戲失其本性　之死靡悔　抑又何故也　此不過財色以誘之　堂獄以愚之　吁亦可哀

也已　父母之愛　童孩之良知　而生不養而歿不祭　則曾烏鳥豺獺之不若也　男女之別　夫婦之造端　而浴同湢而寢同堂　則與狗彘禽犢之同歸　亦何心哉　書曰　不告不迪　顚越不恭　劓殄滅之無遺育　憝憂者　王法之所不容　語曰　不教而殺　謂之虐　教誥者　王政之所先務也　董之用威　戒之用休　卽先王無非敎之義　亦聖人欲竝生之意也　嗚呼　先王之道　坦若大路　聖人之學　煥乎中天　舍而不由　曲逕摘埴　視而不見　昏衢覆盆　今欲拯濟於罟獲陷穽之中　同囿於帲幪廈屋之下　死者固不足論　生者訖可以變　環東土數千里　戴髮噙齒　圓顱方趾者　罔非吾赤子耳　爲民父母　忍見其匍匐入井　而不思所以援之以手乎　肆予沖人　以口舌代斧鉞　開示其牖迷向明之路　惟爾臣僚庶民　尙克時欽　其有沈蠱詿誤　陷溺而不自知者　亟懷好音　革心革面其良善不頗僻者　胥訓胥誥胥教誨胥保惠　群居講磨　敦行孝悌　君子讀書明理　不求新奇之說　小人守分安業　毋底刑憲之科　豈不美哉　予於是　深有所慨歎者　孟子曰　楊・墨之道不息孔子之道不著　又曰　吾爲此懼　閑先聖之道　距楊・墨放淫辭　以此推之　邪教之肆行　實由於正學之不明　耶蘇之禍　有甚於楊・墨　則聖人之道　亦幾乎泯矣　寧不大可懼哉　苟能講明於修己冶人之要　用究其明德新民之效　導迪斯世粹然一出於正人　誦洛・閩之書　士服鄒・魯之訓　淫朋比德　無所依　邪說暴行　無由作　吾道不期明而自明　異學不期斥而自斥　斥此予所以奮蔆蹈厲於燕蠖之中者也　書曰　百姓有過　在予一人　反躬自省　若恫在己　今茲敷心之諭悉暴予哀痛之意　凡厥臣庶　毋遑曰　予不惠若茲多誥　藝文提學申錫禧製進

李興敏(1866. 9. 21/高宗三年八月十三日) ➞ 萬青藜

서양국가와의 통상 불허 방침 전달

관련문서 (1) 이흥민 사함(私函)의 도부(到付)를 알리는 萬青藜 상주문(1866. 11. 21/同治五年十月十五日)

弊邦僻在海隅卽一褊小之壤而儒敎立國尊尙禮樂士惟誦周孔民惟知畊鑿自童髫而白紛不見異物而遷焉曩忽泰西之敎自何吹到或有悖常之類爲其染汚是眞風馬牛之不相及也時則我宣恪王廓揮英斷痛加鋤治無俾易種厥後六十有餘年或者一二萌櫱而旋卽掃淸雖愚夫愚婦皆知其避邪趨正之爲一副義理矣今我國王仁孝睿智方域承德講學日就勵精治理大院君卽國王之親爺而國王承統後國典例崇爲大院君矣方協贊機務而雋偉光明威德竝著典章制度燦然畢擧料事如神畫籌中窾凡有注措大小憚

懷內而羣工率職外而長吏奉法環海八域之內如風行草偃農桑不擾民生樂業此誠東方無疆之會也宜其無邪穢之氣敢干休明而今行歸聞春閒又有怪事一種不逞之徒或在王城之內或在鄕峽之中亦有異樣人藏踪匿影跡其所爲詭祕叵測畢竟發露盡行誅殛國人之伏罪者毋慮數千異人則爲八名此皆自速天誅者而頃覽貴部移咨此事已播於彼邊至有興兵動師之說可知其異類聲氣相應於萬里之外也幸蒙我皇上字小之恩諸大人排解之力俾有以緩其鋒而弭其機此誠擧國臣民感戴頂祝者而閣下方在春官愚生幸託末契有此非常之睠庇實不勝聳喜而與有榮焉月前又忽有異舶來泊於近洋一在畿內一在浿

西始皆以交易爲說而交易大事也非小國所可擅許故據此以拒相持有日畿內所泊者犁然而去浿上之舶一向住碇資之以米肉諭之以事理不惟不知感反肆悖惡拘縶我官員殺害我人民銃礮竝發直有攻城之勢勢到此地無以坐受其毒且衆怒莫遏矢丸所交自致隕滅其中聞有黑鬼子幾個而其亦無甚技勇同歸烏有矣曾聞利於水者不利於陸今見彼輩之束手就勦儻前聞儘然耶月前有二巨舶冒入我平安道鐵山前洋卽洋船之載兵者而乘潮張帆而來忽然黑雲四合雷雨交作水天晦冥霹靂火從空直下俄者二大舶瞥眼震碎勢若山崩地塌船中人幾百無一倖免時適黃海道椒島商販之民船過其近處猝見此光景魂

驚魄褫來傳其懍怖之狀於鄕里親知自諸衙門招問而得其詳卽六月事也雖若適然而豈不異哉其設心行事實爲天神之所厭亦足爲後來者監戒矣蓋前後異船之來者動輒曰交易而絶遠之地國俗與土産不能該悉故也弊邦物産鮮薄畊農漁採

所得僅能自給復安有資送巨舶厭其所求乎且彼舶所賚雖窮極奇巧其於利用厚生都無所須至若雅片煙我東之人亦聞有此個物而咸知爲促生之藥視以鴆毒金屑誰肯以一點近口乎交易云者彼此相資之謂而彼無可資於我我無可資於彼將何所藉而交易乎彼將以上國公文爲脅持之計云而設有上國之飭令交市徒致擾拏而已畢竟是行不得者是故凡屬洋貨自今憲書之行一切禁斷從前自燕市流出者竝令收聚公庭無遺燒爐亦可見弊邦之自爲計者如是而大抵東國之於
西洋隔以幾萬重溟此殆天之所限聲氣所不及恩讐尤何論彼雖以春閒服罪者藉口而莠民異類弊邦之法所不貸孰知爲敎主敎士耶如此尋釁天下無有是理藉使彼動衆而來將以鉛刀蓬矢悉索弊賦以與從事而無端發出殺機使生人肝腦塗地在此之利害無論在彼亦何利而何快以交易則初無可資之貨以交危則終無可據之辭彼若灼知實事實理之如此則亦豈欲運巨艦涉層濤空然侵撓於痛癢不關之地乎閣下旣居訏謨之地與國之憂視同一家入告於內出而與總理諸大人爛相講確以事理之不當然者昭晰開解期使彼人更不置東方一隅於胸中彼此相忘各安其俗此實閣下之賜東國之人其將家家繪像而祝之而僕之於閣下一日受知諒非偶然也
爲暴事委張皇滿紙不勝主臣

【관련문서 1】

禮部尙書臣萬青藜跪奏爲奏聞事竊朝鮮國上年年貢正使李興敏來京臣適官禮部例得接見因與之有一面之識前日有該國領取時憲書使人著人送信一函於臣宅臣自署歸來始行拆閱書內所言乃近時洋舶情形核與該國王咨請禮部代奏之語大略相同臣不敢壅於上聞除將原函封送軍機處外謹照來書原式鈔呈御覽伏祈聖鑒謹奏

同治五年十月十五日

17

高宗(1866. 9. 30/高宗三年八月二十二日) → 禮部

제너럴 셔먼호 사건 전말 통보

歷陳洋舶情形咨

朝鮮國王爲歷陳洋舶情形事同治五年二月十八日據公忠道觀察使申櫶馳啓備海美縣監金膺集呈稱本年二月十二日巳時量異樣船一隻來泊於本縣西面調琴津後洋馳往問情則答英國船主姓馬名力勝在大淸國通商往來請到貴國賣買云又問船中人姓名則答姓戴名拔英國倫頓府商人也姓方名倫同知加一級廣東瓊州府人也程俟林泉其職選知府銜也楊俟永金乃補同知也黃俟名新其職選雲南鹽提舉竝福建厦門廳人也其外行船水工三十餘名也列書貨物大照身鏡一面自鳴鐘兩個西洋琴三個五彩地毡三張五彩擡一張時辰鏢一個千里鏡筒一個謂之敬獻貴國王云答以異國之物不可進獻又請交易故以邦禁斥退矣十五日離船向北而去本年六月二十六日異樣船一隻又泊於海美縣調琴津後洋本縣監金膺集問情答大英國商人戴拔本年二月道經貴國曾請通商因別埠有事不及靜候卽行發輪往業經事畢來此係候貴國王命求請通商云仍抵書於海美縣監申言貨物進獻及交易等事答以外國之物素無進獻法例通商亦係禁令今不必更說也七月初三日發船向西海大洋去本年七月十三日據江華府留守李寅夔馳啓備本月十一日巳時量異樣船一隻來泊於本府月串津鵂巖墩下本府經歷金在獻譯官方禹敍馳往問情則答以英國商人戴拔本年二月道經貴國海美縣專請通商又於前月二十六日到海美轉到貴境伏祈通貨又請貨物數種進獻貴國王云問船中人姓名則答俺們共三十人內英國商人戴拔船主詹仕火淸人馮芝林汪文山謝在田陳其修其餘俱是行船燒火造工也英商曰船到貴國專求通商竝無別情答我國之法上國無許施之公文則不敢擅便英商曰弊國通商之事敢煩貴國代請大淸公文可乎答請于大淸卽我國事無關於貴國英商曰兩國通商度大淸必許施也日間歸去大淸請公文竝貨物前來本月二十日發船向南仍無形影又於本年七月連據平安道觀察使朴珪壽鱗次馳啓備平壤庶尹申泰鼎呈稱異樣船一隻十一日來泊於本府草里坊新場浦口平壤中軍李賢益庶尹申泰鼎馳往問情則其中一人稱解朝鮮言語自言姓崔名蘭軒英吉利國人也姓趙名凌奉北京人也姓趙名邦用盛京穆溪縣人也姓李名八行卽船主但國人也仍曰欲翫平壤兼見省城大人交易物貨云答以交易一款本是皇朝法禁有非藩邦所敢擅許者也崔蘭軒曰六月二十一日自大淸

國有出來咨文則貴國豈可曰不能交易乎俺等於六月二十二日躡後出來又曰貴地因何趕逐大主教人令我耶蘇聖教體天道正人心非同天主教云故答以此兩教俱是我國法禁又曰法國主教及教士竝與貴國習教人何爲殺害答以無公憑而浮遊異國變服藏蹤與我國奸細之民陰謀不軌在法當誅而若我國人民之有罪被誅何關於法國乎仍問爾們同來者爲幾人答洋人五人淸人十三人烏鬼子二人云船中食盡願爲借助故厚給米肉者凡三次而盖此船先入黃州海港願借糧饌自黃州兵營優數贈遺旋又趕到平壤東西閃忽而隨請隨給曲副其意矣十八日彼人六名乘小靑船溯流而上故本營中軍李賢益瞭望次乘小舟隨後矣彼人等督然曳去中軍所乘之船執留中軍於彼船中翌日軍校輩始奪還中軍矣彼人專昧好意一向咆嚇轟砲而窺逼全城放銃而刼掠商船本國人前後殺傷爲十三人之多彼人又曰米一千石及金銀人蔘多數饋遺然後可以解去也誅求無名谿壑難充滿城民人不勝憤忿必欲力居二十四日彼沿向我人亂發銃砲彼銃而我銃彼砲而我砲烈焰延及彼船猛風又助其勢彼船二十人或被爛或落水或中丸盡數就死等因具啓據此竊惟弊邦密邇上國仰蒙我皇朝天地罔極之恩事大之誠自守外蕃字小之渥視同內服凡諸憲章律令條約法禁一遵皇朝勅咨而行之奉若金石毋敢違越上國與弊邦物貨互市立之以程限定之以時月邊圉之犯界者漁採之涉海者上國抵法尙嚴三尺之科況越海幾萬里與一帆乘風之商舶私相貿遷漸通聲氣是豈人臣無外交之義哉弊邦僻在東陸與英國隔以重溟書契之所不通舟車之所不至也謹照道光十二年壬辰忽有該國商船强要市易事關邊情咨陳始末乃蒙皇朝特加恩褒二十五年乙巳又以英國船事陳咨伏蒙勅諭兩廣至有伊國人不復再往朝鮮之命弊邦君臣尙今感戴近年以來亦有外洋過去之舶或請交易而開誠布信曉諭卽還未有如今者江華平壤所到兩船之直入內洋或費辭牢請或殺害逞嚇者也崔蘭軒所云大淸咨文出來時躡後發船之說顯有疑端而爲其遠人也故必欲善辭退送諭以法禁非不屢矣賙以糧資非不厚矣而銃砲之毒殲我人民拘執之辱及於副將教主殺害之說作爲脅喝金蔘討索之計竟出盤托此若舍忍仍置不測之禍有難盡言而無以抑軍民激憤殊死之心則彼船燒爐卽不過自送其死也上國人之混被爛死殊甚慘傷而彼所稱北京人盛京人其眞僞難信弊邦奸民亦有入彼船而和應交易者其打扮作上國人樣英國人樣都未可知設有上國之的實同處者投異國商估之船違皇朝犯越之禁火炎所及玉石難分雖異擅殺之失終有驚悚之心江華所到英船之言亦甚叵測大淸公文之自稱准許豈其必然哉藉令如其言而赴愬天朝冒干崇嚴以我皇上懷保小邦之望念諸大人愛護小邦之高義旣料非小邦所願則夫安有因其言而遽然允許之理乎弊壤卽海隅一彈丸耳民貧貨儉金銀珠玉尙矣無論

米粟布帛未見其嬴一國之産不足以支一國之用矧復流通荒徼耗竭域內則蕞爾區疆將有岌岌難保之憂矣且念弊邦久沐皇朝同文之化其道則堯舜禹湯文武周孔也其學則詩書禮樂也故國中愚夫愚婦之或傳習彼教者一切禁之彼所云趕逐天主教者指此也然彼國自有彼國之教我國自有我國之教有如朔粵之不同枘鑿之不合以其風氣習俗之所隔別也交易之不可許弊邦之事勢卽然異教之不可行弊邦之學術卽然亦所以上遵天朝之典憲恪修海藩之侯度也而洋人之頻年泛海固請不已至有殺害人民之變圖受公憑之計勿論其言之虛實殊切邊防之憂虞玆庸備悉事由謹此咨陳煩乞貴部轉達天廳隨機鎭安開諭排解杜絶交易之說俾小邦獲藉隆庇永藉妥靜千萬幸甚爲此合行移咨云云 同治五年八月二十二日

E. Sandford (1866. 10. 8) ➔ G. F. Seward

제너럴 셔먼호 사건 발생 보고

United States Consulate
Cheefoo, October 8, 1866

Sir:

I have the honor to inform you that the French fleet returned from Corea, October 3rd. On the 4th, it was reported here that the American schooner, *General Sherman* had been wrecked, and all on board murdered by the natives. I immediately wrote to the Admiral, requesting him to furnish me with what information he could, to which he replied, viz:

"In reply to the letter, which you have done me the honor of writing me, I can do no better than send you the exact copy of a note that was sent me by Rev. P. Ridel, apostolic missionary."

"On the 30th of September, we were at anchor near Woody Island, on the coast of Corea. During the night, a Corean boat with two natives on board approached the "Déroulède." Having recognized in one of them one of the sailors who had accompanied me in the spring, on the voyage from Corea to Cheefoo, I succeeded in inducing them to come on board. Among other information, they told me that about the middle of the 7th moon (about the end of the month of August) a small vessel from the country of the West had appeared on the coast of Corea, in the province of Phieng-an-do which is in the extreme northwest of the Kingdom. She was endeavoring to ascend the river, to reach the City of Phieng-iang, capital of this province and had already arrived, almost off this city, when she grounded on a sand bank. The governor at once sent to the King's father for instructions, whether he should put to death those on board or should burn them and the vessel together. The King's father replied, to burn the vessel and all on board. This barbarous order was executed. Such, Sir, is the only information bearing at all, upon the matters to which you allude, that has reached me, &c, &c.

The *General Sherman* left here on the 9th of August. She called for water, and took Mr. Hogarth as supercargo and Mr. Thomas, as interpreter. The owner of the vessel also went with them.

A Chinese junk arrived on the 6th from Corea, and stated that as she made the coast, she was met by another junk, who warned them not to go in, as a foreign vessel had been wrecked and all on board burnt, both foreigners and Chinese. The schooner is overdue, and we fear that it is the *General Sherman*. It might be well to let the Admiral know.

I have the honor to be
Your Obedient Servant
Signed E.S. Sandford: U.S. Consul

Geo F. Seward
U.S. Consul General, Shanghai

E. Sandford (1866. 10. 12) → G. F. Seward

제너럴 셔먼호 사건 경과 보고

U.S. Consulate at Cheefoo
October 12, 1866

Sir:

I have the honor to inform you, that the Chinese junks have arrived from Corea, and make the following reports, respecting the wreck and burning of a foreign schooner, viz: The Captain of one of them was engaged by Mr. Thomas to pilot the schooner up the river Phieng-an-do, as he was acquainted with Mr. Thomas before. He yielded, and took her up four tides. By this time, an alarm had spread amongst the natives, they taking her for a pirate, and would not believe the pilot, when he told them that she was a peaceful trader. (The *General Sherman* was heavily armed, and had a large crew.) All trade was stoped, and the natives began to collect, in large numbers, when his friends on board of the junk, becoming alarmed, refused to allow him to go any further, saying that if he was killed, they would have no face to return to Yentai; He therefore left them opposite little Phieng-an-do, about half way up the river. Those on board the schooner were determined to go farther. This was about the middle of the 8th moon. You will notice here a disagreement, between the date given by the French missionary, and this man. I think this date the most reliable for this reason. The French missionary's informant was no doubt anxious to leave the Steamer as soon as possible, and being flurried by the many questions put to him by Mr. Ridel, may not have been as careful in the replies, as he otherwise would have been, and again Mr. Ridel was more desirous of learning about the Christians, and his colleagues, who were still in the mountains, and may not at the time have felt, the importance of examining him carefully on the date: The other junk, it seems, did not reach Corea, as, on its nearing the coast, a junk put off, and warned them not to go in, as a foreign vessel had been wrecked opposite Phieng-an-do, and all hands with the schooner burnt, on which the junk returned to Yentai. I fear that it may prove too true. There seems no doubt, but that some foreign vessel and crew have been burnt, and the *General Sherman* is the only one know to be on the coast.

I think if not incompatible with public interest, that Admiral Bell would do well to send a vessel to make inquiries. It is true that the vessel ought not to have gone there, but this sad tale should disarm our judgment. The *General Sherman* did not enter at this port, stopping only long enough to take in water, and provisions.

I have the honor to be
Your Obedient Servant
Signed, E.S. Sandford
U.S. Consul

Geo. F. Seward Ex,
U.S. Consul General
Shanghai

S. W. Williams(1866. 10. 23) ➞ 總署

제너럴 셔먼호의 생존자 확인 및 구호 여부 문의

LEGATION OF THE UNITED STATES,
Peking, October 23, 1866

A report has been received here from Chifu that an American schooner, the *General Sherman*, was wrecked last month on the coast of Corea, and burned by the natives; her officers and crew, 24 in all, being captured by them, but it is not certainly known whether they are still alive or not. It is the usage of the Corean government to deliver all such persons at the frontier of China to her officers, to be handed over to their respective consuls at Niuchwang. In the month of June lst a small American vessel was lost on Corea, and her crew were very kindly treated by the people, and handed over to the officers in Manchuria, whose treatment was, on the other hand, in utter contrast with that of the Coreans, very harsh, the poor men not having enough to eat. However, owing to the exertions and expostulations of Père Gillie, a French missionary at Mukten, they were sent to the consul at Niuchwang.

I have to request, therefore, that orders may be immediately sent to the officers in Manchuria that if the Coreans should deliver over these 24 men to them, to treat them with kindness and protect them, and not with the harshness shown to the former company. All expense incurred by the authorities there on account of these men will be repaid by the government of the United States. I have, &c.,

S. WELLS WILLIAMS

【漢譯文】

美國衛廉士信函

逕啓者 現據煙臺報到 八月間有美國兩枝桅船 一隻在高麗國擱淺 被高麗土人將船燒毁 竝捉去船主水手二十四人 未知從來生死如何 照高麗規矩 應送至中國交界 俾中國官轉交營口本國領事 今年五月間 曾有美國小船觸礁擱淺 其高麗人款待極好 後將送至奉天府 該處官刻薄 飲食款待 與高麗大不同 後有法國教師 勸將送至牛莊了事 玆二十四人儻或送至 請貴衙門行飭奉天府官撫卹保護 勿如前時刻薄 或有花去費用及採買糧食等項 本國應當送還 爲此豫聞

S. W. Williams (1866. 10. 24) ➔ W. H. Seward

서프라이즈호 선원 송환 및 제너럴 셔먼호 선원 피살 보고

LEGATION OF THE UNITED STATES
Peking, October 24, 1866

Sir:

I have the honor to bring to your notice the case of the shipwrecked crew of the American schooner *Surprise*, the treatment which they received at the hands of the Corean and Chinese officials, and the kindness extended toward them by a French missionary who met them on their journey. I have condensed the principal facts of their history from the narrative of Captain M'Caslin.

On the 24th of June the crew left the schooner in a sinking condition, and reached an island, whose few inhabitants supplied them with rice, but wished them to leave as soon as they had eaten it, which, however, a storm prevented their doing until the next day. Going on nearly 20 miles toward the northwest, they saw a village on the mainland, which they thought best to reach, if possible, in order to obtain food rest. On approaching it from the beach, they were surrounded by about 200 natives who would not allow them to move until an officer arrived and was ready to receive them. This was done in the open air, and by means of the Chinese cook they were able to make him understand their condition, after which they were comfortably provided for during two-days. Another official then arrived who likewise interrogated them minutely, but would not let them leave the village, keeping the party under a guard of soldiers within a small enclosure. On the fourth day a third officer came from the capital, bringing with him a Chinese interpreter, who henceforth took charge of them, giving them abundance of good food, tobacco, and even medicines for the sick.

After remaining in this village for 24 days, a special courier arrived from the capital to conduct the whole party to the Chinese frontier. The first day's journey of 14 miles on foot, over a rugged mountainous country, brought them to a large city, where they were courteously treated, furnished with suits of clothes, and well fed. From this place, two days' riding brought them to the large frontier town where they were comfortably lodged until notice could be given to the Chinese, and another escort arrived on the tenth day. Meanwhile they were placed in a government building, under a guard, and each man furnished with a suit of clothes. Chickens, beef, corn and rice were served out to them, and on three occasions they were invited to dine with the authorities of the town, when each of them received a catty of tea and a fan.

Two days' journey on horseback from this city, through a wild and uninhabited country, brought the party to a wall about 30 feet long and 20 feet high, in which was the gate that dives Corea from China; they stopped in a town near it that night, and the next morning went to a walled town about 10 miles off, where they were delivered to the Chinese authorities, and remained two days. Their food was insufficient, and of the poorest quality; and during the journey to Mukten, which city they reached after six days' hard travelling, they had only an allowance of millet and corn. The officer at Mukten would give them nothing, and the escort took them to an inn outside of the city, where a French missionary, hearing of their distress, sent for them; but the escort refused to let them go. However, Captain McCaslin and two others did go, and were kindly received and supplied with a good meal. The next day the authorities again declined to receive them, and they all went back to the inn to spend the night; but before going to bed all went on to the Père Gillie's house, who furnished them with a dinner.

Next morning they were again brought before the city authorities, who gave them in charge to four people, one of whom furnished mats for sleeping, and the others took them to a kind of lock-up, where several hundred criminals were detained. The filthiness of the place was unendurable, and some of the men managed to rush about and get outside of the enclosure, from whence they all ran beyond the city gates, and reached Père Gillie's house only a few moments before the policemen came to carry them back. He refused to let them go, until a proper place for lodging was provided, and sufficient food. After two days, he went with them into the city to the authorities, and according to Captain McCaslin's belief, it was entirely owing to his energetic remonstrances and intervention that the party were saved from death through starvation and exposure in Mukten by being immediately sent on to Niuchwan. They were furnished with mules the next days, and reached Yingtsz after seven days' journey, where they were delivered to the United States consul nearly two months after they were wrecked.

On learning the particulars here narrated, I addressed a letter of thanks to the French charge d'affaires in this city, (enclosure A), who has forwarded it to Mr. Gillie. I respectfully request, too, that if you deem it proper, a testimonial of some kind may be sent to him as a mark of approbation for his kind succor to our unfortunate countrymen. The danger they were afraid of in dying from neglect was not imaginary, for travellers visiting Mukten have come across Russian sailors in the streets, who had been living there a twelve month in great destitution, their existence being unknown to the Russian consuls.

In my despatch of August 8th, (No. 37*), I referred to the hostile proceedings of the French naval commander against the Corean government, Before Admiral Rose had sent any vessels to that coast, another American schooner was wrecked, and the hull burned by the Coreans, as is their usual wont; but, according to the reports which have since come here from Chifu, they murdered all her company. This consisted of five foreigners, (three Americans and two British-one a passenger,) and 19 Manillamen, as sailors. I have not been able to learn more than that she had gone over on an experimental trading voyage. The Surprise had very little, if any, cargo on board.

The reports concerning the fate of these men being doubtful and conflicting, I addressed a note (enclosure B) to the Chinese officers, which they promised to send off the next morning to Manchuria. If anybody from the *General Sherman* should be given to the authorities there, I hope they will receive better usage.

I hear that the French have already effected a landing in Corea, but nothing more of importance has been learned of their movements. The force now there consists of six ships. I enclose a copy of the notification of blockade, (enclosure C), and shall apprise the department of the operations that are made public. I suppose the expedition will result in throwing open to the western world the last country which now forbids intercourse with other lands, and whose rulers have jealously guarded their subjects from the least acquaintance with their fellow-men. It is full time that Corea was introduced into the family of nations.

I have, the honor to be, sir, your most obedient servant.

S. WELLS WILLIAMS

Hon. WILLIAM H. SEWARD,
Secretary of state, Washington, D. C.

---

*제1권 90번 문서.

Mem. from Mr. Williams

PEKING, October 29, 1866

Subsequent rumors indicate that the French are pressing on towards the capital of Corea, and that it has been attacked and captured, and the king has fled. There is very little doubt about the death of all the company on board the *General Sherman*. "The Coreans decapitated them all" is the brief account which has just been received.

Enclosure A

LEGATION OF THE UNITED STATES,
Peking, September 15, 1866

Sir:

It affords me very high gratification to the medium of conveying to you the thanks of Captain McCaslin, as given in the enclosed narrative of the humane conduct of the Rev. Père Gillie, who successfully assisted a company of ship wrecked American sailors belonging to the schooner Surprise, late under his command, in their journey across Manchuria to Niuchwang. The consciousness of having been the means of preserving the lives of these unfortunate mariners, as they state was the case, will be of itself a great satisfaction of Père Gillie; and I wish to add my own sincere thanks to him for his kindness to my countrymen in their trouble. Will you sir, oblige me and them by conveying to him this expression of our united thanks, either through Bishop Mouilly or otherwise, as you deem proper, and I shall make known his noble conduct, so congruous to his sacred calling, to the President.

I seized this occasion to renew the expression of the high consideration with which I am, sir, your obedient servant.

S. WELLS WILLIAMS

HENRY D. BELLONET, Esq.,
French Charge d'Affaires

Enclosure B

Mr. Williams to the Foreign Office.

LEGATION OF THE UNITED STATES,
Peking, October 23, 1866*

Enclosure C

Notice of blockade of the river Seoul by the French naval squadron.

The undersigned, rear-admiral and commander-in-chief of the naval forces of his Majesty the Emperor of the French, in the China and Japan seas, in furtherance of the measures which have been deemed necessary in consequence of the murder of many French missionaries by the government of Corea, and by virtue of the powers belonging to me as commander-in-chief, hereby declares, that after the 15th day of this month the river Seoul, by all its entrances, will be held in a state of effective blockade by the naval forces under my command.

All vessels which shall attempt to violate this blockade will be treated according to international laws, and the treaties in force with neutral powers.

G. ROSE.

Given on board the Guerrire, Chefoo roads, October 5, 1866.

---

*제1권 20번 문서.

22

總署(1866. 10. 28/同治五年九月二十日) → S. W. Williams

미국측 요청의 처리 결과 통보

給美國衛廉士信函

本月十五日 貴大臣來署 面交信函一件 內稱八月間 有兩枝桅船在高麗擱淺 一事 當日經本衙門辦信 分致盛京將軍及山海關監督 查照妥爲辦理 知關廑注 特此布聞

H. H. Bell (1866. 11. 30) ➞ G. Wells (1867. 2. 19)

제너럴 셔먼호 사건 경과 및 천주교도 탄압 사실 보고

U.S. Flag Ship *Hartford* (2d Rate)
Lat 26 01′ N: Long 123 47′ E
November 30, 1866

Hon Gideon Welles
Secretary of the Navy
Washington, D. C.

Sir:

I have the honor to inform the Department that on the 19th of November, I received from Vice Admiral King, Commander in Chief of Her Britanic (*Sic*) Majesty's Naval Forces in these seas; information of the shipwreck of the American Schooner *General Sherman* and the murder of all on board of her, on the West Coast of Corea.

This information, was in the form of a letter, from an English house Meadows & Co. of Tientsin, China to the British Consul, at that part; a copy of which letter was forwarded in the above mentioned British Consul to Admiral King; two British subjects having been murdered on board at her.

The following is the substance of this communication.

In July, or August 1866; the American Schooner *General Sherman* was loaded for a trading voyage to the West coast of the Corea; in pursuance of an engagement, between her owner and the firm of Meadows & Co. above referred to. She sailed from Chifu, bearing the following the persons on board: Mr. Preston, her owner, and Mr. Page, her Master, both said to be American citizens; Mr. Neilson, here mate, said to be a naturalized American citizen, Mr. Hogarth, of the firm of Meadows & Co. acting as her super cargo, a British subject; Mr. Thomas, an English Missionary; Mr. Portuguese, who accompanied Mr Thomas; and a crew of Malays and Chinese. The Schooner has not been heard from since her departure from Chifu; till the return of the French Naval forces from the Corea to Chifu, in the last days of September, when, it was rumored, that the Schooner *General Sherman*, had been wrecked, in the Corea, and burnt with all her people on board; by order of the King (Regent, the King being a Minor, his father is Regent.)

The following extract from the letter referred to gives some interesting information of the ill fated vessel, [viz. (accompanied writing from Chifu Oct 7th)] since writing to you yesterday. I have had a long conversation, with the pilot of a junk, belonging to this part regarding the *General Sherman*. It appears that he met the *General Sherman* at the mouth of a very large river, called Ping-Yang. He know, Mr. Thomas very well, and so consented to act as pilot to the *General Sherman*. He conducted her for four tides, which occupied three days, up the river, and then left her to fend her way to Ping-Yang city; a large trading mart on the river, about six days journey, from its mouth, going day and night. It is between five and six hundred miles by land. He left her about midway, between the mouth of the river, and the trading mart above referred to. This was on the final day of the eighth moon (11th Sept. 1866). He has never seen the vessel since. He left piloting the *General Sherman*, because her appearance had created alarm: the Coreans being a simple people; and all trading was stopped, between the Coreans and Chinese. The Coreans asked him about the *General Sherman*, and her intentions. He replied, she was a peaceful trader, but they said he has not come to buy our goods. He goes from Shanghai to Corea, sometimes, three times a year. He is forty three years of age, and has traded for many years with Corea. Mr. Thomas, constantly wanted to land and ramble, but the pilot advised him against doing so. Thomas wished to keep the pilot and let his junk return to Shang-tung, but his junkmen, would not hear of it; saying they could not face his family without him. On the pilot reaching the mouth of the Ping-Yang river, he had some conversation, with the Coreans there; and they told him, that their sovereign would by no means trade with foreigners."

Last spring, some Roman Catholic Missionaries (French) in the Corea, were put to death, by the Coreans. Hearing of this, the French Admiral, with one Frigate, one ship and two small gun boats of the frailest kind, all steamers, repaired to the west coast of that country, and leaving the two large vessels at anchor off the mouth of the Kiang Kang, or Seoul, ascended that river for about fifty miles, with her two gun boats to make a reconnaissance.

Finding the navigation difficult, and also meeting with active resistance from the natives, as he approached near to the Capital, he descended the river, and retired to Chifu, on the coast of China, to await instructions from France; leaving a garrison in a fort, and one vessel to hold the entrance to the river.

The Kiang-Kang, the largest river in Corea, debouches into Bay of Prince Jerome, Lat 37° 30′ North.

After carefully consulting the chart, I am unable to find any river of the name Ping-Yang; given by the Chinese pilot; and as the width of Corea exceeds in no part one hundred and eighty miles. I infer that the pilot has exaggerated the distance from the sea to the Capital; and that when he speaks of the town, as being, five or six hundred miles from the coast; it is probably not more than fifty or sixty miles.

I shall not therefore, be surprised to find that the Ping-Yang, is the same river, that was ascended by the French Admiral, and known as Kiang Kan, or Seoul.

Notwithstanding, that the trade in which the *General Sherman* was then engaged, was irregular, the murder of our countrymen, and their associates, was a most cruel and barbaric outrage; and shall receive my immediate attention.

Not only, should prompt punishment be inflicted on the savage King, and his willing people; but a sufficient guarantee should be extracted to ensure humane treatment to Americans; and all persons under the American flag who may fall into their unchristian hands.

Admiral King, on whom devolves the protection of British subjects; requested me to let him know my determination in the matter; after I shall have obtain more exact information; though he did not indicate what measure he might pursue.

The murder of the French priests, followed so soon after, by the murder of the Americans and English, on board of the *General Sherman*, indicate to the intention of the Coreans, to keep out all foreigners from their country.

I shall upon my arrival at Hong Kong; despatch a vessel of the Squadron to Chifu, for further information; and if possible to the Corea itself. The coast of that country is however described as being very dangerous, in the winter, and much cannot be done before next spring.

In April, I shall go the Corea myself; and I should be happy to hard from the Department on this subject, previous to setting out. In the mean time, I will keep it duly informed.

My despatch No. 57, enclosed herewith, informs the Department of the accident to the engine of the *Hartford*; and the necessity for that vessel to proceed to Hong Kong for repairs.

I have the honor to be, Sir, Very.

Very Respectfully
Your Obedient Servant
H. H. Bell
Acting Rear Admiral
Commanding US Asiatic Squadron

議政府(1866. 12. 11/高宗三年十一月五日 ➞ 禮部

제너럴 셔먼호 생존자설 부정 및 프랑스 군사행위의 부당성

朝鮮國王爲覆陳致謝仍辦洋舶事實事同治五年十月二十七日承准貴部咨節該云云自主客司案呈止疎虞可也見上知會總理衙門相機酌辦咨等因奉此竊念小邦凡有患難疾聲具籲者仰藉天朝字小之春也今此貴部之據情代奏軍機大臣之面奉論旨總理衙門之相機籌辦俾小邦悉心籌畫計出萬全不得稍涉疎虞其所以撫保小邦靡不用極不知小邦何以獲此隆庇也第茲英船焚溺之事法檄悖慢之說法兵退去之由前以具咨詳陳而本年二月七月再到海美縣江華府固請通商以無上國公文不敢擅便許施則謂往大清國請公文竝貨物前来而發船遠去仍無形影者卽自稱英人馬力勝戴拔等也又於七月来泊平壤府拘執將弁殺害人民討索財貨亂放銃砲擱淺而自被焚溺者卽自稱英人崔蘭軒但國人李八行及烏鬼子等也原無美國人兩枝桅船一隻擱淺被燒竝捉去船主水手等二十四人之事則今此衛廉士来凾想因平壤府英船焚溺事而轉相訛傳不究根由也弊邦與英法兩國本不交涉何有失和通商傳敎則以邦禁而拒絶之敎士則以異國莠民變服誑惑而斥除之而已凡天下各國相與征戰必先詳究情實明執釁端始可興兵而今法人之瞰我未備闖入江華府焚毁全城剽攘財貨卽一劫掠殘暴之寇也通商者果如是乎傳敎者果如是乎末乃頭領被殲擧帆而走然伊後踪跡有難料測惟當秉義修備務盡誠信而至若兵費賠償一節伏荷貴部及總理衙門之慮及利害誠萬萬銘感但法人之攫取弊邦帑蓄戎器者其數不貲則弊邦責償於法國猶或可矣法國責償於弊邦安有是也凡係洋夷之通商傳敎賠償諸事小邦之民情國勢雖幾年受困於洋夷斷不可行矣小邦有事輒蒙皇朝之曲賜矜恤茲庸備悉事由謹具覆陳煩乞貴部深軫小邦情實轉達天廳隨機指諭俾底安靖庸究終始之惠千萬達甚爲此合行咨覆云云　同治五年十一月初五日

H. H. Bell (1866. 12. 12) → G. Wells

제너럴 셔먼호 사건 경과 보고

U.S. Flag Ship *Hartford* (2 Rate)
Hong Kong, China
December 12, 1866

Hon. Gideon Welles.
Secretary of the Navy
Washington, D. C.

Sir:

I have the honor to inform the Department that I am here in Hong Kong, on the 3rd Inst. having been forced to come to this port, by the circumstance reported in my dispatch No: 57 1/2 (Dated November 30th 1866,) namely, the breaking of the air pump of the after engine of this ship.

I found the *Wachusett* Commander R. W. Shufeldt in this port. He has been actively cruising between the Island of Hainam to the westward and Amoy to the eastward without falling in with any pirates.

The hull and the decks of the *Wachusett* needing calking, and her copper being off her bottom in several places, I dispatched her on the 7th instant to ["Whumpoa"]; to go into dock there.

She will probably return to this anchorage in about ten days; when I shall dispatch Her to "Chifoo" (as she is the most capable of steaming against the strong N.S. monsoon, which blows on this coast, 'till May); to obtain information as to the American Schooner *General Sherman*, and her people referred to in my dispatch No. 58*; November 30th, 1866. Commander Shufeldt will be directed to proceed thence to the Corea; if not prevented by the ice, which is said to blockade that coast, during the winter months.

I regret to state, although there is an American Consul residing at Chifoo whence the Schooner *General Sherman* sailed for the Corea, and whence come all the reports, as to the murdering outrage upon her people, that all the information I have yet received of that shocking affair, has been from British

*제1권 23번 문서.

authorities. Except from Mr. F. P. Knight, Acting U.S. Consul [at Freed.] [Cherang]. Mr Knight arrived here on the 10th December last and placed in my hands, copies of Shanghai papers, which tend to prove that the *General Sherman* was destroyed in the river "Se'oul" or "Kiang Kang" and that her officers and crew were murdered, by order of the Regent of Corea, but a shadow of doubt is cast over the horrible report, that all the hands were burned to death in the vessel as one of the persons on board is rumored to have escaped to China; and it is therefore hoped that others also, may have escaped. The date of this outrage is fixed at the 2nd of September, 1866.

My despatch No. 58 of November 30th: 1866 informed the Department of some movements of the French Admiral, in the Corea. Since my arrival here, I have learned from the Shanghai papers that the French Admiral, on the 5th of October last; declared a blockade of the mouth of the river "Se'oul," and his intention, of obtaining redress for the murder of the French missionaries (a copy of the declaration of which blockade is herewith enclosed; marked A). In pursuance of which, he landed a force of 600 men, upon the large island of "Koangboa"; at the mouth of the Se'oul River and took possession of the city of the same name; which has a population of about 30,000; [situate] upon this Island.

From thence reconnoitering parties were pushed out upon the mainland, but a determined resistance by the Coreans, and on one occasion, twenty five of the French were killed and wounded.

Finally, a large force of Coreans were landed upon this island and a party of 50 French sent to dislodge them were obliged to retreat with a loss of 35 killed and wounded. Under these circumstances and probably influenced by the fact that the ice would place his vessels in the most critical condition, if he remained, Admiral Roze is said to have re-embarked his forces having first destroyed the city of "Kanghwa" where there were magazines, containing large quantities of cannon, small arms, [jingals] swords, armor, spears, bows and arrows, and other arms; and also, no less than four hundred and fifty tons of powder, and raised the blockade for the present, retiring from the coast. It is not known, whether the Admiral has withdrawn under instructions from France or not.

The capital of Corea, Se'oul, is now ascertained to be situated about twenty six miles from "Koang Hoa" by land, and about fifty miles by the river.

Considering all these circumstances, I hope the Department will deem it expedient to increase the force under my command in these seas. I shall proceed to the Corea in this ship as soon as winter breaks up in that region to ascertain more particularly the fate of our unfortunate countrymen, if the Wachussett should return from Chifoo without any satisfactory tidings of them.

The enclosed excerpts from Shanghai papers, relating to the Corea, may prove interesting to the Department.

I have the honor to be, Sir
Very respectfully
Your obedient servant
H.H. Bell
Acting Rear Admiral
Commdg. US Asiatic Squadron

H. H. Bell (1866. 12. 14) → G. Wells

한양 점령 건의

U.S. Flag Ship *Hartford* (2nd Rate)
Hong Kong China
December 14, 1866

Hon. Gideon Welles
Secretary of the Navy
Washington D. C.

Sir:

The barbarous murder of the people on board of the Schooner *General Sherman*, suggests the terrible fate that awaits such of our countrymen as are lawfully navigating the Japanese Sea, and the Whang Hai of Yellow Sea, which wash the shores of the Corea, and may be as unfortunate as to fall into the hands of that savage people. I trust therefore that the Government of our Country will take this affair in hand without delay, and in anticipation of the French, next spring. It will need as preparations; fortunately the Government is ready with all the material in their hands.

This squadron can be immediately reinforced from the Pacific Coast with light draft vessels; and fifteen hundred or two thousand soldiers can, in the same time, be transported in the Vanderbilt, or, in the Pacific Mail Steam-Ship Company's Steamer running from California to this port, landing them in Hamilton Harbor Latitude 34° 08¢ N Long 127° 20¢ E. Corean Archipelago, with their necessary equipment &c., and I doubt not we could possess ourselves of Seoul the Capital of the Corea, twenty-six miles from the coast; by next June, and humble the King of that Country to our demands.

Only twelve thousand British and French troops marched to Peking.

A blow to [________], promptly and efficiently, followed by a quiet withdrawal of our forces to California, as soon as our demands are satisfied, would awe not only Japan and the Court of Peking into profound respect for American views and interests, but would disclose to the world who are the Master of the Pacific; and make American Diplomacy easy in the East, as well as on the Northern boundary from Vancouver to Newfoundland.

Very little is known of the Coreans, of their government, of their power or of their industrial pursuits, though it is apparent that they desire no intercourse with Christians. While the Japanese carry on some little trade with them on the East, the Chinese traffic with them on the West coast.

Fine harbors abound, particularly in the Archipelago to the South of that promontory. The most attractive of these is Port Hamilton, Lat 34° 03¢ N Long 127° 20¢ E, inhabited by about four hundred fishermen, being easy of access, and easy of defense. This harbor claims the attention of Naval Powers. It is 150 miles from Nagasaki, 240 miles from Van Diemans Straits, 180 from Simonasaki, 300 from the Yangtze River and 330 from the Seoul River.

Chrichton Harbor Lat 34° 20¢, Long 126° 38¢, further west is also regarded as a good harbor. These islands have very little soil, are thinly peopled with a poor race of fishermen who are jealously watched over by a district Corean Mandarin. Good anchorages are found in the Prince [Jerome] Archipelago leading to Seoul River, the rise and fall of tides being twenty-six feel.

I have the honor to be, Sir
Very respectfully
Your obedient servant
H.H. Bell
Acting Rear Admiral
Commanding U.S. Asiatic Squadron

A. Burlingame(1866. 12. 15) → W. H. Seward

제너럴 셔먼호 사건 경과 보고

UNITED STATES LEGATION,
Peking, December 15, 1866

Sir:

It is my painful duty to inform you that the United States schooner *General Sherman*, while on a trading voyage to Corea, was destroyed and all on board murdered by the natives. The news was brought to Cheefoo by Admiral Rose, of the French fleet, the particulars of which please find in Mr. Sandford's despatch, (A). I refer you also to the letter of Meadows & Co., (B) from which you will learn that the schooner was chartered and loaded by them and for what purpose.

As Corea was formerly tributary to China I brought the affair to the attention of Prince Kung, who at once disavowed all responsibility for the Coreans, and stated that the only connection between the two countries was one of ceremonial. I thereupon addressed the letter (C) to Admiral Bell, in which I limit myself to a suggestion as to what action should be taken.

As the French are seeking redress for the murder of their missionaries, (for account of which see Mr. Williams' despatch, No. 37*), it may be that those on board the *General Sherman* were by the Coreans confounded with them; this seems the more probable, inasmuch as the crew of the *Sherman* were heavily armed. Recently an American crew under Captain McCaslin, (see Mr. Williams' despatch, No. 44**), wrecked in Corea, were treated with the utmost kindness. My colleagues have written to their admirals, and I suppose in the spring there will be a large fleet in Corea. The issue of all will be the opening of the country. If my advice can have weight, it will be that our presence there should rather restrain than promote aggression, and serve to limit action to such satisfaction only as great and civilized nations should, under the circumstances, have from the ignorant and the weak.

---

*제1권 90번 문서.
**제1권 21번 문서.

You have seen from my despatch, No. 122*, what passions are aroused and to what their indulgence would lead. I am informed that the French government does not contemplate an expedition against Corea, but after the virtual repulse of Admiral Rose it will be impossible to avoid it.

I have the honor to be, sir, your obedient servant,
ANSON BURLINGAME

Hon. WILLIAM H. SEWARD,
Secretary of State, Washington, D. C.

Enclosure A

Mr. Sandford to Mr. Burlingame

UNITED STATES CONSULATE,
Cheefoo, October 30, 1866

Sir:

I have the honor to inform you that the French fleet returned from Corea, October 3, and on the 4th it was reported here that the American schooner *General Sherman* had been wrecked, and all on board murdered by the natives. I immediately wrote to the admiral, requesting him to furnish me with what information he could, to which he replied:

"In reply to the letter which you have done me the honor of writing, I can do no better than send you the exact copy of a note that was sent me by Rev. P. Ridel, apostolic missionary: 'On the 30th of September we were at anchor near Woody island, on the coast of Corea. During the night a Corean boat, with two natives on board, approached the Déroulède. Having recognized in one of them one of the sailors who had accompanied me in the spring on the voyage from Corea to Cheefoo, I succeeded in inducing them to come on board. Among other information, they told me that about the middle of the 7th moon, (about the end of the month of August,) a small vessel from the country of the West

*제1권 169번 문서.

had appeared on the coast of Corea, in the province of Phienganso, which is in the extreme northwest of the kingdom. She was endeavoring to ascend the river and to reach the city of Phiengiang, capital of this province, and had already arrived almost off this city, when she grounded on a sand-bank. The King's father replied, to burn the vessel and all on board. This barbarous order was executed.' Such, sir, is the only information bearing at all upon the matters to which you allude, that has reached me."

The *General Sherman* left here on the 9th of August; she called for water; took Mr. George Hogarth (British subject) as supercargo, and Rev. Mr. Thomas (British) as interpreter. The owner, W. B. Preston, (American) also went with them. - Page, captain, - Wilson, chief mate, (both Americans). The crew consisted of from 15 to 20, (Malays and Chinse). Cargo, cotton goods, glass, tin plates, &c, &c. On October 7th, two Chinese junks arrived from Corea and made the following reports respecting the wreck and burning of a foreign schooner, viz: The captain of one of them was engaged by Mr. Thomas to pilot the schooner up the river Ping Yangso, as he was acquainted with him previously; he yielded, and took her up four tides. By this time the alarm had spread amongst the natives, they taking her for a pirate, and would not believe the pilot when he told them she was a peaceful trader. (The *General Sherman* was heavily armed). All trade was stopped, and the natives began to collect in large numbers, when his friends on board the junk becoming alarmed, refused to allow him to go any further, saying that if he was killed, they would have no face to return to Yeutai. He, therefore, left them opposite to Little Ping Yangso, about halfway up the river. They were still determined to proceed; this was about the middle of the 8th moon. You will notice here a disagreement between about the dates given by the French missionary and this man. However, the other junk, it seems, did not reach Corea. On its nearing the coast, a junk put off, and warned them not to go in, as a foreign vessel had been wrecked opposite Ping Yangso, and the vessel, with all hands, burnt, on which the junk returned to Yeutai.

On the night of the 27th instant, the two French missionaries, who had been concealed in the mountains in Corea, reached this place. They state that a foreign vessel was wrecked opposite Ping Yangso; after some fighting between the natives and those on board the schooner, the natives succeeded by strategy in drawing the men on shore, when they were surrounded, and their hands tied behind their backs. They were then made to kneel down on the shore, and were decapitated. The missionaries report there were 20 thus put to death.

I have the honor to be, very respectfully, your obedient servant,

E. SANDFORD
United States Consul

Hon. ANSON BURLINGAME,
Minister of the United States, Peking.

Enclosure B

Messrs. Meadows & Co. to Mr. Burlingame

TIENTSIN, October 27, 1866

Sir:

We, the undersigned British firm, beg leave to bring to your excellency's notice the following circumstances, in order to obtain your excellency's assistance in getting redress.

During the latter half of July last the American schooner *General Sherman* arrived at this port, and was consigned to our care by Mr. Preston, the owner, who had come passenger on the vessel for the sake of his health. After we had taken delivery of the inward cargo, Mr. Preston and we came to an arrangement that we should load her with a cargo of foreign merchandise, and despatch her to Corea with a supercargo to sell the goods there. We accordingly loaded her with foreign merchandise, and on the 29th of July last she left Tientsin. Mr. Hogarth, one of our clerks, who went as supercargo, left previously in the steamer Shaftesbury for Cheefoo, in order to have a pilot and shroff ready on the *General Sherman* arriving there, and thus save delay. On the schooner reaching Cheefoo, Mr. Hogarth, accompanied by a Chinese pilot and a Cantonese shroff belonging to our firm, went on board; also Mr. Thomas, who having expressed a wish to visit Corea again, in order to extend his knowledge of the Corean language, went as passenger from the day the vessel left Cheefoo till now we have received no written advices from Mr. Hogarth or Mr. Preston, or, in fact, from any one on board when she left Cheefoo.

On the 8th of October current we received letters from the partners of our firm in Cheefoo acquainting us that the French admiral's vessel had come to Cheefoo, from Corea, with the news that the King of Corea had caused the *General Sherman* to be burnt with all on board, while proceeding up the Ping Yang river.

We immediately addressed Dr. Williams on the subject copy of our letter herewith enclosed.

On the 20th of October current we received further advices from our partner in Cheefoo, informing us that he had seen a junk captain who had piloted the schooner for four tides up the Ping Yang river, when he left her and returned to the mouth of the river to his junk, and finally to Cheefoo. This man stated that the Coreans had told him their king was opposed to foreign intercourse with his country. We imagine that this man, who understands something of the Corean language, knows something more about the vessel than he is inclined to divulge, fearing, Chinese-like, to mix himself up in the matter with the authorities to question him later on the points.

As the act of visiting Corea for the purposes of trade was not an act which could, in the eyes of civilized western nations, justify the Corean government in destroying those who committed it, we, the undersigned, have taken the liberty of addressing you for the purpose of bringing the above matters to your excellency's notice, with the request that you will be pleased to beg his excellency Admiral Bell to make inquiries regarding the destruction of the vessel and her people, and take steps to cause the Corean government to make redress as far as such in the nature of things is practicable.

We have the honor to be, sir, your excellency's most obedient servants,

MEADOWS & CO.

Hon. ANSON BURLINGAME,
United States Minister Plenipotentiary.

P. S.

We beg to enclose copy of our letter to H. B. M.'s consul, Mr. Mongan, on the loss of the *General Sherman*, and requesting the British admiral's assistance in the matter, Mr. Hogarth and Mr. Thomas being both British subjects.

M. & CO.

Enclosure C

Mr. Burlingame to Admiral Bell

PEKING, November 27, 1866

Sir:

I find that the Chinese government disavows any responsibility for that of Corea, and all jurisdiction over its people.

Consequently the occurrences there relating to the *General Sherman* are beyond my jurisdiction. It may, however, strengthen your hands to receive a suggestion from me, that if consistent with your instructions, it may be well to send a vessel of war to inquire into the facts of the case, to the end that they may be reported to the government for its instructions. Having great confidence in your discretion, I leave the matter in your hands, where it properly belongs.

I have the honor to be, sir, your obedient servant,
ANSON BURLINGAME

H. H. BELL,
Acting Rear-Admiral Commanding
U. S. Asiatic Squadron

H. H. Bell (1866. 12. 27) → G. Welles

미국의 단독 조선 침공 건의 및 거문도의 지정학적 중요성 보고

U. S. Flag Ship *Hartford*(2nd Rate)
Hong Kong China
December 27, 1866

Hon. Gideon Welles
Secretary of the Navy
Washington D. C.

Sir:

In connection with my Despatch No 63* of December 14th, 1866, marked confidential, a duplicate of which is herewith enclosed, I have the honor to transmit to the Department for its information the following Documents;

1st: An Extract marked A, from a communication received yesterday, from Captain I.P. Bankhead, commanding U.S.S. *Wyoming* dated Nagasaki December 6th, 1866.

2nd: A copy, marked B, of a letter likewise received yesterday from our Consul at Chifu, from Mr. E. J. Sandford, addressed to Consul General Seward at Shanghai which was forwarded to me by that efficient officer:

3rd: A copy, marked C, of a letter from the Honorable Anson Burlingame, U.S. Minister at Peking, informing me that Corea is outside of his diplomatic boundaries.

4th: Extracts, marked D, from Shanghai newspapers, transmitted to me by Consul General Seward.

The enclosure from Captain Bankhead, and that from our Consul at Chifu, give more exact information, than any yet received, and I am glad to observe, that my own opinion, as expressed in my Despatch No. 63, as to the propriety of attacking the Coreans, by moving a land force upon the Capital Seoul, is sustained by that of the French Admiral.

*제1권 26번 문서.

The situation of Ping-Yang, (or Phieniang), the name of the river and the capital of the Province, is now ascertained; the letter of the diplomacy, the Rev. C. Ridel, quoted by the Consul at Chifu, describing it, as being in the extreme N.W. of Corea, and I also find it on an English atlas, while the river Seoul, the scene of the French operations, is about the middle of the Corea.

The number of the people of the *General Sherman* having been committed, we are led to believe, by the Order of the Regent of Corea; the Capital Seoul, is in my opinion, the proper place to seek redress, and if the Government should consider this a proper occasion for the exercise of force, I take the liberty of saying that this can be more honorably and efficiently done by the United States single-handed, than by any combined movement made with England or France. This would cause the power of the United States to be felt in the East, and the prestige attending the prompt redress of this outrage upon our citizens, would have a great effect, in both China and Japan, where the influence and power of the United States is constantly and systematically disparaged to the natives by the European press and people in these parts.

Considering the resistance which the French encountered, I do not regard the force, at present, under any command, sufficient for any decisive operations, against the Coreans. I therefore repeat my opinion that a land force of about two thousand men is necessary for success, as none of the vessels under my command can ascend these rivers.

The squadron should be supplied with six steam launches, drawing not over four feet; and armed with a rifled howitzer.

If these cannot be promptly sent from California, it is probable that suitable craft may be secured upon this coast.

Port Hamilton referred to, in my Despatch No. 63, is formed by a cluster of three small islands, standing alone, about thirty-five miles from the large island "Quelpart," while Chrichton Harbor is formed by a larger cluster of islands, and more convenient to "Quelpart." Vegetables and bullocks may be supplied from the last named island in sufficient abundance. The position of these harbors is somewhat commanding; and I have little doubt that either one of them would afford the squadron a desirable sanitarium easily obtained at the present time, and whence a profitable traffic might be established with the Coreans themselves.

The *Wachusett* Commander Shufeldt, having completed her repairs in dock, is now nearly ready for sea; at this port she will sail on the 29th of this month for Chifu to obtain in formation with regard to the *General Sherman*, from thence she will proceed to Chien-yang (if not shut out by the ice) to ascertain the fate of the unfortunate persons on board the *General Sherman*, and to demand that the survivors (if there are any) be delivered on board the *Wachusett*.

I have the honor to be, Sir
Very respectfully
Your obedient servant
H.H. Bell
Rear Admiral
Commanding U.S. Asiatic Squadron

29

H. H. Bell (1866. 12. 27) ➞ R. W. Shufeldt

제너럴 셔먼호 사건 경과 전달

U.S. Flag Ship *Hartford*
Hong Kong China
December 27, 1866

Commander R.W. Shufeldt
Commanding U.S.S. Wachussett

Sir:

As soon as the Wachussett under your command is ready for sea, proceed in her to Chifu, and there inquire into the fact and the circumstances of the loss of the American Schooner *General Sherman* in the Corea, and of the murder of the people who were on board of her, namely Mr. Preston (owner), Mr. Page (master) Americans, Mr. Wilson (mate) naturalized American, two Portuguese or Malays, and Chinamen for crew, also Mr. Hogarth supercargo, and Mr. Thomas (missionary) both British subjects and a Chinese Schroff belonging to the latter party. Reports having come from Chifu that the *General Sherman* was loaded at that port some time in last summer by Meadows and Co a British house at Tientsin and dispatched to Corea to trade; that the schooner has not been heard from since the day of her departure except from rumors circulated by the French after their return to Chifu from the Corea in October last, in effect that the Gerneral *Sherman* had been wrecked and all her people murdered. Subsequently Mr. Mackie belonging to the branch house at Chifu of Messers Meadows had an interview with a junk Captain belonging to Shantung, who made three or four voyages a year to the Corea, and who stated that he saw the *General Sherman* in the Corea last summer, and having before known Mr. Thomas the missionary, went on board of the *General Sherman* and piloted her four tides up the Ping Yang River, but finding the natives hostile to the people on board the Schooner, he left her. This is the only authentic information yet received of the Schooner, and it is the only reference to the place of her misfortune.

The Mouth of the Ping Yang or Phiang-iang River is situated in about

Lat 38° N, Long 125° E, on the Northwestern Coast of Corea; ascertain, its approaches, depth of water, rise and fall of tide, at what season it is navigable, and what are its defences. The China Pilot referred to knows doubtless more of the fate of the unhappy people of the *General Sherman* than he has revealed. More exact information could be obtained from him if he could be found; and his services should be secured. French officers if you meet any may give some reliable information.

Having obtained all information in your power at Chifu of the locality of the disaster to the *General Sherman*, proceed to the Phiang-iang River with a Pilot and an Interpreter, rating them both as Pilots and demand of the Chief Authorities the delivery to you on the deck of the Wachussett of such of the unfortunate men of the Schooner *General Sherman*, as may have been spared, whether they be American, British Portuguese, Malays, or Chinamen, and make such further investigation of the case as may be practicable.

Having performed this service proceed to Port Hamilton, and examine into its advantages or capabilities.

From Port Hamilton proceed to Shanghai, and report to me in writing, from there, the result of your investigations.

From Shanghai you will visit Ningpo and the open ports on the Yangtze, (if the water in the river be favorable) for the encouragement and protection of American citizens and interests, giving special attention to the suppression of piracy as per General Order Number Sixteen dated September 11 1866. Shanghai will be regarded as your headquarters.

Please keep me informed of your proceedings after you return to this coast.

If you hear anything new about the loss of the *General Sherman* before going to the Corea, please inform me of it. I am anxious to receive your report as soon as possible in order to communicate it to the Navy Department.

The regular mail being more reliable you will when opportunities offer, send your dispatches by them instead of by private hands.

I am, Sir,
Very respectfully
H.H. Bell
Rear Admiral
Commanding U.S. Asiatic Squadron

While at Chifu you will inquire into the treatment of American missionaries at Tang-Chow, and give to our countrymen and to American interests such protection as may be necessary.

H.H. Bell
Rear Admiral
Commanding U.S. Asiatic Squadron

E. Sandford (1866. 12. 31) ➞ W. H. Seward

제너럴 셔먼호 사건 경과 보고

U.S. Consulate
December 31, 1866

Honble William H Seward
Secretary of State
Washington DC

Sir:

I have the honor to transit my report for the quarter ending December 31 1866. The principal case which has transpired is the case of the American Schooner *General Sherman*.

The French fleet returned from Corea Oct. 3rd, and on the 4th it was reported here, that the American Schooner *General Sherman* had been wrecked on the coast of Corea, and all on board murdered by the natives. I immediately wrote to the Admiral requesting him to furnish me with what information he could, to which he replied as follow.

"In reply to the letter which you have done me the honor of writing, I can do no better, than send you the exact copy of a note that was sent to me by Rev. P. Ridel "Apostolic Missionary." On the 30th of September we were at anchor near Woody Island on the coast of Corea. During the night a Corean boat with two natives on board approached the Déroulède. Having recognized in one of them, one of the Sailors who had accompanied me in the spring, on the voyage from Corea to Cheefoo, I succeeded in inducing them to come on board. Among other informations they told me that about the middle of the 7th moon (about the end of the month of August) a small vessel from the country of the West had appeared on the coast of Corea, in the province of Chiengan-do, which is in the extreme Northwest of the Kingdom.

She was endeavoring to ascend the river and to reach the city of Phiang-iang, capital of this province, and had already arrived almost off this city, when she grounded on a sand bank. The Governor at once sent to the King's father for instructions whether he should put to death those on board, or should burn them and the vessel together. The King's father replied to burn the vessel and all on board. This barbarous order was "executed." Such, Sir, is the only information bearing at all upon the matters to which you allude that has reached me."

The *General Sherman* was chartered by Mess. Meadows & C. of Tientsin, and left here on 9th August ostensibly for Passiett. She called for water, took Mr. George Hogarth as Supercargo, and Rev. Mr. Thomas as interpreter, both of whom were British subjects. The owner, W.B. Preston, Page Captain, Wilson Chief Mate, were Americans. The crew consisted of from 15 to 20 Malays and Chinese, Cargo Cotton Goods, Glass Tin Plates &ca&ca. On October 7th two Chinese junks arrived from Corea, and made the following report, respecting the wreck and burning of a Foreign Schooner viz:

The Captain of one of them was engaged by Mr. Thomas, to pilot the Schooner up the river Ping Yang, so as he was acquainted with him previously, he yielded and took her up four tides. By this time the alarm had spread amongst the natives, they taking her for a Pirate, and would not believe the Pilot, when he told them she was a peaceful trader. (The *General Sherman* was heavily armed) All trade was stopped by order of the Governor, and the natives began to collect in large numbers, when the friends of the Pilot on board the Junk, becoming alarmed, refused to allow him to go any further, saying, if he was killed they would have no face to return to Yentai; he therefore left them opposite to little Ping-yang-so about halfway up the river. They were still determined to proceed up, this was about the middle of the 8th moon. You will notice here a disagreement between the date given by the French Missionary and this man. However, the other Junk it seems did not reach Corea, on its nearing the coast, a Junk put off, and warned them not to go in, as a Foreign Vessel had been wrecked opposite to Ping-Yang-So, and the Vessel with all hands burnt, on which the Junk returned to Yentai. On the night of the 27th instant, the two French Missionaries who had been concealed in the mountains in Corea, reached this place. They state that a Foreign vessel was wrecked opposite Ping-Yang-so; after some fighting between the natives and those on board the Schooner, the natives succeeded by strategy in drawing the men on shore, when they were surrounded, and their hands tied behind their backs. They were then made to kneel down on the shore, and were beheaded. The Missionaries report they were 20, thus put to death.

Inquiry now arises, what has been done with the rest. Mr. Moore informed me, that the crew consisted of nearly 20, while there were in addition 5

Europeans besides their Servants. It may be that the Coreans instead of putting them to death kept them prisoner thinking that they might be enabled to use them in some way, on arrival of the French forces.

A speech made by Dr. McGowan in San Francisco, is one which I feel well merits the attention of the Government, he says "The Government of the United States should follow the example of other great powers and establish at the earliest possible moment naval station on the Coast of China & Japan. In the event of a War between the United States and other Maritime Power, one of the most important points wherein the commerce of that power could be seriously annoyed will be the Indian Ocean and China Seas, but to do this a powerful squadron have to be employed, and this could not be done, if we possess no base of supplies nearer than our nearest home port, which port would be San Francisco, had we however a Naval Station, a depot of Stores and munitions of war, a port whereat our vessels could be refitted and repaired, without the necessity of returning to the distant coast of the United States, we could maintain a fleet on those waters that would harass and annoy the enemy constantly. Even as a peace establishment its importance and great economy would be manifest to everyone. If located far enough North, the port will answer admirably, wherein to give the Crews liberty, and enable them to recruit strength & health after an extensive cruise in the tropics. Of course, a hospital will form a portion of the establishment. Again, if the Vessels commissions had expired, or the time had arrived to relieve the Officers and Crew instead of the Vessel going home, and another coming to take her place, she could be overhauled and refitted, and a new set of Officers and crew could be sent out, thus avoiding the heavy expense of taking the Vessel from the Station."

The French and English have a Naval Station here on the Island at the mouth of the Harbor, but the best position has been left unoccupied by them, I feel fully convinced that Cheefoo offers many inducements to Naval powers desiring to establish a Naval depot in the north. It is accessible all the year, in constant Steam communication with the South, near to Japan & Pekin, the climate is regarded as superior to any of the other ports in China, while provisions can be obtained at a moderate price.

Dr. McGowan's remarks regarding consuls are also worthy of attention. I am sorry to admit that our Consular service is a disgrace to American name. Many who come out are proficient (if common report is to be believed) in tipping the bottle, at least none of them know anything about the language, nor do they attempt to learn it, in many of the ports, they have no time, even if anxious to do so, consequently in their interviews with the Authorities, where no Interpreter is allowed, they are dependent upon the kindness of the same of the Missionaries, also are obliged to depend upon them for translating documents into Chinese, as there is not one Missionary out often, who is up in official language; it is easy to imagine how the letter causes our officials and country to sink in the estimation of the Chinese, our influence is lessened if not wholly destroyed.

Again, if the Consul is engaged in business, he is frequently brought into collision with the Authorities, moreover he depends upon his Compradore to write his Communications to the Chinese Authorities.

I am fully convinced, that there can be no hope of any improvement, until they adopt a plan similar to the English, thus if a young man should be sent out as student interpreter he then fills respectfully the position of interpreter Consul & Vice Consul.

All Vice Consuls & Consuls to be taken from this class, and hold their appointments for life, unless they prove themselves unworthy. A man who has risen to the position of Vice Consul or Consul, would be fitted to act either in China, Corea, or Japan, for while the spoken languages of Corea and Japan differ from the Chinese, yet their official communications are written in Chinese characters. At present Trade is falling off owing to the approach of the Chinese New Year, the prospect of the American Trade next year is good.

I have the honor to be
Sir
Your most obedient Servant
Sandford
U.S. Consul

H. H. Bell (1866. 12. 31) ➞ R. W. Shufeldt

조선 해안 항해시 유의사항 전달

U.S.S. Flag Ship *Hartford*
Hong Kong, China
Dec. 31 1866

Commander R.W. Shufeldt
Commanding U.S.S. *Wachusett*
Shanghai

Sir:

The charts of the West and Northwest coast of Corea being very imperfect, you will be very careful in taking and [recording] soundings as you approach that coast; and also determine the positions in Latitude and Longitude of the entrance of the River Phing-iang and of the Islands in the way, also of as much of the coast line as may come under your observation.

Report upon the same upon your return to Shanghai furnishing me with a diagram or chart embracing all these points. I trust you will not remain longer in Shanghai than is necessary for coaling.

Very respectfully
H.H. Bell
Rear Admiral
Commanding U.S. Asiatic Squadron

Don't forget your Quarter Gunner left in hospital at Shanghai last August.

H.H.B.

R. W. Shufeldt (1867. 1. 8) ➞ H. H. Bell

제너럴 셔먼호 관련 정보 수집 보고

U.S.S. *Wachusett*
Shanghai, Jan. 8, 1867

To R. Admiral H.H. Bell

My Dear Sir:

Since our arrival here, I have been actively engaged in pursuit of "Korean" information.

First, I have seen Capt. Bochet of H.I.M.S. *Primaguet*, which vessel you will remember formed part of the French expedition in that country.

His information in regard to the *Genl. Sherman* seemed to me to be very vague. He supposes that she went up the river "Tai ling Kong" in about the lat. of 88° 10' N. The reasons why she went up this river, as the Missionaries gave them to him, were that the country to the Nth & Wst is all a desert and would offer no inducements for trade.

Second, Capt. Haswell of H.R.M.S. *Pelonis*, when at "Chefoo" saw the Pilot referred to in this matter, and he (the Pilot) stated that the schooner ascended the river "Yalu Kiang." This corresponds with the impressions of Mr. Knight our Consul at "Nienchwang" now here, who informs me that Messrs. Meadows & Co. the charterers of the *Genl. Sherman*, had spoken to him of their desire to explore that river.

Third, I find that among others, the British Steamer "Emperor" has been to the Korea, and ascended the river "Kian Kang," lat. 37° 30′ N. Long. 128° 53′ W. Messrs. Jardine, Matherson & les her owners very kindly gave me a chart of the river, and today I am going to see a Mr. Oppert, who went in the Steamer on this voyage.

Fourth. The American Schooner *Surprise*, Capt. McCaslin, was wrecked in June last while attempting to enter a river in about lat. 39° 18′ N. Long. 128° [36′] West and this Capt. whom I have seen here thinks that the *Genl. Sherman* was attempting to ascend this river, from the fact that he had talked with Capt. Preston of his project of carrying arms into the "Korea" from this point.

Capt. McCaslin, with his crew of eight men, after landing from the wreck of the *Surprise*, was taken charge of by the Korean Authorities and was in their hands for 43 days and transported on horseback to the "Korean Gate," there turned over to the Chinese Officials, and finally found his way here &c. He speaks warmly of the kindness and hospitality of the Korean Officers and people contrasting them very favorably with the subsequent conduct of the Chinese.

It will be remembered that this occurred only two or three months previous to the affair of the *Genl. Sherman* and hence it might be inferred that owing to the lateness of the season, the crew of the *Genl. Sherman* might yet be "en route" to China, and not heard of at the "Korean Gate." The only reason to suppose that their treatment would be different from that received by the men of the other vessel is the course of subsequent events with reference to the French, which may have involved all foreigners at that time in the Country.

Fifth. All of the foregoing persons, whom I have seen unite in saying that this coast is too much unknown and of too dangerous a character where it is comparatively known, to approach in midwinter, added to the fact that even if the coast could be reached, the rivers which are the principal means of communication with the interior would unquestionably be found frozen up.

Conclusions. With all due allowance for hastily formed opinions, and imperfect knowledge, it occurs to me, that if we went to "Khangoa" in order to communicate with the "Korean" Govt. we should identify ourselves or rather be identified with the French, and received from the first in a hostile manner.

If we do not go to "Khangoa," where can we go? There are five rivers, each of which has its advocates, and each of which at this season it is dangerous to approach. My impressions at present, is that were I to act upon my own judgement, I should go to the harbor of "Chosan," and there communicate with the authorities of Korea, thanking them first, as I think we are in duty bound, for their kindness to the crew of the Am. Schr. *Surprise*, wrecked upon their coast while unlawfully engaged in a contraband voyage, and then enquiring and asking for the crew of the *Genl. Sherman*, which until we get more knowledge we might suppose to be still alive and in the Country. Any subsequent proceeding would not be prejudiced by such a course, and in the meanwhile we might avoid a serious difficulty.

Chosan harbor I am told is accessible at all seasons, and from its importance in connection with the Japanese trade, has I have no doubt constant communication with the capital of Korea.

Knowing that you feel an immediate interest in everything pertaining to this matter, I have hastily for today's mail jotted down these impressions, simply as the result of investigations at this port, and I regret that you were not in possession of more definite information before giving me my orders but if in the future I shall diverge from these orders I trust that you will consider the mist in which this whole thing has been involved and the absolute necessity for the exercise of individual judgement when removed so far from superior authority.

We finish coaling tomorrow or next day and then sail at once for Chefoo. The weather here has been very boisterous, so as to render work until today almost impossible. Our Starboard boiler has given trouble from leaks &c. but will be in good order this eve.

Your letter of Dec. 31st has just reached me. The Qr. Gunner referred to rejoined this Ship at Hong Kong.

Very Respectfully
(Signed) R.W. Shufeldt
Commander
Comdg. U.S.S. *Wachusett*

R. W. Shufeldt, Ridel (1867. 1. 9)

Shufeldt와 Ridel 신부의 대화 기록

Memorandum of an interview between Comdr. R.W. Shufeldt of the U.S.S. Wachusett and Father Rydell and another Missionary of the Roman Catholic Church, both of whom were in Korea at the time of the disaster of the General Sherman.

Also questions put to the Korean who piloted the French expedition to "Ile Boisée"&c.

Question to Father Rydell. "Were you in the Korea at the time of the disaster to the *Genl. Sherman*?"

Answer. "We were."

Question. "Are you sure that the crew of the *Genl. Sherman* were murdered? And why?"

Answer. "I am sure that they were murdered because it was the uniform report of the inhabitants of the surrounding country."

Question. "Are you equally sure of the locality of the disaster?"

Answer. "I am, it was in the Tai-Tong Kang river in the province of Ping-An-To. The Korean chart was here produced showing that the river rises in the North and centre of Korea, and running in a S. Westerly direction, empties into the Yellow Sea about 120 miles Nth & Wst from "Saoul" or "Kan-gi-tan" the capital of the country."

Question. "Are these rivers frozen up at this season of the year?"

Answer. "The Saoul river is probably open at its mouth, but frozen at the capital."

Question. "Do you think it possible or probably that a pilot could be procured to take the vessel to the anchorage at "Ile Boisée"?"

Answer. "I do not think it possible under the circumstances, as the natives would all run away, or if taken by force would be beheaded with all of their families, on your departure."

Question. "Is it possible to have communication from the harbor of "Chosan" with the Govt. of Korea?"

Answer. "There is a highway between "Chosan" and the capital, and you could have communication, no doubt, provided you could get anyone to carry the dispatch, the distance is about 70 leagues."

Questions to the Korean pilot through Father Rydell acting as interpreter.

Question. "Is there a good anchorage at the "Ile Boisée" at this season of the year?"

Answer. "Yes, if you have a pilot to take you there."

Question. "How is the weather on the Korean coast in the winter?"

Answer. "About the same as at Shanghai at present but very bad about a month or six weeks later."

Question. "Is it possible to anchor off the river "Tai Tong"?"

Answer. "There is no harbor, it is full of dangerous sand banks, and the river itself is frozen up to the Sea."

Question. "Could I get a pilot on the coast of Korea?"

Answer. "There are plenty of pilots, but they would all run away from the sight of a vessel."

Remark 1. The *Genl. Sherman*, I have ascertained in Shanghai, was a centerboard vessel, drawing not more and probably less than 6 feet of water, and of about 80 tons burden.

Remark 2. I am satisfied from the intelligence of these priests and the appearance of the pilot, that the above information is substantially correct; and that the crew of the *Genl. Sherman* were murdered seems to be established, and in the river before mentioned (the Tai Tong). Also that it is very inadvisable to attempt to reach the mouth of the "Tai Tong" river at this season of the year; and improbably that any communication could be held with the Korean Government at the point of the French operations. Chosan, in view of season of the year, the late operations of the French, and its accessibility in the winter, seems to present the most feasible point for communication with the Korean Government on the subject of the disaster to the *General Sherman*.

R.W. Shufeldt
Com.
Shanghai, China
Jan. 9th 1867

R. W. Shufeldt (1867. 1. 19) ➞ H. H. Bell

上海와 芝罘에서의 제너럴 셔먼호 사건 관련 정보 수집 보고

U.S.S. *Wachusett*
Chefoo, Jan. 19, 1867

Rear Admiral H.H. Bell
Comdg. U.S. Asiatic Squadron

Sir:

In compliance with your order of 27th December, to forward all information in the case of the Am. Schr. *Genl. Sherman* to you, before proceeding to Korea, I have the honor to submit the following brief abstract as the most reliable result of inquiry at Shanghai and at this port.

The *General Sherman* cleared from Tientsin for "Possiete" a Russian port on the N.E. boundary of Korea and Russian possessions. She touched at Chefoo, but at this port it was only indirectly understood that she was going to trade on the West coast of Korea. She did go however, leaving Chefoo on the 9th of August last, and entered the river "Tai tong" in the province of 'Ping Yang' for the purpose of ascending to the capital of that province called "Ping Yang so."

A reference to "Williams mark of China and Korea" which I have compared with a native Korean chart will show this river there called "Ta-ting" running through the Northwestern part of Korea in the province of Ping Yang, thus reconciling all discrepancy as to the point of disaster between the French Missionaries and the Chinese Pilot.

Without referring to an immaterial difference of date between the above authorities, the Schooner got on shore in the river sometime during the last week in August or the first week in September, and according to the French Missionaries, all of the persons on board amounting to 19 or 20 were beheaded by order of the Regent of Korea. According to the Chinese Pilot she had 27 persons on board, and they were murdered by a crowd of natives who were fully impressed, with the idea that the Schooner was a pirate, this impression gained ground and increased the mob the higher she ascended the river. The *Genl. Sherman* was a vessel of 80 tons armed with 2 twelve par. guns on broadside, and from the number of her crew, and her armament might easily have been mistaken by an excited, and ignorant populace. Be this as it may, the difference between the number reported by the French Missionaries to have been beheaded, and the number reported by the Pilot to have been on board, leaves the slight hope that the Americans and Europeans may have been spared, and are now held either in captivity or yet on the way to China delayed by the inclement season.

The Am. Schooner *Surprise* of Shanghai was wreaked on 23rd of June last, while endeavoring to enter the same river (as near as I can ascertain from the Captain) and the crew and officers were taken charge of by the Korean Officials and transferred at Govt. expense, for 43 days, to the "Korean Gate," then turned over to the Chinese Authorities. During this time they received kind treatment from both Korean officers and people.

The Am. Bark *Juan Raltray* bound to "Possiete" entered the port of Chosan, from stress of weather in Sept. last, and although the natives were anxious to have her leave, they manifested no unfriendliness.

It will be seen that these vessels were in Korea, the one before the other after the disaster to the *Genl. Sherman*, and the Raltray was actually in "Chosan" while the French were fighting at "Kang Wha."

These facts leave the impression that the murder of the crew of the *Sherman*, was done by the mob, for the reason stated by the Chinese Pilot, and not by order of the Govt. as reported by the Missionaries, and that the event ought not necessarily to be confounded with the massacre of the French priests and their converts.

Out of the mass of evidence that I have been able to collect from the French Naval Officers, the Missionaries survivors of the Korean massacre, from the Chinese Pilot, the last person known to have been on board the *Sherman*, and from the records of this Consulate, the foregoing seems to be all the points essential and reliable. But it may not be amiss to state that the Missionaries attribute the massacre of Christians in Korea to the encroachments of the Russians across the Northern border of that country. This encroachment, gradual but apparently inevitable, was the source of the greatest dread to the Korean Govt. and with it they had associated the progress of Christianity. The massacre occurred on Feby 6th 1866, included 2 Bishops, 9 Priests and all the native converts who would not apostatize.

The Korean Government is at present in the hands of a Regent, whose son a minor was adopted, by the Queen when she herself a widow married the present Regent, thus making his son the presumptive heir. The capital is at "Kangitao" called by the French "Seoul."

If the Chinese Government disclaims all control over Korea, then the voyage of the *Sherman* was not illegal, for she violated none of the treaty obligations with China, by endeavoring to enter the ports of an independent Government.

This fact, while it might have been unknown to the Capt and Charterers of the *Sherman*, deprives the voyage of the appearance of illegality, and gives to them a more lawful claim, upon the protection of their Government.

I am Sir
Very Respectfully
R.W. Shufeldt
Commander
Comdg. U.S.S. *Wachusett*

35

R. W. Shufeldt (1867. 1. 24) → 高宗

제너럴 셔먼호 생존자 송환 요구

U.S.S. *Wachusett*
Wachusett Bay
Near mouth of river Tai-tong
Jan. 24,1867

To His Majesty the King of Corea,

The Commander of the American Armed Vessel *Wachusett* begs to inform your Majesty that he has come to the border of your Kingdom, not to engage in war, nor any unlawful business, but in obedience to the command of the officer commanding the Armed Vessels of America stationed in these seas; who has heard with great pleasure and thankfulness of the kindness of your Majesty's officers and people to the shipwrecked crew of an American Vessel, in the month of June last, on the West coast of Corea. How your Majesty had them transported to the confines of China, from whence they safely reached their friends. The whole American people cannot but feel thankful and praise your nation for this act of kindness and brotherly love.

The Officer commanding the Armed Vessels of America has since heard with pain and surprise that the people of another American Vessel, wrecked in the Tai-tong river, in the province of Ping-Yang, in this month of September last, were all put to death and the vessel burned, and has ordered me to ask of your Majesty if this report is true, and, if true, to ask of your Majesty what evil these people had done, that they should be made to suffer such cruel treatment.

But if any or all of these people are living, the Officer commanding the Armed Vessels of America has directed me to ask of your Majesty that they may be delivered to me, on board the *Wachusett*, now lying in the Harbour of Ta-Fung, near the [Neu-to] islands, or at any more convenient port your Majesty may select.

This is especially desired, that the peace and friendship, which has hitherto been uninterrupted for many years, may still continue between America and Corea.

A speedy answer is requested to this communication, in order that I may depart in peace.

(Signed) R. W. Shufeldt
Comdg. American Armed Vessel *Wachusett*

R. W. Shufeldt(1867. 1. 25)

제너럴 셔먼호 사후 처리 관련 Shufeldt의 견해

U.S.S. *Wachusett*
Wachusett Bay
Mouth of Tai-tong river Corea
Jan. 25, 1867

Coreans report abundance of gold in the mountains.
"Chang-Yuen" is 30 miles from the sea.
"Ping Yang" will not be clear of ice for two months

This ship cannot ascend more than halfway to "Ping-Yang-so" at any time. You carry 5 fathoms at low water over the bar, and about that water 30 miles up. The pilot has been no farther. The town of "Ping-Yang-so" is the only one of importance on the river. Rise of the tide about 18 feet.

The people here (Ta-tong) all say that the crew of the *General Sherman* were all murdered by the people on the river, and not by order of the Mandarin.

The Coreans report that the Chinese descend upon this coast in junks, and rob the inhabitants. Last year six young men were killed by these plunderers, on the island of ["Now-ts"], opposite our present anchorage.

The head men of two villages have stated that the *General Sherman* was burned in the "Ping Yang" river, in the month of September last, and the officers and crew consisting of 27 persons were murdered by the people, and not by order of the Mandarins. This fact, they state, is known all through Corea.

The gold reported is said to be abundant in the mountains South of "Ta-tong," on the coast, and is found among the rocks; but the Natives have no tools, by which it can be extracted.

The "Ping Yang" river is reported by the Natives as inaccessible at this season of the year, on account of ice, and cannot be entered till about the 1st of April.

The city of "Hae-Chow-Poo" is 50 miles up the Tai-tong river. It is the district city of this province, and is said to be quite a large town.

The Coreans say that ten of the crew of the *Sherman* were Canton Chinamen, and that these people have been in the habit, for years, of coming to this coast to rob & plunder, [to] the great dread of the whole [seaboard]. This is confirmed by our pilot.

Mr. Hogarth, an English subject on board of the *Sherman*, was known throughout China for his reckless character, and his acquaintances suppose that if riot occurred, he would be very likely to be one of the means of causing it.

The *Wachusett* is the first foreign vessel of any description that ever anchored on that part of the Corean coast.

The people of Corea are no doubt primarily responsible for the *Sherman* affair, but they have an excuse in the fact that that whole West coast is annually the scene of depredations and robbery on the part of the Chinese – particularly Canton men – ten of whom were on board the *Sherman*. Our pilot says that, failing to purchase his Corean ponies, the Captain of the *Sherman* had determined – Chinese fashion – to steal them on his return down the river. But the Govt. of Corea will sooner or later have the lesson taught to other Eastern nations that it can no longer maintain that contemptuous exclusiveness, which disdains all explanation or responsibility for its own acts or those of its people.

Signed R.W.S.

37

朴承輝(1867. 1. 27/高宗三年十二月二十二日) ➞ 議政府(1867. 2. 1/高宗三年十二月二十七日)

와츄세트호 출현 및 투서(投書) 보고

一即刻呈長淵縣監韓致容本月二十日辰時成貼馳報內當日辰時量本縣大曲坊陸島洞首羅化兼来告內〇〇〇〇〇〇〇㨾挾船一隻自月乃島来泊本浦而所来人物三十九〇〇〇下陸執捉居民等以一封書而授之曰持此書納于本〇〇〇以来之意萬端威脅故不得已受来此書是如現納是乎旀〇次陸島洞民任允恊未告內以為異㨾挾船授其書封後旋徃月乃島矣居無何異㨾三竹船一隻従其挾船而来碇留於本浦前洋是如故同書封玆以監封上使為乎旀洋船之尚此出沒聞極驚駭為先追逐次縣監多率軍校砲手等登時發行于該浦為乎旀緣由牒報是如為白乎旀鱗次呈水軍節度使鄭志鉉本月二十日戌時成貼謄報內即刻呈吾乂浦僉使丁大薰本月十八日戌時成貼馳報內本鎮西山浦瞭望将李啓得進告內當日申時量異㨾三竹船一隻自西海遠遠外洋泛泛中流而来至薄暮到本鎮前洋水路二十里許月乃島南邊近洋而島山中隔去留形止果未詳察是如為卧乎所僉使聞不勝驚駭即徃浦邊是乎則日已昏黒去留未能瞭察故別定将吏詳察以来次馳送月乃島為乎旀待還来去留形止鱗次馳報伏計是如牒呈為白有旀一時呈地方官長淵縣監韓致容本月十九日巳時成貼馳報內辭緣與該僉使所報同然是白置有亦當此冬節異船去来聞極驚駭去留形止詳探次臣營帶率軍官出身柳桂昇急急定送于吾乂鎮月乃島為白乎旀鱗次呈白翎僉使任景模本月十八日未時成貼馳報內當日午時量頭毛津瞭望将白海玉馳告內異㨾三竹船一隻自西海外洋過去本鎮及吾乂月乃島之中洋是如故聞甚驚惶僉使即率追捕軍人等登高望見則三竹異㨾船一隻或起烟火其疾如飛即向吾乂月乃島近洋海〇爲五六十〇〇〇〇〇體長廣未能的知其在邊情極涉惶悚即為嚴飭瞭察是〇〇白乎所今此白翎鎮過去三竹異㨾船果是吾乂月乃島〇〇者是白乎等以更待瞭察随現馳報之意措辭題飭為白乎旀同異㨾船去留形止待該邑鎮更報連續馳 啓計料事狀啓 謄報是如為等如牒呈是白置有亦當此風高之時異船之闖人內洋已是可駭分叱除良書封之肆然投去尤極而自該縣無嚴不能據理退去既為上使故原本姑留臣營以待問情時還投計料而另以別紙依見㨾謄書上送于議政府為白乎旀水使狀啓謄報中彼人之書封一欵初不舉論者事涉〇忽而水使謄報則今二十日戌時成貼者也長淵縣監所報則乃是二十日辰時成貼者也異船形止先為馳報水營而書封投進之事

未及修報是白加隱喻參互日時反程途事勢似然是白遣彼船既曰碇留則問情一款不可晷刻遲滯乙仍于臣營帶率軍官出身張昌薰登時乫送與水營譯學趙廷孝眼同舉行之意星火題飭于水使鄭志鉉處是白遣沿海各邑鎮瞭察防守之節一體嚴飭為白乎旀嗣後形止連續登　聞計料緣由并以馳　啓為白卧乎事　丙寅十二月二十二日卯時封

朴承輝(1867. 1. 28/高宗三年十二月二十三日) ➡ 議政府

와츄세트호의 동태 및 경계 상황 보고

一今十二月十九日長淵縣月乃島来泊異船書封投去緣由纔已馳　啓為白有在果即刻呈長淵縣監韓致容本月二十一日辰時成貼牒報内縣監發行陸島緣由已為牒報為有在果昨日戌時量始到牧洞浦而自此距陸島不過三帿之地也仍宿本浦今日平朝詳細探察是乎則果是三竹異㨾船碇留於陸島前洋而長可為四十餘把許矣所乘人物俱在船中一不現形問情不得追逐無奈聞其島民所告則○○○○○○○封受荅以来自可退去而若為遅緩浦底居民盡爲○○○○無數恐喝是如是乎旀昨日午時量縱渠挾船尺水於○○○味浦苔灘浦及瓮津地馬蛤等浦是如是乎所縣監○○○○排立軍校武士砲手等觀其動静期於猛逐伏計為乎於稍近邑良中直發關文捉送砲手等以為防守之地是○○○○○鱗次呈該縣監韓致容本月二十一日戌時成貼牒報内○進各邑良中直發關文砲手捉付之由已為牒報為有在○○○虛實探知次使漢語人金里元入送異船矣囬造内遣船制度層層作房而每房所載人物數至為四五百名是乎乙遣軍器則大碗砲與五穴鳥銃鎗釖等物不知其數也彼賊言内曰昨所送書今二十二日内受来囬文是矣雖空紙踏印期於受来而若過限日必動干戈殺害浦邊諸處居民将犯邑府之意萬端威脅是如為卧乎所洋夷之近日倡獗已是痛恨而其言之悖慢胡至此極乎勢将戰破乃已是如乎此時戰器莫如銃手而本縣銃手未滿二十名則以此赴敵勢實難強故玆以擧實牒報各邑砲手等一并定校罔夜押付之意發關各邑教是乎旀為先營底砲手限五百名罔夜送則破賊必矣異船若泊他境是良置縣監親率赴陣計料是如為白有置彼船自月乃島又為移泊于陸島前洋而所送書封期於今二十二日内受来囬文之說其所督迫有若尋事起鬧者然是白分叱除良船上賊類至為四五百名而必欲動干戈犯邑府云云之說尤極痛駭乙仍于附近各邑及臣營下善放砲手等為先限幾哨星火抄送赴敵之意今方三懸鈴知委為白遣水營只在隔江之地嚴防制敵萬萬時急故一體發關另飭于水使鄭志鉉○為白乎旀緣由先此馳
丙寅十二月二十三日未時封

R. W. Shufeldt (1867. 1. 29)

조선 관리와의 대화 기록

Tai Tong River
at Nento Island
Jan. 29, 1867

Comdr. Shufeldt. "Where are you from, and on what business have you come?"

Corean Official. "My name is Lee Ke Yung. I reside in the district of Hae Chow, at Kee Chen (village) where I am ruler. I have come to see your Ship."

Comdr. Shufeldt. "This vessel came here January 24th and sent a letter by the people of Nento island to the officer of Chang Yuen Heen, accompanied with a communication the King, from which no answer has yet been received. Do you know anything about this?"

Corean. "I know nothing about it whatever. On what business have you come?"

Comdr. Shufeldt. "An American vessel was wrecked in the Ping Yang river in the month of Sept., and it is reported that this vessel was burnt and all on board put to death by the Coreans. I have come to investigate this matter, and have sent a dispatch to the King to enquire whether the report is true or false, and whether any of the crew are still living."

Corean "How many li is it to your country? As it does not become your excellency to remain long at this place, I earnestly hope you will speedily depart and return to your own country."

Comdr. Shufeldt. "The Ship is now merely waiting an answer to the dispatch."

Corean. "You ought not to delay, but leave at once."

Comdr. Shufeldt. "Have you heard or do you know anything about the Ship which was wrecked?"

Corean. "I know nothing about it whatever. I only hope you will immediately leave and return to your native country."

Comdr. Shufeldt. "I am anxious to depart speedily but I wish first to ascertain the truth about the Ship wrecked in the Ping Yang river. No answer has yet been received."

Corean. "I do not know whether this report is true or false. Do not delay but leave immediately, by so doing your honorable country will have great praise."

Comdr. Shufeldt. "What objection can there be to our waiting? If I am obliged to leave without an answer to my dispatch many more armed vessels will return to your country."

Corean. "To return with many armed vessels would be exceedingly unjust. To return to your own country would be praiseworthy."

Comdr. Shufeldt. "To allow your country to murder our Men without cause or provocation can not be passed over (uninvestigated)"

Corean. "I do not know anything about this business."

Comdr. Shufeldt. "If you know nothing, I have nothing more to say to you."

R. W. Shufeldt (1867. 1. 30) → H. H. Bell

대동강변 탐사 결과 및 조선 관리와의 접촉 보고

U.S.S. *Wachusett*
At Sea
Jan. 30, 1867

Rear Admiral H.H. Bell
Comdg. U.S. Asiatic Squadron

Sir:

I have the honor to report to you that this Ship anchored on the W. coast of Corea, Lat 38° 4′N., Long. 124° 50′ W. near the mouth of the "Ta-tong" river, on the 23rd inst.

The Ping Yang river is the one up which the Schr. *Genl. Sherman* went and was destroyed. This river enters the sea 50 miles to the N of the above position, a fact which I could not positively ascertain until our arrival somewhere on the Corean coast, but as we found on survey the "Ta-tong" river to be frozen, and as our Chinese Pilot, a man of unusual intelligence, and for twenty years a trader on this coast, expressed decided reluctance to take the Ship to the mouth of the "Ping Yang" at this season of the year, I determined to attempt some sort of official intercourse from our anchorage, more particularly as the Heen city of "Chang Yuen" was said to be about midway between these two rivers. There are no Official cities on the seaboard of the W. coast. We found however quite a number of fishing villages, and after some unsuccessful efforts, the Chief of one of these on "Nien Fo" or Cow island, was induced to send a messenger with a communication to the King of Corea, accompanied by a letter to the Official of "Chang Yuen," copies of which (English and Chinese) are herewith enclosed.

In the meanwhile we endeavored to cultivate friendly feelings with the natives. They seemed to be kindly disposed, but in great dread of their Gov't. and came as little into contact with us as possible.

Apparently they are a rude and barbarous people, unarmed, and the seaboard entirely defenceless. We saw no iron in use, the boats are fastened with wooden pegs or lashed with coarse seaweed cordage. They spoke with great reserve when questioned in reference to the *Genl. Sherman*, but every one of them told the same story, which they said was known all over the country, viz: that the vessel was burned last Sept. up the "Ping-Yang" river, and all of her people, Amounting to 27 persons, were killed in a melée on shore by the natives, and not by order of the Mandarins.

There remains no reasonable doubt of these facts, and no doubt whatever of the locality of the disaster.

A messenger was sent on the morning of the 24th inst. And was to have returned within two days, but up the eve of the 29th he had not made his appearance. On the morning of the 29th however, an Officer, who said that he came from "Hae Chow Poo" the capital city of the Province, 50 miles up the "Ta-Tong" river, was brought on board in one of our own boats, for which they had signaled from the shore, and the interview with him carried on by writing in Chinese, resulted in the unsatisfactory manner, as by a memorandum herewith enclosed.

I have no doubt the man lied systematically from the beginning to the end of our interview, and that he was either the Governor of "Hae Chow Poo" or some high officer in his confidence.

My communication to the King had probably gone to him, as the Official superior to the Mandarin at "Chang Yuen." In all probability too it went and perhaps will go no further. In all events it soon became evident that this Officer was utterly beyond the reach of reason or argument, and furthermore that I need not expect any more intercourse with or through the natives at that point. His presence seemed to inspire the greatest dread, and I fear very much that both our old Chief and the messenger his son, have by this time paid for their friendship towards us, by the loss of their heads.

The manner of this officer was haughty and imperious, and he presented in his person the most perfect type of a vindictive savage.

The latter part of our interview was carried on the island, and seeing how pointless it was growing, I determined to leave him abruptly, with the impression upon his mind that the result of the conference was not at all satisfactory and that it would not be the end of the investigation.

I had earnestly hoped to have found some peaceable and satisfactory solution to the *Sherman* affair, and even to have discovered some of her crew still living, it is therefore with great person regret that I have to report a different result.

If the disaster to that vessel is regarded as an act of the people of Corea, and without sufficient provocation, then it only remains to go up the "Ping Yang" river at the proper season and inflict proportionate punishment at the scene of the outrage, but if viewed as an act of the Corean Govt. which may and ought to influence our policy in the East, it occurs to me that we would punish that Govt. quite as much by assailing them in the South, at Chosan for instance, a point which might eventually be of use to us to retain, rather than by going up the W. coast where the French are already operating, and which if occupied could be of no national or commercial importance.

I am Sir
Very Respectfully
(Signed) R.W. Shufeldt
Commander
Comdg. U.S.S. Wachussett

41

議政府(1867. 2. 1/高宗三年十二月二十七日) ➜ 高宗

와츄세트호의 투서(投書)에 대한 조처

命長淵来泊異船之投書上送議政府

議政府啓言卽見黃海監司 朴承輝狀啓則枚擧長淵縣監 韓致容牒報以爲異樣船一隻来泊於五叉鎭月乃島而三十九人下陸執捉居民授之一封書不能退却故謄書上送原本待問情時還投計料云矣異船之停泊投書雖以求和爲辭叵測情狀亦難料度問情之際務從詳細書封不必退却卽令上送于本府答書依慶興例使該縣監構送彼船形止馳聞各邑鎭瞭望防守之節益加嚴察之意請另飭道帥臣處允之

R. W. Shufeldt (1867. 2. 3) → H. H. Bell

거문도 해역 탐사 결과 보고, 거문도 점령 건의

관련문서 (1) H. H. Bell이 G. Wells에게 보낸 Shufeldt의 거문도 해역 조사 내용(1867. 2. 11)

U.S.S. *Wachusett*
At Sea, February 3, 1867

Rear Admiral H.H. Bell
Comdg. U.S. Asiatic Squadron

Sir:

I have the honor to submit the following report upon the "Nan-Hou" Islands (Port Hamilton) visited by this Ship in obedience to your order of Dec. 27th 1866.

These islands seem to have attracted the attention of English Naval Authorities as early as 1845, since which time they have been twice surveyed, and certainly as a Naval Depot for any Power, they merit attention.

For the hydrographic character of the Port, I refer you to the published plan of the harbor, adding only that the "holding" ground is excellent, and that although there is a rise of 11 ft. tide, it produces no perceptibly current. The entrances are at right angles to the Basin, thus forming a land-locked harbor capable of containing a Navy, and from its shelving shores and smooth water offering every opportunity for repairs &c.

In their physical construction, the Islands form a large natural fort, with sides to the sea, nearly perpendicular from 100 to 200 ft. high, afterward gradually rising to peaks of 600 to 800 ft., then sloping inwards to the basin in the centre.

On the outside the water is deep and steep to, affording no anchorage, except on the Northern face where the hills are more sloping, and shoaler water is obtained.

In a military point of view, if an insular port can be made inaccessible to an Enemy, this certainly presents the most favorable qualifications. The Islands are in fact two Gibralters on a small scale, facing each other and guarding the harbor between them. As a Sanitarium, in addition to their position, the fact that the Islands separate both at the Southern and Northern points, must give a constant current of cool breezes in the summer, which for the very same reason, or rather for the reason that there are no other openings, they are protected in winter from the cold N.W. & N.E. winds. We found the thermometer at 39 on Feby 1st, although we came in from sea in a very cold N.E. storm of snow squalls &c.

Geographically, as the Islands are evidently volcanic, they possess a fertile soil, about 2/5 however only capable of cultivation wheat and millet are the principal products. The winter wheat was just becoming green when we were there, showing a state of the season about equal to the same latitude in our own Country.

The inhabitants live in four villages of about 500 souls each, their occupation is agriculture, with a little fishing. They are a rude, barbarous, but not unfriendly people. The Islands affording them all they need, but not capable of doing much more. They have no animals of any kind for food, neither Bullocks nor Sheep, though both would thrive upon the hillsides. Water is scarce, there are but two small rivulets, and they depend entirely upon the rains to fertilize their crops.

The Government is patriarchal, the oldest men being the heads of the villages, and each village being distinct from the others, but they pay their taxes annually by sending to their "Heen" city, which they call "Khang Tsin," distant 200 miles by water, and which is probably "Chosan" on the main land.

These Islands belong to Corea, and the people resemble in every respect the Coreans we saw at "Ta-tong." Our intercourse with them at both places was by writing Chinese, which the more intelligent men could do readily, although none of them could speak it. They say they have no written Corean languages.

A few Chinese gardeners, and a stock of cattle imported from California or Japan, would soon furnish all the vegetable and stock required for a Naval Station, and water the scarcity of which we noticed particularly in the driest season, could be easily remedied by a small condensing apparatus.

One is impressed with the beauty of "Nan-Hou" even in mi-winter, and fancies how reluctantly he would leave there for the intense heat and sickly climate of the coast of China during the summer months.

I am Sir
Very Respectfully
R.W. Shufeldt
Commander
Comdg. U.S.S. *Wachusett*

【관련문서 1】

U.S. Flag Ship *Hartford* (2nd Rate)
Hong Kong Harbor
February 11, 1867

Hon. Gideon Welles
Secretary of the Navy
Washington D. C.

Sir:

I have the honor to inform the Department that in connection with the visit of Commander Shufeldt to Corea, for the purpose of enquiring into the outrage upon the people of the *General Sherman*, I directed him to examine into the advantages and capabilities of Port Hamilton (Nam Hoo) situate among the Islands to the Southward of Corea, and belonging to the King of Corea, as a Rendezvous and Sanatorium for this Squadron, and also as a Harbor of Refuge in times of danger, for American commerce in those seas.

By the report of Commander Shufeldt, herewith enclosed, marked A, it will be seen that this harbor possess many natural advantages, and it would be very valuable as a base in any operations against the Coreans.

Its central position with regard to the Northern ports is, as I informed the Department in my Despatch No. 63* of December 14th 1866, one of its most important advantages, being 150 miles from Nagasaki, 240 from Nan Diemans Straights, 180 from the Straights of Simonasaki, 300 from the mouth of the Yang Tze River, 360 from Shanghai, 390 from Ningpo, 315 from the "Shantung" promontory at the entrance to the Gulf of Pechili, 350 from Chifu, and 350 miles from the mouth of the Phien Tang River, the scene of the disaster to the *General Sherman*.

I also enclose, marked B, an interesting descriptive sketch of Port Hamilton, made by Mr. Albert S. Bickmore, a naturalist from Boston, who was on board of the *Wachusett*.

The possession of so small a place does not indicate the least ambition for

*제1권 26번 문서.

territorial aggrandizement.

Plans of this harbor are among the Chank in the Department.

The *Wachusett* is now in the Yang Tze River.

I have the Honor to be, Sir
Very Respectfully
Your Obedient Servant
H.H. Bell
Rear Admiral
Commdg. U.S. Asiatic Squadron

A descriptive sketch of [Nan-hu] – called by the [Sir Fish] survey [on/of] Port Hamilton.

Nan-hu is the name of a small group of islands in the archipelago that surrounds the southern end of the peninsula of Corea. It is situated in Lat 34°1′23″ N. Long. 127°28′15″ E. it is composed of two long, narrow; and one small, triangular island, which together enclose a basin one mile wide and two long. This basin is accessible for ships only through two channels on its southeastern side. On its northwesterly side it is also open to sea, for ten [cubles'] length, but a shallow bar prevents any but small boats from passing through and at the same time breaks up all swell rolling in from the ocean. On the outside, these islands rise up abruptly from a depth of twenty to thirty fathoms, and from perpendicular rocky precipices for one and two hundred feet above the level of the sea. From the edges of these precipices they continue up at the steep angle of 35° to a sharp ridge that has a more gentle declivity down the inner side or toward the center of the basin. This is more clearly seen in the accompanying vertical section A – B, which passes through the highest hills [on/of] the two principal islands in a due easterly and westerly direction. The point C is according my barometer 803 feet above half tide level.

In short, the whole is, in my opinion, merely the top of an old extinct volcano, which was nearly submerged by the sea; and the basin where ships at present anchor in ten and twelve fathoms of water, was once an active, burning crater.

This assumption is strengthened by the structure of Quelpart, which although thirty miles long and eighteen wide, is wholly formed of the cone and flanks of a single volcano, now apparently inactive. On its flanks are [___s] of minor cones, in each of which the eruptive force has found vent for a time, and then becoming clogged up, it has broken out in some other place to form another similar elevation.

From a single position I counted forty six of these miniature volcanoes. Their sides are as smooth and regular as if graded by art, and on two tops of those near the sea, square bastion-like lookouts inform the people of approaching danger.

[Montressor] Island, as we saw it in the distance, was exactly the outline of a volcano with a considerable crater, and probably a large part of the whole Corean archipelago will prove of plutonic origin, like many of the neighboring islands of Japan.

On account of the steepness of the outer flanks of these mountainous islands, only their inner declivities or those that surround the basin [have been] brought under cultivation. The parts that are thus improved, form about two-fifths of the whole area. They are divided into rectangular patches which extend two-thirds the way up the mountain sides, and are already green with wheat that was sowed last autumn. There is but little that can be called terracing – such as seen in China and Japan, and consequently no artificial irrigation; yet the people [   ] but little and appear to rely chiefly on their crops, which they say only "sometimes suffer for want of water."

The soil is a fine, dark loam and appears extremely fertile. They raise wheat, Kowliang (a large species of millet common in the north of China), and some cotton.

They have no cattle, horses, sheep, or goats, yet I am confident the small cattle on the promontory of Shantung would thrive well here; and perhaps, the better breeds that could be imported from California and Australia. Large flocks of sheep and goats would find plenty of the richest pasturage on the declivities that are too steep for cultivation, and good breeds of both of these animals are common in the same latitude in China.

They keep hens, but no ducks or geese, though they have every facility for raising the latter, but not the inducement of a ready market.

The only trees I passed on my way to the peak were a few small pines, and the only shrub that grows on the mountain sides is a Camellia bearing a rich, dark crimson flower.

In general, the climate and vegetation may be considered quite like that of southern Japan and all the many kinds of vegetables and fruit that are raised there, may, no doubt, be as successfully cultivated here.

Many kinds of fish could probably be taken in the immediate vicinity, but no men were out fishing when we were there, though the next day we passed several boat off Quelpart.

In the basin and along the outer shores, the sea has a bluish tinge and is remarkably pure and sparkling.

The islands being separated on the N.W. and S.E., breezes from the sea have free access into [this] basin, and must render the air cool and healthy in summer. This, with its isolated position and its latitude, make it an admissible location for a sanitarium, and I suspect that the southern or inner side of the eastern island would prove the most healthy place, if there is any difference.

The inhabitants live in four villages, two on the eastern and two on the western island. They informed us they number four hundred families, and reckoning five persons to a family thus gives two thousand as the total population, a rather low estimate.

Their villages are very compact, and each house is surrounded by a thick, high wall of small stones laid up without clay or cement. A door is made in this wall and a small house built near it, together making a kind of little "compound" as private grounds are called in the east, when [enclosed]. Their houses are all very low, and have walls built of small stones, or a framework of wood with the [interstices] plastered with clay. The roof is a coarse thatching of straw, fastened down by straw ropes which draw each other at right angles. The rooms have wooden floors but are so low one cannot stand up in them.

Through the open doors and a few small paper windows a scanty light is admitted sufficient however to show a complete want of any kind of furniture.

In front there is generally a rude piazza where the people seem to pass most of their time when at home.

They dislike to have foreigners even enter their grounds, and when the magnates of the several villages gave Capt. Shufeldt an audience, we had to sit down on mats of [coil] and straw, while they ranged themselves around us in a semicircle, in true Indian style. During this interview the brought us a fiery fermented liquor, probably made from their millet or wheat. The official who poured it out invariably tasted it before offering it to anyone, to show us, as we thought at first, that it contained no poison, but after he must have satisfied all on that point he was careful not to desist.

Instead of cakes to eat with this wine, they brought us a kind of dried seaweed, which completed the list of refreshments and show what [____] people esteem special luxuries.

Their streets are merely narrow paths, very crooked and abominably filthy; [indeed], the whole appearance of their houses and villages bespoke a degree of poverty and wretchedness surpassing anything commonly seen in China.

They all dress in white. The men wear their hair combed up and twisted into a kind of knot on the top of the head. The women part theirs in the middle and braid it behind. They wear no ornaments and are more filthy and [stupid] than the men.

All our conversation with them was carried on by writing in Chinese but they speak a different language. They stated they were subjects of Corea and belong to the [Lien] district of Khan-tsin. The official wore the thin black Corean hat with a conical crown and broad, straight brim. One dignitary only had on a straw hat of a hemispherical form, full two feet across.

In regard to their religion we were only able to learn that they worshiped "idols of clay," and I suspect that like the Chinese their ideas on this subject are very indefinite. They bury their dead in mounds, frequently high up among the mountains, and like the Chinese seem to prefer the head of a valley, or a place sheltered from "the evil influences" by hills on the right and left that rise somewhat higher than the spot where the body is interred. On the northerly end of the western island there is a considerable cemetery, and near the center a stone slab stands in front of a mound. The upper part of this slab has a slight prolongation to the right, a corresponding one to the left and one upward, so as in some degree to resemble a cross. It is covered with Chinese characters. In front of this slab and at a distance of ten feet on either side there is a small, square rudely carved idol. These may have been intended for images of Buddha, but such a custom I have never seen in the many cemeteries I have visited during my long journeys in China. A little farther in front, and a little farther to the right and left, there rises on either side a small stone column. This is a common custom throughout the Celestial Empire.

H. H. Bell (1867. 2. 16) → G. Wells (1867. 4. 19)

Shufeldt의 제너럴 셔먼호 관련 정보 수집 결과 보고

U.S. Flag Ship *Hartford* (2 rate)
Hong King China
February 16, 1867

Hon. Gideon Welles
Secretary of the Navy
Washington D. C.

Sir:

In my Despatch numbered 65* Series 1866 and dated December 27th 1866, I informed the Department, that I should send Commander Shufeldt in the *Wachusett* to Chifu, and Corea, to investigate the circumstances of the loss of the American Schooner *General Sherman* and the fate of the people on board of her.

I have now to submit to the Department that General Shufeldt reached Chifu on the 14th January last, and having secured the services of the Chinese pilot who was in the *General Sherman* a few days before her loss, and also of the Rev'd Mr Corbett, an American Missionary to act as interpreter, left there on the 21st for the North West Coast of Corea in compliance with his instructions which were to demand of the Chief authorities of the Pin Tang River, "to deliver on the deck of the *Wachusett*, such of the unfortunate men of the Schooner *General Sherman* as may have been spared whether they were American, Portuguese, British, Malays or Chinamen, and to make such further investigation of the case, as was practicable."

Commander Shufeldt, has performed that service with commendable zeal, intelligence and celerity.

His report marked, A herewith enclosed, confirming the rumors of the wreck of the Schooner *General Sherman* and of the burning of that vessel in Ping Tang River and of the murder of all on board of her, numbering twenty-seven persons by the "Coreans."

*제1권 28번 문서.

The enclosed paper marked B is copy of letter addressed by Commander Shufeldt to the King of Corea. C, is memorandum of interview with Corean official. D, is memorandum regarding the wreck of the *General Sherman* and of the Natural history of Corea.

In conclusion, I beg to suggest that until the Government takes efficient action on the case, our countrymen lawfully navigating the seas adjacent to Corea, will be in peril of life and liberty of person from the barbarities of the people, and the authorities of that Country, who aim at the exclusion of strangers.

No surveys of that part of the coast have been yet made and Commander Shufeldt employed the few days he was waiting to hear from the King in making a partial survey of the entrance to the "Ta Ting" River which lies in Lat. 38° 114 N Long 124° 50 W (the chart of which is marked E is herewith enclosed) and about fifty miles to the Southward of the Ping Tang River which the pilot did not consider it safe to approach in the winter months.

As soon as winter breaks up, and I have a gunboat to spare, I shall have that part of the Corean coast examined pending the decision of the Department.

I have the honor to be, Sir
Very Respectfully
Your Obedient Servant
H.H. Bell
Rear Admiral
Commanding US Asiatic Squadron

W. H. Seward (1867. 2. 23) ➞ A. Burlingame

Gillie 신부에 대한 감사 및 제너럴 셔먼호 조사 촉구

DEPARTMENT OF STATE,
Washington, February 23, 1867

Sir:

I have to acknowledge the receipt of a despatch of the 24th of October, No. 44*, which Mr. Williams has addressed to this department relative to the humane conduct of the Rev. Father Gillie, in giving assistance to and successfully aiding a company of shipwrecked sailors belonging to the American schooner Surprise in their journey across Manchuria to Nuichwang. The government of the United States fully appreciating the kind service rendered by Father Gillie to our unfortunate countrymen on the occasion referred to, have caused a suitable testimonial to be prepared, which when completed will be transmitted to you for presentation to Father Gillie.

In the same despatch Mr. Williams informs the department of the wreck of the American schooner *General Sherman*. It is stated that the hull of this vessel was burned by the Coreans, and that the entire crew were murdered by them. I will thank you to make diligent inquiry respecting the fate of these unfortunate seamen, and acquaint me with the result.

I am, Sir, your obedient servant,
WILLIAMS H. SEWARD

ANSON BURLINGAME, Esq.

*제1권 21번 문서.

45

板倉勝静, 稲葉正邦, 小笠原長行(1867. 5. 10/慶應三年四月七日) ➞ R. B. Van Valkenburgh

조미(朝美) 관계 중재 제안

丁卯四月七日

亞墨利加合衆國ミニストルレシテント
ヱキセルレンシー
アルビワルケンヒユルグえ

以書翰申入候然は朝鮮國近時佛蘭西と爭戰の事起り後貴國無辜の商船を殘害せしと聞同國は素より我か接壤舊交の國にて如此無義の擧をなし我か同盟親交の國民を慘害すると聞て我か大君深く痛歎に堪へす且隣義に於て忠告善導せさるを得さるの理あり此度彼國王に國書を投し平山圖書頭古賀謹一郎に命して委曲曉解せしめんとす而して彼舊愆を悔悟して我に就て和を講するに至らは貴國旌旗を回し舊怒を棄て相友善するの道を開かん事を希望す右等之情狀貴國政府え深く周旋を賴入候尤彼の舊習牢として說くへからさるに至れるは難測といへとも隣義に於て我か盡すへきを盡し四海の和平を祈るは我か大君の素志なり諒悉盡力有之度候拜具謹言
慶應三年丁卯四月七日

板倉伊賀守 花押
稲葉美濃守 花押
小笠原壹岐守 花押

【英譯文】

We have heard that recently there was war in Corea with the French, and that a merchant vessel of the United States was treated wit great cruelty in the country.

Corea being the neighbor of Japan, with which friendly relations have been maintained so long, the Tycoon feels much grieved at learning, in view of the sincere friendship subsisting between Japan and the United States, that a wrong has been perpetrated upon American citizens, and he will not fail therefore to tender friendly advice to Corea and to endeavor to induce that country, with the regard to the friendship which should govern the intercourse between neighbors to mend its course in future.

A letter on the subject will be sent to the king of that country, and Hirayama Diurho No [will be directed to address him in accordance therewith.]

And if, on reflection of the wrong that has been committed and through our influence, he should sue for peace, we hope that the flag of the of the United States will return; that retaliation will be abandoned and the means for friendly intercourse (*Sic*) be found.

We now request your excellency to communicate the foregoing to your government.

We have only to add, that it is of course uncertain whether the Coreans will be dissuaded from persisting in their course. Yet it is the wish of the Tycoon that no effort should be left untried, with the object of promoting peace in this part of the world, and we further request your excellency to use your best endeavor in the same direction.

Stated with respect and consideration the 7th day of the 4th month of the 3d year of Keu. 10th May 1867.

ITAKURA EGA NO KAMI
OGASAWARA IKI NO KAMI

His Excellency R. B. VAN VALKENBURGH,
Minister Resident of the United States

R. B. V. Valkenburgh (1867. 5. 18) ➞ W. H. Seward

일본의 조미(朝美) 관계 중재 제안 보고

LEGATION OF THE UNITED STATES IN JAPAN
Osacca, May 18, 1867

Sir:

I have the honor to transmit herewith No. 1, copy of a letter from the Gorogio, announcing the intention of the Japanese government to send envoys to Corea, for the purpose therein set forth. I transmit No. 2, copy of my reply.

This mission is expected to leave within a fortnight, and as soon as the result shall be made known to me, I shall immediately report the same to you.

I have the honor to be, Sir, very respectfully, your most obedient servant,

R. B. VAN VALKENBURGH

Hon. WILLIAM H. SEWARD,
Secretary of State, Washington, D. C.

A*

B

Mr. Van Valkenburgh to Ministers for Foreign Affairs.

LEGATION OF THE UNITED STATES IN JAPAN,
Osacca, May 18, 1867

I have the honor to acknowledge the receipt of your letter of the 10th instant, in which you announce your intention of sending envoys to Corea; a copy of which letter I shall not fail to send to my government by the earliest

* 제1권 45번 문서의 영역문.

opportunity.

With respect and esteem,

R. B. VAN VALKENBURGH,

Minister Resident of the United States in Japan,

Their Excellencies the MINISTERS FOR FOREIGN AFFAIRS,

Osacca, &c., &c., &c.

47

W. H. Seward (1867. 7. 23) ➞ R. B. V. Valkenburgh

일본의 조미(朝美) 관계 중재 제안에 대한 감사 표시

관련문서 (1) Seward의 답변 보고(1867. 12. 17)

Sir:

I have received your despatch No. 24*, dated the 18th of May last. With it you transmit copy of a letter addressed to you by the Gorogio, and of your reply thereto, concerning the proposed sending by the Japanese government of envoys to Corea with the object of preventing for the future such a strong as is represented to have been committed during a recent war in that country upon American citizens.

This friendly proceeding of the Japanese government is highly appreciated, and you are instructed to return suitable thanks therefore. You will also make known to me the result of the Tycoon's laudable efforts to promote peace in that part of the world.

It is deemed proper to add that the government of the United States will feel obliged, should no satisfactory explanation or apology be furnished by corea, to consider how proper reparation can be obtained and honor maintained.

I am, Sir, your obedient servant,

WILLIAM H. SEWARD

R. B. VAN VALKENBURGH, Esq.

* 제1권 46번 문서.

【관련문서 1】

丁卯十一月廿二日
第百〇七號
千八百六十七年第十二月十七日日本に在る合衆國の公使館に於て江戶外國事務執政小笠原壹岐守殿閣下に呈す
本年第五月余謹て御老中の一書翰を我政府へ送りたり但其書翰の意は高麗亞に於て曾て亞墨利加人に爲せる如き曲事を向後なす事を防く趣意を以日本政府より高麗亞へ公使を贈るべき由を述ふる者なり
余より我政府へ贈れる文通の返書に合衆國の大統領は貴政府の懇親なる所置を大に善とすることを余に申來れり是を以て余閣下に之が謝辭を述ふべし〇余又閣下に左件を告くべきを命ぜられたり若高麗亞にて十分の言譯卽ち詫言をなすことなきときは合衆國の政府は如何して其正當なる償を得且其恭敬を失ざるべきや之を考ふるを要すべし
余貴國政府より高麗亞に送ると定めし公使のなせる手續に就きて閣下より其報告を得ば余之を我政府に申送るべし恐惶敬白

日本在留合衆國のミニストルレシデント
アル、ビ、ワン、ワルケンボルグ

R. B. V. Valkenburgh (1867. 11. 20) → W. H. Seward

조선에서 일본의 중재 제안을 거절한 사유 보고

LEGATION OF THE UNITED STATES,
Yedo, November 20, 1867

Sir:

Your no. 23*, under date of July 23d, concerning the purpose of sending by the Japanese government of envoys to Corea, with the object of preventing for the future such a wrong as is represented to have been committed during a recent war in that country upon American citizens, was received by me on the sixth day of the present month. Soon after that I took occasion to call upon the minister for foreign affairs in person, and according to your instructions to return to him suitable thanks for this friendly proceeding upon the part of this government, and to assure him that the laudable efforts of the Tycoon to promote peace in this part of the world were highly appreciated by the President. I also added that should no satisfactory explanation be made, or apology furnished by Corea, the government of the United States would undoubtedly feel obliged to take into consideration the proper means to obtain a reparation for the injury and to maintain its honor.

Hingama Desho No Kami, a member of the second council, was appointed by the Tycoon in May last as his envoy to Corea, and the management of all the matters connected with the embassy was intrusted to him, and from him I learn the following facts: Tso No Tushema No Kami is a Japanese Daimio residing upon and owning the little island of Tsusima, or Tsu, near the coast of Corea. This Daimio has a small settlement on that coast, and through his retainers at that settlement this government has for many years been kept informed of the action of the Coreans.

They have had no diplomatic relations, and, so far as I can learn, no authorized agent of this government has ever been recognized in Corea. Immediately on the appointment of this envoy he sent a messenger to Tso No Tsusima No Kami, and requested him, through his retainers, to procure permission for him to visit Corea, and a promise of his recognition by the

* 제1권 47번 문서.

government. The answer of the Corean government, returned through Tso No Tsusima No Kami, was that the proposition was a new and strange one, and that the government would take it into consideration, and after a determination had been arrived at the Japanese government should be informed.

This government has again sent messengers to Tsusima, urging the importance of the mission, and of their recognition by the Corean government, and asking for an early reply.

I am of the opinion that the Japanese envoy will not be received. Should any new facts become known to me I will not delay in informing you of them.

I have the honor to be, your most obedient servant,

R. B. VAN VALKENBURGH

Hon. WILLIAM H. SEWARD,
Secretary of State Washington, D. C.

E. Sanford (1867. 12. 3) ➞ W. H. Seward

제너럴 셔먼호 사건 관련 정보 보고

U.S. Consulate
Cheefoo, China Dec 3 1867

Hon William H. Seward
Secretary of State
Washington D.C.

Sir:

I have the honor to inform you of the report made to me by Mr. [BranTae] respecting the American Schooner *General Sherman* which was taken by the Coreans in the year A.D. 1866

Vis. as follows.

"During the last of August and the first of September of the present year, I was over in Corea on a trading voyage. I saw the hull of the Schr. *General Sherman* in the Ping Yang river, about fifteen li (five miles) from its mouth. Her masts had been cut away, and her armament removed. On boarding her I found considerable water in the hold. The Coreans stated that the crew had been beaten to death by the villagers. As I was upbraiding them for their treatment of foreigners who came there for trade, a Corean named King Tze Ping stated that four of the crew were still living in confinement at Ping Yang so (Ping Yang so is the capital of the Province situated on the Ping Yang river, about eighty li (twenty eight miles) from its mouth. I then asked him "Why do you wish to deceive me." To which he replied "I am not deceiving you, I saw the men myself, during the second month (April) two Europeans and two Chinese, of the latter, one belonged to Peking and one to [b___][____]." King Tze Ping further stated that they were confined, under charge of an officer, in a garden 棧 at Ping Yang so, where they were well treated and fed with rice. He did not know why they were detained.

Such is the statement of [BranTae] (and Kan Ban Tae as was erroneously reported in my despatch No. 37.) He moreover added that the above was a common report amongst the Coreans at the Ping Yang river, that it was also well known to other Chinese traders to Corea, that King Tze Ping frequently visited the capital of Ping Yang so to dispose of the goods purchased on the coast, that he had business dealings with him for many years and had found him trustworthy and reliable and that this man King Tze Ping could easily be found should he be wanted.

The pilot [BranTae] has been carefully examined by myself and two others. He tells his story in a straightforward manner and I cannot but be impressed with the feeling that there must be some foundation for the report.

As regards the pilot, the testimony of all the Europeans who have had dealings with him, as well as of Capt. Shufeldt of the U.S.S. *Wachusett*, who employed him as pilot last January, all tend to show that the man is to be depended on.

I have the honor to be
Sir
Your Obd. Servant
E. Sanford
U.S. Consul

50

W. H. Seward (1868. 1. 27) → R. B. V. Valkenburgh

일본의 중재 제안에 대한 미 국무성 훈령

DEPARTMENT OF STATE
Washington, January 27, 1868

Sir:

Your dispatch of the 20th of November, No. 66* has been received and submitted to the President. We learn from it, with satisfaction, that the Japanese government has taken measures to open communication, if possible, with the government of Corea, and that we may indulge an expectation that the United States may be able to avail themselves of the good offices of the proposed Japanese legation to impress upon the Coreans the necessity of a due respect to the power of the United States. The wrong we have sustained is unendurable, and cannot be overlooked. We are nevertheless anxious that our proceedings in the case may be conducted with such moderation as shall not bring in question the dignity and liberality of the United States in their intercourse with such communities in the East as are still remaining rude and unorganized. We look forward with much interest to the further proceedings of the Japanese government in instituting diplomatic communications with Corea.

I am, Sir, your obedient servant,

WILLIAM H. SEWARD

R. B. VAN VALKENBURGH, Esq.

*제1권 48번 문서.

S. W. Williams (1868. 3. 3) ➞ 總署

于文泰로부터 제너럴 셔먼호 생존자 정보 입수, 송환 협조 요청

관련문서 (1) 總署의 회신 영역문(1868. 7. 11)

LEGATION OF THE UNITED STATES,
Peking, March 3, 1868

Sir:

Referring to my note to the Foreign Office of October 28, 1866, respecting an American merchant vessel, the schooner *General Sherman*, which had been stranded in Corea in August of that year, at which time I was favored by a reply assuring me that the military and civil authorities of Manchuria should attend to the wants of such of the crew as might be handed over to them, I have now the honor to bring the subject again before your imperial highness, with the request that you would communicate upon it with the Corean government.

It appears, from reports received after the date of my note of October, 1866, that when the *General Sherman* got ashore in Corea the natives of the country flocked about her, and that a quarrel arose between them and the crew, resulting in injury and wounds to both parties, and a fight, in which all the latter were ultimately destroyed. In consequence of this report, the admiral commanding the United States squadron in these seas last summer dispatched one of his vessels to Corea to make inquiries into the matter, and ascertain the real circumstances of the affair on the spot; but this he was not able at the time to do in a satisfactory manner.

A day or two since I received from the United States consul at Chifu the report of a pilot, named Yu Wautai, who last year returned from Corea, and related to him "that he had gone up a stream called Piyang river, and about 10 miles from the sea had seen a foreign vessel lying on the southern bank, without master or sails, and her hull full of water. He had also met a Corean, named Kin Tsz'ping, a native of an island called Tsioh Tau, or Sparrow island, who told him that in March last he had himself seen two foreigners and two Chinese at the magistrate's office at the chief city of the district of Piyang. The rest of the foreigners and Chinese had all been killed by the farmers and people of the country, and not by the Corean authorities or soldiers. He saw these two foreigners walking in the streets without any instruments of torture upon them, followed by policemen to see that they did not get away; but he could not ascertain why the Corean magistrates detained them in this manner."

This report of the pilot Yu Wautai seems to me to possess a degree of truth, and not to be a made-up story, and I therefore lose no time in making it known to your imperial highness, to see whether some plan cannot be carried into effect to secure the liberation of these four men. I have myself also received directions from the government of the United States, in consequence of the report having reached Washington of the destruction of the *General Sherman* by the Coreans two years ago, to ascertain the true facts of the case and report upon them. This order, in connection with the unsuccessful visit for that purpose of the United States man-of-war last year leads me now to make known these particulars to your imperial highness, and respectfully request that a communication be sent by his Majesty's government to the Corean government for them to deliver over the two foreigners and two Chinese to the Chinese authorities.

The government of the United States has no direct relations with that of Corea, but there is something quite inexplicable in the fact that when this American vessel went there her crew should be treated so barbarously, and there must have been some cause for it, which the American government cannot permit to pass by silently, and without full investigation being made into all the circumstances.

The governments of China and the United States have long been on the most friendly terms, and I therefore entertain the strongest expectation that his Imperial Majesty will so represent this affair to the Corean government that they will see the propriety of transmitting a correct account of all the facts connected with the destruction of this American schooner within their territory, in order that I may report the same to the President. This act of courtesy will likewise add another evidence of the friendly relations existing between our respective governments, and will be duly appreciated.

I have the honor to be, with great respect, your imperial highness's obedient servant,

S. WELLS WILLIAMS

His Imperial Highness PRINCE KUNG,
Chief Secretary of State for Foreign Affairs.

【漢譯文】

美國照會

爲照會事 所有函託轉詢高麗一事 查前年九月間 本大臣函內 言八月間 有本國兩枝桅之商船 在高麗擱淺 當經函覆 稱分致盛京將軍 及海關監督 妥辦在案 嗣後風聞該船在擱淺之處 高麗土人與船上人打仗 彼此傷害 洋人死亡殆盡 去年夏間 本國水師提督 派兵船往彼 查察情形虛實 未得底細而回 昨據煙臺美國領事官申詳 有中國帶水人于文泰回來云 伊到高麗 見披陽河南邊 有夾板船一隻 竝無桅棚 船內空空 滿水而已 離海三十餘里 遇有住雀島之高麗商人金子平 說二月間 親眼見有洋人二名 華人二名 在披陽省衙門內 其餘洋人華人 俱被莊農人打死 非高麗官兵所傷 且見洋人在大衢走 身上竝無刑具 卻是後面有人跟緊 不解高麗官留下洋人何故等語前來 本大臣因思帶水人于文泰所說 亦足爲據 非無稽之言 貴親王能設法救出四人否 請轉達高麗國 將洋人二名 華人二名 送交中國官 本國與高麗素無交涉 該商船往入彼境 遽加殘害 有乖情理 其中必有原由 本國斷難隱忍 定欲追尋其故 我兩國多年和好 敢希轉行知高麗 將本國商船在彼如何被害之實在憑據詳述前來 以便本大臣奏知國家 以昭友誼關切 是所感謝

【관련 문서 1】

Note from the Foreign Office

July 11, 1868

When we received that dispatch of March 3 from your excellency, relating to the American schooner *General Sherman*, lost in Corea in 1866, concerning which an American man-of-war had gone to inquire about and had not succeeded in her mission, so that you requested us to communicate with the government of Corea to ascertain who were the two foreigners reported to be held in confinement there, and learn the reasons why they were so treated, that something might be done for their welfare, we replied that measures would be taken to further your wishes.

We accordingly presented a memorial to the throne, requesting that orders might be transmitted to the board of rites, directing its president to address the King of Corea and ask him to inquire whether two foreigners were really detained in his country. We have recently received a dispatch from the board of rites stating that a reply had been received from the King to the following effect:

"A two-masted foreign vessel went ashore in the Ping-jang river, bit this government had no hand whatever in the disasters which happened to her and her crew; nor has any envoy from the United States been here to inquire respecting them. If you have any means of communicating this to him, you can no doubt fully inform him of this fact. It is a fixed rule of this country, moreover, that when unfortunate men are cast ashore they must be rescued and treated kindly, so that if there were at this time any such pitiable cases here of persons who had drifted sown upon us, how could we detain them against their will? This rumor of two foreigners and two Chinese being kept here has no foundations; and it is a point, too, which can easily be ascertained. I shall be obliged if the officers of the board of rites will make these explanations on my behalf to those who may wish them."

It appears to us from the above that the statement by the Corean authorities that none of your countrymen are detained in their boarders has much to confirm it; and in sending this reply we avail ourselves of the occasion to renew to you the expression of our best wishes for your happiness.

Cards of PRINCE KUNG
WANSIANG
PAUYUN
TUNG SIUN
TAN TINGSIANG
TSUNG LUN
SEU KI-YU

總署(1868. 3. 10/同治七年二月十七日) ➞ S. W. Williams

제너럴 셔먼호 생존자 보호 요청에 대한 회신

給美國照覆

爲照覆事 准貴大臣照會 內稱前年九月閒 有本國兩枝桅商船 在高麗閣淺等因 同日又准英國阿大臣照稱 去年大法國兵船前往高麗交戰 嗣後大美國商船一隻 亦赴高麗有通商之意 行至北陽河 被高麗人將船攻打 現有帶水華人一名 告知美國煙臺領事官云 確知該船中洋人華人各二名 在高麗未死等因前來 本爵查前年九月閒 曾據貴大臣函稱 本國船隻 在高麗閣淺 被土人將船燒毀 捉去水手二十四人 儻或送至中國 請飭奉天府撫卹保護等語 卽經本衙門大臣等面告貴大臣 以如果送至該省 自必加意保護 當由本衙門行文奉省 及山海關監督 轉飭查辦 旋據奉省覆稱 前此曾有朝鮮送到外國遭風難民六名 由承德縣護送至營口洋行 交鼐領事收領 嗣後竝無送過外國民人等情 玆准前因 查此事先經貴國兵船前往查詢 未得底細 總因在法國與朝鮮交兵之際 是以訪察爲難 現旣承貴大臣照請設法辦理 本國自當緩爲籌畫 必須於事有益 方可酌量設法 斷難遽爾轉行查問 如或急切不能得有端倪 仍望貴大臣見諒 緣朝鮮雖臣服中國 其本處一切政教禁令 槪由該國自行專主 中國向不與聞 貴大臣諒亦鑒及於此也 除再行文奉省 轉飭地方官隨時查探 竝照覆英國阿大臣外 爲此先行照覆貴大臣查照

【英譯文】

MARCH 10, 1868,(Tungchi, 7th year, 2d moon, 18th day.)

Prince Kung, chief secretary of state for foreign affairs, herewith sends a reply:

On the 2d instant I had the honor of receiving your excellency's dispatch, in which you inform me of the report that two foreigners and two Chinese are now kept in durance by the Coreans, and request that the Chinese government should demand of the Corean government to hand them all over to the Chinese officers, &c.

On the same day that I received this communication the British minister, Sir Rutherford Alcock, also sent a dispatch to the following effect:

"Last year the French admiral took his squadron to Corea, where a collision took place with the authorities; and it was after that occurrence that an American vessel went to Corea with the intention of trading, and was attacked in the Piyang river, which she had entered, by the people. The report that came to me at the time was, that her crew had been entirely cut off; but afterwards many persons reported that some of them were yet alive, and detained in confinement by the Coreans. Recently a Chinese pilot has informed the United States consul at Chifu that he knows that two foreigners and two Chinese belonging to this vessel are still alive in Corea."

On receiving these dispatches I have recurred to the not written by your excellency on the 28th of October, 1866, in which you stated that an American schonner had been wrecked in Corea, that the vessel had been burned, and 24 of her crew carried off, concluding with the request that directions might be sent to the authorities in Mukten that if any of these men were handed over they might be carefully cared for by those officials. The members of the Foreign Office personally assured you at the time that if any persons were thus delivered by the Coreans, those authorities should be directed to do everything necessary for their comfort; and corresponding instruction were immediately forwarded to the general in command at Mukten, and to the collector at Ninchwang. In due course a reply was received from the former officer, in which he stated that the Corean authorities had previously given over to the district magistrate of Ching-tech six distressed foreigners, saved from the wreck of the *Surprise*, a vessel which had been driven ashore in their country; that they had been already sent on to Yingtsz and handed over to Mr. Knight, the United States consul at that port, since which time no foreigners had been delivered to them.

Taking all these considerations together, and reflecting that an American ship of war has already visited Corea, but was unable to ascertain all the real facts about the matter, and that moreover the French and Coreans seem likely to engage in hostilities, it must be acknowledged that it will be rather difficult to learn the truth of the case. In the dispatch under reply you propose that measures be taken by this government to bring about the release of these men; and if I delay a little, to consult as to the best mode of procedure, it is that the affair may get the benefit of the vest deliberations we can give it. It really will not be best to presently send off a mission to Corea asking about the surrender of these prisoners, for it will probably be evasively excused, and the probable success of the effort imperiled; or else, in our hurry, we shall not het at the real and right beginning of the matter; (referring probably to the misconception the Coreans would get of the object of the demand thus suddenly made on them.)

I would further wish your excellency to reflect that, although Corea is in one sense a dependency of China, her authorities are now engaged in eradicating the religion and forbidding its exercise; and their proceedings in this matter are carried on by themselves just as they please, but in what manner his Majesty's officials have not heard. A moment's reflection will no doubt enable you to see the whole bearing of this suggestion.

I have, however, already sent orders to Mukten to require the authorities in Manchuria to learn all they conveniently can upon this matter, and meanwhile send a reply to the British minister and to yourself in regard to it.

His Excellency S. WELLS WILLIAMS,
U. S. Charge d'affaires ad interim.

禮部 → 總署(1868. 3. 12/同治七年二月十九日)

미국과 영국의 생존자 확인 및 보호 요청에 따른 조처

二月十九日 禮部文稱 主客司案呈 准總理各國事務衙門文稱 同治六年二月十八日 本衙門具奏 接據英美兩國照會 請將羈留朝鮮之洋人設法救出 先擬給與照會一摺 奉旨 依議 欽此 查原奏內稱 臣衙門於同治七年二月初九日據美國使臣衛廉士呈遞照會內稱 前年八月間有美國兩枝桅之商船在高麗擱淺 被高麗土人與船上打仗 洋人死亡殆盡 昨據烟台美國領事官申詳 有中國帶水人于文泰回來云 伊到高麗 遇高麗商人金子平說 親見有洋人二名 華人二名 在披陽省衙門內等語 請卽設法救出 請轉行高麗 將本國商船在彼如何被害之實在憑據 詳述前來 以昭關切等因 仝旧又據英國使臣阿禮國照會稱去年法國兵船前往高麗交戰 嗣後英國商船一隻亦赴高麗 有通商之意 被高麗人將船打破 所有船中人盡行殺死 現有帶水人告知烟台美國人事官云 確知有該船中洋人二名在高麗未死 係英國民人 請卽設法救出 轉送至京各等因前來 臣等查前項洋人被留 係在法國與朝鮮交兵之際 彼時朝鮮自未必能辨其爲英美兩國之人 該使臣所云中國越界民人二名 應聽朝鮮查照向來例禁辦理 至現在是否果有洋人被留 可否請旨飭下禮部轉咨朝鮮國王 令其自行酌核之處 伏候聖裁等因具奏 咨行到部 查前年法國兵船往朝鮮接仗 據英美兩國聲稱 未與其事 朝鮮當交兵之際 自不能別其爲何國之人 如果有英美兩國之人被留 不妨就此遣回 以顯兩無仇怨之意 惟于文泰轉據金子平所說 是否確實 無從查悉 除咨行朝鮮國王妥籌辦理外 相應知照總理各國事務衙門可也 (欽命總理各國事務衙門淸檔撫卹外國人民)

54

禮部(1868. 3. 17/同治七年二月二十四日) → 高宗

미국과 영국의 생존자 확인 요청 사실 등을 알림

禮部爲知照事主客司案呈准總理各國事務衙門稱同治七年二月十八日本衙門具奏接據英美兩國照會請將羈留朝鮮之洋人設法救出先擬給與照覆一摺奉旨依議欽此查原奏內稱臣衙門於同治七年二月初九日據美國使臣衛廉士呈遞照會內稱前年八月間有美國兩枝桅之商船在高麗擱淺被高麗土人與船上打仗洋人死亡殆盡昨據烟台美國領事官申詳有中國帶水人于文泰回來云伊到高麗遇高麗商人金子平設親見有洋人二名華人二各在披陽省衙門內等語請卽設法救出并請轉行高麗將本國商船在彼如何被害之實在憑據詳述前來以昭關切等因仝日又據英國使臣阿禮國照會稱去年法國兵船前往高麗交戰嗣後英國商船一隻亦赴高麗有通商之意被高麗人將船打破所有船中人盡行殺死現有帶水人告知煙台美國領事官云確知有該船中洋人二名在高麗未死係英國民人請卽設法救出轉送至京各等因前來臣等查前項洋人被留係在法國與朝鮮交兵之際彼時朝鮮自未必能辨其爲英美兩國之人該使臣所云中國越界民人二各應聽朝鮮查照向來例禁辦理至現在是否果有洋人被留可否請旨飭下禮部轉咨朝鮮國王令其自行酌覈之處伏候聖裁等因具奏咨行到部查前年法國兵船前往朝鮮接仗據英美兩國聲稱未與其事朝鮮當交兵之際自不能別其爲何國之人如果有英美兩國之人被留不妨就此遣回以顯兩無仇怨之意惟于文泰轉據金子平所說是否確實無從查悉相應咨行朝鮮國王妥籌辦理可也云云　同治七年二月二十四日

李敏庠 ➞ 議政府(1868. 4. 14/高宗五年三月二十二日)

셰난도어호 출현 보고

黃海兵使 李敏庠以異船来到許沙鎭前洋馳啓

狀啓以爲豐川府使 任憲榮馳報內今月十八日許沙鎭將所報內非胡船三竹船及艍舠船三隻自南湖来到本鎭前洋松隅浦下碇止宿云聞甚驚駭府使問情次今方發行而異船之出沒沿浦聞甚驚慮問情等節去留形止絡續馳報之意馳啓

李基祖(1868. 4. 15/高宗五年三月二十三日) ➞ 議政府

李基祖, Febiger 문답기

三月二十三日三和懸旗問情記俄者問情之答曰我是美國兵船尋往平壤到平壤後有相問之事今無可答之語云云此何故也三和亦是平壤地則到平壤可問之事何不問於三和乎可問之事何事耶年前美國船在平壤河攔淺被燒事情可以言之矣其時有異國一船到平壤河下流該處地方官意謂漂到求乘船問情船上人大惡官人不與接談閉目偃臥顯示侮蔑我人忍耐羞憤卑辞苦懇始知非漂到也有崔姓人自稱法國人又或稱英國人其言曰法國兵船方大到若許我交易當爲兩國解兵地方官答以此非地方官所可擅許崔姓益肆咆哮平壤河水淺不可行大船彼猶不顧每天乘潮溯上我人或送米肉菜果示以好意則終不回去漸迫首城省城副將所乘船以鉤索引去執置副將及印信於船中或逢往来商船用砲轟碎奪其物而殺其人不知其数滿城数萬軍民不勝忿憤齊出河上奮力搏擊欲奪副將中丸死者又為数十人衆憤齊激勢莫可遏銃砲互發撒柴擲火竟被船中藏藥轟裂黒焰騰空船燒無餘人死無存尚不知此船之為貴國船也彼崔姓無端深入他國惹此事端至今追究不知其為何意也我國法例凡有异國商民漂到者船完則助粮給需候風歸去船不完則從願旱路差官護送以達北京前後不止一再是為體仁上天視隣國之民猶吾民也豈獨於貴國有相厄之舉乎貴國亦俗尚礼讓問於中國細究原事本末不足秋毫置諸疑慮間今此三和地方官亦是平壤地方官則到平壤所問之事問于於三和地方官可也大書大壯紙四張揭于白旂上竪於彼船相望岸

朴珪壽(1868. 4. 16/高宗五年三月二十四日) ➜ 議政府

셰난도어호 문정(問情) 보고

異様三棹大船一隻来泊于三和新南坊避島近境之由已為馳啓為白有在果即接清南水軍防禦使李基祖本月二十三日未時成貼狀啓謄報内本月二十一日卯時量臣領率衙屬馳徃于吾吾里登高看望是白乎則彼船間已移泊於海西長連界而相距量以陸路洽為三十里之遠越境問情有難遽議是白𠰍除良連放大砲来徃船隻莫可近前故為觀動静臣留待本浦其翌二十二日伶俐校吏給問情記一張使之入船以筆談問情是白加尼回告内小人等持問情記一張夜二更量向徃彼船停泊處未及一帿許彼従船一隻飛到迎擊執捉小人船隻不得前進而彼大船上下燈燭煌煌有刀斗聲假量船體長為二十丈許高為四五丈許三帆羅立中有烟桶是乎遣従船所在人数則為六人而狀貌則高準深目頭髮鬈鬆所着服色段俱是黒色以問情記辭意諭之曰爾以何國人緣何事到此何月何日起程由何地方逶迤到此乎風濤萬里舟中一行俱得無恙乎住碇於此地今已経宿其計安在將欲換賣物貨耶周覽山川耶轉向他處耶還歸故土耶雖曰冠巾異制言語各殊天涯比隣四海一家豈無情志相通所懷各陳乎無或隐蔽一一回示幸甚云云則以手搖之頗有不解文字之様請授問情記而直入大船矣不移時稍觧我國言語者一人来到小人船言曰我是美國兵船但欲尋徃平壌而到平壌後有相問之事今無可答之語是如是白遣辭色甚厲大船中連發砲聲終被阻搪不得已還歸是如為白有卧乎所今此異船之東西閃忽極為叵測則其去其留不是異事是白乎矣今以該防禦使所報觀之謂以長連界到泊已過三数日不即問情雖緣事勢之不及揆以擧行極為疎忽待其兵營譯學来到即速詳細問情馳報之意更為題送是白遣沿邊備禦各浦防守等節另加嚴飭於各該邑鎮為白乎旀緣由馳啓為白卧乎事

58

議政府(1868. 4. 17/高宗五年三月二十五日) ➞ 禮部

제너럴 셔먼호 생존자설 부정

回咨

朝鮮國王爲咨覆事同治七年三月十三日承准貴部咨節該云云[自主客司案呈止妥籌辦理可也見上原咨]等因奉此竊念敝邦平壤江洋船肆虐自取燒燬事情曾於同治五年八月二十五日咨內備陳始末今無庸更述嗣於同治五年十二月據黃海道觀察使朴承輝馳啓備長淵縣監韓致容呈稱有異樣船来泊於本縣牧洞浦有自稱登州人于文泰仲允升兩人以美國水師總兵舒富照會朝鮮國邊疆大臣文字招呼土民金大青交付要致官府該照會內稱本總兵駕駛俄柱嘶船在貴境停泊非有動戈爭戰等事實因本國商船報明據在本年夏天之時路經貴國境界遇沙石淺擱幸蒙貴國救護送至中華大國全得平安還家本國人聞此事無不欣美貴國慈愛之恩也茲查又有本國商船一隻於本年秋間停泊貴國之平洋河卽太平河本總兵風聞被貴國百姓將船焚燬船東船夥俱係美國人船客係別國人俱被殘害至今無一人還本總兵蒙本國水師提督委派詳察如果有此等情事否如係屬實屬虛如係本國商船或在貴境有騷擾等事因以忿爭以致斃命或現存幾人仰貴國迅速查明照覆並現存幾人若在蒙交本船是幸否則從此以後但願兩國照前和好無各殘害等因前来據此始知平壤江惹鬧者之爲美國船也此事不可以無答該地方官不能挽留厥船乃致徑歸其失非細已令戴罪留任飭觀察使朴承輝修置回覆文字以待美船之或者再来相問今此總理衙門原奏內美國領事官申詳有中國帶水人于文泰回来云者確是長淵縣曾到之船中人也伊到高麗云者明是曾到長淵縣之謂也遇高麗商人金子平云者未知爲何等人而其曰親見有洋人二名華人二名在披陽省衙門內等語無據無理之謊說而其曰披陽省者必是平壤之訛也當其藏藥轟裂人船俱燬之際華洋四人那能獨脫而衙門之留置安用也至若英國使臣照會所稱法國兵船前往高麗交戰嗣後英國商船 隻亦赴高麗有通商之意被高麗人將船打破盡行殺死等語尤屬孟浪本國江華府法國交兵在於同治五年九月伊後無論法國英國又無論惡意好意並不曾見一隻船来過初無其船何得將船打破初無其人何得盡行殺死苟有是事豈不以此情形早爲咨報貴部乎其爲蜚語做謊不待辨明可知是必有一種奸細樂禍之徒計在搆釁滋擾而然也金子平者旣稱高麗商人方自本國物色詗捉而于文泰係是登州之人伊于何年月到高麗何地方逢見金子平理合徹底查究

使其說落空快破遠人之惑永絶仇怨之端恐不可已平壤江兩桅商船無端肆惡自取燒燬不是本國枉害遠客之事情不可使美國使臣尚未詳悉每致疑怪其黃海道觀察使朴承輝曾所修置回覆美國總兵之文字茲以附呈倘得轉示則曲直所在庶應洞知而漂海遭難之人國有救送之規今若右流落可憐之命何必使之羈留躊踪乎所稱華人二名洋人二名俱屬烏有自可辨之又況英國船打破元無是事不須更論煩乞貴部將此事情轉達天聽特使布示開諭以爲釋疑解惑毋復故尋事端無往非庇覆之洪恩大德不勝祈懇之至爲此合行咨覆云云 同治七年三月二十五日

59

議政府(1868. 4. 17/高宗五年三月二十五日) ➔ 禮部

황해도 관찰사가 미국에 답하는 서신

黃海觀察使答美國文字

朝鮮國黃海道觀察使朴承輝爲照覆事查本月十八日貴總兵駕駛俄柱嘶船在敝境長淵縣海面停泊投送書一封照會一角專要轉達我朝廷且候邊疆大臣回文該地方官理應明告往復程途之稍遠善辭致誠挽留貴船今乃回文未到之前致令遠賓徑歸違禮乖情未有甚焉除該地方官已令戴罪留任外茲修回覆文字以俟貴船或者再来尚祈管照事情本國法例凡有異國商民漂到者船完則助粮給需候風歸去船不完莫可駕海者從願旱路差官護送以達北京前後不止一再是爲體仁上天視隣國之民猶吾民也今貴本照會盛加稱道還切媿怍秋間平洋河事伊時有異國一船到平洋河下流該處地方官意謂漂到前往求乘船問情船上人大惡官人不與接談閉目偃臥顯示侮蔑我人忍耐羞憤卑辭告懇始知非漂到也有崔姓人自稱法國人又或稱英國人其曰法國兵船方大到若許我交易當爲兩國解兵地方官答以交易一事非一個地方官所可擅許崔姓曾不採聽益肆咆哮平洋河水淺不可行大船彼猶不顧每天乘潮溯上數里我人只要事不張大或送米肉菜果柴薪等物答云明日便回而及於明日反又溯上看看漸迫省城省城副將每日乘舟護行以防彼我人褋亂之弊一日自厥船投下鉤索引去副將之船執置副將及印信於船中或逢往来商船用砲轟碎奪其物而殺其人不知其數遠近莫不大駭奔竄相續何曾有兵戈交鋒之事而副將被執其辱已甚然而猶彼卑辭苦懇請還副將則答曰待我入城還送其崔姓者能爲東國言語桀鰲無雙必欲犯入省城又未知其意所在而滿城數萬軍民不勝忿恨齊出河上奮力搏戰欲奪副將中丸死者又爲數十人之多則衆憤齊激勢莫可遏銃砲互發撒柴擲火而畢竟彼船中藏藥轟裂異焰騰空船燒無餘人死無存尙不知此船之爲貴國船也姓崔的無端深入他國惹此事端至今追究不知其爲何意也貴照會內船客係別國人卽姓崔者之謂歟此事始末盡於是矣貴國俗尙禮讓爲合省名邦中國之所知也貴照會內照前和好無各殘害等語原不足置諸疑慮間茲庸奉覆並須諒悉爲此照覆須至照覆者

【英譯文】

The intendant of circuit in the Hwong-Hae District, Corea and ex-officio, Inspector of the Imperial Board of Directors, makes the following reply to the Commander of the Steamer *Wachusett*s, anchored on our coast off the district of Chang Yuen [Vis], that he has examined you letter of the 18th instant forwarding a communication which you simply wish to be transmitted by my sovereign and proposing to wait the reply of the minister of the frontier. The local magistrate of the place was in duty bound to inform you that the road going and returning would be quite long, and to have treated you with kindness and sincerity so detaining your honored vessel for a reply. Now however, before the arrival of the reply, the guest from afar has already departed, so doing how grievously have we offended the rules of propriety and [violated] true friendly feeling. Aside from the fact that this local magistrate has received a demerit mark, I have prepared a dispatch in reply to be kept in readiness in case your honored vessel should return and first I beg to state in general as regards the circumstances of this affair that the legal regulations of our country with reference to the merchant ships of a foreign country driven hither by adverse winds are that in case that the vessel is sound, we are to furnish provisions and whatever is needed while waiting for a wind to depart. In case the vessel is not sound and there is no means of proceeding by sea, then we are to follow their wish in sending an officer to escort them by land to Pekin, which thing has occurred therefore, not merely once. Such a course we look upon as in accordance with true benevolence. He, who is in heaven above, regards the people of neighboring nations as he does ones own. Your worthy communication which I have just received is as exceedingly complimentary as to make me feel quite ashamed. With reference to the affair which transpired last autumn in the Ping Yang River, I would state that at that time there was a foreign vessel entered the lower waters of the Ping Yang River and the local magistrate of that place supposing that the vessel was driven hither by distress of weather and coming in to seeking a vessel to tranship to, proceeded to make inquiries into the matter, but the men on board the vessel became greatly enraged at the messenger and refused to make any reply, shutting their eyes and lying down at their ease clearly intending to offer insult. Our people restrained their anger and by the most humble address and earnest entreaty found out that the vessel was not driven here by storm. There was one man named Tony calling himself a Frenchman and another said to be an Englishman. They said a large number of men of war was about to come to this place and if the local magistrate would suffer them to open trade with the people it would secure the dispersion of the soldiers of the two countries. The local magistrate replied that the opening of trade was not a thing that a local magistrate could assume to promise. The man "Tony" however refused to regard it, becoming more and more unreasonable and violent. The water in the Ping Yang River is shallow and unfit for running large vessels, but he disregarded this and everyday, riding on the tide, went up a few miles farther. Our people were especially anxious that affairs should not become serious, and so presented them with rice, meat, vegetables, fruit and fuel. The man "Tony" replied that they would leave the next day, but when the next day came, instead of leaving they advanced again up the river apparently intending to push their way to the Provincial city. The Adjutant General went out in a vessel and escorted them every day in order to guard against a collision between their people and ours. One day he threw out grappling irons and ropes and captured the vessel of the Adjutant General, seizing him with his official seal and confining him aboard their vessel. In some cases the trading vessels the met coming to and fro, they rent to pieces with their cannon, carrying off the goods and killing their crew. I do not know to the extent how many far and near, all were exceedingly alarmed and fled in continuous streams. How extreme was the disgrace of the Adjutant General to be seized before hostilities had begun nevertheless we still resorted only to mild words and earnest entreaty, requesting that the Adjutant General should be given up, but the reply was, wait till we enter the city and we will restore him. This man "Tsuy" could speak Chinese and was without a match in fierceness and haughtiness, and seemed determined to force his way into the Provincial City though we did not know what his intentions were. The whole city, including several ten thousand soldiers and people, yielding to their indignant rage came out in a mass to the river and commenced an attack with all their might intending to rescue the Adjutant General. Several tens of people were killed by the cannon balls, when all becoming infuriated rushed on in a mass the force of which was irresistible; fire was opened on both sides and five rafts were used, finally the powder stored in said vessel exploded, rending it to pieces and sending the black smoke up to the heavens. The vessel was entirely burnt up, and the men all killed. We still do not know weather this vessel belonged to your honorable country or not. This man "Tsuy" without cause pushed his way into the interior of another country and provoked this affair, and examination had to this time failed to discover his object in acting thus. It appears from your honorable communication that the vessel of our quest is a different nationality from that claimed by "Tsuy." The beginning and ending of this affair amounts to this: That your honorable country is well known to all the provinces as well as our illustrious neighbor China. As to what is said in your honored communication about continuing former relations of friendship without any occasion of mutual injury I will simply say this affair is but as a particle of autumn dust, not worthy to be entertained as a matter of doubt and solicitude. I now respectfully present this reply asking you to make all necessary allowances and for this purpose this reply is made,

A necessary reply addressed to the American Commander
Fifth year of the Emperor Tung Chi
12th month day

60

G. Welles(1868. 4. 17) → S. C. Rowan

제너럴 셔먼호 생존자 관련 정보 보고

Rear Admiral
S.C. Rowan
Commd'g Asiatic Squadron
Hong Kong

Navy Department
April 17. 1868

Sir:

I transmit herewith a copy of a letter from the Secretary of State, dated the 14th inst. accompanied by a copy of a despatch from the U.S. Consul at Chee-foo, China, relative to a report that some of the crew of the American Schooner *General Sherman* which was destroyed in the waters of Corea, still survive and are in captivity among the Coreans.

Your predecessor, the late Rear Admiral Bell, in a despatch of the 30th of December last, apprized the Department of his having received reports, similar to those herewith transmitted, and announced his purpose, and announced his purpose, as soon as the waters of Corea were sufficiently clear of ice, to despatch a vessel to inquire further into the matter.

Very Respectfully
G Welles
Secr'y Navy

朴珪壽(1868. 4. 19/高宗五年三月二十七日) ➞ 議政府

셰난도어호 문정(問情) 보고

異樣三桅大船一隻移泊於三和府元塘坊麻山浦前洋之由已為馳啓為白有在果即接清南水軍防禦使李基祖本月二十六日午時成貼狀啓謄報內本月二十三日巳時量臣書出問情記一張高揭竿上立於彼船近岸處是白加尼從船一隻追到持去其問情記二十六日寅時量出掛其回文一封故拆見是白乎則回文內昨接来札均已閱悉原籍来由緣問直陳吾本西方大美國人去此五十萬里之遥船経廣東上海至烟台矣三月十五日又由烟台行駛至貴國焉非為貿易而来欽奉君主簡派差来為前二年本國之商船在此河口滅没今特備要文書願貴地方官報知以上者將文書層層上達直至貴國君主案前吾此来甚欲敦友愛之情誼且指望貴國君主與諸大人善為辦理使两國長久和睦再者願向貴國人公平買取禽獸食用之物維此奉復専俟回音如有復文直可在上流芋候今早此船已將上提大美國欽命督理選安多火輪兵船水師副將官云云原本段堅封上送于議政府是如為白卧乎所觀此洋船文字則情偽有難測度而彼船之銃砲相加雖難冒入揭旗問情終涉踈忽該防禦使李基祖不可無警是白遣彼人文字中所謂脩妥文書願層層上達者未知別有何文字是白乎喩亦為疑晦連為另飭各邑鎮備禦戒嚴是白遣嗣後形止陸續馳報之意申飭題送為白乎旀縁由馳啓為白卧乎事

J. C. Febiger (1868. 4. 19) ➞ 朴鼎和

셰난도어호 내항 이유 통지

To the District Magistrate of Chang Leen, Corea

U.S. Steamer *Shenandoah* (2nd Rate)
Off Nan Poo, Ping Yang River, April 19 1868

Sir:

I have the honor to acknowledge the receipt of a communicated addressed to Commander Shufeldt of the U.S.S. *Wachusett*s in reply to a letter from him in relation to the destruction of the U.S. Schooner *General Sherman*.

My present object being the recovery of four of the crew of the *Sherman*, three of whom are Europeans and the others Chinese, reported to be still living and held as prisoners at the Provincial city. I shall proceed slowly and peacefully harming no one until I either reach the Provincial city, or the persons of those four people be placed under my authority. I enclose herewith a letter to the King of Corea, which I hope you will forward with as much dispatch as possible, kindly informing me when you dispatch the letter and the probable time that must elapse before I will receive the reply.

Very Respectfully
Your Obedient Servant
Comdr. John C. Febiger
U.S. Navy

【漢譯文】

大美國欽命督理善安多火輪兵船水師副將官費爲照會事

昨接黃海道觀察使都巡察使同治五年十二月照覆弊國督理俄柱嘶船舒之文一封論○敝國枝半桅商船名戰兒阿實兒僾滅沒一事本副將今來之故因風聞一信該船之人尚有四名未斃二名爲中國人二名爲西國人俱在平洋省城獄內本副將務要得四數人焉且主意○定乘潮溯上若不早將四人交付○吾卽將至省城雖如此溯上亦是和睦不令一人受害再者另有附達貴國君王公一角望貴地方官卽爲速呈更○○此公文之時卽爲照覆並示復待幾日可接貴國大君王示履惟此照會須至照會者

右照會

朝鮮國長連縣

梅紅枝名片費米日

63

J. C. Febiger (1868. 4. 19) → 高宗

조선국왕에게 봉정한 Febiger의 조회문

U.S. Steamer *Shenandoah*
Ping-Yang River, Corea, April 19 1868

Your Majesty,

During the month of August of the year 1866, an Amer. trading Schooner named the *General Sherman* entered this river for the purpose of traffic. To this time she has not returned and it is reported that the crew were murdered by mob violence, the cargo stolen and the vessel destroyed. About a year since one of our Government vessels visited the coast of Corea to the south of this river for the purpose of investigating this matter; but did not get into communication with the proper authorities or receive information satisfactory to my Government. Recent information has been received by the Commander-in-chief of the United States Naval Forces in these seas, that a number of the crew of the *Sherman* are living, and held as prisoners by Corean Authorities, I have been therefore directed by him to proceed to this point with the vessel under any command, and to demand that all persons so detained be given up to my authority on the Deck of this ship. I further earnestly request that Your Majesty will appoint a proper officer with full authority to settle this matter. Hoping for a speedy and favorable reply, I have the honor to remain,

Very Respectfully
Your Obedient Servant
(Signed) Commander John C. Febiger
United States Navy

To His Majesty
The King of Corea

【漢譯文】

照會

大美國欽命督理善安多火輪兵船水師副將官費為照覆事松丙寅年七月有美國枝半桅商船一隻名戰児阿實児縵意通商放至平洋下流至今未囬風聞遭不法之徒將人凶殺貨物刼集船隻滅没焉前一年有美國兵船一隻来至平壤河南特意查訪追究其事但所行之文貴國官不覆故未得確信以覆本國也嗣後美國東海水師提督新聞一信云該船之人尚有数名未斃者却被貴國官員囚執下獄故特派本副將率領所督理之兵船來至此處以討索在獄之人務須完全交於船上方可本副將切望大君王揀派人員前來會議辦理此事尚祈順意速覆惟此照會須至照會者

右照會

朝鮮國大君王

大美國欽命督理善安多火輪兵船水師副將官費公文移至大朝鮮國

64

G. F. Seward(1868. 4. 24) ➜ W. H. Seward(1868. 6. 24)

Jenkins로부터 입수한 정보 보고 및 조선과의 교섭 전권 부여 요청

United States Consulate General,
Shanghai, April 24, 1868

Sir:

Mr. Frederick Jenkins, a citizen of the United States, formerly interpreter to this office, gives me the following information:

There are now in Shanghai four Coreans and a bishop for Corea, of the Romish Church. These persons have been sent here by the Corean government. The purpose is to make inquiries concerning the state of feeling existing toward Corea in regard to the alleged murder of French priests and of the crew of the American schooner *General Sherman*, with a view to determine whether it will be wise for the Corean government to send an embassy to America and Europe to explain those occurrences, and to make desired treaties of amity and commerce. Mr. Jenkins expects to sail with these persons for the Corea in a few days, and believes that the result of the report of the commissioners and of his visit will be the sending of an embassy, as proposed. He expects to return to Shanghai in about a month, and that ambassadors, as indicated, will come with him.

Mr. Jenkins further informs me he is told the priests were executed in punishment for schemes of theirs at the court.

The *General Sherman* trouble is explained as follows: That vessel had reached a point in the interior on a river, of which he does not know the name. Several of the crew went ashore and became embroiled in a row growing out of the wrongful treatment of some women, and were arrested. A force was then sent from the *Sherman*, which rescued the men and took them on board, together with two native officers, who, it is supposed, the master intended to hold as hostages. This excited the people, and they attacked the vessel, killing eight persons and capturing the others, who are still held.

Mr. Jenkins says that this information is known only to the ambassadors and himself, to a Jewish merchant who has visited the Corea several times, and by whom the commissioners were brought to him, and to one other person who has necessarily been spoken to in order to arrange for the charter of a steamer to proceed to Corea. He assigns as reasons why he has been approached, the belief of the Corean government that the proposed embassy would be more favorably received in America than elsewhere, and should be sent there first; and the fact that he is familiar with the Chinese language, which is the written language of Corea. He is unable to explain how it happens that the Corean government is now employing confidentially the Romish bishop, one of a class they have so severely treated. He expects to bring back with him those of the crew of the *General Sherman* who are still living.

The *Shenandoah* has lately sailed from Cheefoo for the Corea to make inquiry regarding the crew of the *General Sherman*, information having been previously received which indicated that some of the number are living.

It is difficult to say whether anything will be accomplished by her commander. Mr. Jenkins says that the Coreans now here declare that the visit will be useless.

GEO. F. SEWARD

Mr. George F. Seward to Mr. William H. Seward.

UNITED STATES CONSULATE GENERAL,
Shanghai, April 24, 1868 (Received June 24, 1868)

Sir:

My dispatch No. 281*, herewith, offers information touching the *General Sherman* case, which has heretofore engaged your attention. It is a subject for congratulation that it is also satisfactory, if true, that the Corean government is anxious to enter into treaties with the western powers. The empire is independent, although it sends complimentary tribute to Pekin. The population is said to be about six millions, or one-third that of Japan. The climate is mild for the latitude. The people are described as peaceful and industrious. In my

*이 문건의 전문(前文)을 가리킴.

opinion there is no sufficient object attainable to render it advisable to use force, or even the show of force, to procure a commercial treaty with the Coreans. It may be considered, however, that the interests of our shipping require that at least a treaty providing for the kind treatment of ship-wrecked people should be entered into. But if the Coreans are prepared to go to the extent of opening up their country to our merchants, this opportunity is not one that should be lost.

I respectfully propose, therefore, in case the proposed embassy be not concluded on, and it shall still seem desirable, on the receipt of your instructions, that authority be given me to request of Admiral Rowan the use of two vessels of war, (one like the *Shenandoah* or Iroquois, the other smaller,) to employ one or more interpreters, and to proceed to the Corea in order to ask an official explanation of the *Sherman* affair, and to negotiate, if possible, a treaty of amity and of commerce similar to those now existing with China and Japan, or such other lesser treaty as may be expedient and attainable without the exercise or show of force.

If unsuccessful, and I am inclined to believe that the exercise of a degree of discretion and patience would insure a more or less complete success-the undertaking could do us no harm.

GEO. F. SEWARD

兪初煥(1868. 4. 26/高宗五年四月四日) → J. C. Febiger

이동을 중지하고 조정의 회답을 기다릴 것을 요청

龍岡送彼船照會草

卽者黃海道觀察營示来貴副將抵長連縣照會及附達我朝廷文書謄本備悉貴船來此之由所索未斃四人本屬島有而文書已經上達惟在我朝廷辦理但回覆之際不可不留待幾日貴船或嫌遲滯又欲乘溯上轉恐主客兩失便宜弊境列鎭將官于我朝廷但受防海之命而已不敢溺戢犯罪必不免鎗砲相警矣貴船全是和睦好意安得不見恀乎且此河溯上沙礁甚多利涉維艱萬一擱淺此所謂主客兩失便宜者也但願貴船在風波安穩處碇住以待回覆析物轉生事端以失和氣爲此照會云云

【英譯文】

The Intendant of the Ping An District in charge of the Ching-Nan Naval Guard and Prefect of San Hoa makes the following communication in reply to Captain Febiger.

That he has just received information from the intendant of Hwang Hae district that your Honor has sent a communication to the Magistrate of Chang Leen together with a dispatch for our Emperor, from a copy of which I fully understand the purpose for which your honored vessel has come. The four men said (not to be dead) which are demanded are in fact not in existence, as however the dispatch has been forwarded, it remains with our Sovereign to adjust the matter and as the reply will require time it will be necessary to wait a few days. In case your honored vessel should be dissatisfied with the delay and desire again to ride up on the tide, I fear that both host and guest may be inconvenienced. The Military officers placed on guard at the borders have simply the orders of the King to guard the entrance from the sea and not daring to be guilty of neglecting their duty, could not but fire guns and cannons as a warning. Your honored vessel coming with intentions wholly peaceful, how could you but feel offended. Further going up the river, the sand banks are very numerous, so that a safe passage is exceedingly difficult, ten thousand to one you would run aground, and this is the point of my saying that both host and guest might be inconvenienced. I earnestly hope that your honored vessel will anchor in some place safe from the winds and waves to await a reply, and by that you will not contrarywise stir up any affair which will destroy our peaceful relations.

A necessary communication addressed to Capt. Febiger
Emperor Tung Chi, 7th Year, 4th mon., 4th day
April 26, 1868

J. C. Febiger(1868. 4. 27/高宗五年四月五日) ➞ 李基祖

조선 조정의 회답 대기, 증급 물품 목록

U.S.S. *Shenandoah*
Ping Yang River, April 27, 1868

Sir:

Your two dispatches dated the 25th and 26th inst., have been received. I am happy to learn that my dispatch to His Majesty the Emperor has been forwarded and shall await the reply at some convenient anchorage near the mouth of the river. I have made a report of my boats having been fired upon from a Military Station to your Government, the reply will be forwarded to my Government for its decision in the case. The mistake in regard to the distance of my country in answer to your queries on that subject occurred in translating the original letter into Chinese. The distance we are forced to sail is about 50,000 li, not 500,000.

The dispatch was prepared in haste by night, which probably occasioned the oversight.

I have the honor to remain
Very Respectfully
Your Obedient Servant
(Signed) Commander John C. Febiger
U.S.N.

To His Honer
The Prefect of San-Hoa

【漢譯文】

外封

大美國欽命督理善安多火輪兵船水師副將官費公文移至平安道水軍防禦使三和府使當臺開拆 內二件 外竹簍一個 戊辰四月初五日

內坪

大美國欽命督理善安多火輪兵船水師副將官費爲照覆事玆接到四月初三日未封之文一伻初四日達到之文一封本副將聞得將上達之文已經轉遞不勝欣歡之至於是卽將船停泊平洋河便宜之地等候幾日可也至於鎭內兵人放鎗一車已經報知貴朝廷而貴朝廷若何示覆本副將必陳奏我國君主以斷定焉再者前覆兩國相隔之地言此去五十萬里之遙本係繙漢字之者誤多書十一字論必得經所之路程大約有五萬里而非五十萬里也因當日之照覆係登○愡忙故未免荒唐耳爲此照覆須至照覆者

右照覆

朝鮮國平安道淸南水軍防禦使三和府使

戊辰四月初五日

昨接華翰不勝欽抑但風範未覩適爲懷憾耳況復多厚貺豕三鷄十鷄卵五十塊儘受納未由情謝尙有微物數種特奉

洋刀一把 胰子五塊 剪子一把 小鏡一面 洋伻二包

鑲銀匙二把 小酒一瓶 信封一包 鑲銀叉二把 吷盒一個

洋針三包 琉璃甁一個 鉛筆一支 鋼釦一付 琉璃盃三個

新間伻二張

非物之爲美聊申投報之情已耳伏思高麗伻中乃貴地所出可否將大小麤細各樣子幷已作成之信封皆賜小許囬至敝國則○爲罕見之搸式再者敝國君主構得華屋一處以聚積別國貽種之物凡有至別國者無論何等五穀花卉菜蔬之種必收取捎囬焉倘不見棄望亦各隨其物之多寡賜之則同爲感情無曁矣謹此奉覆幷候陞祺名另具 四月初五日

J. C. Febiger(1868. 4. 29/高宗五年四月七日) ➞ 李基祖

조선 조정의 회신을 기다린다는 답서

大美國欽命督理善安多火輪兵船水師副將官費爲照覆事初七日於島內取得文書一件已知貴大人已將上達之文轉遞矣本副將必然於河內等候貴國大君王之回示爲只因本副將回覆初三初四之公文貴差人總未來取故特將回文與微物幷送至島內以待差人望見取回焉本副將之意定於初八日至道尖埠以東停泊幾日此雖出河口以後必仍回河內相待爲此照覆須至照覆者

右 照 覆 朝鮮國平安道淸南水軍防禦使三和府使

皮封式

大美國欽命督理善安多火輪兵船水師副將官費公文移至者

朝鮮國平安道淸南水軍防禦使三和府使 當臺開拆

內一件 戊辰四月初七日

68

朴承輝(1868. 5. 2~4/高宗五年四月十日~十二日) ➜ 議政府

김자평(金子平)을 대동한 셰난도어호 문정(問情) 보고

今初十日巳時到豊川月串浦瞭望則異船碇留於殷栗淸凉島豊川席島之間而巡營下送燕京咨文及長連回答書使人傳給于彼船于文泰所遇金子平自巡營捉来爾們出来面質云云 問答條目

初十日傳書時彼問金子平此時坐何處浦邊答月串浦沙場彼問此浦去此幾里答水路三十里陸路量之十里彼問金子平何時官將他捉住長連縣監捉任来此欲辨虛實答曰長連縣監將他送来好我不能去答不欲徃見乎天暮不去耶 彼曰大人說不去我金子平長連縣監欲送則送来答以不去之意書給則歸告官長如何不然則 貴船中無論誰某送一二人去答費大人不着人去答子平年七十九老且病不能乘船故等彼浦邊彼人於年老且病下以不信二字書示故仍爲回棹

十一日

我問爾們来專由金子平說理合一面子平老病無以舟行爾們無意徃將甚爲好且萬里東西惟言是信昨日子平老病勿下書以不信抑甚麽意爾們所遇金子平年幾貌何願詳問爾們云問之於金子平而平都無是說云爾們從何處得聞乎今若詳細指言則又當有辨明之道彼答今日是吾等耶穌教之安息日也諸事不理明日早晨着人来領一二人徃見金子平可也又曰吾船上有事請回故因爲回棹

十二日早朝

當日早朝譯學率長連吏二人及水營執事徃接彼人未時量彼小船一隻載十一人来泊浦邊而各自散行四面顧望故使之禁斷曰弊國之法與人接待不得草草早早来坐

問答記

彼問曰那邊坐者何人答地方官豊川府使任問情官長連縣監朴 彼問金子平在何處吾等是爲此人而来等候多時不見何也答子平在此問爾們姓名彼答吾姓李彼二人一姓山一姓狄彼問二位官坐者何有四人答一是水營虞候官崔一是許沙僉使鄭問此果前者所見金子平乎彼答此次所来之人無曾見過者彼曰請着金子平隨吾等至背靜處吾等細問可否答此外別無背靜處有問這這必問彼曰此去二十丈不在 貴國人之目前卽背靜處也問風濤来徃良苦請飮一盃答不答所問何也至于送酒吾等領謝不必過飮問所問飮後卽答 答吾等剛用飦而来只可心

領耳 問相筆護於問情然後可以卞明 右無答又問此行專爲金子平卞明事相何無一言相及彼問金子平作何生理年歲幾何家住何處答漁業生涯年今七十九住長連府六島彼問羣公何日將金子平捉獲答三月二十五日捉得彼問捉得此人来是何以答曰前所傳燕京咨文及長連縣監囬文何不詳細見之麼答所有之文已經看明但是中國禮部與吾等無于 問然則咨文中于文泰前二年冬遇弊國商人金子平有所問答何也 答子平認識于文泰麼見于文泰○時下幾日 金子平前二年十二月念問于文泰船隻到泊於六島時與官人問情次往見彼曰彼時以後又見遇于文泰否子平曰其後則更不相見彼問金子平之大畧已經問明至於當日船滅沒一事必得吾等背後細問可否允情答背後二字未詳彼曰前後所說去此十餘丈背静處而背後就是背着諸公也答何須背静處對衆明明說去彼曰諸公何不直應曰允不允答背静處不允彼曰無事矣見諸公與未見一也答金子平都無是說云四人拘囚事從何處得聞乎詳細指言則又當有卞明之道右無答彼曰日已西斜吾等欲速歸諸公若有欲吐之裏情于明日或後日至船上有費大人一談可也狄先生代費大人請縣公至船上一觀卽不應公事作閑談之相會無不可也答閑談姑舍雖公事各官不得至異國船上弊國之法至嚴不可近問何時囬船麼答事辨異船卽走問所辨何事答費大人来此旣與 大君王通文諸不能代貴 君主定式所由来之事皆可默待耳問所由来之事右無答問碇留弊國今已數十餘日緣何事不卽歸去麼右無答申時量旅卽歸向大船而去

69

J. C. Febiger(1868. 5. 16/高宗五年四月二十四日) ➞ 李基祖(1868. 5. 17/高宗五年四月二十五日)

조회문에 대한 회신 촉구

月之初旬將所奉貴國大君王之文書已交付貴道台即為轉達矣至今二十餘日合平論埋貴道台諒必已收回文祈速速交來是感本副將食用已經見缺必得早走故望貴道台萬勿躭閣早將貴國之回文交付耳為此照會二十四日三和

李基祖(1868. 5. 17/高宗五年四月二十五日) ➞ J. C. Febiger

Febiger의 서신 전달 요청 거부

三和府使李為照覆事貴船所求上達我朝廷文字間經轉達上司以為此非國書臣不敢輕遽遽上且見今長連縣已有照覆文字附呈黃海道觀察使丙寅冬脩置未傳之書備言〇洋河船燒始末貴副將自可燭悉無餘且本年二月二十四日大清礼部咨移内有貴船來此事情我朝廷已於回咨詳辨初無拘留人名等事此係上國之已達之信蹟㕦文也必當轉到貴國使臣矣今無待更煩縷縷所謂金子平空然做謊搆疑至此已經黃海道觀察營提查情狀綻露矣貴副將亦必釋然更不置疑至若兵人放鎗一事貴船乃是兵船也關防師律何敢擅許兵船之入港乎貴船之以此見恠實所未解幸勿以此介意為此照覆云云二十五日

71

朴珪壽(1868. 5. 19/高宗五年四月二十七日) ➞ 議政府

셰난도어호 철수 보고

異樣大船還泊于海西長連地所軍島前洋之由已為馳啓為白有在果即接清南水軍防禦使李基祖本月二十六日午時成貼狀啓謄報内異船中從船一隻同日未時量溯上于廣梁鎮前洋結石島而洋漢十餘名因為上島許久徘徊是白如可仍入大船故臣直入島中則有洋書一封而觀其辭意專為收索回文故臣旗
招洋人給送責諭文一張是白加尼本月二十六日辰時量同異樣大船飛棹出外洋仍没形跡故彼人書封與責諭文堅封上送于議政府是如為白有卧乎所今此異船雖出外洋從此遠遁姑難料度其周密之道有不可遽爾釋慮乙仍于防守瞭望等節另加嚴飭於沿邊各邑鎮為白乎旀緣由馳啓為白卧乎事

J. C. Febiger (1868. 5. 19) → S. C. Rowan

셰난도어호 조사 결과 보고

U.S. Steamer *Shenandoah* (2nd Rate)
Cheefoo, China, May 19, 1868

Sir:

In obedience to the orders of Commodore J.R. Goldsborough dated the [____] of February 1868, to proceed in this vessel to the Ping Yang river, Corea and demand the delivery of four of the crew of the U.S. Schooner *General Sherman*, said to be detained as prisoners in the Provincial city and also to further investigate the case of the said Schooner, I have to report as follows, viz.

Having secured the services of the Rev'd Mr. Mateer (an American Missionary located at Gung-Chan,) and E.G. Sanford (U.S. Consul at Cheefoo,) as interpreters, together with a Chinese pilot, I left Chefoo on the afternoon of the [____] of April and commenced running a line of soundings across the Yellow Sea, at midnight of the 8th, came to another on the coast of Corea; finding that the pilot was not well acquainted with land marks or depth of water, we were compelled to [round] the way amongst the Islands and into the river, not making our first anchorage inside until the 12th commenced at once the survey of the river with the intention of gradually advancing until I could either get into communication with the authorities, or reach the point at which the *Sherman* was reported to have been destroyed. On the morning of the 15th, a communication was found attached to one of our Signal Staffs on Station Island, requesting information as to our Nationality, our purposes for coming &c (enclosed with translation and reply, Marked "A").

On the morning of the 16th, another communication was found attached to the Staff from the Magistrate of San Hoa, giving an account of a vessel [____] entered the River, of her having in opposition to their request made their way to the Provincial city, that while on their way they robbed and destroyed merchant junks and murdered their crews, seized upon an Official personage and confined him on board the vessel, and otherwise behaved as outrageously, that the people in large numbers made an attack upon them, fire arms being used on both sides, the Coreans losing several Gens killed, and the vessel being eventually fired and blown up, all on board perishing (enclosed with translation and marked "B").

On the afternoon of the 19th, a Corean boat came alongside bringing a communication worded by the Magistrate of Chung Leen; this communication is from a High Government Official addressed to Commander Shufeldt of the *Wachusetts* in reply to his Dispatch to the King of Corea in relation to the *Sherman* affair, and in effect the same as that previously received from the Magistrate of the San Hoa marked "B"; acknowledged the receipt of the communication enclosing a Dispatch from the King of Corea, demanding the delivery on board this ship of four (4) of the crew of the *General Sherman* reported to be held as prisoners in the Provincial city of Ping-Yang. (The letter to Comdr. Shufeldt with translation* and my letter acknowledging receipt are marked "C," also a copy of my Dispatch marked No. 1, are enclosed herewith).

On the 21st, the survey of the river had been carried about twenty five (25) miles, the ship dropping up with the tide; on the afternoon of that day the [Third] Cutter while on her return to the ship from establishing [Point] was twice fired upon by Gingalls from a Military Post some three or four miles above her anchorage, fortunately no one was injured, and although the boat was armed, no shots were fired in return; no notice had been given by the authorities of their intention to fire upon us, should we attempt to pass their Post, as had any cause been given by the action of the boat for their as doing (a report of the officers on duty in the boat is enclosed and marked "D"); a Dispatch was received from the Magistrate of Lung-Ching inquiring into our nationality and the purpose of our coming, (the Dispatch, translation and Reply marked "E" are enclosed); a letter was also received from the Magistrate of San Hoa informing me that a Dispatch had recently come from the Chinese Board of Rites to the Corean Government informing them of the object of my mission and complaining of my not allowing his people to come near us to attend the matter &c; acknowledged the receipt of the letter and reported our Boats having been fired upon, and my intention in case of a repetition to recent such outrage by Force of Arms (The letter, translation and reply marked "F" are enclosed).

On the 25th I forwarded through the hands of the Magistrate of San Hoa to the King of Corea a copy of my Dispatch No. 1, and also a report of our Boats having been fired upon without warning or giving cause for their so doing, demanding an apology for the outrage and the punishment of the

*제1권 59번 문서의 영역문.

offender, (Copy enclosed marked Dispatch No. 2); on the 25th and 26th received Dispatches from the Magistrate of San Hoa, the former informing me of the receipt of my letter, reporting the fact of my boat having been fired upon and rather supporting that act of the Military Authorities, the latter stating that he had received information from the Magistrate of Chang Leen of his having forwarded my dispatch No. 1 to its address and also stating that the four men therein demanded, did not exist (These dispatches with my reply marked "G" [are enclosed]).

Finding that the further prosecution of the survey up the River, would in all probability bring on acts of hostility, which I should be forced to retaliate, I got underway on the morning of the 27th, steamed down the river, came too inside its mouth, and commenced the survey seaward. On the 29th received from the Staff on Station Island a letter from the Magistrate of San Hoa, acknowledging the receipt of my Dispatch to the King of Corea, stating that he had forwarded them and requesting me not to leave like the *Wachusett*s before the reply could be received, in answer stated that I would not leave before that time (Letter, translation and answer marked "H" enclosed). On the 30th shifted anchorage to the eastward of Don Chan Island for the purpose of survey. On the 2nd of May received a letter from the Magistrate of Chang-Leen, enclosing a copy of a Dispatch from the Corean Government to the Chinese Board of Rites. In his letter he stated he could not forward my dispatch No. 1 to his Sovereign as it was not from my Government and also that he had under arrest the Man Kin Tsy Ping, who was said to have given the information of four of the crew of the *Sherman* being still alive and held as prisoners, that he would bring him on board this ship that we might interrogate him in reference to that matter (The copy of Dispatch to Chinese Board of Rites and letter of Magistrate with translation and my reply marked "I" are enclosed). On the 3rd a message was received from the Magistrate of Chang Leen that the man Kin Tsy Ping was old and sick and could not come on board, requesting that we would come ashore and interrogate him. On the following day sent [Ministers or Messer] Mateer and Sanford on shore for that purpose; upon their arrival were received by the officials, one of whom represented himself as the Magistrate of Chang Leen, and the other as the Prefect of Chang Yuen. A man whole they called Kin Tsy Ping was produced asa prisoner with a heavy board canage around his neck who stated that he was 79 years of age and was a fisherman at a place called [Leon Faou] in the Prefecture of Chang Yuen and that he had not seen the

Pilot Yu [Wun] Tai since the *Wachusetts* was on the coast. The magistrate not allowing a private examination, no questions were put in relation to the reported survivors of the schooner. I think it probable that this old man is not Kin [_ sz] Ping, but the head man of the village, off which the *Wachusetts* anchored, mentioned by Commander Shufeldt in his report (a statement of the interview by Mr. Mateer marked "J" is enclosed).

On the 16th having finished the survey [seaward] got underway and ran off the mouth of the river in order to communicate with the Magistrate of San Hoa, on the following day received a letter from him stating he had forwarded my dispatches to his Officials Superior, who had not felt authorized to send it to his Sovereign, as it was not from our Government, that I was in receipt of several dispatches, which ought to be satisfactory in relation to the *Sherman* affair, that the so called Kin Tsy Ping had been beheaded and expressing surprise that I should object to the firing on our Boat (Letter and Translation marked "K" enclosed.)

From all the information I have collected I am of the opinion that none of the Crew or Passengers of the Schooner *General Sherman* are now living, but do not think that the statements given by the Corean Authorities as leading to the destruction of the *Sherman* are at all probable. A schooner of 60 tons whose object was trade would hardly care to proceed slowly up such a river as the Ping Yang, destroying and robbing junks and murdering their crews; it is probable they seized upon and confined the Official spoken of for their own protection, and that they were fired upon first, and by retaliating brought on the result.

The firing upon our Boat at the Military Post up the River was unprovoked and without notice of their intention to do so should we attempt to pass and as satisfaction has been given for the outrage.

During the time of our visit we have succeeded in making a fair survey of the Ping Yang river and its approaches, which I will forward as soon as the sheets are finished. On the 18th got underway and started a [____] of deep sea soundings from [Chode] Island, across the Yellow Sea, arriving here this afternoon.

Very Respectfully
Your Obedient Servant
(Signed) John C. Febiger

Commander.

Rear Admiral
Stephen C. Rowan
Commanding U.S. Asiatic Squadron
U.S. Flag-Ship Piscataqua

A*

Mouth of the Ping Yang River
April 15th 1868

The following communication was given by a Corean petty official to Mr. Cotton on Signal Station.

Of what country are you? For what purpose do you come here? On what month and day did you start and from what place did you come all the way here? Are you all well after your journey of ten thousand le (3 le = 1 mile,) through winds and waves? Is it your plan to barter merchandize or is it simply your plan to take a general view of the hills and rivers, or do you rather wish to pass by to other places and so return to your native land? All under heaven are of one original nature; clothes and hats are very different and language is not the same, yet they can treat each other with mutual friendship; what your wish is please make known and do not conceal anything. A particular reply returned to this Island will be very acceptable.

The region of the Yellow Sea
District Magistrate of San-Hoa

C.W. Mateer
Translator.

U.S. Steamer *Shenandoah*
April 15, 1868

*제1권 57번 "셰난도어호 문정(問情) 보고" 참조.

Your communication of yesterday was received and examined, and affords us pleasure to say that we are Americans. Our country lies to the far west so 50,000 le from this. We came by way of Canton, Shanghai and Cheefoo. We left Cheefoo for this place on the fifteenth of the third month. We do not come here to trade, but have been sent here by our government and have important business to transact with the Corean government concerning one of our trading vessels, which was destroyed in this river, some two years ago. We have ready an important dispatch which we wish forwarded to the King of Corea and ask that you will at once inform the proper officer and request him to send a messenger to bear it with all dispatch to the Capitol. We come with feelings of peace and friendship and we hope that your government will so act towards us, as to continue the peaceful relations of the two countries. We wish to buy from the people some fresh provisions for which we are ready to pay a fair price. A reply to this communication will find us a short distance up the river whither we will move today.

B*

The following communication was tied to the Signal Staff on Station Island during the night of April 15th, and brought on board the *Shenandoah* by Mr. Conie.

The Honorable American Open and Examine

Having just made inquiry concerning your purpose and received a reply saying- We are an American man-of-war searching the way to Ping-Yang; after reaching Ping Yang we have an affair to enquire into; for the present we have no communication in reply to yours. What is the occasion of this course? Since San Hoa is also within the bounds of Ping Yang why not ask here at San Hoa? What is this business that you wish to enquire into? As to an American vessel said to have been grounded and burnt in Ping Yang River, the incumbent local magistrate supposed that they were driven here by distress of weather and wished assistance, but being about to enquire into the thing, the men on the vessel became exceedingly hateful, both officers and men refused attention to our words, shutting their eyes and lying down to sleep, clearly wishing to offer

*제1권 56번 "李基祖, Febiger 문답기" 참조.

insult; our people restrained their shame and rage and after the most humble speech and earnest entreaty ascertained that the vessel was not driven hither by adverse winds. There was one man named Tony calling himself a Frenchman and another said to be an Englishman, they declared that France was about to send a large number of war vessels; if you permit us to open trade it will be the occasion of the dispersion of the soldiers of the two countries. The local magistrate replied that it did not pertain to him to promise such a thing, upon which the man Tony became more and more unreasonable and violent. The water in the Ping-Yang River is shallow and unfit for large vessels, but he disregarded this, and everyday riding on the tide, worked his way up the river; our people showed their friendly feelings by supplying meat, vegetables and fruit, but he would not return (is down the river) but on the contrary gradually pushed his way up to the capital of the province, there by means of grappling irons and cables they captured the vessel of the Adjutant General and put him in confinement and by the time an official letter arrived they had shattered to pieces with their cannon, I do not know how many merchant vessels, robbing them and killing the men. The whole city, several ten thousands of soldiers and people could not restrain their indignant rage but came altogether to the river and made an attack with all their might desiring to rescue the Adjunct General. Several tens of men were killed by the cannon balls and all becoming enraged and furious their combined power was irresistible. Guns and cannon were used on both sides and rafts of burning wood were floated (in, against the vessel) and finally the powder magazine exploded, tearing the vessel to fragments and sending the smoke on high, burning up the vessel entirely and not leaving a single man alive. To this time we do not know whether or not this vessel belonged to your honorable country. This man Tony without sufficient cause pushed into a strange country and stirred up this affair and even to this time inquiry has failed to discover his motive. According to the laws of this country, if merchant vessels of a foreign country are driven on our shores, in case the vessel is still bound we are to assist them with provisions and furnish what they need while they wait a wind to depart, in case the vessel is destroyed we are to send them at their pleasure by land, protected by an officer to Pekin, which thing has occurred more than once. We thus act as according with the principles of true benevolence; heaven above treats the people of different nations as all his own people and it is hard to suppose that we should make a special point of maltreating the people of your honorable country. We have heard from the

Chinese that the custom of your country gives special attention to the rules of propriety. Careful examination into the beginning and end of this affair will show it not to be so much as a particle of autumn dust to be kept in mind as a matter of doubt of solitude. The present local magistrate of San Hoa is also the magistrate of Ping-Yang so that what you have to ask when you reach Ping Yang you may also ask here at San Hoa.

Mon Chin, third month, twenty fifth day
San Hoa, District Magistrate, Le

C. W. Mateer
Translater*

C**

D

U.S.S. *Shenandoah* (2nd Rate)
25 miles up the Ping Yang River, Corea
April 21, 1868

Sir:

I have to report that while in obedience to your order, Lieut. Wm. Starr Dana, Lieut. Robert L. Meade U.S.M.C. and myself were out surveying in the 3rd cutter, we were fired upon this afternoon about three miles above this anchorage and the right (East) bank of the river. We had been making some observations of the river near a small town located on the East bank, along which on the high bluffs, and extending from the town to some distance to the NW, is a wall apparently of stone or mud. The boat was pulling down to the ship and we were close to the East bank to escape the force of a strong flood tide, when we were startled by the sound to two bullets fired in quick succession from the cliffs over head. We pulled immediately out into the middle of the

*제1권 59번 문서의 영역문.
**제1권 62번 문서.

stream, and thus escaped a third shot, for we saw one of the natives loading his piece as rapidly as he could and he was deterred from firing only from having while in the act of aiming, lost something upon which the discharge of his depended, for which he stopped to look. The shots were fired by two persons from the limits of what seems to be a military enclosure or government grounds in the presence of 200 or 300 persons any one of whom could have prevented the act had it been an unauthorized one or one committed by persons actuated by individual malice towards us. We had no communication with anyone within several miles of that place; were making no demonstrations of any kind; had not landed; but were passing quietly by on our return to the ship. We had been signaled by people who seemed to be officials, to land at the village just above, but had not done so as we were desirous of returning to the ship as soon as possible. In our bearing towards the natives whom we have met while landing to angle, get bearing or make observations, we have always been kind and considerate, and have never given offence to our knowledge.

Repectfully Submitted

Commander
(Signed) J.C. Febiger
Commanding

(Signed) Charles S. Cotton, Lt. Comdr.
(〃) William Starr Dana, Lieutenant
(〃) Robert L. Meade, 1st Lieut. U.S.M.C.

E

The Lung Ching Magistrate to Capt. Febiger.

The Lung Ching Magistrate having heard of the arrival of your honorable vessel had determined to call himself, but being confined to his bed from the effects of a cold sent a messenger to enquire for what purpose you had come. The messenger learned that your honorable vessel had come from America, which is several ten-thousand le (a le is one-third of a mile) from here. For what purpose do you come so far? If it be that you are driven in here by the winds or waves, it is well; if it be not so for what purpose do you seek to penetrate into a foreign country and to ascend to the source of the Small stream? Do you wish to open trade or simply to view the scenery of our country? The laws of our country are that on the arrival of a foreigner, it is the duty of the local magistrate of each place or district, into which the foreigner may enter to enquire for what purpose he has come, therefore I trust that you will not be annoyed at the trouble of replying to my letter, but will quickly grant a reply informing me for what purpose you have come. This will be satisfactory.

Mon Chin 3d Moon 18th day Lung Ching Magistrate,
April 21st 1868

To the District Magistrate of Lung Ching,

U.S.S. *Shenandoah*
Ping Yang River, Corea
April 21, 1868

Sir:

I have the honor of acknowledging the receipt of your communication of today, asking for what purpose I have come to this place. I beg to say in reply that I am an American, my country lying to the far West some fifty thousand li (10 li, 3 miles) distant. I have not been driven here by adverse winds nor have I come to trade or to see the country but have been appointed and sent here for the special purpose of investigating thoroughly the matter of the destruction of an American vessel in this river two years ago. I have already prepared and placed in the hands of the District Magistrate of Chang Leen a dispatch to be forwarded to the Government and until an answer shall come I intend gradually to ascend the river with the tides peacefully and harming no one.

Very Respectfully
Your Obedient Servant
(Signed) Comdr. John C. Febiger
U.S. Navy

F

To Captain Febiger,

A dispatch has recently come to our Government from the Board of Rites of China from which we have learned the business on which your honored vessel comes, but seeing your honored vessel will not suffer our people to come near for the purpose of inquiry only attending to this matter of working your way up the stream, our people are all in consternations. I have just received your note in reply to mine from which I learn positively that you do not come for any other purpose (than that specified in the note from the Chinese Government). Your note speaks of a dispatch which you have in readiness and wish forwarded, but it does not appear whether this other dispatch is still on board your honored vessel or whether the documents after leaving your vessel and before reaching me, were meddled with; the dispatch being lost and the accompanying note only retained. All this occasion for doubt is caused by your refusing permission to my people to come near to carry on communication. If this is to be the manner of procedure, how can our wishes be made to harmonize. If the dispatch referred to is still on board the vessel, it is quite unnecessary to trouble yourselves further in going on up the river among the shoals but simply remain at anchor in a safe place sheltered from the winds, putting the dispatch in my hand and awaiting the reply. Our seaboard guard acts in the same way in its treatment of all countries, and so at present all the local magistrates are holding their soldiers in strict readiness lest your honored vessel should again give rise to a disturbance of the peace. I now respectfully present this reply, asking that you will make all necessary allowances only adding that in case your provisions are short, we have a fixed custom with reference to the treatment of guests. Why should you speak of buying from the common people so occasioning me mortification. Hoping for a reply I am yours.

Intendant of the Ping An circuit, having charge of the Naval forces stationed at Ching-Nan and Prefect of San-Hoa.

U.S.S. *Shenandoah*
Ping Yang River, Corea
April 21, 1868

To the Intendant of the Ping An circuit having charge of the Naval Forces stationed at Ching Nan, and also Prefect of San Hoa

Sir:

I have the honor of acknowledging the receipt of your communication of today and beg to say in reply that as to my refusing your people the liberty of holding communication with one, you have been misinformed. To every one of your countrymen coming on board of my vessel bearing any communication I have replied, and such as have come not bearing a dispatch I have treated in a friendly manner; as to your inquiry concerning the circumstances under which I came here I have already replied in my dispatch this morning. I have the honor further to inform you that one of my boats while passing a point some three or four miles from my present anchorage, was fired upon twice this afternoon by persons appearing to be soldiers, but fortunately no one was injured, as my mission is a peaceful one the fire was not returned. As such conduct if repeated must be considered hostile I shall be ready to resent it by force of arms, the responsibility resting on those who have authorized this outrage on the flag of my nation. I shall on a proper occasion demand an apology for this offence and that the persons guilty of firing the shots be punished.

I have the honor to remain
Very Respectfully
Your Obedient Servant
Comdr. John C. Febiger
Commander

U.S.S. *Shenandoah*
Ping Yang River, Corea
April 23, 1868

To the District Magistrate of San Hoa
Sir:

I have the honor to transmit herewith a dispatch to the King of Corea, with the hope you will forward it as soon as possible. You will greatly oblige by informing me of the possible time that must elapse before I can receive a reply from your Government.

Very Respectfully
Your Obedient Servant
Comdr. John C. Febiger
U.S.N.

Dispatch No. 2

U.S.S. *Shenandoah*
Ping Yang River, Corea
April 22, 1868

Your Majesty,

I had the honor on the 20th inst. to forward through the hands of the District Magistrate of Chang Leen, a communication in regard to the delivery on board this ship of four (4) persons, part of the crew of the *General Sherman*. I now forward a copy of that dispatch through the hands of the District Magistrate of San Hoa, and also report that on the afternoon of the 21st inst., while one of the Boats of this vessel was pulling quietly in the river, she was fired upon twice by persons appearing to belong to a Military Station, some three miles above my present anchorage, fortunately no one was injured and as I wish for a peaceful termination to my mission, no shots were fired in return from my Boat.

This act of hostility occurring at a Government Military Station without notice, against the flag of a nation disposed to conduct their business in a peaceful manner, must be considered an insult, if supported by the Corean

Government, if unauthorized. I shall expect an apology and the punishment of the offenders. I shall remain in the river as long as my stock of provisions will allow, in the hopes of a final settlement of the business that has brought me here. Should I be forced to leave without such settlement, my Superior Officer will probably be here during the summer with his Squadron to attend to the affair.

Very Respectfully
Your Obedient Servant
(Signed) Comdr. John C. Febiger
U.S. Navy

To His Majesty
The King of Corea

G*

Intendant of the Ping Yang An district in charge of the Ching Nan Naval Guard and Prefect of San Hoa, makes this following reply to Capt. Febiger. I have just received your honor's reply to my last with a note in reply to my former note, acquainting me with the fact that a dispatch has already been placed in the hands of the Magistrate of Chang Leen. It rests with my Sovereign to determine how this matter is to be adjusted. I could not from my position venture to conjecture, but your vessel having professed itself friendly ought in reason to have sought a safe anchorage and there await a reply, but now on the contrary disregarding the danger of getting aground. You keep ascending on the tide causing the minds of the neighboring people to be filled with doubt. Who will believe you have peaceable intentions? The officers in charge of the forts and appointed by the military regulations of the country to guard the river, not having received the orders of the King, how would they dare to relay their guard. We shall deem it a most fortunate circumstance if you will wave taking any offence at the firing of the soldiers. There was information given you

*제1권 65번 문서의 영역문.

already, I will be most happy if you will only anchor in some safe place and await a reply to your dispatch and hope that you will not on the contrary stir up a collision unbecoming the circumstances. The whole earth is not more than 72,000 li in circumference, yet you say that your country is 500,000 li distant, now although the way by sea may be roundabout, yet cannot exceed 72,000 li.

How is it you speak of 500,000 li. If everything is to be done after this style, it will truly nonplus not a little. I sincerely trust you will give me a reply explaining this matter.

A necessary communication addressed to the Captain of the U.S.S. *Shenandoah*

Mon Chin, 4th month, 3rd day,

April 25, 1868

Reply to No. "G"*

H

The intendant of the Ping Yang An district commanding the Naval Guard at Ching Nan and Prefect of San Hoa, makes this following reply to Capt. Febiger.

"This dispatch brought by the men of your honored vessel has been received and the accompanying dispatch addressed to my sovereign I have already forwarded. I hope you will make allowance for the fact that the journey from this place to the capital and back requires over ten days. It is necessary that the matter concerning which your honored vessel has come should receive a distinct reply that so your doubts may be thoroughly removed. Please do not be offended by a little delay, but by all means anchor in a place safe from the winds and waves and await a reply.

Do not by any means I pray you depart as the *Wachusett*s which came to Chang Yuen last year.

A necessary communication in reply, addressed to Captain Febiger.

Tung Chi, 7th year, 4th month, 6th day.

(April 28th 1868)

*제1권 66번 문서.

U.S.S. *Shenandoah*
Ping Yang River, Corea
April 29, 1868

To the Prefect of San Hoa

Sir:

Your unsealed dispatch which was deposited on Station Island has just been received from which I am happy to learn that my dispatch to your Government has been forwarded. Be assured I shall continue to await in this river the reply to the same.

My reply to your dispatch of the 25th inst., inasmuch as your messenger has not come to take it, I have placed together with a small present on Station Island, where it awaits your disposal. It is my intention tomorrow to move this vessel and anchor under Don Chen for a few days, but will afterwards return and await in the river the reply of your Government.

I have the honor to remain
Very Respectfully
Your Obedient Servant
(Signed.) Commander John C. Febiger
U.S.N.*

I**

A copy of a communication from the Corean Government in reply to a despatch sent from the Board of Rites at Pekin.

We beg to forward the following reply to your honorable Board. During the month of April 1868, the dispatch of your honorable Board was received relating to the case in adjudication between host and guest stating that a report of the foreign office had been received, which said that on the 11th of February

*제1권 67번 문서 "조선 조정의 회신을 기다린다는 답서" 참조.
**제1권 24번 문서 "제너럴 셔먼호 생존자설 부정 및 프랑스 군사행위의 부당성" 참조.

1868 they had presented a memorial to his majesty to such and such effect.

Since therefore we have received this (viz. the recommendations of the foreign office in the memorial to the Emperor and approved by him.) We beg humbly to submit that as to the matter of the foreign vessel which by rash violence brought on its own destruction in our bounds in the Ping Yang River; it has already in the dispatch dated the fifth year of the Emperor, Tung Che, 8th month, 22d day (Sept 30th 1866), been fully stated from first to last so that it is unnecessary now to report.

Afterwards in the fifth year of the Emperor Tung Che 12th month, (January 1867), a report was made by Poo-ching Hwuy Intendant of the province of Hwang Hae submitting a representation prepared by Han Che Yung, the District Magistrate of Chang Yuen, in which it was stated that a strange vessel came and anchored off his district at a place called Moo [T]ung Poo and that two men calling themselves Yung Chow men, one named [T]u Wun Tae and the other [Ts]ung Yuin Shing came on shore with a communication from the American Naval Officer Captain Shufeldt, to the frontier officer of the Corean Government and calling to them, one of the natives of the place called Kin [T]a Ching, put this dispatch in his hands to be carried to a Magistrate. This communication was as follows; The commander of the *Wachusett*e, now anchored off your shores does not come to disturb the people or begin hostilities, but in all sin[cer]ity because of the intelligence brought of one of our merchant vessels vis; that during the Summer of this year while passing along the coast of your country, she was wrecked on the rocks and the officers and crew were most fortunate in being rescued by your countrymen and escorted safely within the bounds of China and so all returned in safety home. Our countrymen on hearing this were unanimous in their expressions of pleasure at the good will and favor shown by your countrymen. I have recently received information that another of our merchant vessels during the Autumn of the present year anchored in the Ping Yang River also called the Tai Ping River and I have heard a report that the said vessel was burnt by the people of your country and that all on board (the owner and the crew being Americans and the passengers of other nationalities) were put to death so that to this time not one has returned. I have had the honor to be appointed by the Admiral representing our Government in these seas to make careful examination whether these things are so or not. If true or if false or if this merchant vessel of ours has been guilty of raising a disturbance within your border in consequence of which a quarrel arose, and they lost their lives, or if some may have survived I earnestly request your Government speedily to make investigation and give a reply, and further the survivors if still alive; please oblige me by placing on board this vessel if not alive, then I earnestly hope that hereafter as heretofore the countries may be at peace without any occasion of violence &c. &c.

On the receipt of this dispatch we first became aware that the vessel which provoked a mob in the Ping Yang River was an American Ship. This communication should have been answered but the local magistrate of the said place could not detain the vessel but occasioned its departure, which error was not small. Orders have already been given reprimanding him, and Poo Ching Huy the Provincial Governor has been enformed to prepare and keep on hand a reply that it may be in readiness in case the American Ship should return again to make inquiries.

Again in the report made by the American Consul included in the Memorial of the foreign office, the statement that a certain Chinese Pilot Yu Wun Tai had returned is undoubtedly made of the man who was with the vessel that came to Chang Yuen Heen; the statement that he had been in Corea clearly refers to the time he came to Chang Yuen and as to the statement that he there met with a Corean Merchant named Kin Tsz Ping we do not know to what individual refers. As to this Kin Tsz Ping's saying that he saw two foreigners and two chinese in prison in the Pi Yang Province, the assertion is a falsehood with out proof and with out reason, moreover he speaks of the Pi Yang Province which must be a mistake for Ping Yang. At the time the explosion of the powder rent the vessel to pieces both men and vessel were all destroyed, how then could these four men make their escape, not only so but of what use would it be to us to keep such men in prison. As to the communication of the English Minister stating that after the war ships of the French came to Corea to wage war, an English Merchant vessel came to Corea for the purpose of trade and was destroyed by the Coreans and the men all killed &c, it is still more unworthy of belief (or consideration). Since the 9th month of the 5th year of the Emperor Tung Che (October 1866), when the French came to the District of Kyang Hoa to make war, not a single vessel either French or English either for a good purpose or an evil one has come near us. In the first place no vessel came, how then could it be destroyed. The men never were, how then could they all be killed. And if this affair had taken place could we have done otherwise than immediately report the circumstances to your honorable Board.

That these flying rumors and manufactured lies without even waiting for a clear refutation may be known to proceed from some villainous fellow delighting in evils, whose purpose was to stir up a quarrel and excite confusion may be taken for granted. Since the man Kin TszPing is a Corean it is therefore for us to spy him out from amongst the hetereogeneous multitude of our people and arrest him and Yu Wun Lai being a [T]ung Chew man, it ought in reason to be investigated to the bottom in what year and month he came to Corea and where he met Kin Tsz Ping and so came his assertion to fall to the ground quickly dispelling the doubts of the foreigners, and forever calling off this occasion of enmity, and even this would probably not be the end of it for him.

The fact that the two masted foreign vessel lost in the Ping Yang River did without cause by its outrageous conduct procure its own destruction, and that our people did not unjustifiably injure the strangers, the american officers should not longer be left without the clearest information so causing each one to harbor suspicions. The reply prepared by Poo Ching Hung the Intendant and General Inspector of the Hwang Hai District and hold in readiness for the American Captains, we do now herewith forward. In case this shall be made known (viz, to the American Officials), it ought to be some where near clearly known who has the right and the wrong of this affair.

As to men shipwrecked and in distress our country has its established custom of rescuing and forwarding them so that if there were any spending their lives in pitiful exile, why should we retain them in such solitary loneliness. That there are no such supposed two Chinese and two Foreigners may be made clearly to appear and still more as no English vessel has been destroyed here, so it is useless to discuss that matter further.

We beg to trouble your respected body with a request to communicate this affair to his Imperial Majesty and specially presenting our most importunate entreaty that His Majesty will grant a public proclamation setting forth his mandate for the dissolving of suspicions and double that there may not again be a wilful seeking of difficulty and that we may never be without the protection of His Majesties illustrious grace.

On account of the above, a reply is sent abroad.

Poo Ting Ho, District Magistrate of Chung Leen, Corea makes the following communication in reply to captain Febiger.

"I have examined your two dispatches of the 28th received through my constables, one addressed to myself and one to the King, both which letters have respect to the matters of a vessel belonging to your country destroyed in the Ping Yang River in the year Ping Yiu 7th month (August 1866) and also referring to a vessel of yours which came afterwards and anchored on the coast off the district of Chang Yuen and sent a dispatch and received no reply. Moreover also inquiries are made in consequence of recent information that four of the crew of the said vessel are still alive and in prison at the Provincial city of Ping Yang. How a communication from the Inspector General and Intendant and of Circuit, which in the Winter of the year Ping Yiu (1866) failed to be delivered has already been placed in your hands, as that the affair from beginning to end ought in reason to be already sufficiently ventilated; but now there comes this renewed inquiry at which I cannot suppress my strong suspicions.

Meantime in consequence of a communication from the Board of Rites at Pekin a statement of the facts from beginning to end has been made out and forwarded. That four of the men of the said vessel have not been detained in prison is thoroughly settled (Lit[.] discussed). This account moreover being imperial is reliable and worthy of belief. The communication which was given me not being from your Government, I a frontier officer did not dare to forward it to the King. But if I should forward it, could a reply be any more explicit than this copy of which I now send you to serve as a thorough explanation of this affair. As to the recent information of which you spake in your dispatch since it came from Kin Tsz Ping I have arrested him for the purpose of conveying him at once on board your ship, that so, you may examine the matter to the bottom. The particulars of his false statement will of themselves lead out and so your formed suspicions will be dissipated, even as the quick melting of ice. I earnestly hope for a reply relieving me of this unpleasant business, which favor if I receive I shall be most happy, but if on the other hand you still consider that which is not as if it were, it must be because you are bent on seeking an occasion of difficulty (or hostility). In this case I must assume to know the issue. I beg your indulgence in making this reply

A necessary communication addressed to Captain Febiger
Seventh Year of the Emperor, Tung Che

4 of month ---- day
Date omitted

Received May 2d 1868.

The Intendant of the Ping An District, Commandant of the Naval Guard at Ching Naw and Prefect of SanHoa, makes the following reply to Captain Febiger.

The dispatch which your Excellency requested me to forward to my Sovereign was forwarded in due time to my Superior. In as much however as it was not a government dispatch the frontier officer would not venture to forward it inconsiderably to his Majesty. Moreover the District Magistrate of Chang Leen has already given you a reply and has forwarded to you the undelivered dispatch of the Inspector and Intendant of the Hwang Hai district, prepared during the Winter of 1866, in which the burning of the vessel in the Ping Yang River was fully stated from first to last, so that Your Excellency must be fully enlightened on this subject. On the 24th of the 2d Month (March 17th) of the present year a dispatch was sent by the Board of Rites of the Chinese Government in which the matter of your Excellency's coming here, was stated. In my sovereigns reply to this dispatch it has been clearly shown that such men have never been held in confinement, and this most reliable reply has already been forwarded to the Chinese Government and will certainly be put in the hands of the American Minister. It is quite unnecessary therefore to continue waiting or trouble yourself with the business any further. ---- The individual called Kin Tsz Ping who without foundation told lies and raised suspicions has already been arrested by the Military Officers of the Intendant and Overseer of the Hwang Hai district. Examination has been made, the affair has been brought to light and the man beheaded. Your Excellency will no doubt understand this and be without any further doubt. As to the matter of the firing by the Soldiers I have to say that your Excellency's vessel being a man of war and the garrison of that place having standing orders, how could they dare to suffer you a man of war to pass within the barrier. Why your Excellency should be surprised at this matter I really cannot understand. I hope you will take no notice of this matter.

A necessary dispatch addressed to Captain Febiger Tung Chi, 7th year,

4th month [11]th day. (May 2d 1868)

J

U.S.S *Shenandoah*
Off the mouth of the Ping Yang River, Corea
May 4th 1868

The undersigned has just been on shore in company with Mr. Sanford for the purpose of seeing a man named Kin Tsz Ping declared by the Corean Authorities to be the man from whom the report comes that four of the crew of the *General Sherman* are still alive and held as prisoners. When we landed we found two officers waiting to receive us one calling himself the District Magistrate of Chang Leen and the other the Prefect of Chang Yuen. They presently brought forward a man which they called Kin Tsz Ping a prisoner, when our interview began. They volunteered in advance that we were not allowed to talk directly with the prisoner but must ask through them in writing. I at once asked the privelege of a private interview with Kin Tsz Ping but they answered evasively and without pressing the matter I proceeded to ask some general questions eliciting information to the effect that this said Kin Tsz Ping is 79 years old is a fisherman by profession and lives at a place called Leon Taon in the prefecture of Chang Yuen and province Hwang Hae. He has not seen the pilot Yu Wim Tae since year before last in the 12th month about the 20th at which time the said Yu Wim Tae was at Leon Taon in a ship probably the *Wachusett*e having business with the officers after bandying back and forth various questions of a general kind which failed to elicit anything I returned to my original request stating that I had no more general question to ask and that for the purpose of going into the particulars of the business on hand I must have the opportunity of a short private interview which I earnestly requested. They at first evaded but when held to the point refused. Upon this I declined asking anything further and after some complimentary talk the interview closed. As soon as they saw that I declined any further questions they volunteered to say that Kin Tsz Ping said he never had said that there were four men of the crew of the *Sherman* in prison. Showing too plainly the answer they intended should be given to any question of mine on this point and that they intended to keep the power of making such an answer in their own hands. The man Kin Tsz Ping is bowed down with age and is evidently an unlettered and obscure man. He came before us with a large and heavy wooden board or caug[sor] on his neck and was altogether a pitiable sight. The strong impression made on both Mr. Sanford's mind and my own is that this is not the man at all from whom our information in reference to the *Sherman* comes.

C. W. Mateer

U.S.S. *Shenandoah*
Off Don Cheen Island "Corea."
May 2d 1868

Sir:

Your communication dated the fourth month containing an abstract of a dispatch to the Chinese Board of Rites has been received.

As you state you will not forward my dispatch to your Sovereign dated the 20th Ultimo, there can be no further necessity of a correspondence between us.

Very Respectfully
Your Obedient Servant
Commander John C. Febiger
U.S. Navy

To the Magistrate of Chung Leen, Corea.

73

G. F. Seward (1868. 5. 25) ➞ W. H. Seward (1868. 7. 13)

조선과의 교섭을 위해 무력 사용이 불가피함

Shanghai, May 25, 1868 (Received July 13, 1868)

Sir:

I have the honor to advise you that the United States steamer *Shenandoah*, which left this port for Corea on the 18th of March last, has returned to Cheefoo. The commander had intercourse with officers at different points on the coast, but learned nothing to corroborate the reports which have been prevalent here that some of the crew of the *General Sherman* are still living, and that the government is disposed to send an embassy to western states. Mr. Jenkins has also returned. He had frequent communication with the Corean officers, and virtually confirms the information brought by the *Shenandoah*. Whatever causes may be at work in corea, I am now led to believe that no negotiations, not supported by a considerable show of force, would be likely to be successful.

GEO. F. SEWARD

S. C. Rowan (1868. 7. 24) ➞ G. Welles

조선의 사과가 없을 시 무력 응징 방침 천명

Yokohama July 24, 1868

Hon. Gideon Welles
Secretary of the Navy

Sir:

I have the honour to acknowledge the receipt of your communications of the 17th April last, enclosing copies of letters from the Secretary of State and our Consul at CheeFoo, China, Mr. Sanford. In reply I have to state that Commodore Goldsborough, my immediate predecessor, in compliance with the declared intention of the late Admiral Bell, dispatches the *Shenandoah*, Commander J.C. Febiger, to Corea, to enquire after the survivors of the *General Sherman* reported to be imprisoned or detained in that country.

The enclosed report of Commander Febiger, and his correspondence with the authorities, may be taken as conclusive that there are no survivors of the *General Sherman*, nor is there a vestige of the vessel above water.

I believe these people as to the manner of the destruction of the schooner, how far they are justified in destroying her, remains an open question.

The insult to the flag requires a more unconditional apology than the one already made. If this country becomes settled before the close of the season, so that vessels can be spared, a force will be sent to Corea for that purpose.

Very respectfully
Your obed. servant
SC Rowan
Rear Admiral
Comd. Asiatic Squadron

75

S. W. Williams (1868. 7. 31) → W. H. Seward

청조의 조미 관계 주선 보고

LEGATION OF THE UNITED STATES
July 31, 1868

Sir:

Referring to Mr. Burlingame's despatch No. 124*, of December 15, 1866, and others, relating to the fate of the American schooner *General Sherman* in Corea, I have now the honor to inclose a correspondence (inclosures A, B, C) with the Chinese government, which was commence for the purpose of engaging its good offices in ascertaining, by direct application to the King of Corea what were the real circumstances connected with t he loss of that vessel.

The reason why an earlier application was not made to Prince Kung, after receiving you dispatch, was that it was deemed best to await the arrival of the annual Corean embassy at Peking, when more direct intercourse with the officials from that country could perhaps be obtained. This embassy did not reach the capital till January, and at that time the rumor mentioned in my note to Prince Kung had assumed so much probability that I wished to learn what grounds there were for believing it. This, unfortunately, could not be done till after the Coreans had left for their country, but in any case I could not have asked them directly, as the Chinese officials in this city are particularly careful to keep these tributary nations confined to their own quarters, and they themselves are shy of all intercourse.

I was, however, able to see one of the confidential members of the Corean mission, and ascertained from him privately some particulars relating to the attack on the schooner. He told me that he was not himself in that part of the country at the time she was in the river Pingjang, but he heard that, after the vessel had got ashore, she keeled over as the tide receded, and her crew landed to guard or float her. The natives gathered around the vessel, and ere long some altercation arose between the two parties, which soon led to blows and bloodshed, and a general attack on the foreigners, who were all killed on the spot by the mob of natives, of whom fully 20 were killed. He understood that

*제1권 27번 문서.

the vessel was French, though he knew nothing of the flag which she bore, nor even of the signification or distinction of foreign flag; but he was sure that all her company were dead, and had moreover believed that the wreck still remained in the Pingjang river.

Before the reply from the Corean authorities was received in Peking, the United States corvette *Shenandoah* had returned from her visit to that country, where Captain Febiger went in March to ascertain the truth of the same rumor that I refer to in my note A. From what he learned, combined with the reply given him, and apparently intended for the United States steamer *Wachusett*, when she was there in 1866, there can remain no reasonable doubt that the whole company on board the *General Sherman* were killed about September, 1866, and the evidence goes to uphold the presumption that they invoked their sad fate by some rash or violence acts towards the natives.

I have the honor to be, Sir, your obedient servant,

S. WELLS WILLIAMS

Hon. WILLIAM H. SEWARD,
Secretary of State, Washington, D.C.

A

LEGATION OF THE UNITED STATES,
Peking, March 3, 1868*

B

Prince Kung to Mr. Williams
[Translation]

MARCH 10, 1868 (Tungchi, 7th year, 2d moon, 18th day)**

C

*제1권 51번 문서.
**제1권 52번 문서의 영역문.

Note from the Foreign Office.

July 11, 1868*

*제1권 51번 문서의 관련문서 1번.

F. F. Low(1871. 6. 15) → H. Fish(1871. 8. 21)

조선내 천주교도로부터 입수한 제너럴 셔먼호 사건 관련 정보 보고

ON BOARD FLAG-SHIP COLORADO,
Off Boisée Island, Corea, June 15, 1871 (Received August 21)

Sir:

On the evening of the 10th instant a Corean junk came along side, and from the actions of those on board we concluded that they desired to communicate the ship. The interpreter whom I sent to ascertain their business, reported that the people on the junk were Christians; that three Catholic priests were looked for on the coast, and hearing that a foreign fleet had arrived, they naturally expected the priests would have availed themselves of the opportunity to come. Their business was to ascertain whether any priests were on board our ships, and if so, to put the junk at their service, to convey them to any point they might choose. The coming of these people naturally excited my suspicion, but subsequent questioning fully satisfied me of their good faith. The zeal and religious enthusiasm which had induced them to run such risks to find their priests, impressed me, profoundly with the power which the Romish church is able to exercise over an alien and ignorant people. These men evidently belong to the peasantry, as but few of them have any education. They were quite free to communicate any information they possessed, but owing to their ignorance and the difficulty of acquiring authentic information in such a country as this, their statements cannot be relied upon, except concerning facts that have come under their personal observation.

They represent that there is great discontent among the people generally, caused by the tyrannical conduct of the government and the exactions of the local authorities; that the will of the officials is the only law, and that summary executions is the universal penalty adjudged for its violation. They represent the number of christians in the country prior to the persecutions of 1866 at 30,000, of whom 10,000 were sacrificed at the time the French priests were massacred; that not only the remaining 20,000 Christians, but a large minority, if not a majority, of the people beside, desire the overthrow of the present despotic and tyrannical government, and would join any movement foreign nations might make which would accomplish the result. As failure would involve the certain destruction of the natives who might join foreigners, it could not be expected that the standard of revolt would be raised until success could be reasonably assured. From them we gained considerable information in regard to the principal cities and their relative importance. The most important intelligence, however, was a connected and apparently truthful account of the destruction of the American schooner *General Sherman*, in the Ping Yang River, in 1866. One of the Christians affirms that he resided near the scene of the disaster, and was perfectly familiar with the whole proceeding. His story appears so reasonable when tested by the other information I have been able to gather concerning this people and their acts, that I feel bound to say that in my opinion it is substantially true. He says the people on board the schooner were enticed on drugged spirit, during which they were fallen upon suddenly seized and bound and all massacred. Some were beheaded, and the others were beaten to death with clubs. The cargo was taken out, and the vessel burned to get the iron used in her construction. They further say that the cannon found on board were taken out and sent to the capital, from which patterns were made and guns manufactured. This story was told in a plain straightforward manner without undue questioning. On the *General Sherman* affair, in order to test the good faith and truthfulness of these people. It corresponds so nearly with the account given by the French priests at the time, that I consider it more entitled to credence than the report of the officials made to the commander of the *Shenandoah* or that to the board of rites, Peking. It is unreasonable to suppose that the persons on board the schooner, the owner of which was largely interested in the cargo, would inaugurate hostile proceedings to force the natives to open trade; it is to be presumed rather that, as they were bent on trade and gain, they would endeavor by conciliation to induce the people to purchase the cargo. To be sure, the attempt to open commercial relations with this government of Corea in any way, the entrance of the vessel into Corean waters being in violation of the laws and policy of the country. And while this is the fact, it affords no justification for the action of the government or people in the destruction of the vessel and cargo, and still less for the massacre of the people on board. The statements of the officials which have been reiterated so often and with such persistency are scarcely worthy credence, and should be received with great caution. Were they honest in the belief that their action can be justified, or the truth of their statements substantiated, why did they oppose so persistently and prevent the *Shenandoah* and *Wachusett* from going to the spot where the vessel was wrecked, and making inquiry of the people who witnessed the whole affair, and thus satisfy the Government of the United States of the real facts? And why are the officials of all grades so profuse in their protestations to me of the primary offense of the people on board the schooner, and so anxious lest I should desire to make further inquiries into the facts? The Government, in its communications to the board of rites, Peking, you will observe, takes great pains to throw the whole responsibility for the disaster upon the foreigners, and insists that its statements shall be received and accepted without question by that of the United States. In view of all the evidence, direct and circumstantial, which I have been able to gather, the conviction is forced upon me that the statements of the Corean government in regard to the *General Sherman* case are unreliable and unworthy of belief, and that if the exact facts could be known, it would be found that the vessel was plundered and then burned, and the men on board wantonly and treacherously massacred.

It remains for the Government of the United States to say whether further efforts shall be made to ascertain the facts, and, if the government of Corea is found to be culpable, to demand and enforce means of redress, or whether the statements of this semi-barbarous and hostile people shall be received without question in justification of their acts of robbery and murder, committed upon the property and people of the United States.

I have, &c.,

FREDERICK F. LOW

〖關係資料〗

제너럴 셔먼호 승선기(乘船記) 1866. 7. 18~1866. 8. 31

六月初七日 異樣船一隻 來泊於頭伊浦之意 有箕尹所報 異樣船入來內地 聞甚驚恠 使人往探其虛實之意分付 則初八日乘舟順流 限日暮 到異樣船上泊處 則地是平壤草里坊頭伊浦邊也 翌日朝 登彼異樣船 先問人數與來由 則洋人中所謂崔蘭軒 能通我國語 答曰 我們凡五十餘名 而我國主教七人 爲爾國兩班殺害 故欲探其委折 而不遠萬里 涉大海而來此云矣 東人答以爲 爾國主教 本非我國擅殺 我國邪學之徒 依法禁譏察之際 爾國主教 自然現捉 誇矜奇術 寧死而登天堂 期不欲還歸本國 故勢不得已就死 則豈非自致其死乎 然我是居村商業之人 聞爾們之來 欲爲換買如干物貨 今從容來見 實無關於公事云 則洋人蘭軒 與淸人趙凌峯 或以言語 或以筆談 輒以交易爲第一喜事 果有眞情和答之際 崔哥忽問北京禮部咨文出來指爾國 爾或知之否耶 答曰 居村商業之人 曾未知咨文之何許文蹟 而近聞道路傳說 則法國有興師而東之論 自都京禮部 排和喜事之文蹟出來云云而已 崔哥答曰 我船中物貨 眞銀一萬二千餘兩矣 以爾國別銀紅蔘楮皮等物 處處交物以給 則我從旱路 由義州即入北京 挽止法國出師 不亦好耶 答曰 紅蔘我國禁 別銀亦非我國所産 况我以村商 百無求得之道 設或有之 他國之換買者 與受同戮云 則崔哥曰 然則以紙丈米苞 隨力相換爲好 如是相持 爲數日 自本官大米一石 生鷄二十五首 鷄卵五十介 牛肉五十斤 四色果實 裝載小船 庶尹中軍 同舟下來 並登彼船 慰問遠來後 一一越給 則彼人等稱謝而已 此乃十一日事也 回告此意於甸營 則分付內 交易不可遽然許施 汝以如干贈給委曲獻誠 第爲還送之道至可有教 故大米二石 火柴二十束 生鷄二十首 鷄卵五十介 生猪一首 牛肉三十斤 扇子二把 烟竹二介 一一辦捧 更爲順流而下去 十三日黃昏時也 擧火越給 亦爲如前稱謝而已 少無感回之心 反以換貨之不持來 恐動滋甚 十四日擧帆溯上 到于萬景臺下 而投碇定泊 我亦乘小船 先到萬景臺上端而泊船 以觀動靜之際 本官居於萬景臺佛堂矣 仍乘小船 亦入彼船 交易一事 實非營府擅行 狀聞朝家 待處分施行爲計 往復間限七日 姑俟之云 則洋人輩 以不可時刻遲滯爲答 本官以義理責諭之 則少

有順從之意 爲本官 以多少間 使私換賣 探知於營門次 十五日馳進臺下後 中軍亦以地方官代行 出待萬景臺酒幕矣 彼人六名 乘艇下陸 經夜無動靜矣 十六日潮水 擧碇掛帆 溯閒似亭 而仍泊於普通江口 故小人亦爲行先於彼溯上 艤船圓伊島上端 中軍亦乘小船 追後行船 期入普通江口之際 彼人五名 乘其從船飛追 中軍勇奪其纜 旋到大船 中軍從船二隻 亦不得已從到彼船之邊矣 彼人輩 使中軍携上其船 搜探從船 奪取印信 中軍下人 一並驅逐 小人觀此景光 仍爲棄船下陸 馳予營門矣 本官限日暮 亦爲出于西山書院 馳書于彼船 請還中軍 要請下陸約會 而彼人輩 終不聽從 十七日潮水 亦爲未及閒似亭而止泊矣 本官來坐於閒似亭 馳書于彼船 要請約會 則洋人崔哥與同國船主及貨主淸人趙凌峯 各持短銃與環刀 來會于閒似亭 與本官同坐酬酢 責其交易之失信 本官亦以義里 責之諭之者 凡爲一時間矣 迨此時 使營門出待軍校圍所 執留相換中軍 然後放還彼人 似可生還中軍之道 而不此之爲 護送彼人於本船 以待中軍之出送 而彼輩去益跳踉 不還中軍 漸漸溯上 將近烏灘 勢將到鍊光亭乃已 中軍執留 凡爲四日 終不放送 大小民 每每憤痛 且彼船到涙 則先自城外民 必將渙散乃已 亦未知何狀變恠 出於何地 更以臺下軍校 各執兵器 排立土城 以示軍威 則伺彼船中 先放鳥銃 亦放火碇口 則我邊軍校 亦爲應接放砲 此是十九日也 如是相持之間 我船艤待於彼人之傍 中軍所屬陪行中軍者 乘其彼船中 遑遑之際 使中軍跳下 我軍仍爲放船還歸 中軍之傔人 與新延通引 亦爲跳下 而無船可救 自爲溺死 如是之間 光景慘然 事勢駭惡 一城內外之愚夫愚婦 孰不憤痛乎 彼人輩 或不無下陸搶奪之慮 使出待軍校 防守於羊一角島閒似亭以上 而爲四日矣 爲彼人之所殺我人 爲四五名矣 轉轉激憤 期欲屠滅彼人爲計 而黠彼胡船 知進不知退 亦無小惻 究其猖獗 殺之無惜 而防守四日 泛在中流 放銃不及 發矢不到 無計可施 以待彼船之自盡 然見今漸生潮水 行船任意 則彼必順風而下矣 彼船中崔哥 自稱四十四國言語 無難皆通 句句言言 欲見平安監司而來此而已 非爲交易之取利也 前監司洪氏與中軍 已爲遞歸 吾已聞之矣 今監司朴氏 四日到任 而吾去北京 爲其使臣入朝時 數次相見 故今來欲見 而平壤城中 亦有親者數人 相見後 我從旱路 入北京云云 小人答曰 監司即我國之重臣 爾到大同江 萬無進見之道 且城內親知之人 未知其誰 而從容指其姓名 則吾當爲汝請來矣 崔哥答曰 北京恭親王 時時來見我處 則汝國監司 焉敢不來見乎 且爾城中親人 曾未相面 但聞其姓名居住 一見則好矣 不可以姓名 先通於汝云云 且交易多多爲之 必受監司憑文 然後還歸

云云 且同來我船八隻 分送于汝國京城近處 想有早晩得聞云云 且我非天主教 尊崇耶蘇教之道源 勝於天主云云 耶蘇學 題其新約全書 逢人輒給一冊 欲爲給價而不捧 每每目覩事也 船漢之五十名 自恐其數 其非煽動荒唐之說 且法國犯我 有難推知乎 以彼中原之大 不能制其師 況於日本朝鮮之小乎云云 船長爲二十三把 廣爲七把 高爲三丈 比我國江華中船 則無大矣 船人合爲二十名 而洋爲五名內 一是崔哥 一是船主 三是貨主 淸人爲十五名 所謂趙文良趙凌峯 能爲筆談 或爲我國語耳 船中兵器 則鳥銃十四柄 而銃頭兼備鎗刃 環刀四柄 其光射日 而別無利銳 銃四柄 洋人各持者也 而無火放聲遠不過百步 其長未滿六寸 其制甚巧耳 小人與彼船相從 九十餘日 其中淸人趙凌峯 似有心契 暮夜無知之間 同趙哥 請來我船 質異船之來歷 則趙哥言內 此船即洋人之商船也 留在山東烟台江 貿物裝載 將欲興販於南 遑遑之際 去六月二十九日洋人崔哥 自北京而來 言於船主及貨主輩 自都京禮部馳咨文於朝鮮 過此時 行船到朝鮮 交易可通 換物大利 船主與貨主 甘聽其說 七月初一日 自烟臺江發船 順風涉海而矣云云 所謂緣何而出來我國 爾是淸人 何登於賊船乎 趙曰 洋人今爲盤居中原 每於衆船興販 雇得中原人然後 可以之南之北 即其例事 吾亦貧寒之勢 受雇登船 而早知此船來朝鮮則豈可登此船乎 追悔莫及也 彼洋人暴悍莫甚 雖死地 知進而不知退 故中原不得已通交易矣 此船必到平壤城乃已 如有交易許給之論 則速速多多許賣 不然則即擇要路 以備橫濫爲好云云 故以此事情 備告于營府 而至於交易勢難 營府擅便亦難 發兵防捍 捱過多日 遽到閒似亭以上 箕城內外之人民 聞風圖生 使其家屬 移送村底 或逃走峽中 便同亂離樣者 爲近十日 與受不通 愁擾日甚 此將奈何且聞洋人崔哥之言 則渠以喪服 潛行朝鮮 凡爲三次 家住京城東水口 多有親人於爾國緣於他事 來見家屬 爲三年云 崔哥之能知監司姓氏 如非我人之相通 豈能如是分明耶 崔哥之今番來船 爲交易之取利也 以動靜以言語 必探我國物情 欲傳耶蘇教之意也

一. 海伯狀啓(二十一日所聞) 水使吳夏泳謄報 則八月初四日 呈康翎縣監趙東恒馳報內 昨日申時量 異樣船九隻 自外洋 泛向海州延坪島是如爲有置 時當風高 異船之多數出沒 聞極驚駭 臣營帶率軍官黃順紅 將校朴耆澤 急急定送于康翎等地是白遣 沿海各邑鎭 各別防守瞭望之意 發關嚴飭爲白乎旀 今此異船之泛向近洋 聞不勝驚駭 探察次 臣營帶率軍官吳益順 譯官崔鍾淵 爲先定送于海州康翎等地爲白遣 沿海各邑鎭 嚴加團束 盛備防禦 使不得任意向往之意 星火關飭事

一. 各宮各衙所存導掌 永爲革罷 其所出條 各邑軍器修正云

一. 異様船來到富平等地 捕將出去云耳二十二日聞

一. 異様船近泊於龍山等地 五營出去 而城中倉庫空虛 五六日之內 都民盡爲飢餓 空家逃避者 不知其數 汲水軍都無 乘轎軍 每十里雖給二三兩 而四求不得云云

제2부 병인양요

E. Verrolles (1866. 6. 28) → G. Roze

조선에서의 천주교도 박해 보고

†N.D. des Neiges, Province du Leatong, 28 Juin 1866

Monsieur l'Amiral,

Vous êtes en cet extrême Orient pour nos chers compatriotes, pours nos néophites (*Sic*), pour nous tous, après Dieu, la raison de notre espérance.

Voici la nouvelle qui m'arrive de Corée. Je transcris : "Corée, 10 Mars 1866_ …… nous sommes en persécution. Mg[r] Berneux vicaire apost. de Corée a été pris le 23 février, et depuis, 5 confrères, M.M. Pourthié, Petit Nicolas, de Bretennières, Beaulieu, Dorie. Tous les autres vont être pris incessamment ; impossible d'y échapper. On parle déjà d'exécuter les 6 Européens pris, et je crois qu'il en sera ainsi, malgré les passeports français-chinois. Injure à la France, injure à L'empereur de Chine. Quoiqu'il en soit, fiat voluntas ! …… Mon tour va venir aussi, et je prie Dieu de me soutenir dans l'arène …… On a pillé la maison de Mg[r] Berneux où se trouvaient réunis l'argent et tous les objets de la mission, perte de bien près de 100,000 [f]……. Adieu …… priez pour moi ……

†Antoine Ev. Coadjuteur de Corée."

Les 2 courriers coréens qui m'ont remis cette lettre de Mg[r] Daveluy ont attendu longtemps sur la Côte avant de pouvoir prendre la mer, et ils n'ont pu quitter la Corée que le 17 du courant. Ils affirment que Mg[r] Berneux a été décapité le 24 de la 1ère lune — 15 mars —; que les 5 missionnaires pris avec lui, l'ont été le 8 avril ; que Mg[r] Daveluy a été pris vers la fin d'Avril, et, avec lui, encore 3 missionnaires ; que depuis S. Gr. avait été conduit à la capitale, mais que le Roi, sur les instances de sa mère qui est cathécumène (*Sic*), accordant un sursis l'avait renvoyé au Mandarin qui l'avait pris à 30 lieues de la capitale.

Ils ajoutent — et ce sont les conclusions naturelles de telles prémisses — que partout les chrétiens sont pillés, traqués, massacrés ; qu'ils s'enfuient sur les montagnes où dénués de tout, ayant tout perdu ils meurent de faim et…

Le Roi actuel âgé de 15 ans a été adopté par la mère du feu Roi; elle a entouré son fils adoptif de ministres de g^{ds} mandarins ennemis de la Religion et des Européens — car en ces pays c'est tout un —; ce sont eux surtout qui ont provoqué ces sauvages massacres de nos compatriotes et des chrétiens. Et que dire aux Français quand ils viendront nous demander raison de tout cela, disait à l'un d'eux le père du Roi? — Je m'en charge, répondit-il.

Déjà, c'était en septembre 1839, ces mêmes Coréens faisaient expirer dans les tourments Mg^{r} Imbert, M.M. Chastan et Maubant. Depuis, transis de peur, ils étaient disposés à travailler avec nous — à tout prix; puis attribuant notre abstention indéfinie ou à l'oubli ou à la faiblesse, leur instinct sanguinaire a repris le dessus.

Helas! En présence de tels actes, de cette boucherie scélérate, toute réflexion devient superflue. Amiral, vous avez tout compris; les moments sont comptés; plusieurs de nos compatriotes sont encore dans les fers, sous le couperet des assassins et chaque jour ils attendent, eux et leurs néophites (*Sic*), l'arrivée ...... l'apparition de notre drapeau, ce drapeau devenu, ces années dernières surtout, si glorieux en cet extrême Orient, mais que ces barbares viennent d'insulter encore une fois, et de rougir dans le sang français.

Je suis, etc...

Signé: Emm. Verrolles év; vic. apost. de la Mandchourie, et...

P. S. En 1845 M. l'Amiral Cécile demandait dans une lettre au Roi de Corée raison de l'assassinat de nos 3 compatriotes. Il devait bientôt, disait-il, revenir pour chercher la réponse. En 1847, l'Amiral Lapierre revenait en effet, mais ayant échoué du même coup ses 2 navires frégate et corvette, il n'entama aucune négociation, et se borna, lui aussi, dans sa lettre au même Roi de Corée, à répéter le mot de l'amiral Cécile, que bientôt il reviendrait demander la réponse. Depuis *la Virginie* est venue sur ces Côtes, et a fait, je crois, de l'hydrographie pendant plusieurs mois; mais elle n'a entrepris aucune relation officielle avec le Gouvernement.

Pour copie conforme

Le C. Amiral Commandant en chef la Division navale de la Chine

G. Roze

G. Roze(1866. 7. 10) → P. de Chasseloup-Laubat

2명의 주교와 7명의 선교사 처형 보고 및 보복 건의

À Bord de *la Guerrière*, Tientsin, le 10 Juillet 1866

Monsieur le Ministre,

Au moment où j'arrive à Tientsin, en revenant de Pékin, je trouve un missionnaire français, le Père Ridel, qui vient d'y arriver lui-même et nous apporte de la Corée des nouvelles de la plus haute gravité. Deux évèques, sept prêtres-missionnaires et un grand nombre de chrétiens indigènes ont été massacrés par ordre du Roi de Corée. La persécution contre les chrétiens s'exerce avec la plus odieuse rigueur et deux Français missionnaires sont encore en ce moment poursuivis, et n'ont dû jusqu'ici leur salut qu'au dévouement de quelques uns de leur coreligionnaires. Le Pére Ridel a quitté la Corée sur une jonque du pays pour nous apporter la nouvelle de ces événements et il a abordé à Tchefou où il a laissé sa jonque coréenne et d'où il s'est rendu en toute hâte à Tientsin, par le courrier à vapeur dans la pensée de donner ces informations à M[r] le Chargé d'affaires de France à Pékin.

La jonque qui l'a condit à Tché-fou est montée par quelques chréstiens coréens qui possèdent, m'a-t-il dit, des connaissances nautiques sur des parages dont nous n'avons que des renseignements très incomplets et dont nous ne possédons aucune carte pouvant inspirer la moindre confiance.

Dans cette conjoncture, il me semble de toute necessité de ne pas laisser sans une réparation éclatante un attentat barbare dont nos compariotes ont été les victimes et dont la perpétration émane de la volonté royale. Mais avant de prendre un parti sur ce que je dois faire, j'ai besoin de connaitre, aussi exactement que possible, quels sont les moyens d'action que je peux employer, et c'est pourquoi je me rends immédiatement à Tchefou où j'emmène avec moi le Père Ridel et où, je trouverai les chrétiens Coréens qui sont restés sur la jonque et qui me renseigneront sur les abords d'une côte si peu fréquentée jusqu'ici. Dans tous les cas, je n'entreprendrai rien qui puisse compromettre la sécurité de nos bâtiments et le Gouvernement de l'Empereur.

Voici la liste des missionnaires massacrés ou plutôt exécutés, liste que je tiens de l'Abbé Ridel :

Monseingeur Berneux, évêque de Capse, vicaire apostolique de Corée;
Mr Petit Nicolas, missionnaire;
Mr Pourthié, missionnaire;
Mr De Bretennières, missionnaire;
Mr Dorie, missionnaire;
Mr Beaulieu, missionnaire;
Mr Daveluy, évêque d'Acône, coadjuteur de Monseigneur de Capse;
Mr Aumaître, missionnaire;
Mr Huin, missionnaire.

Les six premiers ont été exécutés à Séoul, Capitale de la Corée où ils habitaient.

Les trois autres ont été exécutés dans un bourgade, à environ 30 lieues dans le Sud de Séoul, et tous ont été condamnés par une sentence royale.

Jusqu'au mois de mars dernier le séjour de ces missionnaires avaient été à peu près toléré par le Gouvernement de la Corée qui les laissait remplir leur mission sans cependant leur accorder la moindre protection. Mais à cette époque, sans que j'en connaisse exactement la cause, le Gouvernement de la Corée conçut un redoublement d'ombrage contre les chrétiens et nos missionnaires furent accusés de chercher à ouvrir l'accès du pays aux étrangers, c'est du moins le prétexte qui fut donné à leur condamnation et la sentence du Roi fut exécuté avec un certain apparat, suivant le cérémonial réservé aux personnes nobles du pays frapées de la peine de mort.

Le Père Ridel qui n'a pas habité la capitale de la Corée et qui vivait dans une province du Sud n'a pas pu me donner des renseignements bien circonstanciés sur la cause de ces événements déplorables dont l'authenticité est cependant parfaitement établie. Je lui ai demandé, cependant, un rapport, non seulement sur les faits qu'il nous a déclarés, mais encore sur la constitution d'un pays qui est encore si ignoré des Européens et je m'empresserai de le communiquer à Votre Excellence.

En ce moment, le Roi qui règne est un jeune homme de 14 ans. Il est dirigé par quatre ministres qui se sont montrés les ennemis les plus acharnés des étrangers, et ce sont eux qui ont fait rendre la sentence contre nos missionnaires.

J'écris cette lettre très à la hâte pour profiter du courrier et avant d'avoir obtenu toutes les informations que je désire recueillir. Mais j'ai tenu à vous instruire le plutôt possible de ces événements dont je n'ai pu apprendre encore que la substance et qui auraient pu venir à votre connaissance par une autre source que la mienne. De Tchefou, j'aurai l'honneur de vous envoyer une dépêche plus détaillée.

Signé: Roze

G. Roze (1866. 7. 11) → P. de Chasseloup-Laubat

Saïgon 출동 보고

À Bord de *la Guerrière*, Takou, le 11 Juillet 1866

Monsieur le Ministre,

Je viens de rejoindre *la Guerrière* à Takou et j'y ai trouvé mon courrier arrivé de la veille.

L'Amiral de *la Grandière* m'écrit à la date du 23 Juin et me fait part des événements malheureux survenus à Tay-Ninh. Bien que sa lettre soit officieuse, j'y ai vu de sa part le désir de recevoir le concour de *la Guerrière* à Saïgon.

Devant une telle situation, il m'a semblé que c'était pour moi un devoir impérieux de me rendre à son appel, et quoiqu'il m'en coutât, j'ai dû renoncer aux projets que j'aurais formés, suivant les circonstances, dans le but de venger de sang de nos missionnaires odieusement mis à mort en Corée.

Je crois devoir mettre sous vos yeux la lettre de l'Amiral de *la Grandière*, et Votre Excellence, j'en ai le ferme espoir, approuvera ma résolution, et les sentiments qui l'ont dictée. Je vais donc à Saïgon en faisant toutes diligences possibles pour me mettre, ainsi que *la Guerrière*, à la disposition du Gouverneur de la Cochinchine. Je fais les vœux les plus ardents pour trouver la colonie dans la position de prospérité où l'avait placée l'Amiral de *la Grandière* et pour que mes services lui soient inutiles. Mais dans l'incertitude où je suis, sur le degré d'importance que peut avoir acquis l'insurrection dont était menacée la Cochichine, à la date de la lettre de l'Amiral de *la Grandière*, il ne m'est pas possible d'hésiter à lui apporter mon contingent de forces.

Je vais à Tchefou où je ne passerai que le temps nécessaire pour y renouveler mon approvisionnement de charbon et me mettre en mesure d'entreprendre le long voyage que je dois faire contre la mousson de S.O.

Avant de quitter le centre de mon commandement, je laisse la direction des affaires à M. le Commandant Bochet, le plus ancien des officiers supérieurs restant dans le Nord. De plus, dans le but de vous tenir au courant des événements qui pourraient se produire, je lui donne l'ordre de correspondre directement avec Votre Excellence toutes les fois qu'il y aura quelque intérêt à le faire, à charge de m'en rendre compte immédiatement. Je donne pareil ordre à M. Commandant du *Laplace*, en ce qui concerne le Japon.

J'espère que ces mesures suffiront pour assurer la service en mon absence et ne laisser aucun intérêt en souffrance.

Signé : Roze.

P. S.

Je joins ici un duplicata de la dépêche que je vous ai adressée de Tientsin, au sujet des missionnaires de la Corée, pour le cas où le primata ne serait pas parvenu à Votre Excellence. Je vais m'occuper de rassembler tous les documents qui pourront m'éclairer sur la situation de ce pays, et j'aurai l'honneur de vous les transmettre aussitôt que je les aurais recueillis.

H. de Bellonet(1866. 7. 13) ➞ 恭親王

조선에 대한 청조의 종주권 부정, 조선 국왕 폐위 및 조선 침공 선언

Pékin, le 13 Juillet 1866

Mg[r] — J'ai la douleur de porter officiellement à la connaissance de V. A. I. un horrible attentat commis dans le petit Royaume de Corée que des liens de Vassalité rattachaient autrefois à l'Empire de la Chine, mais que cet acte de barbarie sauvage en sépare à jamais.

Dans le courant du mois de mars dernier, les deux Evêques français qui évangélisaient la Corée et avec eux neuf missionnaires, sept prêtres coréens, et une foule de chrétiens de tout sexe et de tout âge ont été massacrés par ordre du Souverain de ce pays.

Le Gouvernement de S. M. ne peut laisser impuni un aussi sanglant outrage. Le jour où le Roi de Corée a porté la main sur nos malheureux compatriotes a été le dernier de son règne. Il a proclamé lui-même sa déchéance que je proclame aujourd'hui solennellement.

Dans quelques jours nos forces militaires vont marcher à la conquête de la Corée et l'Empereur mon Auguste Souverain a seul aujourd'hui le droit et le pouvoir de disposer suivant son bon plaisir du pays et du trône vacant.

Le Gouvernement Chinois m'a déclaré à plusieurs reprises qu'il n'avait aucun droit, aucune puissance sur la Corée et s'est couvert de ce prétexte pour refuser d'appliquer à ce pays les traités de Tien-Tsin et de donner à nos missionnaires les passe-ports que nous lui demandions. Nous avons pris acte de cette déclaration et nous déclarons aujourd'hui de notre part, ne reconnaître au Gouvernement Chinois aucun droit quelconque sur le Royaume de Corée.

J'ai l'honneur d'être, etc, …

Signé : H. de Bellonné (*Sic*)

Pour copie conforme

Le C. Amiral Commandant en chef
la Division navale des mers de Chine et du Japon
G. Roze

【漢譯文】

法國照會

爲照會事 照得本大臣近接朝鮮來函 言於本年三月間 高麗國王突發一令 將該處法國主教二人 及傳教士九人 並本地傳教士七人 其習教之男婦老幼無數 盡行殺害 如此殘暴 自取敗亡 因其係屬中國納貢之邦 是以本國命將興師 以討有罪 理合知照貴親王 宜有此妄行 本國自應與被殺教衆聲罪致討 是該國殘殺之日 實卽其國喪失之日也 理所必然 故特明言 所有本國各路兵船 不日卽可齊集朝鮮 暫取其國 後來再立何者爲王 以守此土 仍請本國諭命施行 再本大臣曾有數次 於貴衙門請發路照於傳教士 前赴朝鮮 均經推脫 據言雖高麗於中國納貢 一切國事 皆其自主 故天津和約 亦未載入 玆當本國於高麗交兵 自然中國亦不能過問 因與彼國原不相干涉也

【英譯文】

July 13, 1866

Sir:

I grieve to bring officially to the knowledge of your imperial highness a horrible outrage committed in the small kingdom of Corea, which formerly assumed the bonds of vassalage to the Chinese empire, but which this act of savage barbarity has forever separated from it.

In the course of the month of March last, the two French bishops who were evangelizing Corea, and with them nine missionaries, seven Corean priests, and a great multitude of Christians of both sexes and of every age, were massacred by order of the sovereign of that country.

The government of his Majesty cannot permit so bloody an outrage to be unpunished. The same day on which the King of Corea laid his hands upon my unhappy countrymen was the last of his reign; he himself proclaimed its end, which I in my turn solemnly declare to-day. In a few days our military forces are to march to the conquest of Corea, and the Emperor, my august sovereign, alone, has now the right and the power to dispose, according to his good pleasure, of the country and of the vacant throne.

The Chinese government has declared to me many times that it has no authority or power over Corea; and it refused on this pretext to apply the treaties or Tientsin to that country, and give to our missionaries the passports which we have asked from it. We have taken note of these declarations, and we declare, now, that we do not recognize any authority whatever of the Chinese government over the kingdom of Corea.

I have, &c.,

H. DE BELLONET

His Imperial Highness PRINCE KUNG.

81

H. de Bellonet (1866. 7. 13) → G. Roze

Bellonet의 해군 병력 동원 지시

Pékin, le 13 Juillet 1866

Monsieur le Contre-Amiral,

En recevant la nouvelle du massacre général des chrétiens et des missionnaires en Corée, vous avez, sans doute, pensé, comme moi, que le moindre retard dans la punition de ce sanglant outrage, pouvait faire courir un danger sérieux aux 500 missionnaires qui évangélisent la Chine, tant la contagion de l'exemple peut être terrible dans ces pays de l'extrême Orient.

Je n'hésite donc pas, Monsieur le Contre-Amiral, à faire appel aux forces navales dont vous avez le commandement ; à remettre entre vos mains, sous ma responsabilité, le soin de tirer une vengeance éclatante de l'attentat dont 2 Evêques et neuf missionnaires français sont tombés les victimes, et à vous prier d'user de tous les moyens en votre pouvoir, sans plus tenir compte des demandes dont les Consuls ou la Légation de Sa Majesté auraient pu vous entretenir, pour commencer le plus rapidement possible les hostilités contre la Corée.

Des liens de Suzeraineté d'une part, de vassalité de l'autre, ont longtemps réuni l'Empire de la Chine et le Royaume de Corée. Il était de mon devoir de m'assurer de leur existence et de savoir jusqu'à quel point la puissance suzeraine entendait prendre la responsabilité de l'outrage qui nous était fait. Mais les explications échangées avec le Gouvernement Chinois m'ayant appris qu'il renonçait à réclamer ses droits, j'ai adressé au Prince de Kong la note dont vous trouverez ci-joint copie, et dans laquelle j'ai déclaré officiellement l'ouverture des hostilités, la séparation définitive de la Corée, la déchéance de son Roi, et le droit exclusif de l'Empereur notre Auguste Souverain, à disposer suivant son bon plaisir du pays et du trône vacant.

Vous voudrez donc bien, Monsieur le Contre-Amiral, ne traiter avec personne, ne reconnaître aucune autorité quelconque en Corée, jusqu'à ce que la Capitale, le Roi déchu et la Régente, mère du feu Roi, aient été remis entre vos mains. Il n'y a plus en Corée d'autre pouvoir que celui qui représente Sa Majesté l'Empereur des Français.

Lorsque vous aurez plus tard à reconstituer le pouvoir que nos armes vont détruire, je pense, Monsieur le Contre-Amiral, que vous trouverez comme moi que les efforts courageux que le père du Roi déchu, a toujours tentés pour faire triompher la cause de la Religion et de la civilisation, le désignent tout naturellement pour remplacer sur le Trône les personnes indignes qui l'occupaient. Mais je regarde, et vous regarderez, sans doute, également, comme une condition indispensable au succès comme à l'honneur de notre cause, à l'avenir de la civilisation dans l'extrême Orient, que le Prince auquel seront confiées les destinées de la Corée, sous la protectorat de Sa Majesté l'Empereur des Français, fait profession de la Religion Chrétienne, et sous ce point de vue encore, l'ami et le disciple des vénérables martyrs, l'époux d'une de leurs cathécumènes (*Sic*), me semble désigné d'avance et n'hésitera pas je l'espère à se prononcer ouvertement.

Je ne doute pas, Monsieur le Contre-Amiral, que vous ne fassiez punir d'une manière exemplaire tous les serviteurs du pouvoir déchu qui ont contribué au massacre des missionnaires et des chrétiens. Mais pour que l'expiation fût complète, pour qu'elle frappât surtout l'opinion populaire, je voudrais que les biens de tous les condamnés fussent distribués aux familles de leurs victimes, et que le Trésor royal lui-même contribuât pendant un certain nombre d'années, par le versement de la moitié de ses remboursements à ce grand acte de justice et de réparation.

Tous les frais de l'expédition, Monsieur le Contre-Amiral, comme ceux de l'occupation subséquente seront nécessairement à la charge du Trésor Coréen et je ne vois pas de meilleur moyen d'arriver à ce résultat que de vous inviter à conserver entre vos mains jusqu'à parfait paiement, les douanes que vous aurez à établir, lorsqu'après la cessation des hostilités vous ouvrirez la Corée Nouvelle au Commerce de toutes les Nations.

Agréez, etc ……

Signé : de Bellonnet

Pour copie conforme

Le Contre-Amiral Commandant en chef

G. Roze

G. Roze (1866. 7. 14) ➜ P. de Chasseloup-Laubat

조선에 관한 자료 송부

관련문서 (1) 조선 정부의 선교사 처형에 관한 Ridel 신부의 보고문

À bord de *la Guerrière*, Tche-fou, le 14 Juillet 1866

Monsieur le Ministre,

J'ai l'honneur d'adresser sous ce pli à Votre Excellence la note qui m'a été remise par le R. P. Ridel, au sujet des événements qui ont accompagné le massacre de nos missionnaires en Corée. J'y joins une copie des renseignements que j'ai recueillis dans le but de m'éclairer sur les difficultés militaires et nautiques que les bâtiments de ma Division auraient pu rencontrer en remontant jusqu'à la Capitale de la Corée. Ces notes succintes fournies par les matelots qui montaient la barque du P. Ridel m'ont confirmé dans la pensée qu'aucun obstacle sérieux ne m'eût empêché de mettre à exécution le projet que j'avais formé d'aller venger, au cœur même du pays, la mort de nos missionnaires et je n'avais pas hésité à entreprendre cette expédition, si les nouvelles venues de Cochinchine n'avaient attiré mon attention sur ce point et ne m'avaient obligé à me rendre à Saïgon d'après le devoir qui m'en a été exprimé par Mr. Amiral de *la Grandière*.

Je suis......

Roze

【관련문서 1】

"Le 7 juillet au matin, nous vîmes le port, et à midi nous jetions l'ancre au milieu des navires européens. Nous descendîmes entourés d'une foule de chinois qui nous faisaient cortège et regardaient avec étonnement notre étrange costume."

Les nouvelles que M. Ridel apportait produisirent une grande sensation dans la colonie européenne, où il trouva le meilleur accueil. Il était à peine débarqué, qu'un riche commerçant catholique, M. Fergusson, lui offrit la plus cordiale hospitalité. Les matelots coréens étaient dans le ravissement; ils ne lassaient pas de contempler cette maison européenne nouvellement bâtie. "Si le roi de Corée, disaient-ils, avait un palais semblable! Père, est-ce que les églises sont plus grandes... ?"

Mais leur admiration ne connut plus de bornes quand ils eurent pénétré à l'intérieur ; les lits, les chaises, les fauteuils, dont il fallut leur apprendre l'usage, étaient pour eux des merveilles. Pourquoi, demandaient-ils avec étonnement, pourquoi des ponts pour se coucher et pour s'asseoir, mais la terre n'est pas percée ? Une armoire à glace obtint le plus grand succès; ce fut une véritable mystification; les uns avançaient, reculaient, ou bien gesticulaient en riant de tout leur cœur, tandis que les autres s'assuraient qu'il n'y avait aucune chambre par derrière, ni aucun personnage de caché.

Quelques jours plus tard, à Tien-tsin, l'amiral Roze était bien étonné, en voyant venir à lui un homme habillé en coréen, dont les traits amaigris annonçaient de longues privations. Son étonnement redoubla quand il entendit cet homme vêtu d'une façon si étrange, lui parler le langage de sa patrie et lui dire: "Amiral, je suis Français, missionnaire de Corée. Sur l'ordre de mon supérieur j'ai fui ce pays sur une petite barque, pour vous annoncer que, par le commandement du roi de Corée, neuf Français, mon Evêque, son coadjuteur et sept de mes confrères, ont été massacrés, sous le seul et unique prétexte qu'ils étaient Européens et chrétiens. De toute la mission de Corée il ne reste que trois missionnaires, les Pères Féon et Calais, traqués en ce moment comme des bêtes fauves, et celui qui a l'honneur de vous apporter cette douloureuse nouvelle."

Les officiers entourèrent le missionnaire de respect et de soins; l'amiral l'accueillit avec la plus grande bienveillance et lui promit d'aller immédiatement au secours des deux missionnaires français qui étaient exposés à la mort.

Il se disposait au départ, lorsque le commandant de l'escadre, M. de la Grandière, le manda en Basse-Cochinchine pour réprimer une révolte qui venait d'y éclater. Néanmoins, il promit de faire à son retour l'expédition projetée.

M. Ridel revint à Tché-Fou, où il séjourna jusqu'à la mi-août. A cette époque, les Coréens qui l'avaient amené manifestèrent le désir de retourner dans leur pays. Il en laissa partir huit, et avec les trois autres se rendit à Chang-Haï pour attendre les événements. Trois semaines plus tard, l'amiral Roze ayant appris que l'insurrection était apaisée, l'invitait à se rendre à Tché-Fou et à se tenir prêt à l'accompagner en Corée.

Il partit en toute hâte, et arriva le 10 septembre à bord de la frégate *la Guerrière*. Quelques jours après il reprenait le chemin de Séoul.

Pauvre missionnaire ! sa vie est agitée comme l'écume à la surface du flot, comme la feuille desséchée que le vent d'automne pousse et repousse. De nouveau il s'éloigne des rivages de la Chine ; il va revoir sa mission bien-aimée. Son cœur alors se dilate, s'épanouit et trouve ces inimitables accents : "ô ma Corée ! terre bénie, terre arrosée du sang des martyrs ! Je t'ai quitée un instant pour le bon Dieu, je reviens. Puissé-je, à mon tour, devenir pour toi un holocauste d'agréable odeur !"

Hélas ! il devait bien des fois approcher du rivage et saluer de loin les montagnes de cette terre inhospitalière avant d'y pénétrer.

總署(1866. 7. 16/同治五年六月五日) ➞ C. H. M. Bellonet

프랑스 함대의 조선 원정 계획 통보에 대한 회신

給法國照覆

爲照覆事 昨准貴大臣照會 內稱朝鮮國突將法國主教及傳教士竝本地傳教習教多人 盡行殺害 本國命將興師 因其係屬中國納貢之邦 理合知會等因前來 本爵查朝鮮國僻處海隅 素知謹守 現在未知何故 有殺害教民之事 今貴大臣以貴國興師緣由 知照本爵 足徵貴大臣敦睦之誼 惟兩國交兵 均關民命 本爵旣知此事 自不能不從中排解 該國果有殺害教衆等事 似可先行據理查詢 究因何故 不必遽啓兵端 爲此照覆貴大臣酌奪可也

【佛譯文】

Pékin, le 16 Juillet 1866

J'ai reçu la dépêche que le Noble Chargé d'affaires de France m'a fait l'honneur de m'adresser pour m'apprendre le meurtre des Evêques des missionnaires ainsi que des chrétiens qui vient d'avoir lieu en Corée ce qui a motivé de la part de la France l'envoi de troupes, faits qu'il a cru devoir porter à ma connaissance, la Corée étant considérée comme un des pays tributaires de la Chine, etc. etc.

Moi, prince, j'ai remarqué que le petit pays de Corée, relégué sur le bord de la mer, a de tout temps rempli fidèlement tous les devoirs qui lui incombaient Qu'elles (*Sic*) peuvent être aujourd'hui les raisons qui l'ont porté à massacrer des chrétiens. (c'est ce que j'ignore).

Mais en me notifiant les motifs pour lesquels la France y envoie des troupes, le Noble Chargé d'Affaires m'a donné une preuve évidente du cas qu'il fait des bons rapports existant entre nos deux pays.

Toutes les fois que deux Etats en appellent à la force ils mettent par cela même l'existence du peuple en danger. C'est pour cela que bien que prévenu je ne puis m'empêcher dans cette circonstance de venir m'interposer pour séparer les deux partis.

Bien qu'il soit avéré que la Corée a mis à mort des individus appartenant à la religion catholique on peut néanmoins légalement faire une enquête préalable sur les véritables motifs qui ont pu amener ce massacre sans pour cela débuter par des hostilités et c'est ce qui me fait en référer à V. E. pour qu'après mûre réflexion Elle (*Sic*) prenne une décision à cet égard.

Tel est le but de la présente.

Veuillez agréer etc. etc.

Pour troduction conforme

Signé : [____] Fontanier.

【英譯文(美國)】

July 16, 1866

Sir:

I had the honor, yesterday, to receive your excellency's dispatch, in which you inform me that the authorities of the kingdom of Corea had suddenly killed several French bishops and priests, together with a great number of native teachers and Christians, in consequence of which the French government had ordered the commander-in-chief to move his forces; and that seeing that Corea is a dependency of China, and sends tribute, it was proper that I should be informed of these things.

I may here observe, that as Corea is an out-of-the-way country, lying in a secluded corner, and as is well known, has always strictly maintained its own regulations, I am quite unaware what has led them to put these missionaries and Christians to death. Still, I am sensible of the friendly feelings which have led your excellency thus to communicate to me the reasons for the French government in moving its forces [against that country].

Seeing, however, that when two countries come to war it involves the lives of their people, as it well in this case and, therefore, I cannot but endeavor to bring about a solution, of the difficulty between them — as the Coreans have killed a number of the missionaries, it seems to me that it would be best to inquire beforehand this step, so that, if possible, a resort to arms may be avoided. I make this reply for the purpose of suggesting such a course to your excellency's consideration.

I have. &c.,

KUNG

M. DE BELLONET

【英譯文(英國)】

THE Prince had the honour to receive yester the Chargé d'Affaires' despatch, information him of the sudden murder by Corea of some French bishops and priests and a large number of native teachers and convers; that France (or the French Government) had ordered the Commander-in-chief to move up forces (to Corea); and that, as Corea was a tributary State to China, he had considered it his duty to inform the Prince of the matter.

The Prince does not understand what cause can have led to this Christian massacre by (a country like) Corea, which is an out-of-the-way, unimportant place, at the corner (or edge) of the ocean, and which has hitherto evinced a sense of prudence and a due regard to what is right.

The Prince fully recognizes the friendly desire to maintain peaceful relations shown by M. de Bellonnet in his informing his Highness of the reasons which have induced France to take military action. But as a hostile collision between the two countries will affect the lives of the people, the Prince, having been informed of the affair, cannot but (offer) as an intermediary to arrange the difficulty.

If, as it appears, Corea has put Christians to death, his Highness would propose that the affair might first be inquired into peacefully, and that arms should not be rashly had recourse to.

The Prince offers this suggestion, in reply to the French Chargé d'Affaires, for his consideration.

A necessary communication, &c.
6th moon, 5th day (July 1866)

總署(1866. 7. 18/同治五年六月七日) ➡ 同治帝

프랑스의 조선 원정에 대한 중국의 입장 보고

六月初七日 本衙門奏稱 爲接據英使照會 擬派輪船至朝鮮察看海岸形勢 幷法使照會 朝鮮殺害該國主教教士等 欲與該國交兵 謹將現辦情形 恭摺仰祈聖鑑事 竊臣衙門於四月二十日 據英使阿禮國照會內稱 本國擬派輪船一隻前赴中國海面迤北等處 察看海岸形勢 丈量靠岸海水深淺 繪圖載明 俾嗣後行船來往 均可預防危險 至朝鮮海邊一帶 預須協力說法 使該輪船行抵該國等因 查上年法國前使臣柏爾德密 曾經以該國教士欲往朝鮮傳教 請先行文知照 經臣等告以朝鮮向祇遵奉正朔 歲時朝貢 所有該國願否奉教 非中國所能勉强 碍難行文 竝勸其毋庸前往 當卽罷議 續於九月間 英國威妥瑪呈送照會內開 英國水師輪船近沿朝鮮境內迤西海邊遊歷 隨時欲買伙食 朝鮮民人不敢售賣 請轉爲勸諭等語 維時正値英國新舊使臣交替 威妥瑪旋卽卸事今阿禮國照會 輪船前赴中國海面迤北 幷復申擬往朝鮮前說 臣等以輪船行駛中國洋面 原爲條約所有 碍難駁斥 當經咨行迤北濱海督撫將軍查照 至欲往朝鮮一節 卽酌擬以從前答覆柏爾德密之言照覆 告以未便行文 致涉兩岐正在核辦間 又於本月初三日 接據法使伯洛照會稱 朝鮮國王將法國主教二人 及傳教士九人 幷本地傳教士七人 其習教之男婦老幼無數 盡行殺害 本國兵船不日齊集朝鮮 暫取其國 自然中國亦不過問等情 臣等查去年伯洛內請臣衙門行文朝鮮 是法國欲往朝鮮傳教 蓄志已久 本年三月間 朝鮮將該國主教人等殺害 其中顯有情節 該使旣經照會前來 若向該使攔阻 而固執之性未必遽肯允從 若任該使所爲 而朝貢之臣 何忽聽其受害 臣等公同商酌 當此勸禁兩窮 惟有照覆該使 以中國旣知此事 自不能不從中排解 不必遽爾稱兵 於調處之中 暗戢其虛憍之氣 此後該公使等有無異說 除由臣衙門隨時察看情形 相機開導 竝行知禮部外 謹先將辦理緣由 恭摺具奏 竝將英使威妥瑪 阿禮國照會各一件 法使伯洛內照會一件 臣等給予英法公使照覆各一件鈔呈御覽 伏乞皇太后皇上聖鑑 謹奏

85

崇厚 ➞ 總署(1866. 7. 19/同治五年六月八日)

조선에서 탈출한 프랑스인의 입항 보고

六月初八日 三口通商大臣崇厚文稱 同治五年六月初五日 據東海關監督登萊青潘道稟稱 本年五月二十五日申刻 據海關委員面稟 有高麗船一隻駛進煙臺海口 遙望該船兩道桅桿 船身甚小 不過裝一百餘擔 當經諭令地方員弁前往確探 卽據覆稱 該船上水手共有八九名 均係高麗人 內有法國人一名 身穿高麗衣服 有滋大洋行商人發達生專人送去水萊 竝不上岸滋事 竝探聞法國人在高麗國傳敎共十二人 因至王京地方 不知何故被該國人殺去九名 不知下落者二名 今逃出一名 係用洋錢八百圓僱船來煙 所有法國人一名 同高麗人一名 於二十六日附南潯火輪前往天津等語 復經職道與兼法國領事李蹕良相晤 查詢情形 大略相同 且稱伊雖兼理法國領事 其到高麗國傳敎非伊所管之事 可不豫聞等語 除仍飭該員弁等探明確情 竝法國人是何姓名 再行稟報外 擬合將法國人一名僱高麗國船進口 旋附輪船赴津緣由 稟請察核 俯賜咨明總理各國事務衙門查考等情 據此 除稟批示外 理合咨呈 爲此咨呈王大臣 請煩查照施行

總署(1866. 7. 24/同治五年六月十三日) ➜ 禮部

프랑스 공사와의 교섭 경과 통보

六月十三日 行禮部文稱 前因法國公使屢向本衙門請發給傳教士護照 持往朝鮮傳教 竝請先爲行文知照等因 當經本衙門告以習教非朝鮮所願 自未便稍事勉强 碍難發照行文等語在案 本年六月初三日復據法國公使照會內稱高麗國王將該處法國主教二人 及傳教士九人 竝本地習教男婦老幼 盡行殺害 是以本國命將興師 兵船不日卽可齊集朝鮮 特此照會等因前來本衙門 查中國原不能勉強朝鮮習教 爲之發照行文 然亦不能因該國搆兵 不爲排解 因給予照覆 告以兩國兵爭 彼此俱有傷損 中國既知此事 自不能不從中排解如果朝鮮有殺害教士等情 亦可先行據理查詢 不必遽啓兵端等因 竝將現辦情形恭摺具奏 爲此咨行貴部查照可也

87

總署(1866. 7. 28/同治五年六月十七日) ➞ 南洋大臣

프랑스 공사와의 교섭 경과 통보

六月十七日 致上海通商大臣函稱 六月初三日 據法國伯洛内照會内稱 朝鮮國王將法國主教二人 及傳教士九人 竝本地傳教士七人 其習教之男婦老幼無數 盡行殺害 本國兵船不日齊集朝鮮 塹取其國 自然中國亦不過問等語 查上年法國公使伯爾德密在京時 曾以該國教士欲往朝鮮傳教 請先行文知照 經本處告以朝鮮向祇遵奉正朔 歲時朝貢 該國願否奉教 非中國所能勉强 碍難行文 竝勸其勿庸前往 該使旋卽作爲罷論 本年四月間 英國公使阿禮國呈遞照會 亦敍及該國擬派輪船一隻前赴中國海面察看海岸形勢 丈量海水深淺 繪圖載明 俾嗣後行船來往 均可預防危險 請爲協力設法 從優幫助 不致遇有留難之事 竝稱去年九月 前署公使威 因本國水師輪船一隻 行至朝鮮海邊遊歷 欲買伙食用物 據該民人云不敢售賣 恐官究治等情詳細照會 今本國所派輪船前往朝鮮海邊等處 務希行文咨致 以免再有失禮等因 本處查阿使所云輪船行駛中國洋面 原係載在條約 自難駮斥 是以通行盛京吉林黑龍江各將軍 直隸山東督撫 竝咨貴處各在案 至英人欲往朝鮮一層 卽酌擬照覆 按從前回答柏爾德密之言 聲明未便行文 致涉歧異 玆伯洛内又以朝鮮殺害主教等人欲與交兵 照會本處 其中顯有情節 中國斷難坐視 第值此時勢 勸禁兩窮 再三商酌 先給伯使照覆一件 略云朝鮮國僻處海隅 素知謹守 未知何故有殺害教民之事 令貴大臣以興師緣由知照前來 足徵敦睦之誼 惟兩國交兵 均關民命 中國旣知此事 不能不從中排解 該國果有此事 似可先行據理查詢究因何故 不必遽啓兵端云云 當卽一面照覆該使 一面將現接該使照會情形奏聞 竝行文禮部 密爲籌辦 洋人性情詭譎 該使自收本處照覆後 數日來竝未提起 是否虛聲恫喝 抑或該國兵船由西洋而來 尚需時日 均未可定 第中國各沿海地方不可不知此事 爲此抄錄本處奏稿 密致閣下 卽希(密致沿江沿海各將軍督撫密致盛京吉林黑龍江等處及沿海督撫) 查照 切勿稍有宣露 除由本處隨時察看 竝禮部作何辦法 再爲知照外 一切未便形諸公牘 專泐布達 卽頌近綏不一

G. Roze(1866. 7. 28) → P. de Chasseloup-Laubat(1866. 10. 11)

조선 원정의 승인 및 인력과 물자 지원 요청

À Bord de *la Guerrière*, Hong-Kong, le 28 Juillet 1866

Monsieur le Ministre,

J'ai eu l'honneur de vous adresser récemment de Tche-foo les renseignements que j'ai pu recueillir auprès du Père Ridel sur la Corée. Ces renseignements sont vagues et nécessairement incomplets, car l'existence que mènent nos Missionnaires, les précautions qu'ils sont forcés de prendre pour se soustraire aux poursuites des Mandarins, l'obligation pour eux de ne voyager en général que pendant la nuit et de vivre presque toujours cachés, sont autant de raisons pour les empêcher de connaître, aussi bien qu'on pourrait le désirer, un pays qui, de lui-même, d'ailleurs, est disposé à s'envelopper de mystère.

Les renseignements que j'ai transmis à Votre Excellence ne peuvent donc être que des données peu détaillées et, sans doute, problématiques sur la situation actuelle de la Corée, sur son organisation militaire, sur sa constitution civile et sur ses ressources commerciales. En cela, pourtant, nous n'avons pour le moment, d'autres indications que celles que nous tenons de nos missionnaires. Une reconnaissance de la côte par une ou deux canonnières eût pu nous instruire sur l'accès de ces parages, sur la configuration des rives, sur la navigation du fleuve auprès duquel est bâtie la ville de Séoul, capitale de la Corée. Mais lorsque j'ai parlé au Père Ridel de mon désir d'effectuer cette reconnaissance, il m'a prié instamment de m'en abstenir jusqu'au jour où elle pourrait être immédiatement suivie d'une force expéditionnaire capable d'intimider le Gouvernement Coréen.

Sa crainte était que l'apparition sur ces côtes d'un ou deux bâtiments seulement ne redoublât la persécution contre les chrétiens et ne fût le prétexte de nouveaux massacres. Cette reconnaissance, d'ailleurs, pourra toujours avoir lieu dès qu'il s'agira de faire une expédition et son but principal sera d'éclairer la marche de nos navires, d'indiquer le mouillage le plus convenable pour les bâtiments qui ne pourront pas remonter dans la rivière, de faire des sondages précis pour faciliter la navigation des canonnières dans le fleuve de Séoul.

A Tche-foo, je me suis empressé de faire venir chez moi les marins

Coréens qui avaient amené le père Ridel. Quelques uns de ces hommes m'ont paru intelligents et m'ont affirmé qu'ils seraient capables de conduire *la Guerrière* à travers les lignes de récifs qui entourent la baie indiquée sur nos cartes sous le nom de golfe de Prince Jérôme, et dans laquelle débouche le fleuve qui passe auprès de la capitale de la Corée. Votre Excellence sait que l'hydrographie de ces parages est tout à fait incomplète, et que nous n'en possédons ici aucune carte digne de confiance. Il est possible, cependant, que le Dépôt des cartes et plans à Paris ait quelque document plus précis sur les côtes de la Corée. Je lui serai reconnaissant, dans ce cas, de vouloir bien m'en faire l'envoi.

Mais en nous faisant précéder par des bâtiments d'un faible tirant d'eau et en nous aidant, à l'un des renseignements des pilotes coréens cette navigation peut être facilement accomplie avec succès.

De toutes les assertions recueilles tant auprès du Père Ridel qu'auprès des marins Coréens, il paraît ressortir:

1º Un mouillage sûr, pour un grand nombre de bâtiments, et du plus fort tirant d'eau, existe près de l'embouchure de la rivière de Séoul. L'accès de ce mouillage à travers les récifs est très praticable et on y trouve 10 mètres de profondeur à marée basse. La mer marne de 7 à 8 mètres sans que cependant les courants y soient bien forts; ils sont, en général, d'un mille et demi à deux mille;

2º La rivière n'a pas de barre; elle a environ trois encablures de largeur. Sa profondeur, à marée basse est de 4 à 5 mètres, un banc seulement existe à près de 3 à 4 milles en aval de l'endroit le plus rapproché de la capitale. Il n'y reste que 1 mètre 50 centimètres à marée basse; mais à mi-marée la navigation redevient libre sur toute la rivière. Elle gèle, en partie, pendant l'hiver.

3º La capitale de la Corée, Séoul, est à environ 30 milles en amont dans la rivière; elle est à 5 kilomètres de la rive droite. De là des accidents de terrain en cachent la vue; elle est dominée par deux collines, l'une à l'Ouest, l'autre au Sud, deux chemins praticables aux charrettes y conduisent.

La ville est entourée d'une muraille continue et de forme à peu près circulaire de 6 à 7 mètres d'élévation sur un ou deux mètres d'épaisseur. Elle a 12 à 15 kilomètres de contour. Sa population est de 80 à 100 mille âmes; sa garnison militaire est de cinq mille hommes armés en partie de fusils à mèches, de flèches et de lances; elle a sept portes.

Les pilotes coréens n'y ont pas vu de fortifications et pas de canons. Ils pensent que le peuple de la Corée est susceptible d'instincts guerriers.

La distance à laquelle se trouve la capitale des rives du fleuve empêche les bâtiments d'agir directement contre elle. Pour la réduire un débarquement est donc indispensable. Les premiers efforts devront tendre à s'emparer des deux collines qui dominent la ville, de conserver la possession des deux routes qui y conduisent et d'assurer les communications avec la flotille. (*Sic*) Aussitôt [____], les deux collines devront être armées de pièces de montagne, au moins six sur chacune d'elles, pour forcer la ville à se rendre, et, s'il le faut, on y devra transporter des pièces d'un plus gros calibre pour battre en brèche et faciliter l'assaut.

Les données que nous possédons sur les forces résistantes de la Corée sont si vagues, la connaissance du caractère des habitants, celle de leur esprit national, l'influence que l'autorité peut exercer sur eux sont autant de questions encore tellement ignorées, qu'il est assez difficile à priori, de fixer le chiffre du personnel nécessaire pour entreprendre une expédition ou même exécution coups de main.

Cependant, en supposant que, s'attendant à une entreprise contre eux, les Coréens se soient préparés par quelques travaux de défense, tant à terre que sur le fleuve, je pense qu'il suffirait pour faire face aux éventualités de la défense de 1200 à 1500 marins de débarquement. La Division Navale de Chine peut en fournir 600 ; ce serait donc 600 ou 900 marins fusiliers à envoyer de France par un des transports de Cochinchine. A cet envoi, il faudrait ajouter celui d'une batterie de 8 obusiers de 4 rayés de montagne avec son personnel ; la Division de Chine n'en possédant que quatre.

La température de la région dans laquelle se trouve la capitale de la Corée est très froide en hiver ; le fleuve gèle en partie. Une expédition pourrait être entreprise dès le mois d'Avril ou le mois de Mai. C'est le moment où le changement de mousson faciliterait la navigation du transport qui devrait venir directement à Tche-foo, porter les hommes de débarquement. Il serait opportun d'avoir deux canonnières en sus de celles de la Division en Chine qui ne possède que les canonnières *le Tardiff* (*Sic*) et *le Le Brethon* et les avisos *le Déroulède* et le *Kien-chan*. Ces six bâtiments légers au moins seraient indispensables pour le transport des hommes et le remorquage des embarcations dans le fleuve. La Cochinchine pourrait en prêter deux et le rendez-vous général serait à Tche-foo d'où nous partirions tous à la fois pour les Côtes de la Corée.

Tels sont les renseignements que j'ai l'honneur de soumettre à Votre Excellence en attendant ses ordres et ses instructions. La Division Navale de Chine serait glorieuse d'avoir à venger le sang de nos missionnaires morts en Corée, et permettez-moi d'ajouter combien je serais fier et heureux d'être jugé digne de remplir une aussi belle mission.

Signé : G. Roze

禮部(1866. 8. 1/同治五年六月二十一日) ➞ 同治帝

프랑스 함대의 원정 계획을 조선에 통지할 것을 상주(上奏)

戊申 禮部奏准總理各國事務衙門咨開 法國與朝鮮搆兵等因前來 臣等查朝鮮之於中國 奉朔稱臣 數百年以來 至爲恭恪 玆與法國將有搆兵之釁 雖經總理各國事務衙門排解 似應行知該國 使之熟思審處 計出萬全 臣等共同商酌 擬由臣部行文朝鮮國王查照 以示朝廷眷顧藩服之意 軍機大臣面奉諭旨依議

S. W. Williams (1866. 8. 8) → W. H. Seward

프랑스 함대 및 조선 조정의 동정 보고

LEGATION OF THE UNITED STATES,
Peking, August 8, 1866

Sir:

It has been reported that a dreadful execution of two Roman Catholic bishops and nine priests, belonging to the mission in Corea, together with a large number of native Christians, took place in March last, attended by circumstances of great barbarity, and under the direct instigation of the highest authorities of that country. Three priests escaped arrest by hiding in the mountains, on of whom, named Ridel, afterwards succeeded in escaping, in a shallop manned by this native friends and co-religionists, to Chifu. The other two are supposed to be still alive in their retreats.

The French admiral was at Chifu at the time, and learned all the particulars of this affair from the refugee party. He has since determined to visit Corea at the head of all his available land and naval force, and obtain satisfaction from what seems to have been an unnecessary outrage, for it was very easy for the Coreans to have sent the missionaries over their borders. He has already despatched a gunboat or two to survey the coasts and channels leading up to the capital, and has himself gone to Shanghai (and Saigon if necessary) to prepare his expedition and return in October.

The full account of the proceedings of the Corean authorities, and what previous acts aroused their fears, or stirred their anger, to suddenly resort to these severe measures, to repress the new faith, will, I suppose, be known by and by; but enough has been done to furnish an excurse to the French authorities to interfere in the behalf of their countrymen living in Corea. It will probably result in opening and establishing the dominant influence of Christian nations throughout the entire globe, if nothing worse to the independence of the Corean peninsula.

It is rumored there that the Coreans have applied to the Chinese for help to oppose the French, but they can receive no aid from the middle kingdom.

I have the honor to be, Sir, your obedient servant,

S. WELLS WILLIAMS,
Charge d'Affairs

Hon. WILLIAMS H. SEWARD,
Secretary of State, Washington, D.C.

91

禮部 ➞ 高宗(1866. 8. 16/同治五年七月七日)

프랑스와의 교섭 과정 통보 및 방비 권고

丙寅 禮部知會因法國教士殺害等情排解搆兵仍行查照咨

禮部爲知照事主客司案呈本部謹奏爲請旨事同治五年六月十三日准總理各國事務衙門咨開前因法國公使屢向本衙門請發給傳教士護照持往朝鮮傳教並請先爲行文知照等因當經本衙門以習教非朝鮮所願自未便稍事勉强礙難發照行文等語在案本年六月初三日復據法國公事照會內稱高麗國王將該處法國主教二人及傳教士九人並本地習教男婦老幼盡行殺害是以本國命將興師兵船不日卽可齊集朝鮮特此照會等因前來本衙門查中國原不能勉强朝鮮習教爲之發照行文然亦不能因該國搆兵不爲排解因給予照覆告以兩國兵爭彼此俱有傷損中國旣知此事自不能不從中排解如果朝鮮有殺害教士等情亦可先行據理查詢不必遽起兵端等因並將現辦情形恭摺具奏爲此咨行禮部查照等因前來臣等查朝鮮之於中國奉朔稱臣數百年以來至爲恭恪玆與法國將有搆兵之釁雖經總理各國事務衙門排解似應行知該國使之熟思審處計出萬全臣等公同商酌擬由臣部行文朝鮮國王查照以示朝廷眷顧藩服之意爲此謹奏請旨一摺同治五年六月二十一日准軍機處交片軍機大臣面奉諭旨依議欽此欽遵知照到部爲此鈔錄原奏知照朝鮮國王查照可也云云 同治五年 月 日

高宗(1866.8.20/高宗三年七月十一日) ➡ 禮部

천주교도 처형 배경 설명

回咨

朝鮮國王爲歷陳情形咨覆事同治五年七月初七日承准貴部咨節海云云自主客司案呈止查照可也見上原咨等因奉此竊念小邦偏荷聖朝天地覆燾之恩報答無階北望攢頌廼又諸大人仰體皇上字小之德俯諒弊邦事大之誠既紆總理衙門之排解至蒙貴部行文查照感極涕零罔知攸謝茲具事實本末冒瀆私悃弊邦自昨冬以來有凶徒匪類聚黨糾結潛圖不軌遂乃掩捕則異國人八名不知何歲冒越衣冠言語與東國無別甚至姦昵婦女幻形匿跡其久處弊境推可量會藉曰傳習其教安用此秘詭爲哉異國人之漂到弊國者盡行護還至若無公憑潛越者一切置辟原係金石之成憲此所以竝施當律者也假使弊邦之人潛入他國冒禁煽訛民國與受其害則他國必鋤誅之無遺弊邦亦不當一毫致憾靖封疆嚴邦禁易地則皆然矣弊邦與法國隔以重溟不痛書契仰有何舊然夙嫌不思所以全歸之方忍行此誅殛之擧乎蓋藩臣無外交闢市譏異言尤係守邦之彝典小邦粗知義分恪守候度而今此法國之執言尋釁誠圖慮之所不及也弊國僻遠全昧機會而幸蒙諸大人之排難解紛敎之以熟思萬全之計此誠格外眷佑之盛德至意也冀藉隆庇永獲妥靖環東臣庶相與聚首抃祝客俟前頭使行稱謝忱悃茲先備悉事由有此覆陳煩乞貴部深軫弊邦情實免有不虞釁端庸究終始之惠合行咨覆爲此專差司譯院前正吳愛錫齎咨前去請照詳轉奏施行云云 同治五年七月十一日

93

G. Roze (1866. 8. 28) → P. de Chasseloup-Laubat (1866. 10. 8)

원정을 위한 조선 해안 사전 탐사

À Bord de *la Guerrière*, à Hong Kong, le 23 Août 1866

Monsieur le Ministre,

L'Amiral de *la Grandière* m'ayant informé que ma présence n'était plus utile en Cochinchine par suite de la sincérité et du calme dont jouissait de nouveau le pays, j'ai quitté Saïgon le 16 du courant pour remonter dans le Nord; je viens de toucher à Hong Kong où j'ai renouvelé mon approvisionnement de combustible, et aussitôt que sera arrivé le courrier d'Europe qui est attendu vers le 27, et que, dans les circonstances actuelles pour nous apporter des nouvelles d'une haute importance, je partirai pour rejoindre le centre de ma station. J'ai embarqué sur *la Guerrière* à Saïgon les quatre canons du *Primauguet* ainsi qu'un grand nombre de munitions et d'objets d'approvisionnement pour les bâtiments de la station de Chine. J'ai l'intention en quittant Hong Kong de faire route directement pour Tchefou où *le Primauguet* va recevoir l'ordre de se rendre afin d'y prendre le chargement que j'ai pour lui; un séjour d'ailleurs dans ce port sera très favorable à son équipage après avoir subi les fortes chaleurs de Shanghaï. Je retrouverai, je l'espère, à Tchefou le Père Ridel et les marins Coréens que j'y avais laissés lors de mon départ pressé pour Saïgon. Je compte profiter des beaux jours de l'automne, si le temps le permet, pour aller moi-même sur *le Primauguet* accompagné de deux canonnières faire une exploration de la côte de Corée dans le golfe du prince Jérôme. J'ai hâté de connaître par moi-même ces parages et de voir si l'accès de la rivière de Séoul est praticable pour nos canonnières ainsi que l'ont avancé les marins Coréens. Je pourrai ainsi juger des moyens qui seraient nécessaires soit pour tenter un coup de main, soit pour entreprendre plus tard une expédition; mais malgré mon immense désir de venger le massacre de nos missionnaires, V. E. peut être assuré que dans l'exploration que je compte faire, j'agirai avec les plus grandes précautions et en assurant à ma navigation toute chance de réussite. J'emmènerai avec moi, bien entendu, le Père Ridel et ceux des marins coréens qui pourront m'être les plus utiles et j'ai la ferme confiance que cette tournée dirigée par moi-même, qu'elle qu'en soit la nature, ne pourra qu'être favorable aux intérêts des chrétiens en Corée et servira utilement au but que je me propose.

J'ai l'honneur d'être avec un profond respect,
Monsieur le Ministre,
Votre très obéissant Serviteur,
Le C. Amiral Commandant
G. Roze

P. S.

Le Courrier du Nord qui arrive à l'instant et qui va repartir pour l'Europe m'apporte une lettre de Monseigneur Verrolles, vicaire apostolique de la Mantchourie dont je mets la copie sous les yeux de V. E.

G. Roze

P. de Chasseloup-Laubat (1866. 9. 7) → Moustier

7월 10일자 조선에서의 선교사 살해에 관한 Roze의 보고* 전달

Paris, le 7 Septembre 1866

Monsieur le Ministre et cher collègue; J'ai reçu de M^r le commandant en chef de notre Division navale des Mers de Chine un rapport daté de Tien-tsin, le 10 Juillet dernier, et qui contient des informations de plus graves au sujet de la mise à mort en Corée de deux évêques et de sept missionaires français.

Ces informantions m'ayant paru de nature à être portées à la connaissance de Votre Excellence, j'ai l'honneur de lui comminiquer le rapport de M. le C. Amiral Roze en la priant de me renvoyer ce document, lorsqu'elle en aura pris connaissance.

Agréez Monsieur le Ministre et cher collègue,
l'assurance de ma haute considération,
Le Ministre, Secrétaire d'Etat de la Marine et des Colonies,

P. Chasseloup-Laubat

*제1권 78번 문서.

G. Roze (1866. 9. 7) → H. de Bellonet

Roze와 Bellonet의 조선 원정 주도권에 관한 논쟁

À Bord de *la Guerrière*, Tche-foo, le 7 Septembre 1866

Monsieur le Chargé d'affaires,

J'ai l'honneur de vous accuser réception de votre dépêche datée du 13 Juillet 1866.

Je n'ai pas ressenti moins vivement que vous l'outrage fait à la France et à la Civilisation par le meurtre de neuf de nos missionnaires en Corée, et soyez assuré qu'il n'a fallu rien moins que des devoirs impérieux pour m'empêcher de me rendre sur les lieux aussitôt que ce fait odieux m'a été connu, afin d'en tirer une vengeance éclatante. Cela posé, Monsieur le Chargé d'affaires, permettez-moi, dans le but d'éviter tout malentendu ou toute équivoque, d'établir nettement nos situations respectives en cette grave occurence.

Par votre long séjour en Chine et par les études que vous avez faites de l'Extrême Orient, vous avez sans doute, sur la Corée, des informations qui pourraient m'être utiles et peut-être même faciliter mes projets. Si, pour le bien commun et dans l'intérêt des armes de l'Empereur, vous étiez assez bon pour me les communiquer, je les recevrais avec une grande reconnaissance et en ferais tout le cas qu'elles méritent. Mais votre intervention, purement officieuse, ne saurait aller au delà, sans donner à vos pouvoirs diplomatiques une extension que rien ne nécessite et sans m'enlever, à moins une initiative et une responsabilité que j'ai le droit d'assumer en entier.

La Corée est, en effet, un pays absolument nouveau et demeure fermé, jusqu'ici, à toutes relations Européennes. Si, longtemps, des liens de suzeraineté l'ont uni à la Chine, ces liens, affaiblis par les années, ont aujourd'hui complètement cessé d'exister: la réponse faite par S. A. I. le prince Kong, à votre note, ne laisse aucun doute à cet égard.

D'un autre côté, il est notoire qu'aucun Agent diplomatique n'a encore jamais été accrédité auprès de la Cour de Séoul.

Dès lors, les négociations à entamer avec cette nation, les opérations navales et militaires qu'il y aura lieu d'entreprendre, la nature et l'étendue des réparations à exiger pour le passé, les concessions et les garanties à obtenir pour l'avenir, voilà autant de points que je me réserve d'apprécier seul, suivant la situation des esprits et des choses, jusqu'au moment où j'aurai pu recevoir des instructions de notre Gouvernement.

Monsieur l'Amiral Rigault de Genouilly, en 1858, et Monsieur l'Amiral Charner, en 1860, se sont trouvés dans le même cas, vis-à-vis de la Cochinchine dont la vassalité était et encore revendiquée par la Chine. Néanmoins l'un et l'autre, ont agi de leur propre mouvement et ont dirigé, sous leur seule responsabilité, cette expédition beaucoup plus importante que celle dont il s'agit aujourd'hui.

Veuillez croire, Monsieur le Chargé d'affaires, qu'en vous faisant cette notification, je ne cède point à une vaine susceptibilité qui n'a jamais été dans mon caractère. Comme vous, je n'ai en vue que l'honneur de la France, et, ce but, nous l'atteindrons d'autant plus sûrement que chacun de nous restera mieux dans les limites de ses attributions et de ses droits.

Je viens d'arriver à Tche-foo avec *la Guerrière*. J'ai l'intention de me rendre de ma personne, avec une ou deux canonnières, sur les côtes de la Corée pour en faire l'exploration et voir ce qu'il me serait possible de faire.

Dès que je me serai arrêté à une résolution quelconque, je m'empresserai de la porter à votre connaissance, de même que je me ferai un devoir de vous tenir au courant de tout ce qui pourra survenir d'intéressant, si je me décide à recourir à la force.

Veuillez recevoir, etc, etc, ….

Signé : G. Roze

Pour copie conforme

Le Contre-Amiral Commandant en chef
G. Roze

G. Roze (1866. 9. 7) ➜ P. de Chasseloup-Laubat (1866. 11. 4)

Bellonet의 월권적 행위 인정 불가

À Bord de *la Guerrière*, Tche-foo, le 7 Septembre 1866

Monsieur le Ministre,

Comme j'ai eu l'honneur de le faire connaître à Votre Excellence le 23 août dernier, de Hong-Kong j'ai fait route pour Tche-foo où je suis arrivé hier.

Le massacre de nos missionnaires a soulevé au plus haut degré l'opinion publique dans les différents ports de la Chine. Les journaux se sont faits les organes de cette réprobation universelle et, de toutes parts, on demande une satisfaction complète.

Dans quelques jours je compte voir arriver ici les petits bâtiments qui font partie de ma Division et alors je pourrai donner suite à l'idée que je vous ai déjà soumise, c'est-à-dire aller de ma personne faire une exploration des côtes de la Corée et juger si un coup de main pourrait s'exécuter à la fois rapidement et sûrement. Votre Excellence peut être assurée que je n'entreprendrai rien qu'à bon escient et que si les difficultés étaient trop au-dessus de nos forces j'attendrais ses instructions avant d'agir.

J'ai reçu, il y a quelques jours, une lettre de M[r] le Chargé d'affaires à Pékin par laquelle il me notifie que, de sa propre initiative et sans m'avoir consulté, il a officiellement déclaré l'ouverture des hostilités contre la Corée, la déchéance du Roi, etc., etc. Ces mesures prématurées ont été portées à la connaissance du Cabinet de Pékin qui n'en aura pas, sans doute, fait mystère. Les Coréens sont donc, très probablement, informés de nos intentions et ils peuvent en profiter pour augmenter les difficultés de l'attaque.

Je n'attache pas à ce fait plus d'importance qu'il ne convient et, tout en le regrettant, j'espère être à même de conjurer les fâcheux résultats qu'il pourrait avoir.

Ce qui m'a le plus particulièrement frappé dans cette communication, dont Votre Excellence trouvera, ci-joint, une ampliation, c'est l'attitude prise vis-à-vis de moi par M[r] le Chargé d'affaires de France. Non seulement il requiert les forces navales que je commande mais il précise et limite mon action, il en détermine, à l'avance, les conséquences et les résultats, en un mot, il se substitue entièrement à moi et pour me mettre, sans doute, encore plus à l'aise Mr de Bellonné (*Sic*) veut bien ajouter qu'il prend le tout sous sa responsabilité. Une telle manière d'envisager sa situation et la mienne m'a paru inadmissible et j'ai dû la repousser.

La Corée est un pays tout à fait neuf et indépendant. Il est certain qu'il n'existe plus entr'elle et la Chine aucun lien de vasselage : le prince Kong l'a déclaré lui-même.

Dès lors l'agent diplomatique, accrédité spécialement auprès du Cabinet de Pékin, sortirait de ses attributions s'il intervenait, en quoi que ce soit, dans les affaires d'un pays qui n'a jamais eu de représentation au dehors et qui jamais, non plus, n'a admis aucun Représentant étranger auprès de lui.

Dans ces circonstances, c'est au Commandant des forces navales présent sur les lieux, il me paraît du moins, qu'incombent le droit et le devoir de prendre en main les évènements et de leur donner la direction la plus propre à faire valoir les intérêts de la France.

J'ai écrit dans ce sens à Mr de Bellonné (*Sic*), afin de bien établir ma situation dès le début et d'éviter ainsi tout malentendu entre nous.

Permettez-moi, Monsieur le Ministre, d'espérer que Votre Excellence voudra bien partager mon opinion à ce sujet. Dans tous les cas, je la prie d'être bien convaincue que, dans cette circonstance, je n'ai été mû par aucun sentiment personnel. Quand il s'agit du Service de l'Empereur, on ne peut avoir qu'un seule mobile, celui de le satisfaire, et je n'en aurai jamais d'autre.

Je suis avec un profond respect
Monsieur le Ministre,
De Votre Excellence,
Le très obéissant Serviteur

Le Contre-Amiral Commandant en chef
G. Roze

G. Roze (1866. 9. 11) ➞ P. de Chasseloup-Laubat

조선 공격을 위한 함대 사령부의 芝罘 회의 보고

A Bord de la *Guerrière*, Tche-foo, le 11 Septembre 1866

Monsieur le Ministre,

J'ai l'honneur d'informer Votre Excellence que *le Primauguet* est arrivé à Tche-foo le 8 de ce mois, de retour d'une excursion qu'il était allé faire à Swatow, province de Kwan-tung, dans les circonstances suivantes:

En me rendant à Saïgon, je reçus le 24 Juillet, à Hong-Kong, une lettre du capitaine du navire de Commerce français *le Léon*, par laquelle il m'informait que des rixes sanglantes s'étaient élevées entre deux villages voisins de Swatow. Dans l'un de ces villages, nommé Oo-tau, réside un missionnaire français nommé le père Tardy. Très vivement impressionné par les scènes de violences auxquelles il venait d'assister et craignant pour sa sûreté, ce missionnaire avait écrit au Capitaine d'un autre navire français, le Bankok, une lettre qu'il terminait par ces mots: Un condamné à mort. De plus, profitant du désordre, des maraudeurs s'étaient introduits dans sa maison et lui avaient volé 300 piastres.

Les affaires de la France sont gérées en ce moment à Swatow par le Vice Consul anglais, Mr Cooper, mais je n'avais reçu de lui aucune communication au sujet de ces affaires.

Sur la foi des renseignements de Mr le Capitaine du *Léon*, je m'empressai de donner l'ordre au *Primauguet* de se rendre sur les lieux, afin de s'enquérir exactement de tout ce qui s'y était passé.

Comme Votre Excellence le verra par le rapport de Mr le Commandant Bochet, ci-joint, les choses n'avaient pas autant de gravité qu'on aurait pu le supposer. De vieilles animosités avaient mis, il est vrai, les armes à la main à deux villages, mais il ne paraît pas qu'il fut question des Européens.

Le vol dont le père Tardy avait été la victime était un fait isolé et il avait été déjà réparé sur la demande de Mr le Vice Consul anglais et par le soin des autorités Chinoises.

Quoi qu'il en soit, l'apparition du *Primauguet* a été du meilleur effet : il y a plus de 10 ans qu'on n'avait vu un bâtiment de guerre français dans les eaux de Swatow, bien que notre commerce y ait une certaine activité. Une moyenne de 12 navires de notre nation fait, en permanence, l'intercourse entre ce port et les petits ports voisins. Le sucre et les tourteaux pour engrais sont les deux articles principaux d'exportation et d'importation. M[r] le Vice Consul Cooper a exprimé le désir que notre pavillon se montrât un peu plus souvent dans ces parages. Je m'associe complètement à ce vœu et j'y donnerai satisfaction autant que me le permettront les ressources dont je dispose.

Dans le peu de jours que *le Primauguet* est resté à Swatow, M[r] le Commandant Bochet s'est mis en relations avec les autorités locales et leur a rappelé, en termes énergiques, que la France ne demandait qu'à vivre en bons rapports avec la Chine, mais qu'on la trouverait toujours prête à venger les injures ou les dommages qui seraient faits à aucun de ses enfants.

Le Mandarin de la ville s'est montré plein de déférence et d'empressement. Il s'est rendu, en grand cérémonial, à bord et a donné l'assurance des meilleures dispositions à notre égard.

Je me félicite d'avoir fait faire ce voyage au *Primauguet*, car, en attestant notre vigilance, il ne peut manquer de rassurer nos nationaux missionnaires et commerçants. Ce voyage avait, d'ailleurs, l'avantage de rentrer dans mes idées au sujet de la répression de la piraterie et encore, à ce point de vue, le passage d'un bâtiment de guerre sur les Côtes de Formose n'a pas dû être sans utilité.

Comme je l'ai dit en commençant, *le Primauguet* est arrivé le 8 à Tchefoo où je lui avais donné l'ordre de se rendre aussitôt après avoir rempli sa mission. C'est avec cette corvette que j'ai l'intention de faire l'exploration des côtes de Corée, dont j'ai déjà eu l'honneur d'entretenir Votre Excellence à diverses reprises. Je me ferai, en outre, accompagner, dans cette reconnaissance, par *le Déroulède* qui se trouve ici et par la canonnière *le Tardif* que j'ai rappelée de Ning-Po.

Cette exploration n'a, pour le moment, d'autre but que de me faire connaître un pays sur lequel il n'existe aucune donnée et de me renseigner sur les moyens de venger, s'il est possible, le massacre de nos missionnaires. Mais si, après examen, il m'était démontré qu'un coup de main contre Séoul pût s'exécuter sûrement et vite, il m'en coûterait beaucoup, Monsieur le Ministre, de temporiser et d'ajourner une réparation qui me semble impérieusement commandée par la dignité et par les intérêts de la France.

Dans cette pensée, j'ai donné l'ordre au *Laplace*, au *Kien-chan* et au *Le Brethon* de me rallier; je fais venir, en outre, 150 fusiliers de Yokohama. J'aurai ainsi tous mes moyens d'action sous la main et serai à même d'agir, si les circonstances me paraissent propices.

Que Votre Excellence veuille bien être convaincue que j'apporterai dans mes résolutions toute la mesure et toute la prudence dont je suis capable. Si j'en viens à un engagement, c'est que le succès m'aura paru assuré et que j'y aurais vu une occasion de plus, pour la marine, de montrer ce qu'elle sait faire quand l'intérêt du pays est en cause.

Des nouvelles arrivées, il y a quelques jours, m'avaient fait craindre que *le Laplace* ne pût pas se rendre à mon appel; mais je viens de recevoir un rapport de M^r^ le Commandant Amet qui m'ôte toute inquiétude à cet égard.

Après une tournée fort intéressante dans la mer Intérieure avec notre Ministre, Mr Léon Roches, *le Laplace* rentrait à Yokohama le 13 août quand tout à coup il s'échoua sur la pointe de Kanon-Saki. De prompts secours lui arrivèrent de toutes parts: Anglais et Italiens offrirent leurs services avec un égal empressement, la frégate de S. M. le Roi d'Italie, *le Magenta*, en particulier, a montré dans cette circonstance une confraternité dont je ne saurais trop faire l'éloge. Je me propose d'en adresser tous mes remerciements à son honorable Commandant.

Bref, après s'être allégé le plus possible, *le Laplace*, puissamment aidé par *le Magenta*, fut renfloué dans la soirée du 14 et bientôt après il avait repris son poste accoutumé dans la baie de Yokohama.

Le rapport de Mr Amet que je joins ici montrera à Votre Excellence que les avaries résultant de cet échouage sont presque nulles, un bout de fausse quille enlevé, une vergue d'hune cassée, un grelin perdu, voilà à quoi se réduit un évènement qui m'avait inspiré les plus graves inquiétudes et qui pouvait avoir des conséquences beaucoup plus sérieuses.

G. Roze

G. Roze (1866. 9. 16) ➞ Lieutenant de vaisseau de *la Guerrière*

*Guerrière*함 함장에게 보낸 Roze의 훈령

À Bord de *la Guerrière* à Tché-foo, le 16 Septembre 1866

Monsieur le lieutenant de vaisseau de *la Guerrière*

Après mon départ pour l'exploration que je compte faire sur la Côte Ouest de Corée avec *le Primauguet*, *le Déroulède* et *le Tardif* vous resterez avec *la Guerrière* à Tché-foo où vous serez chargé de la Direction de Services.

Je laisse à bord de *la Guerrière* le chef d'Etat Majors et le Commissaire de Division pour recevoir les bâtiments de guerre et de commerce qui doivent apporter les hommes, le matériel, les vivres et le charbon que j'ai demandés.

Les officiers et les hommes appelés de Yokohama par *le Laplace*, seront à leur arrivée mis en subsistance sur *la Guerrière* où ils apporteront leurs armes, leurs sacs et leurs effets de couchage qu'ils pourraient avoir avec eux.

Le matériel de campement, les munitions et les pièces de montagnes apportées par *le Laplace* (et peut-être par *le Kien-chan*) resteront provisoirement en dépôt sur ce bâtiment jusqu'à ce que j'ai donné de nouveaux ordres.

J'attends deux bâtiments de commerce l'un Hollandais (déjà, je crois parti de Shanghai) l'autre Anglais chargé de vivres et de charbon. Les vivres étant en dessous du chargement, les deux navires doivent d'abord aller à Yentaï ou les denrées seront emmagasinées dans le local que j'ai loué à Yentaï et dont nous prenons possession à compter du 15 Septembre. Le magasinier passager sur *la Guerrière* à destination de Yokohama sera mis à terre à Yentaï pour garder le magasin sous la surveillance du chef du service administratif. Quatre hommes de confiance pris sur *la Guerrière* lui seront adjoints.

Vous donnez à ces marines de commerce toutes les facilités possibles au moyen des corvées pour que leur chargement de vivres soit mis en magasin avec ordre et célérité. Quand ils auront fini, ils devront se rendre à Kung-tung pour y déposer le charbon, et pour que ce mouvement se fasse sans perdre de temps, vous les aiderez dans leur appareillage pour ce (*Sic*) rendre à ce point les faisant remorquer s'il est nécessaire. De même vous aurez à leur fournir des corvées pour accélérer le déchargement.

Si par hasard pendant le temps que je serais absent, il se présentait des occasions, je vous écrirais pour vous mettre au courant de la situation où je me trouverais en Corée. Dans tous les cas, je vous enverrais *le Primauguet* dès que je saurais au juste ce que nos moyens nous permettent d'entreprendre.

Pendant mon absence vous recevrez et ouvrirez toutes les lettres officielles, plis de service [____] qui arriveraient à mon adresse, et je vous autorise et même vous prescris. Si vous receviez des nouvelles de quelque événement important dans les limites de ma station, d'écrire directement à ce sujet, à Son Excellence le Ministre de la Marine en l'informant qui je suis encore sur la Côte de Corée, dans le but de l'explorer avec plusieurs bâtiments de la Division.

Signé G. Roze

99

G. Roze (1866. 9. 17) → E. Verrolles

선교사 처형에 대한 Roze의 의견

À Bord de *la Guerrière* à Tche foo, le 17 Septembre 1866

Mg[r] Verrolles Vicaire apostolique de la Mandchourie

J'ai reçu la lettre que vous m'avez fait l'honneur de m'écrire. Le Massacre de nos Missionnaires en Corée, m'était déjà connu et m'avait profondément ému. Je ne sais encore ce que le temps et les circonstances me permettront de faire, mais vous pouvez être assuré qu'autant qu'il dépendra de moi, un tel forfait ne restera pas impuni.

Comme vous le dites avec raison, Monseigneur, la Marine est le protecteur naturel de la Religion et de la civilisation dans les pays lointains, et cette fois, comme toujours, elle saura se montrer digne d'un si honorable mandat.

Signé : G. Roze

奇正鎭(1866. 9. 24/高宗三年八月十六日)

시무상소(時務上疏)

副護軍奇正鎭疏曰 仄聞日者洋胡猖獗 凶圖狼藉 至有北京移咨之來 其辭意殊常 半涉虛喝 半涉調停 船隻亦或犯泊西海 蓋此賊之懷狼心於吾東 非一朝一夕之故 特以舟路多淺 海山多峻 狐疑而不敢登陸 今雖以殺害彼人 爲執言 其實 削之亦反 不削亦反也 今其旣來者之登陸肆凶 不可保其必無 復來者之有無多寡 又非料度所及 要之肆凶與否在彼 應變之善不善在我 不可恃彼之不我犯 而不爲應變之圖也 廟堂之深謀長策 竊計靡不用極 有非草野愚淺之臣 所可懸想者 而微臣漆嫠之過慮 尙恐其機事之或失 後悔無窮 衷情所迫 平日之私分 有不暇顧矣 敢以數條 錄在下方 冒昧陳達 其一 廟算不可不先定 自古有國家者 必先有一定不易之算 定於君相之心而後 萬人精神 灌注歸一 三岐兩端 最事之病也 咨文以後 里巷愚妄 以爲北京已行之事將不免復在吾東矣 異時百僚之中 有以此說 疑亂四聽者 則臣以爲此妖言也 外國相通 非曰無之 此胡 乃非常妖氣 計行意得 一天之下 盡入其彀中 差爲乾淨者 獨靑邱一片耳 彼以此 爲眼中之釘 百方鑽隙 必欲交通而乃已 豈有他故哉 其無厭之溪壑 欲附庸我國家 帑藏我山海 奴僕我衣冠 漁獵我少艾 禽獸我生靈耳 萬一交通之路一開 不出二三年 殿下赤子 不化爲西洋者無幾 斷然自任 無或饒恕 近日豪華輕薄 喜蓄洋物 貪服洋布 最爲不祥 殆海寇東來之兆 命中外官 搜括廛人 所儲洋物 焚之通衢 嗣後貿來者 施以交通外冦之律 其二 先修辭令 古者兩國相攻 使在兵間 辭令屈則斂兵而退 彼以濫殺問我 而我之答辭 若不光明直截 則問者氣伸 答者氣縮 氣之伸縮 卽勝敗所決也 其答大義 當云我國 待外國人本自不薄 告飢則賜食 告病則賜藥 告舟船傾漏則給材木 哀矜救活之意 豈有遠近之別乎 若或不告地方官變形潛入 出沒城府閭巷間 則此乃窺覘之奸細 寇賊之先導也 隨現捉而加刑誅 乃天下有國之恒典 何足疑乎 況此人等 旣犯此一罪 又嘯聚無賴 誘以反君背父之敎 瀆亂男女 計口收貢 衆惡兼備 此非徒我國之罪人 乃汝國之羞恥 彼必無辭可答 竊見龍岡縣問答一紙 彼醜有問 而我人元無所答 其阻縮之氣可想 令善爲辭令者 作答爲一通 頒布沿海鎭邑 其三 審地形 利於水者不利於陸 制彼之法 恐不過據險邀擊四字 其四 練兵 其五求言 其六內修外

攘 節日甚繁 要歸則不過結人心三字 用人行政之際 以結人心三字 念念不舍焉 答曰 省疏具悉 所陳諸條 明白痛快 可使洋醜 足以破膽 爾其益進良猷 副此至意

高宗, 時原任大臣 등(1866. 9. 26/高宗三年八月十八日)

프랑스 함대에 대한 대처 방안 논의

丙寅八月十八日酉時 上御重熙堂 時原任大臣・各營將臣・兵判・左右捕將引見入侍時 承旨鄭雲龜 假注書金秉鍵 記事官權命菊・趙潚 判府事趙斗淳領敦寧李景在 左議政金炳學 訓鍊大將李景夏 禁衛大將李周喆 御營大將李顯稷 摠戎使申觀浩 兵曹判書金炳湚 左捕將申命淳 右捕將李周喆 以次進伏訖 上曰 史官分左右 上曰 大臣進前 斗淳進前問候 各殿問候訖 上曰 予有可詢之事 故有此入侍之命矣 仍教曰 幺麼小醜 闖入京江 無所忌憚者 尤極忿痛 其剿滅之道 大臣・將臣商確定算 不日奏凱 以安生民 斗淳曰 洋夷之入江深矣 而旣命將出陣 至於制勝之策 臣等方爛熳籌度 宜不致拖日徯時過貽聖心之憂慮 水剌寢睡 以至講學 一如平常之時 此爲鎭安之第一務矣景在曰 洋船二隻已過內洋 至入京江 行止之閃忽 情狀之叵測 尤爲痛惋矣旣命訓局中軍 領軍出往 如欲剿滅 似可非難 但緣何來泊 姑未能詳細問情則彼輩起釁之前 先加攻伐 恐欠柔遠之意 第觀動靜 隨機應接 似好矣 斗淳曰 廟堂之議 以隨機應變 有所爛商矣 炳學曰 船數不過二隻 而人名亦不過數百 則其所殄殲 當隨機應變矣 寢睡・水剌諸節 莫如舒泰 是臣區區之望上曰 如此之時 可見向上忠義之誠 自廟堂 掛榜城門 如有應募奏功者 當不次擢用矣 炳學曰 聖教誠切當矣 忠義激勸 秉彝攸在 而應募之才 似必隨現矣 斗淳曰 自古憂慮之時 人才可見 無事之時 雖有人才 未易知也 上曰 如此之時 或有城內城外無賴之輩 犯分搶竊之患 各別禁戢事 分付左右捕廳炳學曰 此時各門把守 不可疎忽 令各該營 另加團束 多數排立 崇禮・昭義・敦義三門 多數排立 以外沿江直路 亦定軍數 各持器械 嚴加把守之意分付 何如 傳曰 各別申飭 上曰 史官就座 又教曰 大臣以下先退 諸將以次退出

102

議政府 ➡ 高宗(1866. 9. 28/高宗三年八月二十日)

동진(東津) 수비 강화책 건의

議政府啓曰 蠢兹小醜 深入跳浪直敢行稱亂耳 今雖偸命退去 彼情亦旣叵測 則百里之內 尤當戒嚴 而時且潮落 其與陸路有異矣 許多軍卒之曠日露處 亦屬可悶 西江出陣之馬步軍兵 姑令解嚴 各門與京江上下之把守 一體撤還之意 分付 何如 傳曰 允 惟彼小醜 不知我國軍容 無嚴無憚 闖入京江 雖以柔遠之意 許其寄命回帆 而出陣軍卒之露宿喫苦 甚庸矜悶 訓將出往行陣 勞問後乾犒饋分給 各處把守軍兵 亦令該營 一體分給

又啓曰 卽見平安監司朴珪壽狀啓 則曰本道急水門設防之論 自前有之 而今番異船事過之後 詳察形便 則其西岸 卽龍岡東津也 其東岸 卽黃州鐵島也 竝置鎭守 尤極完備 設施方略 後錄仰陳 請令廟堂稟處矣 其一 東津淤泥處可築土城 而中有民田柴山 則不可不給價 至於鎭廨墩臺之創建物力 設鎭後廩料支放 竝別般措劃事也 其一 鎭廨創建材木 斫取於海西長山串事也 其一 兵船數隻 依漁網大船樣 另爲造置事也 其一 募置別砲手五十名 自驚蟄入防 至小雪收防 而居接鎭底 每朔施賞事也 其一 城山·龍淵·金城 本非關防 便屬閒謾 一竝革罷 而三鎭之從前自辟 難廢激勸之方 慈母·保山兩鎭 許屬本營 黃龍別將 亦爲革罷 以其四鎭年例劃給米 與排朔錢 移屬新鎭 而厥數零星 不可不另爲措劃事也 其一 鎭將 以有地望聲績人差送事也 其一 鐵島之設鎭備豫 惟在海西道帥臣之另加商度事也 急水軍設防之論 其來久矣 今此東津形便 已有古城之址 則其爲前人之先得地利也審矣 道臣之籌度講究 極有條理 且城山·龍淵·金城·黃龍四鎭之減此屬彼 實合隨行變通之政 而第許多所入 不可以四鎭零碎之移劃者 擬論於新設之費 令道臣爛加商確 從長啓聞 鐵島便否 關問海西道帥臣 更爲稟處 何如 傳曰 允

總署(1866. 10. 1/同治五年八月二十三日) ➜ 同治帝

프랑스 회신 미접수 사정을 조선에 통지할 것을 상주(上奏)

己酉 總理各國事務恭親王等奏 本月二十一日 軍機處交出禮部奏朝鮮國王李熙咨請代奏謝恩一摺 軍機大臣面奉諭旨 該衙門知道 欽此 查法國使臣伯洛内自接臣衙門照覆 力爲排解後 已閱數月 未據照覆 是否願與罷兵 抑尙憑藉師船觀釁 臣等無從臆揣 第事關軍務 朝鮮國自應妥爲處置 不可稍有大意 貽誤事機 除將現在未據法使照覆緣由 密咨禮部行文朝鮮國王知照外 理合具奏 御批 依議

104

禮部(1866. 10. 2/同治五年八月二十四日) ➡ 議政府(1866. 10. 18/高宗三年九月十日)

조선 원정과 관련된 프랑스 회신의 미접수 통보

禮部知會洋船前往均未可定咨

禮部爲知照事主客司案呈八月二十二日准總理各國事務衙門咨稱本月二十一日軍機處交到禮部奏朝鮮國王咨請代奏一摺欽奉諭旨該衙門知道欽此欽遵抄錄前来本衙門公同閱看原咨所述事實本末係因法國人冒越伊境幻形匿跡等情將其置辟並因法國聞知欲與搆衅曾經中國爲之排解教以熟思萬全之計是以遣官賫咨到部請爲轉奏等因本衙門查法國使臣伯自接照會後已閱數月未據該使臣照覆是否願與罷兵抑尙仍有師船前往均未可定查此件事關軍務朝鮮國王自應妥爲處置未可稍有大意貽誤事機除由本衙門奏明外相應咨行禮部飛咨朝鮮國王查照等因又於八月二十三日准該衙門咨稱本衙門具奏法國欲與朝鮮搆兵已咨禮部轉咨該國王妥籌辦理一摺八月二十三日奉旨依議欽此相應鈔錄原奏知照禮部等因前来相應飛咨朝鮮國王遵照可也云云 同治五年八月二十四日

G. Roze (1866. 10. 5) → B. de Montmorand, H. de Bellonet 등

강화도부터 서울까지의 해안 탐사 고려

Guerrière, Tche-foo, le 5 Octobre 1866

M^r le Consul général de France à Shanghaï
M^r le Ministre de France à Yokohama
M^r le chargé d'affaires à Pékin

J'ai l'honneur de vous informer que j'ai quitté Tche-foo le 18 du mois dernier avec la corvette *le Primauguet* et les 2 canonnières *le Déroulède* et *le Tardif* dans le but d'explorer les atterrages de la Corée et les abords de la rivière de Séoul. Nous avons eu la bonne fortune de trouver dès les premiers jours un mouillage offrant toutes les sécurités pour nos bâtiments grands et petits. Ce mouillage est situé à la partie sud d'un bras de mer étroit qui sépare l'Ile de Kang-hoa de la terre ferme. Après avoir consacré 2 jours à reconnaître ce chenal hérissé de bas-fonds dangereux et sillonné par des courants violents, je résolus de tenter avec les 2 canonnières la montée de la Rivière de Séoul dont nous avions reconnu l'embouchure dans le Nord du Canal de Kang-hoa (Baptisée par nous Rivière Salée).

Je n'entrerai pas dans le détail des difficultés nautiques sans nombre que nous avons eu à surmonter pendant cette pénible navigation de 8 jours : grâce à Dieu nos bâtiments en sont sortis sains et saufs. Le 26 au matin, nous étions à quelques milles de Séoul et nous mouillions à une heure de l'après midi en face de la ville, après avoir rencontré un semblant de résistance qui s'est manifesté par une estacade de jonques que nos boulets ont dispersés, et par quelques coups de canon et de fusils à mèche tirés des 2 rives sur nos bâtiments.

Après un séjour de 24 heures devant Séoul, je redescendis la rivière ; mon but n'était pas d'entrer en pourparler avec le Gouvernement Coréen, mais de m'assurer de la vulnérabilité de la Capitale et de la possibilité d'une attaque par eau. Cette possibilité est aujourd'hui un fait acquis et je compte agir vigoureusement contre Séoul aussitôt qu'on aura mis à ma disposition, les bâtiments d'un faible tirant d'eau et les renforts que je demande en France.

Je suis de retour à Tche-foo depuis le 2 ; j'y suis venu chercher le restant de ma division et compte en repartir sous peu pour Kang-hoa dont j'ai l'intention de m'emparer. Son occupation me permettra de bloquer la capitale et d'arrêter les convois de riz qui servent à l'alimentation de la population.

Tout me fait espérer que j'aurai sou (*Sic*) peu un nouveau succès à vous annoncer.

Signé : G. Roze

G. Roze (1866. 10. 5) → 상하이 주재 각국 공사 등

한강 봉쇄 통고

À bord de *la Guerrière* Tché-foo, le 5 Octobre 1866

Son Excellence Monsieur le Ministre des Etats-Unis à Pékin
M[r] le Ministre de France,
M[r] le Ministre d'Angleterre,
M[r] le Ministre de Russie,
M[r] le Ministre de Prusse,
M[r] le Ministre d'Espagne,
M[r] le Ministre de Belgique,
M[r] le Ministre d'Italie,
M[r] le Ministre de France à Yokohama,
M[r] le Consul général de France à Shanghaï

J'ai l'honneur de vous informer qu'à la suite du meurtre de neuf missionnaires français, ordonné par le gouvernement Coréen, j'ai résolu de poursuivre par tous les moyens en mon pouvoir, les légitimes réparations auxquelles nous avons droit; j'ai, à cet effet, déclaré le blocus de la Rivière de Séoul et je m'empresse de vous en adresser la notification officielle.

Votre Excellence trouvera sans doute opportun de la porter à la connaissance de ses nationaux.

Signé: G. Roze.

Notification du Blocus de la Rivière de Séoul par la Division navale Française. Je soussigné Contre-Amiral Commandant en Chef les forces navales de Sa Majesté l'Empereur des Français dans les mers de la Chine et du Japon.

Voulant poursuivre les réparations qui nous sont dues à l'occasion du meurtre d'un grand nombre de missionnaires français ordonné par le Gouvernement de la Corée, et en vertu des pouvoirs qui m'appartiennent comme Commandant en chef.

***Déclare*:**

À partir du 15 du courant, la Rivière de Séoul et toutes ses issues, seront tenues en état de Blocus effectif par les forces navales placées sous mon commandement.

Il sera procédé contre tout bâtiment qui essayerait de violer le Blocus conformément aux Lois internationales et aux traités en vigueur avec les Puissances neutres.

Signé: G. Roze

【英譯文】

Notice of blockade of the river Seoul by the French naval squadron.

The undersigned, rear-admiral and commander-in-chief of the naval forces of his Majesty the Emperor of the French, in the China and Japan seas, in furtherance of the measures which have been deemed necessary in consequence of the murder of many French missionaries by the government of Corea, and by virtue of the powers belonging to me as commander-in-chief, hereby declares, that after the 15th day of this month the river Seoul, by all its entrances, will be held in a state of effective blockade by the naval forces under my command.

All vessels which shall attempt to violate this blockade will be treated according to international laws, and the treaties in force with neutral powers.

G. ROSE

Given on board the Guerrire, Chefoo roads, October 5, 1866.

G. Roze (1866. 10. 6) → P. P. M. Grandière

조선 해안 탐사에 대한 의견, 원정을 위한 군수물자 보급 요청

Guerrière, Tché-foo le 6 Octobre 1866

Monsieur le Vice-Amiral Gouverneur et Commandant en Chef de la Cochinchine à Saïgon

J'ai l'honneur de vous informer que j'ai quitté Tché-foo le 18 du mois dernier avec la corvette *le Primauguet* et les 2 canonnières, *le Déroulède* et *le Tardif* dans le but d'explorer les atterrages de Corée et les abords de la Rivière de Séoul. Nous avons eu la bonne fortune dès les premiers jours de trouver un mouillage offrant toutes les sécurités pour nos bâtiments grands et petits. Ce mouillage est situé à la partie sud d'un bras de mer étroit qui sépare l'Ile de Kang-hoa de la terre ferme. Après avoir consacré deux jours à reconnaître ce chenal hérissé de bas-fonds dangereux et sillonné par des courants violents, je résolus de tenter avec les deux canonnières la montée de la Rivière de Séoul dont nous avions reconnu l'embouchure dans le Nord du Canal de Kang-hoa (Baptisée par nous Rivière Salée).

Je n'entrerai pas dans le détail des difficultés nautiques sans nombre que nous avons eu à surmonter pendant cette pénible navigation de huit jours : grâce à Dieu, nos bâtiments en sont sortis sains et saufs. Le 26 au matin, nous étions à quelques milles de Séoul et nous mouillions à 1 heure de l'après midi en face de la ville, après avoir rencontré un semblant de résistance qui s'est manifesté par une estacade de jonques que nos boulets ont dispersés, et par quelques coups de canon et de fusils à mèche tirés des deux rives sur nos bâtiments.

Après un séjour de 24 heures devant Séoul, je redescendis la rivière ; mon but n'était pas d'entrer en pourparler avec le Gouvernement Coréen, mais de m'assurer de la vulnérabilité de la Capitale et de la possibilité d'une attaque par eau. Cette possibilité est aujourd'hui un fait acquis et je compte agir vigoureusement contre elle aussitôt qu'on aura mis à ma disposition, les bâtiments d'un faible tirant d'eaux et les renforts que je demande en France.

En attendant, mon intention est de m'emparer immédiatement de l'Ile de Kang-hoa, qui est la première place forte de la Corée et dont l'occupation me permet de bloquer Séoul et d'arrêter les convois de riz qui servent à l'alimentation de la population. À cet effet je suis revenu à Tchéfou depuis le 2 de ce mois pour chercher le restant de ma Division, dans quelques jours nous reprendrons la mer et j'aurais peu de temps après, je l'espère, un nouveau succès à vous annoncer.

Vous savez, Mr le Gouverneur, combien mes moyens sont restreints. Aussi m'a-t-il fallu les appeler tous à moi et pour cela, dégarnir, sans exception, tous les points où nos intérêts m'obligent à entretenir des stations. Si, à la rigueur, cette situation n'a pas de raison de me préoccuper pour ce qui concerne la Chine, il n'en est pas ainsi pour le Japon. Ce malheureux pays est, depuis longtemps, en pleine guerre civile et la mort du Taïcoun, arrivée récemment, en ouvrant le champ aux ambitions, va, sans doute, réveiller de vieux partis et peut faire naître de grands événements.

Dans l'intérêt de nos nationaux et de notre influence, je considérais comme un grand bien qu'un bâtiment de guerre restât en permanence à Yokohama à la disposition de notre Ministre. Mr Léon Roches m'en a, d'ailleurs, exprimé le désir dans les termes les plus pressants.

Dans l'impossibilité où je suis d'apprécier l'époque ou les affaires de Corée me permettent de confier cette mission au *Laplace* ou *le Primauguet*, je prends la liberté, Mr le Gouverneur, de vous demander s'il ne vous serait pas possible d'y affecter temporairement *le Monge*.

Le Ministre, dans les instructions qu'il m'a remises au moment de mon départ de France, m'a autorisé à vous faire appel en cas de besoin. Mais je ne parle de cette faculté que pour mémoire, m'en rapportant en cette circonstance bien plus aux sentiments de bienveillance que vous avez bien voulu me témoigner qu'a une requête officielle.

En raison du calme dont jouit votre colonne et surtout de la saison, il serait possible que *le Monge* ne vous fût pas en ce moment d'une grande utilité. Ce serait, au contraire, un auxiliaire précieux pour nous pendant quelque temps, car, en m'enlevant toute préoccupation pour le Japon, il me permettrait de me consacrer avec toutes mes forces, aux affaires de Corée, jusqu'à leur complet règlement.

Cette demande, Monsieur le Gouverneur, n'a pour but que le bien général, cependant, permettez moi de vous assurer que je vous serais personnellement très reconnaissant si vous voulez bien y donner la suite que je désire. Dans cette expérience, j'ai l'honneur de vous envoyer des instructions pour Mr le

Commandant Scheverer, à qui vous auriez la bonté de les remettre.

Nous avons aussi besoin d'une assez grande quantité de munitions dont le détail est ci-joint, je vous prie, M^{r} le Gouverneur de vouloir bien donner des ordres pour qu'elles soient envoyées au Service administratif de Woo-sung le plus tôt possible. Si, comme j'ose l'espérer, *le Monge* vient, il pourrait s'en charger et dans ce cas il relâcherait à Woosung et de là ferait route, sans retard pour Yokohama,

Signé: G. Roze

Note des munitions demandées ci-dessus			
Détail des munitions	**Espèces des unités**	**Quantités**	**Observations**
Sachets remplis de poudre pour canons rayés de 12	Nombre	800	
Obus de guerre pour canons rayés de 12	nbr	800	
Boîtes à mitraille pour canons rayés de 12	nbr	100	
Sachets remplis de poudre pour canons rayés de 4 de montagne	nbr	1200	
Obus de guerre pour canons rayés de 4 de montagne	nbr	1200	
Boîtes à mitraille pour canons rayés de 4 de montagne	nbr	150	
Etoupilles à friction pour canons rayés de 12 et de 4	nbr	2000	
Capsules pour carabines	nbr	20.000	
Cartouches à balles pour carabines transformées	nbr	120.000	
	Signé: Roze		

G. Roze (1866. 10. 6) → P. de Chasseloup-Laubat

조선 해안 탐사 보고

La Guerrière, baie de Tche-foo, le 6 Octobre 1866

M^r le Ministre,

Dans mes dépêches en date du 23 août et du 7 septembre derniers, j'ai eu l'honneur d'informer V. E. que j'avais l'intention d'entreprendre, si le temps le permettait, l'exploration des côtes de la Corée qui avoisine la capitale. Le retentissement qu'avait eu le massacre de nos missionnaires, l'émotion que ce grave évènement avait causé parmi les populations de l'extrême Orient, me faisaient regarder comme une nécessité de tenter, par tous nos efforts, les moyens de punir un Gouvernement barbare qui, à l'abri de son isolement absolu, et au mépris de toutes les lois de l'humanité, avait si odieusement mis à mort nos compatriotes. C'est dans cette pensée qu'après avoir quitté Saïgon où j'avais été appelé momentanément, j'ai pris sur le champ la résolution de réunir à Tche-foo les bâtiments de la Division de Chine, afin de me mettre en mesure d'exécuter mon projet, si les circonstances m'en donnaient la possibilité.

Le 18 septembre, au point du jour, j'ai quitté Tché-foo sur *le Primauguet* qui portait mon pavillon et qui avait pris à la remorque l'aviso *le Déroulède* et la canonnière *le Tardif*, arrivée récemment de Ning-po. J'avais seulement à ma disposition la carte que M. le Contre Amiral Guérin avait levé en 1856, dans son excursion au milieu des récifs du golfe de Prince Jérôme. C'était le seul document qu'il me fut possible de consulter, et j'ignorais encore sur quelle partie de la côte se trouvait l'embouchure du Han-Kiang, fleuve qui conduit auprès de Séoul, capitale de la Corée. L'aspect de la côte, le mouvement actif des jonques dans le golfe du Prince Jérôme, des récits de marins indigènes avaient fait supposer à l'armiral Guérin que la capitale était peu éloignée des parages où il se trouvait, et que l'embouchure du Han-Kiang devait aboutir à l'extrémité d'une anse profonde dont il avait marqué les abords sur sa carte, sans avoir eu le temps de la faire explorer en entier. J'avais longtemps partagé cette supposition, et, bien que j'eusse auprès de moi un marin du pays, compagnon du Père Ridel, je n'avais pu savoir par lui, d'une manière claire où gisait le passage qu'il m'importait si grandement de connaître. Dans le doute sur sa vraie position, je pris le parti de me rendre tout d'abord, dans le golfe du Prince Jérôme où je fus guidé par l'excellent travail de M^{r} le Contre-Amiral Guérin, travail dont j'ai pu apprécier la complète exactitude, tout en admirant le talent et la hardiesse que cet honorable Amiral avait déployé, pour retracer ainsi les sinuosités et les points importants de ces difficiles passages.

Le 19 vers midi, j'avais connaissance des îles Ferrière, je fis gouverner aussitôt pour les contourner à petite distance, et dès ce moment, les remorques furent larguées et les canonnières vinrent se placer sur l'avant du *Primauguet* pour éclairer sa route. Nous entrâmes ainsi dans l'intérieur du Golfe, en laissant à notre gauche les îles innombrables de l'Archipel du Prince Impérial. Nous nous dirigeâmes vers l'île Fernande avec les précautions usitées pour une navigation de ce genre ; nous la laissâmes à droite, et aidés par la clarté de la lune, nous pûmes continuer notre route même pendant la nuit, pour aller chercher un mouillage praticable par des fonds moindres que ceux annoncés par la ronde et qui, dans la plus grande partie de notre parcours, n'ont pas été moindres de 55 mètres. À minuit, je fis mouiller par 38 mètres de fond de gravier, après avoir dépassé l'île Fernande de 5 miles environ.

Le 20 au point du jour, nous changeâmes de mouillage, et nous pûmes trouver un plateau d'une profondeur de 15 à 20 mètres à marée basse, auprès d'une île qui nous offrit un excellent abri. J'ai donné à cette île, dont le nom n'est pas marqué sur la carte de M^{r} l'Amiral Guérin, celui d'Eugénie, en souvenir respectueux de notre Auguste Souveraine.

M^{r} le Commandant Bouchet, dont le zèle est infatigable, et auquel j'avais adjoint MM^{r} Hermann et Desfossés, mes aides de camp, ainsi que tous les officiers du *Primauguet*, s'occupa de coordonner tous les relèvements et documents nautiques que nous avions pu prendre la veille, et fit compléter les sondages de manière à lever une carte aussi détaillée qu'il nous était permis de le faire, de la partie du golfe que nous avions traversée. Nous fîmes établir à terre une échelle de marée pour constater le mouvement des eaux qui est si considérable au milieu de ces îles ; des croquis nombreux des points les plus saillants furent dessinés, et le travail réparti entre chacun des officiers et exécuté avec le plus grand entrain par eux tous, nous a donné les éléments d'une carte qui pourra, en partie, compléter cette dessinée par l'Amiral Guérin. ce (*Sic*) même jour 20, sans perdre de temps, j'expédiai *le Déroulède* avec la mission d'aller rechercher l'embouchure du Han-Kiang. Mr Hermann, mon aide de camp, passa sur ce bâtiment pour assister le capitaine Richy dans ses nouveaux travaux ; le Père Ridel lui fut donné comme interprète, et le marin coréen qui ne nous avait guère été utile jusqu'alors, reconnut les île auprès desquelles nous étions placés, et se chargea de guider *le Déroulède* dans sa nouvelle exploration. Le 21 *le Déroulède* revint auprès de moi, et m'annonça qu'il avait réussi dans sa mission. En contourant la partie nord des côtes qui touchait à celle du Prince Jérôme, il avait pu trouver un bras de mer resséré qui conduit à l'embouchure de la rivière de Séoul : il avait découvert à l'entrée de ce canal, un mouillage assez vaste et parfaitement sûr qui pouvait même abriter *la Guerrière*, mouillage qui commandait l'un des accès principaux du fleuve, et avait en conséquence l'extrême importance de nous rendre au besoin, les maîtres de la plus grande partie du mouvement commercial du Han-Kiang. Il avait poussé ses recherches jusqu'à l'île de Kang-Hoa l'une des quatre places les plus fortifiées, et réputée la plus importante de la Corée, qui se trouve à environ 20 milles de l'entrée du canal, et vis-à-vis l'entrée du flueve de Séoul. Cette île est, en effet, garnie de fortins sur lesquels, à notre passage, surtout en revenant, nous avons vu une multitude de soldats. Pendant l'expédtion du *Déroulède, le Tardif* qui m'avait signalé une avarie assez grave dans le moyen de son hélice pour aller s'échouer sur une magnifique plage de sable vis-à-vis l'île Eugénie, et là, laissé à sec par les grandes marées qui ne sont pas de moins de 7 à 8 mètres, il exécuta complètement sa réparation et revint, dès le soir même, mouiller auprès de nous.

Dès le lendemain, 22, de très bonne heure, je partis sur *le Primauguet*, précédé du *Déroulède* et du *Tardif*. Je sortis du golfe du Prince Jérôme, et, après une navigation de quelques heures, accomplie avec de minutieuses précaution, j'arrivai au mouillage qui m'avait été signalé par le capitaine du *Déroulède* ; je n'y passai que le temps nécessaire pour le visiter et m'assurer, en effet, par moi-même, que *la Guerrière* y serait en parfaite sécurité, et je remontai immédiatement vers l'île de Kang-hoa, en prenant le canal (baptisé pour nous Rivière Salée) qui avait été exploré la veille par *le Déroulède*. Les canonnières nous signalèrent les sondages et déjà nous avions franchi les deux tiers de la route, quand un changement de fond nous fût aussitôt annoncé ; le *Primauguet* arrêta subitement sa marche, essaya de reculer, mais quelque célérité qu'on apportât à sa manœuvre, il ne put assez tôt marcher en arrière pour éviter de tomber sur un banc de roches qui était à environ 6 mètres sous l'eau, profondeur qui équivalait à peu près au tirant d'eau de la corvette. *Le Primauguet* resta quelques instants immobile, et, au bout de quelques minutes, la marée qui montait avec force le fit flotter de nouveau et lui permit de s'éloigner. Cependant, quelque faible que fût cet échouage, plusieurs morceaux de la fausse quille avaient été arrachés. Les sondages annoncés par les canonnières me prouvant que le fond était trop inégal, même à marée haute pour y risquer de nouveaux *le Primauguet*, je donnai l'ordre de revenir sur nos pas, pour aller prendre un mouillage un peu plus en aval près d'un village appelé Sirou, et c'est là que nous passâmes la nuit.

Le lendemain 23, j'embarquai sur *le Déroulède*, et j'envoyai *le Primauguet* au mouillage de l'entrée du canal, que je nommerai désormais mouillage de l'Ile Boisée, à cause d'une île qui se présente à l'entrée comme un véritable bouquet d'arbres. Le bâtiment recevait la mission d'en lever le plan, d'en étudier les marées, et d'en faire exactement les sondages. En même temps, je partis sur *le Déroulède*, suivi du *Tardif* avec l'intention de remonter aussi près que je le pourrais de Séoul. Les marées étaient très fortes et les courants excessivement violents. Les conditions rendaient la navigation très difficile et exigeaient de bien grandes précautions pour éviter les bancs nombreux que nous allions rencontrer. Les canonnières eurent à subir un échouage de quelques minutes, entraînées par des rapides qui, par moments paralysaient l'effet du gouvernail. Heureusement la nature des fonds qui, dans cette partie, étaient de sable fin, empêchèrent toute avarie, et bientôt les canonnières purent flotter encore et continuer leur marche en entrant tout à fait dans la rivière de Séoul. L'île de Kang-hoa domine cette entrée et peut être considérée comme une sentinelle avancée qui commande complètement le fleuve dont le cours ne commence à proprement parler qu'à ce point. C'est ainsi que les indigènes appellent tout le canal qui mène de l'Ile boisée à Kang-Hoa, rivière de mer, et à partir de Kang-Hoa jusqu'à Séoul, rivière de terre. L'inspection des croquis que j'ai l'honneur d'envoyer à V. P., pourra mieux faire comprendre la configuration générale de ces parages, que la description que je pourrais en faire. C'était pour la première fois que des bâtiments de guerre montraient leur pavillon sur ces rives, et dès ce moment, nous pourrions penser que le voile mystérieux dont s'entourait ce pays allait être arraché, car le chemin de Séoul était ouvert devant nous.

Ce même jour, vers 9 heures du soir, nous avons laissé tomber l'ancre devant un petit village appelé Ptoué, auprès d'une plage qui nous a paru très convenable, avec un fonds suffisant pour nous assurer de flotter quand la mer serait basse. La nuit a été paisible, nos canotiers que nous avons envoyés à terre pour établir une échelle de marée ont communiqué avec les indigènes qui, comme tous ceux que nous avons vu jusque-là, ont paru doux et sociables, mais fort craintifs ou plutôt réservés, et disposés sans doute, à frayer avec les étrangers, si leur mandarins ne les en empêchaient. Leur curiosité est excessive : partout sur le passage des canonnières qui défilent très près des rives, la foule se presse, et se groupe sur les collines pour jouir du spectacle qui pour la première fois frappe ses yeux.

Le 24, à 9 heures du matin, au renversement de la marée, nous appareillâmes de nouveau, et après avoir pris les mêmes précautions pour assurer notre navigation, nous vînmes mouiller près du village de Seuk-Kol, agréablement situé au milieu de bouquets de verdure ; là, à peine arrivés, un bateau d'indigènes se détache de la rive, et vient à bord. Les Coréens d'abord défiant ne tardent pas à s'enhardir, et demandent la permission de monter à bord ; ils ont la curiosité des enfants, ils regardent partout, touchant à tout ce qu'ils aperçoivent, prennent nos lunettes et nos binocles, et cherchent à y voir, avec des éclats de rire et une joie enfantine. Ils paraissent gais, mais toujours très craintifs à l'égard de leurs mandarins ; ils répondent à voix basse à nos demandes d'échange en nous disant qu'ils nous satisferaient volontiers s'ils n'étaient pas surveillés par leurs Mandarins. Nous leur demandons à acheter des provisions, mais ils ont besoin pour cela d'une permission ; ils vont à terre pour la demander ; ils reviennent bientôt après et nous rapportent que leur Mandarin ne veut y consentir que si nous prenons l'engagement de nous éloigner. Je réponds aussitôt avec force que nous, nous avons l'habitude de traiter en amis les étrangers qui viennent chez nous, et que nous sommes empressés à leur fournir ce dont ils ont besoin ; j'exige donc qu'ici, ils agissent de même à notre égard ; j'ajoute, que s'ils se montrent si peu hospitaliers, je les traiterai en ennemis, et que je ferais enlever leur Mandarin. Ils se dépêchent d'aller porter cette réponse à leur chef, et ils reviennent bientôt avec un approvisionnement complet : un bœuf, un porc, des volailles et des légumes en assez grande quantité pour les équipages des deux canonnières. Une bonne découverte que nous faisons en même temps, c'est que l'eau du fleuve avec jusant, à partir de ce village est tout à fait douce et potable. Je fais donner aux Indigènes des piastres en paiement de leurs provisions, mais ils refusent d'abord et ne paraissent pas comprendre la valeur de la monnaie ; sur mon insistance, ils finissent par accepter avec la restriction cependant que leur Mandarin les leur permettra. Pendant la nuit, nous avons établi à terre une échelle de marée ; les courants sont très forts, et la marée marne environ de six mètres ; durant toute la nuit, les Coréens restent en groupes nombreux accroupis sur la plage à nous regarder, et allument de grands feux ; des ordres sont évidemment arrivés de Séoul, pour nous surveiller avec soin.

Le 25, à 6 heures du matin, dès que la marée devient favorable, nous nous mettons de nouveau en route pour remonter le cours du Han-Kiang. Les difficultés de navigation semblent plus grandes, les précautions sont les mêmes ; les canots sondent sur l'avant pour éclairer le chemin ; cependant, entraîné par le courant, *le Déroulède* ne peut éviter un banc de sable sur lequel il reste échoué pendant une demi-heure environ ; la marée étant sur le point de renverser, je me décide à revenir sur nos pas pour aller prendre un mouillage convenable par 8 mètres de fond. L'inégalité des profondeurs de l'eau est une des plus grandes difficultés de la navigation du fleuve ; les marées étant très fortes, on ne peut laisser tomber l'ancre que par des fonds où l'on puisse flotter à mer basse, ce qui est souvent très malaisé. Comme toujours, dans ce nouveau trajet, les populations curieuses s'établissent dans les collines et sur les plages pour nous voir passer ; sur le parcours du fleuve, elles paraissent très nombreuses et je pense que la plupart de ces villages sont beaucoup plus peuplés sans doute que ceux qui sont dans l'intérieur du pays. Plusieurs fois des embarcations d'indigènes sont venues accoster le bord ; un mandarin entr'autres, envoyé probablement par le G$^{\underline{nt}}$ et arrivant de Séoul, nous questionne par les mêmes phrases que celles qui nous ont été dites depuis notre départ de l'Ile Boisée. Que venez-vous faire ? De quel pays êtes-vous ? Quels sont vos projets ? Je fais répondre invariablement à ces demandes par le Père Ridel. Nous sommes Français, nous allons où nous voulons et nous tenons à voir le pays. Les réponses n'ont pas l'air de satisfaire les mandarins, car leur physionomie témoigne une vive inquiétude. Cependant, vers le soir, sur notre demande, ils nous apportent des provisions, bœufs, volailles, œufs et légumes, et ils en reçoivent très bien le prix en piastres, bien qu'ils n'aient pas l'air de connaître cette monnaie.

Cette station n'est plus qu'à trois milles environ de la rive la plus voisine de Séoul. Le 26, de grand matin, au moment où nous la quittions pour continuer notre exploration, nous apercevons un changement complet dans l'apparence générale de la côte ; la polpulation qui la veille encombrait les plages et les hauteurs est devenue invisible : les collines couronnées naguère d'une foule curieuse sont complètement désertes ; plus un seul indigène ne paraît. Un contraste aussi opposé dans les allures de ce peuple doit avoir une signification et doit être l'effet d'un ordre du G^{nt}. De plus, une grande quantité de jonques sont venues pendant la nuit se placer sur la route que nous devons suivre pour arriver au mouillage de Séoul, et dans le but certainement de former une estacade pour nous barrer le passage. Tenant à tout prix à me rendre devant Séoul, et à ne pas laisser croire que je cède aux injonctions si souvent renouvelées des Mandarins, je fais dire à ces jonques, par une embarcation indigène d'un village voisin, que je leur donne une heure et demie pour se dissiper, et que si après ce délai elles n'ont pas obéi à mon ordre, je me faierai (*Sic*) un passage au millieu d'elles à coups de canon. En même temps je fais arrêter des trains de bois considérables qu'il serait très facile de les couler en les chargeant de pierres dans un défilé fort étroit et très difficile par lequel il nous faut passer pour aller à Séoul. Bientôt après, je m'engage dans ce même passage où nous nous étions échoués la veille, mais cette fois grâce aux sondages pris avec un soin infini par le C^{nt} Bochet, lui-même, nous le franchissons sans accident. Le délai que j'avais fixé étant expiré et les jonques ne faisant aucun mouvement pour s'écarter, je me décide immédiatement à exécuter ma menace, bien convaincu qu'elles ne sont placées ainsi sur ma route que par l'ordre du Gouvernement. Je me rends avec mon Etat major dans *le Tardif* que j'avais fait mettre en téte de ligne, mon pavillon y est arboré, et je fais envoyer quelques coups du canon de 30, qui fort bien pointés, jettent un trouble inexprimable devant nous. Les équipages de ces jonques s'enfuient en toute hâte dès le premier coup de canon sur la rive voisine ; je peux passer tout auprès d'elles, et tandis que je prolonge leur ligne, une espèce de projectile comme une fusée à la congrève nous est lancée de chacune des deux rives, et vient tomber à une assez grande distance de nous. Des coups de fusil en assez grand nombre sont également tirés sur nous ; aussitôt les canons de 12 du *Tardif* et ceux de 12 et de 14 du *Déroulède* envoient rapidement quelques obus vers l'endroit d'où les coups sont partis ; les fusiliers font en même temps un feu de mousquetterie sur les quelques soldats Indigènes qu'ils peuvent apercevoir de ce côte. Mais après quelques instants une panique immense s'empare de ces hommes qui fuient à toutes jambes et désertent complètement la plage. Je fais cesser immédiatement le feu et j'arrive très tranquillement au mouillage de Séoul. Cet exemple aura produit certainement un salutaire effet en montrant la puissance et la portée de nos canons. Il était bon d'ailleurs, d'assurer notre prestige et de prouver au Gouvernement de la Corée, si confiant jusque là dans son isolement et dans la position que la nature lui avait faite en l'entourant d'une aussi innombrable quantité d'écueils, qu'il n'était plus inviolable, et qu'il était à la merci de nos boulets. Des milliers d'Indigènes ont envahi toutes les hauteurs qui dominent les rives, et sont demeurés avides de curiosité en ne cessant de nous regarder. C'était une foule immense, dont il eut été bien difficile d'apprécier le chiffre et qui répandue partout dans la campagne donnait par ses vêtements invariablement blancs un aspect des plus pittoresques au paysage. Un très grand village qui prolonge la rive droite enserre le chemin qui conduit à la Capitale; un village semblable est placé tout à fait vis-à-vis le premier sur l'autre rive. L'esprit de cette population m'étant complètement inconnu, il ne m'a pas été possible d'envoyer une reconnaissance à Séoul qui s'étend au pied d'une haute montagne à environ 8 kilomètres de la rive la plus rapprochée et d'où la vue ne peut l'atteindre. Nous avons pu cependant distinguer une partie de ses murailles. Mais j'ai fait prendre tous les sondages qui pouvaient compléter un croquis très suffisant du mouillage. Le Gouvernement ne m'a envoyé aucun Mandarin, et, de mon côté, la mission que je m'étais donnée, se bornant pour le moment à une exploration, je n'ai pas cherché à entrer en relation avec ceux des Mandarins qui probablement habitent le grand village auprès duquel nous sommes mouillés. Les événements du matin étaient d'ailleurs de nature à leur imposer une grande réserve. J'ai eu l'occasion cependant là, comme dans toutes les stations où j'ai séjourné, de faire savoir à la population que nous ne venions pas pour la châtier, qu'au contraire nous étions les amis du peuple de Corée et que les Français étaient connus dans le monde pour leur générosité et leur désintéressement; mais j'ai tout lieu de penser que ce peuple est fort ignorant en géographie, et qu'il ne connaît guère les délimitations de l'Europe; pour lui, toutes les nations qui ne sont pas la Chine ou la Corée n'existent que dans les ténèbres de son imagination.

Au mouillage de Séoul, vers le milieu de la rivière, il existe un banc de roche, où *le Tardif* est resté fortement échoué pendant toute la journée dans une position à me donner de vives inquiétudes. J'espère que la population ne s'en est pas aperçue bien que *le Tardif* ait été obligé de se béquiller pour soutenir ses flancs. Vers le soir, la marée de flot l'a renfloué tout naturellement, et heureusement sans la moindre avarie. Ces accidents d'échouage devaient être très fréquents dans une navigation constamment accomplie en découverte, entraînées comme l'étaient les deux canonnières par un courant rapide et ne pouvant pas toujours gouverner d'après les indications des canots que nous n'avons jamais négligé de mettre en éclaireurs devant notre route. Cette exploration malgré toutes ces difficultés a pu réussir sans malheur à déplorer, et le mérite en revient au zèle incessant qu'ont déployé les officiers que j'avais appelé à me seconder. Le Commandant Bochet du *Primauguet* que j'avais détaché momentanément de son bâtiment pour le charger des travaux hydrographiques, s'est acquitté de cette mission avec l'intelligence et la passion dévouée qu'il a l'habitude de mettre aux travaux qui lui sont confiés. Il a été parfaitement assisté, d'ailleurs par M.M. Hermann, Desfossés, mes aides de camp, et M. de Marlione, aspirant de 1ère classe, attaché à mon état major général, ainsi que par tous les officiers du *Primauguet*, du *Déroulède* et du *Tardif*. Chacun d'eux dans cette campagne a acquis des droits à ma gratitude et à la haute bienveillance de V. Ex. M.M. Richy et Chanoine, capitaines du *Déroulède* et du *Tardif*, ont conduit leurs bâtiments avec l'aplomb et le talent de marins consommés ; ils ne se sont jamais lassés un instant de chercher à vaincre les difficultés presque incessantes qui surgissaient devant eux. Les équipages parfaits comme ils le sont toujours dans les circonstances importantes, ont redoublé de force et d'énergie et nous sommes tous heureux d'avoir ainsi accompli une exploration qui peut avoir d'aussi grands résultats dans l'avenir et qui intéresse à un si haut point la géographie.

Après avoir passé 24 heures au mouillage de Séoul, j'ai donné l'ordre du retour ; nous sommes revenus avec les mêmes précautions en mouillant sur plusieurs autres points où nous avons pu faire des observations de latitude et de longitude, ainsi que des travaux de triangulation pour déterminer le mieux possible les positions exactes et les contours de la rivière. Grâce à ces soins, nous en avons aujourd'hui une carte très satisfaisante. Enfin, après bien des échouages et plusieurs jours d'une navigation toujours aussi difficile, nous sommes arrivés le 30 septembre au mouillage de l'Ile Boisée.

Pendant mon absence, *le Primauguet* mouillé cependant par 14 mètres de fond en marée haute était resté échoué à marée basse dans la journée du 29 septembre ; la mer avait marné de 9 mètres 50 c. C'était, à la vérité, l'un des jours des grandes marées de l'équinoxe. *Le Primauguet* avait été obligé de se béquiller, mais il n'avait nullement souffert dans ce nouvel échouage. Après avoir écrit très à la hâte la relation sommaire du voyage si rempli d'intérêt que je m'étais promis d'effectuer, je voudrais pouvoir donner à V. E. des renseignements détaillés et surtout exacts sur la politique et la constitution du pays que j'ai parcouru ; mais en cela j'en suis encore à l'ignorance des premiers jours, car, à part le Père Ridel qui est en ce moment auprès de moi et qui ne peut connaître un pays dans lequel il est resté constamment caché, je n'ai vu personne qui puisse me donner les informations que je désirerais me procurer, on m'avait annoncé qu'à notre apparition sur ces côtes, les chrétiens se lèveraient et viendraient en foule à nous; Je n'en ai pas vu encore un seul et je ne sais seulement pas dans quelle partie de la Corée se trouvent les chrétientés les plus importantes. Le Père Ridel n'a pas même trouvé le moyen de faire savoir aux deux missionnaires qui ont survécu au massacre de leurs collègues, notre arrivée sur ces côtes, ils me seraient cependant bien utiles pour me servir d'interprètes. La légation de Pékin m'avait écrit que le Père du Roi était désigné par le parti chrétien comme très sympathique à la population, et comme devant remplacer son fils sur le trône, si une révolution venait à y éclater par suite notre présence en Corée. De son côté, le Père Ridel m'assure que ce Père du Roi est un homme détestable qui s'est associé aux trois ministres les plus coupables, pour ordonner le meurtre des missionnaires. Du milieu d'opinions aussi contradictoires, il est bien difficile de savoir où est la vérité. Cela ne serait donc que par un séjour plus prolongé et surtout par des communications avec des hommes influents dans le pays que je pourrais savoir à quoi m'en tenir à ce sujet, mais encore cela serait-il bien difficile, tant est excessive la crainte que le Gouvernement inspire à ses sujets, car chacun d'eux tremble de se compromettre par indiscrétion qu'il pourrait payer de sa tête.

Mon explication étant terminée, comme je le désirais et avec un succès complet j'ai quitté le 1er Octobre le mouillage de l'île Boisée, sur *le Primauguet* et suivi de deux canonnières et suis arrivé à Tchefou le 3 octobre.

V. E. a vu par le récit suivant de notre navigation combien il est difficile de parcourir avec sécurité toutes les sinuosités de ce fleuve avec des bâtiments du tirant d'eau de nos canonnières qui ne dépasse pas pourtant 2m. 20c. Nous avons eu beaucoup de peine à les diriger seules et nous n'avons pu éviter de fréquents échouages sur ces bancs dont nous avons cherché à déterminer avec notre carte le gisement et l'étendue mais qui se déplacent fréquemment par les alluvions que les courants entraînent. Cette difficulté eut été bien plus grande encore s'il nous avait fallu remorquer un certain nombre d'embarcations chargées d'hommes comme cela serait nécessaire pendant plusieurs jours s'il s'agissait d'une expédition. C'est pourquoi je ne pense pas qu'il soit possible de tenter une entreprise de ce genre avec les seuls moyens dont je dispose et de conduire environ 500 hommes de débarquement à la remorque de 4 canonnières de ma Division, *le Déroulède*, *le Tardif*, le *LeBrethon* et *le Kien Chan*. L'envoi de ces hommes nécessiterait le transport d'approvisionnement considérable de vivres et de munitions et cette armée bien peu nombreuse aurait à agir à une distance encore assez grande, à environ 8 kilomètres des canonnières mouillées sur la rive.

Bien que j'aie toujours pensé que l'opération nautique fut la plus difficile à exécuter, celle qui touche à la question militaire demande aussi beaucoup de soin, d'autant plus que nous avons affaire à un peuple que nous ne connaissons pas encore et dont les instincts guerriers peuvent se révéler en voyant les étrangers fouler le sol de leur patrie. D'après ce que j'ai pu voir, je pense que pour aller jusqu'au Séoul et pour obtenir un résultat assuré sans courir les chances incertaines du hasard, il serait opportun d'avoir un grand nombre de petites canonnières démontables comme celles de Cochinchine, au moins 6, plus 6 canonnières du tirant d'eau que j'ai signalé plus haut, et environ 6 à 8 chaloupes à vapeur en bois comme celles qui ont été envoyées au Mexique. Les plus grandes de ces canonnières, comme *le Tardif* pourraient aller devant Séoul, seules sans avoir à remorquer par des courants rapides, soit des jonques soit des embarcations chargées d'hommes. Elles porteraient les approvisionnements de vivres et les munitions et je crois que 1900 hommes de débarquement, plus deux batteries de 6 obusiers de 4 rayés, seraient suffisants pour soumettre Séoul surtout s'il s'agissait de s'y établir pendant le temps nécessaire pour peser sur le pays. Les Jonques des Indigènes et un certain nombre de chalands plats, remorqués par des chaloupes à vapeur et les petites canonnières serviraient au transport du personnel. Je ne peux tracer ici qu'un aperçu très rapide des moyens qui me semblent nécessaires pour entreprendre une expédition jusqu'à Séoul; Je n'ai pu constater que les difficultés nautiques et je n'ai encore aucun renseignement sur les forces actives du pays et ses projets de résistance.

Quant à présent, sans engager le Gouvernement de l'Empereur, dans une entreprise qui peut ne pas être certaine, il me semble nécessaire de frapper de terreur le Gouv[t] de la Corée et je suis sûr que l'apparition des forces dont je dispose en prouvant que ses côtes sont accessibles aux plus grands bâtiments, produira un effet assuré pour prévenir désormais la persécution contre les chrétiens. Je compte donc profiter des beaux jours qui restent encore dans cette saison pour me rendre avec *la Guerrière* et mes autres bâtiments au mouillage de l'île Boisée. Là je serai à portée de l'île de Kang-hoa, dont l'occupation peut être d'un grand intérêt et qui ainsi que j'ai eu l'honneur de le dire à V. E. peut par sa position importante et fortifiée être considérée comme la clef de Séoul.

Je suis

Signé : Roze

P. S.

Devant partir demain ou après demain pour Kang-hoa j'ai cru nécessaire de déclarer le blocus de la rivière de Séoul pendant tout le temps que je resterai dans les parages. J'en ai fait en conséquence la déclaration officielle aux représentants des différentes nations résidant en Chine.

崇厚 ➞ 總署(1866. 10. 11/同治五年九月三日)

조선에 대한 미국, 영국, 프랑스의 연합 공격 가능성 보고

九月初三日　三口通商大臣崇厚函稱　朝鮮與法國興兵一節　現據東海關潘道寄来探報一紙　玆特照錄呈覽

照錄淸摺

敬稟者　日昨稟報法國兵至高麗情形　計蒙鈞鑒　本日密詢稅務司　據稱新有輪船自彼回煙云　煙台對面五百餘里卽高麗山島　前往兵船經此島時　爲其開砲擊沉夾板船一隻　傷去二十五人　內有敎士托馬浂密妥士　商人胡賈　現英法美三國各因本國人被害　共圖報復　証兵三千　調集大小輪船十八隻　不日在煙台取齊　法國水師提督昨已到煙　明日駛往東行等語　復據稱高麗槍砲無多　其現在所用之砲上安火箭　式樣頗奇　而運用甚不靈便　鳥槍自用火繩點葯　亦不如外國之捷速　惟海口皆高山暗礁　不易進攻　近探得有小港一處　可小舟通入大河　經探路者棹舟偵視　見高麗屯兵甚衆　開放火槍　卽紛紛逃散　由此進兵　看来不難速破各等語　查得前此兩國搆怨　英美竝未出師助戰　今因傷及本國之人　合意復仇　以兵力而言　蕞爾海邦　實非其敵　俟密探情形隨時稟報外　合先據此啚稟憲台鑒核　肅此　恭請福安　職道霨謹稟

高宗, 時原任大臣 등(1866. 10. 16/高宗三年九月八日)

프랑스 함대에 대한 대처 방안 논의

丙寅九月初八日未時 上御重熙堂 時原任大臣率兵曹判書各營將臣 請對入侍時 左承旨宋熙正 假注書趙秉鎬 記事官趙㦓·金性均 行判中樞府事趙斗淳 行判敦寧府事李景在 左議政金炳學 右議政柳厚祚 行兵曹判書金炳湫 禁衛大將李周喆 御營大將李顯稷 以次進伏訖 上曰 史官分左右 斗淳進前 奏曰 日候稍冷 聖體 若何 上曰 一樣矣 斗淳曰 寢睡·水剌之節 何如 上曰 一樣矣 大王大妃殿氣候 何如 上曰 一樣矣 斗淳曰 王大妃殿氣候何如 上曰 一樣矣 斗淳曰 大妃殿氣候 何如 上曰 一樣矣 斗淳曰 中宮殿氣候 何如 上曰 安順矣 斗淳曰 洋夷若是猖獗 至犯保障重地 其爲駭憤 容有其極 禦遏防守 事係時急 相率請對矣 景在曰 洋夷之各持兵器 毋難下陸不但痛惋 出於惡意 推可知矣 則備禦之策 不容少緩矣 炳學曰 洋船事 去益憤惋 而有稟定事 相率請對矣 厚祚曰 洋醜凌犯如此 不勝驚惋 剿滅之策不容少緩 敢此仰達 上曰 洋夷之侵犯內洋 莫近日若 防守備禦之策 唯恃諸大臣及諸將臣矣 須爛加商確 務盡措劃之方也 炳學曰 江都保障之地 有此洋夷之猖獗 其爲憂虞 無所止届 訓鍊大將李景夏 巡撫使差下 使之卽速設營 先送中軍 領率精兵幾哨 隨機應變 嚴加備禦 何如 上曰 依爲之 嚴加團束 不日奏凱 可也 出榻教 炳學曰 各殿宮南廟動駕 既有成命矣 更待他日下教恐好 故敢達矣 上曰 依爲之 出榻教 炳學曰 左右捕將 多有防務之事竝姑許遞 其代 知宗正卿李東鉉 宗正卿李章濂差下 城內城外凌逼竊發之患 使之另爲禁斷 何如 上曰 依爲之 都下人心 極爲騷訛 多有犯分掠奪之弊 嚴加禁戢 可也 出榻教 炳學曰 摠戎使申觀浩 方守鹽倉項矣 訓局馬軍一哨 步軍二哨 兩營牙兵各三十人 標下軍各三十人 使之領率 沿江上下 巡察防守 軍餉令度支舉行 何如 上曰 依爲之 出舉條 炳學曰 前掌令李恒老文學經綸之士也 此時獎用恐好 故敢達矣 上曰 同副承旨除授 使之乘馹斯速上來 出榻教 炳學曰 向日洋船之來 有幾人應募者矣 今亦當不無其人 隨其來告 使之白衣赴陣 何如 上曰 應募而若有成功者 當不次擢用矣 以此意揭榜于通衢四門 可也 出舉條 炳學曰 禁將有所仰達事云 雖大臣就座前 使之奏達 何如 上曰 依爲之 周喆曰 將家後裔之勸武奬進 多有已例 而當此

之時 人器可合者 尤不可不收用 閑良具德喜 別薦施行 何如 上曰 依爲之 出榻教 熙正曰 新除授左邊捕盜大將李東鉉 右邊捕盜大將李章濂 卽爲牌招傳授命召大將牌·傳令牌 何如 上曰 依爲之 出榻教 炳淅曰 別薦人具德喜先付軍門 哨官 使之赴陣 何如 上曰 依爲之 出榻教 炳淅曰 永宗僉使沈永奎 年老身病 海防鎭守 恐有疎虞之慮 改差 前兵使白樂莘 勿拘常格差下使之當日給馬下送 何如 上曰 依爲之 出榻教 仍教曰 今日筵說 當日頒布可也 上曰 史官就座 仍命大臣先退 又命退 諸臣以次退出

111

高宗(1866. 10. 17/高宗三年九月九日)

척사윤음(斥邪綸音)

諭京外大小民人 王若曰 惟予小子 沖齡嗣服 上不能寅畏天命 下不能慰答民心 蚤夜厲厲 惟不克負荷我列聖朝全付之重 太母殿下期勉之隆 是懼是怵 錦玉靡安 淵氷若涉 乃者外寇之警 近薄於沁都保障之地 備禦疎虞 全城失守 士民駭竄 畿輔繹騷 嗚呼 此何等時也此何等變也 靜言思之 一則寡躬之咎 二則寡躬之咎也 政不足祖述先憲 德不足以懷綏方域 恬嬉頹惰 駸駸然馴致此境矣 我國介在東海之東 與極西幾萬里之地 曾是風馬牛之不相及 非有疆界之互爭 釁隙之可修 踔重溟歷風濤 何爲而涉吾地哉 是必有我邦奸細之類 或失志怨國 或畏罪亡命 糾結旣久 聲氣潛通 越海遠引 公然犯臨 噫嘻 尙忍爲此 尙忍爲此 天理孔昭 王法至嚴 從當一一鉤覈 快雪神人之憤 而然彼愚迷造變之徒 喪倫蔑紀 不覺自陷於罔赦之科 以予視之 皆吾赤子也 亦皆我列聖化育之餘 則庇覆不廣 綏馭失宜 使不得安生樂業 以致此不率不軌之行者 果誰之咎 書曰 百姓有過 在予一人 撫躬自訟 予固愧恧之不暇 又何責於蚩蠢悖詟之輩也 言之痛心 不必多誥 咨爾京外有司之臣 咸悉此意 宣布朝家哀痛之諭 使之革心革面 偕底大道焉

G. Roze(1866. 10. 18/高宗三年九月十日) ➞ 高宗

선교사 살해 책임자 처벌 및 전권대표 파견 요구

回檄皮封前面 呈高麗統司台前安啓 後面上封

大法欽命全權大臣 統帶各哨勇軍羅爲剴切曉諭事 爾華陽土司悉知 予以本朝大皇帝命 護庇本國軍民人等 在此方寓者 其所以於本年在此邦無辜遭誅者 係我國傳教士推重之人也 爾司不仁 弑之不義 極宜攻罰 然傳教士仁義光明 毫無過犯 殺之之違天悖理 此等諸惡 世法全不能容矣 不聞乎中國前數載 伊行不仁 犯此凶行 我本大國 征之輒之 俾不得不俯首尊命而行 今大法全權大臣 主定征代高麗不仁不義之邦 若不傾耳受教 全無饒處

一 因有三員唆弄其司爲源由 殺我朝傳教士者嚴辨

一 爾司宜早差全權一員 披星戴月 來此面議 永定章程 災害凶患 今以臨近矣 爾欲避之 宜早回言 果受教 若不欽命 本大臣先期與爾是諸患難 爾民受災之根 勿謂言之不先也

救世壹仟捌百陸拾陸年洋十月十八日

113

巡撫營(1866. 10. 19/高宗三年九月十一日) ➞ G. Roze

선교사 처형의 정당성 강조, 프랑스 군의 군사 행위 비난

巡撫營傳檄洋舶都主

夫逆天理者必亡 違國法者必誅 天降民人 理以順之 國分封疆 治以守之 所順者何 仁之而不害 所守者何 犯之者罔赦 是所以逆則必亡 違則必誅也 然交隣柔遠 自古有道 而在於我國 尤用寬仁 凡不知國名不知道里者 每有漂泊我境 則命守土之臣 迎接問情 如修舊好 飢則賜食 寒則與衣 告病則調藥以救之 告歸則齎糧以送之 此我國世守之規 而至今行之 故天下之號我者莫不曰禮義之國也 若或夤緣我人 潛入我境 換我衣服 學我言語 罔我民國亂我禮俗 則國有常法 隨現必誅 此通萬國畫一之規也 我行常法 汝何怒焉易地行之 我當無問 而今汝之執此爲言 已極違理 日前汝船之入我京江也船不過二 人不滿千 則苟欲屠戮 何患無術 而旣與潛入差別 則其在懷遠之義 不忍加兵相害 故過境牛鷄 隨請輒饋 扁舟往來 以言相問 則受其饋而不受 其回者 汝自負我 我何負汝 猶且不足 去益行悖 今此犯我城府 殺我民人 掠貨攘畜 罔有紀極 逆天違法 未有甚於此也 天旣厭之 人得誅之 且聞汝輩 欲以行敎於我國云 此則尤爲大不可也 車書不同 各有所尙 正邪曲直尙矣勿論 我崇我學 汝行汝學 殆若人人之各祖其祖 而曷敢敎人以捨其祖而祖人祖乎 此若免誅 可謂無天 我之待汝 殷湯之於葛伯也 汝之暴我 玁狁之於周宣也 雖以我之至仁至德 不當任他泯默 故千萬大兵 今玆臨海 要伸奉天行討之義 先馳詰朝相見之約 師曲師直 勝敗決矣 汝勿退避 俯首聽命

丙寅九月十一日戌時 朝鮮國巡撫營著押踏印

【佛譯文】

Il est ordonné de transmettre cette lettre au Maître des Navires Européens.

Quiconque renie la loi divine doit mourir, quiconque renie la loi de son pays mérite d'être décapité. Le ciel a crée les peuples pour qu'ils obéissent à la raison. Les royaumes sont séparés par des frontières et sauvegardés par des lois. A quoi faut-il obéir ? A la justice et sans restriction aucune. Tout homme qui la viole est indigne de pardon. D'où je conclue qu'il faut mettre à mort celui qui la renie, qu'il faut décapiter celui qui la viole.

De tout temps les relations avec les voisins, les secours accordés aux voyageurs ont été de tradition ; dans notre Royaume, nous faisons preuve de plus de bienveillance, de plus d'amour encore. Souvent, en effet, il arrive que les navigateurs ignorant la position et le nom des pays abordent sur nos côtes. Les mandarins de nos villes reçoivent alors l'ordre de les recevoir avec bienveillance, mais leur demandent s'ils viennent dans de bonnes et pacifiques intentions, donnent des vivres à ceux qui ont faim, vêtissent ceux qui sont nus, soignent les malades. Il est même d'usage de donner la viatique aux mourants. Telle est la règle qui a toujours été mise en pratique dans notre Royaume sans avoir à souffrir aucune offense, aussi la Corée est-elle pour le monde entier le Royaume de la Justice et de la civilisation. Mais s'il se trouve des hommes qui viennent séduire nos sujets, pénétrent chez nous clandestinement, changent leurs vêtements, étudient notre langue, corrompent notre peuple, bouleversent nos coutumes, l'antique loi du monde veut qu'ils soient mis à mort ; telle est la règle commune à tous les Royaumes, à tous les Empires. Pourquoi m'en voulez-vous donc de l'avoir toujours observée ? N'est-il pas suffisant que nous ne vous demandions pas compte du motif qui vous amène ici de lointains pays ? Vous, au contraire, vous occupez notre sol comme s'il était le vôtre et par ce seul fait, vous violez odieusement la raison.

Quand dernièrement vos navires ont remonté le fleuve impérial, ils n'étaient qu'un ou deux, les hommes qui les montaient ne dépassaient pas le nombre de mille. Si nous avions voulu les détruire n'avions-nous pas des armes ? Mais par bonté à l'égard des voyageurs, nous n'avons souffert ni qu'on leur fit du tort, ni qu'on fit acte d'hostilité contr'eux. C'est ainsi qu'en franchissant nos frontières, ils prenaient ou recevaient selon leur volonté des bœufs et des poules, allant et venant en enbarcation, ils étaient interrogés en termes pacifiques; bien plus, on leur faisait des présences sans les inquiéter en aucune façon.

Vous vous montrez donc ingrats envers moi tandis que je ne le suis pas envers vous. Cela ne vous suffit pas, vous aviez besoin de vous retirer; votre rentrée est inconvenante maintenant vous bouleversez nos cités, vous tuez mon peuple, vous détruisez mes denrées et mes troupeaux. Jamais on ne vit d'une façon plus grave, violer et le ciel et les lois.

Comme le Ciel poursuit de tels hommes de sa haine, il convient de les mettre à mort lorsqu'on les prend! Bien plus, on a dit que vous vouliez répandre votre religion dans mon Royaume. C'est un crime. Les livres différents ont leurs sentences propres qui présentent le vrai et le faux, qu'importe que je suive ma Religion, vous la vôtre?

S'il est blâmable de renier ses ancêtres, pourquoi venez-vous nous apprendre à abandonner les nôtres pour en adopter d'étrangers? S'il ne fallait pas mettre à mort de tels hommes, mieux vaudrait nier le Ciel!

Je vous traite comme Yn et Tan traitèrent l'impie Ko-pe et vous vous révoltez comme Ngien Yeou l'a fait contre Tcheou-Onen. Quoique je n'ose pas me comparer à ces Rois illustres, on ne saurait, je l'avoue, passer ma générosité sous silence.

Vous paraissez ici maintenant avec une armée nombreuse comme si vous étiez les instruments de la Justice Céleste, venez à la cour, ayons des entrevues et nous déciderons s'il convient de réunir ou de renvoyer les troupes, de tenter la victoire ou la défaite. Ne fuyez pas, inclinez-vous et obéissez.

La 5e année de reigne de Tong-Tchy, la 9 lune, le 11e jour.
Pour traduction.
Le Contre-Amiral Commndant en chef

G. Roze

大院君(1866. 10. 19/高宗三年九月十一日)

척화문(斥和文)

是時大院君致書于廟堂曰 人死國亡 古今天地之常經也 洋夷侵犯 列國亦自有之 于今幾百年 此賊不敢得意矣 伊自年前中國許和之後 跳踉之心 一倍叵測 到處施惡 皆受其毒 惟獨不行於我國 實是箕聖之在天陰騭也 到此之地 所知者禮義也 所恃者衆心成城也 今日上下 若有疑怯 則萬事瓦解 國事去矣 我有三件劃定于心者 諒此血誓 隨我躡後焉

一. 不耐其苦 若和親則是賣國也

一. 不耐其毒 若許交易則是亡國也

一. 賊迫京城 若有去邠則是危國也

115

鄭雲龜 ➞ 議政府(1866. 10. 19/高宗三年九月十一日)

프랑스 군과의 교전 상황 보고

鄭雲龜 以畿輔巡撫營言啓曰 卽見先鋒中軍李容熙 今月初十日戌時 成貼馳報 則大陣當日申時量 行到通津境陽陵橋 則該府使李公濂 囊齎印符 單身來待 具道事狀曰 昨日午時量 洋賊五十餘名 各持銃劍 突入邑村 掠奪民財牛畜衣服 了無餘存 轉入官舍 公私錢六七百兩 沒數持去 至於官服諸具 亦皆無遺 而官隷則吏屬俱逃 閭閻則男女全空 至於外村民人 莫不聞風逃散府使則隻身孤立 不宜坐受殺害之患 故不得已徒步登山 暫避經夜於五六里外民家 今纔來此云云 故聞甚驚憤 爲先急發數校 使之微服先行 詳察前路左右 以探賊情之虛實伏兵之有無 又發數校先行 自左右村落 以至邑底 而使之以安心還巢之意 逢人輒諭 大陣仍卽前進 酉時量 到該府前街 結成方陣 以待機變 而大軍旣到 衆情咸悅 三三五五 民皆稍集 其中有一二民 來告曰 昨日洋賊 自邑村 轉上文殊山城 或上或下 若有據險之意云 故問其遠近 則距邑爲十里許 而行將飼馬饋卒 一以盡防患之策 一以盡制變之方云矣敢啓 傳曰 知道

G. Roze (1866. 10. 19) → H. de Bellonet

작약도(芍藥島) 탐사에 관한 Roze의 보고

À Bord du *Déroulède* Mouillage de Kang-hoa, le 19 Octobre 1866

À notre arrivée à l'île Boisée, vous prendrez le commandement supérieur de ce mouillage qui vous sera donné par Monsieur le Commandant du *Laplace* que vous inviterez à vous communiquer les instructions que je lui ai laissées en partant. Je n'ai que peu de choses à y ajouter.

Vous aurez à faire prendre toutes les précautions nécessaires contre les mauvais temps qui peuvent se faire sentir en cette saison ainsi que nous venons d'en faire l'apprentissage au commencement de la semaine.

Toutes les mesures usuelles en temps de guerre contre une surprise ou une attaque devient (*Sic*) être également prises sur les trois [_____] [_____] dans votre direction.

Monsieur le Commandant de *Laplace* m'a demandé de faire mettre sur l'île Boisée, les bœufs qui sont maintenant à bord des navires. Il a noué des relations amicales avec les habitants d'un village voisin et selon lui la mise à terre de ces bœufs serait urgente. Les animaux seraient bien mieux, les navires seraient dégagés et on n'aurait pas l'inconvénient d'aller [_____] sur une assez grande quantité de fourrage à une longue distance des bâtiments. Je [_____] d'ici bien juger la question, je la laisse à votre appréciation vous invitant à faire ce que vous jugerez le plus convenable. Il me semble nécessaire que les bœufs soient gardés par quelques hommes [_____] qu'il y aurait à installer, sur l'île dans une cabane facile à faire il me semble avec des branchages.

Vous maintiendrez autant qu'il vous sera possible le [_____] de la Rivière, empêchant de passer ceux qui tenteraient de remonter. Pour les jonques, il est probable que plusieurs d'entre elles [_____] à s'échapper [_____] [_____] [_____] fastidieux, surtout à marée haute. Il est difficile d'empêcher celles-là de s'enfuir mais arrêtez [_____] celles qui passeraient dans votre voisinage.

Je n'ai pas besoin de vous recommander l'excursion du Mouillage de l'île Boisée au point de vue des ressources qu'il peut offrir et sur les rapports hydrographiques. Ces travaux importants que vous avez fait il y a peu de jours encore sont pour moi des garants que tout ce qui sera possible dans cette voie sera fait.

Signé : G. Roze

117

巡撫營 ➞ 議政府(1866. 10. 20/高宗三年九月十二日)

프랑스 군 철수 보고

巡撫營以先鋒中軍李容熙姑留通津啓

該營啓言卽見先鋒中軍李容熙馳報則結陣探賊形止昨已馳報而更發校卒詳細偵探則洋酋之入文殊山城者昨聞大軍先聲皆已撤還渠舶不復向犯通津一步之地而戒嚴一依對敵故天明後更擧詳察或登山瞭望或沿海搜探則通津 境內果無一箇洋酋而只有雙帆竹二隻船碇留於甲串前洋雙帆竹一隻則起煙逆風向南而去雙帆竹一隻碇留於月串前洋則大抵有船然後可以渡江接戰而沿海上下了無一葦是所謂無用武之地欲造筏木則寸木尺葛末由求得極爲悚悶姑仍留于通津府云又啓言通津府使 愼我芝以本營軍官仍置臣營幕下之意草記蒙允而此時不得不使之赴任請仍兼軍官而下送

李恒老 ➞ 高宗(1866. 10. 20/高宗三年九月十二日)

척사상소(斥邪上疏)

同副承旨李恒老疏曰 伏以 臣於今月九日 伏奉承政院八日成帖 以臣爲同副承旨 使之斯速上來者 臣聞命驚惶 罔知攸措 臣實空空一野人耳 少治功令 才拙不售 略涉性理 病廢因循 老矣無聞 甘爲棄物 忽於憲廟庚子 虛名上徹 誤恩下降 傴僂悸恐 不敢就職 哲廟壬戌 誤出賊招 雖蒙睿燭 得保首領 俯仰慙駭 不敢自同平人 不謂殿下嗣服之初 大僚筵薦 驟加清顯 一歲中超遷至掌憲 此在宿德名儒 不敢容易承膺 況在臣身 何異木偶之華衮 瓦缶之黃流也 卽因徑遞 未得封疏陳情 似若儻來者然 臣罪萬死 況今洋賊猖獗 正當危急存亡之秋 凡繫庶官 尤宜遴選 而以臣萬萬不似之物 畀之納言之重任 臣愚竊以爲過矣 且臣犬馬之齒 七十有五 百病侵凌 坐起須人 尋常應接 七顚八倒 喉舌供職 決非可強 不獨負乘之爲憂也 但今賊情叵測 艱虞溢目 而召命之降 出尋常萬萬 臣非木石 何以爲心 茲不敢在家辭免 扶曳癃疾 敢膺有旨 而來籲此惶悶之情 伏乞聖明 哀矜垂察 將臣所帶職名 亟命遞去 以重公器 以安私分焉 抑臣竊有所懷 不忍不冒死一陳焉 恭惟我殿下 以沖齡膺受祖宗丕丕基 霜豕積漸 禍亂猝發 宵衣旰食 將伯無地 謂草萊之愚 猶或有千慮之一得 庶幾有以傾否扶顚於萬一 有此馹召之擧 臣自上道以來 夜不成寐 食不知味 實不知仰酬聖心之一二也 臣本章句腐儒 無經濟之術 加以老病垂死 精神昏耗 日用瑣細 前忘後失 不得逆探賊情 條論時事 鑿鑿符合 然姑擧其大概 則今日國論 兩說交戰 謂洋賊可攻者 國邊人之說也 謂洋賊可和者 賊邊人之說也 由此則邦內保衣裳之舊 由彼則人類陷禽獸之域 此則大分也 粗有秉彝之性者 皆可以知之 況以殿下之明聖 豈容左腹之入也 但恐宗社危急之禍 迫於呼吸 而計利徼倖之論 乘間抵隙 則未知聖明 果能持之如一 剛決鎭壓 如孫討虜斫案之勇否也 此愚臣之所大懼也 其主國邊之論者 又有兩說 其一 戰守之說也 其一 去豳之說也 臣謂戰守常經也 去豳達權也 常經人皆可守 達權非聖人不能也 何者 蓋有太王之德則可 無太王之德 則無歸市之應矣 百姓一散 不可復合 大勢一去 不可復來 此愚臣所以先事深憂 願殿下 脫有事變 寧守常經 而毋遽以聖人之事自況也 殿下若於戰守之說 堅定聖志 雖萬夫沮撓 不動毫髮 則暗聾跛躄 且增百倍之氣矣 況

簪纓世臣之族 草野忠義之人 孰不願激勸小民 爲殿下効死哉 臣願殿下 亟下哀痛之敎 自訟致寇之由 明示善後之意 十行絲綸 丁寧懇惻 足以泣鬼神而動木石 則其鼓發民情之端 得之於此矣 敬信大僚 以尊體統 三司之外 廣開言路 選將繕武 極用人望 八道之內 又各擇本道人望所歸者一人 爲號召使 假之以盛權 示之以尊寵 爵祿之榮 及於副貳 使之收拾忠孝氣節之人 以爲義旅 與官軍相爲應援 賊來則折衝禦侮 以衛王室 賊去則修明彛倫 以息邪敎 則其轉禍爲福之幾 又得之於此矣 昔者隋煬帝 以百萬之衆 來攻高句麗 其大小强弱之勢 不翅若萬斤之壓鳥卵也 然而乙支文德 能以褊師 敗衂其衆 隋以不振 唐太宗之英武 天下無敵 而自將擊安市城 城守不克 天師摧敗 爲天下笑 麗氏之末 紅巾賊率貔貅熊羆之師三十餘萬 來陷松都 我太祖及鄭世雲 一擧而破其二十萬 斬其魁關先生 逐破頭藩 於是乾淸坤夷 麗室復安 今我朝雖當文恬武嬉 不識兵革之餘 凜凜若不保朝夕 然地方千里 山海險固 財粟之出 魚鹽之利 雖在戰國之世 猶當伯仲於趙・魏・燕・韓 決非高句麗丸泥之比也 殿下自今伊始 夙興夜寐 君臣相誓 戒宴安之鴆毒 致勤儉之實德 私意不萌於心術之微 文具不設於政事之著 則群臣百姓 莫不精白其心 丕應徯志 何事之不可濟哉 雖然臣竊聞之 水所以載舟 亦能覆人之舟 民所以衛國 而亦能亡人之國 故曰 人心險於山川 殿下歷覽古史 興邦之慶 孰不本於人心之歸嚮 喪邦之禍 孰不由於人心之離叛也 臣願殿下 謀及聖心 謀及卿士 內自輦轂 外至遐荒 凡經術道德 足以爲殿下之師友 面折廷爭 足以正殿下之闕失 孝廉氣節 足以勵殿下之風俗 淸白政事 足以活殿下之赤子 武學才智 足以敵殿下之所愾 與凡小善一藝 可備殿下之器使 而擯棄淪落者 卽命有司悉心推訪 拔茅連茹 使之于于洋洋 來列庶位 而凡懷利忘義 遺君後親之輩 漸次疎遠 則朝著淸明 士林相慶 而皆願爲殿下致身矣 停土木之役 禁歛民之政 去侈大之習 卑宮室菲飮食惡衣服 而盡力於民事 如大禹之爲 養好生之德 充不忍人之心 如皐陶之謨 孟子之訓 表裏一致 孚信傍達 則民力大紓 物情洽然 而仰之如父母矣 率致身之臣 以遺其君 率孝順之子 以攻其父 古今天下必不成之事也 如此然後洋賊可逐 國家可保 苟爲不然 上失君子之心 下結小人之怨 日往月來 不知所以反之 則雖使猛將如雲 謀臣如雨 前知預計之士 日効其能 無補於土崩瓦解矣 老臣受國厚恩 一息尙存 決不爲無理之妄言 以負我聖明也 耿耿此心 神明可質 伏願殿下 赦其狂妄之罪 而深留睿念焉 臣無任云云 省疏具悉 所陳諸條 莫非藥石之論 予當體念矣 爾其勿辭 卽爲肅命

H. de Bellonet(1866. 10. 21) → 恭親王

한강 봉쇄 통보

Pékin, le 21 octobre 1866

Le Chargé d'Affaires de France au Prince de Kong

J'ai l'honneur de porter à la connaissance de V. A. la notification officielle du blocus de la rivière de Séoul et des Côtes Occidentales de la Corée par les Forces Navales de S. M. l'Empereur des Français. Je prie V. A. de vouloir bien donner à ce document toute la publicité possible afin que nul n'en ignore, et que les intérêts des Chinois qui trafiquent avec la Corée soient entièrement sauvegardés.

J'ai l'honneur d'être etc.

Henry de Bellonnet

【漢譯文】

法國照會

爲照會事 照得本大臣現准本國水師提督來文 移送該員所出告示一張 以高麗西海沿通該國京城之河各口 經該員所領之兵船 均爲堵塞 因不日攻打交兵 暫止別國船隻前往 玆本大臣將所接告示字樣 繙譯漢文 合送貴親王查閱 卽請出示曉諭 貴國商船俾各知曉 免致冒進受損 爲此照會

【英譯文】

OCTOBER 24, 1866

Sir:

I have the honor to bring to the knowledge of your imperial highness the official notification of the blockade of the river Seoul, and the west coast of Corea, by the naval forces of his Majesty the Emperor of the French. I beg your imperial highness to be pleased to give this document all the publicity possible, to the end that none may be ignorant of it, and that the interests of the Chinese who trade with Corea may be entirely safe.

I have, &c.,

HENRI DE BELLONET

His Imperial Highness PRINCE KUNG.

G. Roze (1866. 10. 22) → P. de Chasseloup-Laubat

강화도 도착 및 점령 보고

À bord du *Déroulède*, Rade de Kang-hoa, le 22 Octobre 1866

Monsieur le Ministre,

Dans ma dépêche qui rendait compte à Votre Excellence des résultats de mon exploration sur les côtes de Corée, j'avais l'honneur de vous informer que mon intention était de me rendre au mouillage de l'île Boisée avec *la Guerrière* et les bâtiments de ma Division. Mon but était de frapper un coup aussi rude que possible aur l'île de Kang-hoa qui est la place la plue fortifiée de la Corée et qui, par sa position géographique, domine la rivière de Séoul. Au retour de mon exploration, en passant auprès de cette île, tandis que mes deux canonnières étaient entraînées par un courant rapide de Jusan, j'avais aperçu un grand nombre de soldats coréens avec leurs drapeaux déployés garnissant les murailles qui défendent l'accès de l'île, ainsi que les forts construits sur les deux rives de la rivière Salée. Ils avaient même tiré quelques coup de canon et de fusil, quand nous étions déjà beaucoup trop éloignés pour pouvoir leur répondre. Ces indices me faisaient donc supposer, avec raison, que l'île de Kang-hoa était une place forte, conformément aux renseignements qui m'avaient été donnés et je pus dès lors acquérir la certitude qui frapper (*Sic*) rigoureusement sur elle, était un moyen certain d'humilier le Gouvernement de la Corée qui, justqu'à ce moment, à l'abri de ses innombrables écueils avait compté sur son invulnérabilité.

Ainsi que je l'ai signalé à Votre Excellence, j'avais reconnu, dans l'exploration qui m'avait conduit à la rive la plus rapprochée de Séoul, qu'il ne m'était pas possible de tenter une attaque contre cette Capitale avec les simples moyens à ma disposition, mais un coup de main contre Kang-hoa me semblait de nature à pouvoir être effectué, malgré les grandes difficultés de navigation qu'offrent ces parages que nous avions été les premiers à visiter.

En conséquence, aprés avoir pris à Tché-fou toutes les dispositions les plus minutieuses pour assurer la réussite de mes projets, je partis le 11 Octobre avec *la Guerrière, le Primauguet, le Laplace*, les avisos *le Déroulède* et *le Kien-Chan* et les canonnières *le Tardif* et *le LeBrethon*. *La Guerrière* avait pris à la remorque *le Kien-chan* et une chaloupe pontée, provenant de notre occupation de Takou, et dont je comptais me servir pour le transport de nos approvisionnements dans mon trajet de l'île Boisée à Kang-hoa. *Le Primauguet* remorquait *le Déroulède* et *le Tardif*; enfin *le Laplace* trainait derrière *le LeBrethon*. Le lendemain 2, vers 6 heures du soir, j'avais la chance heureuse de conduire toute ma Division au mouillage de l'île Eugénie dans le golfe du Prince Jérôme. Le 13, sans perdre de temps, je fis appareiller tous mes bâtiments pour l'île Boisée, où nous pûmes arriver vers 11 heures du matin. Je m'occupai immédiatement des derniers préparatifs par un ordre du jour très détaillé, j'avais indiqué le rôle que chacun devait avoir dans le débarquement d'opération dont nous avions déjà fait une répétition la veille de notre départ de Tché-foo sur l'île de Kung-Tung, en présence de M$^{\underline{r}}$ l'Amiral King qui se trouvait auprès de moi à son retour de Pékin et qui voulut bien passer à mes côtés la revue de nos compagnies. J'avais la ferme confiance que tout réussirait à souhait, en effet, le 14, à 6 heures et demie du matin, avec la marée favorable, nous quittâmes l'île Boisée. *Le Tardif* avait pour mission d'éclairer la route, *le Déroulède* où j'avais mis mon pavillon venait après en remorquant huit embarcations contenant les compagnies de débarquement du *Primauguet* et du *Laplace. Le Kien-Chan* suivait avec cinq embarcations de *la Guerrière* portant les companies de la frégate. Venait ensuite le canot à vapeur remorquant deux chaloupes chargées de vivres et de munitions, et enfin *le LeBrethon* fermait la marche pour servir d'arrière-garde et porter secours aux canots en cas d'accidents. Nous parcourûmes ainsi les dix-huit milles de la rivière Salée qui nous séparaient de Kang-hoa. En approchant de la place, les forts étaient occupés par des soldats qui paraissaient pointer avec soin leurs canons, mais aucun ne fit feu et nous arrivâmes vers midi au mouillage que j'avais assigné aux bâtiments. Les embarcations quittèrent aussitôt les remorques et les divisions de dèbarquement sautèrent à terre avec une rapidité remarquable; nous n'avions essuyé aucune résistance. Dans son trajet, *le Kien-Chan* s'était échoué sur un banc à une distance assez rapprochée de sa destination, ce contretemps le força de confier les embarcations qu'il remorquait au *LeBrethon* qui les conduisit promptement auprès de nous. En un instant les hauteurs furent couronnées par nos hommes et n'apercevant pas d'ennemis à proximité, je m'occupai immédiatement du cantonnement de tout mon monde qui fut logé dans les cases du Gouvernement sur le rivage et sur les forts voisins. Cette précaution fut heureusement prise à temps, car à peine étions-nous à terre depuis une heure que la pluie vint à tomber par torrents et le temps devint excessivement mauvais; mais nos hommes avaient déjà trouvé un abri et ils n'eurent plus à travailler qu'à leur installation. Quoique bien gênés par la pluie qui continua à tomber avec la même persistance pendant toute la nuit et une partie de la journée du lendemain, le service fut parfaitement réglé à terre et les distributions de vivres ne subirent aucun retard. Les compagnies de débarquement de *la Guerrière* formant la première colonne étaient sous le commandement du Capitaine de frégate d'Osery, celles du *Primauguet* et du *Laplace* réunies étaient commandés par le Capitaine de frégate Bochet et composaient la deuxième colonne, enfin une troisième colonne formée par les 150 fusiliers du détachement de Yokohama était sous les ordres de M[r] le Lieutenant de vaisseau de Thouars. Les trois colonnes avaient été placées sous le commandement supérieur du Capitaine de vaisseau Olivier de *la Guerrière*.

Partis le 11 de Tché-foo, j'avais la satisfaction de voir dans la matinée du 14, toutes mes compagnies de débarquement parfaitement établies sur l'île de Kang-hoa. Le soir du même jour, un Mandarin de rang inférieur fut conduit auprès de moi et me demanda quelles étaient mes intentions. Je lui repondis que chargé par l'Empereur de Français de veiller aux intérêts de ses sujets dans l'extrême Orient, je venais punir le Gouvernement de la Corée qui avait ordonné le massacre de nos missionnaires et que puisque l'île de Kang-hoa avait tiré sur mes bâtiments, quelques jours auparavant, j'avais cette nouvelle offense à venger. Je le congédiai en lui disant de faire part de ma résolution au premier Mandarin de l'Ile. Il est très difficile dans ce pays de pouvoir entrer en relations avec les Mandarins d'un rang élevé, car les chefs sont les premiers à s'enfuir et laissent ainsi le vide après eux. Aussi les rapports officiels avec le Gouvernement sont-ils à peu près impossibles et personne ne se chargerait de lui porter une communication qui à ses yeux pourrait être compromettante.

La ville de Kang-hoa est à 5 kilomètres des positions que nous occupions sur le bord de la rivière Salée. Cette ville est assise sur un vaste terrain entouré de hauteur; les maisons n'y sont pas disposées régulièrement, elles sont éparses au milieu de bouquets d'arbres. Une muraille, crénelée, d'environ 4 mètres de hauteur, entoure complètement la ville en passant sur les crêtes. Les points culminants ont des forts circulaires qui flanquent les murailles. Les portes sont voutées et surmontées par des corps de garde en pierres.

Le 15, j'ordonnai une reconnaissance de la ville qui fut exécutée par cent hommes de *la Guerrière* sous le commandement du Capitaine de frégate d'Osery. Cette colonne, après avoir parcouru les crêtes qui dominent la partie droite, s'approcha d'un fort qui défend l'une des portes de la ville. Elle fut accueillie par un feu assez vif de mousquetterie et par celui de deux canons de petit calibre. Nos hommes repartèrent aussitôt et après un engagement de quelques minutes, ils escaladèrent la muraille et en chassèrent les défenseurs. Ces derniers s'enfuirent en laissant un drapeau qui me fut rapporté.

Le Commandant d'Osery qui avait lui-même escaladé la muraille à la tête de ses hommes aurait pu entrer dans la ville, mais n'ayant eu pour mission qu'une simple reconnaissance, il revint bientôt après dans nos cantonnements. Cet officier supérieur, dont le sang froid et le courage ont été signalés dans bien des circonstances antérieurs, a montré dans cette nouvelle occasion son intelligence et la fermeté habituelles. Ses hommes l'avaient secondé avec leur entrain ordinaire ; il m'a cité particulièrement l'Enseigne de Vaisseau Fournie qui lui avait été adjoint pour dessiner le terrain et qui, pendant l'action avait continué à prendre les croquis de la ville au milieu des balles avec le calme le plus parfait. Il a remarqué également quelques hommes de son détachement dont la conduite a été des plus dignes d'éloges, entr'autres le gabier Jounaux qui s'est emparé d'un drapeau dont le défenseur coréen gisait blessé tout auprès.

Le 16, dès 8 heures et demie du matin, je rassemblai mes trois colonnes et me mettant à leur tête, je les conduisis vers la porte principale de la ville. Arrivé à une centaine de mètres, quelques coup de fusil furent tirés sur nous, des bastions qui dominent cette porte. Les murailles furent aussitôt escaladées au cri de Vive l'Empereur, et, en un instant, les soldats coréens mis en fuite, nous laissèrent maîtres de la place ; plusieurs de leurs drapeaux furent enlevés et restèrent en notre pouvoir. J'aurai l'honneur de vous les adresser comme un trophée qui, quoique dû à un succès facile, n'en est pas moins important. Nos hommes ne demandaient du reste qu'à rencontrer un ennemi plus digne de leur valeur. Pas un seul Mandarin, pas un seul soldat ne restait dans la ville dont nous venions de nous emparer. Tous avaient fui avec la plus grande précipitation et nous n'avons même pas pu suivre leur trace. A peine entrés dans cette cité où nul Européen, sans doute, n'avait encore pénétré, mon premier soin fut de rassurer les habitants inoffensifs et d'empêcher toute espèce de sévices contr'eux. Je leur fis lire une proclamation qui était de nature à les ramener à la confiance. La discipline la plus sévère fut, en effet, observée parmi nos marins et nous n'eûmes aucun désordre sérieux à réprimer. Je parcourus immédiatement la ville et je me rendis au Yamoun de premier Mandarin, édifice très élégant qui était entouré de tous les magasins appartenant à l'Etat et qui à eux seuls formaient une seconde ville dans la premières. Les recherches que j'ordonnais nous donnèrent la preuve de l'importance militaire de la place nous trouvâmes des poudrières en grand nombre une grande quantité de canons et de gingoles en fer et en bronze, des magasins considérables remplis d'armes et de munitions de toute sorte, plus de dix mille fusils, des sabres en quantité, ainsi qu'un grand nombre de flèche et de carquois et des aumures excessivement bizzarres par leur forme et leur variété. Nous avions déjà découvert la veille trois grandes poudrières pleines de poudre et de munition dans le voisinage de nos cantonnements. A n'en pas douter, l'île de Kang-hoa devait avoir été choisie par le Gouvernement de Séoul, comme le boulevard militaire de la Corée. Dans l'un des magasins, on trouva également dix-neuf caisses remplies de lingots d'argent; je nommai immédiatement une commission pour les compter, en prendre possession régulièrement et les acheminer ver nos cantonnements. La Commission a reconnu qu'il y en avait pour une valeur de 195,217 francs. Toutes ces caisses seront envoyées à Votre Excellence par une prochaine occasion. Nous mîmes aussi la main sur les Archives de l'Etat, et je reconnus des ouvrages très curieux qui peuvent éclaircir bien des mystères sur l'histoire de la Corée, ses légendes et sa littérature. J'en ai fait faire un inventaire en règle et je me propose d'adresser cette précieuse collection à Votre Excellence qui jugera, sans doute, utile de la transmettre à la bibliothèque Impériale. Aucun de ces documents n'est devenu la propriété particulière de qui que ce soit dans la Division, tout ce que nous avons trouvé appartenant ainsi à l'Etat a été inventorié avec soin et recueilli par procès-verbal. J'attachai une scrupuleuse importance à ce qu'aucun détournement n'avait lieu et, d'ailleurs, je dois le dire, ces sentiments sont partagés par tout le personnel sous mes ordres.

Il me reste, M. le Ministre, à recommander à Votre Excellence les officiers et marins qui, dans le cours de cette expédition, se sont fait remarquer entre tous par leurs services. J'ai l'honneur de vous adresser à ce sujet divers états de propositions que je supplie Votre Excellence de vouloir bien accueillir favorablement.

Je suis avec un profond respect,
Monsieur le Ministre,
De Votre Excellence,

Le très obéissant Serviteur,

Le Contre-Amiral Commanant en chef
G. Roze

Annexes:
Proclamations de l'Amiral aux officiers et Equipages.

Officiers et Equipages,

Un grand crime a été commis en Corée ; plusieurs missionnaires, nos compatriotes ont été odieusement massacrés par les ordres du Gouvernement de ce pays. Il nous appartient à nous qui avons reçu la noble mission de faire rayonner au loin le drapeau de la Patrie de frapper ceux qui ont commis un semblable forfait et de montrer à un gouvernement barbare que le sang innocent des enfants de la France est à jamais sacré.

Je vous conduis donc sur les rivages de la Corée. Nous ferons nos efforts pour arriver au cœur du pays et pour venger les hommes de bien qui ont été mis à mort par ceux auxquels ils venaient enseigner la charité et la vertu. Je n'ai pas besoin de faire appel à votre courage et à votre dévouement, je les connais ; mais dans notre juste vengeance nous ne confondons pas ceux qui ont ordonné le meurtre de nos compatriotes avec les habitants paisibles qui ne demandent qu'à nous tendre la main.

Nous saurons nous montrer digne de la France et de notre grand Souverain dont le cœur magnanime veille sur ses enfants partout où ils se trouvent et, en nous inspirant du souvenir de la patrie, nous marcherons au cri mille fois répété de Vive l'Empereur.

Signé : G. Roze.

Proclamation de l'Amiral au Peuple de la Corée.

En paraissant sur vos rivages, en pénétrant au sein de votre pays, nous ne venons ni vous châtier, ni vous soumettre ; nous sommes vos amis, et nous voulons que vous soyez heureux : toute notre colère est contre votre Gouvernement qui, au mépris des lois les plus saintes de l'humanité, a mis impitoyablement à mort un grand nombre de nos compatriotes, de nos frères qui n'étaient venus parmi vous que pour vous apporter des paroles de paix et de vertu. Ces hommes de bien que votre Gouvernement a fait si impérieusement massacrer appartenaient comme nous au puissant pays de France dont le Souverain est le grand Empereur Napoléon III. Les Français sont ses enfants et sa sollicitude s'étend sur eux partout où ils se trouvent. C'est donc en obéissant à ses ordres paternels que nous venons punir ceux qui ont massacré nos frères, mais en nous disant de frapper sans pitié les coupables, notre Magnanime Empereur veut que nous protégions le peuple de Corée qui est innocent de ce crime et qui est aussi la victime de ceux qui l'ont commis.

Rassurez vous donc, peuple de Corée, vos propriétés, vos biens seront respectés, accueillez nous comme des amis qui vous tendent la main, mais rappelez-vous que ceux d'entre vous qui se montreront nos ennemis, attireront sur leur tête la plus implacable rigueur.

Signé : G. Roze

G. Roze (1866. 10. 22) → P. de Chasseloup-Laubat

강화도 획득 물품 보고서

Marine et Colonies

Division Navale de la Chine et du Japon, Commandé par le Contre-Amiral Roze

Procès-Verbal d'Inventaire de divers objets trourés à Kang-hoa (Corée)

Aujourd'hui vingt Octobre mil huit cent soixante-six, les corps de débarquement de la Division Navale de la Chine occupant la ville de Kang-hoa (Corée).

Nous Jouan, Capitaine de frégate, chef d'Etat-major, et La Vieille, sous-commissaire, Commissaire de Division. Nous sommes réunis, conformément aux ordres de M^{r} le Contre-Amiral Commandant en chef, dans le Yamoun du Mandarin de la dite ville pour recueillir les objets qui pourraient intéresse (*Sic*) l'histoire, la science et les arts.

Aprés examen des divers locaux qui composaient cette habitation nous n'avons trouvé que les objets ci-après qui nous aient paru susceptibles d'offrir quelque intérêt;

Savoir:

300 grands volumes brochés,

9 petits volumes brochés,

13 petits volumes renfermés dans une boite en boîs blanc,

10 petits volumes ______ D^{o} ______

8 petits volumes ______ D^{o} ______

1 carte de la Chine, de la Corée et du Japon,

1 Planisphère céleste,

7 rouleaux portant des Inscriptions diverses,

3 tablettes en marbre gris avec inscription en caractères chinois,

3 petites caisses renfermant chacune des tablettes en marbre blanc

articulées, avec charnières en cuivre,
3 armures de guerrier avec casque,
1 masque.

A défaut d'interprète, il nous a été impossible de préciser la nature des divers ouvrages ci-dessus, mais il y a lieu de croire qu'ils sc rapportent à l'histoire du pays, à sa littérature, et à ses légendes. Quant aux tablettes en marbre elles seraient, d'après quelques renseignements recueillis sur les lieux, destinées à perpétuer certains faits mémorables.

Tous ces objets ont été renfermés dans caisses sous nos yeux, du N° au N° inclus, pour être envoyés à la disposition de Son Excellence Monsieur le Ministre de la marine, conformément aux ordres du Contre-Amiral Commandant en chef.

Fait à Kang-hoa, le 22 Octobre 1866.
Les membres de la Commission.

Vieille

Vu:
Le Contre-Amiral Commandant en chef.

G. Roze

G. Roze (1866. 10. 22) → P. de Chasseloup-Laubat

강화도 점령, 조선 국왕의 서신 접수 및 회신 발송 보고

À bord du *Déroulède*, Rade de Kang-hoa, le 22 octobre, 1866

Monsieur le Ministre,

J'ai eu l'honneur dans un rapport spécial, en date de ce jour, d'entretenir V. Exc. des faits maritimes et militaires qui ont accompagné la prise de Kang-hoa. Il me reste maintenant à vous préciser la situation dans laquelle je me trouve au point de vue politique.

Le Blocus de la rivière de Séoul qui, en arrêtant les nombreux convois de riz qui ont lieu à cette époque de l'année, menace d'affamer la Capitale et l'occupation de Kang-hoa, doivent avoir sérieusement frappé le Gouvernement Coréen. Ce peuple, si cruel et si fier, a vu tomber les barrières qui semblaient le séparer au reste du monde, et il est trop intelligent pour n'avoir pas compris toute la portée de notre apparition sur ces côtes.

Les Mandarins de Kang-hoa avaient fui à notre approche et il est présumable qu'ils s'étaient rendus à Séoul pour rendre compte d'un événement aussi grave et si inattendu.

Depuis mon arrivée j'avais fait de vains efforts pour me mettre en rapport avec le Gouvernement, quand le 19 au matin, on vit apparaître sur la rive gauche de la rivière un homme à cheval portant un pavillon blanc, le pavillon parlementaire. C'était un soldat de la milice royale qui m'apportait une lettre du Roi, dont vous trouverez ci-joint la traduction fidèle. Cette lettre qui, à l'instar de toutes les productions orientales, commence par des considérations générales et des espèces d'aphorismes philosophiques, ne contient, sans doute, rien de concluant. Mais elle semble empreinte, dans son esprit général, d'une certaine humilité. C'est l'œuvre d'un homme qui, se sentant accusé, se justifie et se défend. Si l'on tient compte de l'orgueil des nations orientales, cette première ouverture faite spontanément et à une assez grande distance de nos canons, est un fait important qui atteste l'impression que nous avons produite et permet, peut-être, d'espérer une conclusion plus prompte qu'on ne devait attendre. J'y ai répondu immédiatement et j'attends une nouvelle communication qui ne fera connaître, sans doute, la suite donnée à mes légitimes demandes. Nous saurons bientôt, je l'espère, à quoi nous en tenir.

Je ne pourrais marcher sur Séoul, ainsi que je l'ai déjà dit, avec le peu de forces dont je dispose et j'ai précédemment exposé à V. Exc. quels seraient les moyens qui me paraîtraient nécessaires pour effectuer une semblable entreprise. Aussi, ce que je désire maintenant c'est que le Gouvernement Coréen, comprenant bien ses intérêts, se rendre à mes injonctions et nous dispense d'aller plus loin. Si je parvenais à conclure un traité basé sur les immunités habituelles entre nations civilisées, le coup de main de Kang-hoa aurait rendu, sans coûter un homme, un signalant au commerce et à la civilisation.

Quoi qu'il arrive, le but que je m'étais proposé est atteint : celui de punir le meurtre de nos missionnaires en détruisant la place la plus fortifiée du Royaume et en montrant à ce pays qu'il n'était pas invulnérable.

La Corée est un pays extrêmement accidenté, ce n'est qu'une succession de plaines et de montagnes. Ces dernières sont généralement arides et peu boisées, mais les vallées sont d'une prodigieuse fertilité et cultivées avec un soin infini. Entre les mains d'un Gouvernement moins despotique, l'agriculture seule suffirait pour donner un tel pays la plus grande prospérité. On affirme, d'un autre côté, que ses richesses minéralogiques sont aussi nombreuses que variées : l'or, le cuivre, le fer s'y trouveraient en abondance. Sur ce dernier fait, je n'ai que des données vagues, mais quelques observations recueillies sur les lieux permettent de ne pas les considérer comme trop hasardées.

Le climat y est d'une salubrité qui rappelle les points les plus renommés en Europe et, par certains exemples que j'ai vu de mes yeux, l'existence humaine y atteint une longévité très remarquable.

En un mot, Monsieur le Ministre, le Royaume de Corée est un admirable pays pour lequel la nature a tout fait et que ses institutions ont seules arrêté dans son développement.

V. Exc. sait que toutes les tentatives faites jusqu'ici pour y pénétrer avaient échoué. M[r] l'Amiral Guérin était venu jusque dans la baie du Prince Jérôme et, dernièrement, un navire de la Maison Jardines de Shang-haï, était allé un peu plus loin. Les uns et les autres avaient pu constater l'impossibilité de se mettre en relations avec les habitants qui, se fondant sur des ordres formels de leurs chefs, refusaient de fournir aucune provision. Plus récemment encore une goëlette de Commerce Américaine, *le Général Schermann*, ayant à son bord le Révérend Père Thomas, de l'Eglise Anglicane, qui m'avait été recommandé par Notre Chargé d'affaires à Pékin, a essayé cette difficile entreprise et il paraît que ce navire, arrêté dans une rivière, a été brulé et tout le monde mis à mort. C'est donc nous, M^r le Ministre, qui avons forcé ce redoutable pays et qui en avons découvert la route. Nous pouvons dire, sans crainte, que la Corée est désormais ouverte car quelles que puissent être ses lois et ses prohibitions, il ne lui est plus possible d'échapper au mouvement contre lequel ses puissants voisins, la Chine et le Japon, ont vainement résisté. Tout l'honneur en reviendra à la France.

Signé : G. Roze

Lettre du Gouvernement de Séoul à l'Amiral Commandant en chef.
Ordre de transmettre cette lettre au maître des navires Européens.

Quiconque renie la loi divine doit mourir, quiconque renie la loi de son pays mérite d'être décapité. Le ciel a créé les peuples pour qu'ils obéissent à la raison. Les royaumes sont séparés par des frontières et sauvegardés par des lois. À quoi faut-il obéir ? À la justice et sans restriction aucune. Tout homme qui la viole est indigne de pardon. D'où je conclue qu'il faut mettre à mort celui qui la renie, qu'il faut décapiter celui qui la viole.

De tout temps les relations avec les voisins, les secours accordés aux voyageurs ont été de tradition ; dans notre Royaume, nous faisons preuve de plus de bienveillance, de plus d'amour encore. Souvent, en effet, il arrive que les navigateurs ignorant la position et le nom des pays abordent sur nos côtes. Les mandarins de nos villes reçoivent alors l'ordre de les recevoir avec bienveillance, mais leur demandent s'ils viennent dans de bonnes et pacifiques intentions, donnent des vivres à ceux qui ont faim, vêtissent ceux qui sont nus, soignent les malades. Il est même d'usage de donner le viatique aux mourants. Telle est la règle qui a toujours été mise en pratique dans notre Royaume sans avoir à souffrir aucune offense, aussi la Corée est-elle pour le monde entier le Royaume de la Justice et de la civilisation. Mais s'il se trouve des hommes qui viennent séduire nos sujets, pénétrent chez nous clandestinement, changent leur vêtements, étudient notre langue, corrompent notre peuple, bouleversent nos coutumes, l'antique loi du monde veut qu'ils soient mis à mort ; telle est la règle commune à tous les Royaumes, à tous les Empires. Pourquoi m'en voulez-vous donc de l'avoir toujours observée ? N'est-il pas suffisant que nous ne vous demandions pas compte du motif qui vous amène ici de lointains pays ? Vous, au contraire, vous occupez notre sol comme s'il était le vôtre et par ce seul fait, vous violez odieusement la raison.

Quand dernièrement vos navires ont remonté le fleuve impérial, ils n'étaient qu'un ou deux, les hommes qui les montaient ne dépassaient pas le nombre de mille. Si nous avions voulu les détruire n'avions-nous pas des armes ? Mais par bonté à l'égard des voyageurs, nous n'avons souffert ni qu'on leur fit du tort, ni qu'on fit acte d'hostilité contr'eux. C'est ainsi qu'en franchissant nos frontières, ils prenaient ou recevaient selon leur volonté des bœufs et des poules, allant et venant en embarcation, ils étaient interrogés en termes pacifiques ; bien plus, on leur faisait des présences sans les inquiéter en aucune façon.

Vous vous montrez donc ingrats envers moi tandis que je ne le suis pas envers vous. Cela ne vous suffit pas, vous aviez besoin de vous retirer ; votre rentrée est inconvenante maintenant vous bouleversez nos cités, vous tuez mon peuple, vous détruisez mes denrées et mes troupeaux. Jamais on ne vit d'une façon plus grave, violer et le ciel et les lois.

Comme le Ciel poursuit de tels hommes de la haine, il convient de les mettre à mort lorsqu'on les prend ! Bien plus, on a dit que vous vouliez répandre votre religion dans mon Royaume. C'est un crime. Les livres différents ont leurs sentences propres qui présentent le vrai et le faux. Qu'importe-t-il que je suive ma Religion, vous la vôtre ?

S'il est blâmable de renier ses ancêtres pourquoi venez-vous nous apprendre à abandonner les nôtres pour en adopter d'étrangers ? S'il ne fallait pas mettre à mort de tels hommes, mieux vaudrait nier le ciel !

Je vous traite comme Yn et Tan traitèrent l'impie Ko-pû (*Sic*) et vous vous révoltez comme Ngiên Yeoù l'a fait contre Tcheou-Onen. Quoique je n'ose pas me comparer à ces Rois illustres, on ne saurait, je l'avoue, passer ma générosité sous silence.

Vous paraissez ici maintenant avec une armée nombreuse comme si vous étiez les instruments de la Justice Céleste, venez à la cour, ayons des entrevues et nous déciderons s'il convient de réunir ou de renvoyer les troupes, de tenter la victoire ou la défaite. Ne fuyez pas, inclinez-vous et obéissez.

La 5ème année du Règne de Tong-Tchy, la 9ème lune, le 11e jour.

Dépêche de Siam, vice-Roi militaire du Royaume.

Réponse de l'Amiral au Gouvernement de Séoul.

Je soussigné C. Amiral Commandant en chef les forces françaises fais savoir au Chef du Gouvernement de la Corée que, chargé par le Grand Souverain qui règne sur la France de protéger ses sujets dans l'extrême Orient, il vient demander réparation du meurtre des Missionnaires français qui ont été mis à mort dans le courant de cette année par ordre du Gouvernement.

Les Missionnaires français étaient des hommes de paix et de vertu et nulle loi humaine ne pouvait excuser le crime odieux qui leur a arraché la vie.

Il y a peu d'années, la Chine a été conquise par le Grand Empire de la France parce qu'il avait à venger un semblable forfait.

Le C. Amiral Commandant en chef est disposé à recourir aux moyens de la plus extrême rigueur envers le Gouvernement de la Corée, si les satisfactions qu'il demande ne sont pas immédiatement accordées.

Il exige :

1° La punition sévère des trois Ministres qui ont pris la plus grande part au meurtre des missionnaires français.

2° L'envoi auprès de lui d'un ambassadeur muni de pleins pouvoirs pour arrêter de concert les bases d'un traité ;

Si le Gouvernement de la Corée est désireux d'éviter les malheurs qui menacent son pays, qu'il se rende aux injonctions ci-dessus.

Si non, le Contre-Amiral Commandant en chef rend le Gouvernement de la Corée responsable de toutes les conséquences qui pourront résulter de la guerre.

Signé : G. Roze

123

G. Roze (1866. 10. 22) → B. de Montmorand

통역 파견 요청

À Bord du *Déroulède*, Rade de Kang-hoa (Corée) le 22 octobre 1866

M^{r} le Consul général de France à Shang-haï

L'absence de tout Interprète est une des plus sérieuses difficultés que j'éprouve dans ce pays. Vous savez que si les Coréens parlent une langue à eux, ils se servent, pour le langage écrit, des caractères chinois.

Un lettré chinois lisant et écrivant couramment ces derniers caractères et parlant le français me serait d'une absolue nécessité. Je viens vous demander, M^{r} le Consul Général, si vous auriez la bonté de m'en procurer un à Shang-haï et de me l'envoyer par *le Laplace*. On m'assure que les Pères Jésuites seraient peut-être plus à même que personne de vous fournir un sujet d'élite. Afin d'éviter toutes difficultés, je vous prierais de fixer vous même ses gages.

Les lettrés chinois parlant français sont peut-être plus rares que ceux parlant l'anglais. À la rigueur, je me contenterais d'un de ceux-ci.

Veuillez me pardonner, M^{r} le Consul G^{al}, de vous donner cet ennui. Mais vous m'éviterez de sérieuses difficultés en me fournissant un moyen sûr d'entrer en relations courantes avec le Gouvernement Coréen, de répondre à ses communications et de lui faire connaître mes volontés.

Signé : G. Roze

P. S.

Au lieu d'un seul Interprète, je vous prierais, M^{r} le Consul G^{al}., de vouloir bien m'en envoyer, si c'est possible, deux, dont un très habile pour moi. Quant au second, il pourrait, sans inconvénient, être moins fort.

G. Roze (1866. 10. 22) → H. de Bellonet 등

강화도 공격 결과 보고

À bord du *Déroulède*, Rade de Kang-hoa (Corée), le 22 Octobre 1866

M.M. le Ministre de France à Pékin, Yokohama;
M[r] le Consul Général de France à Shang-haï;
M[r] le Gouverneur de la Cochinchine à Saïgon

Je m'empresse de vous informer que nous occupons militairement, depuis le 16 de ce mois, la ville de Kang-hoa, une des places les plus considérables de la Corée.

Parti de Tche-foo avec tous les bâtiments de ma Division, nous arrivions le 12 à l'île Eugénie dans le golfe du Prince Jérôme; le 13 nous étions à l'île Boisée et enfin le 14 dans la soirée, nous avons mouillé dans la baie de Kang-hoa. Immédiatement je fis jeter à terre les corps de débarquement qui s'emparèrent des hauteurs sans difficultés.

Le lendemain une reconnaissance eût lieu jusque sous les murs de la ville située à 6 kilomètres de là. Notre colonne fut accueillie par un feu de mousqueterie assez nourri. La ville eût pu probablement être prise dès ce moment, mais comme je n'avais prescrit qu'une simple reconnaissance, on se contenta d'escalader les murailles et on revint aux cantonnements en me rapportant un drapeau.

Le 16, je pris moi-même le commandement de toutes nos forces. À onze heures du matin nous nous trouvions en face de la porte principale, quelques minutes après Kang-hoa nous appartenait après un échange de quelques coups de feu.

La ville avait été abandonnée par ses habitants et j'ai pris toutes les dispositions nécessaires pour que les propriétés particulières ne reçussent aucun dommage. Les Etablissements publics sont nombreux et forment pour ainsi dire une ville officielle à côté de l'autre ville. Le Yamoun du grand Mandarin est situé sur le versant d'une colline au milieu d'un beau parc et se compose d'une nombreuse réunion d'édifices fort élégants. Dans les environs se trouvent des magasins d'armes dont il ne nous a pas encore été possible d'apprécier au juste l'importance. C'est par dizaines de mille que l'on peut compter les fusils, les sabres, les arcs, les casse-têtes que nous y avons trouvés et dont on a commencé la destruction. Partout des canons et des gingoles en bronze et en fer.

Enfin, Mr le ...... (*Sic*) les renseignements qui m'avaient été donnés étaient exacts, Kang-hoa était vraiment la citadelle du Royaume et en l'occupant nous avons frappé la Corée jusqu'au cœur.

Bien que ce succès ait présenté peut-être peu de difficultés il n'en a pas moins une sérieuse importance. Le Gouvernement de Séoul ne peut manquer d'avoir compris que son pays n'était pas aussi invulnérable qu'il le pensait et j'ai bien d'espérer que la France et toutes les Nations civilisées retireront de précieux résultats de ce rapide coup de main.

Le Roi m'a envoyé une Lettre à laquelle j'ai répondu en faisant connaître mes intentions. (paragraphe supprimé pour le Ministre de Pékin)

En attendant je continuerai à occuper Kang-hoa et à bloquer la Rivière de Séoul. Je me ferai un véritable plaisir de porter à votre connaissance tout ce qui nous arrivera encore d'intéressant.

Signé : G. Roze

高宗(1866. 10. 24/高宗三年九月十六日)

척사윤음(斥邪綸音)

王若曰 嗚呼 咨爾中外臣庶暨軍民耆老 明聽予一人誥 予以沖年 叨承丕緖 慄慄危懼 若將隕于深淵 惟不克負荷是懼 早夜孜孜 思免厥愆 而治不徯志 德不足以撫綏方域 惠不足以懷保民生 至于洋賊之變 而生民之塗炭 又極矣 靜念厥由 罪在寡躬 百姓何辜 嗚呼 洋夷之窺闖我海防 蠱惑我民心 所由來者漸矣 非一朝一夕之故 而原其所以爲說 則鬼蜮而狐魅也 麀聚而瀆倫也 至於矯誣上天 殄絶祭祀 自有天地以來 所未有之至妖至憯不可方物者也 東俗 自箕聖 以來 所尊崇者 五帝三王周公孔孟程朱之道 所服習者 父子君臣夫婦長幼彝倫之敍 而我朝立國五百年來 一是皆以先聖人之道爲道 而不幸人心陷溺 世道交喪 自六七十年以來 怨國失志之徒 凶險邪慝之輩 糾結七八萬里外凶醜異類 思欲以易天下 前後朝家之所以鋤治而殄滅之者 非不至矣 而種下生種 滋蔓不已 至于今春鍾三之獄而極矣 嗚呼 尙忍言哉 今此輩 乃敢眉語頷瞬 跡祕計憯 呼吸相通 暗地輸情 鴟鳴梟應 蛇盤蚓結 乃敢掛帆海洋 直指京城 是豈隔重溟屢萬里醜類凶種之所可爲也 思之及此 寧欲無言 今者江都失守 中外戒嚴 方以宿將重兵 開府出陣 期於不日掃淸 而江都則方大集舟航 直搗巢穴 俾無一箇凶種 接跡於此地 而昇平日久之餘 我民之猝罹鋒鏑 念之哀矜 錦玉靡安 豈忍重困我民力 以蹈死亡之患哉 諸道召募 纔已罷休 凡所徵斂 當次第蠲免 咨爾臣庶 各安其業 勿爲浮言所撓騷訛所動 各保爾父母妻子村堡閭里 其間 亦必有忠義奮發爲國家效力之人 各陳備禦之策 鼓發衆庶之心 期底廓淸妖氛 同我太平 則朝家所以酬忠奬節之方 當無所不用其極 而村閭之間 易致望風而潰 聞聲而逃 如此則所在騷擾 迄無底定之日 雖白挺短鋤 奔突擊賊 使不敢肆其凶鋒 則勇氣自倍 賊不敢嚮邇 里正村長 各自率領 無敢離次 而今此致賊之由 皆朝廷處置之不能得宜 則予方痛自刻責 將有大奮發大振作之擧 而先將十行敷心之諭 布告中外 咨爾大小臣庶 咸須知悉

李恒老(1866. 10. 27/高宗三年九月十日)

척사상소(斥邪上疏)

工曹參判 李恒老疏陳病狀乞遞仍陳時務賜批

疏略曰日者賜批悶臣老病以調理行公爲敎而實病萬無何強之勢方將治疏重籲副總管新命又至瀝血陳情反成虛套更加矜察竝命遞改臣伏讀朝紙十行絲綸令人感泣足以仰見大聖人罪己責躬收拾人心之盛節也第今中外物情下不信上痼瘼已久徒言無實不足以濟事孟子曰仁言不如仁聲之入人深也所謂仁聲者如亟罷土木之役悉禁斂民之政大開從諫之門深講用賢之方不留一毫私意文具吝執使擧國曉然知聖意必信不疑然後乃所謂仁聲也不然而斟酌其中稍減分數而無拔本塞源之實粗能收用而無貫始徹終之實則百姓至愚而神彼其怨咨離叛又非奉天一詔所能回也惟聖明念哉若夫信賞必罰之說則前疏亦旣微發其端矣左攻于左右攻于右御以其馬之正者不可不賞于祖左不攻左右不攻右御非其馬之正者不可不戮于社此則帥臣之所當講也尊君親上盡伏節死義之忠者不可無五服之章懷利忘義有偸生苟免之罪者不可無五刑之誅此則朝廷之所當講也惟聖明察焉抑又有一獻焉洋夷之禍至於今日人獸之關存亡之機決於呼吸誠不可少緩也然徒治其末不治其本則根本之崩雖善者亦無如之何矣朱子曰正其本者雖若迂緩實易爲力救其末者雖若切至而實難爲功然則迅掃洋氛之本在殿下之一心不爲外物所牽制所謂外物者事目甚多不可枚擧而洋物爲最甚臣願殿下斷自睿衷凡服食器用一有洋物悉行搜出聚之闕庭而燒之昭示好惡之有在則宮闈宗戚莫不從志而殿下之家正矣內自朝廷外至遐裔莫不從志而殿下之國正矣洋物無所用之而交易之事絶矣彼之奇技淫巧不得售矣旣不得售其欲則彼必無所爲而不來矣此與誅捕征伐本末相資不可不加之意也臣平生身不着洋織家不用洋物以成一家之政願殿下行此一着快示中外使知大聖人之作爲焉批以卿其勿辭調理行公尾附事所陳切切正當當體念矣

鄭雲龜 ➜ 議政府(1866. 10. 27/高宗三年九月十九日)

문수산성 교전 경과 보고

鄭雲龜 以畿輔都巡撫營言啓曰 卽見先鋒中軍李容熙今十八日申時成貼馳報 則兼差哨官韓聖根 率領執事池弘寬別破陣五十名 防守文殊山城矣 當日巳時量 文殊別將馳報內 小洋船四隻 乘潮直向山城南門 故急發一哨軍 使之赴救矣 未及中途 池弘寬·韓聖根 以蓬頭短衣 先後來到曰 二船當前先泊之際 韓聖根 挺身大呼 先自放銃 一發數丸 則賊漢之應響仆船者 爲幾名 而五十銃手 隨卽齊發 二船賊漢 太半僵仆者 假量爲五六十名 於焉之間 後二船賊漢 一時登陸者 無慮爲百餘名 而未遑粧藥 遽中彼丸而死者 爲三人 中肩中臂者 又爲二人 衆寡不敵 回身走還 而行且顧眄 則賊漢 衝火山城南門 旋卽還渡云 賊旣入境 未盡殲滅 反致傷我軍燒我門者 職在出征 惶恐待罪 被火形止 行將詳探 馳報計料云矣 敢啓 傳曰 知道 勿待罪 斯速奏凱也

128

巡撫營 ➞ 議政府(1866. 10. 29/高宗三年九月二十一日)

프랑스군과의 교전 후 피해 상황 보고

又以畿輔都巡撫營言啓曰 卽見先鋒中軍李容熙成貼馳報 則今十八日兼差哨官韓聖根 執事池弘寬 及別破陣砲手等所告內 我軍死者三名 傷者二名 而踵後方來者又爲二名云 故依所告先報矣 所謂踵後者 終不現形 當日黃昏多發校卒 一邊搜探 一邊舁來矣 賊船迫近 火勢益烈 不得搜覓而還 故翌早 又發伶俐校卒 終日搜探 僅得三屍 侵夜舁來 而二名則仍無形跡 未知死入灰燼 生被捕捉 不敢指的 而舁來三屍 爲先厚斂 被傷二名 到底調治 文殊山城別將申道赫所報內 十八日衝火時 鎭民一名 亦爲被死 斂葬之具 從厚以給 公廨被燒 爲五十四間半 民家被燒 爲二十九戶 而死傷者姓名 竝爲馳報云矣 被死四名廣州別破陣崔長根・金達城・吳俊成 文殊鎭民吳乭仲段各其本家 錢十兩・木三疋式 自本營題給 以爲運葬之地 而仍無形跡之二名更加廣探 生死間期於推覓 傷者 亦加各別調治事 另飭之意 敢啓 傳曰 知道

巡撫營 ➞ 議政府(1866. 10. 31/高宗三年九月二十三日)

프랑스 함대 정황 보고

又以畿輔都巡撫營言啓曰 卽見先鋒中軍李容熙今二十一日戌時成貼馳報 則當日申時到付通津府使愼㦲芝牒呈內 以爲本府初境瞭望吏吳裕善馳告內 永宗馬嶼前 昨日碇留異大船一隻 今日潮水上去 而二隻船 則尙留馬嶼前 德浦鎭僉使馳報內 異大船一隻 今日辰時量 過本鎭前洋 而向于甲串津 異船中賊徒四五十名下陸 由甲串津城邊 而下來廣城鎭 衝火門樓 仍向德津 文殊別將申道赫所報內 昨日申時量 賊漢衝火於玉浦江邊人家及龍津火藥庫 今日午時量 異樣飛船一隻 及小船一隻 往祖江放大碗口二丸 而衝火於我船 仍到康寧浦 又放大碗口三聲後 還泊甲串津 鱗次祖江浦本陣防守軍急告內 異樣中船一隻 及小船一隻 當日午時量 來逼本浦 放大碗口二次 丸落於執待之我船 幸免全傷 故急發一哨軍 使之往救矣 賊船先卽還去 被傷船則只一隻 而修改次 曳置江邊 防守之節 嚴加申飭云矣 敢啓 傳曰 知道

高宗(1866. 10. 31/高宗三年九月二十三日)

군민(君民) 단결 및 내응자 엄벌을 지시하는 교서(教書)

傳于趙秉世曰 國有患難之時 或以召募 或以倡義 而終底戡定者 卽上下相須之道也 見今洋夷之磐據江都 已至旬餘日 四方之向義募赴者 尙此零星 八域之內 其眞無義勇智略之士而然乎 抑因予之否德 有所過失 不能激感而然歟 反覆推究 莫曉其由 而雖以在朝之縉紳言之 俱是喬木世祿之家也 何忍有後其君之心 而彼之一時猖獗 卽往古來今所未有之變也 我朝 自檀·箕以來 上之所教導 下之所服習 皆先聖遺訓 而未嘗與法國 有聲氣相通 恩怨可論 則今此尋釁動兵 來侵於隔海幾萬里之外者 非徒兵出無名 洵是慢天虐民 古人云 師直必勝 在我 抑有何驚怯之端 而不思所以各陳碩劃 卽圖掃滅之方 徒懷全軀保妻子之計 先送家眷者有之 而無知小民 從而和之 都下騷訛之患 日甚一日 今則城內便是空虛云 其在同休戚之義 寧有如許道理乎 誠爲之萬萬慨然 且念奸細輩 潛通和應於醜類 同謀助勢者多矣 苟能各司摘發 亟施當律 則彼亦知我國君臣至死不變之義 而必不能强其所不可强者 此豈非目下急務 而一切任他 徒事玩愒而止乎 噫 彼小酋 渠雖乘虛侵掠 終當有殪殄無遺之日矣 朝野之間 苟有敵愾之人 皆輸智而陳策 出義而赴陣 同心同力 刻期討平 則是豈予一人之幸也 實宗社無疆之休 予言止至 咸須知悉

H. de Bellonet(1866. 11. 1) → Moustier(1867. 1. 7)

조선 원정이 청국 정부에 미친 영향 보고

Pékin le 1er Novembre 1866

Monsieur le Ministre,

Les négociations entre la Chine et l'Italie ont été heureusement terminées par la signature d'un traité qui donne aux sujets du Roi Victor Emmanuel tous les droits de la Nation la plus favorisée. Le Gouvernement Chinois un peu ému de notre expédition en Corée a montré beaucoup plus de laisser aller, qu'il ne l'avait fait avec les autres Puissances, et l'article qui concède au Ministre d'Italie le droit de résidence à Pékin, n'a soulevé aucune des impossibilités qui accueillaient d'ordinaire sa présentation.

Plusieurs indices me prouvent aussi que ce fait matériel d'une exécution militaire en Corée, a fait impression sur le Gouvernement Chinois, en lui faisant prendre au sérieux mes réclamations. Des ordres ont été expédiés partout où les affaires restaient en suspends, et les Mandarins qui se confiaient jadis en notre faiblesse, semblent aujourd'hui se remuer pour nous donner satisfaction. La Tsong-ly-ya-men m'a donné avis de plusieurs restitutions d'églises, mais j'avoue qu'avant d'avoir reçu des Vicaires Apostoliques, la confirmation de ces heureuses nouvelles, je crois devoir me retrancher dans une incrédulité que n'excusent que trop les mécomptes que nous avons subi depuis cinq ans! Ce qui me semble certain maintenant, c'est qu'il est possible de tout obtenir en ce pays par l'envoi sur les lieux d'un bâtiment de guerre et que je ne puis trop engager le Gouvernement de Sa Majesté à entrer résolument dans cette voie.

Veuillez agréer les assurances de la respectueuse considération avec laquelle

J'ai l'honneur d'être,

Monsieur le Ministre

De Votre Excellence

Le très humble et très obéissant serviteur.

Henry de Bellonnet

P. S.

Les dépêches de l'Amiral Roze devant parvenir à Paris près d'un mois avant cette dépêche, j'ai pensé qu'il était inutile de rapporter ici les nouvelles de sa première expédition en Corée, nouvelles que Votre Excellence aura reçues directement.

鄭雲翼 ➞ 議政府(1866. 11. 3/高宗三年九月二十六日)

프랑스 함대의 내습(來襲) 보고

京畿水使 鄭雲翼以洋賊衝火我船五隻馳啓

狀啓以爲二十五日洋賊從船二隻自江華下來于臣境連放大碗口臣與中軍李祉秀領率防守軍兵方欲追捕之際洋醜初不下陸來卽衝火於前洋泛留船五隻還爲上去亦發大碗口丸落於臣營前三門階砌崩頽相距可爲三百步而直向昌陵浦其疾如飛不能防備惶恐待罪教以勿待罪事回諭

133

總署(1866. 11. 4/同治五年九月二十七日) ➜ C. H. M. Bellonet

무력 행위 자제 및 사전 진상 조사 제안

給法國照會

爲照覆事 六月初五日 本爵以朝鮮國殺害教衆一事 似可先行據理查詢 不必遽啓兵端 照覆貴大臣在案 至今未荷覆知 玆於本月十六日 接據貴大臣照會內稱現准本國水師提督來文 移送該員所出告示一張等因 檢查條約第三十一款 內開載甚明 無庸深辨 至兩國交兵 均關民命該國僻處海隅 向知謹守 此次何以殺害教民 貴國是否曾經查詢 可否先行詳究情由 無庸遽行攻戰 以全兩國民命之處 統希貴大臣查察可也

【佛譯文】

Pékin le 4 novembre 1866

Le Prince de Kong au Chargé d'affaires de France

Dans la 6e lune de la présente année j'écrivais à V. E. qu'avant d'entrer en opérations de guerre avec la Corée il y avait peut-être lieu de rechercher avec soin qu'elles (*Sic*) causes avaient pu amener le massacre des chrétiens de ce pays. Je ne reçus pas de réponse à cette observation.

Le 6e jour de la présente lune, V. E. m'écrivait pour m'annoncer le blocus des Côtes de Corée par la division navale française et me transmettait copie de la notification faite à ce sujet par le Commandant de vos forces navales.

Moi, Prince, je trouve que l'art. 31 du traité parle assez clairement des cas de blocus pour qu'il ne soit pas besoin d'en discuter les termes.

Quant à la guerre entre les deux pays c'est une affaire de Grande conséquence pour la vie des sujets de chacun. La Corée est un petit État retiré et paisible. La France a-t-elle recherché les motifs qui l'ont pu conduire au massacre des chrétiens. N'y aurait-il pas lieu de les (*Sic*) de chercher scrupuleusement à les connaître avant d'agir ; ne pourrait-on pas éviter une guerre si funeste aux populations. C'est ce que nous vous prions de vouloir bien examiner.

Dépêche importante.

Le 27e jour de la 9e lune de la 5e année de Tong-tje
Pour traduction conforme
Le 1er Interprète de la Légation

G. Lemaire

【英譯文(美國)】

NOVEMBER 4, 1866

Sir:

On the 16th of July last I had the honor of replying to your despatch respecting the murder of missionaries and others by the Coreans, and suggested the desirableness and propriety of first inquiring into the circumstances attending the affair, that hostilities might, if possible, be avoided; but up to the present time I have not been favored with an answer. I have, however, to acknowledge your despatch of the 24th ultimo, in which you state as follows:

"The commander-in-chief of the French naval forces has sent me a notice of blockade(of which a copy is enclosed) of all the ports and rivers leading to the capital of Corea, on its western coasts, by the ships of his squadron; and as he will soon attack that country, he has for the present forbidden the vessels of all other nations from going there," &c., &c.

Your despatch and the notice of blockade are entirely in accordance with the provisions of article XXXI of the treaty, and I have no wish to discuss their purport. But when two countries resort to arms it involves the lives of their people; and as Corea is a very secluded country, lying away from others, and keeping itself aloof by strict regulations, it is not improper to inquire, whether the French government has made any investigation into the circumstances connected with the Christians; and if not, whether such as mode is not desirable as a first step. There may not, after all, be an absolute necessity of a resort to hostilities, and thus human life on both sides will be preserved. On a review of the whole subject, I hope your excellency will also see it in the same light.

I have , &c.,

KUNG

M. DE BELLONET, &c., &c.

【英譯文(英國)】

On the 5th day of the 6th moon of the 5th year of Tung Chih (July 16, 1866). the Prince addressed a despatch in reply to the French Chargé d'Affaires, in which he suggested that the affair of the massacre of the Christians by Corea might be first inquired into peacefully, and that arms should not be had recourse to rashly. To this (suggestion the Prince) has not yet had the honour to receive a reply.

The Prince has now to acknowledge the receipt on the 16th day of the present moon (October 24, 1866), of M. de Bellonnet's despatch informing him that the French Admiral had forwarded to him officially a copy of a proclamation issues by that officer, announcing the blockade of all the ports on (or mouths of) the river leading from the western shore of Corea up to the capital of that State, and prohibiting, as active operations are about to commence immediately, the vessels of other nations proceeding thither for the present.

With reference to the closing of the ports of Corea by vessels of war, the Prince will not dwell upon the clear provisions of Article XXXI of the (French) Treaty. But as a hostile collision between the two countries will seriously affect the lives of the people, and as it is unintelligible what reasons Corea, an out of the way country on the verge of the ocean, that has hitherto evinced a sense of prudence and a due regard to what is right, could have had in putting the Christians to death, (the Prince would ask) if France has made inquires yet (into the cause of the affair), and would suggest, with a vies to the preservation of the lives of the subjects of both countries, that the circumstances of the outrage should be first carefully ascertained, and that France need not hostilely proceed to active operation.

The Prince hopes M. de Bellonnet will give these suggestions due consideration.

A necessary communication, &c.

9th moon, 27th day.

P. de Chasseloup-Laubat (1866. 11. 6) ➔ Moustier

Bellonet의 월권적 행위 비판

Paris, le 6 Novembre 1866

Monsieur le Marquis et cher Collègue, par une dépêche du 7 Septembre dernier, j'avais communiqué à M. le Mis de Lavalette un rapport de M. le Commandant en chef de notre Division Navale des Mers de Chine, du 10 Juillet précédent, contenant des informations concernant la mise à mort en Corée de deux Evêques et de sept missionnaires Français.

Aujourd'hui, j'ai l'honneur d'envoyer, sous ce pli, à Votre Excellence la Copie d'un nouveau Rapport que M. le Contre-Amiral Roze, m'a adressé de Tchefou, le 7 Septembre, et dans lequel, en m'entretenant de son projet d'exploration de la côte de Corée, cet officier général me signale l'attitude prise, dans cette grave circonstance, par M. le Chargé d'Affaires de France à Pékin. Ce rapport est accompagné, au surplus des copies des lettres écrites à ce sujet par M. de Bellonnet au Prince Kong et au Contre-Amiral Roze, et de la réponse faite, par ce dernier.

Je ne saurais dissimuler à Votre Excellence que les lettres de M. Bellonnet prononçant la déchéance du Roi de la Corée, et déclarant que cette contrée doit être considérée comme placée sous le protectorat de S. M. l'Empereur, enfin, imposant en quelque sorte d'avance les conditions de la satisfaction à réclamer, me paraissent d'une extrême gravité.

Je ne m'arrête pas à ce qu'il peut y avoir de plus ou moins régulier dans ce fait de M. le Chargé d'Affaires de France à Pékin donnant des instructions semblables à M. le Contre-Amiral, Commandant en chef de la Division des Mers de Chine et du Japon, lorsqu'il s'agit d'actes accomplis sur un territoire qu'il déclare lui-même ne point dépendre de l'Empire de Chine mais il m'est impossible de ne pas me préoccuper de l'effet que pourraient produire ces instructions sur le public en France et sur les Gouvernements qui n'ont pas vu avec indifférence nos succès au Japon et notre Etablissement en Cochinchine; il m'est impossible de ne pas me préoccuper aussi de la situation dans laquelle la publicité donnée à ces instructions placerait notre Division Navale qui, par sa composition et le petit nombre d'hommes dont elle dispose, sera peut-être dans l'impuissance d'obtenir une satisfaction sérieuse du Gouvernement de la Corée.

Lorsque j'ai été instruit des tristes évènements qui ont amené le meurtre des missionnaires, j'en ai entretenu l'Empereur, et j'ai dû faire connaître à Sa Majesté combien il nous serait difficile d'agir sans un déploiement de forces qui nous entraînerait peut-être dans une entreprise bien sérieuse.

C'est après cet entretien avec l'Empereur que j'ai été amené à écrire de ma main au Contre-Amiral Roze une dépêche dont je vous envoie un extrait. Vous verrez combien elle est éloignée des dépêches de M. Bellonnet.

Quoiqu'il en soit, Monsieur le Marquis et cher Collègue, je désire avoir votre opinion sur toutes ces choses; il importe que nos deux Départements marchent d'accord.

Agréez, Monsieur le Marquis et cher Collègue, l'assurance de ma haute considération. Le Ministre, Secrétaire d'Etat de la Marine et des Colonies.

P. Chasselouplaubat

1ère annexe à la dép. de la Marine du 6 Novembre 1866

Pékin, le 10 juillet 1866

Légation de France en Chine

Monsieur le Contre Amiral,

En recevant la nouvelle du massacre général des chrétiens et des missionnaires en Corée, vous avez sans doute, pensé comme moi, que le moindre retard dans la punition de ce sanglant outrage, pouvait faire courir un danger sérieux aux 500 missionnaires qui évangélisent la Chine, tant la contagion de l'exemple peut-être terrible dans ces pays de l'Extrême-Orient.

Je n'hésite donc pas, Monsieur le Contre-Amiral, à faire appel aux forces navales dont vous avez le commandement; à remettre entre vos mains, sous ma responsabilité, le soin de tirer une vengeance éclatante de l'attentat dont deux évêques et neuf missionnaires Français sont tombés les victimes, et à vous prier d'user de tous les moyens en votre pouvoir, sans plus tenir compte des demandes dont les Consulats ou la Légation de Sa Majesté auraient pu vous entretenir pour commencer le plus rapidement possible, les hostilités contre la

Corée.

Des liens de suzeraineté d'une part, de vassalité de l'autre, ont longtemps réuni l'Empire de la Chine et le Royaume de Corée. Il était de mon devoir de m'assurer de leur existence et de savoir jusqu'a quel point la Puissance Suzeraine entendait prendre la responsabilité de l'outrage qui nous était fait. Mais les explications échangées avec le Gouvernement Chinois m'ayant appris qu'il renonçait à réclamer ses droits, j'ai adressé au Prince de Kong la note dont vous trouverez, ci-joint, copie, et dans laquelle j'ai déclaré officiellement l'ouverture des hostilités, la séparation définitive de la Corée, la déchéance de son Roi, et le droit exclusif de l'Empereur, notre Auguste Souverain, à disposer, suivant son bon plaisir, du pays et du trône vacant.

Vous voudrez donc bien, Monsieur le Contre-Amiral, ne traiter avec personne, ne reconnaître aucune autorité quelconque en Corée, jusqu'à ce que la capitale du Roi déchu, et la Régente, mère du feu Roi, aient été remis entre vos mains. Il n'y a plus en Corée d'autre pouvoir que celui qui représente Sa Majesté l'Empereur des Français.

Lorsque vous aurez, plus tard, à reconstituer le pouvoir que nos armes vont détruire, je pense, Monsieur le Contre-Amiral, que vous trouverez, comme moi, que les efforts courageux que le père du Roi déchu a tenté pour faire triompher la cause de la Religion et de la civilisation, le désignent tout naturellement pour remplacer sur le trône les personnes indignes qui l'occupaient. Mais je regarde, et vous regarderez sans doute également, comme une condition indispensable au succès, comme à l'honneur de notre cause, à l'avenir de la civilisation dans l'Extrême-Orient, que le Prince auquel seront confiées les destinées de la Corée, sous la protectorat de Sa Majesté l'Empereur, fasse profession de la Religion Chrétienne, et sous ce point de vue encore, l'ami et le disciple des vénérables martyrs, l'époux d'une de leurs cathécumènes (*Sic*), me semble désigné d'avance, et n'hésitera pas, je l'espère, à se prononcer ouvertement.

Je ne doute pas, Monsieur le Contre-Amiral, que vous ne fassiez punir d'une manière exemplaire tous les serviteurs du pouvoir déchu qui ont contribué au massacre des missionnaires et des chrétiens. Mais pour que l'expiation fût complète, pour qu'elle frappât surtout l'opinion populaire, je voudrais que les biens de tous les condamnés fussent distribués aux familles de leurs victimes, et que le Trésor Royal lui-même contribuât pendant un certain nombre d'années par le versement de la moitié de ses revenus à ce grand acte de justice et de réparation.

Tous les frais de l'expédition, Monsieur le Contre-Amiral, comme ceux de l'occupation subséquente seront necessairement à la charge du Trésor Coréen et je ne vois pas de meilleur moyen d'arriver à ce résultat que de vous inviter à conserver entre vos mains jusqu'à parfait paiement, les douanes que vous aurez à établir, lorsqu'apres la cessation des hostilités vous ouvrirez la Corée nouvelle au commerce de toutes les nations.

Agréez, etc.

Signé : Henry de Belloné (*Sic*)
Pour copie conforme :
Le C. Amiral Commandant en chef de la Division navale des mers de Chine et du Japon
Signé : Roze

2e annexe à la dép. de la Marine du 6 Novembre 1866

Pékin, le 13 Juillet 1866*

3e annexe à la dép. de la Marine du 6 Novembre 1866

A bord de *la Guerrière*, Tche-Foo, le 7 Septembre 1866**

4e annexe à la dép. de la Marine du 6 Novembre 1866
En marge : Division navale des mers de Chine

A bord de *la Guerrière*, Tche-foo, le 7 Septembre 1868***

5e annexe à la dép. de la Marine du 6 Novembre 1866

*제1권 80번 문서.
**제1권 95번 문서.
***제1권 96번 문서.

Paris, le 8 Septembre 1866

J'éprouve une hésitation bien grande pour ce que vous samblez vouloir faire dans la Corée.

C'est sans coute un grand malheur que le meurtre de ces hommes dévoués qui s'en vont au milieu de populations inconnues porter avec la croix les germes de notre civilisation. Missionnaires de la religion la plus sainte, la plus libérale, qui ait jamais existé sur la terre, ils ont droit à tous nos respects, à notre admiration même dans bien des circonstances.

Mais lorsque, pour venger leur mort, il nous faut peut-être lancer notre pays dans des aventures dont il nous est difficile de calculer les chances, alors, mon cher Amiral, il ne nous est point permis de n'obéir qu'au sentiment qui nous entraîne, et notre devoir est de nous rendre compte des conséquences que pourrait avoir un échec dans l'entreprise, même légitime, que nous ferions.

J'ai lu avec grand soin la note que vous avez remise le R. P. Ridel. Cette relation, simplement faite, et qui, au point de vue des faits accomplis m'inspire toute confiance, est loins, je vous l'avoue de faire naître dans mon esprit une assurance aussi grande lors qu'il s'agit de l'expédition à faire pour remonter jusqu'à la capitale <u>le Séoul</u>. Je ne puis oublier que nous avons perdu des bâtiments sur ces côtes peu connues de la Corée et quand je vais dans cette note que "les pilotes Coréens se font forts de conduire la frégate dans un mouillage bien abrité où l'on trouverait dix mètres d'eau à marée basse, et que d' [____] les renseignement de ces gens, la [____] des eaux serait de sept à huit mètres." J'avoue que je trouve ces renseignements bien peu digne de nous inspirer une confiance absolue. Je dirai autant des facilités qu'on présente pour remorter la rivière et pour "s'emparer des personnages qui ont été les instigateurs de l'assassinat de nos missionaires."

Lorseque je vois que <u>le Séoul</u> est à neuf lieues du mouillage qu'on vous propose, que cette capitale est éloignée d'environ <u>une lieuc</u> des rives du fleuve, je me demande si vous avez les moyens suffisants pour faire ce qu'on réclame de vous.

De la meilleure foi du monde, les missionaires voient souvent les choses comme ils les désirent. Lorsque l'Amiral Rigault de Genouilly s'est rendu à Tourane et ensuite à Saïgon, il est loin d'y avoir trouvé et les <u>facilités</u> et les <u>adhésions</u> qu'on avait annoncées: nous devons donc nous mettre en garde contre des renseignements qui nous viennent d'hommes qui n'ont pas été d'ailleurs à même de constater par eux-mêmes les faits qu'ils nous font connaître par les récits que leur font les gens qui les entourent.

Pour donc, si vous pouviez avec une certitude de succès punir le meurtre de nos missionaires; si, comme à Simonoseki, vous pouviez trouver un point accessible à nos navires sans être obligé de faire d'expédition à terre, vous devriez y montrer votre pavillon et exiger des réparations, enfin venger ces assassinats. Mais autrement, mon cher Amiral, vous devez n'entreprendre que ce que vous serez absolument certain de conduire à bonne fin.

Pour donc proscrire d'une manière formelle ce que vous pouviez méditer, ce que l'éloignement où je suis placé des lieux et l'ignorance des conditions ne me permettent pas d'apprécier suffisamment, je ne puis que vous inviter à [___] rien entreprendre qui soit de nature à nous engager. Votre responsabilité comme la mienne ne nous permettent pas d'entraîner le Gouvernement de l'Empereur dans des entreprises qui exigeraient d'autres forces que celles dont vous disposez.

Or, comme j'ai déjà eu l'occasion de l'écrire à votre prédécesseur pour les affaires du Japon, l'acte maritime, quelque soit le plus ou moins de [_____] n'entraîne guère après celle que les conséquences que le Gouvernement peut vouloir en faire sortir ; mais il n'en est pas de même de tout engagement qui, dans l'intérieur d'une contrée amènerait un échec et laisserait après lui l'obligation pour nos armes de le venger.

Je pense au surplus que le premier courrier m'apportera de vous quelques nouveaux documents sur toutes ces choses.

Je suis…

Signé : P. de Chasseloup-Laubat

135

李恒老(1866. 11. 9/高宗三年十月三日)

시무상소(時務上疏)

護軍 李恒老疏陳時事仍乞遞金吾之任賜批

疏略曰臣日者以癃疾垂死之狀冒昧鳴號何幸聖慈矜悶許遞未幾日又奉金吾之命臣老而不死欺世盜名濫叨匪分至此甚也使臣疾病可強不敢承膺者其亦有說臣本腐儒無他奇謀少從師友略聞經傳先儒之說此世俗所謂常談死法然朱子曰常談之中有妙理死法之中有活法臣篤信此訓思以獻之君父之前卽前疏之所陳是也書曰民惟邦本本固邦寧傳曰德者本也財者末也外本內末爭民施奪又曰國不以利爲利以義爲利也朱子推明其說曰仁者散財以得民不仁者亡身以殖貨臣嘗以此數言爲百王不易之訓而適見近日洋賊猖獗苟求其故則實由於我民之內應我民之內應由於民心之怨叛民心之怨叛由於恒産之罄竭恒産之罄竭由於聚斂之不息聚斂之不息由於土木之張大夫驅怨叛之民以充卒伍使之赴湯蹈火固已難矣若此不已則舟中皆敵國蕭墻皆顓臾豈但洋賊之爲可憂哉臣深憂永歎不量其力溯本而論之請罷土木之役止斂民之政此老臣滿腔熱血之所瀉也殿下但下體念之敎而迄未聞施行之實反見其科目益廣是以已叛之民心日益叛已驕之賊勢日益驕此臣之未解一也書曰天命有德五服五章哉天討有罪五刑五庸哉旣曰五服五章則德之高下不可以分寸顚倒旣曰五刑五庸則罪之大小不可以毫髮僭差也臣於前疏再陳信賞必罰之說蓋有所指而發也夫國家數百年保障之地何等重大而守疆之臣一遇小賊棄城圖免使國勢危如一髮制刑論辟死有餘罪殿下過於寬仁罪止屛裔誠如是也凡封疆之臣出戰之帥彼獨無全軀保妻子之心哉風聲鶴唳在在效尤則殿下將誰與爲守乎此臣所以不量其力再發其端冀悟宸衷而殿下不之省至於三司合啓大臣聯箚而殿下不之聽此臣所未解二也自古異端蠱人心術者何限而莫甚於洋敎夷狄禍人國家者何限而亦莫甚於洋賊蓋潛入我國廣傳邪學者欲以植其黨與表裏相應偵我虛實率師入寇糞穢我衣裳奪掠我貨色以充谿壑之慾也然則內修外攘之擧如根本技葉之相須不可闕一也明矣枝葉雖不可緩根本尤所當急所謂根本者在殿下之一心克己從善而已殿下立志居敬當爲卽爲有雷厲風飛之勇當去卽去有斬釘截鐵之斷則聖智日明無氛翳之弊聖德日剛無撓奪之患收拾士類講明正學誅鋤奸細遏絶內應而爲外攘之田地矣雖然察其機要又在禁絶洋物夫洋物之來其目甚多要皆奇技淫巧而於民生日用不惟

無益爲禍滋大揆以召公戒獒之義則正使洋夷歲貢此物如聘享之禮且不可受況潛洩我國衣食之原以易之哉況彼之爲物生於手而日計有餘我之爲物産於地而歲計不足以不足交有餘我胡以不困以日計接歲計彼胡以不贍是以生生自用往來無常或雜處民間移易民俗或出沒海澨焚掠城邑至於今日爲國家之膏育矣然救之有道凡洋物之用於家而鬻於市者竝抵重刑使群臣百姓無一人用之者則彼之所恃便同章甫之入越而不售於我矣故禁絶洋物爲內修之機要而不本於殿下之身心則是猶治其末而塞其流也故臣於前疏敢請殿下服食日用之間一有洋物則悉聚闕庭而燒之使中外上下知聖意所在如靑天白日洋賊之來可絶其根源此非高遠難行之事在聖明克己從善之實心而已殿下循例賜批迄無施行之實臣之所未解三也其餘所陳未蒙施行者今不暇一二焉大抵天下之義理無窮一己之明睿有限故智者千慮必有一失愚者千慮必有一得是故堯舜之聖猶曰稽于衆舍己從人曰好問而好察邇言隱惡而揚善執其兩端用其中於民仲虺告湯曰好問則裕自用則小伊尹告太甲曰有言逆于汝心必求諸道有言遜于汝志必求諸非道孔子曰悅而不繹從而不改吾末如之何也已殿下親御經筵日接儒臣所講者何事而今此緊要去處疏脕乃爾者何歟苟如是殿下之所以召臣於草萊之中者何意歟不用其言而徒褻命德之器在聖朝失擧措之宜在臣身毁廉義之防不可冒沒承膺故瀝血陳情仍及殿下之闕失雖以此獲蒙天怒萬被誅戮有所不辭也伏乞亟收成命以重公器批以此時此言實是光明正大可不體念乎

巡撫營 ➞ 議政府(1866. 11. 10/高宗三年十月四日)

정족산(鼎足山) 전투 승전 보고

巡撫營以鼎足山守城千總 梁憲洙報捷請援啓

該營啓言卽見先鋒中軍李容熙今初三日戌時馳報則鼎足山守城千總 梁憲洙手本內當日午時量賊將騎馬率數百兵分入東南門我軍發銃一放或中或未中彼亦發放遠及城內船頭堡別將及邑民車再俊中丸而仆哨官一名中丸而死賊漢則致死者爲六名而皆收屍而去彼有餘氣我無齊進之銃且藥與丸俱盡豈有如許罔措者乎賊漢未乃退走謂以請援復進云我軍則無器械可修故玆急手本丸與藥卽刻越送平壤 海西砲手沒數越送救此孤城 京營牙兵砲手及藥丸與在陣砲手連續下送以爲救援之地云矣又啓言卽見先鋒中軍李容熙今初三日亥時馳報則鼎足山守城千總 梁憲洙馳告內俄者捷報大戰方收百擾交叢未能詳陳蓋此城卽必守之地而今月初一日彼漢六十餘名入此城詳察四勢破僧徒器皿而去其夜我軍潛渡而入彼實不知今日則彼以別占守城之計頭領騎馬牽驢携輜重酒食無疑而來分入東南門之際我軍左右埋伏齊發彼死者六我死者一而船頭堡別將中丸而臥賊未敢入城輜重器械多有棄去我軍拾取而來故竝使僧徒留置以待後日詳閱錄報我軍旣經一場驚恸藥丸俱盡有口者皆請援兵而明日彼若加兵復來則將不知至於何境砲手限三百名明日未明前越送助勢之地云矣

Moustier(1866. 11. 10) → H. de Bellonet

Bellonet가 취한 조치의 무효화 주장

관련문서 (1) *Le Moniteur universel* 1866년 12월 28일, 29일, 1867년 1월 8일자 보도문

Paris le 10 Novembre 1866

Monsieur, J'ai reçu la dépêche que vous m'avez fait l'honneur de m'adresser sous le n° 16 au sujet des missionnaires françaises massacrés dans la Corée et à laquelle se trouve jointe la correspondance que vous avez échangée avec M^r l'Amiral Roze. J'ai vu avec une profonde surprise que vous ayez cru pouvoir, sans aucune instruction qui vous y autorisât, engager au point où vous l'avez fait la responsabilité de la Légation que vous dirigez, en proclamant, de votre autorité privée, la déchéance du Roi de Corée, en lui déclarant solenellement la guerre et en prescrivant au commandant de nos forces maritimes dans les mers de Chine de commencer les hostilités. Je n'ai pas à examiner en ce moment si la Corée est ou non un pays vassal de l'Empire Chinois; mais en décidant négativement cette question dans la communication si irréfléchie que vous avez faite au G^ce de Kong, vous traciez en quelque sorte vous-même des limites à votre juridiction et vous ôtiez par ce raisonnement à la Légation de S. M. à Pékin le droit d'intervenir directement dans les affaires de la Corée. Sans m'arrêter au surplus, à cette contradiction et, sans rechercher les motifs de votre conduite, je dois désapprouver entièrement la marche que vous avez suivie, et je vous prie de considérer comme nuls et non avenus les déclarations que vous avez faites ainsi que les ordres que vous avez donnés. M^r le C. amiral Roze est [_____] d'instructions de M. le M^tre de la Marine qui détermine le caractère de la mission dont cet officier G^al est chargé, et il lui appartient de les exécuter sous sa seule responsabilité jusqu'à ce que je me sois entendu avec mon Collègue sur les résolutions nouvelles qu'il pourrait y avoir à prendre en commun. Je suis du reste convaincu d'avance que l'amiral saura concilier ce que réclament les devoirs de l'humanité et la protection de nos missionnaires avec la nécessité de ne pas entraîner la France dans une entreprise lointaine; qu'il se bornera pour le moment, à se renseigner sur l'état des choses et des lieux, enfin qu'il n'aura recours aux moyens d'intimidation matérielle que s'il a la certitude de pouvoir mesurer exactement la portée de ses opérations et d'obtenir un résultat immédiat sans engager pour l'avenir l'action du G[t] de l'Empereur.

【관련문서 1】

Journal officiel de l'Empire Français.

Vendredi 28 Décembre 1866

Le ministre de la marine et des colonies a reçu du contre-amiral Roze, commandant en chef la division des mers de Chine, des dépêches annonçant la prise de Kang-hoa, ville fortifiée située au nord de l'île de ce nom, et à l'embouchure du fleuve sur les bords duquel se trouve Séoul, capitale de la Corée.

Parti de Tche-fou le 11 octobre, avec la frégate *la Guerrière*, les corvettes à hélice *le Laplace* et *le Primauguet*, les avisos *le Déroulède* et *le Kien-chan*, les canonnières *le Tardif* et *le Lebrethon*, le contre-amiral Roze mouillait, le 13, avec sa division, devant l'île Boisée, à 18 milles de Kang-hoa. Le lendemain, les canonnières remontèrent la rivière Salée, remorquant les embarcations qui portaient les compagnies de débarquement de *la Guerrière* et des corvettes, ainsi qu'un détachement des marins-fusiliers de Yokohama. A peine débarqués, nos marins occupèrent les hauteurs sans rencontrer la moindre résistance et campèrent à 5 kilomètres de Kang hoa. Le 15, une reconnaisance fut exécutée par une colonne commandée par M. le capitaine de frégate comte d'Osery; arrivée près d'un fort qui domine la ville, elle fut accueillie par un feu bien nourri de mousqueterie et par celui de deux canons de petit calibre. Après un engagement de quelques minutes, le fort fut occupé, et les Coréens s'enfuirent, laissant un drapeau entre nos mains.

Le 16, dès huit heures du matin, le contre-amiral Roze, à la tête de toutes ses forces, se présentait devant la ville, qu'entourait une muraille crénelée de 4 mètres de hauteur. Parvenues à une centaine de mètres de la porte principale, nos troupes furent reçues par une fusillade assez vive, mais la muraille fut bientôt escaladée au cri de *Vive l'Empereur*! et l'ennemi nous laissa maîtres de la place.

Un grand nombre de canons, plus de 10,000 fusils, des munitions de toute sorte, ont été trouvés dans d'immenses magasins, et démontrent l'importance de la place de Kang-hoa au point de vue de la défense de la capitale de la Corée.

Le contre-amiral Roze a fait inventorier avec soin les magasins dont il a pris possession au nom de l'Etat, et qui contenaient également dix-huit caisses remplies de lingots d'argent et des archives officielles.

Une proclamation adressée aux habitants leur a fait connaître le but que l'amiral s'était proposé en venant châtier le gouvernement coréen et leur a assuré la protection la plus complète.

Le blocus de fleuve de Séoul, qui a été notifié aux consuls des puissances européennes en Chine, et la prise de Kang-hoa, devaient produire une profonde impression sur le gouvernement coréen. En effet, la ville de Kang-hoa étant, comme on vient de le rappeler, située à l'embouchure du fleuve de Séoul, commande ainsi la principale voie que le commerce de la capitale est obligé de prendre, particulièrement pour assurer ses approvisionnements de riz.

Aussi, dès le 19, le contre-amiral Roze recevait une lettre du roi à laquelle il s'est empressé de répondre, en faisant connaître les satisfactions qu'il réclame au nom du Gouvernement de l'Empereur.

La dépêche qui renferme ces détails est datée du 22 octobre ; à cette date, le contre-amiral Roze était encore dans la ville de Kang-hoa, où il attendait les interprètes qu'il avait fait demander à notre consul de Shang-haï.

Journal officiel de l'Empire Français.

Samedi 29 Décembre 1866

Partie Non Officielle

Paris, le 28 Décembre

Bulletin

Le département des affaires étrangères a reçu par le dernier courrier de l'extrême-Orient une dêpèche de Shang-hai, en date du 6 novembre, qui confirme sur tous les points les informations relatives à la prise de Kang-hoa, adressées le 22 octobre au ministre de la marine par le contre-amiral Roze, commandant en chef la division navale des mers de Chine, et insérées au Moniteur d'hier. M. Brenier de Montmorand, consul général de France à Shang-hai, annonce que la colonie française a accueilli avec la plus grande satisfaction la nouvelle de l'heureuse issue de l'expédition du contre-amiral Roze dans le royaume de Corée, dont le premier effet sera de mettre fin aux actes fréquents de piraterie que le commerce européen avait à redouter dans ces parages.

Journal officiel de l'Empire Français.

Mardi 8 janvier 1867

Le ministre de la marine et des colonies a reçu du contre-amiral Roze, commandant en chef la division navale des mers de Chine, des dépêches en date du 17 novembre.

Après l'occupation de Kang-hoa par les compagnies de débarquement des bâtiments de la division, cet officier général s'est établi dans une position fortement retranchée, en ayant soin de faire parcourir par des détachements les environs de la ville et explorer les rives opposées de la presqu'île de Corée, en détruisant toutes les jonques qui se trouvaient dans le canal.

Dans l'une de ces exploration, la chaloupe de *la Guerrière*, au moment d'aborder la côte, a été accueillie, presque à bout portant, par une décharge de mousqueterie qui tua trois matelots : nos marins autant à terre débusquèrent les Coréens qui, cachés dans les broussailles, avaient fait feu, et, conduits par l'aspirant de 1ère chasse Châtel, les mirent en fuite, après leur avoir tué quelques hommes.

Le contre-amiral Roze ayant voulu s'assurer de l'état du pays, un détachement commandé par le capitaine de vaisseau Olivier sortit de Kang-hoa et rencontra à quelques kilomètres de la ville des Coréens en grand nombre, retranchés dans une pagode fortifiée ; l'ennemi, qui avait d'abord fait une sortie, fut repoussé et se hâta de rentrer dans ses retranchements en abandonnant ses morts.

Après une fusillade très-vive, dans laquelle nous n'avons eu aucun homme tuè, mais qui malheureusement nous a quitté quelques blessés, la colonne rentra le soir même à Kang-hoa.

Quelques jours après, le contre-amiral Roze, voyant que le gouvernement coréen ne donnait pas suite aux ouvertures auxquelles il avait dû croire en recevant une lettre du roi, se décida à quitter Kang-hoa : les approches de l'hiver se faisaient d'ailleurs déjà sentir, et il était à craindre que toute navigation dans la rivière Salée ne fût bientôt interrompue : alors il ordonna la destruction de tous les établisements du gouvernement, ainsi que celle du palais du roi, et nos matelots retournèrent à bord des bâtiments mouillés devant l'île Boisée.

Les caisses renfermant des lingots d'argent représentant une valeur de 197,000 francs, des manuscripts et des livres qui peuvent offrir quelque intêrèt pour la science, ont été dirigées sur Shang-hai, d'où elles seront transportées en France.

Le contre-amiral Roze annonce également que les deux missionnaires qui étaient restés en Corée sont venus le rejoindre, après avoir réussi à se faire débarquer à Tche-fou.

La destruction de Kang-hoa, place de guerre importante, des poudrières et des établissements publics que cette ville renfermait, a dû prouver au gouvernement coréen que le meurtre des missionnaires français ne restait pas impuni.

Olivier(1866. 11. 10) → G. Roze

전등사(傳燈寺) 전투 경과 보고

Île de Kang-hoa, le 10 Novembre, 1866

Amiral,

J'ai l'honneur de vous rendre compte de la reconnaissance que vous m'aviez chargé de faire dans la journée du 9 novembre. Je devais visiter la pagode de Tchiong-tung-sa situé à cinq lieues environ dans le S.S.O. de la ville de Kang-hoa, et aperçue par les marins de nos cannonières, dans une exploration qu'ils avaient faite la veille. Je suis parti à sept heures du matin, à la tête de quatre pelotons, deux de Yokohama, et deux du *Primauguet*. J'ai suivi un grand chemin, à travers des plaines de rizières et dans quelques gorges de collines boisées, dans un pays accidenté, le long de hautes montagnes dont la chaîne principale s'étend vers le S.O.

J'ai questionné en vain, à l'aide du Père Ridel, les gens de la campagne. Les reseignements que vous avez cherché à vous procurer, Amiral, depuis le commencement de l'expédition ont été nuls ou trompeux et les reconnaissances que vous envoyez chaque jour dans toutes les directions, pour étudier le pays que nous occupons servent seules à nous le faire connaître.

Après avoir fait 18 kilomètres, nous sommes arrivés vers onze heures au pied du massif montagneux de Tchiong-tung-sa ; c'est un amas de plusieurs collines rocailleuses, aux pentes les plus abruptes dominant la plaines de 80 à 100 mètres. Les différents sommets de ces collines laissent entr'eux une sorte de vallée en partie boisée, dont les deux flancs sont fortement inclinés du côté du S.E. Cette vallée, d'un kilomètre et demi ou deux kilomètres de tour, représente l'étendue de la place. On y distingue une pagode, divers magasins aux toits en tuile et une muraille intérieure la coupant en travers, de l'Est à l'Ouest, et la protégeant ainsi contre un envahissement. Les fortifications extérieures se composent, selon le système du pays, d'une muraille crénelée, toute en maçonnerie, épaisse de plus d'un mètre, haute d'environ trois mètres, très ancienne et ébranlée dans plusieurs endroits, suivant les crêtes d'une colline à l'autre. Cette muraille est renforcée à chaque angle saillant, c'est-à-dire à chaque sommet, d'un massif carré en maçonnerie de même hauteur, et forme une plate-forme pour l'artillerie, deux portes se trouvent placées vers le sud, aux angles rentrants de l'enceinte et à la partie la plus [_______].

Aucun indice ne me faisait supposer la présence de l'ennemi. Cependant je voulus agir avec prudence. Je fis halte à quelques centaines de mètres de la porte du S.O. hors de la portée que je supposais aux armes coréennes, et j'envoyai deux petits détachements gravir les arêtes pour choisir un passage et reconnaître l'intérieur. Ils arrivent à quelques mètres des murs, lorsque tout à coup une grèle de projectiles tombe sur eux. Les remparts se garnissent instantanément de soldats coréens ayant à côté d'eux un approvisionnement de fusils chargés, pour continuer le feu sans interruption. En même temps une sortie nombreuse fait irruption par la porte. Nous accourons au secours de nos hommes et nous repoussons l'ennemi, qui, loin de nous attendre, se sauve dans ses retranchements, en laissant ses morts sur la route. Mais par tous les créneaux les balles et les biscaïens pleuvent sur nous avec une telle intensité, que c'eût été compromettre ma petite troupe de garder cette position et de combattre contre des hommes retranchés derrière des murailles, dans des conditions si inégales.

Je profitai d'un repli de terrain qu'était à cinq cents mètres des points d'attaque, pour venir m'y établir et continuer la lutte avec plus d'avantage, par la justesse et la portée de nos armes. Nous recueillimes nos blessés au milieu du feu et nous les logeâmes provisoirement dans une petite case, non loin de nous.

Le combat dura pendant une demi heure. Nos hommes visaient avec sang-froid, étaient pleins d'ardeur, exécutant promptement tous les ordres qu'ils recevaient. J'étais heureux de voir leur belle contenance.

J'avais atteint un double but : recconnaître cette importante place et intimider sa garnison que nous pûmes estimer, d'après divers aperçus, s'élever à plus de douze cents hommes.

Je devais revenir le soir. Nous n'avions pas de vivres pour le lendemain et nous étions à 18 kilomètres de nos cantonnements, ayant une trentaine de blessées à transporter. Il ne restait plus aux hommes que trois ou quatre paquets de cartouches qu'il fallait réserver pour le retour. Je fis faire l'appel, compter les armes, et quand je fus certain que je ne laissai rien entre l'ennemi et nous, j'envoyai d'abord les blessés derrière deux mamelons situés à mille mètres des forts, et je viens ensuite occuper ces deux mamelons. Là nous essayâmes avec succès quelques coups de nos carabines avec les meilleurs tireurs. Les Coréens faisaient feu de leur côté, mais sans nous atteindre.

Je chargeai Mr. de Thouars de disposer avec sa division le transport des blessés. A une heure nous étions en marche. Je fis éclairer nos flancs et les défubler. Nous ne fûmes inquiétés nulle part. L'ennemi avait éprouvé de grandes pertes et appris qu'il ne pouvait se mesurer avec nous qu'à l'abri de ses murailles.

Nous fîmes quelques courtes haltes, indispensables pour le soin de nos blessés, et vers six heures du soir, à l'entrée de la nuit, nous arrivâmes dans notre camp, où nous trouvâmes toutes les ressources d'ambulance dont nous avions besoin. Nos braves matelots avaient fait dans la journée près de 40 kilomètres soutenu un combat où ils s'étaient vaillament conduits, et porté pendant tous le retour ou des blessés ou deux carabines.

Les Coréens ont dû se servir de cannons de divers calibres et de longues coulevrines à mêche portant jusqu'à 600 mètres. Leurs coups semblent avoir été dirigés de préférence sur nos officiers, qui étaient, il est vrai, au premier rang.

Ils ont montré une certaine énergie et un instinct guerrier que je ne m'attendais pas à rencontrer chez eux, d'après les renseignements fournis par nos missionnaires. C'étaient sans doute les meilleurs troupes régulières qui avaient été expédiées de Séoul et qui avaient franchi la rivière par les nombreux passages, soustraits à notre surveillance, de l'île de Kang-hoa qui a plus de 45 milles de côtes, et qui dans presque tout son pourtour n'est séparée que par un espèce étroit du continent ou d'îles successives y conduisant Tchiong-tung-sa est placé forte de Kang-hoa, le chef de l'île qui est elle-même le poste militaire avancé de la Corée et qui renfermait un nombre considérable de magasins d'armes et de munitions que vous avez fait détruire. Il faudrait un siège en règle, avec au moins 500 hommes et une batterie d'artillerie de campagne, pour nous emparer de cette citadelle, et à la distance où elle est de Kang-hoa, nous serions obligés de l'évacuer aussitôt après.

La présence d'un ennemi qui jusqu'ici ne s'était pas montré en nombre, exige de notre part un système de guerre à établir dans l'île, au lieu d'une simple occupation militaire parmi des populations que tous nos efforts ont inutilement appelées à nous. Les simples reconnaissances que nous avons faites jusqu'ici doivent devenir de véritables expéditions. Les signaux qui se multiplient jour et nuit sur toutes les hauteurs, les mouvements de troupes que nous apercevons en face et la désertion du pays par les habitants, prouvent assez que le gouvernement de Séoul ne veut traiter avec nous que dans sa capitale en présence de nos baïonnettes.

Nous pouvons rester encore longtemps sur l'offensive, mais c'est à la condition de désarmer entièrement nos bâtiments, comme ils le sont en ce moment, à quinze milles de distance, ne pouvant communiquer avec eux qu'à certains moments de la marée, par un cours d'eau très étroit qu'on pourrait facilement couper.

Je ne saurais assez vous dire, Amiral, combien j'ai été satisfait des 150 hommes que je commandais. Permettez-moi de vous citer Mr. de Thouars, officier d'une rare énergie, à qui je dois la prompte et intelligente organisation du convoi des blessés. M.M. Delasalle et Zuber, qui dans leur élan sont arrivés jusqu'aux remparts, le premier était grièvement blessé. Mr. Laguerre accourru au secours de Mr. Delasalle, Mr. de Chabannes, plein d'intrépidité, malgré sa blessure au genou. Le quartier-maître Nédellec, blessé au bras, pendant qu'il soutenait Mr. de Chabannes et qui n'a pas voulu l'abandonner. M. Suenson, officier danois, qui a deployé un beau courage et qui a été blessé à la jambe. M. Chatel animant sa compagnie avec beaucoup d'entrain.

Je termine mon rapport. J'aurais trop de noms à vous donner, Amiral. J'aurais l'honneur de vous adresser les états de proposition que vous m'avez demandés, en faveur des officiers et marins qui se sont les plus particulièrement fait remarquer par leur bravoure, et que je vous prie instamment de recommander à la bienveillance du ministre. J'y joindrai la liste des blessés qui s'élève au nombre de 29 dont 5 officiers.

Je suis …

Le Capitaine de vaisseau, Commandant Supérieur des Compagnies de débarquement,

Olivier

巡撫營 ➞ 議政府(1866. 11. 11/高宗三年十月五日)

프랑스 함대 정황 보고

巡撫營以甲串津碇留異船沒數下流向于富平境千總 梁憲洙使之移陣該府啓該營啓言卽見先鋒中軍李容熙馳報則月串津碇留異大船一隻下來與甲串津三隻船碇立分在洋船忽聚一處抑何意思大陣戒嚴之節倍前審愼云矣又啓言卽見先鋒中軍李容熙馳報則當日辰時甲串津碇留異大小船沒數擧碇下流向德浦鎭前洋而去鱗次到付德浦僉使馳報內體大異船四隻及從小船等今日辰時下來本鎭前洋向于富平境云如彼凶賊不卽勦滅任其恣意生還憤惋之餘不勝悚惶今方執捉船隻於近浦委送別軍官于江華府看審後摘奸形止馳報則異大船二隻碇留於富平境異船所留之傍二隻則仍向于細於島之外而不見其形江華府城內城外摘奸次分送別軍官 朴鼎和 申錫範而當此一府空虛之時亂民作梗亦所當念故使哨官 秋正旭領率一哨軍姑爲防守而賊旣逃矣安民爲急亦爲傳令于鼎足山守城千總 梁憲洙處使之移陣入府揭榜各處慰撫居該府留守來到之前姑留陣之意申飭云矣

140

巡撫營 ➞ 議政府(1866. 11. 11/高宗三年十月五日)

정족산(鼎足山) 전투 후 양측 사상자 보고

巡撫營以鼎足山賊漢致死實數啓

該營啓言卽見先鋒中軍李容熙馳報則鼎足山守城千總 梁憲洙手本內賊酋昨既見敗今必逞毒故益加戒嚴以待之昨日戰死砲手卽楊州尹 興吉而千總撫屍痛哭以白木斂殯被傷者卽船頭堡別將 金聲豹 洪川砲手李邦元 春川砲手李長成而金聲豹則千總親自吮之至於唇泡尙難必生李長成等使諸校扶護藥治亦在死生未分中矣關西砲手九十三名遊擊將崔慶善前五衛將 洪錫斗領率海西砲手五十名兵曹佐郎 韓性根領率到陣稍慰軍心而彼既衆強有不敵之歎竊聞江邊砲手五百名不日內到大陣云到卽越送俾振軍勢昨戰時彼漢六名之死在南門之外我軍目見分明只以六名報達矣昨夜村民四五人來告陣上曰彼漢敗歸時詳見于中路則行且死者爲四十餘僵屍相續彼皆束屍作幾駄而去云然則彼之致死無慮爲五十餘所獲彼物之輸來者第竢到陣一一考閱輸上計料云矣

H. de Bellonet ➞ 恭親王(1866. 11. 11)

總署의 사전조사 제안의 거절 사유 및 조선 침공의 정당성 주장

Pékin 11 Novembre 1866

Mg[r]

Je regrette beaucoup que V. A. n'ait pas su deviner les réponses qui m'ont engagé à garder le silence après les offres qu'elle me faisait dans Sa Communication du 16 juillet dernier. Puisqu'elle revient avec insistance sur ce sujet, je crois devoir lui opposer les motifs de ma conduite en la priant de vouloir bien se rappeler que j'ai évité, tant que j'ai pu, de faire une communication aussi désagréable au Gouvernement Chinois.

En premier lieu, le massacre des missionnaires français est un de ces crimes irrémissibles que rien ne peut excuser. Pour nous importe donc de connaître les raisons qui ont poussé les Coréens à commettre cet exécrable forfait. Le fait est là, il nous suffit de le connaître pour que ceux qui s'en sont rendus coupables en soient punis d'une manière éclatante ; les Ministres qui ont donné les ordres et les mandarins qui les ont exécutés, par la perte de leurs têtes et la confiscation de leurs biens qui seront distribués aux familles de leurs victimes, le Roi, qui a toléré, commandé ou même n'a pas empêché ces armes pour la perte de son trône et peut-être pire encore.

J'ai déjà donné les instructions les plus précises pour que les mandarins coupables dont j'ai pu me procurer les noms soient jugés et exécutés aussitôt qu'ils tomberont entre nos mains. Quant au sort de l'ancien Roi de Corée, il est soumis en ce moment à la décision de l'Empereur, mon Auguste Souverain.

En second lieu, j'ai le regret d'être forcé d'avouer à V. A. que les rapports qui depuis cinq mois, me sont parvenus ou qui ont été envoyés à Paris sur les évènements de Corée, font preuve de bien lourdes suspicions de complicité sur le Gouvernement Chinois. Il est affirmé dans plusieurs que l'ambassade coréenne venue l'hiver dernier, a porté à Pékin le projet de massacre, et en a remporté une approbation tacite et l'approbation de quelques membres du Gouvernement Chinois. L'avis qui nous en fut donné au passage de la mission coréenne par le Lioatong fut reçu assez légèrement et considéré comme une de ces rumeurs populaires auxquelles il ne faut point prendre garde: les évènements ont trompé notre confiance. Le mystère qui a enveloppé ensuite les 3 missions coréennes qui se sont succédées à Pékin depuis le mois de juillet, l'envoi en Corée d'un ambassadeur chinois publiquement annoncé dans les gazettes, les bruits de mobilisation des troupes tartares qui nous sont venus de l'autre côté de la Grande Muraille, cette insistance même à chercher une excuse aux Coréens au lieu de leur montrer [___] de l'horreur de leurs crimes, toutes ces choses contraires aux usages que malheureusement V. A. ne connaît pas encore, [___] sans nul doute une [___] impression en Europe et vont faire considérer avec défiance la conduite du G[t] chinois.

Comme tout le monde n'a pas les mêmes raisons que moi de croire à la sincérité et à la bonne volonté de V. A. I., on aurait trouvé pour le moins étrange que je confiasse le soin d'une enquête à ceux-là même qui auraient eu intérêt à ne pas découvrir la vérité.

En troisième lieu, nous avons été deux fois les dupes d'une enquête conduite par les autorités chinoises seules, et nous ne recommencerons pas. La comédie qui s'est jouée au Sse-tchouen autour de Tien-ching cheou, celle qui dure encore aujourd'hui au sujet du meurtre de l'abbé Mabileau nous ont donné de trop dures leçons sur la manière impudente dont les autorités provinciales abusaient de notre confiante loyauté pour que nous puissions l'oublier de longtemps.

V. A. ne doit plus douter elle-même de la manière dont beaucoup de mandarins comprennent le devoir de dire la vérité à l'Empereur, après les preuves matérielles que je lui ai fait présenter dernièrement, et elle doit comprendre qu'ayant depuis plusieurs mois déjà ces preuves dans les mains, et n'attendant qu'une occasion pour les faire connaître, il m'était difficile d'entrer de gaieté du cœur dans une nouvelle enquête qui aurait infailliblement amené les mêmes résultats.

En quatrième lieue, V. A. ignore probablement que la guerre, qui pour nous est un plaisir que les Français recherchent avec passion, est loin d'être dommageable aux populations. Nous combattons et nous cherchons à détruire le Gouvernement et son armée, nous lui faisons tout le mal possible dans ses établissements publics et militaires aussi bien que dans ses propriétés Royales mais nous respectons le bien du pauvre et le peuple gagne à notre présence. Nos armées ne vivent pas comme les armées chinoises en pillant le pays qu'elles traversent et en malmenant les habitants. Au contraire nos soldats, bien payés et bien disciplinés font la richesse du paysan en achetant ses denrées et en gagnant bien vite l'amitié des populations paisibles.

D'ailleurs, ce que V. A. ignore aussi peut-être, c'est que le peuple de Corée loin de nous être hostile, loin de défendre un Gouvernement qui l'opprime et le réduit à la misère, nous appelle comme ses libérateurs. Ce sont des Coréens, et pas des Coréens chrétiens, qui ont fourni au seul missionnaire qui ait échappé au massacre, les moyens de nous en porter la nouvelle en lui disant: "Allez chercher les étrangers et revenez avec eux." Ils savent que nous ne faisons pas la guerre aux populations inoffensives, que nous allons les délivrer de tous les petits tyrans qui les gouvernent, que nous allons leur donner la liberté et la richesse en ouvrant leur pays au commerce et à l'industrie de toutes les nations; que nous ferons régner l'ordre, la justice et la prospérité. Aussi, je le dis très sincèrement à V. A. I., nous aurons pour nous tout le peuple, qui nous aidera au lieu de nous nuire, et c'est lui qui nous livrera le pays, les autorités, et la famille Royale, dès qu'il verra qu'il peut le faire sans danger.

Enfin, que V. A. nous permette de lui faire observer que le massacre des Missionnaires Français était un outrage au G^{t} de l'Empereur, et qu'un outrage ne se discute pas, il se punit.

Je crois, du reste, que cette punition éclatante aura pour le G^{t} Chinois de très grands avantages. Elle fera réfléchir les autorités provinciales de la Chine sur les inconvénients de trop écouter leurs passions personnelles sans tenir compte des intérêts généraux de l'Empire, ni des idées nouvelles que représentent les étrangers et qu'ils sont prêts à soutenir par les armes s'ils ne peuvent les faire adopter autrement. Notre expédition en Corée évitera peut-être à la Chine une intervention militaire que les efforts conciliants de V. A. n'auraient probablement pas empêchée.

Je dois, en terminant, faire observer à V. A. que les opérations militaires une fois commencées comme elles le sont aujourd'hui, je n'ai pas le pouvoir de les arrêter avant que nous n'ayons atteint le but que nous nous proposions. Toute tentative de conciliation serait donc maintenant inutile à moins que l'ancien Roi de Corée ne se rendit à discrétion et n'implorât la clémence de l'Empereur, notre Auguste Souverain en se remettant à sa générosité. C'est à V.A. de voir si elle peut donner ce conseil au G^{t} Coréen.

Je suis etc.

Henry de Belloné (*Sic*)

【漢譯文】

法國照會

爲照會事 接准來文 內開朝鮮國殺害教衆一事 似可先行據理查詢 不必遽啓兵端 本應隨時照覆 因有格外情由難覆 玆旣備丈催覆 不能不逐一說明 儻有逆耳之言 統冀原諒 當念先不遽覆之意 查朝鮮國殘殺本國主教竝傳教士及教衆多命 斯實萬不容赦之罪 不論有無緣故 本國不屑查詢 有此兇擧 卽應興師征勦所有授意之大吏 及同謀加功之屬員 定須治之死罪 竝將其家産變價 分給被殺教衆之家 以補所受之害 至於該國國王不問係伊自出諭令 或從該國大員兇行 應暫罷其王爵 聽候本國大皇帝降旨辦理 再本大臣探聽 有該國於未擧行之先曾通意於貴國 又有言及去歲高麗官至京師 亦未瞞貴國知曉此事 復查去歲朝鮮官赴京 其跟役中有天主教一人 行至遼東地方 尋見本處法國人 再三說高麗立有此意 特爲來京相商 查高麗國行兇之後 三次派官來京 又見貴國降旨 派官前赴高麗 又聞巷議街談 言貴國在口外挑兵 前往朝鮮幫同會戰 及准貴親王屢次來文 似有包庇之意 難免疑猜 本大臣若請貴國代爲查詢 恐令疑者驚訝 况兇聞甚遙 貴親王亦必知查詢匪易 如四川前辦田興恕 及現今本國教士瑪弼樂被殺二案 可知外省官員 不能實心查詢矣 更有平空揑造假印各等弄虛之事 本大臣豈能放心 特請代爲查詢 貴親王勸不必遽啓兵端 有憐恤兩國民人之意 但法國向來與別國交兵 從無毒害敵國民人之處 兩國不睦 搆怨興兵 多由該員辦理不善所致 竝非因民而起 故用兵專與敵國官兵打仗 若地方官物 或攻或取 皆可任便 若民地民業 一概無犯本國兵丁糧餉日發 一時不能短乏 萬不致於路搶刦民人食物 致令鷄犬不甯且所需各等全係價買 爲令敵國民人 漸知敬重 朝鮮民人 本無怨恨外洋之心該國官員 性情殘暴 其國苛政 民久苦之 私望援救 如盼雲霓 此次殺害主教竝傳教士 實無民人同謀 且救護一位教士 民人設法逃躲 幸脫虎口 是該國人明知外洋風俗 無害良民之意 又知外洋人到伊國 無非爲通商貿易起見 更屬彼此有益之事 揣高麗民人 定無與本國相敵者 大約欲相幫本國者 容或有之 豈能驚訝 總之朝鮮殺法國主教竝傳教士數員 實與法國有重大之恨 萬不能不興師征勦 復何理論 且此次用兵 實有益於貴國不淺 因中國外省官員多讎恨外國人 祗圖一時得意 竝不念其所爲 遺累國家 本大臣甚望此等官員 知法國與高麗交兵之情 早爲酌量 如何免中外國早晩失和 至法國與朝鮮國用兵 早已交鋒 本大臣實不能阻止 除非該國國王自行投順本國大皇帝前

求恕 聽候降旨辦理 至解和戎事 暫難相講 不知貴親王可否勸該國王 爲此
照覆

【英譯文】

M. de Bellonet to Prince Kung

NOVEMBER 11, 1866

Sir:

I regret greatly that your highness could not divine the reasons which constrained me to keep silence after the offers you made to me in your communication of the 16th of July motives of my conduct, begging you to be pleased to remember that I have avoided as much as possible making a communication so disagreeable to the Chinese government.

In the first place, the massacre of the French missionaries is one of those unpardonable crimes which nothing can excuse. It is no consequence, therefore, for us to know the reasons which led the Coreans to commit this execrable offence; the deed is done' it is sufficient for us to know that they have thereby rendered themselves culpable, and may be punished for it in a signal manner: the ministers who gave the orders, and the mandarins who executed them, by the loss of their heads and the confiscation of their property, which will be distributed among the families of their victims' the King who tolerated or commanded, or who did not even prevent the crime, by the loss of his throne, and perhaps still more. I have already given the most precise instructions that the culpable mandarins, whose names I have been able to procure, shall be tried and executed as soon as they fall into our hands. As for the fate ci-devant King of Corea, it is now subject to the decision or the Emperor, my August sovereign.

In the second place, I regret to be forced to declare to your imperial highness that the reports that have reached us these five months, and which have been sent to Paris, upon the events in Corea, force upon us very serious suspicions of complicity on the part of the Chinese government. It is affirmed by many that the Corean embassy, which came last winter, brought to Peking the project of the massacre, and carried back a tacit authorization and the approbation of some members of the Chinese government. The notice which was given us of the transit of the Corean mission, through Liantung, was received very lightly, and considered a sone of those popular rumors which need not put one on his guard. Events have deceived our confidence.

The mystery which later surrounded the three Corean missions which came to Pekin in the month of July' the sending to Corea of an ambassador, publicly announced in the Gazete' the reports of the recruiting and mobilization of Tartar troops, which came to us from the other side of the great wall' this very eagerness to seek an excuse for the Coreans, rather than to show themselves horror-stricken at their crime-all these thins, contrary to usages which, unhappily, your highness is not yet acquainted with, will, without a doubt, produce a painful impression in Europe, and will tend to cause the conduct of the Chinese government to be regarded with suspicion. As every one has not the same reasons which I have for believing in the sincerity and good will of your imperial highness, it will be less strange that I should confess some anxiety for an inquiry to those very ones who might have an interest in not discovering the truth.

In the third place, we have been twice the dupes of an inquiry conducted by the Chinese authorities alone, and we shall not begin again. The dissimulation which was practiced in Sz'chula in regard to the affair at Chun-chia-chan, and that which still continues in suspense respecting the murder of Abbe Mabileau, have given us too severe lessons regarding the insolent manner in which the provincial authorities have abused our confiding fidelity, to prevent our forgetting it for a long time. Your imperial highness ought not yourself to be ignorant of the manner in which many of the mandarins understand the duty of telling the truth to the Emperor, after the material proofs which I have lately presented to you' and you should understand that, having already, during many months, these proofs in my hands, and only waiting for an occasion to make them known, it has been difficult for me to enter with lively interest into a new inquiry, which would, without fail, lead to the same results.

In the fourth place, your imperial highness is probably ignorant that war, which for us is a pleasure, which the French passionately seek, is far from being detrimental to the people at large. We fight against and seek to destroy the government and its armies' we do all the harm possible in its military and public establishments, as well as in the royal property' but we respect the property of the poor, and the people gain by our presence. Our armies do not live like the Chinese armies by pillaging the countries they traverse, nor in maltreating the inhabitants' on the contrary, our soldiers, well paid and well disciplined, add to the riches of the country by spending their money, and very quickly gain the friendship of the peaceable. That which your highness is, perhaps, also ignorant of, is that the people of Corea, far from being hostile, far from defending a government which oppresses them and reduces them to misery, address us as their deliverers. It was some of the Coreans, and not the Christian Coreans, who furnished to the only missionary who escaped the massacre the means of bringing us the news saying to him, "go, seek the foreigners, and return with them." They know that we do not make war upon inoffensive people, that we are going to deliver them from all the petty tyrants who govern them, that we are going to give them their liberty and riches by opening their country to the commerce and industry of all nations, and that we shall inaugurate the reign of order, justice, and prosperity. And, I tell your imperial highness, very sincerely, we shall have on our side most certainly all the peopole, who will aid instead of injuring us' and it is they who will deliver up to us the country, the authorities, and the royal family as soon as they see that they can do it without danger.

Finally, your imperial highness will permit me to bring to your notice that the massacre of the French missionaries was an outrage against the government of the Emperor, and such as outrage, it is evident, as cannot be discussed. Moreover, I believe that this conspicuous punishment will be of great advantage to the Chinese government. It will lead the provincial authorities to reflect upon the inexpediency of listening too much to their personal prejudices, without taking into consideration the general interests of the empire nor the new ideas which foreigners bring forward, and which they are ready to support by arms if they cannot otherwise cause them to be accepted. Our expedition in Corea will, perhaps, avert in China a military intervention, which conciliatory efforts of your imperial highness would not probably prevent.

I ought, in closing, to bring to the notice of your imperial highness that military operations once commenced, as they now are, I cannot stop them before we shall have attained the end we have set for ourselves. Every attempt at conciliation will now be useless, unless the cidevant king of corea surrenders at discretion, and implores the mercy of the Emperor, our August sovereign, trusting to his generosity. It is for your highness to see if you can give this advice to the Corean government.

I have, &c.,

HENRI DE BELLONET

巡撫營 ➞ 議政府(1866. 11. 12/高宗三年十月六日)

강화도 피해 상황 및 조곡(漕穀) 탈환 보고

巡撫營以沁都內外城被燒形止及向日見奪漕穀遺在數爻馳啓

該營啓見卽見先鋒中軍李容熙馳報則鼎足山守城千總 梁憲洙手本內沁都摘奸別軍官 朴鼎和 申錫範回告內經劫敗局滿目慘痛而內城則長寧殿 萬寧殿客舍及各公廨竝入灰燼而貳衙政堂只餘三間作廳則完校宮忠烈祠 閱武堂中營及捕廳完民戶則不可一一計數而灰燼過半東西門完南門門隻及懸板女城盡爲毁破城上左右分列我國鎗十二柄外城則鎭海樓內民家一戶被燒鎭海寺前禁營庫訓局 御營兩庫燒燼人定鍾運到外城內路上我國大碗口二坐落在於甲串浦邊銃筒四坐散在於外城內外向日見奪漕運米遺在甲串浦民家假量爲四百餘石而漕船一隻掛岸中又有二百石而人民空虛日勢且暮未及照數故使領軍哨官秋正旭卽爲收拾守直云矣六百餘石之米係是稅穀請令廟堂稟處允之又啓言卽見先鋒中軍李容熙馳報則所獲彼物輸來之際適失水站今始來到故輸上云矣卽自臣營捧上一一照驗則無非麤雜亦多破傷姑俟鼎足城接戰軍上來查問先後放次第分給計料

143

巡撫營 ➞ 議政府(1866. 11. 12/高宗三年十月六日)

덕포(德浦) 매복 작전 성공 보고

巡撫營以洋船去路別軍官 李基祖督軍交戰凶酋逃走啓

該營啓言卽見先鋒中軍李容熙馳報則洋船去來之路擬設伏兵今初四日使 別軍官 李基祖率別武士崔養崙砲手五十名別破陣三名往德浦埋伏於該鎭浦邊矣今日辰時量異大船四隻齊到埋伏處我兵放砲發銃則異大船四隻一時放砲飛礮兩下李基祖躬冒直入拔劍督軍一場交戰之際洋舶四面煙焰昏黑其疾如飛凶酋之被傷幾許未能詳知從可遁魄逃走而我軍別無傷損實爲萬幸云矣

G. Roze (1866. 11. 13) → P. de Chasseloup-Laubat

강화도에서 전사한 프랑스 해병 3인의 인적사항 송부

Guerrière, mouillage de l'Ile Boisée, le 13 novembre 1866

J'ai l'honneur d'adresser à V. Exc. en double expédition, les actes de décès des sieurs :

Goaziou, Paul-Marie, Sergent d'arme de 2e classe,
Pallier, Gilber, Quartier-Maître de manœuvre de 2e cl,
Et Grosselin, Jean-Marie, Matelot de 2e classe,

Tous les 3 morts le 26 octobre dernier des suites de blessures reçues devant l'ennemi à Kang-hoa (Corée).

J'y joins les certificats exigés par l'ordonnance du 26 janvier 1832, pour établir les droits à la pension des familles de ces marins. Une expédition de ces dernières pièces a été, d'ailleurs, transmise par Goaziou au Conseil d'admon de la Don de Brest ; pour Pallier à Mr le Commissaire de l'inscription maritime du même port, et pour Grosselin, à Mr. le Commissaire du quartier de St Brieuc.

Deux de ces braves gens laissent des enfants en bas âge, Grosselin et Pallier ; l'autre était le soutien de ses vieux parents. Je prends la liberté de les recommander à la sollicitude de V. Exc. et la prie de vouloir bien leur accorder un secours, sur la caisse des Invalides, en attendant que le travail de la pension ait pu être établi.

Signé : G. Roze

145

巡撫營 ➡ 議政府(1866. 11. 15/高宗三年十月九日)

프랑스 함대 정황 보고

巡撫營以富平碇留異船三隻向于細於島啓

該營啓言卽見先鋒中軍李容熙馳報則到付德浦僉使　李斗鉉所報富平境碇留異大船五隻中三隻今日開東向于細於島外本鎭瞭望則阻山不見一時到付富平府使　趙秉老牒呈以爲煙筩船一隻初八日午時下去于八尾島又啓言卽見先鋒中軍今初八日戌時馳報則當日酉時到付通津府使　愼哉芝及德浦僉使所報今日午時富平境碇留六隻異大船中一隻向永宗而去又啓言卽見平安道雲山郡赴陣砲手齊訴則以爲本邑出身安樂豊乃壬申軍功人故加德僉使如坤之子也自聞洋賊之變奮發忠義自願赴陣之際巧値身病不得遂意賣其所居之家辦錢一百五十兩而使其子追及該邑砲手等於黃州地傳給以助糧資云錢雖不多顧其慷慨發憤誠可謂世濟其美矣如此之類另施褒奬之典恐好請令廟堂稟處允之

G. F. Seward (1866. 11. 15) ➞ W. H. Seward

프랑스 함대의 한강 봉쇄 보고

U.S. Consulate General
Shanghai, Nov. 15 1866

To His Excellency,
Honorable William H. Seward,
Secretary of State,
Washington.

Sir:

I transmit herewith inclosed a copy of a notification regarding the blockage of the Seoul River in Corea by the French Admiral made by me this day.

I have the honor to be
Sir
Your Obedient Servant
Geo F. Seward

Notice of blockade of the river Seoul by the French naval squadron*

*제1권 106번 문서의 영역문.

147

G. Roze (1866. 11. 15) → 북경 주재 각국 공사*

한강 봉쇄의 해제 선언

À bord de *la Guerrière*, mouillage de l'île Boisée (Corée) le 15 Novembre 1866

J'ai l'honneur de porter à votre connaissance qu'après avoir occupé militairement Kang-hoa, une des principales placcs de la Corée, et atteint le but que je m'étais proposé, j'ai décidé que le Blocus de la Rivière de Séoul, que j'avais établi, serait levé à partir du 18 de ce mois.

J'ai l'honneur de vous en transmettre la notification officielle que je vous prie de vouloir bien porter à la connaissance de (vos ou nos) nationaux.

Signé : G. Roze

Notification de la cessation du Blocus de la Rivière de Séoul

Nous soussigné Contre-Amiral Commandant en chef les forces Navales de Sa Majesté l'Empereur des français en Chine et au Japon, déclarons que le Blocus de la rivière de Séoul établi par notre déclaration du 11 octobre dernier, sera levé à partir de ce jour.

À bord de *la Guerrière*, le 18 Novembre 1866

Signé : G. Roze

*수신자 명단: M.M. le Ministre de France, d'Angleterre, de Russie, de Prusse, des Etats-Unis, d'Espagne, de Belgique, d'Italie à Pékin ; Le Ministère de France à Yokohama, Le Consul Général de France à Shanghaï, Monsieur le Gouverneur de Cochinchine

G. Roze (1866. 11. 15) → 상하이 주재 총영사 외*

강화도 점령과 서울의 공격을 위한 추가병력 지원 요청

À bord de *la Guerrière*, mouillage de l'île Boisée (Corée), le 15 Novembre 1866

Le Ministre de France à Pékin

Monsieur le Consul Général,

J'ai eu l'honneur de vous informer par une dépêche spéciale, N° 392, que les corps de débarquement de ma Division avaient pris, le 16 octobre dernier, la ville de Kang-hoa, l'une des places fortes les plus considérables de la Corée. Depuis ce jour cette ville a été occupée militairement par les forces françaises.

Le Gouvernement de Séoul m'avait fait des ouvertures qui sont demeurées sans résultats. La saison avançant, je me suis décidé à me retirer le 11, de ce mois après avoir fait raser et détruire tout ce qui appartenait à l'Etat, brûler des quantités immenses d'armes et de munitions.

Dès ma première exploration, j'avais reconnu l'impossibilité pour moi de remonter jusqu'à la Capitale à cause des moyens restreints dont je dispose et je m'étais, dès ce moment, arrêté à l'idée d'un simple coup de main sur la côte.

Les troupes nombreuses réunies dans les environs par le Roi de Corée, les préparatifs de défense qui m'ont été annoncés, les instincts belliqueux du peuple qui ne peuvent êtres révoqués en doute, n'ont fait que me confirmer dans mon premier sentiment et j'ai fait connaître à Son Excellence Monsieur le Ministre de la Marine les forces que je considère comme indispensable pour aller jusqu'au cœur du pays et l'amener à traiter avec nous.

L'expédition que je viens de faire si modeste qu'elle soit, en aura préparé une plus sérieuse, si elle est jugée nécessaire, et l'a rendue possible en lui frayant la route et en lui fournissant de précieuses indications. Elle aura, d'ailleurs, profondément frappé l'esprit de la nation Coréenne en lui prouvant que sa prétendue invulnérabilité n'était que chimérique. Enfin, la destruction d'un des boulevards de Séoul et les pertes considérable que nous avons fait éprouver au Gouvernement Coréen, en le frappant dans ses richesses et ses

*수신자: M.M. le ministre de France à Pékin, Le ministre de France à Yokohama, Le consul Général de France à Shanghai, Le Gouverneur de Cochinchine

approvisionnements, ne peuvent manquer de le rendre plus circonspect à l'avenir.

Le but que je m'étais proposé a donc été complètement rempli et le meurtre de nos missionnaires a été vengé.

Il ne me reste plus maintenant qu'à attendre les ordres de l'Empereur et les renforts qui me seront envoyés, si les opérations contre ce pays doivent être continuées.

Comme je vous le fais connaître par une déclaration officielle, j'ai décidé que le blocus de la Rivière de Séoul serait levé le 18 de ce mois, jour où nous quitterons la Corée pour nous rendre au Japon. Signé : G. Roze

Permettez-moi, Mr. le Ministre, d'appeler votre attention sur un fait qui pourrait se produire ; le Gouvernement de Corée, redoutant une nouvelle attaque pourrait peut-être s'adresser au Gouvernement Chinois pour lui demander de secours en armes. Vous jugerez, sans doute, utile de veiller, autant que cela vous sera possible, à ce qu'un semblable contrat ne puisse se produire ni recevoir son exécution.

Signé : G. Roze

W. H. Seward(1866. 11. 16) ➞ S. W. Williams

8월 8일자 Williams의 공문에 대한 회신

DEPARTMENT OF STATE
Washington, November 16, 1866

Sir:

Your despatch of August 8, No. 37,* has been received.

The information it gives of the execution of two Roman Catholic bishops and nine priests, together with a large number of Christians, in March last, in the Corean peninsula, is, indeed, painful and singularly exciting.

The proceedings of the French admiral, as indicated in your communication, will be regarded with great interest throughout christendom.

I shall expect that you will keep me well advised concerning the same.

I am, Sir, your obedient servant,
WILLIAM H. SEWARD

S. WELLS WILLIAMS, Esq.

*제1권 90번 문서.

150

總署(1866. 11. 16/同治五年十月十日) ➞ H. de Bellonet

조불(朝佛) 중재 시도에 대한 해명

給法國照會

爲照覆事 接准貴大臣照會 大意以中國有包庇朝鮮之意 本爵閱之 深爲駭異 查本年六月九月間 致貴大臣照覆 本爵不過因貴國與朝鮮搆兵 兩國均有損傷 斷無坐視之理 不得不從中排解 冀以保全兩國民命 在本爵係屬一番美意 今閱貴大臣來文 忽以跟役一面之詞 及巷議街談毫無影響之言 遽見猜疑 竝且顯然形之筆墨 是本爵此番美意 貴大臣全未理會 反疑另有別情 本爵心中不快實甚 來文所謂朝鮮遣官來京 及中國派員前往一節 查朝鮮與中國往來歷有成案 竝不始於今日 本年該國使臣來京 與中國派員前往 皆自來應行典禮不得因貴國與該國搆兵 遂爾廢棄 至所稱中國挑兵幫同會戰一層 查國家如果用兵 乃係人所共知共見之事 其有無此事 不待辯而自明 而來文亦據以爲詞 更屬有心誣指 且來文明言得自風聞 風聞者無據之謂也 以無據之言爲據 此豈各國相交之理乎 貴大臣於本爵之美意 旣不能理會 且復隨意誣指 本不必再相計較 惟來文相關彼此和好 是以仍據理照覆貴大臣查照可也

【佛譯文】

Pékin le 16 novembre 1866

Le 4e juin de la 10e lune j'ai reçu du V. E. une dépêche dans laquelle la pensée dominante est que la Chine cherche à excuser la Corée. La lecture de cette lettre m'a causé la plus grande surprise.

Dans les reponses officielles que j'adressai à V. E. dans les 6e et 9e lunes ma pensée était que Votre noble pays s'engageant dans une guerre avec la Corée les deux parties devaient naturellement en éprouver de grands dommages. Je pensai qu'il n'était pas convenable de rester spectateur indifférent et que mon devoir était d'offrir mes bons offices pour ramener les choses à une entente cordiale et éviter ainsi aux deux pays la perte de beaucoup de leurs sujets.

Certes c'était là de ma part une fort bonne pensée.

En lisant la lettre que vous m'écrivez je vois que sur les seuls dire d'un suivant (de la mission Coréenne), sur des rumeurs courant les rues et les carrefours, toutes paroles dépourvues d'une apparence quelconque de verité (litt. sans son ni ombre) V. E. se crée des doutes et encore ne se fait aucun scrupule de me les faire connaître par écrit, non seulement elle n'a pas compris le bon sentiment qui me faisait agir mais encore ce dernier n'a servi qu'à exciter dans son esprit le doute et la défiance.

Quant à la venue de plusieurs missions coréennes en Chine et à l'envoi en Corée d'un fonctionnaire chinois dont parle la lettre de V.E. je dirai que les rapports de la Chine avec la Corée sont depuis longtemps établis et réglés et que ce n'est pas d'aujourd'hui qu'ils commencent.

La venue de la Mission Coréenne à Pekin et la nomination d'un Envoyé Chinois en Corée sont deux faits résultant de lois anciennes que l'état de guerre entre la Corée et la France ne saurait en rien modifier ou détruire.

Quant aux troupes levées en dehors de la muraille pour aider la Corée je répondrai que si l'Empire Chinois se préparait à la guerre tout le monde le verrait et le saurait. Je ne crois pas qu'il soit nécessaire d'attendre que j'ai discuté avec V.E. l'existence réelle ou non d'un pareil état de choses pour qu'elle sache à quoi s'en tenir et quand elle met dans sa lettre une insinuation basée sur de pareils bruits c'est qu'elle a évidemment le désir de nous trouver des fautes.

D'autant plus qu'elle dit dans sa dépêche "fong ouen" "(Nous avons appris par les rumeurs ou les bruits publics) Or la rumeur publique est un bruit dénué d'aucune preuve et prendre pour preuves des dires qui en sont dénués n'est certainement pas avoir pour nous les égards que se doivent entre elles deux nations amies.

Puisque V.E. n'a pas voulu faire attention à la bonne intention qui me faisait agir et qu'au contraire elle nous accuse selon son bon plaisir je devrais m'abstenir de la faire ressortir d'avantage en la discutant mais comme sa lettre intéresse les bons rapports existant entre les deux pays je ne puis m'empêcher d'y faire une réponse basée sur la raison.

Tel est le but de la présente
10e jour de la 10e lune
Pour traduction conforme le 1er Interprète de la Légation
******

【英譯文】

Sir:

I have the honor to acknowledge the receipt of your excellency's despatch of the 11th instant, in which you intimate, in general terms, that it is the intention of the Emperor's government to screen and protect the Coreans-a most strange and surprising assertion! In my two former replies to your despatches I simply observed that if the French and Coreans came to blow both countries must necessarily suffer injury. There certainly was no desire on my part to become the arbiter, or to interfere [in the quarrel], but I could hardly do otherwise than urge the propriety of getting at a full explanation of the affair, and with the laudable desire of thereby preserving the lives of the people of both countries.

In the despatch under reply, the story told by an official attendant of the Coreans, together with the gossip of market places-things of which there is not the shadow of evidence-are all at once brought forward to cast suspicion on me, and obtain a sort of evidence by being put into words in your despatch. Seeing that my laudable desire [to promote peace] does not meet your excellency's views, but that, on the contrary, you make it a ground for suspecting me of other designs, I cannot but feel very highly dissatisfied.

You remark in your despatch that the Coreans have sent officers to Peking, and that China has despatched her agents to Corea; but this practice is of very long standing, and no recent thing. The officers who came from thence, and ours who went thither the present year, came and went on affairs of ceremonial, and in accordance with long-established usage' having no reference to the quarrel between France and Corea, they were not to be set aside or abrogated.

The remark that you make that China is preparing troops to take part in the conflict is sufficiently answered by simply stating that if his imperial majesty had decided to levy and prepare his forces, everybody would have heard or seen it. That there is nothing of the kind intended is so plain that it is needless to argue the point further; but its insertion in your despatch indicates a design to avail your self of such talk in order to implicate and embarrass others. You mention whence these rumors have come, and yet from such unproven reports you proceed to argue as if they were true. Is such a procedure compatible with friendly relations between nations? Sewing, therefore, that my efforts in the interests of peace do not at all meet your views, but that you rather make it an occasion of calumny, no room is left for any further discussion or arrangement of the matter' but it seemed to be incumbent on me, in view of the friendly relations which should be maintained between our governments, to make a reply to your present communication.

I have, &c.,

KUNG

M. DE BELLONET, Charge d'Affaires, &c.,

G. Roze(1866. 11. 16) → Primauguet 함장

강화도에서 탈취한 현금 상자 수송에 관한 지시

관련문서 (1) Laplace 함장에게 보낸 Roze의 현금상자 수송 지시(1866. 11. 16)

À bord de la frégate *la Guerrière*, le 16 novembre 1866

J'ai l'honneur de vous informer que je donne l'ordre de faire embarquer sur *le Primauguet* 19 Caisses numérotées de 1 à 19 et contenant des lingots d'argent estimés à une valeur de 197,231 francs 36 centimes.

Dès notre arrivée à Shanghaï vous voudrez bien vous entendre avec l'administration des Messageries pour que ces caisses soient transportées en France par le premier paquebot de cette administration qui partira et qu'elles soient remises et à Monsieur le Ministre de la Marine.

Vous aurez soin de retirer un connaissement que vous adressez en mon nom à Son Excellence.

Je vous envoie aussi une autre caisse contenant des objets en marbre et ayant la même destination. Vous ferez pour elle ce que je viens de dire pour les caisses d'argent et vous voudrez bien m'informer de la date de départ du tout de Shanghai.

Signé: G. Roze

【관련문서 1】

À Bord de la frégate *la Guerrière*, le 16 novembre 1866

Monsieur le Commandant du *Laplace*

J'ai l'honneur de vous envoyer une caisse contenant des syccès (*Sic*) et adressée à Mr. L'aide Commissaire Le Cardinal à Tche-foo. Ayez la bonté de la lui faire remettre dès votre arrivée. Il est bien entendu que vous ne prendrez cette caisse qu'en cours de transport.

Signé : G. Roze

G. Roze (1866. 11. 17) → P. de Chasseloup-Laubat

서울 공격이 불가능함을 보고

À bord de *la Guerrière*, le 17 novembre 1866, mouillage de l'Ile Boisée.

Je viens vous remercier avec effusion de la lettre que vous avez daigné m'adresser et par laquelle V. E. veut bien approuver la résolution qui m'avait conduit en Cochinchine.

En répondant à l'appel de l'Amiral de la Grandière, je n'ai accompli qu'un devoir bien naturel, mais je suis heureux et flatté tout à la fois du témoignage de haute satisfaction que je reçois de votre bienveillance. Quand je suis arrivé à Saïgon, l'insurrection était mineure, mes services ne pouvaient plus y être utiles. Je me suis hâté d'en partir pour retourner au centre de ma station où m'appelaient des devoirs nouveaux. Il n'était bruit en ce moment que des nouvelles apportées de la Corée où nos missionnaires avaient été mis à mort. Le retentissement de cet acte odieux avait produit une vive émotion parmi les étrangers résidant dans l'Extrême Orient, et, sous la coupe de ces impressions, j'ai pensé qu'il m'appartenait de chercher, par tous les moyens en mon pouvoir, à punir un crime qui avait été commis dans le rayon de mon commandement. Je me considérais avec raison comme un satellite envoyé au loin par la France pour veiller sur ses sujets et je regardais comme une obligation de faire au moins une tentative pour renseigner le Gouvernement de l'Empereur et lui donner la possibilité de venger le sang de nos missionnaires, quand le moment lui paraîtrait convenable. C'est animé de ces sentiments que j'ai fait ma première exploration et que je suis allé devant Séoul dont la position géographique était encore ignorée ; au point de vue maritime, cette exploration n'a pas été sans valeur et j'ai la confiance que vous avez bien voulu en apprécier les résultats.

Ainsi que j'ai eu l'honneur de l'écrire à V. E. dans mes dépêches officielles, ma préoccupation la plus constante a été de n'engager en rien le Gouvernement de l'Empereur et d'agir avec la plus extrême prudence pour mener à bonne fin l'entreprise que j'avais projetée.

J'ai compris en pénétrant au cœur de la Corée sur ce fleuve dont l'accès présente tant de difficultés à la navigation, qu'une attaque contre Séoul était impossible avec les seuls moyens dont je disposais, mais comme j'ai eu le soin de l'écrire à V. E. dès le principe je pouvais avec mes forces réunies frapper le Gouvernement de la Corée en détruisant le boulevard de sa puissance militaire que je pouvais atteindre sur l'Ile de Kang-hoa, je n'avais en vue qu'un coup de main et je prouvais en l'accomplissant, que chargé par le Gouvernement de l'Empereur de veiller sur les intérêts de ses sujets, je comprenais l'étendue de la mission qui m'était confiée.

Mon programme a été rempli de tous points. Kang-Hoa, la place la plus forte du Royaume a été présque complètement anéantie. Les établissements officiels, y compris la demeure du Roi, ont été rasés, et le Gouvernement de la Corée a vu que nous avions su trouver le chemin qui, dans un moment donné, pouvait conduire les Français jusqu'à Séoul. Comme je le dis dans mon rapport officiel, cette œuvre étant accomplie et le but de ma mission étant atteint, je suis parti à mon heure, sans y être forcé par les circonstances, et ayant exécuté l'opération que j'avais en vue, c'est à dire un coup de main dont le caractère était essentiellement maritime.

Les renseignements qui m'avaient été donnés ont été bien souvent en désaccord avec la réalité, mais j'avais appris à m'en défier et j'ai constamment agi en me mettant en garde contre des récits infidèles qui, dans bien des circonstances analogues et dans d'autres pays, avaient trompé la bonne foi des chefs d'expédition. Pour conquérir en effet un royaume aussi étendu que la Corée, ce ne sont pas quelques compagnies de débarquements qui seraient nécessaires, mais bien une armée de 3 à 4 mille soldats.

Je peux le dire en toute sincérité, au point de vue maritime, notre excursion en Corée a découvert un pays inconnu jusqu'ici aux navigateurs ; au point de vue militaire, nous n'avons eu que des succès, car même la reconnaissance exécutée par le Commandant Olivier vers la forteresse de Tchiong-tong-sa, malgré les blessés que nous y avons eus a prouvé une fois de plus aux Coréens la valeurs de nos marins, et nos ennemis restés retranchés derrière les murailles qui les abritaient, n'ont pas osé se mesurer en rase campagne avec une troupe dont ils avaient pu mesurer le nombre. Ils ne l'ont pas suivie dans son retour qui n'a été que la continuation de la reconnaissance du matin, et cette poignée d'hommes est rentrée dans nos cantonnements dans le même ordre qu'elle était partie.

Je peux donc dire avec raison que notre coup de main sur la Corée a réussi de toutes les manières. Les résultats ne peuvent être douteux, et je me suis retiré quand j'en ai jugé le moment convenable, après avoir entièrement rempli mon but et sans avoir engagé le Gouvernement de l'Empereur dans une entreprise dont le moment pouvait ne pas lui paraître opportun.

Nous avons pu nous livrer à des travaux d'hydrographie qui seront précieux dans l'avenir et grâce à l'habileté de nos capitaines nous avons eu le bonheur de n'avoir à subir aucun funeste accident dans ces parages dont l'accès avait paru impossible avant nous. J'ai donc lieu de me flatter, Monsieur le Ministre, que vous daignerez apprécier la résolution que j'ai prise en venant en Corée, et je serais bien heureux si vous vouliez bien assurer à mes efforts une approbation à laquelle j'attache tant de prise.

Signé : G. Roze

G. Roze (1866. 11. 17) ➜ P. de Chasseloup-Laubat

강화도 점령을 위한 군사 활동 및 조선으로부터의 철수 보고

À bord de *la Guerrière*, Mouillage de l'Ile Boisée (Corée) le 17 novembre 1866

Ainsi que j'ai eu l'honneur de l'écrire à V. Exc. le but que je m'étais proposé en débarquant à Kang-hoa, en détruisant cette place de guerre, la plus forte de la Corée, en bloquant rigoureusement la Rivière de Séoul, était de punir et d'humilier dans les limites des seuls moyens fournis par ma Division, un Gouvernement qui, dans la confiance de son impunité, avait osé faire massacrer nos missionnaires. Ce but est, à mes yeux, complètement atteint et bien que ce Gouvernement n'ait plus donné suite aux ouvertures qu'il m'avait adressé dès mon apparition, il n'en a pas moins ressenti profondément les effets du traitement sévère que je lui ai infligé. En prenant ainsi l'initiative d'une opération de guerre qui rentrait dans les prescriptions de mes devoirs, ma préoccupation la plus constante a été de n'engager en rien le gouvernement de l'Empereur. C'est ainsi que la campagne que je viens de faire en Corée a conservé son caractère essentiellement maritime; elle a été accomplie avec les seules ressources de la Division Navale, avec ses compagnies de débarquement et sans coûter au budget le moindre surcroît de dépenses. J'ose espérer que ces résultats seront jugés favorablement et qu'ils mériteront la haute approbation de V. Exc.

L'île de Kang-hoa, qui mesure 18 milles de longueur sur une largeur de 8 milles est d'une assez vaste étendue pour ne pouvoir être gardée et surveillée d'une manière complète par le personnel restant que j'avais pu réunir et dont le chiffre s'élevait à environ 400 bayonnettes depuis le départ du *Laplace*. Dans l'impossibilité de multiplier les points d'occupation qu'il m'eût été utile de conserver, j'ai dû m'attacher à nous retrancher aussi fortement que possible dans nos cantonnements et de rayonner au loin par l'envoi fréquent de quelques colonnes en reconnaissance. Cette mesure était d'autant plus nécessaire que les renseignements m'ont constamment fait défaut en Corée et que j'avais pu me convaincre combien ceux qui m'avaient été donnés, dès le principe, étaient erronés. Par cette raison, je n'ai jamais pu connaître ni l'esprit de la population ni ses sympathies, ses craintes ou ses espérances. Tous les villages des environs sont restés complètement déserts aussitôt après notre arrivée et les habitants qui fuyaient ainsi à notre approche paraissaient souvent éprouver des sentiments hostiles à notre égard. Je n'ai rien négligé cependant pour les ramener à nous, pour empêcher mes hommes de les molester, et pour attirer leur confiance ; je leur ai fait offrir maintes fois, de venir établir un marché aux portes de nos cantonnement en leur donnant l'assurance que tout ce qu'ils nous fourniraient leur serait scrupuleusement payé. Mais, soit par intimidation de leurs Mandarins, soit par un éloignement traditionnel contre les étrangers, ils sont restés constamment sourds à mon appel et c'est ainsi que nous sommes demeurés dans un isolement complet pendant notre séjour en Corée.

J'appris pourtant quelques jours après notre arrivée, par un chrétien, venu de Séoul, que l'apparition de nos bâtiments avait produit une vive agitation dans la Capitale et que le Gouvernement avait décrété aussitôt des mesures de toute sorte pour nous combattre. Une armée de 30,000 hommes fut créée et organisée dès le premier moment, un appel fut adressé aux volontaires et un millier y répondirent, des jonques devaient être armées en guerre pour venir attaquer nos bâtiments. La confection de brûlots fut ordonnée, enfin une colonne de 2 à 3 mille hommes dû se réunir dans l'île de Sonto, vis à vis la côte Ouest de Kang-hoa avec la mission d'y opérer une descente et marcher contre nous. Je ne sais si toutes ces mesures furent conçues et mises à exécution, mais elles n'avaient rien de surprenant et ce fut une raison pour moi de penser à nous établir plus fortement encore dans nos cantonnements. Cependant, je laissai la compagnie de *la Guerrière* sous le commandement de Mr d'Osery, dans la ville de Kang-hoa, où elle occupa les logements officiels du gouvernement parmi lesquels se trouve le palais du Roi, inoccupé depuis longtemps, fort jolie résidence que le souverain s'était réservé à côté du Yamoun du premier mandarin de l'île. Ce poste était à 3 kilomètres de nos positions.

La côte vis à vis celle que nous occupions et qui, dans cette partie en est séparée par une distance de 500 mètres, avait été quelquefois explorée par de faibles détachements de nos marins qui, dans les premiers temps, n'y avaient jamais aperçu un soldat ennemi. C'est là que la porte de Séoul est construite ; elle domine la tête du chemin qui, en suivant la rivière douce et dans quelques-unes de ses sinuosités, conduit jusqu'à la Capitale. Une porte semblable que nous avions vue dans notre première exploration termine la route sur la rive près de Séoul. Ces portes sont de structure assez monumentale, de forme ogivale et surmontées d'une toiture en pagode chinoise. Celle vis à vis de Kang-hoa est entourée de plusieurs maisons dont quelques unes font partie du Domaine du gouvernement et les autres appartiennent à la population. Nos détachements y avaient abordé plusieurs fois et y avaient rencontré, comme ailleurs, une absence complète d'habitants.

Le 26 octobre vers 7 heures ½ du matin, deux pelotons sous le commandement de M[r] le Lieutenant de V[eau] de Thouars furent envoyés pour examiner, comme par le passé, les environs de la plage opposée. Nos hommes étaient massés dans la chaloupe de *la Guerrière*, remorquée par le Canot à vapeur. Ces embarcations étaient sur le point d'accoster au môle, quand une décharge de mousqueterie fut envoyée à la distance de 15 à 20 mètres par des soldats coréens cachés derrière les maisons et les murailles. Bien que ne s'attendant pas à cet accueil, nos hommes ripostèrent aussitôt par un feu très vif de leur carabines et sautèrent immédiatement à terre pour se précipiter sur les ennemis. Mr Chatel, aspirant de 1e classe, fut le premier à leur tête; en détournant l'arme d'un soldat coréen, qui tirait sur lui, il fut blessé légèrement à la main, mais il put décharger son revolver sur ce soldat qui fut en même temps transpercé par la bayonnette de l'un de nos hommes. Les ennemis furent poursuivis à outrance. Je m'empressai d'accourir sur le lieu du combat, mais déjà nous étions maîtres de la place quand j'arrivai à terre et les Coréens dispersés fuyaient au loin sur le haut des montagnes qui dominent la rive. Ils avaient laissé un grand nombre de leurs morts sur les routes avoisinant. Malheureusement, cette affaire qui fait tant d'honneur au courage de nos marins, nous a coûté 3 hommes tué dans la chaloupe et 2 blessés. Dans cet engagement M[r] l'aspirant Chatel, s'est particulièrement distingué en s'élançant le premier sur l'ennemi: aussi ai-je l'honneur de solliciter auprès de V. Exc. la croix de la Légion d'honneur pour ce jeune officier qui s'est toujours fait remarquer par ses bons services et qui, dans cette dernière circonstance, a reçu une blessure en déployant la valeur.

Après 3 heures de courses dans les environs qui furent ainsi fouillés de tous côtés, je fis rallier mes hommes qui se rembarquèrent pour rejoindre leurs cantonnements.

Les Coréens que nous venions de culbuter formaient l'avant garde d'un rassemblement de troupes arrivées la veille de Séoul et qui, avait-on dit au Père Ridel, s'élevait au nombre de 2 à 3 mille hommes. Ces troupes avaient formé un camp près de la ville de Dondinn située à quelques kilomètres de la rive opposée et nous étaient cachés par des élévations de terrain. Souvent des groupes vinrent se montrer à nous sur les pentes des collines vu sur les hauteurs ; mais quand ils s'approchaient à distance, un obus envoyé à propos et quelquefois plusieurs coups de nos carabines les dispersaient aussitôt.

Ainsi que je l'ai déjà fait remarquer à V. Exc. le défaut de renseignements exacts ainsi que l'absence à peu près complète d'interprètes ont été pour moi la source de grandes difficultés. Aussi ayant accompli avec tout le succès désirable le coup de main que j'avais projeté sur Kang-hoa, après avoir bloqué rigoureusement Séoul précisément au moment où les Jonques chargées de riz arrivent des provinces du Sud pour alimenter la Capitale et avoir causé par ce fait un grand préjudice au gouvernement qui, dans ce pays, s'est institué le fermier général de presque toutes les productions, ressentant déjà les approches de l'hiver par des gelées et des coups de vent, désirant d'ailleurs ne pas m'absorber en Corée au détriment de mes autres obligations, j'avais formé le projet d'évacuer au premier jour l'île de Kang-hoa où aucun nouvel intérêt ne pouvait me retenir. Sur ces entrefaites, j'avais appris par les capitaines des canonnières que des renforts de troupes coréennes se trouvaient répandus autour de nos côtés et que leur nombre augmentait journellement. Bien que je n'eusse nullement à les redouter, je pouvais penser qu'elles pourraient me gêner au moment de l'évacuation, opération si difficile quand il s'agit d'un rembarquement en pays ennemi. Un corps nombreux, dont je n'ai pas su le chiffre exact, venait de débarquer sur l'Ile de Kang-hoa à l'un des points qui, par son éloignement, pouvait échapper à notre surveillance. Cette île qui a une grande étendue de côtes est en communication très facile et très rapprochée avec la terre ferme sur tous les points de son littoral. Ce qui permettait à un corps de troupes de débarquer à notre insu et sans que nous ayons la possibilité de nous y opposer. Le père Ridel sut d'une manière très vague que le rassemblement de soldats qui venait de passer sur l'île devait occuper une pagode à quelques kilomètres de nos cantonnements. Informé de ce fait, je donnai l'ordre au Commandant Olivier de prendre 4 pelotons, ce qui composait un effectif de 150 hommes et d'aller reconnaître la position exacte de cette pagode. En général les pagodes que nous avions vues autour de nous étaient entourées d'une faible muraille construite plutôt dans la pensée de servir au prestige de ces établissements religieux que dans l'intention d'en faire des réduits fortifiés. Il y avait lieu de croire qu'il en était de même pour celle qui nous était indiquée et dont nous avions ignoré l'existence. Le commandant Olivier fit 18 kilomètres de marche avant d'y arriver, ce qui était déjà une distance bien éloignée de nos cantonnements, devait surtout rentrer le soir même. Cette obligation de rentrer avant la nuit était indispensable pour ne pas dégarnir notre position sur la plage qui était restée sous la garde de 2 pelotons seulement, environ 70 hommes. Le Commandant Olivier trouva que la pagode qu'il venait reconnaître était située dans une position excessivement fortifiée et qu'elle était entourée de hautes et épaisses murailles bâties sur des crêtes de collines très abruptes qui la défendaient de toutes parts. N'entendant aucun bruit qui put lui révéler la présence d'un corps d'occupation et n'apercevant personne sur ces remparts, il s'en approcha avec précaution cependant à une distance de 300 à 400 mètres et envoya un détachement pour la reconnaître de plus près. Il s'apprêtait même à y pénétrer quand tout à coup un feu excessivement violent fut ouvert contre cette petite troupe ; cette première décharge à si courte distance, atteignit plusieurs de nos hommes qui furent plus ou moins blessés. Le commandant Olivier fit aussitôt marche en avant et l'engagement devint alors très vif, mais notre détachement, malgré toute son ardeur et son élan valeureux, fut obligé de faire quelques pas en arrière et de s'abriter derrière des replis de terrain pour tirer sur des ennemis qui restaient parfaitement retranchés derrière les remparts. Il eût fallu une artillerie de siège pour réduire cette position qui, aux yeux des officiers les plus compétents présents à cette action, était inexpugnable avec les moyens dont nous disposions. Les obusiers de 4 que nous possédions eussent été impuissants contre de semblables murailles et, d'ailleurs, nous n'avions pas de bêtes de somme pour les y porter. La veille encore nous avions essayé de charger une de ces pièces de 4 sur des bœufs mais ceux-ci tous très petits et très faibles avaient plié sous le fardeau et n'avaient pu servir à cet usage pour un aussi long trajet. Le commandant Olivier n'avait donc emmené avec lui que de la mousqueterie. Après quelques minutes d'un engagement aussi inégal, 29 de nos hommes étaient déjà blessés. C'était beaucoup pour un effectif aussi peu nombreux. Une seul fois l'ennemi fit un semblant de sortie mais elle lui coûta cher, et il se hâta de rentrer dans ses retranchements. Le Commandant Olivier prit une position à environ 1,000 mètres de la place ; tout en continuant le feu sur les Coréens, il fit travailler aux moyens de transporter pour les blessés. Après une heure environ consacrée à ce soin, il prit la route du retour et arriva le soir dans nos cantonnements en ordre parfait, après avoir fait 36 kilomètres dans la journée, sa petite troupe toujours prête à combattre et ramenant avec les blessés les armes de ces derniers dont pas une ne fut égarée ; personne des nôtres n'avait été tué. La contenance de nos hommes avait certainement assez intimidé l'ennemi pour l'empêcher de faire un retour offensif et le dissuader d'inquiéter leur marche. Dans cette affaire, dont le but n'était qu'une simple reconnaissance et qui, par l'entraînement naturel des circonstances, est devenue un combat, chacun des nôtres a fait noblement son devoir et s'est vaillamment conduit. Les officiers ont donné, comme toujours, les premiers, l'exemple de l'ardeur et du courage à la tête de leurs hommes et 5 d'entre eux ont été blessés. En mettant sous les yeux de V. Exc. le rapport du commandant Olivier qui fait un si juste éloge de tout le personnel que j'avais placé sous ses ordres, je dois vous signaler la belle conduite de cet officier supérieur qui a montré le sang froid et le courage habituel à son beau caractère. C'est avec un profond sentiment de justice, et je peux dire d'admiration, que j'ai l'honneur de vous recommander ceux qui se sont distingués entre tous et qui ont tant de titres à une récompense.

Je citerai en première ligne Mr le Lieutenant de vaisseau de Thouars, vaillant officier, homme de guerre, qui commande avec la plus grande distinction le détachement de Yokohama et dont les services ont été des plus utiles pendant notre expédition,

Mr Delassalle, enseigne de vaisseau qui a déployé une grande valeur dans l'attaque de la forteresse et qui a été très grièvement blessé en s'élançant un des premiers sur les remparts,

Mr de Chabannes, enseigne de vaisseau, qui, plein d'entrain et de courage, a été blessé d'un coup de feu,

Mr Suenson, officier danois, dont j'avais déjà apprécié les services et qui a reçu une blessure grave en combattant parmi nous,

Mr La Guerre, lieutenant de vaisseau, officier énergique et résolu, commandant les compagnies du *Primauguet*,

Mr Chatel, aspirant de 1ère classe, dont j'ai déjà signalé la valeur dans l'attaque du 26 octobre et qui s'est encore distingué dans cette dernière circonstance par son courage et son élan,

Le nommé Nédellec, matelot du *Primaugue*t qui, voyant Mr de Chabannes blessés l'a pris dans ses bras sous le feu violent de l'ennemi et qui, blessé à son tour d'un coup de feu dans le bras, a continué à le porter avec un héroïque dévouement. Comme le dit le Commandant Olivier dans son rapport, il faudrait citer tous les noms car chacun s'est montré homme de cœur.

Malgré mon immense désir de retourner moi-même à cette place forte, je n'ai pu donner suite à ce projet dont l'exécution n'était certainement pas possible; j'aurais voulu attirer l'ennemi en rase campagne, bien sûr que dans ces conditions il n'eût pas résisté à notre attaque, mais j'avais l'assurance de ne l'y jamais décider jusqu'au jour où son nombre eu fait toute sa force. Cependant, je dois ajouter que le peuple coréen que l'on m'avait dépeint, dès le principe, comme une nation timide, craintive et tout à fait étrangère au métier des armes, n'est pas aussi méprisable qu'on avait voulu le dire ; je les crois, au contraire, susceptible de sentiments guerriers et bien supérieurs à beaucoup d'égards aux races voisines de l'extrême Orient. L'immense quantité d'armes, de munitions de toutes sortes, le soin avec lequel tous ces articles de guerre étaient conservés, prouvent suffisamment que l'esprit national a des tendances militaires. Les Coréens sont un peuple de montagnards ; ils en ont l'agilité et supportent sans fatigues les longues marches ; ils doivent avoir surtout une grande aptitude à la guerre de partisans. Mais dans ce pays, pour les hommes comme pour toutes choses, il nous a fallu cheminer toujours à la découverte et apprendre par nous mêmes ce que nous ne pouvions savoir par renseignements. Quoiqu'il en soit, en venant en Corée par une initiative que justifiait la nature de mes devoirs, je tenais à ne pas me laisser entraîner au delà du but que je voulais atteindre et surtout à ne pas engager le Gouvernement de l'Empereur dans une entreprise qui eût pu contrarier ses intentions et ses projets. Le but que je m'étais proposé était atteint depuis le jour où j'avais frappé dans Kang-hoa le Gouvernement Coréen, et où je lui avais montré que nous avions trouvé la route qui conduit au cœur de son pays. Cette route pourra être suivie quand le moment sera jugé opportun par le Gouvernement de l'Empereur, car la Corée n'est plus désormais une terre inconnue.

L'Ile de Kang-hoa, ainsi que je l'ai dit déjà, est entourée, dans sa plus grande étendue, par les rives de la terre ferme et elle n'en est séparée que par une très courte distance. Le canal qui est appelé Rivière Salée est formé d'un côté par les rives de cette île et de l'autre par une multitude de petits îlots très voisins et, dans certains endroits, par le continent lui même. Ce canal a 18 milles de longueur. Vers le milieu se trouve un coude très aigu qui rend le passage fort difficile ; à marée basse, il est complètement impraticable. Le courant y est toujours très rapide et renverse instantanément d'une marée à l'autre. Lorsque la marée est basse, le courant, par suite d'un dénivellement dans le fond, devient un torrent ; une embarcation même peut y courir de grands dangers. Dans presque tout leur parcours les deux rives, celle de Kang-hoa et de la terre ferme, n'y sont séparées que par une distance de 400 à 600 mètres. Pendant la nuit et sur bien des points pendant le jour, l'ennemi pouvait communiquer d'une rive à l'autre sans être vu par nous. Pour l'en empêcher, il nous eût fallu occuper les deux bords ainsi que la multitude de forts ou fortins qui les défendent. C'est ce qui sera indispensable de faire si plus tard, une expédition venait en Corée. Nous nous sommes donc trouvés au nord de Kang-hoa, séparés de nos bâtiments, par un canal d'environ 20 milles de longueur dont les bords restaient à la disposition presque entière de l'ennemi du moment où il avait pris la résolution d'y accumuler ses forces. Du côté de Kang-hoa les forts avaient été tous désarmés par nous, mais dès que nous les avions abandonnés, les Coréens venait les occuper de nouveau, quitter à s'éloigner quand nous y revenions pour y retourner ensuite. Bien que nous eussions également détruit toutes les Jonques que nous avions aperçues dans le canal, il pouvait en venir d'autres par des [____] qui nous étaient cachés.

Cependant, ma préoccupation n'était certainement pas dans le nombre des ennemis qui pouvaient débarquer dans l'île, ni dans la quantité de Canons qu'ils avaient apportés sur les rives opposées et qu'ils avaient répandus sur toute sa longueur, je pensais bien plus tôt à la facilité qu'ils pouvaient avoir de fermer le passage par des Jonques coulées qu'ils auraient chargées de pierre et aux conséquences que pourrait entraîner pour nous l'empêchement de communication avec l'île Boisée: en multipliant ces obstacles, ils auraient pu nous mettre dans l'impossibilité de les détruire et notre situation en eût été forte gênée. Ces considérations et surtout ma conviction d'avoir atteint le but qui m'avait conduit en Corée, durent m'inspirer la résolution de terminer mon excursion dans ce pays et de quitter Kang-hoa pour retourner sur nos bâtiments que j'avais laissés depuis un mois avec un personnel bien réduit. J'ai donc fait embarquer les Compagnies de débarquement sur les deux avisos et les deux canonnières et le 11, je revenais au mouillage de l'île Boisée, après avoir fait détruire complètement le palais du Roi et les Etablissements du Gouvernement. Je suis parti avec la satisfaction d'avoir rempli de tous points le programme que je m'étais tracé à l'avance et sans avoir engagé, en quoi que ce soit, le Gouvernement de l'Empereur.

Au milieu de nos préoccupations de guerre, nous n'avons pas négligé ce qui pouvait intéresser particulièrement la Marine: nous avons poursuivi, sans interruptions nos travaux hydrographiques. Les cartes et les plans qui ont été levés, avec tout le soin désirable, resteront comme un document d'une extrême utilité et éclaireront, désormais, la navigation de ces parages restés inexplorés jusqu'ici. Ce travail, accompli avec persévérance et souvent non sans danger, fait honneur aux officiers qui en ont été chargés.

Pour me résumer, M[r] le Ministre, l'apparition de nos bâtiments en Corée, l'occupation de l'île de Kang-hoa, la destruction de cette place de guerre, nos rencontres avec l'ennemi, sont autant de causes qui ne peuvent manquer de produit une profonde impression sur l'esprit des hommes de ce Gouvernement, et si la vengeance que méritait le massacre de nos missionnaires n'a pu être aussi complète qu'elle le sera un jour, la Corée a vu du moins pour la première fois, ses portes ouvertes aux étrangers ; elle a senti que notre bras pourra s'étendre sur elle quand la France le voudra et cette seule crainte sera de nature, j'en ai l'assurance, à prévenir le retour des forfaits dont elle s'est rendue coupable.

Je suis, etc., …

Signé : G. Roze

G. Roze (1866. 11. 17) → P. de Chasseloup-Laubat

강화도에서 획득한 서적, 은괴 등 물품 발송 보고

À bord de *la Guerrière*, mouillage de l'Ile Boisée (Corée) le 17 novembre 1866

Monsiur le Ministre,

Dès mon arrivée à Kang-hoa, j'avais chargé une commission de rechercher et de recueillir les objets qui pourraient offrir de l'intérêt au point de vue historique ou scientifique.

J'ai l'honneur d'adresser à votre Excellence le procès verbal qui m'a été remis par cette commission.

La Ville assez pauvre d'apparence ne contenait rien qui méritât de vous être envoyé. Mais la résidence que le Roi de Corée y possédait, et qu'il n'habitait que rarement, renfermait une bibliothèque riche d'un assez grand nombre d'ouvrages qu'il est permis de croire fort important. La commission a réuni 340 volumes qui ont été soigneusement emballés et que j'expédierai en France par la première occasion de l'Etat qui se produira. Je regrette que le poids énorme qu'ils représentent ne me permette pas de les envoyer par les Messageries Impériales.

À défaut de tout interprète sérieux, je n'oserais rien assurer à Votre Excellence. Cependant j'espère que ces ouvrages jetteront un grand jour sur les Annales, la Religion, la littérature et les légendes d'un pays qui est resté inconnu jusqu'ici.

Parmi les quelques autres objets recueillis encore dans la même résidence, se trouvent trois boîtes contenant des tablettes articulées, en marbre, avec des caractères d'or. Je vous les adresserai en même temps que les dix-neuf caisses d'argent.

Ces tablettes, propriété du Roi, seraient destinées à perpétuer un événement ou un fait mémorable quelconque particulier à la personne Royale. L'une d'elles surtout est richement habillée de soie et c'est presque avec terreur qu'un Coréen s'en est approché tant étant grand le respect que sa vue lui inspirait.

Je prends la liberté, M[r] le Ministre, de vous prier de vouloir bien l'offrir à Sa Majesté l'Empereur. C'est la Division navale de la Chine toute entière qui la met à ses pieds comme un gage de son dévouement et de sa fidélité.

J'ose espérer que votre Excellence voudra bien accepter aussi, pour elle même, une de ces tablettes que chacun de nous est heureux de lui offrir respectueusement.

Signé : G. Roze

G. Roze (1866. 11. 17) ➜ P. de Chasseloup-Laubat

은괴 발송 보고

À bord de *la Guerrière*, Mouillage de l'Ile Boisée le 17 novembre 1866

Monsiur le Ministre,

En rendant compte à Votre Excellence de l'occupation de la ville de Kang-hoa(Corée) par les Corps de débarquement de ma Division, j'ai eu l'honneur de l'informer que nous avions trouvé dans un local appartenant au Gouvernemnet dix-neuf caisses d'argent évaluées ensemble à la somme de 197,231.f 36.

Je m'empresse de vous adresser le Procès-verbal qui a été dressé par la commission que j'avais chargée de prendre régulièrement possession de cet argent. Je vais faire diriger les dix-neuf caisses sur Shang-haï, où elles seront embarquées sur les paquebots des Messageries Impériales pour être mises à Votre disposition.

Votre Excellence appréciera si cette somme doit faire retour à l'Etat ou considérée comme prise et comme telle, répartie entre les différents ayant droit.

G. Roze

Marine et Colonies

Division Navale de la Chine et du Japon, Commandée par le Contre-Amiral Roze

----

Procès Verbal de prise par les Equipages de la Division Navale de la Chine à Kang-hoa (Corée)

Aujourd'hui seize Octobre mil huit cent soixante-six, sur l'avis donné à Mr. le Contre-Amiral Commandant en chef que des caisses contenat de l'argent devaient d'être découvertes dans un quartier de la ville de Kang-hoa occupée par les Corps de débarquement de la Division.

Nous Jouan : Capitaine de frégate, chef d'Etat-Major,

Et La Veille, sous-commissaire, commissaire de la Division.

Nous sommes transportés sur les lieux pour en faire la reconnaissance et l'inventaire, conformément aux ordres du Comm. en chef.

Arrivés aux point indiqué, nous avons pénétré dans un hangar en bois où nous avons trouvé dissimulées, sous une foule d'objets divers, des caisses empilées les unes sous les autres et ayant toutes les mêmes dimensions,

savoir: Longueur 0.68
Largeur 0.31
Hauteur 0.26

Ces caisses comptées par nous se sont trouvées être au nombre de 19 dont 4 étaient ouvertes et le restant en bon état.

Nous avons pris possession de tout, au nom de Mr. le Contre-Amiral Comm. en chef, et nous avons ensuite procédé à l'ouverture et au passage de chacune d'elles.

Nous avons constaté qu'elles contenaient toutes des rondelles d'argent avec une quantitié variable de petits morceaux du même métal qui semblaient être l'appoint d'un compte déterminé.

Les pesées ont donné les résultats suivants.

No. 1--26, rondelles, plus un appoint en petits morceaux
pesant ensemble 48. k 740
2--25--Do .... Do 47. 660
3--26--Do .... Do 47. 750
4--26--Do .... Do 48. 890
5--26--Do .... Do 48. 980
6--26--Do .... Do 48. 400
7--26--Do .... Do 48. 600
8--26--Do .... Do 48. 900
9--26--Do .... Do 48. 600
10--26--Do .... Do 48. 710
11--26--Do .... Do 48. 700
12--26--Do .... Do 48. 470
13--26--Do .... Do 48. 710
14--26--Do .... Do 48. 540
15--26--Do .... Do 48. 200
16--26--Do .... Do 48. 429
17--26--Do .... Do 47. 990

No. 18--26--Do .... Do ....47. k 709

19--9 --Do .... Do 16. 460

Total … 426, rondelles plus les appoints, le tout pesant

887. k 550

Nous n'avions pas le moyen de nous assurer du titre de cet argent, mais d'après les reseigements qui nous ont été donnés nous avons lieu de le croire pur tout alliage. Dans ce cas, le kilogramme valant 222.f 22 (Bouillet-dictionnaire des sciences) la prise dont il s'agit représenterait une somme de 197,231^{f}, 36.

Immédiatement après le pesage, toutes les caisses ont été refermées, clouées, cerclées et numérotées pour être envoyée à bord de *la Guerrière* et expédiées ultérieurement à M. le Ministre de la marine et des colonies.

Fait à Kang-hoa

les seize octobre 1866

Les Membre de la Commission Vieille

Vu : Le Contre-Amiral Commandant en chef.

G. Roze

156

巡撫營 ➡ 議政府(1866. 11. 19/高宗三年十月十三日)

프랑스 함대 팔미도(八尾島) 철수 보고

巡撫營以異船沒數出去八尾島外啓

該營啓言卽見先鋒中軍李容熙今日未時馳報則德浦僉使馳報富平境碇留異船五隻移停於馬嶼島前洋今日巳時一齊擧碇下去永宗境前洋瞭望則更無一隻船所見又啓言卽見右先鋒將金善弼巳時馳報則卽接富平府使 趙秉老所報異樣船七隻今日辰時沒數出去于八尾島外

高宗 ➞ 議政府(1866. 11. 21/高宗三年十月十五日)

서양 선박 관련 전말을 일본에 통지할 것을 지시

관련문서 (1) 대마도주에게 서양선박의 침입에 대비할 것을 권고하는 예조참의의 서신

命我國所經洋舶顚末修書契送于萊館轉致東武

議政府啓言向以洋舶情形已有咨報於北京而第念日本自講和以後凡事係邊政者互相通報曾於庚申以緊防洋教事島主因東武意書通我邦矣今此洋夷之猋往倏來情狀叵測且統營外洋出沒之舶有事於日本難保必無其在交好之道似合先事通知亦以我國近日所經詳述顚末修書契送于萊館仍令轉致東武請以示警邊防敦隣好之意允之

【관련문서 1】

丙寅 禮曹參議以畿沿各邑洋舶情與島主書

云云玄英弭節緬惟啓居珍毖慰溯並摯竊以弊邦與貴國講信修好垂三百年凡係邊圉之政疆場之事未有不陳述因由開示方略如庚申貴國書契者卽所以申舊約而敦隣誼也西洋英佛諸國遠涉重溟來請交易於弊邦者不止一再而竟至於兵刃相加則其毒愈憯矣本年春間有南鍾三洪鳳周者或簪紳邇列或衣冠遺裔傳習邪教糾結匪類潛引洋人奉爲教主薰染旣久煽惑益廣奸跡掀發於緝捕之際悖黨駢就於刑辟之下夏秋間洋舶一艘先泊於湖西海美縣前洋次泊於畿內江華府近地乍往旋來懇請通貨弊邦嚴辭牢拒終不聽允則彼乃缺望而退又於此際洋舶一艘自西海轉入平壤府羊角島剽掠商貨殺害人畜道臣設計火攻盡行勦滅八月十六日洋舶二艘自南洋直入京江三宿而返言語不通情款相阻行止莫詰堨來自恣乃於九月初六日洋舶大小三十餘艘又到京畿或留碇於富平府前洋或直向江華府甲串津打破樓櫓焚毁廨宇殺害人民攘奪牛畜宬籍輓漕盡爲剽刼着巡撫使李景夏開營戒嚴於輦下先鋒中軍李容熙陣于通津府左先鋒將鄭志鉉陣于濟物鎭右先鋒將金善弼陣于富平府遊擊將韓聖根陣于文殊山城游擊將梁憲洙陣于鼎足山城游擊將李基祖陣于廣城鎭摠戎使申觀浩召募使李元熙陣于楊花津召募使鄭圭應陣于西江隘口御營中軍權○京畿中軍白樂贇陣于幸州隘口楊州牧使林翰洙陣于礪峴隘口招討使韓應弼陣于延安府防禦使柳晥陣于坡州牧都護使申櫶陣于長湍府移檄請戰期日相見賊盡幷其衆聚保港議無意交兵沿浦舟楫沒數燒燼間或潛襲文殊鼎足諸城輒被守將擊却弊邦方敵敕器仗修繕戰艦又令三路舟師合勢進攻十月十二日大小洋舶仍卽捲還退向外洋而去此爲弊邦被兵之大略也弊邦昇平日久戎政弛而武備疎未能長計制勝使片帆不還則雖有數三克捷多小勦殪固不足爲耀威武而讋遠人且夷情叵測進退無常未可以日下之紓急永蠲方來之憂虞也又有一事之不容不據實相報者弊邦之瀕海東南與貴國諸州涯涘可辨牛馬境界殆聞雞狗而自夏秋至于近日無數帆檣自西而南者出沒於煙雲島嶼之間封疆之臣飛報日至未知彼夷將欲起釁而貴國設備而待變歟未知貴國已與搆兵而彼夷左此而敗衂歟又未知彼方恣睢潛伺磨牙鼓吻而貴國或未覺悟其閃秘之情狀逆折其猋發之氣勢歟弊邦用是憂慮不印自恤茲以控擧顚末修牘展布幸將右項事由轉達東武是所深望統惟崇照肅此不備　丙寅年十月　日 式見 憲宗乙巳邊禁

總署(1866. 11. 23/同治五年十月十七日) ➜ 북경주재 각국 공사

조불(朝佛) 문제의 국제 공론화 시도

給英美俄布各國照會

爲照會事 查自中外換約以來 本爵王大臣辦理各國一切交涉事件 無不出自信誠 以期共敦和好 今夏法國有與朝鮮國搆兵之事 准法國伯大臣兩次照會前來 當經前後照覆 爲之從中排解 以冀保全兩國民命 在本爵王大臣乃係一番美意 不料頃接伯大臣來文 乃以跟役一面之詞 及巷議街談 毫無影響之言遽見猜疑 是本爵王大臣此番美意 伯大臣全未理會 反疑中存袒護 另有別情本爵王大臣閱之不快實甚 且伯大臣來文 明言得自風聞 風聞者無據之言也以無據之言責人 本爵王大臣斷不心服 因同係和好之邦 特將此件前後法國照會三件 及本衙門照覆三件 鈔錄附覽 想貴大臣閱之 自必有公論也 除照會各國住京大臣外 爲此照會

【佛譯文】

Pékin le 23 Novembre 1866

Son Altesse le Prince de Kong au Ministre d'Angleterre

Depuis que la Chine et les pays Etrangers ont échangé des traités moi Prince chargé de la Direction des Affaires Extérieurs j'ai toujours agi avec bonne foi et sincerité voulant ainsi maintenir et fortifier la bonne harmonic qui existe entre nous.

Depuis que, dès le commencement de l'automne, la France et la Corée se sont trouvées en hostilités j'ai reçu du Chargé d'affaires de France deux dépêches auxquelles j'ai répondu selon leur date d'arrivée en essayant de ramener la concorde et dans l'intéret de l'existence des sujets des deux pays.

C'était là réellement une très bonne pensée de ma part et je n'aurais pas prévu que je recevrais une dépêche du chargé d'affaires dans laquelle il est visible que se basant sur les seuls dires d'un suivant (de la Mission Coréenne) et sur des bruits sans consistance circulant dans les rues et les carrefours, il se met à concevoir des doutes, n'accorde aucune attention à la bonne pensée qui me faisait agir, prétend que je cherche à excuser la Corée et croit que j'ai des sentiments différents de ceux que j'exprime. Mr de Bellonnet dit très clairement que ce sont des bruits qui lui sont revenus (fong ouen) or des bruits sont des choses sans preuves et je ne puis admettre que l'on s'appuie là dessus pour dire aux gens des choses désagréables (litt. gronder). Comme nous sommes en bonnes relations je vous envoie Copie des deux dépêches reçues précédemment de la Légation de France et de la troisième que j'ai reçue dernièrement ainsi que des trois réponses de notre Yamen. Je vous prie de les lire sachant très bien que vous les apprécierez avec toute justice.

J'écris en outre oux autres Ministres Etrangers résidant à la Capitale.

Veuillez agréer.

Le 14e jour de la 10e lune de la 9e année de Tong-tzé

Pour traduction conforme

Le 1er Interprète de la Légation

G. Lemaire

【英譯文(美國)】

Prince Kung to Mr. Burlingame

Prince Kung, chief secretary of state for foreign affairs, herewith makes a communication.

It is well known that since the ratification of the treaties between China and western countries, I have endeavored, by a constant adherence to truth and good faith, in every transaction connected with those countries, to maintain amicable relations with them. A serious quarrel having arisen last summer between the French and Coreans, M. de Bellonet, the French charge d'affaires, addressed two communications to me respecting it. In my replies to them, I endeavored to act as a mediator, and so to explain the points of the affair that there might not, after all, be any loss of life to either party. This laudable desire was my only motive. Much to my surprise, I have just received a despatch from M. de Bellonet, in which he quotes the verbal statement of a Corean attendant, together with the gossip of market-places, for the truth of which there is not the shadow of evidence, and brings them up to cast suspicion on me. Seeing, therefore, that he does not meet my laudable desire [to prevent a collision] with the same spirit, but, on the contrary, throws out a suspicion that I am screening and excusing the Coreans, and even have other designs in view, I cannot but be exceedingly dissatisfied with him. He expressly states in his despatch that he thus obtained these rumors, and yet to make from such unsupported rumors charges implicating and upbraiding others, is certainly what I cannot assent to or see the justice of.

I have been on friendy (*Sic*) relations with both these countries, and have deemed it best to copy the three despatches of M. de Bellonet. with their replies, and enclose them for your excellency's information. From them you will no doubt see the merits of the case' copies of the same are also sent to the other foreign ministers resident in Peking.

His Excellency ANSON BURLINGAME,
United States Minister to China.

NOVEMBER 21, 1866 (Tungchi, 5th year, 10th moon, 14th day)

【英譯文(英國)】

November 20, 1866

THE Prince of Kung makes a communication.

Ever since China and foreign nations exchanged the ratification of their Treaties, the Prince, in the management of all questions in which foreign countries have had a common interest with China, has in every instance acted with perfect good friendly relations would be strengthened.

In the summer of the present year hostilities broke out between France and Corea, and the Prince received first one and then another despatch on the subject from M. de Bellonnet (Chargé d'Affaires of France).

To these despatches replies were at the time severally sent. The Prince's object (in the replies) was, as an intermediary, to arrange the difficulty in the hope of preserving the lives of the subjects of both countries. The Prince was actuated by none but the best of motives; he has read, therefore, with excessive grief a despatch just received from M. de Bellonnet in which (the Chargé d'Affaires gives expression to) certain suspicions he has hastily formed, based upon the one-sided statements of a menial attendant, and the totally groundless gossip of the streets and lanes.

M. de Bellonnet completely ignores the goodness of the Prince's intentions, and even suspects (the Chinese Government) of a desire to favour and defend (Corea), and of having other designs besides.

M. de Bellonnet states distinctly in his despatch that his information is based on rumour. Now a rumour is a statement destitute of proof, and that a person should be censured on statements destitute of proof (is a principle) the Prince can by no means acquiesce in.

As China and the Powers (represented in Peking) are all in relations of amity and friendship with each other, the Prince herewith incloses, for the perusal of the British Minister, copies of the three French despatches on this subject and of the three replies of the Yamên. His Highness has no doubt that when his Excellency reads them he will express a just opinion on the matter. ["Kung lun," just opinion, may also imply a general and impartial discussion of the questions by all the Ministers].

The Prince is writing at the same time to the other foreign Ministers in

Peking.

A necessary communication addressed to Sir R. Alcock, K. C.B., &c. &c.
Tung Chih, 5th year, 10th month, 14th day.

159

H. de Bellonet(1866. 11. 25) ➞ 總署(1866. 12. 20)

공문을 왜곡하여 각국대신에게 조회문을 발송한 것에 대한 항의

Péking (*Sic*), le 25 Novembre, 1866

J'ai déja eu plusieurs fois l'occasion de dire à vos Excellences que leur ignorance des usages diplomatiques et internationaux leur faisait faire des démarches qui étaient mal interprétées en Europe. Celle qu'elles viennent de faire en déférant notre correspondance au sujet de la Corée aux Représentants des Puissances à Péking rentre dans cette catégorie. Je n'ai assurément aucune objection à faire à ce que le Gouvernement Chinois communique mes dépêches à mes collègues. Cette publication sera interprétée en Europe dans le sens d'un dernier effort en faveur de la Corée, et par suite prouvera que je n'avais pas tort en écrivant ce que j'ai écrit. Mais les usages diplomatiques exigeaient que dans ce cas je fusse prévenu par le Gouvernement Chinois, et que copie de la lettre circulaire adressée à mes collègues me fût envoyé. Cela n'a pas été fait et j'ai le droit de m'en formaliser. Je préviens donc vos Excellences que je soumets leur procédé à l'appréciation du Gouvernement de Sa Majesté en lui demandant s'il ne juge pas convenable d'en exiger satisfaction; et j'avoue que je ne comprends guère pourquoi, puisque le Gouvernement Chinois croit que je cherche à le trouver en faute, il m'a donné une si belle occasion de satisfation mon penchant.

Puisque mes dépêches sur la Corée deviennent publiques, j'envoie à vos Excellences les expéditions officielles en Français exigées par les Traités, et dont j'avais cru pouvoir me dispenser depuis quelques temps par suite du départ de plusieurs employés de la Légation. Je les ai de même envoyées à tous mes collègues, et comme il me semble par la dernière dépêche du Prince de Kung que le Gouvernement Chinois n'a compris ni les idées que je lui exposais, ni les sentiments qui me faisaient agir, je charge M. Lemaire de lui expliquer mot à mot chacune de mes idées.

J'espère que cette leçon prouvera une fois de plus à vos Excellences le besoin d'avoir des Interprètes Européens, en leur démontrant l'impossibilité de parler d'affaires politiques en employant une langue aussi imparfaite que la langue Chinoise.

Je saisis, &c.

(Signé) HENRI DE BELLONNET

【漢譯文】

本大臣屢次說貴衙門不知萬國交涉往來彼此相待之規矩 不免令歐羅巴諸國聞知怪異不服 如貴衙門將本署論議高麗公文 移送各國住京大臣閱覽 實類於是 此於本大臣毫無妨礙 不過歐羅巴地方想幫高麗 無可如何 而益顯明本大臣公文內所有之詞 爲不枉論萬國往來交涉之例 貴衙門照會各國住京大臣 應來文與本大臣通知其意 合卽詳明本國 以定可否 貴衙門旣欲免本大臣有猜疑之舛 卽不應與以可疑之端 本大臣已將此法文鈔送各國住京欽差大臣矣 查恭親王來文 似有不曾洞徹文內之言及行文之意 因此特委本署繙譯官李親詣貴署 將文內之言隨句解明 以免含混 竝希諸位大臣從此早知中國應得熟習外國語言之通文官 而漢文實非中外辦理交涉事件之融洽語也

【英譯文】

PEKING, November 25, 1866

I have already many times had occasion to say to your excellencies that your ignorance of diplomatic and international usages has caused you to take steps which have been wrongly interpreted in Europe. That which you have just done, in submitting our correspondence on the subject no objection to make to the Chinese government 's communicating my despatches to my colleagues. This publication will be interpreted as a last effort in favor of Corea, and, consequently, will prove that I have not been wrong in writing what I have. But diplomatic usages demanded that in this case I should have been previously informed by the Chinese government, and that a copy of the circular addressed to my colleagues should have been sent to me. This has not been done, and I have a right to find fault. I, therefore, inform your excellency that I submit your proceedings to the appreciation of his Majesty's government asking them if they do not think proper to demand satisfaction; and I confess that I do not exactly understand why, since the Chinese government believe that I seek to find fault, it has given me so good an occasion to satisfy my desire.

Since my despatches regarding Corea are made public, I send to your excellencies the official copies in French required by the treaties, and with which I had thought it possible for me to dispense, on account of the departure of many of the employes of the legation. I have sent the same to all my colleagues; and as it seems to me, from the last despatch of Prince Kung, that the Chinese government has comprehended neither the ideas which I expressed nor the sentiments which made me express them, I instruct Mr. Lemaire to explain each of my ideas to them word for word.

I hope that this lesson will prove once for all to your excellencies the need of having European interpreters, by showing you the impossibility of speaking of political affairs while employing a language as imperfect as the Chinese.

H. DE BELLONET

His Imperial Highness PRINCE KUNG

高宗, 議政府堂上官, 巡撫使 등(1866. 11. 26/高宗三年十月二十日)

외양(外攘)과 관련한 선후책(善後策) 논의

召見大臣政府堂上巡撫使以下于春塘臺

予命景夏等曰跨月結陣無恙往來風餐露宿之餘軍卒亦無疾病乎景夏等曰無頉往還而軍卒亦無病還來矣命容熙等曰無病往來乎容熙等曰無病往來矣

領敦寧 金左根陳禦寇及節財之方賜批

左根啓言洋匪回帆官軍方撤跨月戒心之餘上下始安何幸何幸正陰之月不令不寧之災又何爲而至也修省之要又不當少緩第安不忘危不但此時爲然凡係備禦之策專意講究可無疏虞所謂講究者非別件事也迺士有器械金穀舟船之屬以今番事觀之該營軍容一不入量倉卒召募未免苟且如是而何以應外至之寇乎自今諸凡兵家所需一一繕治儲待團束軍伍敵至則禦宜無臨時窘跆之歎批以所陳切實另當服膺矣又啓言用之節無當於民聖人必曰節用而愛民而民生財之謂也不節則重斂重斂則傷民傷民則本不固本不固則國將奈何國將奈何則無可言之言是故明君制民之産仰事父母俯畜妻子樂歲終身飽凶年免於死亡者意豈徒然而已哉今殿下春秋漸盛智慮日進聖王用心設教處庶幾見得於方冊之間則上所云節用愛民等事可以理會矣苟爲節用而愛民內而倉廩之歲計外而營壘之日用何患乎不足也哉批以所陳切實當服膺矣

判敦寧 李景在陳勉賜批

景在啓言洋船纔退雷異適發恐懼修攘之道尤不可以少忽也昨伏見四條責躬之教則惻怛懇摯有足以孚格玄穹古語曰多難興邦殷憂啓聖此殆天所以警發睿智將期大有爲之兆也夫外攘末也內修本也內修之本在於安民安民之本在於節用若其端本出治之方又在於講學而已第念病加於少愈戰狃於少勝天下之大戒也朱子所謂大人事業皆從戰兢臨履中出來伏願殿下益加儆省恒若敵國外患之至則轉災回危太平萬世亶在於是批以所陳切實當服膺矣

左議政 金炳學辭免兼陳沁府拊循之方及勉聖學賜批

炳學啓言臣之冒據三事已數歲于茲邇來洋賊之滋擾直從臣中書視務之初訖今爲終始矣藉使臣才器威望有足以服遠人而讋狡夷則朝廷無人之歎勿生邊釁之戒古今人豈相遠哉且況聖主勤勞於上生民蕩析於下而臣無以仰紓主憂俯鎭民心閱月府坐與無一言一事之所裨益此已爲萬殞難贖之罪而今於寇退之後補漏

船而整欹器非如臣不肖所可擔夯做去且青臺告警咎在輔相災異策免亦所以式遵故事也伏願亟賜斥退以幸民國千萬血祝批以今此辭免萬萬過當更勿以此事言之又啓言江華一府卽王都陪京而刼後餘民罔有定極寇賊雖退而疑惻之心猶存眷屬不保而事育之資又乏捿遑道路景色愁慘所以哀痛之音慰諭之命繼降發帑存恤回眺爲笑矣第念民業一匱則不可以復畜民志一散則不可以復聚分付守臣凡係安集拊循之方悉心措劃如有不可以便宜從事者這這狀聞以爲實效誠爲今日急務故敢達批以自廟堂關問於該守臣從長措劃又啓言凶醜遠去大陣雖還方來之憂亦不可不念而繕械治艦今其設都監擧行矣士馬精強兵甲之堅利未始非外攘之急務而若夫內修之要明天理正人心而已崇正學闢邪說爲其本耳臣聞人君一心萬化之原崇之闢之之道亦惟在於聖學之勤不勤此所以大小臣民之日夜顒祝也惟殿下日開講席頻接臣僚討論得失諮訪治道則天理自明人心自正正學崇矣邪說闢矣西洋小寇將不敢復肆其凶此之謂內修外攘也伏願懋哉懋哉批以所陳切實可不服膺乎

右議政 柳厚祚陳時務仍辭免賜批

厚祚啓言蠢玆洋醜今已遠遁實爲目前之幸而賊情叵測難保其必無後慮陰雨之備不容少緩而惟在於嚴防守簡軍實繕器械峙糇糧而已且騷訛之餘中外民心波蕩末由收拾則亦思所以鎭安之方愼擇守令使之懷保安集實爲今日之急務至於治邪之道靡不用極而若不鋤治其本則外寇之來其將磁鎭而相引猶復如前更加嚴防搜捕俾無漏網之患焉臣之蠢愚湔劣百不如人非但臣自知甚明實是淵鑑之所燭悉則以此無狀不可久冒匪據自速伴食之譏而纔復萬里之命適値艱虞之會遽爾丐免者義分之所不敢趨赴府坐之末粗效奔走之勞矣見今匪舶退去大陣告班旰憂稍紓群情胥欣此正臣必辭之日也伏乞亟遞臣政府之職以重公器以安私分焉批以所陳切實當服膺而至於辭免實非此時可言之事諒之焉

161

G. F. Seward (1866. 11. 27) → W. H. Seward

프랑스 함대 원정 관련 기사 송부 및 조선과의 통상 조약 필요성

U.S. Consulate General,
Shanghai, Nov. 27 1866

To His Excellency,
Honorable William H. Seward
Secretary of State, Washington

Sir:

A considerable degree of attention has lately been drawn to Corea. Which has been the scene of the murder of two Romanist Bishops and seven Priests and probably of the crew of the American Schooner *General Sherman*. With about twenty men, two of whom, passengers were British subjects and men of high standing.

To avenge the murder of the missionaries, the French Admiral undertook an expedition to Corea that has apparently resulted unfavorably.

Instead of attempting a resume of these several matters I inclose to you slips cut from the public press of this port which contain substantially all the information that has been received. The slips marked with the plain letters are taken from the issues of the "Shanghai Recorder" and those followed by an X from those of the "North China Daily News" and the dates are noted.

The slip marked "Y" contains, I think, the most authentic information that has been made public touching the French Evacuation.

This account however is unsatisfactory as it does not fully explain the motive which influenced the French Commander and leaves him as if he has withdrawn from a position deliberately taken upon the first appearance of trouble.

My own idea is that the whole expedition was undertaken without authority from Paris and that the Admiral uncertain as to the prospect of being supported caused him to take a step which must have been distasteful to him.

I am inclined to suppose that the French Government will, if it has not already, propose a joint expedition to the Corea on the part of France, England, and the United States. There is perhaps no reason to hope for any immediate advantage to trade from opening Corea. But doubtless a considerable traffic would grow up in the course of a few years. Corea is, however, so situated that the commerce of the Gulf of Petcheli of Eastern Siberia and Western Japan flows along the coasts and whether it would be of advantage to make a Commercial Treaty, or not, it certainly is desirable to require of the Coreans security for the kind treatment of Shipwrecked persons.

I have the honor to the,
Sir
Your obedient Servant
Geo F. Seward.
U. S. Consulate General Shanghai

H. de Bellonet(1866. 11. 28) ➞ Moustier(1867. 2. 8)

조선 문제에 미온적인 청조의 태도 비난

관련문서 (1) Bellonet와 恭親王 간 왕래한 조선 문제에 관한 서신을 번역한 *Shanghai Evening Courrier*의 기사(1867. 1. 12)

Pékin le 28 Novembre 1866

Monsieur le Ministre,

Ainsi que j'avais l'honneur de le faire pressentir à Votre Excellence par une dépêche du 30 Juillet dernier le Gouvernement Chinois a tenté de faire accepter sa médiation et de remplacer une éxécution militaire en Corée par une enquête qui ainsi que toutes les enquêtes conduites par les Chinois aurait produit de gros bénéfices pour ceux qui en auraient été chargés, aurait découvert d'excellentes raisons pour justifier le massacre de nos missionnaires, et fait disparaître toutes les preuves qui pourront nous montrer un jour la complicité, par moi presque certaine de la Cour de Pékin, et surtout aurait rassuré les Mandarins engagés dans cette persécution cauteleuse et voilée qui nous est signalée de partout contre les Etrangers et les idées qu'ils apportent en démontrant qu'il suffit de quelques mots du "Grand Empereur chargé par le ciel de régir l'univers" pour que les "Barbares" suspendent leur vengeances et s'inclinent "[____] et respectueux" devant la volonté suprême du maître des nations.

J'ai naturellement repoussé ainsi que j'en avais annoncé l'intention à Votre Exellence une proposition qui me semblait dérisoire, alors que nos troupes occupaient l'Ilc et la ville de Kan-hoa (*Sic*) et qui m'était faite en réponse à la notification du blocus. Je saisis même cette occasion pour écrire au Gouvernement Chinois ce qui lui avait été répété vingt fois, et ce qu'il n'avait pas voulu comprendre que les renseignements qui m'arrivaient de tous cotés faisaient peser sur lui de graves soupçons.

Le Gouvernement Chinois n'avait plus qu'une ressource, et il l'a tentée, un appel à l'intervention des autres puissances. Seulement au lieu de le faire franchement, il l'a fait à la Chinoise "en sous entendu[,"], sous le prétexte ostensible de se défendre contre mes soupçons. Or, d'une part, je savais par le Ministre de Russie lui même qu'il avait demandé au Tsong-ly-ya-men pourquoi il n'offrait pas sa médiation je savais que des conseils plus ou moin accentués étaient venus de la Légation de la Reine, et que des pourparlers au sujet de la Corée s'échangeaient, en ce moment même entre nos deux Gouvernement, d'autre part le Prince sans réfuter aucun de mes soupçons se bornait à se lamenter sur leur injustice et à prétexter de sa bonne foi. Mais a-t-on oublié le pays où nous sommes, et n'est ce pas avec les mêmes phrases, avec les mêmes protestations qu'il y a six ans à peine les Ambassadeurs et les Armées Alliées et aux de nos malheureux compatriotes qui en ont été les victimes étaient attirés dans le guet-à-pens (*Sic*) de Tong-tcheon.

Je me suis empressé de remettre aux Représentants des Puissances le texte français de mes dépêches, et j'ai pu m'assurer de l'impression très vive produite sur eux par un langage qui s'écarte passablement des tournures pacifiques qu'ils se croient obligée (*Sic*) d'employer, et par la découverte qu'il était difficile de s'immiscer dans l'affaire de Corée, sans une entente préalable avec le Gouvernement de Sa Majesté.

Quant au langage en lui même il a sa raison d'être dans l'inutilité des efforts tentés diplomatiquement depuis quatre ans pour amener une solution à nos affaires, et sa justification dans le succès qui couronne son emploi. Ainsi que j'avais l'honneur de l'expliquer à Votre Excellence dans ses dépêches des 20 et 25 Juillet dernier il devenait indispensable "de mettre un terme à une politique de conciliation trop longtemps prolongée" or pour nous faire prendre au sérieux puisque je n'avais pas encore la permission d'employer la force, j'ai voulu essayer de la contrainte morale, sans croire pourtant, "à la puissance d'une dépêche sur le Gouvernement Chinois.[”]

Je suis contraint d'avouer, Monsieur le Ministre, que ma parole a eu plus de poids que je ne le pensais. Ce que quatre années de Négociations diplomatiques et courtoises [____] pu obtenir, quatre mois d'un langage violent, cassant, soldatesque, appuyé il est vrai sur l'écho lointain du canon de Corée l'ont obtenu. Le Vice Roi Li, le Roi du Sud qui avait [____] dédaigneusement repoussé nos réclamations et les ordres de Pékin a perdu subitement la confiance qu'il mettait dans les sept ou huit cents pièces de canon dont il a orné les remparts de Nankin, et il a plié. Il vient de rendre les terrains de l'église à l'Evêque, et de régler avec lui les autres questions religieuses en suspens. Au Heo-nan, au Chen-si les restitutions viennent également de se faire, parait-il, mais le Gouvernement Chinois, que les Affaires du Sse-tchuen ont rendu méfiant, a [____] avant d'en écrire officiellement à la Légation, un satisfait en français des Evêques. Ici les deux affaires dont je parlais à Votre Excellence, sont en pleine voie d'arrangement, et je puis dire dès à présent, que sauf pour le règlement des affaires du Sse-tchuen, je n'ai plus besoin de l'assistance des forces navales de Sa Majesté.

Votre Excellence sait que dans ce pays momifié sous les bandelettes dont l'entoure un rituel qui date de quatre mille ans, j'amais (*Sic*) une mauvaise nouvelle ne doit arriver jusqu'à l'Empereur et lui faire penser que tout n'est pas pour le mieux dans le meilleur des mondes.

De là ce système de mensonges officiels qui présente toujours l'état des affaires comme excellent et qui dissimule avec soin tout ce qui arrive de fâcheux. De là, la satisfaction sans mélange que goûtait le Prince de Kong et son Gouvernement quand il a vu que les Barbares dont il avait bien fallu accepter la présence à Pékin, se soumettaient de bonne grace à l'ilotisme auquel on les condamnait, et répondaient avec une mansuétude courtoise aux vexations qui ne leur étaient point ménagées. Il n'avait pas compris que si les Représentants des Puissances Etrangères se contentaient si facilement de paroles et de promesses, c'est que la guerre civile pour les Etats-Unis, les intérêts du Commerce Anglais que cette guerre compromettait gravement et pour la France la perspective d'une guerre Européenne nous faisait à tous un devoir d'éviter à tout prix les complications, il n'avait pas compris que cet état devait avoir un terme et que ce terme était arrivé, aussi l'impression produite par mes dernières dépêches a-t-elle été profonde et les renseignements que je reçois des provinces sur la façon dont a été accueillie la nouvelle des premières opérations de l'amiral Roze, m'a prouvé que j'avais eu raison de prendre cette grave détermination.

Une chose encore reste à obtenir, Monsieur le Ministre, et j'espère que Votre Excellence voudra bien donner sur ce point des instructions précises au nouveau Ministre de l'Empereur, et s'entendre avec les différentes Puissances pour que leurs Représentants, agissant de concert, imposent au Gouvernement Chinois leur volonté. Je veux parler de la réception des Ministres Etrangers par l'Empereur de la Chine qu'on n'obtiendra jamais par de simples négociations. Les faits ont prouvé combiens M.M. Bruce et Bourboulon s'étaient trompés en croyant que l'affaire se ferait d'elle même, et qu'elle (*Sic*) faute ils ont commise en n'insistant pas pour l'affirmative les deux fois que la question leur fût posée par le Prince Kong. Il est pour moi certain que c'est à cette exclusion systématique que nous devons le mépris avec lequel on nous traite, que le prestige qui entoure encore en Chine tout ce qui approche de l'Empereur vaudra pour nous, lorsque nous serons reçus par lui comme les Représentants de ses égaux plus que tous les canons de nos escadres et nous permettra mais seulement alors de conduire pacifiquement la Chine dans les voies de la Civilisation.

Mais je le répète, il faut pour cela une entente préalable entre les Puissances, et l'intention bien arrêté de ne pas admettre de discussion sur une formalité que nous considérons comme indispensable pour valider l'entrée en fonctions d'un Diplomate étranger. Les Chinois me semblent vivement impressionnés et du présent et de l'avenir, et je ne mets pas en doute que l'année prochaine ne voie la solution de cette affaire, si les Gouvernements Européens le veulent sincèrement. L'Empereur commence à être assez âgé pour avoir envie de nous voir, pour qu'il ne soit pas ridicule de notre part de demander à être admis devant lui. Le Prince de Kong, les Princes, ne mettraient pas je crois une grande ardeur à s'opposer à notre volonté une fois qu'elle serait nettement exprimée. Les obstacles viendront des Mandarins, et seront puisés dans les Rites. "Comment voulez vous, disait Ouen Siang que nous puissions admettre que vous soyez assis ou debout en présence de l'Empereur alors que nous serions à genoux." Votre Excellence peut se rappeler qu'en Père nous avons eu à vaincre les mêmes difficultés et que la volonté bien arrêtée de M. Bourée a seule triomphé de l'opposition de [______]. Ici ce sera le même, il faudra imposer une solution qu'il est absolument impossible de nous accorder de bonne grâce, et si Votre Excellence le permet je répéterai ici les paroles que me disait un jour Ouen-siang dans une conversations à ce sujet: "La guerre nous tirerait d'embarras."

Veuillez agréer les assurances de la respectueuse considération avec laquelle

J'ai l'honneur d'être

Monsieur le Ministre de Votre Excellence

Le très humble et très obéissant serviteur

Henry de Bellonnet

P. S. 2 Decembre.

L'Amiral Roze m'annonce qu'il a évacué la Corée. J'ignore quelles peuvent être les raisons militaires qui ont pu le décider à se rembarquer immédiatement après avoir été battu, mais je dois à la vérité de protester contre les conclusions qu'il tire de sa malheureuse expédition. Ce n'étaient point les Coréens mais bien les Européens qui croyaient à l'invulnérabilité de la Corée; la destruction de quelques magasins et le pillage de Kang-hoa n'ont produit aucun effect favorable sur le gourvernement du pays, bien au contraire, et le meutre de nos missionnaires est si peu vengé que tous les chrétiens sont mis à mort sans exception. Je ne sais si le but de l'Amiral avait été simplement de faire de l'hydrographique en Corée, mais quant au but politique, il est absolument manqué. A Pékin, les Envoyés Coréens répètent dans tous les Yamens qu'ils ont "battu l'amiral, tué des soldats, et forcé le reste à se rembarquer." L'effet produit en est en ce sens déplorable, et je ne serais pas étonné de voir massacrer cet hiver dans les provinces lointaines, bon nombre de missionnaires et de chrétiens. J'essayerai de combattre cette dangereuse éventualité en parlant hautement d'une expédition sérieuse pour le printemps prochain.

Henry de Bellonet

Au moment de fermer cette dépêche arrive une longue lettre d'excuses du Tsong ly yamen à propos de la communication de notre correspondance aux différentes missions. Je l'enverrai par le prochain courrier.

1er annexe à la dép. pol. nº 21 de Pékin, 28 Novembre 1866

Pékin, le 13 juillet 1866*

Le Chargé d'Affaires de France au Prince de Kong

2e annexe à la dép. pol. nº 21 de Pékin, 28 Novembre 1866

*제1권 80번 문서.

Pékin le 16 Juillet 1866*

Le Prince Kong au Chargé Affaires de France

3e annexe à la dép. pol. n° 21 de Pékin, 28 Novembre 1866

Pékin, le 21 octobre 1866**

Le Chargé d'Affaires de France au Prince de Kong

4e annexe à la dép. pol. n° 21 de Pékin, 28 Novembre 1866

Pékin le 4 novembre 1866***

5e annexe à la dép. pol. n° 21 de Pékin, 28 Novembre 1866

Pékin le 11 novembre 1866****

6e annexe à la dép. pol. n° 21 de Pékin, 28 novembre 1866

Pékin le 16 novembre 1866*****

---

*제1권 83번 문서의 불역문.
**제1권 119번 문서.
***제1권 133번의 문서의 불역문.
****제1권 141번 문서.
*****제1권 150번 문서의 불역문.

7e annexe à la dép. pol. n° 21 du 28 novembre 1866

Pékin, le 23 novembre 1866*

*제1권 158번 문서의 불역문.

【관련문서 1】

Correspondance entre le Prince Kung et M. de Bellonet, chargé d'affaires de France à Pékin au sujet de la difficulté de Corée

Traduit de "Shanghaï Evening Courrier" du 12 Janvier 1867

Le Prince Kung aux Ministres étrangers (Extrait d'une traduction)

21 Novembre 1866

Une sérieuse querelle s'etant élevée l'été dernier entre les Français et les Coréens, M. de Bellonet le Chargé d'affaires de France m'a adressé deux communications à ce (*Sic*) relatives. Dans ma réponse je me suis efforcé d'agir comme médiateur -------- de manière à ce qu'il pût n'y avoir en fin de compte aucune perte de vie d'un côté ou de l'autre. A ma grande surprise je viens de recevoir une dépêche de M. de Bellonet dans laquelle il cite la déposition verbale d'un Coréen ainsi que les cancans des marchés, pour la véracité desquels il n'a pas l'ombre d'une preuve, et il s'en sert pour jeter un soupçon sur moi --------

J'ai été en termes d'amitié avec ces deux pays et j'ai cru que ce qu'il y avait de mieux à faire c'était de copier les trois dépêches de M. de Bellonet, avec leurs réponses et de les joindre à la présente pour l'information de Votre Excellence. Elles suffiront sans aucun doute à vous faire apprécier l'affaire. Des copies sont également envoyées aux autres Ministres étrangers résidant à Pékin. (14e jour de la 10me lune de la 5e année Tung-che-[B] annexer à la dépêche du Prince Kung.)

M. de Bellonet au Prince Kung.

Mr, je regrette de porter officiellement à la connaissance de Votre Altesse Impériale, un horrible attentat commis dans le petit royaume de Corée qui était autrefois rattaché à l'Empire de Chine par les liens de vasselage mais que cet acte de sauvage barbarie a séparé pour toujours de ce dernier.

Dans le cours du mois de Mars dernier les deux Evêques Français qui évangélisaient la Corée et avec eux neuf Missionnaires, sept prêtes coréens, et une grande foule de chrétiens des deux sexes et de tout âge, ont été massacrés par l'ordre du Souverain de ce pays.

Le Gouvernement de Sa Majesté ne peut pas permettre qu'un aussi cruel attentat reste impuni. Le jour où le Roi de Corée a mis la main sur mes malheureux compatriotes a été le dernier de son règne, lui-même en a proclamé la fin qu'à mon tour je viens déclarer solennellement aujourd'hui. Dans peu de jours nos forces militaires marcheront à la conquête de la Corée et l'Empereur, mon Auguste Souverain, a seul maintenant le droit et le pouvoir de disposer, d'après son bon plaisir, du pays et du trône vacant.

Le gouvernement Chinois m'a déclaré plusieurs fois qu'il n'a ni pouvoir ni autorité sur la Corée et il a refusé sous ce prétexte d'appliquer les Traités de Tientsin à ce pays et de donner à nos missionnaires les passeports que nous lui avons demandé (*Sic*). Nous avons pris note de ces déclarations et nous déclarons maintenant que nous ne reconnaissons aucune autorité que ce soit du Gouvernement Chinois sur le royaume de Corée.

J'ai l'honneur etc.

(signé) H. de Bellonet.

Réponse du Prince Kung à M. de Bellonet

(après avoir accusé réception de la lettre ci-dessus). Je puis faire observer ici que comme la Corée est un pays en dehors des autres qui s'étend dans un coin isolé et qui a toujours strictement maintenu ses propres règlements, comme on le sait bien, je suis tout-à-fait ignorant de ce qui les a conduit à mettre ces Missionnaires et ces chrétiens à mort. Cependant, je suis sensible aux sentiment d'amitié qui ont amené Votre Excellence à me communiquer les raisons pour lesquelles le Gouvernement français met ses forces en mouvement (contre ce pays).

Voyant toutefois que quand deux pays en viennent aux mains il y s'agit de la vie de leurs peuples -------- Je ne puis que m'efforcer d'amener une solution des difficultés qui existent entre eux -------- Il me semble qu'il vaudrait mieux s'enquérir préalablement des preuves et des mérites de l'affaire et s'assurer des raisons qui existent pour prendre cette mesure, de manière à ce qu'on pût éviter si possible de recourir aux armes. Je fais cette réponse en vue de suggérer cette manière de faire à la considération de Votre Excellence.

J'ai l'honneur, etc.

(signé) Kung

M. de Bellonet au Prince Kung (contenant avis du blocus avec demande de la promulguer dans l'intérêt du commerce, etc.)

Avis traduit du Chinois.

(le texte original de cette déclaration de Blocus est déjà connu)

Le Prince Kung à M. de Bellonet.

4 Nov. 1866

Il accuse réception de l'avis ci-dessus ainsi que de la dépêche du 24 octobre, et suggère de nouveau qu'on devrait examiner l'affaire en vue d'empêcher la guerre. Il mentionne qu'il n'a pas reçu de réponse à sa dépêche du 16 Juillet.

M. de Bellonet au Prince Kung

11 Novembre 1866

M^{r}, Je regrette que Votre Hautesse n'ait pas pu deviner les raisons qui m'ont forcé de garder le silence après les offres que vous m'avez faites dans votre communication du 16 Juillet dernier. Puisque vous insistez pour me faire revenir sur ce sujet je pense que je dois expliquer les motifs de ma conduite, en vous priant de vouloir bien vous souvenir que j'ai évité autant que possible de faire une communication si désagréable au Gouvernement Chinois.

En premier lieu le massacre des Missionnaires français est un de ces crimers impardonnables que rien ne peut excuser -------- J'ai déjà donné les instructions les plus précises pour que les mandarins coupables dont j'ai pu me procurer les noms soient jugés et exécutés aussitôt qu'ils tomberont entre nos mains. Quant au sort du ci-devant Roi de Corée, il est maintenant soumis à la décision de l'Empereur mon Auguste Souverain.

En second lieu je regrette d'être forcé de déclarer à Votre Hautesse Impériale que les rapports qui me sont parvenus durant ces cinq mois et qui ont été envoyés à Paris, sur les événements de Corée nous obligent à admettre de très sérieux soupçons de complicité de la part du Gouvernements Chinois. Beaucoup affirment que l'ambassade Coréenne qui est venue l'hiver dernier a apporté à Pékin le projet de massacre et remporté une autorisation tacite et l'approbation de quelques membres du Gouvernement Chinois -------- Le mystère dont ces derniers ont entouré les trois Missions Coréennes qui sont venues à Pékin au mois de Juillet, l'envoi en Corée d'un ambassadeur publiquement annoncé dans la Gazette, les nouvelles du recrutement et de la mise en mouvement de troupes Tartares qui nous sont parvenues de l'autre côté de la grande muraille, cet empressement singulier à chercher une excuse pour les Coréens plutôt que leur montrer l'horreur produite par le crime, toutes ces choses … tendront à faire regarder la conduite du Gouvernement Chinois avec soupçon.

En troisième lieu nous avons été deux fois les dupes d'enquêtes conduites par les autorités chinoises seules. La dissimulation qu'on a montrée à Sz-chula par rapport à l'affaire de Chun-chia-chan et celle que l'on montre encore relativement au meurtre de l'abbé Mabileau nous ont donné de trop sévères leçons sur l'insolente manière dont les autorités provinciales ont abusé de notre confiante fidélité, pour nous empêcher de l'oublier pendant longtemps.

En quatrième lieu Votre Altesse Impériale ignore probablement que la guerre qui pour nous est un plaisir, que les Français recherchent passionnément, est loin d'être préjudiciable au peuple en général -------- Ce que Votre Hautesse ignore peut-être enfin, c'est que le peuple de Corée loin d'être hostile, loin de défendre un Gouvernement qui l'opprime et le réduit à la misère s'adresse à nous comme à ses libérateurs -------- Notre expédition en Corée empêchera peut-être une intervention militaire en Chine que les efforts conciliatoires de Votre Altesse Impériale n'empêcheraient probablement pas -------- Toute tentative de conciliation sera maintenant inutile à moins que le ci-devant Roi de Corée se rende à discrétion et implore la merci de l'Empereur notre Auguste Souverain en se confiant à sa générosité. C'est à Votre Altesse Impériale à voir si Elle (*Sic*) peut donner cet avis au Gouvernement Coréen.

Signé : H. de Bellonet

Le Prince Kung à M. de Bellonet.

(Il accuse réception de la lettre ci-dessus du 11 Nov. Et exprime sa grande surprise des termes qui y sont contenus etc., etc.)

Dans la dépêche à laquelle je réponds l'histoire racontée par une personne officielle de la suite des Coréens ainsi que les cancans des marchés — choses pour lesquelles il n'y a pas l'ombre d'une preuve — servent à jeter un soupçon sur moi et à fournir une sorte de preuve par leur énonciation dans votre dépêche. Voyant que mon louable désir (dans la paix) ne s'accorde point avec les vues de Votre Excellence, mais qu'au contraire vous en faites un prétexte pour me soupçonner d'autres dessins, je ne puis que me sentir profondément mécontent -------- L'officier qui vint de la Corée et les nôtres qui y allèrent, le firent pour des affaires de cérémonial et conformément avec l'usage établi depuis longtemps : sans aucun rapport avec la querelle, etc -------- Si Sa Majesté Impériale avait résolu de lever et de préparer ses forces tout le monde l'aurait entendu ou l'aurait vu. Il est si évident qu'il n'y a rien de ce genre qu'il est inutile de discuter ce point plus longtemps mais son insertion dans votre dépêche trahit un désir de vous emparer de tels bruits pour gêner et embarrasser les autres -------- Une pareille manière de faire est-elle compatible avec les relations amicales entre nations ?...

M. de Bellonet au Ministère des affaires Etrangères Chinois.

Pékin 25 Nov. 1866

(Il se plaint de ce que sa correspondance ait été communiquée aux

Ministres étrangers et dit qu'il aurait dû en être préalablement informé, etc.) "Cela n'a point été fait et j'ai le droit d'y trouver une faute. J'informe en conséquence Votre Excellence que je soumets vos procédés à l'appréciation du Gouvernement de Sa Majesté, en lui demandant s'il ne juge pas convenable d'en réclamer satisfaction, et je confesse que je ne comprends pas pourquoi, depuis que le Gouvernement Chinois croit que je cherche à le trouver en faute, il m'a donné une si bonne occasion de satisfaire mon désir. (Il envoie M. Lemaire pour expliquer ses sentiments qui, dit-il, ont été mal compris.)

J'espère que cela prouvera une fois pour toutes à Votre Excellence le besoin d'avoir des Interprètes Européens en vous montrant l'impossibilité de parler d'affaires politiques tandis que vous employez un langage aussi imparfait que l'est le chinois.

Signé : H. de Bellonet, au Prince Kung

Réponse à la lettre ci-dessus
Le Ministère des affaires Etrangères à M. de Bellonet.

M[r], — J'ai l'honneur d'informer Votre Excellence que M. Lemaire, l'Interprète de la Légation de France, m'a apporté votre note du 25 Nov. avec les textes originaux (de la correspondance antérieure). Je les ai placés les uns à la suite des autres.

En vérité si les allégations que Votre Excellence a mises en avant contre ce Gouvernement avaient été tenues secrètes et si nous n'avions rien dit publiquement pour expliquer nos vues, cela fût devenu sûrement un grand sujet de reproche contre la réputation de Sa Majesté Impériale. C'est un point évident et qui n'a pas besoin d'être discuté ici, de savoir si une telle démarche était de nature à vous être préjudiciable ou non.

-------- Nous ne nous sommes pas considérés comme obligés de vous laisser connaître notre intention (de communiquer les dépêches) et de les envoyer ensuite (comme si vous les permettez).

Signé : Wausing et 5 autres membres du Ministère des affaires Etrangères

議政府(1866. 11. 30/高宗三年十月二十四日) ➞ 禮部

프랑스 함대와의 교전 경과 및 결과 보고

歷陳洋匪侵擾咨

朝鮮國王爲歷陳洋匪侵擾形實事本年九月洋匪入據江華府其回檄悖慢之由已有所具咨仰陳矣嗣後敵勢轉益猖獗有不可一一盡述而江華不但爲敝邦保障之重地也敝職先祖僖順王莊順王眞幀亦妥於行宮洋匪入城之日守臣倉黃移奉於僻處而殿宇廨署幷入灰燼以至驅刼男婦攘殺牛畜攫去椿留之銀掠取綱運之米武庫先被放燹利器多歸藉冦緣江列堡有龍津廣城等鎭而燒燬殆盡甲串鎭上下分船遮住以斷赴援之路鄕紳知宗正卿李是遠居在城外及聞城陷與其弟憂憤仰藥死之故已施褒隱之典巡撫中軍李容熙住陣于江華府越岸通津府未及交鋒矣九月十八日巡撫哨官韓聖根率銃手守文殊山城彼人乘四小船自甲串津來泊將欲上山聖根奮不顧身一發數丸則彼人應聲落水銃手隨卽齊發彼人多震仆而死者而船中人蠭涌登山放火於城門及公廨而去十月初四日巡撫千摠梁憲洙潛師由廣城津而入鼎足山城城在江華之東南將以爲憑高直擣如建瓴之勢也彼人又欲據此城其頭領騎馬悉帶銃卒上山不知憲洙已在城中也憲洙盡力捍禦齊放銃砲一場鏖戰其騎馬者應丸而墮彼兵相繼僵死者如麻輿尸而走器械輜重委棄路側初五日江華城中所在彼人紛紛輸器物於船中而甲串津碇留四隻一時解纜出往富平前洋與前留三舶同住而城中無一敵憲洙自鼎足山城整軍而下克復府城撫輯兵民而富平前洋碇留七舶本月十二日出外洋向南而去噫彼法國人人之强欲尋釁涉我海疆毁我關防創殘我民人偸竊我蓄貯是豈弊邦有所失而然哉特以其谿壑無厭之慾作一海浪賊耳弊邦地狹力弱不嫺戎政而惟玆禮義之俗秉彝攸存故上自朝廷卿士下至軍卒氓黎莫不扼腕裂眥誓死防守或有沫血倡義者或有捐軀殉難者衆心成城庶可藉此而獲保藩維然彼夷去來無常情跡叵測未可以釋慮而弛備矣竊伏惟我大朝字育之澤曠絶千古前後恩造山海崇深藐玆冲年遭此大難兢兢業業罔知攸措其在緩急安危之際籲告情實固臣分之當然而凡係小邦之患難每蒙大朝之捄恤玆具被兵事由修咨詳陳煩乞貴部轉達天聽導示備禦之機略使蕞爾屬國永底安靖恭備候度千萬幸甚爲此合行移咨云云 同治五年十月二十四日

164

H. de Bellonet(1866. 11. 30) ➔ P. de Chasseloup-Laubat

원정에 참여한 선박의 귀항 보고

À bord de *la Guerrière*, Nagasaki, le 30 Novembre, 1866

Monsieur le Ministre,

J'ai l'honneur d'informer Votre Excellence que, le 18 du courant j'ai quitté le mouillage de l'Ile Boisée avec les bâtiments de la Division. J'ai navigué avec toutes les précautions d'usage au milieu des bancs et des écueils qui sont parsemés sur la route qui sépare ce mouillage du golfe du Prince Jérôme et nous avons tous franchi sans accident ce passage difficile. La brise d'Ouest s'étant élevée avec violence et afin de ménager les bâtiments légers qu'il eût été imprudent de lancer au large avec cette apparence de temps, je suis allé prendre un mouillage qui m'avait été désigné quelques jours auparavant par le *Kien-chan*. Cet aviso que j'avais chargé de compléter nos travaux hydrographiques avait découvert dans l'Est de l'île Fernande un mouillage convenable par la nature du fond et présentant un abri suffisant contre les vents de la partie de l'Ouest. Cést là que j'ai conduit les bâtiments de la Division et bien que la mer y fût agitée par un ressac assez dur, nous y avons supporté très bien l'effort des grandes brises d'Ouest et de N.O. qui ont soufflé sans interruption pendant trois jours.

Dans la matinée du 21, la brise étant tout à fait tombée et toutes les indications tant du baromètre que de la mer m'annonçant une complète amélioration dans le temps, J'en ai profité pour sortir du golfe du Prince Jérôme et quitter définitivement les côtes de la Corée. J'ai expédié *le Laplace* à Tchéfoo, pour y rétablir, comme par le passé, le service de l'île de Kung-tung et y conduire deux chaloupes qui provenaient de l'occupation de Takou et dont j'avais eu besoin pour le transport des vivres et des munitions de l'île Boisée à Kang-hoa. *Le Primauguet* a fait route pour Shanghai, escortant *le Déroulède* qui y resta en station, *le Le Brethon* qui ira reprendre sa station de Han Kaw et *le Tardif* qui retournera à Ning-Po pour continuer la surveillance de cette partie de la côte et la répression des pirates. Enfin, j'ai pris avec *la Guerrière le Kien-chan* à la remorque et le 24 de ce mois j'arrivais à Nagasaki.

J'ai prescrit au *Laplace* de venir me rejoindre à Nagasaki et j'ai l'intention de mettre mon pavillon sur ce bâtiment pour aller visiter la mer intérieure et me rendre ensuite à Yokohama où j'enverrai en même temps *la Guerrière* par le détroit de Van-Diemen.

Les relations entre le nouveau Taïcoun et le Prince de Nagato ne sont pas encore rentrés dans l'ordre régulier, cependant un armistice de deux mois a été conclu et l'on espère arriver, avant son expiration, à un arrangement qui mettra fin à la guerre civile.

Je suis avec un profond respect,
Monsieur le Ministre,
De Votre Excellence,
Le très obéissant Serviteur
Le Contre-Amiral Commandant en chef

G. Roze

165

禮部(1866. 12. 3/同治五年十月二十七日) ➞ 高宗

Bellonet, Williams 등과 왕래한 조회문 전달

禮部知會總理衙門相機酌辦仍示法美往復書函

咨

禮部爲知照事主客司案呈本月初八日准摠理各國事務衙門謹奏爲朝鮮國咨請禮部代奏歷陳近日洋舶情形擬將臣衙門酌辦緣由仍由禮部咨照朝鮮俾其相機設法以免疏虞恭摺密陳仰祈聖鑑事本月初二日軍機處交出禮部奏據朝鮮國王咨覆洋舶情形請轉達天聽一摺軍機大臣面奉諭旨該衙門知道欽此欽遵鈔錄原奏並朝鮮國原咨知照到臣衙門臣等公同閱看該國王原咨大意以英國人馬力勝等强欲在該國地面通商藉稱中國曾有咨文並詰責其殺害教民教士該國不願習教並深知中國斷不給以咨文强其通商因該國將弁被擄見辱英船開砲遂亦開砲還擊人船均經焚溺緣有中國北京盛京廣東厦門等處人在內深自引咎並聲明洋人頻年泛海固請不已至有殺害民人之變茲備具事由請爲隨機鎭安開諭排解杜絶交易之說俾獲永底安靜等因臣等查上年法國前使臣栢尒德密曾經以該國教士欲往朝鮮傳教請先行文當經臣等拒絶並勸其毋庸前往卽經罷議本年夏間據英使阿禮國照會稱擬派輪船一隻至朝鮮海邊一帶請協力設法使該輪船行抵該國並據法使伯洛內照會稱朝鮮將法國主教傳教士人等殺害法國兵船不日齊集朝鮮暫取其國等情當於六月初七日將臣衙門向該兩國照復排解阻止各情形奏報並行知禮部各在案嗣因朝鮮國咨請禮部代奏法國搆兵一事復經臣衙門於八月二十三日將未據法使照復緣由奏請先由禮部咨復朝鮮亦在案伏思英國前請派輪船赴中國海面迤北並申擬前往朝鮮臣等以輪船行駛中國洋面列在條約未便駁斥而於欲往朝鮮一節曾酌擬照會復知阿禮國聲明礙難行文並阻其毋庸前往業於前奏內詳細具陳該國王接到禮部咨文想已洞悉原委今稱自七月以後英國人馬力勝等迭泊朝鮮屢地等情查英國志在通商自係蓄謀已久然在中國只有隨時阻止寔無准令朝鮮通商之文英人所云中國咨文躡後發船之說顯係揑造該國王自可毋庸顧慮惟臣衙門自照復阿禮國之後迄今四閱月並未復有照會前來昨據美使衛廉士函稱八月內有兩枝桅船一隻在高麗擱淺被高麗將船燒燬並捉去船主水手等二十四人未知後來生死如何高麗倘或送至中國請飭奉天府官撫

恤等語臣等隨給衛廉士復函允爲致信盛京將車及山海關監督查照妥辦今朝鮮所稱擊燬之船是否另自一事無從懸揣臣等風聞法國興兵前往朝鮮英美兩國曾經勸阻法國雖未聽從而朝鮮亦當分別核辦庶免多樹之敵至原咨所稱此次擊斃英船人等二十名內有聲稱中國姓名十三人查中國人民私出邊境例禁綦嚴若甘附敵船脅喝屬國斃于槍砲無從分別寔屬咎由自取朝鮮並無不合自可毋庸引咎其請爲隨機鎭安開諭排解一節臣等查英法兩國屢請輪船駛赴朝鮮臣衙門迭經給予照會妥爲擱阻迨教士被害法國用兵明知非空言所得而爭在臣衙門不得不隨時隨事力爲排解是以於法使照會兵船堵塞朝鮮海口時復給照覆仍令先行詳究情由毋庸遽行征戰以全兩國民命臣等查法國自與朝鮮用兵之後其與從前只求傳教局面不同英美雖聞前有勸阻之言頃又復與朝鮮搆衅將來通商之說勢必持之愈堅且既經用兵如欲講解勢必又有兵費之議三國駸駸乎已有相合之勢就目下而論則法爲甚而英次之此時若由臣衙門再給英法二國照會措詞之間稍露痕跡該二國未必遽就範圍卽使能有轉圜亦必以通商傳教賠償三事相責今朝鮮原咨旣深以通商傳教爲必不可行是亦曾慮及利害特賠償一節其害亦復相等臣衙門亦斷不能於朝鮮稍涉勉强相應請旨飭下禮部應如何咨照朝鮮國王計出萬全之處務須妥爲處置不可稍有大意除由臣衙門隨時相機酌辦外謹再恭摺密陳並照錄法國來往照會各一件美國來往信函各一件恭呈御覽伏乞皇太后皇上聖鑑謹奏一摺本月初六日奉旨依議欽此鈔錄原奏恭錄諭旨咨行禮部遵照辦理等因前來本部相應鈔錄該衙門原奏知照查照辦理除由總理各國衙門隨時相機酌辦外該國王仍當悉心籌畫分別核辦計出萬全不得稍涉疏虞可也云云　同治五年　月　日

法國照會

爲照會事照得本大臣現准本國水師提督來文移送該員所出告示一張以高麗西海沿通該國京城之河各口經該員所領之兵船均爲堵塞因不日攻打交兵暫止別國船隻前往茲本大臣將所接告示字摞繙譯漢文合送貴親王查閱卽請出示曉諭貴國商船俾各知曉免致冒進受損爲此照會須至照會者　九月十六日

法國告示

大法欽命前來中海日本等海統領本國水營兵船提督軍門羅爲曉諭事照得高麗國王殘暴不仁擅殺本國主教並傳教士數員及敎民男婦老幼多命揆度情理髮指難容因此本軍門聲罪致討先帶本營水軍前往該國征剿所有西海沿通該國京城

之河各口早經本營兵船堵塞把守一切別國船隻暫停前往倘有故違强進者應卽按照各國軍例嚴辦爲此特示

給法國照會

爲照覆事同治五年六月初五日本爵以朝鮮國殺害教衆一事似可先行據理查詢不必遽啓兵端照覆貴大臣在案至今未荷覆知玆於本月十六日接據貴大臣照會內稱現准本國水師提督來文移送該員所出告示一張以高麗西海沿通該國京城之河各口均經兵船堵塞因不日攻打交兵暫止別國船隻前往等因前來本爵查來文兵船堵塞該國各口等因檢查條約第三十一款內開載甚明無庸深辨至兩國交兵均關民命該國僻處海隅向知謹守此次何以殺害教民貴國是否曾經查詢可否先行詳究情由無庸遽行攻戰以全兩國民命之處統希貴大臣查察可也　九月二十七日

衛廉士來函

逕啓者現據烟台報到八月間有美國兩枝桅船一隻在高麗國擱淺被高麗士人將船燒燬並捉去船主水手二十四人未知後來死生如何照高麗規矩應送至中國交界俾中國官轉交營口本國領事今年五月間曾有美船小船觸硏擱淺其高麗人款待極好後將送至奉天府該處官刻薄飲食與高麗人大不同後有法國教師勸將送至牛莊了事玆二十四人倘或送至請貴衙門行飭奉天府官撫邮保護勿爲前時刻薄或有花去費用及採買粮食等項本國應當送還爲此預聞卽頌日祉　九月十五日

給美國衛廉士信

逕覆者本月十五日貴大臣來署面教信函一件內稱八月間有兩枝桅船在高麗擱淺一事當日經本衙門辦信分致盛京將軍及山海關監督查照妥爲辦理知款㕓注特此奉聞　九月二十日

H. de Bellonet (1866. 12. 8) ➔ G. Roze

Roze의 한강 봉쇄 해제에 대한 항의

Pékin, le 8 Décembre 1866

Monsieur le Contre Amiral,

J'ai reçu la lettre que vous m'avez fait l'honneur de m'écrire pour m'annoncer que vous aviez levé le blocus de la rivière de Séoul et complètement évacué la Corée. Mais celle qui devait m'annoncer, paraît-il, la prise de Kang hoa ne m'est jamais parvenue.

Je n'ai pas à discuter, Monsieur le Contre Amiral, les raisons militaires qui ont pu vous décider à prendre aussi brusquement et dans des circonstances aussi défavorables une détermination à laquelle j'étais loin de m'attendre ; mais je ne puis m'empêcher de regretter de n'avoir pas été mis à même, par quelques confidences de votre part, de préparer l'opinion publique à ce dénouement fâcheux qui a produit ici le plus déplorable effet. Vous me faites l'honneur de me dire que le but que vous vous proposiez a été atteint : je dois le croire, d'autant plus que j'ignore quel pouvait être ce but ; mais je dois aussi protester auprès de vous, comme je l'ai fait auprès du Gouvernement de l'Empereur, contre les conséquences politiques que vous tirez de vos opérations. Bien loin de frapper l'esprit de la Nation Coréenne, comme il vous plaît de le dire, ce rembarquement précipité après un échec qu'on n'a même pas cherché à réparer, a exalté l'orgueil de la Cour de Séoul. Les Coréens répètent dans tous les Ya-mens de Pékin "qu'ils vous ont chassés, et que s'ils avaient eu quelques soldats de plus pas un de nos hommes n'aurait pu se rembarquer." La mise à mort de tous les chrétiens sans exception a été décidée, et je proteste, au nom de la vérité, contre l'idée que vous paraissez avoir que le meurtre de nos missionnaires a été vengé. Je regarde au contraire la situation comme identique à celle de 1859 après le désastre de Takou.

Agréez, Monsieur le Contre Amiral,
l'assurance de ma haute considération,

Henry de Bellonet

P. S.

J'ai eu l'honneur de vous prévenir que vous recevriez probablement des instructions au sujet d'une démonstration [_____] [_____].

La restituition des terrains de l'église et le déplacement du Vice-Roi Li rendent aujourd'hui cette démonstration inutile et les instructions que j'avais demandées pour vous à Paris doivent être considerées comme non avenues.

Roze

高宗(1866. 12. 11/高宗三年十一月五日) ➔ 禮部

總署에 감사 표시와 함께 서양선박 관계 사실 통보

覆陳洋舶事實仍謝總理衙門相機酌辦咨

朝鮮國王爲覆陳致謝仍辦洋舶事實事同治五年十月二十七日承准貴部咨節該云云[自主客司案呈止疎虞可也見上知會總理衙門相機酌辦咨]等因奉此竊念小邦凡有患難疾聲具籲者仰藉天朝字小之眷也今此貴部之據情代奏軍機大臣之面奉諭旨總理衙門之相機籍辦俾小邦悉心籌畫計出萬全不得稍涉疎虞其所以撫保小邦靡不用極不知小邦何以獲此隆庇也第玆英船焚溺之事法檄悖慢之說法兵退去之由前以具咨詳陳而本年二月七月再到海美縣江華府固請通商以無上國公文不敢擅便許施則謂往大淸國請公文並貨物前來而發船遠去仍無形影者卽自稱英人馬力勝戴拔等也又於七月來泊平壤府拘執將弁殺害人民討索財貨亂放銃砲擱淺而自被焚溺者卽自稱英人崔蘭軒但國人李八行及烏鬼子等也原無美國人兩枝桅船一隻擱淺被燒並捉去船主水手等二十四人之事則今此衛廉士來函想因平壤府英船焚溺事而轉相訛傳不究根由也弊邦與英法兩國本不交涉何有失和通商傳敎則以邦禁而拒絶之敎士則以異國莠民變服誑惑而斥除之而已凡天下各國相與征戰必先詳究情實明執釁端始可興兵而今法人之瞰我未備闖入江華府焚毁全城剽攘財貨卽一劫掠殘暴之寇也通商者果如是乎傳敎者果如是乎末乃頭領被殲擧帆而走然伊後踪跡有難料測惟當秉義修備務盡誠信而至若兵費賠償一節伏荷貴部及總理衙門之慮及利害誠萬萬銘感但法人之攫取弊邦帑蓄戎器者其數不貲則弊邦責償於法國猶或可矣法國責償於弊邦安有是也凡係洋夷之通商傳敎賠償諸事小邦之民情國勢雖幾年受困於洋夷斷不可行矣小邦有事輒蒙皇朝之曲賜矜恤玆庸備悉事由謹具覆陳煩乞貴部深軫小邦情實轉達天廳隨機指諭俾底安靖庸究終始之惠千萬達甚爲此合行咨覆云云　同治五年十一月初五日

168

P. de Chasseloup-Laubat (1866. 12. 11) → Moustier (1866. 12. 12)

향후 조선 원정 계획에 대한 질문

Paris, le 11 Décembre 1866

Monsieur le Marquis et cher Collègue, j'ai l'honneur de vous communiquer sous ce pli un rapport que M. le Commandant en chef de notre Division navale des Mers de Chine m'a adressé de Tche-Fou, le 6 Octobre, à la suite d'une exploration qu'il a faite sur la côte de Corée.

Malgré les difficultés que présentait cette exploration, M. le Contre Amiral Roze a remonté le Han-Kiang jusque devant Séoul, Capitale de la Corée, et il a pu se rendre compte des moyens qu'il conviendrait d'employer si une expédition devait être entreprise pour venger le massacre de nos missionaires.

Votre Excellence pensera sans doute comme moi que, dans la situation actuelle, on ne saurait engager le gouvernement de l'Empereur dans une expédition qui nous forcerait à envoyer dans ces parages 1500 ou 2000 hommes, et exigerait des moyens d'action considérables en dehors des forces dont se compose la Division navale des mers de Chine.

Je vous serai obligé, Monsieur le Marquis et cher Collègue, en me renvoyant le rapport dont il s'agit, de vouloir bien me faire connaître votre avis sur cette question et sur les mesures prises en dernier lieu par M. le Contre Amiral Roze.

Agréez, Monsieur le Marquis et cher Collègue, l'assurance de ma haute considération.

Le Ministre, secrétaire d'Etat de la Marine et des Colonies

P. Chasseloup-Laubat

A. Burlingame (1866. 12. 12) → W. H. Seward

조선 문제 관련 恭親王과의 면담 결과 보고

LEGATION OF THE UNITED STATES
Peking, December 12, 1866

Sir:

I have the honor to inform you that, on the 20th of November last, I had an interview with Prince Kung, at the Tsung li Yamen, of more than ordinary interest.

After the usual formalities and felicitations, the Prince dismissed, with the exception of his official suite, his attendants, and proceeded in a disturbed manner to speak of this relations with foreigners. He said they were excellent with all but the French, but that with these, in spite of all he could do, they were not such as he desired. The causes of irritation were their claims on account of their missionaries, and the nature of a correspondence touching affairs in Corea; that the missionaries, not content to spread their faith, to which there was no objection, were political agents, and undertook to absolve their Chinese converts from obligations to their own government, and that they were supported in their pretensions by their diplomatic representatives at Peking; that when he sought, on behalf of a kindred and once tributary people, (the Coreans), to secure, in the interests of peace, an investigation into facts, before proceeding to extremities, he had been charged with complicity with them, and his own people menaced with attack.

I replied, as I had often done before, that I could not interfere between them and others, more than to proffer my good offices when they might serve to restore friendly relations. I urged the Prince strongly to instruct his officials in the provinces to treat the missionaries with the utmost kindness, so as to avoid all occasion for armed intervention. I said to him that my colleague, M. Berthemy, the French minister, now absent on leave, had said to Sir Frederick Bruce and myself that he did not, nor did his Emperor, sustain any such pretensions as those mentioned by the Prince on the part of the missionaries; that he had informed them that he, and the officials under him, alone represented the political and diplomatic power of France in China, and that I thought, with patience and caution, an amicable solution of their difficulties might be reached.

With regard to Corea I said that, if the Prince had done no more than to proffer his friendly offices, I did not see that he had done more than his duty; and that, if such action called forth menaces, he could rest strong in the consciousness of good intentions, and submit, with confidence, the correspondence to the impartial judgment of the civilized world.

That very evening the despatch marked A, covering a long correspondence with M. de Bellonet, French charge d'affaires, was sent to each one of the foreign legations, and I submit it (with the subsequent despatches marked B) without one word of comment.

I have the honor to be, Sir, your obedient servant,
ANSON BURLINGAME

Hon. WILLIAM H. SEWARD,
Secretary of State, Washington, D. C.

[Enclosure A-Translation]*

[Enclosures in Prince Kung's despatch]

CORRESPONDENCE, BETWEEN PRINCE KUNG AND M. DE BELLONET, FRENCH CHARGE D'AFFAIRES. RELATIVE TO THE MASSACRE OF FRENMISSIONARIES IN COREA.

No. 1

M. de Bellonet to Prince Kung**

No. 2

Reply of Prince Kung to M. de Bellonet

[Translation]

*제1권 158번 문서의 영역문(美國)

**제1권 80번 문서의 영역문

July 16, 1866*

No. 3

M. de Bellonet to Prince Kung**

[Enclosure translated from Chinese]

Rose, rear-admiral and commander-in-chief of the French naval forces in the Chinese and Japanese seas, herewith issues a notification to all concerned:

Whereas the King of Corea, in a spirit of of (*Sic*) inhuman barbarity, having seized and killed several French bishops and missionaries, together with many native Christians, male and female, old and young, I think that his numerous crimes cannot be suffered to pass with impunity. I have determined to proceed against him for his notorious crime, and shall take the forces under my command to attack and subdue his country. All ports and embouchures on the western shores of Corea, leading to the capital, are immediately to be blockaded by the ships under my command, and the vessels of all other nations are for the present forbidden to resort there. If any of them attempt to violate this order and break the blockade, they will be dealt with according to the laws acknowledged among nations in such cases. A special notice.

OCTOBER 5, 1866; (or, Tumgchi, 5th year, 8th moon, 27th day.)

No. 4

Prince Kung to M. de Bellonet***

No. 5

M. de Bellonet to Prince Kung****

No. 6

---

*제1권 83번 문서의 영역문.
**제1권 119번 문서의 영역문.
***제1권 133번 문서의 영역문.
****제1권 141번 문서의 영역문.

Prince Kung to M. de Bellonet*

No. 7

M. de Bellonet to the Foreign Office

[Translation]**

No. 8

From Foreign Office to M. de Bellonet

[Translation]

[No date]***

*제1권 150번 문서의 영역문.

**제1권 159번 문서의 영역문.

***제1권 176번 문서의 영역문.

R. Alcock (1866. 12. 13) → Stanley (1867. 3. 8)

조선 문제 관련 청불(淸佛) 관계 및 양국 교섭 과정 보고

Peking. December 13, 1866

My Lord,

THE inclosed correspondence between the Prince of Kung, the Ministers of the Tsung-li-yamen, and M. de Bellonnet, the French Chargé d'Affaires, arising out of the Corean massacre of Roman Catholic missionaries and their converts, has been forwarded to all the Legations by his Imperial Highness, as a protest, apparently, against the language of M. de Bellonet and the injurious charges conveyed in his letters to the Prince accusing the Chinese Government or certain of its members of complicity in the acts of the Coreans.

The Prince, in his covering letter, after recapitulating the substance of M. de Bellonet's correspondence, particularly refers to the absence of all proof of any foundation for the injurious charges, and appeals to the other Representatives of Treaty Powers at Peking, inviting an expression of their opinion.

Neither I nor my colleagues, the Representatives of America, Russia, and Prussia, have felt it expedient to take this course. Whatever judgement may be formed of the grave charges brought by M. de Bellonnet or the language employed, any formal intervention at the request of one party in a matter of dispute without the consent of the other would only serve to envenom the discussion. I have, however, had some conversation with the French Chargé d'Affaires on the subject, which satisfied me that he believed credit was to be attached to various rumours conveyed to him, through the missionaries or their converts chiefly, as to the complicity of the Chinese Government. He conceived this was shown by indications of previous knowledge that a massacre of Romanist missionaries and their converts was contemplated, and he was determined to adhere to the line of policy which his letters indicate.

What that policy is, and how far it may be sanctioned or is likely to be carried out by the French Government, are questions of such serious importance to the interests of all the other Treaty Powers that I deem it essential to put your Lordship in possession of whatever tends to throw light upon them.

M. de Bellonnet makes no secret of what his view are or the policy he advocates. He has often, in conversation with Mr. Wade and his colleagues, declared his conviction that the dismemberment of the ere is inevitable: and he thinks that the sooner it takes place the better, because only then can any reconstruction on a better basis take place, for nothing is to be hoped from the existing dynasty and effete system. He has no scruple, therefore, in precipitating the event by insisting upon decide progress and changes for which those at the head of affairs are wholly unprepared, and with little heed as to what may be the immediate consequences or danger to the Government and its rule over the provinces. Nor does he seem to regard with any fear the possible contingency of an indefinite period of anarchy consequent on the fall of the present Government and dynasty. One or more of the European Powers, with a handful of troops, and a few Sous-Lieutenants to preform the function of Government in the provinces, might suffice, he conceives, to maintain order, recognize the whole system of government, and administer it over the empire, with its eighteen provinces, each larger and more populous than many European kingdoms.

In close connection with these sweeping views for the regeneration of China-the first element of which is the destruction of all existing forms-note must be taken of a standing grievance in the perpetual contravention of Treaties by the provincial authorities, and the impossibility of obtaining redress from the Central Government. This applies, it is true, to all the Treaty Powers, but with France, the assumed protectorate of the Roman Catholic missionaries, scattered far and wide through the Empire, with fixed habitations in the interior far away from all supervision of Consuls, introduces and additional and exceptional class of grievances, bringing their own peculiar conditions of mutual wrong and irritation. Other Governments have ever-recurring complaints of injury to their subjects in their material interests, and feel in common the hopelessness of removing the grounds, as well as the weariness of vain efforts to obtaining redress by diplomatic means. M. de Bellonnet does not stand alone, therefore, in his dissatisfaction at the folly of those who, instead of smoothing the way for the gradual progress of change by reasonable and safe concessions, treat it as if it could be permanently kept at bay, and meet it with an opposition of which the only effect can be to hurry it on too quickly and too far. But there is this essential difference, even as regards material wrongs, between the French Representative at Peking and his colleagues. Delays and tergiversations prolonged from month to month and from year and year, have undoubtedly an exasperating effect on all; only with M. de Bellonnet, as he wrote to me some time ago, "Pour nous Francais, qui sommes un peu moins patients que les Chinois, six mois de silence est l'équivalent d'un refus;" whereas his colleagues, feeling that great material interests are at stake, and that a vast commerce is bound up with the maintenance of peaceable external relations and a fixed Government within, are less disposed to regard delay as a refusal to do justice, and to peril all by prompt recourse to violence and coercion. The sense of responsibility, which sobers them and keeps in check all important impulses, is unfortunately wholly wanting in the case of the French, who have no large trade to injure or to risk, and no material interests of any real importance in China. Their grievances are nearly all of a putative character, and exclusively due to the voluntarily assumed protectorate of Roman Catholic missionaries and their converts. I say of their converts advisedly; for it is impossible to doubt that these missionaries do in effect, if not avowedly, seek to establish under the ægis of France a veritable protectorate over the thousands of Chinese subjects whom they claim as converts. Not content with their own exemption from the jurisdiction of the Chinese authorities, under an exterritorial clause, which is in itself a source of constant humiliation to the country, they strive unceasingly to withdraw their converts and protégés from the legitimate authority of the territorial sovereign. Thus a struggle full of bitterness and hostile feeling is constantly maintained on both sides: the one trying to obtain a right of interference and protection over large classes of Chinese subjects, and the other stoutly contesting an encroachment on their rightful authority by all means at their command-sometimes by craft, and at others by violence, according to their weakness or their strength, but always with a consciousness of right, and no question except as to a choice of means. The Central Government at Peking is probable more sensitive than the distant provincial authorities to the danger and responsibility of acts tending to embroil them with the great Protecting Powers so constantly invoked in aid by the Romanist missions. But who can doubt what it approves in secret of all resistance to the priestly domination sought to be established, to the subversion of all territorial sovereignty and independence of a foreign Power?

This same battle, with some little modification in form, has been waged in our own and every Protestant country in Europe in times past, and has not ceased even at the present day. It seems, indeed, to be inevitable wherever the two forces are in presence. It has been well and truly remarked that, "among a people so careless of religion and religious faith as the Chinese, the attempt to inculcate a dozen new religions would be regarded with callous indifference did the missionaries confine themselves to the simple apostolical routine of proselytism. It is only when they awaken jealously by mixing in matters temporal that they become objects of dislike and suspicion to the governing power."

To this desire to obtain temporal influence as a means to spiritual ends, under the belief that the minds of people would be more easily swayed if political power were brought to the aid of argument, is to be traced the present danger to all peaceable relations. The Romanist missions think to strengthen their own cause, by showing that they have power to protect their converts from all action of their own authorities. That the latter should resist such attempts is in the nature of things, and unavoidable. To this and no other cause is to be attributed the extermination of Romanism in Japan nearly three centuries ago, with the massacre of thousands of converts; and the similar persecution and expulsion which took place about the same era, and later, in Chinese. The more recent massacres in Saigon, about it was annexed, and in Corea, read very much like chapters out of the same book.

The Roman Catholic missions are provoking precisely the same results now, trusting to France to avert the catastrophe by drawing the sword in their defence, and revolutionizing the country if not conquering it. It cannot be matter of surprise, therefore, that these grievances of missionaries, alleged spoliations and oppressions of their converts, and even acts of violence directed against their own persons, and occasionally costing a life, should meet with tardy recognition, and still more reluctant reproval or redress from the Government here. And it is precisely these cases that create the greatest exasperation at the French Legation, not the less that there is known to be a certain national pride in the protectorate assumed by France, and a very considerable party in that country who sympathise entirely with the aims and work the missionaries. It is said, I know not with what truth, that 7,000,000 French subjects, exclusive of large numbers in Belgium, Italy, and Spain, subscribe funds to maintain the Romanist missionaries in China.

The prestige and honour of France, as the avowed protector of these pioneers of the Roman Church, are engaged to shield them; and armed with the consciousness of this, and their own zeal in the propagation of the faith, I fear it is too true that, in the spirit of the crusaders, they look more to the sword than the cross to remove all obstacles and make their way clear, quite willing themselves to incur all the risks of martydom in establishing a new order of thins more consonant with their hopes and aims.

It requires no accumulation of details and facts to show how pregnant with danger the operation of these causes must be throughout a vast Empire like China, torn by civil dissensions, badly governed, under the weak administration of a child Emperor, and still further paralyzed by the ever-present fear of foreign aggression and forcible interference.

It is easy to understand, under such conditions, how, in the case of the priest murdered in Kuei-chow, five years ago, and another in Sze-chuen last year, no promise given with regard to the punishment of the guilty has been kept; and, no less easy to comprehend, that each post brings a fresh crop of complaints and grievances, from every quarter, of missionaries on collision with local authorities, of persecutions directed against their isolated congregations, and of wrong and injury suffered by the one or the other. How far these may be well or ill founded it must, in the majority of cases, be exceedingly difficult for the Chinese Government to ascertain, were they ever so well-disposed to arrive at the truth; and hardly less so for the French Representative at Peking, or to establish his conclusion upon satisfactory evidence. Where one party is eager to find or to make causes of offence, and the other equally ready to resent and resist pretensions, it may be safely concluded that the wrong is not always on one side.

Mr. Wade in the memorandum of a conversation with Wēnseang which I inclosed in my despatch No. 7 of September 7 last, dwelt much upon the irritation felt by the French on account of the ill-treatment of the Romish missionaries, and on the natural increase of this irritation consequent on the Corean massacres; and even admitting the unreasonableness of the missionary complaints in many cases, the excusableness of anger where the Chinese Government had behaved as in the cases already cited of two missionaries put to death, the Minister, without denying that some of the missionary complaints might be well founded, obviously felt that little account was taken by the foreign Legations of all the deeper grounds of complaints his Government had against these fomentors of discord and subversive action; and I think that it is only fair in reference to the endless complaints which find their way to Peking from the Roman Catholic missionaries of wrong and ill-treatment in all parts of the Empire, to call attention to the inclosed brief account of a journey of 900 miles by two English Protestant missionaries through the western provinces, so lately the scene of civil conflicts and disturbance. It is certainly a significant fact that in all this prolonged journey, extending over several weeks, in regions rarely visited by foreigners, they never once met with serious ground of complaints, and, when they had occasion to appeal to the local authorities they invariably met with attention and civility.

It is not necessary, however, to assume that the Romanist missionaries have no bonâ fide ground of complaints. How far they provoke any injuries suffered by unwarrantable pretensions and usurpations of authority not properly attaching to their mission, is another thing. If it were a question of tolerance, even Protestant Powers might be willing to incur some risk and damage in their material interests for an object so highly appreciated by all. But it is not tolerance which is denied them, but something quite different and thoroughly antagonistic. It is too much therefore to expect that Protestant nations, or Russia with its Greek Church, should submit to have all their interests imperilled in order that ultramontane doctrines and Papal rule should be established in China under a French Protectorate. That which France herself steadily resists at home cannot with any show of consistence be imposed on other nations, either by missionaries or her troops. Still less can England. America, or Prussia, all Protestant States which have maintained the opposite principle through centuries of war and effort, see with equanimity an enemy no longer able to find a resting-place in Europe make a safe lodgment in in the Far East with the aid of French bayonets, at the expense of every interest they possess in those regions. It is not a question of theology, or the relative merits of Protestantism and Papacy. Whether the latter, cleared of some of its non-essentials and corruptions, might not exercise a more beneficial influence among Asiatic races, and be more readily accepted by them than any existing form of Protestantism, amy fairly be considered a matter of opinion, in which most earnest and sincere believers in the divine origin and authority of Christianity may entertain different views. It is not the spiritual but the temporal bearing of ultramontane theories and operations which affects Government.

And as regards this country more especially, apart even from the ulterior tendencies and schemes of the Romanist missions, there can be no doubt, I think, that when M. Lagréné, the first French Minister in China, introduced a clause in his Treaty stipulating for the restoration of all land or houses which, on the expulsion of the Roman Catholic missionaries in the beginning of the eighteenth century, were confiscated to the State as having belonged to the different missions all over the country, he planted the seed for a plentiful and never-failing crops of contentions and heart-burning with the Chinese authorities, by which in the end I believe all the property they may acquire in virtue of the Treaty will have been dearly purchased. But apart also from this fruitful source of ill blood and popular hostility, the special feature attaching to the Romanist pretensions lies in the fact that it is impossible for the Chinese Government ever to satisfy them. To yield to their claims for authority, and a protectorate over Chinese subjects, would be for the Emperor to abdicate in effect, and renounce the rights of sovereignty over his own people. Therefore, so long as a powerful foreign State like France undertakes to support these Romanist missions, and fight their battles, there can be neither peace nor security.

The grievances of other foreign Powers, those more especially who have large commercial interests engaged, are of a very different type, and would seem to admit of far easier redress, although none can be obtained, or only of so tardy and imperfect a character that it amounts almost to a total denial of justice. If there were any question of coercion and the policy of restoring to it, it would surely be in such cases that the strongest argument might be found where the wrong or injury is undeniable, and the benefit any success would be common to all.

I happened lately to have occasion to refer to the correspondence of my predecessor Sir Frederic Bruce, in 1863, with the Prince of Kung, and I could not help being struck with the stereotyped forms of complaint reiterated then for the twentieth time, year after year, and as applicable now as them without the alteration of a word. In a memorandum of the substance of observations addressed to the Prince of Kung by Sir Frederic Bruce on the 5th of June, 1863, the following passages occur, and are so entirely to the point that I cannot forbear quoting them as they stand : -

"These expectation have not been realized. At several of the parts the Treaty is daily broken in matters great and small, and the Central Government, if not unwilling, shows itself unable to enforce a better order of thins. The orders sent by the Foreign Board when Sir Frederic Bruce complains are not carried out, either because the local authorities do not stand in awe of the Foreign Board, or because they do not believe that the Foreign Board issues them in earnest.

Questions of this sort have again and again been brought forward by Sir. F. Bruce. The Foreign Board has gone through the form of issuing instructions thereupon, but causes of complaint remain as they were, either because the local authorities do not fear or because the Foreign Board do not care. Seeing that none of the authorities whose conduct has been complained of have been punished or removed; that officials notoriously hostile to foreigners have been appointed to place where they have increased opportunity of indulging their anti foreign tendencies, while in one or two instances, as at Canton, Newchwang, and Foochow, officials of friendly dispositions have been withdrawn, Fir F. Bruce is induce, however, reluctantly, to infer that if the Imperial Government be not adverse to foreign intercourse, it is, at all events, indisposed to do what is necessary to teach the people and local authorities that China is sincerely desirous of friendly relations with foreign Powers."

And again, in a letter dated June 16 of the same year, Sir Frederic remarks: "Complaints are incessant from almost every port of entire indifference on the part of the authorities to the provisions of the Treaties affecting transit duties, passports, the free employment of Chinese, the acquisition of building sites, and the recovery of debts."

"I do not deem it worth while to go more into detail, because there is no case before me in the catalogue of those still unsettled which could not have been disposed of without reference to the capital and which could not now be disposed of in a few days were the local authorities persuaded of the fact that the Treaties form part of the law of the land, and that neglect or violation of their provisions will be denounced and punished as breaches of the law."

This is in fact the summary of a whole series of despatches, and were I to write as many more on the present state of out relations I could nor more completely or accurately describe it. And this was more than three years ago.

The Government of the United States of America and of Great Britain are the most seriously aggrieved, because their commerce and material interest of various kinds are so immeasurably greater than those of other nations in China. Russia has no doubt large interest territorial and commercial on the northern and western boundary, and, as I learn from its Representative, they are not without grounds of complaints, aggravated by the same inertness or indisposition to do justice. But the greatest amount and multiplication of cases requiring redress fall necessarily to the share of Great Britain and America, from the greater magnitude of interests and more numerous points of contact with the Chinese. On them also, therefore, is laid in the present state of affaires the greatest burden of patience and forbearance.

And it is this long animity which is made a subject of reproach to their Representative by French Chargé d'Affaires. Impatient of delay and eager to strike as the readiest means of obtaining the satisfaction he despairs of otherwise securing, and strong in the belief that it is only by such action China can be either promptly or effectually shaken out of the rut of old prejudices and retrograde ways, he condemns all reliance on milder means as lamentable weakness as well as the worst policy.

To Great Britain more especially he disposed to attribute, by her willingness to add to the difficulties of the present Government by any action calculated to weaken its power or influence with its own subjects, and her generally conciliatory spirit, the resistance which he meets with in all his efforts to obtain prompt redress; and he conceives our moral support to the existing Government is not only a mistake but a main cause of an indisposition to change or progress, which all, nevertheless, are pressing upon it as necessary to its own security and advancement. That he should also attribute our caution or reluctance to force them on in the paths of innovation against their will and before they are satisfied of its prudence or wisdom, to an all-engrossing and sordid care for our own interests to the prejudice of all civilization or progress in this country, will hardly be matter of surprise. Nor should I allude to it not that undoubtedly these opinions are communicated to his Government, and whatever may be the degree of influence they may be calculated to exercise upon the French Executive, it is only right that Her Majesty's Government should be in a position to act upon the knowledge of the views and motives attributed to them, as well as those maintained by the French Representative in support of a policy diametrically opposed to that which they desire to see followed in this country.

I can only say in conclusion that I consider the Romanist missions, and the action of the French in their support, the greatest danger to our interests in China and the continuance of good relations with either people or Government; and no less certainly, in my opinion, the most serious impediment to any improvement in material civilization. It is impossible to follow the conversation with the Chinese Minister Wēnseang, the most intelligent and liberally-disposed member of the Yamēn for Foreign Affairs, and not see that the one predominant idea which presented itself to his mind whenever railroads, telegraphs, or other European innovations were in question, was the fear of opening a door to further interference and dictation on the part of the French under pretext of vested interests.

M. de Bellonnet may possibly believe that it would only require firmness and resolution on the pert of the Treaty Powers, or even one of them if the others did not by their support and sympathy neutralize the effect, to compel the Chinese Government to enter at once on a course of reform and innovation, and to render prompt justice in all cases of wrong inflicted on foreigners by the provincial authorities. He may think that, without any resource to arms, all the calamities with which the empire is threatened by the continuance of abuses and vain efforts to perpetuate a feeble and utterly corrupt administration might thus be averted to the great benefit of Chinese and foreigners alike. And if not, yet the best and safest policy would be to dictate, not to temporize, and, other means failing, to use coercion and put the whole empire under tutelage, as dependent States are in India. He has certainly so expressed himself on more than one occasion when speaking on the subject to me and to others.

That a French Minister should deem such a system as France might establish an undoubted again to any other nation is not perhaps unnatural; but the Representatives of other Powers may be excused if they place less implicit trust in a régime of Sous-Lieutenants or Prefects for the government of 400,000,000 of an Eastern race, whose language there are not twenty Frenchmen can either speak or understand.

There is no empire in the world with so vast a population or so entirely homogeneous in race, language, customs, and religion, and it may well seem strange that France, which in the recent declaration of her Emperor proclaims the indisputable right of nationalities to form themselves in unity, should be the most active agent, by her Representative here, for the disintegration or dismemberment of China as a means of advancing good government and civilization.

But, as I have already remarked, the interests are too great for a hazardous or experimental policy; and the field of operations is on too vast a scale. We have nearly as strong reasons as the Chinese for being very slow in departing from the status quo, unsatisfactory as this may be; for any great change during the minority of the Emperor, as I have already pointed out in a recent despatch, is sure to be attended with equal risk to all material interest. It is much more difficult than many suppose to improve an Oriental Government, owing to the badness of the instruments by which improvement is to be carried out. And this, if all others were wanting, is a strong argument in justification of their obstinate adherence to custom and routine in preference to innovation.

On the other hand, it is impossible to deny that great and tangible benefits accrue to foreign nations under existing Treaties, however imperfectly in many instances their conditions are fulfilled. These advantage, it is quite true, are not without certain drawbacks; but it is impossible to maintain that the injury resulting is either very great in extent or serious in its bearing on the whole results. And the endeavour to remove them by the summary action advocated by the French Representative in connection with views and aims of the Romanist missions in the interior, would be simply to sacrifice a great and substantial good to escape a comparatively small evil, and for at best a very doubtful future gain. It would be, above all, to abandon every hope of improvement in this generation, or of progressive changes by more rational modes of proceeding.

This is the view equally entertained by my colleagues and myself, who see more to fear than to hope from any innovations forced upon either the people or the Government by foreign influence. We are of in opinion, that the more immediate result of any such attempts would be anarchy and revolution, with the total destruction of a valuable and flourishing trade, which, notwithstanding all shortcomings of the existing Government, and many real and constantly recurring grounds of complaint, continues to prosper and increase. However small the hope of any rapid or spontaneous improvement, or poor the chances of progress either in civilization or good government in the present aspect of affairs, we are satisfied they would be infinitely less under the pressure of foreign coercion or dictation, while the injurious effects to be anticipated are altogether incalculable.

The one question, therefore, is, which policy shall prevail? If the Romanist missionaries in the interior and the French Representative at Peking are allowed to pursue the course they deem best, it will very certainly not be a policy of forbearance or non-interference, but one of menace and coercion, leading rapidly to acts of war, and possibly to dismemberment. It rests with the other foreign Powers to determine how far such action on the part of France is compatible with their common interests, or the preservation and enjoyment of Treaty rights in China; and if judged to be adverse to both, by what means a more temperate and pacific line of conduct may be secured.

I have, &c.

(Signed) RUTHERFORD ALCOCK

Inclosure 1

The Prince of Kung to Sir R. Alcock*

Inclosure 2

M. de Bellonnet to the Prince of Kung**

Inclosure 3

The Prince of Kung to M. de Bellonnet***

Inclosure 4

M. de Bellonnet to the Prince of Kung

Monsieur,

Peking, le 21 Octobre, 1866

J'ai l'honneur de porter à la connaissance de votre Altesse Impériale la notification officielle du blocus de la rivière de Séoul et des côtes occidentales de la Corée par les Forces Navales de Sa Majesté l'Empereur des Français. Je prie votre Altesse Impériale de vouloir bien donner à ce document toute la publicité possible afin que nul n'en ignore, et que les intérêts des Chinois qui trafiquent avec la Corée soient entièrement sauvegardés.

*제1권 158번 문서의 영역문.
**제1권 80번 문서.
***제1권 83번 문서의 영역문(英國).

J'ai, l'honneur d'être etc.

(Signé) Henry de Bellonnet*

Inclosure 5

The Prince of Kung to M. de Bellonnet**

Inclosure 6

M. de Bellonnet to the Prince of Kung***

Inclosure 7

The Prince of Kung to M. de Bellonnet

(Translation.)

THE Prince has read with great astonishment the despatch received from M. de Bellonnet on the 4th day of the 10th moon (November 19, 1866), charging in its general purport the Chinese Gorvernment with a desire to take the part of and protect Corea.

In the 6th and again in the 9th moon the Prince addressed two despatches in reply to the Chargé d'Affaires of France. The Prince's reasons for writing as he did in those replies were, that as France and Corea could not engage in hostilities without both sides suffering loss and injury to life and property, his Highness could not sit by and watch the proceeding without moving. He could not but (endeavour) as an intermediary to arrange the difficulty in the hope of preserving the lives of the subjects of both countries.

The Prince was actuated by the best of motives; he is excessively grieved, therefore, to read the despatch under acknowledgment, in which the Chargé d'Affaires openly, and in writing, gives expression to certain suspicions he has been pleased to form, founded on the one-sided statements of a menial

*제1권 119번 "한강 봉쇄 통보"와 같음.
**제1권 133번 문서의 영역문(英國).
***제1권 141번 문서.

attendant, and the totally groundless (lit., shadowless, soundless) gossip of the streets and lanes. The Chargé Affaires completely ignores the goodness of the Prince's intentions, and even suspects (the Chinese Government) of having other designs(i.e., moving troops to the aid of Corea),

With reference to the remarks in the despatch under acknowledgment on the sending of officials by Corea to Peking, and by the Chinese Government to Corea, the Prince has to observe that this intercourse between Corea and China is a usage of long standing, and not simply an affair of to-day. The Envoys sent by Corea this year to Peking and the officer sent by China to Corea were commissioned to perform certain ceremonial duties that have obtained from of old, which China could not now renounce because France was at war with Corea.

As to the statement that China is selecting troops to assist Corea and fight on her side, the Prince would remark that if the State were employing troops (for this purpose) the circumstance would be publicly known and perceived by all.

Whether China is or is not acting as alleged is a point patent in itself, without the need of argument to establish it. But the despatch under acknowledgment asserts as a fact (that China is so acting), thus deliberately, in addition (to the other statements) casting wrongful imputations (on the Prince).

M. de Bellonnet also states distinctly in his despatch that his information is derived from rumor. Now, a rumor is a statement without proof; and is it a proper principle of international intercourse to take as proofs of a charge statements destitute of proof?

M. de Bellonnet's inability to recognize the Prince's good intentions, and his casting imputation at will (upon his Highness) are points it is unnecessary to dispute further about; but as the despatch under acknowledgment seriously concerns the peaceful relations of the two countries, the Prince has to make this reply, setting forth what is right in the case.

A necessary communication, &c.

(No date)

Inclosure 8

The Ministers of the Yamên to Sir R. Alcock

(Translation)

A Short time ago the despatches that had passed between this office and

M. de Bellonnet, the French Chargé d'Affaires, on the Corean affair, were forwarded in copy to the British Minister. A further letter on the same subject has just been received from M. de Bellonnet, to which the Yamên has replied.

Copies of this letter and of the reply the Yamên begs to forward herewith to the British Minister for his perusal. The Ministers are also writing to M. de Bellonnet, informing him (of the step now taken), and are sending at the same time a copy of the two letters to all the other Foreign Ministers.

With best wishes and compliments, &c.

10th moon, 25th day(December 1, 1866).

Inclosure 9

M. de Bellonnet to the Minister of the Yamên*

Inclosure 10

The Minister of the Yamên to M. de Bellonnet**

Inclosure 11

Memorandum by Mr. Brown of a Voyage in the North of China made by Messrs. Williamson and Lees

Mr. WILLIAMSON, of Chefoo, a missionary agent of the Bible Society, and Mr. Lees, of Tien-tsin, a member of the London mission, have recently returned from a trip which they have made in company to Si-ngan-fu, the capital of the Province of Shensi.

Si-ngan-fu is distant from Peking, their point of departure, about 900 miles, in a south-westerly direction. The journey was performed all the way by land, and with the ordinary covered carts of North China. It occupied some seventy days going and returning.

The chief object the missionaries had in view in reaching Si-ngan-fu

*제1권 159번 문서의 본문서

**제1권 176번 문서의 영역문(英國).

was to examine in what state the famous tablet of the Nestorian Christians, erected towards the end of the eighth century A.D., at present was. Rumours had reached Peking and the coast that it had been recently destroyed by the Mahometan rebels; but Messrs. Williamson and Lees found it still existing in a perfect state of preservation. The figure of the Cross and the Syriac characters on the tablet were still perfectly distinct. The temple in which the monument formerly stood was situated outside the walls of the city, and had been completely destroyed by the Mahometan brigands; but the monument itself had been spared, and left standing in its original place.

The travellers passed in a diagonal line through the Province of Shansi, which lies on the western side of Chihil, the Province in which Peking is situated. Shansi is intersected by ranges of hills, which leave broad fertile valleys between them; coal and iron being everywhere most abundant. Indeed, the whole province, both hills and valleys, seems to rest on beds of coal. It was sold everywhere at a copper cash a "catty"-say, about 7s. to 8s. a ton. Both bituminous and anthracite coal was seen, and the quality appeared excellent.

Shensi, separated from its eastern neighbour, Shansi, by the Yellow River, has been thoroughly laid waste by the Mahometan rebels, but was showing faint signs of recovery. The population is sparse, compared with Shansi and Chihli.

Messrs. Williamson and Lees were everywhere informed, and they made constant inquiries both of natives and of the Roman Catholic missionaries they occasionally met with, that the Mahometans who devastated Shensi were without organization or political motive. They consisted simply of bands of brigands, each under its own independent head. The capital, Si-ngan-fu, had never fallen into their hands.

Messrs. Lees and Williamson travelled throughout their journey without molestation or other inconvenience than what arose from the curiosity of the inhabitants, who had never before seen a foreigner in foreign costume. Any little difficulty or delay, such as will be met with on a route not hitherto openly travelled over by foreigners, bringing with them all their peculiarities of dress, habits, and mode of living, were easily got over by the production of the Consular passport, or an interview with the local officials, who, as a rule, were readily accessible and civil.

Their chief object being to do missionary work, Messrs. Lees and Williamson lost no opportunity of publicly preaching in every town and populous village they passed through. They were invariably listened to with perfect good temper by crowds of people, and no interference was met with on the part of either the people or the officials.

They further succeeded in selling (not in giving away) over 20,000 volumes of Christian books in the Chinese language.

The travellers had intended returning through the province of Honan by the city of Kai-fêng-fu, where the settlement of Chinese Jews was discovered some years ago. They found, however, that all communication south of the Yellow River was cut off by the Nienfei rebels; they were obliged, therefore, to return by their original route.

The above is the substance of a statement made by Mr. Lees on the evening of the 26th November, a few days after his return, to his missionary brethren in Peking, at which I was present.

(Signed) J. McL. BROWN

Peking, December 1, 1866

Moustier (1866. 12. 14) → P. de Chasseloup-Laubat

12월 11일자 Chasseloup-Laubat의 서신에 대한 답신

Paris, le 14 Décembre 1866

M. le M$^{\underline{quis}}$ et C.C.

Vous avez bien voulu me communiquer le rapport dans lequel M. le C. Amiral Roze Com$^{\underline{ant}}$ en chef de la D$^{\underline{on}}$ navale des mers de Chine vous rend compte de l'exploration qu'il a faite du Han Kiang jusque devant Séoul, Capitale de la Corée.

J'ai lu ce travail avec beaucoup d'intérêt et j'en conserve une copie. Je vous renvoie ci-joint l'original avec tous mes remerciements pour l'empressement que vous avez mis à m'en donner connaissance. Ainsi que vous en exprimez l'opinion il me paraîtrait inopportun d'engager le Gouv$^{\underline{ent}}$ de l'Empereur dans une expédition qui exigerait l'emploi de moyens plus considérables que ceux dont dispose en temps ordinaire notre station navale dans ces parages. M. l'amiral Roze lui-même me semble marquer dans son rapport la limite où doit s'arrêter notre action lorsqu'il indique comme seule possible et raisonnable l'occupation qu'il allait effectuer de Kang-Hoa située à l'entrée de la rivière de Séoul où il comptait établir un blocus temporaire si [_____] il [_____] en terminant son rapport l'apparition de nos bâtiments dans ces eaux réputées jusque-là inaccessibles a produit un effet suffisant pour prévenir désormais la persécution contre les Chrétiens, il me semble que dans les circonstances actuelles il conviendrait de s'en tenir à ce premier succès.

高宗(1866. 12. 15/高宗三年十一月九日) ➜ 禮部

프랑스 함대의 강화부 침입과 회격(回檄) 내용 보고

관련문서 (1) 조선 자문의 禮部 상주문

朝鮮咨文

朝鮮國王爲歷陳洋檄事 本年八月十六日 法國船三艘 來泊於京畿富平府前洋 一舶留碇 二舶直到西江口距王城十里之地 一宿而退 仍與留碇之舶還出外洋 不知去向矣 九月初四日 洋船七艘 又爲闖入 三舶留碇於舊泊處 四舶直向距王城一百二十里江華府 事在倉卒 府城失守 著巡撫中軍李容熙領率馬步軍兵出陣 於江華府越岸通津府津頭 移檄請戰 伊國回檄 辭意悖嫚 汚衊罔極 至有侵偪上國之語 不聞乎以下三十一字 目可見而口不可道 讀之未竟 骨顫膽掉 北向涕泣 憤不欲生 洋人之故尋事端 必欲啓釁 已爲上國所照燭 而猋發之勢 忽起於呼吸之頃 侵陵之患 方棘於迫近之域 敝邦受困 不遑自恤 而竊念敝邦自祖先以來 承藉洪庇 恪修侯度 爲藩爲屛 自效於疏附禦侮之義 不虞今日因屬國有事 貽辱大邦 至此之極 一國君臣 由是驚慟 衷情所激 不容隱忍 玆將法國回檄原本 仍具事由 謹此咨陳 煩乞貴部轉達天聽 千萬幸甚 爲此合行移咨 請照驗轉奏施行

【관련문서 1】

禮部奏 接到盛京禮部咨送朝鮮國公文 臣等公同拆閱 係因本年八月十六日有洋船三艘 泊於富平府前洋 旋卽退出 九月初四日 又有洋船七艘 闖入前洋 其四艘直抵距王城一百二十里江華府 事在倉卒 府城失守 朝鮮現於江華府越岸之通津府 領兵出陣 竝將法國原檄咨送到部 懇請代奏前來 臣等查閱原咨 甚形忠憤 應如何相機酌辦 以示朝廷懷遠之意 而堅藩邦嚮化之忱 應由總理各國事務衙門察覈辦理 軍機大臣面奉諭旨 該衙門知道

A. Burlingame (1866. 12. 15) ➜ W. H. Seward

조불(朝佛) 교전 경과 보고

UNITED STATES LEGATION
Peking, December 15, 1866

Sir:

I have the honor to inform you that the French fleet, of six vessels and 600 men, under the command of Admiral Rose, left Cheefoo on the 11th of October for Corea, for the purpose of obtaining satisfaction for the murder of the French missionaries. It arrived on the 13th at the mouth of a river on which is situated Seoul, the capital of Corea; ascending this to Kang-hoa, a city of 20,000 inhabitants, on the 14th the admiral landed his force, and on the 15th and 16th captured the city without loss. Great preparations had been made by the Coreans to meet the French all along the river, but the French arriving before the completion of their works they abandoned them at first without a struggle

A deputation arrived from the capital, 26 miles from Kang-hoa, complaining of the conduct of the missionaries, but ending with a request that the admiral should go to the capital and discuss the affair in a friendly manner. The admiral conceived this to be a ruse to entrap him and refused to go, but invited them in return to come to him. In the mean time large forces began to gather about Kang-hoa. On the 26th a reconnoissance was made with 150 men, near the river, along the road leading to the capital. These when near the landing on the river side were fired upon, and two men were killed and 25 wounded.

On the 27th another reconnoissance was made with 150 men, who, upon nearing a pagoda, were fired upon by 500 Coreans, and at the first volley three were killed and 32 wounded, whereupon a retreat was made, and Admiral Rose, probably finding that nothing could be done with his limited force, left Corea to recruit it, with which he cannot return until next spring or summer.

I have the honor to be, Sir, your obedient servant,

ANSON BURLINGAME

Hon. WILLIAM H. SEWARD,
Secretary of State, Washington, D.C.

H. de Bellonet (1866. 12. 16)

프랑스 고시문(法國告示)

大法欽命全權大臣統帶各哨勇軍羅爲剴切曉諭事

予以本朝大皇帝之命 護庇本國軍民人等在此方寓者 本年在此邦無辜遭誅者 係我國傳教士推重之人也 傳教士仁義光明 毫無過犯 殺之違天悖理 不能容矣 不聞乎中國前數載伊行不仁 犯此凶行 我本大國征之厄之 俾不得不俯首尊命而行 今大法全權大臣主定征伐高麗不仁不義之邦 若不傾耳受教 全無撓處

一. 因有三員唆弄殺我朝傳教士者 嚴懲究辦

一. 早差全權一員來此面議 永定章程 災害凶患近矣 爾欲避之 宜早回言 若不領命 勿謂言之不先也

總署(1866. 12. 20/同治五年十一月十四日) ➞ 同治帝

프랑스의 장정 체결 등 요구와 관련하여 조선에 철저한 대비를 촉구하도록 상주(上奏)

恭親王等又奏 本月初九日 准禮部咨稱轉奏朝鮮國王歷陳洋檄事實一摺 奉旨該衙門知道 欽差 先後由軍機處暨禮部鈔錄原奏 及該國原文 法國回檄知照前來 查此案於初接法使照會內稱 因與朝鮮構兵 堵塞港口 暫禁商船前往 當經臣等酌給照覆 極欲從中排解 而法使照覆 詞氣之間 竟牽及中國 又經臣衙門給予照覆詰責 竝照會英俄美布各國使臣 以伸公論 當於十月二十日奏明在案 旋接法使來函 大致謂中國不曾洞徹文內之言及行文之意 特委繙譯官李梅 親將文內之言逐句解明 竝有漢文與洋文不能融會之處各等語 雖未遽認前送照會詞氣之非 而言外歸咎所譯漢文不無舛錯 復經臣等酌給覆函 與之辯析 仍將來往信函分致各國使臣查照 自此案照會信函分致各國之後 聞各國使臣以法國興師動衆於前 又無端牽連中國於後 雖未遞有照覆 公議頗以爲非 嗣後法使亦未再來爭論 僅於十月二十五日 遞來照會一件 內稱頃接本國水師提督文稱 本國添派弁兵 再期深入重勦 暫住日本過冬 所有前經本國兵船堵塞該國通京三河各口 由今日以至來春 已算開解 臣等公同商酌 給予照覆 以開解之說 業經具悉 絶不下一贅語 於本月初十日照覆在案正在籌商間 適准禮部咨送朝鮮國王原咨 及法國檄文等件 查法國檄文中 仍有牽及中國之語 頗爲無理 但事已多年 業經議和 該國不知中國文義輕重不値與之計較 其餘所稱各情 雖不免仍以用兵爲說 惟內有欲朝鮮早差全權一員面議 永定章程一條 似亦頗注意於和解 現在朝鮮已失一郡 兵事恐難驟弭 如欲因法國面議章程 藉解兵患 則通商傳教賠償兵費三事 法國必持之益力 朝鮮是否願從 中國斷不能稍有勉强 查從前琉球因法國許烈 咱㘞嚷在該國傳教 懇中國代爲阻止 經臣衙門照會前法國使臣阻其前往 法國亦卽撤回彼此均無傷損 今朝鮮启釁之由 及法國蓄意之處 與前事迥不相同 總之中國從中排解 法使迄未應允 而法國欲定章程 亦遽難代議 是相持之勢 要在朝鮮之自爲熟計 查法國文內 旣有欲朝鮮差員面議一節 相應請旨飭下禮部詳加酌覈 應否知照朝鮮國王 將來法國如再有兵船前往 可否由該國自行妥籌辦理 總期計出萬全 是爲至要 御批 依議

總署(1866. 12. 20/同治五年十一月十四日) ➞ H. de Bellonet

조불(朝佛) 문제 조회문을 각국 공사관에 발송한 것에 대한 해명

給法國伯洛內信

貴國與高麗交兵一事 中國毫無偏袒 亦無勉强 前因貴大臣照會 遽以無據之言爲據 詳閱通篇詞意 竟謂中國包庇高麗 本衙門不能任受此語 是以恭親王於照覆貴大臣後 竝將往來公文移送各國住京大臣閱覽 以期表明心跡 俾知中國和解兩國美意 貴大臣未達本衙門表明心跡之意 轉於此次來函內稱 公文送與各國大臣閱看 於本大臣毫無妨礙云云 查貴大臣前次照會 以中國包庇高麗 尙稱得自風聞 此次來函 謂想幫高麗 竟直斷以己意 明言爲不枉論是中國和解兩國美意 始終不明其實 本衙門現在竝未聞各國有疑中國想幫高麗之說 本衙門斷不肯隨意誣指 遽謂各國有疑中國之意 中國是否包庇高麗及貴大臣之論枉與不枉 所有三次來往公文 業已分送各國大臣閱覽 本衙門亦無須多論 即此可知本衙門移送各國大臣閱覽之意 不過意欲表明心跡 誠以貴大臣誣指中國各節 若隱忍不言 以致不能公同部白 實於中國國家大有妨礙 殊難計及於貴大臣之有無妨礙 此亦不辨自明 恭親王前次照會 勸貴大臣先向朝鮮查明教民被害緣由 毋遽動兵 自係排解美意 是否可行 貴大臣久未照覆 經恭親王照會催覆 始據覆稱早已交鋒 不能阻止等因 貴大臣若早將此言聲覆 本衙門亦不至再爲復催 至貴大臣補照條約送到法文照會三件 內十月初四日一件 經貴國繙譯李老爺逐層講解 融會大意 與漢文相符 李老爺深通漢文 於中外辦理交涉事件 實能融洽 當將此件補送法文照會 歸入十月初四日漢文卷內存案 其補送六月初三日法文照會一件 補送九月十六日法文照會一件 亦分歸各漢文卷內存案 此次來往信函 仍係敘述前次分送照會緣由 自應仍前分送各國大臣 俾可詳知端委 至前次將往來照會移送各國大臣閱覽 本衙門以爲貴大臣自無不知之 原無須先向貴大臣告知 再行移送 今貴大臣來文 以爲當先通知其意 所有此次來往信函仍行分送緣由 即照來意明告貴大臣查照

【英譯文(美國)】

Sir:

We have the honor to inform your excellency that Mr. Lemaire, the interpreter of the French legation, brought your note on the 25th of November with the original texts in French of your several despatches of July 14, October 24, and November 10, which you furnished to this office in accordance with Article III of the [French] treaty. We have put them on file.

In regard to the quarrel between France and Corea, we may observe again, that China has shown neither a desire to be unjustly partial, nor to constrain either party. From your previous despatches, in which you so hastily quoted certain rumors, and acted upon them as if authentic, we could only infer, after the most careful examination of their contents, that you wished to charge this government with the design of screening and protecting Corea. Being wholly unwilling to rest quietly under this imputation, his imperial highness Prince Kungm after his last reply to you, sent copies of the entire correspondence to all the foreign ministers resident in Peking, in the hope thereby of showing them his real purpose, which is to do all that China can do to preserve the peace between those two countries. It appears as if your excellency did not entirely appreciate our motive in doing so; for in the note under reply you say, "I certainly have no objection to make to the Chinese communication my despatches to my colleagues; but such a publication will be regarded in Europe in the light of a last effort in favor of Corea, and consequently it will be thence inferred that I was not wrong in writing what I did."

In your former despatch you observed that China designed to protect the Coreans, and acknowledged that this assertion was founded on a rumor: and now in the present note you sat that this government is aiding them. This charge is certainly one of your own making, and yet you tell us plainly that you are asserting nothing which is unfounded.

It appears to us that you have altogether misapprehended the laudable desire of this government throughout to preserve the peace between Corea and France. We have, indeed, not yet learned what the other foreign ministers say respecting the charge made against us, that we are aiding the Coreans; but on our part we certainly are not inclined to admit such an unfounded aspersion. You said that these ministers all have a suspicion that China intends to protect the Coreans; and it was for the purpose of enabling them to judge for themselves whether your words were well founded or not, that we sent them the whole correspondence. We were desirous of avoiding a long discussion upon the point with you; and you yourself can but see that our only desire in doing so was to clearly make known to them our real intentions.

In sooth, if the allegations which your excellency has brought against this government had been kept quiet, and we had said nothing publicly in explanation of our views, it would surely have worked a great reproach to his imperial Majesty's fame. It is a plain point, and need not here be discussed, whether such a step was likely to prove detrimental to you or not.

When his imperial highness urged you to send to Corea and have careful inquiries made first into the reasons why the Christians had been maltreated and not immediately proceed to hostilities, it was done with the sincere desire to see if it was possible to bring about a clear understanding upon the affair; but as you delayed answering him for a long time, he deemed it only respectful to request a reply; the more so, as your despatch [announcing the blockade] intimated that hostilities would ere long commence, and that you had not then power to stop them. If you had sooner informed him that such was the case, there would of course have been no need of requesting a reply.

The original texts of your three despatches (including that of November 10), which you have sent to this office, according to the provisions of the treaty, have all been clearly explained by the interpreter, Mr. Lemaire, and shown to be in accordance with their Chinese translations. He is well acquainted with the Chinese language, and fully competent to manage and arrange to mutual satisfaction such things as arise between us. The French text of your despatch of the 10th of November, which he brought, has been placed with its translation; and so have the texts of those of the 14th of July and 24th of October. It will be proper to communicate your present note and our reply, also, to the other ministers, as they relate to and explain the previous despatches, and each of them can then clearly understand the merits of the case for himself. In sending the copies to them of the first correspondence we did nothing which we were unwilling to have you know; but we did not consider ourselves required to let you know our intention to do so, and then forward them, [as if by your leave]. As the present note from your excellency is to be understood only by reading the previous despatches, the reason for furnishing others with copies of this reply, and that note, are now fully stated for your information.

Availing ourselves of this occasion to wish you every happiness, we enclose our cards.

WAUSIANG,

His Excellency M. DE BELLONET, &c., &c., &c.

【英譯文(英國)】

On the 19th day of the 10th moon (November 25, 1866), M. Lemaire, the French Interpreter, came to the Yamên with a letter from M. de Bellonnet; and on the same day was forwarded, in accordance with Treaty, the French texts of the Chargé d'Affaires' three despatches of the 3rd day of the 6th moon (July 14, 1866), the 16th day of the 9th moon (October 24, 1866), and the 4th day of the 10th moon (November 10, 1866). These, which had not been forwarded at the time of writing the despatches, the Yamên has received and placed in its archives.

In the matter of the hostilities between France and Corea, the Chinese Government had, as a matter of course, not the slightest leaning towards of favour for Corea, and when the Chargé d'Affaires, taking as evidence statements without proof, manifestly both from the tone and letter of his despatches, charged China with taking the part of and defending Corea, this office could not rest under such an imputation, and the Prince of Kung, therefore, after replying to M. de Bellonnet, forwarded the correspondence to all the foreign Minister for their perusal, with a view to make manifest the motives of the Imperial Government and enable (the Ministers) to know that China had none but the best intentions, namely, to repair the breach between the two countries. This desire to make manifest its motives M. de Bellonnet has not comprehended, but goes so far as to state in the letter under acknowledgment that the steps taken by the Yamên in forwarding the correspondence to the foreign Representatives is Peking, while it does not affect himself in the slightest, will only be looked upon by Europe as a desperate expedient resorted to by the Chinese Government in its desire to assist Corea, and as proving more clearly that the Chargé d'Affaires was not wronging China in what he said in his despatches.

M. de Bellonnet in his previous despatches charged China with taking the part of Corea, stating that his proofs for this charge were derived from common rumour. In his present letter he still adheres to this his own opinion, which he considers decisive of the question, and says that China has a desire to aid Corea. He also asserts distinctly that he was not wronging the Imperial Government in his (previous) statements. He has thus from first to last misapprehended the good intentions of the Chinese Government which were to heal the breach between the two countries.

The Yamên has not heard that the other Powers suspect China of a desire to assist Corea, and this office would not deliberately taken upon itself to impute such suspicious to them.

The questions as to whether China is or is not taking the part of Corea, and whether M. de Bellonnet has or not maligned the Imperial Government in the statements he has made, need not be dwelt upon at length by the Yamên, as it has already submitted to the foreign Representatives the three (paris of) despatches interchanged on the subject. It will be understood from them that the Yamên, in submitting the correspondence to the foreign Minister, could have had no other desire save to make its motives manifest to all; for it requires no arguments to show that had the Chinese Government kept dark the imputations cast upon it by M. de Bellonnet, and thus prevented the questions being cleared up and understood by all, the consequences to the Government of His Chinese Majesty would have been very injurious. As to whether (the submitting of the correspondence to the Minister) would or would not injuriously affect M. de Bellonnet, was a point very difficult for the Yamên to estimate.

The Prince in his pervious communication recommended M. de Bellonnet to ascertain first from Corea the circumstances of the murder of the Christians, and not rashly to have recourse to arms. In doing so his motive was to arrange the difficulty; but M. de Bellonnet for a long time made no reply as to whether such an inquiry would first be made or not. It was only when the Prince wrote again pressing for an answer that he learned form M. de Bellonnet's answer that hostilities had been commenced for some time and could not be put a stop to. Had the Chargé d'Affaires replied in these terms earlier the Yamên would not have been led to write again pressing for an answer.

As to the French texts of the three despatches forwarded by M. de Bellonnet, according to Treaty (which had not been sent with the Chinese translations), M. Lemaire, the interpreter, has explained (to the Ministers) paragraph by paragraph the French text of the despatch of the 4th day of the 10th moon (November 10, 1866), and its general purport, taken as a whole, seem to agree closely with the Chinese version. M. Lemair understands the Chinese official language extremely well, and in the conduct of international questions is both highly intelligent and successful. The French text of the third despatch has been placed amongst the records with its Chinese version, as have also been those of the previous two.

As this letter and the one to which it is a reply, repeat or refer to the reasons for sending the previous despatches to the foreign Representatives, it is the duty of the Yamên to forward copies of them also to the foreign Ministers that their Excellencies may inform themselves fully of the particulars of the affair from first to last.

When (the Prince) submitted the previous correspondence to the foreign Ministers, the Yamên considered that M. de Bellonnet would as a matter of course know that his Highness was doing so, and therefore did not think it necessary to inform him of their intention beforehand. As M. de Bellonnet, however, in the letter under acknowledgment, considers that he ought to have been previously told, the Ministers of the Yamên now beg to inform him, in accordance with his wish, that they are about to forward copies of this letter and of the one to which it is a reply (to the foreign Ministers), as they did with the previous correspondence.

With the usual compliments.

(No date)

長崎奉行(?) (1866. 12. 23/慶應二年十一月十七日) ➞ 幕府

병인양요 이후 서양 열강의 재침략 풍문

丙寅十一月十七日出長崎來狀寫

此度佛狼西軍艦罷越風聞仕候ニは此程朝鮮え戰爭ニ罷越候處初てハ敗軍いたし候へとも其後之戰には殊之外勝利ニて棹銀箱三十二其外筋入大砲二三挺種々之もの戰爭中に奪取罷歸候趣右軍艦一ト先本國へ引取數艘之軍艦を以再戰爭可仕候ニ付朝鮮ハ日本清國兩屬之國に候へハ自然日本清より加勢等も可致哉之段前以承り度旨申來候よし右軍艦ハ殊之外大船ニて凡乘組七百餘人大砲二段に備筒數七十門計り小砲數多仕組誠に見事之船ニて御座候當湊に日數廿日計滯船之處跡より前同斷軍艦一艘外に少し小形軍艦三艘相揃進ミ神奈川港へ相廻り一應本國へ引取其上數艘ニて再朝鮮へ押寄候よし英吉利亞墨兩國よりも數艘ニて佛郎西え加勢致し共に朝鮮を攻掠之專用意致居候よし然るに當港ニ先頃より來泊之魯西亞人此風聞を聞や否や一夜之內ニ三艘共出帆致し申候全く淸國魯西亞兩國之勢ニて朝鮮へ加勢致し候よし定て淸國ハ右加勢之相談ニ罷越候儀と被察候誠に六ヶ國之大戰爭とも相成候ハヽ實に如何成行可申哉煩敷儀ニ御座候右風聞承り候儘不取敢奉申上候以上

178

禮部(1866. 12. 24/同治五年十一月十八日) ➞ 高宗

조선국왕의 자문 접수 후 상주(上奏) 처리했음을 알림

禮部知會歷陳洋儆轉奏咨

禮部爲知照事主客司案呈本部據咨轉奏朝鮮國王歷陳洋儆事實一摺於同治五年十一月初九日具奏本日准軍機處交片奉旨該衙門知道欽此相應鈔錄原奏知照朝鮮國王可也云云 同治五年十一月十八日

原奏

禮部謹奏爲據咨轉奏事同治五年十一月初六日接到盛京禮部咨送朝鮮國王公文臣等公同折閱係因本年八月十六日有法國洋船三艘泊於朝鮮富平府前洋旋卽退出九月初四日又有法國洋船七艘闖入前洋其四艘直抵距王城一百二十里江華府事在倉卒府城失守朝鮮現於江華府越岸之通津府領兵出陣移檄請戰竝將法國原檄咨送到部懇請代奏前來臣等查閱原咨甚形忠憤應如何相機酌辦以示朝廷懷遠之意而堅藩邦嚮化之忱應由總理各國事務衙門察覈辦理除將朝鮮所呈法國曉諭原文封送軍機處外謹鈔錄原咨竝所稱洋儆恭呈御覽伏祈聖鑒謹奏

大島友之允(1866. 12. 24/慶應二年十一月十八日) ➡ 平田主殿, 森川玉城, 相良丹藏, 早田作左衛門, 仁位格之介, 內野廣之允

병인양요 후 大島友之允의 화의사절 제안

관련문서 (1) 大島友之允와 長崎奉行의 제1차 대담(1867. 1. 3/慶應二年十一月二十八日)
(2) 大島友之允와 長崎奉行의 제2차 대담(1867. 1. 11/慶應二年十二月六日)
(3) 大島友之允와 長崎奉行의 제3차 대담(1867. 1. 13/慶應二年十二月八日)

以內狀令啓上候殿樣御隱居樣益御機嫌克被遊御座恐悅御同意奉存候小子儀去ル九日長崎表着いたし蒸氣船其外御用向專取調罷在候付委細近日歸國之上可達御聽候尙亦今度佛夷朝鮮國江亂入之傳聞過日長崎役より申上越ニ爲相成儀と存知候處其筋一向慥成儀相知不申右者御役職被爲取不容易事柄ニ付出崎之上尙情實探索罷在候處此程定役格通詞賀禮之介より別帳上海橫文之新聞志和解差出候付則差上之候外ニ漢文之新聞志寫且ツ傳聞之趣至り是又別帳ニ集メ送り差上候朝鮮國之儀者從來之御家役殊ニ外夷邊之事より相起り御重用被仰出置當時御用中之御事ニ茂有之右之涉ハ朝鮮國之情實委曲御探索御屆不被仰立候而難叶御事ニ相見彌來春大擧戰爭之時宜ニ至候節舊來之御隣誼ニ於而御傍觀可被爲在御事共不奉存候旣ニ寬永年唐國兵亂之砌御援兵御差渡之公命も有之候程之儀ニ而今日之御時機如何御所置可被爲在哉萬一茂說之通魯西亞より仲入取扱抔申ニ至候節者向來之御國害限も無之第一御隣好之御實意薄ニ茂相當り旁を以勘考仕候時者此度社朝鮮國危急存亡之秋到來共可申此場ニ付孰とか御和談を以兩國解兵脣齒萬世相保之御誠意致貫徹候樣御明斷之御一策有御座間布哉右者御一己なあさる御事ニ而神州一般ニ致關係候事柄ニ付廟堂之御建議何レニ出可申哉乍恐是等公邊御屆之上孰とか御指揮被爲蒙度御事ニ奉存候右一條尙專探索中ニ付時宜ニ依候ハヽ當所御奉行御面談をも相賴公邊御模樣を茂相伺度差含罷在候ニ付何事も歸國之上委情申上候樣可致候右之趣不取敢得御意候條可然被仰上可被下候此段爲可申述如是御座候恐惶謹言

十一月十八日　　大嶋友之允

平田主殿樣　森川玉城樣　相良丹藏樣　早田作左衛門樣　仁位格之介樣　內野廣之允樣

【관련문서 1】

朝鮮國之儀ニ付長崎奉行能世大隅守殿德永石見守殿江及御應答候口上大意
長崎奉行支配地組頭東條八太郎殿より明廿八日兩奉行御面談可申ニ付四ツ半時西役所江罷出可申趣以手紙申來
但八太郎殿ニ者過日罷出及御面談朝鮮一條ニ付追々之御手續を茂申述御同人よりも承知之次第有之候事
同日刻限西役所江罷出候處兩尹列座被申聞候者朝鮮國之儀ニ付此程組頭迄被申聞候趣一ト通致承知猶委細直話致承知度無伏意申聞候樣との事
御答　此度佛朗西朝鮮國江及爭戰一先休兵來春再擧之聞も有之御承知之通朝鮮國之儀者御創業以來御隣好之國柄一朝一夕ならさる御由緒も有之殊ニ方今宇內之形勢外夷之情態ニ依四年前 將軍家御上洛中彼國御手附之御廷議相決對馬守儀國情探索之蒙御內命引續幕府御役向御下向御談判御取懸り可至御沙汰之處其砌より御邦內彼是不容易御形勢ニ立至御役向御下向之儀茂御遲緩其內御掛之御役々追々御交代ニ至朝鮮國御用件全御廢止同樣之姿ニ被成只樣於機會相後其內萬一外夷先制之勢ニ乘候時者千悔不及之時機顯然ニ有之皇國之御爲遺憾不少次第ニ付乍微力對馬守一藩之見込を以御用邊糸口取開然上追々蒙御差圖度當度於京坂橋府幷板倉閣老江奉申上候品ニ依友之允儀以公命歸國被仰付直樣朝鮮江も罷渡御用件相運可申處小官渡館方彼國向少敷驅引も有之兼而彼國熟知之者先問として差渡御用邊精々爲相運時宜次第渡海之內決ニ有之然處右御用ニ付而者外國御條約御交際之御規則等得と相心得置不申候而難叶都合も有之小官渡館方猶豫之內其邊取調も仕度此程出崎之處韓佛戰爭之說始而承及果而外夷先入今日之時機ニ至候段歎息有余義ニ奉存候乍併是迄御手後と相成候段御邦內之御形勢不得止儀と申今更不復儀ニ付此上之御良策ニ至而者乍恐禍を被轉福とせられ候外茂無之就夫此度韓佛之取合魯英抔各仲入取扱候儀を相心掛居候說茂有之萬一說之通り外夷より仲入抔申ニ至候而者朝鮮國忽彼之所有と相成候儀者眼前ニ有之然者皇國之御大害限茂無之其上從來御隣好之國柄今日之國難御傍觀可被爲在御事共不奉存旣ニ寬永六年唐國兵亂之砌時宜次第御援兵可被差渡哉之公命御布告ニ至居候先蹤も有之素り此度佛國ニおゐて者矢張御條約之國柄と申殊ニ御邦內御多端之折柄御援兵等之御沙汰ニ出可申儀と者不奉存候得

共孰ニ茂差向候危急御救不被下候而者御信義も相立不申事と奉存候加之佛國ニ至候而も萬里之波濤を經大軍を海外ニ相發候儀實不可好之儀ニ付近比分を超候申上事重々恐入候得共此度我國より先立御和談御取扱ニ至候ハゝ兩國君臣是を利スルノミナラス數萬生靈之幸不過之此一擧外ニしてハ此度神州朝鮮舊交之國たる事公然と各國ニ致貫徹候ハゝ以來各國より朝鮮江手を附候儀我國ニ對し大ニ相憚候意味可有之内ニしてハ被對朝鮮國從來之御信誼相立彼國上下御仁恩深感戴仕往々國家依賴之意念を茂相生可申然時者力を不用して彼國御取開之御用件も自ら其内ニ相運ひ數年之後不知不識我版圖ニ歸候樣成行可申事候樣奉存候尤我國より御仲入と申儀者乍憚當御奉行所限之御決評ニ出候御事とも不奉存知又對馬守より差極候而申上候筋合ニ茂無之孰京坂東武之御賢斷ニ出不申候而難叶段勿論ニ有之然者小官等尚更可容喙之事ニ無之候得者朝鮮國御用件ニ付而者追々幕府御要路向ニ於而御應接申上置候次第も有之此度之儀實ニ不可失之詩會と恐考仕見込丈之處不顧前後達御内聽之儀ニ付此儀全御別段ニ御聞達被下度何れ當節歸國之上委情對馬守江申達候ハゝ朝鮮掛合向者素り幕府御屆方ニ至主人存意茂可有之然處大體此節之儀只此元之傳聞而已ニ而朝鮮國より何等之儀も不申立候付他之傳聞を以表立幕府江御屆申上候時宜ニも難至然者此場朝鮮國之情實國論等篤と取糺其狀情を得候而幕府江申上何分之御沙汰可奉待之處同國之儀國事向善惡となく致隱密候國風ニ付此度之儀例之陋習を以談判之初其國情事實相秘候歟も難斗然者兎哉角舌戰時日を送り候内兵機相迫り兩國刃を交候ニ至而者折角之御誠意も空敷且ツ者唇亡齒寒之憂目下ニ相生候段顯然至候此節之談判實寸刻分陰を爭迅速ニ其情實を得不申而難協隨而過日佛國より兵艦を向候始末表立幕府江申立居候儀有之候歟且ツ來春再擧等之說ニ至朝鮮國江向確證と可相成事件御聞取も候ハゝ御内々承知致し置度自然同國談判向ニおゐて國情致壅蔽候機會も候時者其證記を以及詰問情實委曲承糺候而幕府江御屆中上有無之蒙御指揮度奉存候

兩尹　被申立候趣一々尤承り候然處差向朝鮮國之談判ニ取り確證と可申程之事無之候得共過日佛蘭西軍艦當浦來着之砌其船江我々乘込見候節戈之如キ見馴サル物五六本有之候付相尋候處提督より是者朝鮮ニ而分捕イタシ候而旗也と相答簱ハ花色ニ而白キ形有之樣相見卷キ有之文字共模樣共不相分候事其外吹銀或者玩具樣之物有之兵器其外ニ見當不申

但肥藩伊東外記右船江乘込候節朝鮮より奪來居候大小砲餘程爲有之由砲者

唐金之菅筒小銃ハ和筒ニ似奇タル品之趣外記直和承候定而兩鎭臺ニ者大小砲有之場所江ハ参り合不申事と相考候事一體朝鮮之模様承度提督江相尋掛候處不圖何か存付候顔色ニ而其期を餘事ニ轉シ一向朝鮮之儀不相答申サハ不都合之儀を申出候と可申振ニ相考夫より我々ニも强而不相尋就夫是ハ拙者共全之考ニ候得共惣體外國之風他ニ而戰爭分捕ニてもいたし候時者大ニ誇候而渠より頻ニ其說を鳴ラシ候勢ニ候處右之如一言相發候候期を取消候者自然日本朝鮮舊好之國ニタル事存付此振合ニ至候事ニ無之哉其後手筋を替爲相探候得共一向委敷儀不申出併朝鮮ニ而分捕と申儀者兩人親敷見聞前之儀故是又證據之一端と存候先比石見守東武相發候時分横濱ニ而佛と朝鮮江兵を向候と申風說承り其次第出崎掛坂地ニ而閣老江申立置是も全體鳴咄同様ニ而確證と申程之儀ニ無之併今日被申聞候通從來御隣誼之國柄何分御傍觀被成候御譯ニ無之尙又表向取調見候ハヽ朝鮮掛合向ニ取り何歟勘考と可相成事柄も可有之事故吟味之上重而面談可致候付其含ニ而暫滯崎有之度
右一條佛國コンシユル當所居合候得者此者者學力も有之頗ル人物ニ付談判いたし見候ハヽ彼是勘考と可相成儀可多敷當時横濱出張中ニ而殘念存候
右ニ付是非精々御取調被下候様申述置退座

【관련문서 2】

十二月六日

今日立山御奉行所江罷出可申旨其筋より聞役江申來候付四ツ時罷出候處大隅守殿御逢有之此程被申聞候譯ニ付朝鮮應對向ニ付證據共可相成事柄其筋取調見候得共何分是と申程之義も無之此書面丈其筋より差出候付相渡置候迚書面二通御渡有之

但一通ハ軍艦之名同提督船將之名前等相認有之壹通者初端何禮之助より差出候上海横文之新聞志和解ニ候事

大隅守　右書面さしえ確證共相成申間敷候得共戰爭之模様等者餘程委敷相見居御手前渡海之上者前日相咄置候次第も有之右等之廉々を以對談有之候ハゝ朝鮮ニもヨモヤ此上致隱密候儀も有之間敷走海之往來千萬苦勞ニハ候得共此場折角盡力有之度尙又我々共ニも致評議此度之儀御隣誼ニ於て決て御傍觀可有之御筋合と相心得不申孰とか御所置有之度尙委細對州家より申立ニも可相成趣閣老江申上候樣書面をも相仕立罷在隨而拙者共考ニてハ此度御手前朝鮮江被罷渡彼國情實趣糺然後上坂幕府江被申立候運順序ニ取り至當之儀ニ候得共東西往返時月を經候内自然佛國兵艦を發し戰を始候ニ至而者機會相後候付是より直ニ上坂當所傳聞之次第并見込之趣ニ至具ニ閣老江被申立御和談御取扱之御決定ニ至候ハゝ然上御指揮を以朝鮮江被罷向公命を奉し御用被取扱候方却而急便ニ可有之然時者東武ニても佛國公使江應接兵機を被駛候御所置ニも可至其内朝鮮國江も說得兩國解兵事故無之相治候時者御内外ニ取無差上時宜と存候付氣附之趣申試候

大嶋　　御賢慮之次第御尤ニ奉存候過日東條樣よりも右邊之御內意有之小官是より直ニ上坂閣老方へも御屆申上候儀御沙汰之通急便無相違相見候處朝鮮國之儀對馬守從來之家役ニも有之然を根本韓地之情實をも不取調只外國よりの傳聞を以表立御屆申上候儀他家より者格別對州家ニをゐてハ御役儀ニ對致兼候儀ニ有之此度各樣より閣老方へ被仰立候趣も有之彌御和談御仲入等之御時宜ニ至候節萬一渠自國陋習泥ミ國之大小强弱をも不相弁一意固守之決心を以我意ニ募候得者彼國社稷之亡滅不旋踵而已ナラス幕府御和談之事ニ於而御不都合無限次第ニ奉存候自然彼國右樣頑固之意見挾ミ居候ハゝ弊藩も幾重ニも申諭渠保國之長策結局神州ニ致倚賴之外別術無之次第

彼國君臣肺腑ニ徹候樣無御座候てハ折角之御和談御熟調之程も無覺束奉存候第一此度之儀對馬守見込如何可有之哉一應主人存意相伺不申候而者小官豫斷を以幕府ニ向表立彼是被申上候筋合ニ無之其上小官儀兼而公命之次第も有之旁是非一應歸國朝鮮表江罷渡國情探索御屆不申上候て難叶行掛も有之是等之事情御明察被爲下此度小官當所より直ニ上坂難仕次第御賢察奉希候尤東西往返之間御機會相後候時者是又第一不相濟儀ニ付領分田代表ニハ家老共相詰居候付申談京坂詰方之者江及書面候ハ勿論時宜ニ依役向爲差登此節之始末委細申達京坂ニ於て閣老方へ及御內意置候樣致度相考居候儀も有之隨而近比恐入候儀ニ候得共此節御和談御取扱之儀各樣ニも御內々御尤ニ御評議有之閣老方江被仰立之御次第柄も被爲在候趣ニ付可相成者弊藩より朝鮮國情取糺御屆申上候迄ハ自然來春ニ至佛國兵艦を向候機會有之候共從來之御舊好を押立東武ニおゐて御談判ニ至是非御押留被爲下候樣各樣御分を以被仰立被下如何可有之哉若當所ニ而其機會御座候時者素御油斷可被成下樣無御座兎角朝鮮者朝鮮ニ運を付上方ハ上方ニ而御運置被成下然內雙方御熟談際克御取扱ニ至候儀御兩全之策と奉存候付是等可然御賢評被爲下度奉賴候前申上候通京坂詰方之者より閣老方江及御內意候儀も可有之候得共佛兵御押留之儀等者表立弊藩より申上兼候事情先ニ御承知通之儀ニ付此儀ニ吳々各樣ニ而御盡力被爲下度奉願候

大隅守　此度之儀御傍觀可被成譯柄ニ無之孰とか御所置ニ至候樣との矣閣老方江之書面相仕立居尙又今日被申聞候趣尤之御事ニ付石見守申談重而可及返答候(하략)

【관련문서 3】

十二月八日

一昨六日大隅守殿御應答之品ニ依り今四ツ時御暇乞旁参殿之處卽刻御逢有之此程承置候朝鮮江兵艦差向候儀横濱ニ而者佛公使石見守江直對申聞候譯ニ無之東武出立時分横濱ニ而其說を承り候事と相聞其次第者今般朝鮮國不法之取計方有之軍艦差向候付自然者長崎江寄船等致候儀も可有之其節ハ何か世話ニも可相成と申樣之事ニ而聢と申立候事ニも無之併し其趣者坂地ニ而石見守より閣老江申上置候由佛公使之名者ローシと申者之趣

但右一條一昨六日風說云々を以隅州殿江及尋候次第ハ兼而東條八太郎殿より內密承り居候儀有之候其事柄自然兩鎭臺隱密被致候共ニ無之哉相下墨候付風說と申ニ而相尋候處前之返答ニ有之其譯者江戶ニ而支配組頭中臺信太郎殿江佛公使より申問候ハ此度宗門之事ニ付朝鮮國不法相働候付近々兵艦差向候筈ニ有之就夫長崎者最寄之場所往返立寄船修理等取計候儀可有之自然ハ入用之物品等御心配ニ可預候付其段長崎奉行江御通知置被下候樣申述候趣其節德永者旣ニ横濱より上船ニ臨被居中臺態々出張石州江被申通候付石州より閣老江も被申出置候趣ニ相聞兩鎭臺東條之說大同小異東條之說慥ニ有之併兩鎭臺ニもさして其儀を被秘候振合ニも無之只少之意味淺深有之候樣相考候尤右一條閣老方御聽ニ入候ハゝ何とか對州家江ハ御內意可有之儀勿論ニ而其儘御打過ニ至候段些落附兼候次第候事(중략)

大隅守　今般朝鮮國之一條御手前此許より直ニ上坂閣老江被申立候方急便ニ相見候得共朝鮮之儀他より者兎もあれ對州家之儀者御役義も有之根本彼國を閣キ外よりの傳聞を以表立御届も不相成候付彼國情實得と探索之上有無之御差圖可被蒙との儀尤ニ有之然處東西往返之間時日相後再兵端ニ至候而者折角之御信義も空敷相成候付萬一朝鮮之運取レ不申內佛蘭西より兵を向候機會も候ハゝ關東ニ而是非御差押ニ相成度此許ニ而者拙者共無油斷相心得居可申孰之道朝鮮江對し御信義相立往々皇國之御爲ニも相成候樣有之度然者此場何分御和談御取扱無之候而難協事故右之趣我々より委細閣老江も申上候事ニ致治定候間是又含迄ニ相咄置候尤御手前朝鮮江被罷渡候次第篤も申上候筈候處右者我々應對之末被罷渡候都合ニ候哉素り朝鮮江者被罷渡候筈ニ候哉强而拙者共差圖ニて被罷渡候と申譯ニハ有之間布候

大嶋　　朝鮮表江罷渡方之儀聊各様御差圖と申譯ニ無之彼國御用筋ニ付而者渡海方兼而蒙公命罷在敏ニも相越可申之處過日申上候通彼地之驅引ニ依り渡海方當時猶豫仕居候付其内外國御條約等取調仕度暫時出崎之處此度之一擧始而承及終ニ今日之時宜ニ至候事故此上者一日も速ニ歸國不取敢朝鮮江も罷渡候様決定罷在候

大隅守　過日相咄候佛國コンシユル近日ニ者罷歸可申然時者時宜を以朝鮮一條談判ニ及可申其都合ニ儀御手前渡海被居候趣爲申聞候時强而差支無之哉

大嶋　　愚意少しも差支無之様奉存候希ハ日本朝鮮舊好之國たる事者成丈各國江相示置度事ニ付御時宜次第御應接御座候而不苦様奉存候

大隅守　佛國コンシユル談判之驅引も有之自然來春再擧之勢等當所ニ而相考候時者是非差留候含ニ付朝鮮國之情態一々我々ニ茂心得居不申候而難協候付追々之模様逐一爲御知被下度其内差掛候儀者封書ニ而手前ニ向直ニ被申越候而不苦尚此後當所ニ而探索相屆候儀者委細申通候様可致就夫御手前朝鮮より歸國之上者直ニ上坂ニも可至處上坂掛此許江被立寄候而者格別偏土ニ相成候哉希ハ朝鮮之模様直面ニ而承候得者其上無之候

大嶋　　上坂之海路此許にハ方角相違候尤御用之儀候得者假令偏土ニ相成候時御當所江寄船罷登候ても不苦乍併何レ此邊りハ朝鮮國江相越候上上坂方其緩急も可有之兎も角も時宜次第相心得成丈御當所より罷登候様仕度候

大隅守　彌上坂掛當所江立寄被申時者朝鮮之事情も委細承り尙其時分迄ニハ此許探索方も行屆可申然時ハ兩地之事情打合御手前上坂之節我々存寄をも閣老江申上候様可致此許よりハ東武大坂共蒸氣船之往來屢有之候付當所迄被參候得者上方江被罷登候儀者蒸氣船之方速ニ有之候事故右便船之儀ハ我々より何時も可及差圖成丈當所より被罷登候都合可然存候

大嶋　　仰之趣奉畏委細歸國之上對馬守江申達得差圖候様可仕候

大隅守　朝鮮より歸國上坂之都合ニ至候節何ツ比被罷登候時宜ニ可至哉

大嶋　　此儀彼國談判向之駈引ニ而豫難相測儀ニ候得共三月迄ニハ是非相運度奉存候

大隅守　右邊之都合時宜ニ依閣老へ申上置候儀も可有之何分一日も速ニ相運候様至急之事候此節朝鮮一條ニ付而者御役儀ニ取り對馬守様ニも嘸以心配ニ可有之宜敷申上呉候様との事

宗義達(1866. 12. 29/慶應二年十一月二十三日) ➞ 幕府

병인양요 대응 방안 건의

口上書

朝鮮國情探索警衛筋之儀追々御達ノ次第モ御座候處卽今彼國不穩事件相聞難安儀ニ付年來ノ御位儀モ有之事故從來ノ古法ニ付不拘近年五ヶ國交際取扱之法則準處置ヲ加御國威相立候樣厚相心得可申段御沙汰奉願度御座候已上

十一月廿三日

外ニ左ノ題號ノ帳面二册差出

佛蘭西朝鮮國襲來新聞書

長崎探索書

G. Roze (1867. 1. 15) → P. de Chasseloup-Laubat

Bellonet의 강화도 원정 실패 평가에 대한 반박

À bord de *la Guerrière*, Yokohama, le 15 Janvier 1867

Monsieur le Ministre,

Votre Excellence sait maintenant dans tous ses détails les événements qui viennent de se passer en Corée. Dans mes lettres successives du 23 Août, du 11 Sept., du 6 Octobre, du 22 Octobre et du 17 Nov. 1866, j'ai eu soin de lui faire connaître mes intentions, mon but et plus tard les opérations que j'ai dirigées contre ce pays pour remplir ce que je considérais comme un devoir, comme une des obligations de mon commandement. Je ne lui ai rien tu et en relisant ma correspondannce, il me semble n'avoir rien à y ajouter pour vous permettre d'apprécier ma conduite en pleine connaissance de cause. J'attendrais donc avec confiance le jugement de l'Empereur et le vôtre, si une lettre que je viens de recevoir de Notre Chargé d'Affaires à Pékin et je vous envoie ne m'obligeait à revenir sur ces faits et à repousser certaines impressions dont M. de Bellonnet s'est fait trop facilement l'écho. Je me serais abstenu d'en entretenir V. Excellence s'il ne m'avait annoncé que ces impressions étaient reproduites par lui auprès du Gouvernement de l'Empereur. Avant d'examiner cette lettre dont le ton et la forme ne peuvent s'expliquer, il est nécessaire de bien préciser la politique que l'agent diplomatique a voulu m'imposer de celle que je me suis cru obligé de suivre. De ce rapprochement ressortira, j'ai lieu de le croire la raison, sinon la justification de l'amertume dont je ne puis m'empêcher de me plaindre.

Les idées de M. de Bellonnet se trouvent exposées dans la dépêche qu'il m'a écrite le 13 Juillet dernier et que j'ai communiqué à Votre Excellence le 7 Septembre suivant. A peine le massacre de nos missionnaires lui fut-il connu qu'il prononça la déchéance du Roi de la Corée et qu'il en fit la notification officielle au Cabinet de Pékin, il prit même sur lui de nommer son successeur. Je dirais en passant que le choix n'était pas heureux car le successeur ainsi désigné n'était autre que le père du Roi régnant, l'auteur de la persécution, l'ennemi irréconciliable des chrétiens. Les biens de la famille royale devaient être confisqués, de même que ceux des principaux mandarins, Séoul devait être prise et nous ne devions l'abandonner qu'après avoir amené le Gouvernement à traiter avec nous. En attendant, les Douanes devaient être confisquées des notre arrivée, car il importait de nous faire rembourser de toutes nos dépenses. Il eût été peur-être difficile de trouver une Douane dans un pays isolé, sans relations, ni commerce avec l'extérieur, mais j'ai dû citer ce détail pour prouver que rien n'avait été oubié. Tel est en résumé le plan qui fut arrêté dans le Cabinet de M. le Chargé d'Affaires, livré à la pubicité et qui me fut ensuite transmis pour l'exécution. C'était une déclaration de guerre en forme, une expédition contre le pays tout entier, avec ses chances bonnes ou mauvaises, ses complications et ses hasards M. de Bellonnet avait en même temps il est vrai, la bonté de m'informer qu'il assumait toute la responsabilité de ces entreprises, mais quand il s'agit d'opérations de cette importance, un Commandant en chef, comme Votre Excellence a eu soin de me le dire elle-même dans ses instructions, a sa part d'initiative et d'appréciation qu'il ne lui est pas permis d'abdiquer. Le meurtre de nos compatriotes m'avait profondément ému. Quelque soit le respect et l'admiration que je professe pour nos missionnaires, ce ne fut pas la question religieuse qui me parût en cause, ce fut la France elle-même outragée dans ses enfants. A un tel forfait, il fallait une vengeance soudaine et éclatante, mais si pour l'obtenir il m'eût fallu suivre M. le Chargé d'Affaires jusqu'au point où il voulait me conduire, je n'hésite pas à déclarer que je n'aurais rien commencé avant de recevoir les instructions de Votre Excellence. Heureusement le but pouvait être atteint sans aller ni si vite, ni si loin. Comme représentant le bras de la France j'avais, je le répète, un devoir à remplir: Venger la mort de nôtres, mais je devais m'arrêter à la limite rigoureuse de ce que je pourais (*Sic*) faire avec les moyens dont je dispose. Aller au delà, c'eût été dépasser mes obiligations et engager, peut-être, la politique de l'Empereur, ce que je devais éviter à tout prix.

L'apparition de toute ma Division sur les côtes de la Corée et la destruction du premier point important que je reconnaîtrais sur ma route me parurent devoir remplir le but quc j'avais en vue. Après y avoir mûrement réfléchi, ce fut le programme auquel je m'arrêtai et je ne crains pas de dire que je l'ai entièrement accompli. Il avait loin de là, sans doute, aux plans ambitieux de Monsieur le Chargé d'Affaires mais encore aujoud'hui je me félicite de m'être arrêté aux modestes propositions d'une action purement maritime que j'ai engagée à mon heure et que j'ai terminée à mon gré.

Quoiqu'il en soit, Monsieur le Ministre, cette divergence d'opinions a été le point de départ de la Division qui s'est élevée entre M. de Bellonnet et ma Division que je déplore et qui me vaut aujourd'hui des appréciations dont la forme n'a pas même le mérite d'atténuer l'injure. Si ces récriminations n'atteignaient que moi, fort de ma conscience, je n'aurais garde de m'y arrêter; mais comme elles intéressent la vérité et qu'elles pourraient fausse, le jugement public, je me dois à les relever avec toute l'énergie dont je suis capable.

Dans la lettre qu'il m'a écrite et par laquelle il m'informe qu'il proteste contre mes actes auprès de son Département, M. le Chargé d'Affaires se demande si le meurtre de nos missionnaires a bien été vengé et il se prononce, sans hésitation, pour la négative. Si M. de Bellonnet veut dire que quelle que soit la satisfaction que nous ayons obtenue, elle n'équivaudra jamais à la perte de neuf hommes de cœur et de vertu, je suis de son avis. Mais s'il entend contester la sévérité de la leçon que nous avons infligée à la Corée et les effets qu'on doit en attendre, on ne peut l'attribuer qu'à son éloignment des lieux et aux renseignements interéssés qu'il a dû recevoir. La prise, l'occupation et la destruction de Kang-hoa sont des faits qu'il ne peut révoquer en doute. Est-il vrai qu'ils puissent être sans résultats? Kang-hoa était une des principales villes, un des boulevards de la Corée. Placée à l'entrée de la rivière qui mène à la Capitale qu'on protège, sa conservation intéressait, au plus haut point, la sécurité et l'honneur du pays. Abondamment pourvue d'approvisionnements de toute espèce, d'armes et de munitions de toute sorte; passé dans une résidence royale et de splendides demeures officielles, elle représentait une valeur dont il serait difficile de dire l'importance. En le détruisant, nous avons frappé le Gouvernement Coréen dans sa force, dans son prestige et dans ses richesses. Au seul point de vue matériel, n'est-ce pas une vengeance capable de faire réfléchir celui qui l'a subie? Au point de vue morale l'humiliation qui en est la suite n'est-elle pas faite pour abaisser l'orgueil le plus intraitable? Poser ces questions, Monsieur le Ministre, c'est les résonances à moins d'être aveuglé par la colère et la passion. Dire que la Corée est vaincue et soumise serait sans doute, aller au delà de la vérité, mais ses murailles détruites, ses forts renversés, ses palais ruinés resteront longtemps comme un enseignement qui préviendra, j'en ai l'espérance, le retour des cruelles persécutions qui ont si souvent ensanglanté ce pays.

Contester la portée de tels événements, refuser toute espèce de mérite et de valeur à mes opérations, ce n'est, après tout, qu'une opinion individuelle dont je pourrais laisser au temps le soin de faire justice. Mais M. de Bellonnet va plus loin et se livrant à des insinuations que je me refuse à qualifier, il laisse croire à un échec qui intéressait les armes de la France. C'est ici surtout, Monsieur le Ministre, que je proteste de toutes mes forces contre une pareille appréciation et que je m'élève, avec indignation contre le sentiment qui l'a dictée. Dès le principe, mon programme a été connu de tous : frapper un coup sur un point quelconque et nous retirer ensuite, notre rembarquement n'a point été précipité ni forcé ; il a eu lieu, quoiqu'on puisse dire M. le Chargé d'Affaires, librement et à l'heure que j'avais fixée en dehors de tous préoccupations. Nous avons pris Kang-hoa le 16 Octobre et dès le lendemain, je pensais au retour, convaincu que mon but était atteint. Si, après réflexion, je me décidai à différer de quelque temps, c'est que je crus indispensable de faire explorer l'île pour me procurer quelques renseignements sur les mœurs, les coutumes, les produits et l'industrie du pays. Il me paraissait, d'ailleurs, nécessaire de compléter les travaux hydrographiques qui avaient été entrepris depuis l'île Boisée jusqu'à la rivière de Séoul. Le commerce, la navigation et les entreprises que l'avenir pourrait amener étaient également intéressées à l'accomplissement de ces travaux. Un incident qui se produisit le 19 Octobre vint encore ajouter une raison de plus à cet ajournement. Un émissaire se disant envoyé de Séoul m'apporta une lettre du Roi. Cette lettre me donna des espérances qui ne se sont pas réalisées et m'oblgeait à attendre l'effet de la réponse que je dus y faire. C'est ainsi que nous atteignîmes la fin d'Octobre et comme je n'avais reçu aucune nouvelle communication du Gouvernement et que l'hiver se faisait déjà rigoureusement sentir, je décidai d'une manière irrévocable que notre départ aurait lieu dans les premiers jours du mois de Novembre. On commença aussitôt la destruction de toutes les propriétés de l'Etat. Plus de 200 jonques furent coulées ; on fit sauter les poudrières et d'innombrables Magasins, avec tout ce qu'ils contenaient, furent mis à feu. Bientôt, il ne resta plus debout que la résidence royale et le Yamoun du Mandarin qui servaient de logement à une partie de nos hommes et qui, pour cette dernière raison, ne devaient être rasés qu'au dernier moment. C'est dans ces entrefaites que j'appris l'existence d'une citadelle dont personne ne m'avait parlé jusque-là et qui, disait-on, était presque inexpugnable. On assurait que Corps de soldats indigènes avait passé le bras de mer, les jours précédents, et était y prendre ses logements. Nous étions du 8 Novembre et tout prêts à lever la campagne. Cependant je voulus savoir à quoi m'en tenir et je décidai qu'une dernière reconnaissance serait faite de ce côté. A cet effet, le 9, du matin, une colonne de 150 hommes se mit en route sous le

Commandement de M. le Capitaine de vaisseau Olivier; elle n'avait d'autre mission que de reconnaître position, si elle existait et de compléter ainsi les renseignements sur les fortifications du pays. Je lui donnai l'ordre formel de rentrer le soir même. Vers 11 heures du matin, la colonne arriva en vue d'une fortresse dont les proportions dépassaient ce qu'on nous avait dit d'elle. Si Votre Excellence veut bien se reporter mon rapport du 17 Novembre dernirer, elle y trouvera des détails qu'il est inutile de reproduire ici. Le Commandemant Oliveir s'approcha d'une distance de trois à quatre cents mètres après avoir pris toutefois les précautions commandées en pareille circonstance. Rien ne faisait supposer la présence de l'ennemi et nos hommes se disposaient à pénétrer dans l'enceinte, quand une grêle de balles vint tout à coup les assaillir. Les remparts se garnissent comme par enchantement de soldats. Les témoins les plus véridiques portent leur nombre à trois mille au moins. En même temps, une masse considérable fait éruption au dehors. Un instant surprise par cette attaque inattendue, la petite troupe du Commandant Olivier se réforme sous la valeureuse impulsion de son chef et refoule l'ennemi dans ses retranchements.

Cent cinquante hommes luttant à découvert contre 3,000 et forçant ces derniers à rentrer précipitamment derrière leurs murailles, voilà un spectacle que l'on ne saurait trop admirer et dont on peut être justement fier. Cependant notre Colonne ne se replia pas. Dans l'impossibilité où elle était d'entamer des murailles, puisqu'elle n'avait pas d'artiller, elle choisit une position et continua bravement à harceler la garnison qui encombrait les parapets intérieurs. Elle espérait une nouvelle sortie mais il n'en fut rien. Bien convaincu de son infériorité, l'ennemi n'entendait combattre qu'à l'abri de ses remparts. C'est seulement après une heure d'un audacieux défi que l'on se décide à l'abandonner la place. Le Commandant Olivier régla tous les détails de la marche et notre petit corp défila, tête haute, sous les yeux des Coréens avec autant d'ordre qu'au sortir de ses cantonnements, nous ne laissons pas une bayonnette derrière nous!

Cette affaire était-elle de nature à modifier mes projets? Je ne le pensai pas, ja ne le pense pas encore. Nous avions eu, il est vrai, vingt-neuf hommes de blessés, tout légèrement; mais le chemin par lequel les Coréens avaient tenté leur sortie était littéralement couvert de cadavres et toutes nos tentatives pour les amener au combat avaient été inutiles. Fidèle à ma programme, je fis achever la destruction de la partie officielle de la ville de Kang-hoa dans la journée du 10 et 11, chacun avait repris à bord des bâtiments son poste accoutumé.

Voilà le récit fidèle de cette rencontre ; libre à M. de Bellonnet de la considérer comme un échec. Pour tout esprit non prévenu, elle fait le plus grand honneur à nos marins et elle atteste une fois de plus leur courage, en même temps qu'elle prouve la terreur que nous avons su inspirer aux soldats coréens.

L'honneur de la France, Monsieur le Ministre, m'est plus cher que ma propre réputation et si j'avais eu le malheur, comme on ne craint pas de l'insinuer, de l'engager dans la plus modeste mesure, aucune considération ne m'eût empêché de vous en faire l'aveu et de supplier Votre Excellence de me donner les moyens de laver une telle injure. Mais grâce à Dieu il n'en est rien ! ...... Loin d'être engagée, la France doit être satisfaite ; vengée et libre de son action, et elle peut s'arrêter là, ou poursuivre jusqu'au bout l'œuvre que nous avons commencée ; mais dans cette grave question elle n'aura à s'inspirer que de ses intérêts seuls.

L'exagération de M. le Chargé d'Affaires ne s'est pas arrêté là et le rapprochement qu'il fait entre la journée du 29 Juin 1859 en Chine et la journée du 9 Novembre en Corée, est une preuve des erreurs que peut être faire (*Sic*) commettre la passion quand on la prend pour conseillère. Dans le désastre du 25 Juin, les Anglais perdirent 400 hommes et 3 bâtiments. Obligés de battre en retraite et de se rembarquer à la hâte sous le feu de l'ennemi, ils laissèrent derrière eux une quantité d'armes et de munitions. Là, certainement l'honneur de l'Europe était en jeu et sa peine de renoncer à toute considération et à toute influence dans l'Extrême Orient, il fallait frapper un grand coup. C'est ce qui décida l'expédition de la France et de l'Angleterre en 1860. Y-a-t-il rien de semblable dans ma situation ? Non seulement nous n'avons perdu ni un bâtiment ni un homme ; mais encore nous n'avons pas eu à déplorer le plus léger accident ; j'ai accompli tout ce que je voulais et réalisé tout ce que je m'étais promis. M. l'Amiral Hope, arrêté à l'entrée du Peïho, est forcé de rétrograder après un combat sanglant. En Corée, au contraire, nous avons pénétré jusqu'au cœur du pays, nous y avons tenu garnison pendant près d'un mois et nous ne l'avons quitté que quand il ne nous était plus utile d'y rester. Encore une fois, Monsieur le Ministre, peut-on trouver la moindre similitude entre ces deux dates rapprochées avec une si fâcheuse intention ? Quant aux discours que M. de Bellonnet attribue à quelques Coréens dans le Yamoun de Pékin, il leur a donné certes plus d'importances qu'ils ne méritent. C'est bien peu connaître l'esprit des nations orientales que d'exiger d'elles de la sincérité et l'aveu d'une défaite. Les puissances Européennes n'ont pas eu des succès en Chine qui n'ait été l'occasion par la gazette officielle des plus incroyables récits. Même après la signature du Traité de Pékin, tout le monde sait que les Mandarins se vantèrent de nous avoir chargés et que des placards répandus partout l'annoncèrent aux divers parties de l'Empire.

J'ai la ferme confiance, Monsieur le Ministre, que Votre Excellences apprécie toutes ces récriminations à leur juste valeur ne me jugera que sur des rapports véridiques et complètement désintéressés. Je n'ai pu suivre M. de Bellonnet dans une politique qui m'a paru contraire à mes devoirs, j'ai temoigné de l'éloignement pour des relations particulières qui ne me semblaient point enviables. Plusieurs lettres officieuses que m'a écrites cet agent diplomatique ont laissé percer des tendances et une tournure d'esprit qui n'allaient point à mon caractère; je n'y ai répondu que par des témoignages non douteux d'indifférence; ce sont là, sans doute, ses griefs contre moi. Je regrette, pour lui, que dans des circonstances aussi graves il ait laissé ses susceptibilités ou ses rancune personnelles l'emporter sur les intérêts de la justice et de la vérité. Quant à moi, si pénible qu'il me soit de parler de mes actes, je répète que mon excursion en Corée a été suivie d'un plein succès. Commandé par d'impérieuses circonstances, exécutée avec des moyens infiniment réduits et terminée dans les limites de temps et d'importance que je m'étais tracés à l'avance, cette expédition, je ne crains pasde le dire, si modeste qu'elle soit, fait honneur à Notre Marine. Grâce à elle, la France a pénétré la première dans un pays resté jusqu'ici fermé à la lumière et si jamais ses intérêts l'y ramènent de nouveau elle n'y trouvera que des souverains dignes d'elle et dont chacun de nous est fier.

Je suis avec un profond respect, Monsieur le Ministre,
De Votre Excellence, Le très obéissant serviteur
Le Contre-Amiral Commandant en chef,

G. Roze

P. S.

J'ai eu l'honneur de joindre à mon premier rapport une carte à grands points de la route suivie dans le golfe du Prince Jérôme, ainsi que la carte du canal de Kang-hoa et de la rivière de Séoul jusqu'à la rive la plus rapprochée de cette capitale. Ces cartes pouvaient suffire à l'intelligence de nos opérations;

cependant pour plus de facilités, j'adresse aujourd'hui à Votre Excellence un nouveau corquis réduit où les positions sont mieux déterminées. Les officiers chargés de soin s'occupent, sans interruption, de dresser les cartes rectifiées d'après nos dernières observations et j'espère que je serai bientôt en mesure d'adresser à Votre Excellence l'ensemble de nos travaux hydrographiques qui les accompagnent.

G. Roze

P. de Chasseloup-Laubat(1867. 1. 18) → G. Roze

Roze의 조선원정 결과 평가

Paris le 18 Janvier 1867

Monsieur le Contre Amiral Roze,
Commandant en chef la Division navale
des Mers de chine,

Monsieur le Contre Amiral,

Lorsque vos dépêches m'annonçant le meurtre des missionnaires français en Corée, et contenant le récit que vous avait remis le R. P. Ridel me sont parvenues, je me suis empressé par une lettre de ma main, en date du 8 Septembre, de vous faire part des observations que me suggérait le projet dont vous m'entretenez de vous rendre sur les côtes de cette contrée pour obtenir du Gouvernement Coréen la satisfaction que nous avions légitimement droit de prétendre pour l'acte cruel dont il s'était rendu coupable. Mais, pendant ce temps, les événements avaient marché, vous aviez reçu de M. de Bellonet, chargé d'Affaires de France à Pékin, l'invitation de venger le merutre des missionnaires, et cet agent diplomatique avait même par des actes que je n'avais pas examiné ici, prononcé la déchéance du Roi de Corée, mais, par des réponses auxquelles j'ai donné mon entière approbation, vous aviez fait connaître à M. de Bellonet que la Corée étant indépendante, d'après ses propres affirmations, du Gouvnt de Pékin, il appartenait uniquement au Commandant en chef de la Division navale d'examiner ce que les forces dont il disposait lui permettaient de faire pour la protection de nos nationaux, et que dès lors à vous seuls dans ces parages était remis le soin de décider.

Quoiqu'il en soit, invité à agir par M. le Chargé d'Affaires à Pekin, ému sans aucun doute des récits de R. P. Ridel enfin, ayant comme Commandant en chef des forces navales françaises dans l'extrême Orient à protéger tous les sujets de l'Empereur et à maintenir l'influence de notre pavillon, vous vous êtes décidé à vous porter sur les côtes de la Corée. Apèrs une navigation pleine de périls, vous êtes arrivé à l'embouchure du Han-Kiang que vous avez remonté jusque devant Séoul.

Cette reconnaissance, M. le C. Amiral, vous fait le plus grand honneur ; conduire avec autant de hardiesse que de prudente intelligence, votre navigation dans une mer presque entièrement inconnue, sans cartes, et sur ce fleuve rempli d'écueils qu'aucun navire européen n'avait, que je sache, jamais parcourir, enfin vos travaux hydrographiques, tout cela mérite de sincères éloges, et je suis heureux d'avoir à vous les adresser.

Toutes fois, ne pouvant, avec les moyens que vous aviez, rien tenter de sérieux contre la Capitale de la Corée placée à quelques kilomètres des rives du Han-Kiang, vous avez dû vous retirer, il eut été imprudent d'agir autrement. Mais, revenu à Tché-fou, vous y avez réuni toutes vos forces, vous vous êtes préparé à l'expédition que vous méditiez. Vous avez donc conduit vos navires au mouillage de l'Ile Boisée et, après avoir parcouru une partie de la Rivière Salée, vous avez mis à terre vos compagnies de débarquement, et, par un coup de main aussi brillant qu'heureux vous vous êtes emparé de la ville de Kanghoa.

Jusque là, M. le C. Amiral, il n'y avait lieu que de se féliciter de tout ce que vous aviez fait sans doute lorsque vous mettiez à terre vos compagnies de débarquement et que vous vous dirigiez sur Kang-hoa, vous vous éloigniez de vos cannonières, vous ne pouviez plus être protegé par leur feu ; mais enfin si vous rencontriez un ennemi qui vous forçat à vous retirer, vous pouviez regagner le rivage, et dans ce cas même un succès ne pouvait pas avoir de conséquences trop graves.

Mais lorsqu'après la lettre du Roi reçue, vous ne voyez autour de vous que le vide fait par ordre du Governement Coréen, vous restez vingt jours à terre, lorsque vous envoyez des reconnaissances à des distances conidérables, lorsqu'un détachement de 180 marins, placé sous le commandement d'un Capitaine de vaisseau s'en va à, à 18 kilomètres, attaquer une pagode fortifiée, et revient avec une trentaine d'hommes blessés. Ayant ainsi parcouru 36 kilomètres en une journée — je ne puis, je vous l'avoue, m'empêcher de vous témoigner mes regrets qu'on se soit ainsi écarté de tous les principes qu'il importe à la Marine d'observer d'abord pour ne pas engager le Gouvernement de l'Empereur au delà de ce qu'il entend faire, ensuite pour que la Marine elle-même ne soit pas exposée à de singuliers mécomptes.

Si, au lieu de rester aussi longtemps à terre le surlendemain de la prise de Kang-hoa vous aviez annoncé au Roi de Corée que la ville serait détruite dans le cas où une journée s'écoulerait sans qu'il vous eut donné satisfaction ; si, ne voyant rien venir, vous aviez immédiatement opéré la destruction que vous avez réalisée, plus tard, et si vous aviez après cela embarqué vos compagnies, alors vous auriez frappé de stupeur toute la Corée et son Gouvernement qui se seraient crus sans cesse exposés à vos coups; vous auriez pu même proclamer que vous vous reviendriez quand vous le voudriez et peut-être vous eût-on fait des offres si l'année prochaine ou eût vu vos bâtiments venir au moment des arrivages de riz, bloquer le Han-Kiang.

Je crains, au contraire, que votre départ opéré après l'affaire de la pagode, et quand des troupes déjà nombreuses étaient parvenues à franchir la rivière Salée, n'ait singulierement affaibli l'effet qu'a pu produire la destruction de Kang-hoa. Sans doute, il n'y avait pas à hésiter dans les circonstances où vous vous trouviez, il fallait quitter la Corée; mais aux yeux des popultions de ces contrées et devant les proclamations que le Gouvernement Coréen n'aura pas manqué de répondre, nous aurons dû paraître contraints à la retraite.

Des dépêches télégraphiques qui sont venues de Chine par la voie de la Russie, et qui ont procedé de plusieurs semaines l'arrivée de la lettre par laquelle vous m'annonciez la prise de Kang-hoa, et votre seconde lettre me faisant connaître que vous aviez embarqué vos compagnies avaient présenté cette affaire comme une sorte d'échec à notre influence. Je ne pense pas qu'il en puisse être ainsi, mais vous comprendrez combien la situation eût été différente si vous n'aviez pas prolongé votre séjour à terre après votre brillant coup de main.

Enfin, M. C. Amiral, vous comprendrez dans quelles graves difficultés se trouverait placé le Gouvernement de l'Empereur si ce détachement de 180 marines envoyé à 18 kilomètres, et qui est revenu si maltraité, avait été détruit, comme cela eût pu arriver au milieu d'un pays inconnu, rempli d'ennemis que vous-même considérez comme loin d'être sans valeur.

Quoiqu'il en soit, le Gouvernemnet de l'Empereur a dû, dans une note que vous trouverez au Moniteur du 8 du ce mois, rendre compte de tout ce qui s'est passé. Vous remarquerez que cet article se termine par ces mots: "la destruction de Kang-hoa a dû prouver au Gouvernement coréen que le meurtre des missionnaires français ne restait pas impuni."

C'est vous dire, M. le Contre Amiral, que le Gouvernement de l'Empereur ne se croit pas dans l'obligation de dépasser, quand à présent, ce que vous avez fait, et que dès lors, vous n'avez rien à entreprendre, sans que de nouvelles instructions vous aient tracé la ligne de conduite à suivre. Je pense d'ailleurs, que vos premières dépêches me donneront de nouveaux renseignements sur toutes ces choses.

Je vous envoie la liste de récompenses que l'Empereur a bien voulu accorder à votre Division.

....

....

Recevez ....

183

G. Roze (1867. 1. 31) → P. de Chasseloup-Laubat

조선원정 결과의 비난에 대한 반박

À bord de *la Guerrière*, Yokohama, le 31 Janvier 1867

Monsieur le Ministre,

Les détails que j'ai donnés à Votre Excellence sur notre excursion en Corée pourraient me permettre de ne pas revenir sur cette affaire. Mais il n'est peut être pas inutile d'appeler votre attention sur le langage que la Presse Anglaise de la Chine n'a cessé de tenir depuis notre retour, avec un parti pris de dénigrement et dans un but qu'il est facile de saisir.

Votre Excellence a connu le programme que je m'étais tracé après mon exploration de la rivière de Séoul. Ayant reconnu l'impossibilité d'aller, avec les seules forces dont je disposais, venger dans la Capitale de la Corée, le meurtre de nos missionnaires, j'avais conçu la pensée de frapper le Gouvernement de ce pays dans l'île de Kang-hoa, place forte que je rencontrais sur ma route et qui, par son importance ainsi que par les richesses militaires qu'elle renfermait, méritait de fixer mon attention. Là s'arrêtaient mes projets et l'attaque que je méditais restait ainsi dans le cercle moins étendu, mais plus certain, d'une opération essentiellement maritime. Ce plan a été exécuté comme ja l'avais conçu et la destruction des Etablissements de Kang-hoa est là pour l'attester.

Cependant le commerce étranger de la Chine qui s'était flatté qu'un pays nouveau allait être ouvert à ses convoitises, et qui attendait la réalisation de cet espoir comme un résultat certain de notre expédition, fut deçu en apprenant que je m'étais arrêté à Kang-hoa et, oubliant les motifs plus élevés qui avaient dicté ma détermination, ne vit en jeu que ses intérêts méconnus.

Aussitôt la Presse Anglaise de Shang-haï se fit l'écho de ses doléances et animée, en outre, de cet esprit triste rivalité qui l'a portée, de tout temps, à dénigrer ce qui peut procurer quelque honneur à la France, la Presse Anglaise, dis-je, s'éleva contre les résultats de notre entreprise et s'attacha par des insinuations sciemment injustes à dénaturer les faits avec l'intention bien évidente de laisser croire que notre œuvre devait être continuée.

Votre Excellence, j'en ai la ferme confiance, ne se sera pas méprise sur le calcul d'un pareil système qui chercherait inutilement à cacher le but vrai d'un désir intéressé.

Depuis longtemps déjà la spéculation avait les yeux impatiemment tournés vers la Corée ; elle en attendait des éléments de fortune qu'elle avait vainement poursuivis. Dans la seule année de 1866, l'Emperor, petit navire à vapeur appartenant à la Maison Anglaise Jardines et Co, s'était approché des côtes et en était revenu sans avoir pu entrer en relations avec ses habitants, un autre bâtiment, *le Général Shermann*, portant le pavillon des Etats-Unis, l'avait suivi à quelques mois de distance et plus malheureux encore, arrêté à l'entrée d'une rivière située à plusieurs milles du Nord de Kang-hoa, il fut incendié après d'être échoué et, bientôt après, tout son équipage, m'a-t-on assuré, fut impitoyablement mis à mort. Ces tentatives furent désastreuses ou restèrent sans succès et le commerce n'en attendit, qu'avec un désir plus ardent, l'ouverture de la Corée par nos armes.

Dans le principe la Presse confidente de ses arrières pensées, avait affecté, avec une apparence de désintéressement, de ne parler que de la nécessité de venger le meurtre de nos missionnaires mais plus tard, quand elle apprit la rapidité de nos opérations et les limites que je m'étais imposées, son déchaînement ne connut plus de bornes et elle ne put dissimuler le vrai sentiment qui inspirait ses regrets.

Mais ces vaines clameurs me laissent calme et, fort de ma conscience, je dédaigne ces appréciations malveillants au dessus desquelles je cherche à m'élever. Dans un autre ordre d'idées quelques impatiences ont pu se traduire et des personnes intéressées à voir la liberté religieuse s'étendre sur la Corée, ont regretté, de concert avec les hommes voués aux affaires commerciales, que ce pays n'ait pas été ouvert à leurs aspirations. J'ai encore (*Sic*) je ne pouvais me prêter à la réalisation d'espérances aussi prématurées ; un tel progrès ne se conquiert pas en un jour. Voilà bientôt neuf ans que nous sommes au Japon en vertu d'un Traité, notre influence s'y développe rapidement et cependant le prosélytisme y est encore formellement interdit. Du reste, tel n'était pas mon but : je le répète, je n'avais voulu qu'une chose, tirer une vengeance éclatante de la mort des nôtres, sans me laisser entraîner au delà de ce qu'il m'était possible de faire et surtout sans engager le Gouvernement de l'Empereur dans des opérations dont il aurait pu ne pas juger l'opportunité. Mais, quoiqu'on de dise, sous le rapport religieux même, la leçon sévère que j'ai infligée au Gouvernement Coréen ne peut manquer d'avoir d'heureuses conséquences, car il est en toute évidence qu'elle le disposera, par crainte, à des sentiments plus humains et qu'elle préviendra le retour des forfaits dont il s'est rendu coupable.

D'ailleurs, je n'ai quitté Kang-hoa qu'après avoir acquis la certitude que les deux seuls prêtres français qui étaient restés dans le pays, après le Père Ridel, étaient parvenus à le quitter et je suis en droit de croire que l'intimidation causée par notre présence n'a pas été étrangère à la facilité de leur fuite. Si quelques Missionnaires se décident, plus tard, à y rentrer il reconnaîtront eux-mêmes, j'en suis convaincu, que leur condition, loin d'avoir perdu à notre intervention, y aura sérieusement gagné. Mais je dois le dire encore l'amertume et les regrets, qui se font aussi jour de ce côté, viennent à la fois d'une déception qu'il ne dépendait pas de moi d'épargner à ceux qui l'ont ressentie et du besoin qu'ils ont de faire croire à la nécessité d'une nouvelle expédition.

Je ne m'arrêterai pas plus longtemps sur des récriminations dont la cause est évidente. Je les repousse comme dépourvues de sincérité et j'ai la ferme confiance que Votre Excellence ne s'y méprendra pas. Aussi je ne doute pas qu'elle en sanctionne de sa haute approbation une entreprise que j'ai accomplie sous ma seule responsabilité, il est vrai, mais qui, en donnant satisfaction à la partie des intéressés de l'opinion, laisse le Gouvernement de l'Empereur absoulument libre de son action pour l'avenir.

Je suis avec un profond repect,
Monsieur le Mnistre,
De Votre Excellence,
Le très obéissant serviteur.
Le Contre-Amiral Commandant en chef,

G. Roze

A. Burlingame (1867. 1. 31) ➞ W. H. Seward

프랑스의 2차 조선 침공 가능성 및 각국 동태 보고

Leagation of the United States
Peking. Jan'y 31, 1867

Hon. William H. Seward
Secretary of State

Sir:

In the Spring or early Summer the French will probably make a demonstration against Corea, which will result in a treaty and the opening of the country to commerce. Sir Rutherford Alcock, the British Minister, informs me that he shall probably represent his country on that occasion, and be present with the British Admiral to look after British interests. Mr. Vlangaly, the Russian Minister, agrees with me that our countries by contiguity and future prospects are as much interested in the questions involved, as are the English and French.

We have therefore agreed to request from our respective Governments full power to act as may be best for their interests. We shall strive to prevent bloodshed, and to establish amicable relations with the Coreans who command by position one of the principal passes for our future trade.

The Chinese will be much pleased to have us present. We are on the spot and have full knowledge of the questions to be considered. Admiral Bell, who has sufficient force, will be in the gulf of Petcheli in the Spring, and we can in a few hours go over to Corea. He has already sent Captain Shufeldt with the *Wachusett* to enquire for and bring away those who may possibly survive the massacre on board of the *General Sherman*. In the absence of a Russian war vessel I have taken the liberty to write Mr. Vlangaly, the Russian Minister, to accept of the United States' hospitality, and go with me.

If you approve of this dispatch and confer the power requested, be so kind as to confide a telegram stating the facts to the Russian Government to be communicated to me and also send one by the way of California; and at the same time give the necessary instructions to our Naval Officers in China.

It will be well to send a duplicate of your full dispatch in reply to this, as the mails are not certain between Shanghai and Peking.

I have the honor to be, Sir,
Your obedient Servant,
Anson Burlingame

高宗 ➡ 禮部(1867. 2. 1/高宗三年十二月二十七日)

조불(朝佛) 교전 경과 통보

照錄原咨

朝鮮國王爲歷陳洋匪侵擾形實事 本年九月洋匪入據江華府 具回檄悖慢之由已有所具咨仰陳矣 嗣後敵勢轉益猖獗 有不可盡述 而江華不但爲敝邦保障之重地也 敝職先祖僖順王莊順王真幀亦妥於行宮 洋匪入城之日 守臣倉皇移奉於僻處 而字廨署竝入灰燼 以至驅刼男婦 攘殺牛畜 攫去樁留之銀 掠取綱運之米 武庫先被放燹 利器多歸藉寇 緣江列堡有龍津廣成等鎮 而燒燬殆盡 甲串津上下分船遮住 以斷赴援之路 鄉紳知宗正卿李是遠居在城外 及聞城陷 與其弟憂憤仰藥死之 故已施褒隱之典 巡撫中軍李容熙住陣於江華府越岸通津府 未及交鋒矣 九月十八日 巡撫哨官韓聖根率銃手守文殊山城彼人乘四小船自甲串津來泊 將欲上山 聖根奮不顧身 一發數丸 則彼人應聲落水 銃手隨卽齊發 彼人多震仆而死者 而船中人蠭涌登山 放火於城門及公廨而去 十月初四日 巡撫千總梁憲洙潛師由廣城津而入鼎足山城 城在江華府之東南 將以爲憑高直搗如建瓴之勢也 彼人又欲據此城 其頭領騎馬 悉帶鋭卒上山 不知憲洙已在城中也 憲洙盡力捍禦齊放銃礮 一場鏖戰 其騎馬者應丸而墮 彼兵相繼僵死者如麻 輿尸而走 器械輜重 委棄路側 初五日 江華城中所在彼人紛紛輸器物於船中 而甲串津碇留四船 一時解纜出往富平前洋與前留三舶同住 而城中無一敵 憲洙自鼎足山城整軍而下 克復府城 撫輯兵民 而富平前洋碇留七舶 本月十二日出外洋向南而去 噫 彼法國人之强欲尋釁 涉我海疆 毁我關防 創殘我民人 偸竊我蓄貯 是豈敝邦有所失而然哉 特以其谿壑無厭之慾 作一海浪賊耳 敝邦地狹力弱 不嫺戎政 而惟玆禮義之俗秉彛攸存 故上自朝廷卿士 下至軍卒氓黎 莫不扼腕裂眦 誓死防守 或有沫血倡義者 或有捐軀殉難者 眾心成城 庶可藉此而獲保藩維 然彼夷去來無常情跡叵測 未可以釋慮而弛備矣 竊伏惟我大朝字育之澤 曠絶千古 前後恩造山海崇深 藐玆冲年 遭此大難 兢兢業業 罔知攸措 其在緩急安危之際 籲告情實 固臣分之當然 而凡係小邦之患難 每蒙大朝之捄恤 玆具被兵事由 修咨詳陳 煩乞貴部轉達天聽 導示備禦之機略 使蕞爾屬國 永底安靖 恭備候度 千萬幸甚 爲此合行移咨 請照驗轉奏施行

吉川主計(1867. 2. 1/慶應二年十二月二十七日) ➞ 幕府

제너럴 셔먼호 사건과 병인양요 직전의 조선상황 탐문 보고

丙寅十二月廿七日
一覽仕候
卯正月 小栗上野介
小栗下總守
羽田十左衛門
一覽仕候
卯正月 外國奉行
外國掛
大目付
御目付 承之

今般朝鮮國え外夷侵入不穩之次第彼國え差置候役目之者及探索別紙之通國許より申越候に付不取敢於京地御老中板倉伊賀守様え及御届候依之右別紙寫奉添
御內聽置候以上

十二月廿七日 宗對馬守家來 吉 川 主 計

表書
朝鮮國え外夷侵入御屆書寫
訓導俊卿安僉知申出之次第
當年七月平安道平壤之邊海え異樣船四艘來泊竟に同所江之內え乘込小船を乘廻上陸村民を驚し候ニ付土官是を制候處渠より砲發我土人拾貳人被打殺手負數十人に及候ニ付京司え伺打果候に決し折柄深霧に乘し小船筏等に火攻之支度調四艘之內壹艘先水上より燒立候處其船之異賊何れも水中に入游泳致し候を召捕或は打果其內には切に降を乞候者も有之放還せ

しめ候處拾歩餘を不過内最前被殺或は被傷付候我土之者之父兄子弟暗雲追掛悉く打果大數凡七拾余名にも及其内清國之者三拾人計異人四拾余人爲有之由に候殘る三艘は右之勢を見掛何れも令退帆候

一夫より又三日目異船三艘平壤間近乘掛洋には夥數相見候様に有之時偶風雨甚く右間近く乘掛居候三艘之内壹艘横様に左之方え駈離壹艘は跡に少し後れ居候處殘壹艘に折節震電落打かと見へ候處忽燃上り候故我土人船を出し見候へは悉く燒焦居右横に駈離候壹艘跡に續居候船共悉く行方不相知夫切に平壤之地えはいまた參り不申候

此燒候船中凡三尺計申さは矢竹を見候如き程頃之鐵串を百本五拾本或は三拾貳拾を手把に致し大分積載居候由

其後當八月十二日京城之近海江華邊え參段々漢江近く乘込候に付京中も騷敷有之候得共是と申手入にも不相成十八日に退帆致し夫より九月初に貳艘參り兩三日滯留退帆又同月七日七艘同所え參り洋にも大分相見候說も有之候處乘込候儀はいまた承不申小子同十二日京地出立其後十四日迄之便を承居候處夫迄はいまた繫泊致し居候由今程如何哉全体之擧動難閣振合に相聞是等を打候は不難事に候得共北京和交あるに對し强て不法を不咎其儘に見流し有之事に候彼之者水軍砲術に妙なる而已力量極甚微弱なる者共に候小子先年北京に參り候節渠と清人立會候を見物致し候處清人より頭を手にて被打其儘被打倒候ゆへ其相手之清人え相尋候處全体彼之者力量と申は更に無之由申聞候此節迚も邊浦え上陸は致し候得共只其水邊而已を立廻陸地深く立入不申船を以家とし城とし候もの共と相見候

一去春異人九人我國之服を著國中え紛れ入天主學を專と致し候事露顯何れも被刑候事有之候處平壤え參り候異人共其難題を申聞候江華え參り候異人共は此國山川好き由承り候ゆへ見物に參候と申幾日も滯留いたし候ニ付此方より山川之見物も最早多日に及候故退帆せしめ候様申向候得共何ゆへに歸る事を催促致し候哉此國清國共交日本共交候事ゆへ我共通交せよと頻に申聞應對之人より清國に咨して可答と云候處彼直に一書を出し爰に清國之令書有清に屬するの國は悉く我議に從へと令せり是を證とし我か言に隨んやと云答曰假令清國此令書ある共我に未た令する之書なく故に我か知る所に非すと答候由全体右異人之内に朝鮮詞を申候者も有之候

一來泊滯留數日之間小船より水邊村里に上陸鷄犬之類を奪取候位之事に候得共渠等素遠大之深意有之事と相見へ去春參り候九人之ものも何方より

紛入候哉一向相分不申於我國專相察候は黃海道之海邊は淸國に近く年分此邊りえ淸人靑魚を漁り候事有之其場所水上之事ゆへ彼是と定界迚ハ無之我國之者水家を踰へ淸海に往て漁り淸國之者も又越て我黃海近く漁り候者有之間々互に界を爭ひ喧嘩等之事にも及ひ候樣之場所柄に候處其所え先年異人參り人參を潛商せしめ候事有之若は右之邊より右九人之者紛入候共には無之哉と被相察候

一全体近年渠等屢近海え出沒覬覦威劫之意念深く相見實に可惡之限に御座候旣先年忠淸道之邊海え異船參候節禮曹より書契を以御告知に及候譯も有之則右樣之船乘廻候に付ては御互に堤防を堅く相備輕侮を不受樣致し度存事候此後に至必手入之儀可押及勢に相聞御隣國之儀其節に臨候ハヽ從來之御好誼も有之何分宜御心添被下度希申候

右之通に御座候處此外別說に承候得は諸道より海士を被召登候由にて東萊郡より海士數多登候由に御座候右異船乘込候場所々々浦口或は江尻等に難見込樣要備取設候爲之役夫に召使候譯にも候哉未た其能用相分り不申候

一海士召使候儀は燒討之役夫に當て候哉之說も仕候事

右は訓導俊卿九月十二日京地發足迄之儀申出候所に御座候其後之模樣風聞探索仕候得は又々大分之爭戰も仕候哉に相聞候得共數說難取留猶追々相探委細可申上候事

總署(1867. 2. 27/同治六年正月二十三日) ➞ 同治帝

조불(朝佛) 교전 경과 및 향후 대응 방안 정리

正月二十三日 本衙門正摺奏稱 爲朝鮮國咨請禮部代奏 覆陳上年洋船情形擬請仍由禮部咨照朝鮮預爲籌畫 竝請將法國條約三十一款抄交該國閱看 恭摺密陳 仰祈聖鑒事 竊臣衙門於本月十二日准禮部咨稱 轉奏朝鮮國王覆陳上年洋船情形等因一摺 奉旨 該衙門知道 欽此 先後由軍機處曁禮部抄錄原奏 及該國咨文三件 別錄一件 知照前來 査法國與朝鮮用兵一案 臣等於上年十一月十四日奏陳續籌辦理情形 請飭禮部知照朝鮮國王妥爲籌備 旋准禮部咨稱 閱時已久 情形不同 擬將原奏暫存 俟朝鮮續有咨文到日 再行核辦等因咨覆在案 臣等公同閱看此次該國王來咨大意 以該國與法國本不交涉何有失和 去歲搆兵 實因法國尋衅 該國惟有秉義修備 衆志成城 庶可保護藩維 其通商傳教諸事 民情國勢斷不可行 竝聲明使臣李興敏僭陳私書 已施譴罷之典 仰蒙皇朝曲賜矜恤 玆具被兵各事由 請爲隨機指諭 俾底安靖各等因 臣等査朝鮮前失江華郡城 旋經該國整軍克復 法國兵船亦卽退駛 惟法國是否從此寢息 抑尙銳意興兵 均未可必 前此朝鮮錄送法國回檄 內有欲朝鮮差員面議一節 似亦注意於和解 第通商傳教諸事 朝鮮旣稱邦禁綦嚴 是否願從 中國斷不能稍有勉强 該國應如何悉心籌辦 不致稍涉疎虞之處 相應請旨飭下禮部 詳加酌核 迅卽咨照朝鮮國王自行先事妥籌 總期計出萬全 毋稍大意 至該國王別錄所稱 未知三十一款條約何時所成 開載甚事等語 査去歲臣衙門接據法使照會內稱 因於朝鮮搆兵 堵塞港口 暫禁商船前往 臣等以法國條約第三十一款內開 將來中國遇有與別國用兵 除敵國布告堵口不能前進外中國不爲禁阻法國貿易 及與用兵之國交易 凡法國船從中國口駛往敵國口所有進口出口各例貨物 竝無妨礙 如常貿易無異等語 竝無因兩國用兵 禁止商船前往之條 當經酌給照覆 引及此條 以明不應禁止中國商船之意 至此項條約係於咸豐十年定議 所有法國條約全款 及他國所立條約各款 亦祇言中土而未及外藩 竝無絲毫牽涉朝鮮之處 應請一倂由禮部將前經咨發該部之法國條約第三十一款 抄錄咨行朝鮮國王査閱 俾其洞悉原委 除由臣衙門隨時相機酌辦外 謹將現籌辦理情形恭摺密陳 伏乞皇太后皇上聖鑒 謹奏

禮部(1867. 3. 9/同治六年二月四日) ➜ 高宗(1867. 3. 30/同治六年二月二十五日)

프랑스조약(法國條約) 제31관을 초록하여 발송

丁卯 禮部知會鈔錄法國條約咨

禮部爲知照事主客司案呈准總理各國事務衙門咨稱同治六年正月二十三日本衙門具奏朝鮮國咨請禮部代奏覆陳上年洋舶情形擬請仍由禮部咨照朝鮮預爲籌畫並將法國條約第三十一款鈔交該國閱看一摺軍機大臣奉旨依議欽此應恭錄諭旨鈔錄原奏咨禮部查照欽遵等因前來相應鈔錄該衙門原奏知照朝鮮國王預爲籌畫毋稍大意並將前准總理各國事務衙門咨送法國條約三十一款鈔送該國王閱看可也云云 同治六年二月初四日

原奏

謹奏爲朝鮮國咨請禮部代奏覆陳上年洋舶情形擬請仍由禮部咨照朝鮮預爲籌畫並請將法國條約三十一款鈔交該國閱看恭摺密陳仰祈聖鑒事竊臣衙門於本月十二日准禮部咨稱轉奏朝鮮國王覆陳上年洋舶情形等因一摺奉旨該衙門知道欽此先後由軍機處暨禮部鈔錄原奏及該國咨文三件別錄一件知照前來查法國與朝鮮用兵一案臣等於上年十一月十四日奏陳續籌辦理情形請飭禮部知照朝鮮國王妥爲籌備旋准禮部咨稱閱時已久情形不同擬將原奏暫存俟朝鮮續有咨文到日再行核辦等因咨覆在案臣等公同閱看此次該國王來咨大意以該國與法國本不交涉何有失和去歲搆兵實因法國尋衅該國惟有秉義修備衆志成城庶可保護藩維其通商傳教諸事民情國勢斷不可行並聲明使臣李興敏僭陳私書已施譴罷之典仰蒙皇朝曲賜矜恤玆具被兵各事請爲隨機指諭俾底安靖各等因臣等查朝鮮前失江華郡城旋經該國整軍克復法國兵船亦卽退駛惟法國是否從此寢息抑尙銳意興兵均未可必前此朝鮮錄送法國回檄內有欲朝鮮差員面議一節似亦注意於和解第通商傳教諸事朝鮮旣稱邦禁綦嚴是否願從中國斷不能稍有勉强該國應如何悉心籌辦不致稍涉疏虞之處相應請旨飭下禮部詳加酌核迅卽咨照朝鮮國王自行先事妥籌總期計出萬全毋稍大意至該國王別錄所稱未知三十一款條約何時所成開載甚事等語查去歲臣衙門接據法使照會內稱因於朝鮮搆兵堵塞港口暫禁商船前往臣等以法國條約第三十一款內開將來中國遇有與別國用兵除敵國布告堵口不能前進外中國不爲禁阻法國貿易及與用兵之國

交易凡法國從中國口駛往敵國口所有進口出口各例貨物並無妨礙如常貿易無異等語並無因兩國用兵禁止商船前往之條當經酌給照覆引及此條以明不應禁止中國商船之意至此項條約係於咸豐十年定議所有法國條約全款及他國所立條約各款亦只言中土而未及外藩並無絲毫牽涉朝鮮之處應請一併由禮部將前經咨發該部之法國條約第三十一款鈔錄咨行朝鮮國王查閱俾其洞悉原委除由臣衙門隨時相機酌辦外謹將現籌辦理情形恭摺密陳伏乞皇太后皇上聖鑒謹奏

法國條約第三十一款

將來中國遇有與別國用兵除敵國布告堵口不能前進外中國不爲禁阻法國貿易及與用兵之國交易凡法國船從中國口駛往敵國口所有進口出口各例貨物並無妨礙如常貿易無異

189

G. Roze (1867. 3. 12) → P. de Chasseloup-Laubat

강화도에서 입수한 군기의 발송

À bord de *la Guerrière*, Yokohama, le 12 Mars 1867

Monsieur le Ministre,

J'ai honneur de vous informer que, par suite de la promotion de M. le Comte d'Osery au garde de Capitaine de vaisseau, je vais le diriger sur France par le prochain paquebot des Messageries Impériales. Il sera provisoirement remplacé dans ses fonctions de Second de *la Guerrière* par M. le Lieutenant de vaisseau Forget, le plus ancien officier de la frégate.

Ce n'est pas sans regret que je me sépare de M. d'Osery dont j'ai eu tant de fois l'occasion d'apprécier les brillantes qualités, mais j'en suis dédommagé par l'avancement que Votre Excellence a bien voulu lui accorder.

Je profite du départ de cet officier Supérieur pour vous envoyer les quatre drapeaux que nous avons pris à Kang-hoa et dont j'ai déjà eu l'honneur de parler à Votre Excellence dans mes précédents rapports.

Je suis avec un profond respect …

G. Roze

徳川慶喜, L. Roches (1867. 3. 12/慶應三年二月七日)

조불(朝佛) 분쟁 중재에 관한 제안

同 二月七日於大坂御城佛公使ロセスえ 御對話ノ一節

大君　朝鮮へ其國より討伐の事ありと承り候も始末抦(*Sic*)承り舊交の國故和議爲取扱へく哉被存候に付其人を選可差遣候間事情細示可有之候

公使　アドミラールより戰爭場之地圖戰爭之模様認候壹冊差出申候右は差上候間御慰にも相成候哉と爰に持參仕候
同國極鎖國之風にて近來弘法法師九人永々在留致居候を一朝慘剋に殺害いたし候に付アドミラールの權を以復讐いたし候其後亞船へ英人二人乘組居候を燒之壹人も不殘燒討にいたし候同國は大閤討伐已來御舊交之由大君右之通無名之師を起し候を御說得和議御取扱も被仰付朝鮮承服仕候はゞ佛にて引受聊御不都合無之様取計可申候

大君　何れ其人物は選可遣候猶宜周旋賴入候

公使　支那を萬々一賴上にては面白からず候間探索之上可申上候

191

板倉勝靜, L. Roches (1867. 3. 13/慶應三年二月八日)

조불(朝佛) 분쟁 중재에 관한 대화

관련문서 (1) 막부의 중재 재안에 대한 프랑스 공사의 견해

同　二月八日於大坂佛公使旅寓伊賀守殿縫殿頭殿御應接ノ一節

閣老　昨日被申立候朝鮮一件若支那にて取扱居候はゞ手を引可然旨被申候得共支那我と同意ならば力を合せ候不同意或は誤解等有之候はゝ北京迄も使節を遣し支那をも說諭し到底公平に調和爲致候ては如何

公使　支那とて外國を禦候方え力を入候事は萬々無之候朝鮮一條は已初め北京在留佛國ミニストル王城え罷出朝鮮は何レ之所屬に候や云々之旨懸合候處同國は支那に於て相搆(*Sic*)不申段相答候に付水師提督事を擧候事に及候乍併其後又再考して手を入調和を取扱候哉も難計候

閣老　若其後に至り手を入候とも入れず候とも何れとも此方より取扱彼より渡合有之候節は同心合力候て其事整候様致し候ては如何

公使　支那にて手を入居候はゞ御搆(*Sic*)無之方と奉存候支那にて取扱候節は都て北京在留佛公使之懸にて私之關り候所に無御座候若支那にて取扱候節者口出しは不仕候且支那は自ら尊大にして御國を東夷抔と今以鄙しめ候風儀ゆへ彼手を入居候處へ彼是御心配被成候ても却て心持を惡敷被成迄にて寸益も有之間敷哉に奉存候乍去彼國若御國之所屬に候はゞ支那の取扱を御斷御引受被成候て宜候

就ては間諜之ものえ御委任伏御授被遣能々偵探致しいまだ支那にても手を不入候はゞ往復等之日間を省き直に御委任狀を以彼國を御說諭夫々運被付可然奉存候

【관련문서 1】

朝鮮國之義見込

朝鮮國ニテ去年中本國人ヲ殺害シ亞米利加船ヲ燒亡シ其他種々ノ暴行有之何分不被捨置我國ニテ彼一都府ヲ破リ猶追討モ可致ノ處本國政府ノ命令モ無之全ク我水師提督ノ一存ニテ復讎致シ候迄ニテ相濟候得共亞船ニ乘組居候英人モ殺傷被致候事故英亞兩國ニテモ近々復讎ノ擧可有之御國ニテハ舊交ノ國ト申御取扱ニテ和議御取計有之候方格別ノ御信義相顯レ御威光海外ニ耀キ候美事ニ御座候若可然モ思召候ハヽ御取扱振ハ兼テ方寸ニ蓄藏罷在候間猶委細ニ取調ヘ篤ト事情可申上候同國ニ於テ意ヲ屈シ支那等ヘ相賴旣ニ和議相調候事ニ至リ候ハヽ御捨置可然候右樣ノ模樣モ無御座候ハヽ前文ノ義此節御奮發御處分被成候好機會ニ御座候

G. Roze (1867. 3. 16) ➞ P. de Chasseloup-Laubat

강화도 체류 연장에 대한 해명

Guerrière, à Yokohama, le 16 Mars 1867

Monsieur le Ministre,

J'ai l'honneur de vous accuser réception de la dépêche que vous m'avez adressée en date du 18 Janvier, et par laquelle V.E. me fait des observations qui lui ont été suggérées par mon expédition en Corée.

V. E. veut bien apprécier les motifs qui m'ont engagé à aller venger le meurtre de nos missionnaires, et approuver la manière dont j'avais compris à cet égard les devoirs qui, comme commandant de la Division navale, m'imposaient l'obligation de protéger nos nationaux placés dans le rayon de mon commandement. V. E. a la bonté de donner des éloges à mon exploration dans la rivière de Séoul et veut bien accorder également son approbation au coup de main par lequel je m'étais emparé de la ville de Kang-hoa.

Les témoignages de satisfaction me sont infiniment précieux et j'en remercie V. E. Mais à partir de ce moment, V.E. voit avec regret mon séjour prolongé à Kang-hoa, et pense que j'aurais dû quitter la Corée après la destruction de cette place. Elle ajoute qu'après avoir reçu la lettre du Roi, et voyant le vide fait autour de nous par ordre du Gouvernement Coréen, j'ai eu le tort de rester aussi longtemps dans les positions que j'occupais, et qu'en envoyant des reconnaissances au loin, j'avais méconnu tous les principes qu'il importe à la Marine d'observer.

Je m'incline devant ces reproches et j'y suis douloureusement sensible. Par mes dépêches antérieures, V. E. est à même du juger mes actes en toute connaissance de cause, et je n'ai rien à ajouter à mes précédents rapports pour me disculper à ses yeux.

J'ai eu l'honneur d'exposer à V. E. par quel enchaînement de circonstance, les événements s'étaient succédés depuis mon arrivée à Kang-hoa, et comment j'avais été entraîné à attendre l'issue des négociations dont le Gouvernement de la Corée m'avait fait l'ouverture. Lors de mon arrivée sur les côtes de la Corée, deux missionnaires échappés au massacre de leurs collègues s'y trouvaient encore et rusaient exposés aux représailles du Gouvernement que je venais punir; il m'avait semble que je ne devais m'éloigner qu'après avoir employé tous les moyens en mon pouvoir pour les soustraire aux persécutions dont ils pouvaient être l'objet. Ce fut l'une des principales raisons qui m'ont engagé à différer mon départ; et j'ai eu la satisfaction en effet de savoir ces deux missionnaires hors de toute atteinte avant de m'éloigner des côtes de la Corée. En outre, le pays dans lequel je me trouvais et qui jusqu'alors avait été fermé à la navigation devait être exploré; j'ai pensé qu'il importait de prolonger assez longtemps mon séjour dans ces parages pour les mieux connaître et en faire une hydrographie aussi complète que possible. Sous ce rapport, mon apparition en Corée aura été profitable à la géographie, car nous en avons rapporté des cartes qui seront d'une utilité incontestable.

D'un côté, tout me faisait un devoir de chercher à tirer une vengeance éclatante du massacre de nos compatriotes, et de l'autre j'étais dominé par la préoccupation constante de ne pas en ager (*Sic*) le Gouvernement de l'Empereur. Je me suis efforcé d'atteindre ce double but et je peux affirmer en toute sincérité que l'honneur des armes de la France qui m'importe plus encore que ma propre réputation a été sauvegardé en tous points. Je peux le répéter avec conviction, la reconnaissance du 9 Nov. n'est pas un échec; la colonne conduite si vaillamment par le Commandant Olivier n'avait pas la mission de s'emparer de la pagode; elle avait à l'examiner et à me rendre compte de sa position; l'engagement qui s'en est suivi est un de ces événements comme il en arrive si souvent à la guerre et il fait d'ailleurs le plus grand honneur à nos marins. Il n'a donc pu ajouter qu'à notre prestige, puisque l'ennemi après avoir été repoussé par trois fois avec une grande perte d'hommes, a été contenu dans ses retrenchements, et n'en est plus sorti, tandis que notre petite troupe défilait fièrement sous ses yeux.

Avant de faire réembarquer nos compagnies, j'ai fait compléter l'œuvre de destruction des établissements officiels de la ville, et ce n'est que le lendemain du jour où les flammes avaient dévoré cette place et avaient proclamé à la Corée que notre vengeance était accomplie que j'ai fait évacuer nos cantonnements à quelques kilomètres d'une armée coreénne qui n'a pas osé se montrer pour inquiéter notre départ, opération toujours assez délicate en pays ennemi.

Je ne saurais donc supposer que les résultats de mon expédition puissent être considérés comme ayant porté atteinte à notre influence, je suis au contraire en droit d'affirmer qu'ils auront produit un effet salutaire sur l'esprit de la population et du Gouvernement de la Corée.

Ce n'est pas sans un profond sentiment de tristesse que je viens de vous parler de mes actes, et qu'en entretenant V. E. de ce qui m'est personnel, j'ai pris un langage auquel ma nature plus modeste ne m'a pas habitué ; mais je conserve le ferme espoir que votre bienveillance continuent à m'être acquise comme par le passé, et cette confiance seule peut apporter un adoucissement au chagrin de n'avoir pas su mériter votre complète approbation.

Avant de terminer cette lettre, que V. E. veuille bien me permettre de lui exprimer ma reconnaissance pour l'accueil qu'Elle a faite à mes propositions en faveur d'un personnel aussi méritant. A cette occasion, je la prie de me laisser recommander à toute sa bienveillance le digne Commandant Olivier mon Capne de pavillon dont je lui ai déjà si souvent signalé les excellents services et qui dans l'affaire du 9 a deployé une conduite si brillante et si courageante à la tête de la colonne dont je lui avais confié le commandement.

J'ai l'honneur ……

G. Roze

Moustier (1867. 3. 29) → W. H. Seward

미국의 공동 출병 제안에 대한 프랑스 외무성 훈령

Ministry of Foreign Affairs
Paris 29 March 1867

Sir:

You did me the honor of informing me on the 3rd instant that, the government of the United States planning an expedition in order to avenge the burning of the American merchant vessel *General Sherman* and the murder of her crew by the inhabitants of Corea,

Mr. Berthemy

the Secretary of State had enquired from you if we should be disposed to take part in it in order to obtain on our side a more complete satisfaction for the murder of our missionaries and to oblige the Coreans afterwards to accept a treaty similar to those made with China and Japan.

His Majesty's naval forces in the month of October ultimo inflicted on that people a lesson of which we entertain the hope that they will keep the memory and which we look upon as a sufficient punishment, as you have moreover given it to understand and indicated before hand in your conversation with Mr. Seward. This coup-de-main, for the expedition conducted by admiral Roze possessed no other character, was executed in all conditions of opportunity that could be desirable, I mean, immediately after the guilt from which it had originated. It provided to what we desired. Our interests in Asia being henceforth considered as safe the only motive for an action in common would be therefore to affirm, by the union of both flags, the mutual and constant sympathy that draws towards each other the French and the American people. So our first impulse would have induced us to accept with the most cordial eagerness Mr. Seward's proposal, which answers so well to all the most intimate of our feelings. But the government of the Emperor has not only to take his impressions and his impulses into consideration. He has also to weigh with maturity the resolutions that could bring to account in a considerable measure his responsibility towards public opinion. The spirit in France is not at the present day in favor of enterprises whose distant object and undetermined character could not allow to specify from the beginning their extent and duration. His Majesty's government does not therefore believe to be in measure of engaging himself is an expedition of which the result could not be immediately obtained which in the first moment would not perhaps be accepted with all the favor it does undoubtedly deserve. In a country where public opinion is of so great a weight in all matters, and with a Minister of so elevated a mind and so much practical sense as Mr. Seward, such consideration have chance of being immediately understood.

We nevertheless appreciate the kind intention that has inspired Mr. Seward's proposal and we look upon it as a testimony of cordiality for which I request you to present him my thanks. You will also please let him know that we make wishes for the good success of the intended expedition and to state, if by punishing a barbarous deed, the arms of the United States succeed in accomplishing in those distant countries a new progress and to bring civilization one step further, we will be the first to greet it with our applause.

You are authorized to read this despatch to the Secretary of State.

Receive, etc.

Signed (symbol) Moustier

平山敬忠(1867. 3/慶應三年二月) ➜ 幕府

화의중재사절 正使 平山敬忠의 건의서

관련문서 (1) 건의서에 대한 幕府의 회신
(2) 위임장 요청 및 위임장안
(3) 사절 호위 병력 2대대 요청을 철회하는 平山敬忠의 건의서

丁卯二月

對州表御用被仰付候ニ付心得方之儀相伺候書付

平 山 圖 書 頭

一對州表御用被仰付候に付彼地え罷越候上事体に寄朝鮮王城迄えも罷越夫々引合仕候に付ては信義御武威共に兼備仕候様御仕向に無之ては御旨意柄模通兼候儀も可有之哉に奉存候間大砲其外御備付有之候嚴重之御軍艦拜借被仰付且兵隊二大隊附屬被仰付候様仕度尤其段陸軍奉行海軍奉行え被仰渡被下候様仕度

一御用向之儀は總て機密之事に關り候儀に付御手前様方御直宛にて申上候様可仕哉

一朝鮮通詞儀は對州表に數年罷在候趣に御座候間差支有之間敷候得共談判中萬々一外國船罷越彼是之儀有之候ては一体之御旨意柄にも相障り一と通掛合向相遂候共通辯無之候ては差支候間通辯之もの壹人召連候様仕度

一彼地之模様次第には候へ共談判纏り候ハヽ一旦歸朝言上之上横濱表え罷越佛英亞等え引合又々彼國え罷越候儀に付往返滯留其外共六ヶ月之見込を以出立仕候様可致哉

一當節柄遠國御用御手當等口々御減相成候哉奉承知候へ共御國內而已共譯違ひ海外禮文之國え引合候御用柄之儀に付格別之譯を以支配向御暇拜領物其外御手當取越米請取方等惣て昨冬博覽會に被差遣候もの共幷當正月向山隼人正え附添罷越候者共之振合を以同様被下置候様仕度奉願候

一此余對州表之儀は是迄之遠國爲御用罷越候もの朝鮮表之儀は是迄海外え被遣候もの共相伺候振合に相心得可相成御手數不相掛候様可仕哉

一萬々一談判相調朝鮮官人罷越候様相成候節は急便を以申上兵庫表え歸帆同所え暫時上陸爲致私幷御目付は上京言上仕直様同港より出帆横濱え罷

越夫々取計候様可仕左候ハヽ江戸表朝鮮人旅館并兵庫表旅宿御賄其外共
其筋え被仰渡向々掛り被仰付候様仕度

一大目付御目付并同役共右御用取扱被仰渡置候様奉願候

一私儀伺相濟次第歸府早々支度仕被遣候御目付一同乘船兵庫表より上陸上
京相漏候儀奉伺猶被仰含候儀も奉伺候様可仕哉

右差向候廉々奉伺候猶相漏候儀は追て歸府之上可奉伺猶差掛り候儀は臨機之取計可仕哉此段奉伺候以上

卯二月

【관련문서 1】

覺

伺之通可被心得候尤附屬兵隊之儀は於江戸表可相達候

御委任狀且向山隼人正同様之達等是亦於江戸表相渡候筈に候御手當向之儀は令承知候間歸府之上可被申立候朝鮮人來朝之節旅宿等は兼て手筈致置可申候役々掛り之儀令承知候且又對州表爲御用被差遣候御目付は於江戸表被仰付候筈に候事

【관련문서 2】

丁卯三月十三日

御委任狀被下方之儀相願候書付

平山圖書頭

古賀謹一郎

對州表え被差遣時誼に寄朝鮮國えも可被差遣積に付ては是迄御條約濟各國え被差遣候御使之者共え被下候振合を以て朝鮮國政府え引合向之儀其外別紙案文之通御委任狀被下置候様仕度此段奉願候以上

卯三月

御委任狀案

平山圖書頭

古賀謹一郎

朝鮮國政府え御交誼上之儀は勿論條約濟各國え之諸談判筋其方共え令委任もの也

慶應三卯年三月

【관련문서 3】

丁卯四月五日

陸軍士官之内對州表え召連度儀ニ付申上候書付

平 山 圖 書 頭

對州表御用被仰付彼地え罷越候上は事体に寄朝鮮國王城までえも罷越候儀に付信義御武威とも兼備不仕候ては旨意柄模通り兼候儀も可有之哉心配仕候間兵隊二大隊附屬被仰付候様仕度旨京師表於て伊賀守殿え奉伺候次第も御座候得共尚勘辨仕候處兵隊附屬之儀は御手重にも可有御座候間右は相止め對州表え罷越候上同藩之もの附屬いたし朝鮮國え召連候様可仕就ては同藩儀未た砲術修業等行届不申趣に付陸軍士官之内にて可然人物兩人程彼地え召連教授爲致候様仕度右は陸軍奉行於て歩兵差圖役又は同並之内にて早々人選いたし申上候様同奉行え被仰渡可被下候依之此段申上候以上

卯四月

195

幕府(1867. 4. 5/慶應三年三月一日) ➞ 宗義達

화의중재사절 파견 통보

宗對馬守え

外國奉行

平 山 圖 書 頭

御目付

古 賀 謹 一 郞

右對州表え爲御用被差遣候間可被得其意候

月

平山圖書頭歸府次第可達事

高宗(1867. 4. 7/高宗四年三月三日) ➞ 禮部

3월 9일자 禮部 자문에 대한 회신

回咨

朝鮮國王爲咨覆事同治六年二月二十五日承准貴部咨節該云云自主客司案呈止閱看可也見上原咨等因奉此除將貴部咨內事意承領而鈔示條約曾非頒行天下之事至若小邦民情國勢斷不可行仰冀部堂諸大人具由導達以存終始之澤千萬幸甚爲此合行咨覆云云 同治六年三月初三日

197

W. H. Seward (1867. 5. 6) → A. Burlingame

1월 31일자 Burlingame 보고에 대한 회신

Sir:

Your dispatch of the 31st of January No. 127* has been received. In that communication you state that in the spring or early summer the French will probably make a demonstration against Corea, which will result in a treaty and the opening of the country to commerce. In connection with that statement you observe that Sir Rutherford Alcock, the British Minister, informs you that he shall probably be required to represent his country, on the occasion of the proposed expedition, together with a British Admiral, to look after British interests, and that Mr. Vlangaly, the Russian Minister, agrees with you that it will be desirable that the United States and Russia be represented on that occasion by their representatives at Peking.

Upon these grounds you ask that Admiral Bell may be instructed to be present on the occasion anticipated, and you also ask instructions for yourself to attend, and you propose that the hospitalities of a vessel in Admiral Bell's squadron be tendered on the same occasion to the Russian Minister.

Finally you ask that duplicate instructions on these points may be sent by telegraph.

We have reason to believe that the French government is not intending to make such a demonstration against Corea, at least in the next spring or summer, as you have supposed. On the contrary, we have grounds for supposing that the Emperor's government understands that the chastisement which was inflicted by a French expedition upon the Coreans last autumn will suffice at least for the present as a vindication for the wrongs which France has hitherto sustained in Corea. At the same time, we are satisfied that France, as well as the other Western Powers, would cordially agree with the United States in desiring that the Corean peninsula should be open to social and commercial intercourse with all nations.

Under these impressions the special instructions and powers which you have requested for your own participation in the conjectured proceeding of the French government are withheld.

*제1권 184번 문서.

I am, Sir, your obedient servant,

William H. Seward

198

稲葉正邦(1867. 5. 10/慶應三年四月七日) ➞ 對馬藩京都留守居

조선 중재사절 파견계획 통보 지시

丁卯四月七日

在京稲葉美濃守宅え宗對馬守留守居御呼出左之書付渡之

宗 對 馬 守

對州表え爲御用外國奉行平山圖書頭御目付古賀謹一郎被差遣時宜に寄爲使節朝鮮國へも御差渡相成候は畢竟彼國舊來之交誼を深く被思召其國之禍亂近きに在るを轉して安寧に歸せしめ人民業を安ん唇齒相保たしめんか爲め彼國王へ之御書簡前兩人え御渡被遣委曲之談判筋は御委任相成候に付前以彼國へ申通事態に應し候樣斟酌を加へいつれにも御信義之程相徹使節歡待いたし候樣取扱尙彼國挨拶振幷委細之情狀可被申聞候使節對州着帆之上は速に手續相運候樣可致候事

G. Roze (1867. 5. 15) → P. de Chasseloup-Laubat

미국의 조선원정 소문에 대해 부정적 견해 표명

Guerrière, Oasaka le 15 Mai 1867

Monsieur le Ministre,

En réponse à la dépêche de Votre Excellence en date du 7 Mars dernier, je m'empresse de vous informer que les forces navales Américaines en Chine se composent actuellement de quatre corvettes *le Hartford* bâtiment Amiral, *le Shenandoah*, *le Wachussette* (*Sic*), *le Wyoming*, de deux grandes canonnières, *le Monocacy* et *l'Ashusloh* et enfin de deux transports à voiles. Le tableau dont je fais suivre cette dépêche fait connaître l'armement de ces divers bâtiments.

Les quatre corvettes sont dans ces mers depuis longtemps déjà, on parle même du retour prochain du *Wyoming* aux Etats-Unis. Quant aux deux canonnières, elles sont arrivées récemment dans le but de concourir avec les forces françaises et anglaises à la répression de la piraterie si active et si redoutable, comme Votre Excellence le sait, sur les côtes du Céleste Empire. Mr. l'Amiral Bell, avec lequel j'entretiens des relations de la plus extrême courtoisie, a eu l'occasion de me le dire lui-même.

Je serais étonné que l'expédition contre la Corée, annoncée par Mr. le Consul Général de Shang-haï, fut maintenant en question. Mr. l'Amiral Bell m'a assuré n'avoir reçu de cet égard aucune instruction de son Gouvernement et comme il n'aurait, ce me semble, aucun intention à en faire mystère, je suis porté à penser que ce bruit est dénué de tout fondement. *Le Wachussette* s'est rendu, en effet, dans le mois de février dernier sur Côtes de la Corée, dans le but de reconnaître les lieux où *le Général Shermann* a disparu. Il est allé jusqu'à la hauteur de Peling-Tao à l'entrée d'un petit golfe où ce navire de Commandant paraît-il, a été arrêté et détruit. Mais il ne put entrer en relations avec les habitants et revint à Shang-haï quelques jours après sans avoir recueilli aucun éclaircissement nouveau sur cet événement. Ce résultat était probable car, comme j'ai eu l'honneur d'en informer Votre Prédécesseur dans un de mes rapports, j'avais essayé moi-même d'obtenir des Coréens des informations sur les circonstances qui avaient entouré la destruction du *Général Sherman* et sur les lieux où elle avait eu lieu et je n'ai pu recueillir que des données très indécises et très vagues, tant il est difficile de se procurer des renseignements précis dans ce pays. Le voyage du *Wachussett* n'a donc eu aucun résultat, mais il a pu donner naissance au bruit qui est parvenu jusqu'au Département des Affaires Etrangères, bruit qu'a encore confirmé l'arrivée récente des deux canonnières auxquelles on a, sans doute, prêté une destination qu'elles semblent n'avoir jamais eue.

D'ailleurs, Monsieur le Ministre, en dehors même des assurances qui m'ont été données par M. l'Amiral Bell, la Division Américaine, telle qu'elle est constituée aujoud'hui, ne pourrait guère engager des opérations sérieuses contre la Corée. Ses bâtiments sont trop forts; *le Monocacy* et *l'Ashelot*, elles-mêmes, tirent trop d'eau pour pouvoir aller jusqu'aux points où elles devraient se rendre pour agir efficacement. J'ajoute que, pour une telle entreprise, il ne paraît indispensable d'avoir des troupes de débarquement que M. l'Amiral Bell ne possède pas.

Toutes ces raisons me donnent la conviction que, pour le moment du moins la Division Navale des Etats-Unis ne pense point à attaquer la Corée. Elle pourra, peru-être, le faire plus tard mais il me paraît pas qu'elle s'y dispose et que cela soit aussi prochain que le pense M. le Consul Général de Shang-haï.

Dans tous les cas, Monsieur le Ministre, si des faits de cette importance venaient à se présenter, je prie V.E. de vouloir bien croire que je les suivrais avec tout l'intérêt qu'ils méritent et que je les porterais sans retard à votre connaissance.

Je suis avec un profond respect,
Monsieur le Ministre,
De Votre Excellence,
Le très obéissant serviteur,
Le Contre-Amiral Commandant en chef.

G. Roze

A. de Lallemand (1867. 5. 27) → Moustier (1867. 8. 8)

조선 원정의 결과에 대한 평가 및 청조와의 교섭 훈령 요청

Péking (*Sic*), le 27 Mai 1867

Monsieur le Marquis,

Ce n'est pas sans un peu d'embarras que je viens entretenir un moment Votre Excellence des événements de Corée, de l'expédition qui en a été la suite, des conséquences qu'elle a eues et de celles qu'elle aurait pu avoir, si elle eût été plus heureusement conduite. Mais ce que j'ai à en dire il me paraît nécessaire que Votre Excellence le sache afin de pouvoir juger, en parfaite connaissance de cause, s'il n'y a pas quelque chose à faire pour atteindre, en le définisant (*Sic*) mieux, le but qui a été manqué, l'année dernière. Je dis en parfaite connaissance de cause, car il me semble que les éléments nécessaires à un jugement mûr et définitif n'ont pas tous été mis sous les yeux de Votre Excellence ; ce qui m'autorise à en appeler du Gouvernement de l'Empereur mal ou imparfaitement instruit au Gouvernement de l'Empereur mieux informé.

Je n'examinerai pas s'il eut été possible de fermer les yeux, même temporairement, sur le meurtre de neufs sujets de Sa Majesté, de neufs prêtres qui semblaient couverts de la protection de nos traités avec la Chine, mais j'ai dû me préoccuper, et sur ma route et à mon arrvée ici, de savoir en quoi notre entreprise sur la Corée et l'échec, si léger qu'il soit, qui l'avait terminée, avait pu modifier dans un sens ou dans l'autre, la situation en face de laquelle j'allais me trouver à Pékin. Je le devais d'autant plus que la correspondance de la Légation, pendant les années 1865 et 1866, telle que je l'avais lue à Paris, avant mon départ, était peu encourageante et révélait un état de choses qui semblait n'avoir plus rien à perdre.

Je me suis donc attaché à savoir, auprès des personnes capables d'en juger sainement, tant parmi nos agents qu'en dehors d'eux, si notre échec en Corée et notre retraite avaient eu plus d'effet et de retentissement que la résolution même qui nous y avait conduits. En cas d'affirmative, ce serait le dernier trait d'une situation déjà mauvaise, dans le cas contraire, il y avait évidemment un parti à tirer de cette opinion répandue que la France n'était pas disposée à souffrir de sanglantes violations de ses traités et qu'elle accourait, même mal préparée, pour châtier les meurtriers.

Les réponses, fort peu différentes, si ce n'est unanimes, que j'ai reçues, peuvent se résumer ainsi : on ne croit pas que la France puisse échouer en Corée, même avec des moyens d'action médiocres, du moment qu'elle agira résolument et avec la prévoyance nécessaire. On se persuadera difficilement, Chinois et Coréens, que la retraite de l'Amiral Roze soit le dernier mot de cette affaire et l'on craint un retour offensif de la France auquel il ne serait pas possible de résister. Mais cette crainte une fois dissipée, ferait place à un sentiment contraire et la position des Européens, celle de la France notamment, vis-à-vis de la Chine et dans tout l'extrême Orient, ne pourrait qu'en souffrir.

Je tiens cette opinion pour vraie et fondée et, dès lors, je dois non seulement ne rien faire qui puisse dissiper les appréhensions salutaires qui subsistent encore, quant aux desseins ultérieurs de la France sur la Corée, mais encore les entretenir, s'il est possible, sans engager toutefois le Gouvernement de l'Empereur. Dans ce but, j'ai jugé qu'il y avait quelque parti à tirer de l'offre de médiation qui fut faite par le Prince Kong au Chargé d'affaires de l'Empereur par une communication du 16 Juillet dernier, renouvelée le 4 Novembre en termes plus pressants et qui fut rejetée par Mr. de Bellonet. Cette offre était inacceptable, il est vrai, dans les termes où elle était conçue ; mais ce n'était qu'un premier mot et, d'ailleurs, il n'est pas question de l'accepter. Je veux seulement en prendre texte pour donner à entendre que l'occasion se représentera, peut-être, pour le Gouvernement Chinois de renouveler cette offre et pour la Légation de la discuter. Je vais donc faire, d'ici à quelques jours et dès que le Prince Kong, malade en ce moment, sera sorti de sa retraite, une communication dans ce sens au Tsong-Ly-Yamoun, soit par écrit, soit par l'organe du premier interprète de la Légation. J'aurai soin de ne parler de notre retour en Corée que comme d'une chose purement éventuelle et hypothétique que je ne suis nullement chargé d'annoncer, mais je demanderai si, dans cette hypothèse, le Gouvernement chinois maintiendrait son offre de médiation, en ajoutant que je ne m'engagerais point à l'accepter dans les termes où elle a été offerte.

Cette communication suffira, ce me semble, pour le but modeste, mais pratique, que j'ai défini plus haut et n'aura aucun inconvénient. Car, si le Gouvernement de l'Empereur ne veut décidement pas agir, les raisons de son inaction ne seront ni pires, ni meilleures, ni autrement appréciées qu'elles ne sont aujourd'hui et la situation restera la même. En attendant, je verrai venir le Gouvernement Chinois par sa réponse et lui donnerai quelque peu à penser pour quelque temps.

Il est, d'ailleurs, certain, Monsieur le Marquis, qu'il ne nous offrirait une médiation acceptable et efficace que si une démonstration sérieuse, par exemple, la réunion, dans la rade de Chéfou, de tous les bâtiments de la station, sous les ordres de l'Amiral français, et les mouvements de ces bâtiments lui faisaient croire que nous nous apprêtons à agir vigoureusement contre la Corée. Ce n'est jamais que sous l'empire d'une contrainte morale analogue à la contrainte par corps et plus efficace que la Chine se décidera à nous accorder ce qu'elle nous doit et à payer sa dette aux nations de l'Europe.

J'ai dit, en commençant, que le but que nous poursuivions en Corée aurait besoin d'être mieux et plus largement défini qu'il ne l'a été. Voici comment je le définis : ouverture, au moins, par deux ou trois de ses ports principaux, de cette contrée jusqu'à présent fermée et sur laquelle la Russie a jeté les yeux, j'en suis persuadé ; poursuite, par conséquent, d'un but plus général et plus étendu que ne le seraient de simples réparations pour les crimes commis contre nos missionnaires. Ces réparations deviendraient ainsi l'occasion ou le prétexte, fort légitime assurément, d'une entreprise d'une portée plus considérable et qui, en profitant aux autres nations, se ferait plus aisément accepter, si ce n'est de la Russie, peut-être, qui, d'ailleurs, n'aurait rien à y voir.

Si Votre Excellence approuve ces vues et si elles lui paraissent dignes de l'attention du Gouvernement de l'Empereur, je vous prie instamment de m'autoriser à en poursuivre l'exécution. Je crois qu'on peut le faire à peu de frais et à peu de risques et j'accepte, en cas d'échec, le désaveu et le rappel comme peines de ma présomption. Mais j'ai l'ambition, je l'avoue, de rétablir notre crédit et nos affaires sur le pied où ils étaient, où ils auraient dû être, du moins, en 1861, après la seconde expédition de Chine, de le faire sans déclarer la guerre à la Chine et, peut-être, par l'intermédiaire même du Gouvernement Chinois agissant comme médiateur. Il ne me reste plus qu'à faire part à Votre Excellence des moyens d'action qui devraient être mis à ma disposition.

Avant tout je réclamerais la faculté d'être présent à bord d'un des bâtiments de notre station et le droit d'être consulté par l'officier général chargé de la direction de l'expédition sans avoir la prétention de la diriger moi-même, mais en conservant la direction exclusive de la partie diplomatique de l'entreprise.

Puis les forces de la station du Japon et de la Chine, sans augmentation aucune mais sans exception non plus, devraient concourir soit à l'expédition, le cas échéant, soit à la démonstration projetée. Elles se composent d'une frégate, de deux corvettes et de trois ou quatre bâtiments inférieurs, avisos et canonnières. Deux ou trois compagnies d'infanterie de marine prises à Saïgon et une demi-batterie d'obusiers à joindre à l'artillerie des bâtiments constitueraient une force suffisante pour l'action et pour le but que je propose.

Que Votre Excellence veuille bien ne pas m'accuser de présomption, lorsque j'entre dans des détails qui semblent étrangers à ma compétence. J'ai recueilli auprès d'officiers qui ont pris part à l'expédition de l'automne dernier des renseignements précis et soumis à une discussion contradictoire et je connais aussi les causes de l'échec, peu important en lui-même, mais fâcheux, que nous avons éprouvé. Je suis donc en mesure de savoir ce que je dis.

Un des fruits de cette campagne et du succès que j'ose me promettre, si Votre Excellence m'autorise à l'entreprendre, serait une facilité plus grande pour le renouvellement de notre traité dans de bonnes conditions et avec des clauses favorables. Toutefois, comme je ne pourrai recevoir la réponse de Votre Excellence avant le mois d'octobre et qu'il faudrait encore un peu de temps, dans le cas où elle serait affirmative pour réunir les moyens d'action nécessaires, ce n'est pas avant la fin de l'hiver prochain que je puis espérer l'exécution du plan que je viens de soumettre à Votre Excellence.

L'arrivée de l'ambassade Coréenne qui vient, chaque année, à Pékin, vers la fin de Janvier, faire acte de déférence et de vassalité offrirait une occasion peut-être favorable de se servir de la médiation du Gouvernement Chinois, sinon l'on pourrait agir militairement dès le milieu de Mars.

Je suis avec respect,
Monsieur le Marquis,
De Votre Excellence
Le très humble et le très obéissant serviteur,

A. de Lallemand

Post-scriptum

Réflexion faite, je prends le parti de ne faire aucune communication ni verbale, ni écrite. Je me bornerai dans mon premier entretien avec le Prince Kong à lui parler incidemment de la Corée, et de la médiation Chinoise comme d'une pure éventualité. Cela suffit et cela me paraît plus sûr. L.

G. Roze (1867. 5. 27) → P. de Chasseloup-Laubat

미국의 공동 조선원정 제안에 대해 부정적 견해 표명

Guerrière, Nagasaki, le 27 Mai 1867

Monsieur le Ministre,

J'ai l'honneur d'informer V. E. que j'ai quitté Osaka le 18 de ce mois pour me rendre à Nagasaki où nous avons mouillé le 21 après une traversée de trois jours qui s'est accomplie avec des vents favorables et pendant laquelle *la Guerrière* a pu faire un tir à feu et à boulets qui a donné les résultats les plus satisfaisants. Notre équipage qui compte actuellement 28 mois de campagne est, en effet, parfaitement exercée et son instruction ne laisse rien à désirer. La discipline est aussi telle qu'elle doit être, ferme et bienveillante et les punitions sévères sont, en général bien rares.

Les détails des conférences d'Osaka étaient déjà connues à Nagasaki au moment de notre arrivée et elles y avaient produit l'excellent effet que nous en attendons. On y avait appris l'entente qui s'était établie entre le Gouvernement du Taïcoun et les Représentants étrangers et ces nouvelles bien vite propagées, avaient été accueillies avec une vive satisfaction par les résidants autant que par la population japonaise. Il n'est pas douteux qu'elles ne réagissent également sur l'esprit des Daïmios hostiles qui comprendront combien il serait inutile à leurs intérêts et préjudiciable à la tranquilité de leurs pays de persister plus longtemps dans leurs projets de rebellion.

Le Capitaine du *Kien-Chan* m'écrit de Yokohama, à la date du 18 ni *l'Orne*, ni *le Laplace* n'y étaient encore arrivés ; les nouvelles que je reçois de Chine ne signalent aucun fait important. *Le Primauguet* avait conduit M. le Comte Lallemend à Nankin et s'y trouvait à la date du 29 avril, M. le Ministre de France y avait donné rendez-vous à M. Dabry, notre Consul à Hankow, qui venait d'y arriver sur la canonnière le *Le Brethon*. J'avais déjà reçu du Capitaine de cette canonnière, M. le Lieutenant de vaisseau de Cintré, des informations très détaillées que je lui avais demandées sur les fortifications de Nankin, leur amènent tant au personnel qu'au matériel, ainsi que sur les manufactures d'armes qui sont établies dans cette ville et qui sont dirigées, pour la plupart, par les Anglais. M. de Cintré n'a envoyé à ce sujet des renseignements aussi complets que possible, avec un plan de toutes les fortificaions de Nankin. Ces documents sont pleins d'intérêts et je crois devoir en mettre la copie sous les yeux de V.E. Le Vice Roi de Nankin est le fameux Sanko-faï, beau frère du précédent Vice Roi, lequel a reçu la mission d'aller combattre les Mahométans du Houpé. Ces deux hauts fonctionnaires ont la réputation d'être fort ambitieux et on leur prête à tort ou à raison l'arrière pensée de vouloir un jour se rendre indépendant dans le Sud, en faisant de Navire la capitale de la Chine méridionale et laissant Pékin, celle du nord.

L'Amiral américain Bell est arrivé peu après moi, à Nagasaki sur le *Hartsford*, escorté du *Wyoming*. Il compte repartir sous peu et se rendre à Shang-haï pour aller de la visiter le Nord de la Chine, comme je l'ai fait l'année dernière ; il ira peut être à Pékin, mais, ainsi que j'ai l'honneur de l'écrire à V.E. par ma lettre du 15 de ce mois, No 128, je ne pense pas que les Américains mettent à exécution aucun projet contre la Corée du moins dans le courant de cette année.

Je suis avec ……

G. Roze

G. Roze (1867. 6. 15) ➔ de Genouilly

미국의 공동 조선원정 제안에 대한 Roze의 거부 의사

Frégate *la Guerrière* à Yokohama 15 Juin 1867

Monsieur le Ministre,

J'ai l'honneur de vous accuser réception de la Dépêche confidentielle en date du 8 Avril par laquelle V. E. veut bien me donner communication de la réponse de M. le Ministre des affaires étrangères à la proposition que lui avait adressé le Governement des Etats-Unis, de s'associer à lui dans l'expédition que ce gouvernement projetait contre Son Excellence M. l'Amiral, Ministre de la Marine et des Colonies, etc. la Corée, à l'occasion de la disparition du *Schooner* américain *Général Shermann*.

En me transmettant ce document, V.E. m'invite à m'inspirer des recommandations qu'il contient dans l'hypothèse où le Comm. des forces navales américaines dans les mers de Chine et de Japon m'entretiendrait lui-même de cette affaire.

Dans sa réponse au Gouv. des Etats-Unis M. le Marquis de Moustier a exposé avec une parfaite justesse la situation actuelle de la France vis-a-vis de la Corée par suite du coup de main que j'avais accompli contre ce pays en Octobre dernier. Le châtiment a bien été celui que je m'étais proposé de lui infliger, et cet exemple a produit un effet considérable, j'en ai l'assurance, non seulement en Corée mais encore dans les contrées voisines de l'extrême Orient. La France a donc le droit d'être satisfaite, et elle n'a plus à intervenir pour le même motif.

C'est ce que j'aurais répondu à l'Amiral Bell, s'il m'avait proposé de m'unir à lui dans une nouvelle expédition, et dans ce cas, j'en aurais immédiatement informé Votre Excellence, mais ainsi que j'ai eu l'honneur de vous l'écrire dans une précédente dépêche, je ne pense pas que le Gouv. Américain puisse mettre à exécution ses projets, du moins dans le courant de cette année, car il lui faudrait dans ces mers des bâtiments d'un moindre tirant d'eau que ceux dont sa Division Navale puit disposer en ce moment.

J'ai l'honneur ……

G. Roze

G. Roze(1867. 6. 28) → A. de Lallemand

Lallemand의 지역 순회 및 미국의 공동 원정 제안 등 보고

Paris, 28 Juin 1867

Mr. le Comte de Lallemand

Mr. Le Comte, j'ai reçu les dép. que vous m'avez fait l'honneur de m'écrire le 20 et le 22 avril sous les no. 1 et 2, dans lesquelles vous m'annoncez votre arrivée à Shanghaï et vous me rendez compte des motifs qui vous ont engagé à passer dix jours à Hong Kong, et à Canton. Je pense comme vous que cette station bien naturelle du reste après un aussi long voyage, ne pouvait qu'être utile aussi à la mission que vous allez remplir, en vous mettant à même de recueillir de nos Consuls, de nos missionnaires et des principaux résidents dans ces villes beaucoup de données sur les diverses questions dont vous aurez à vous occuper. Je ne puis par conséquent qu'approuver la détermination que vous avez prise et dont vous me faites part dans votre P. S. du 3, de compléter cette tournée avant de vous rendre dans le nord, par une visite à Nanking sur la corvette de S.A. «*le Primauguet*».

M. de Bellonet m'a transmis en dernier lieu quelques documents intéressants dont vous voudrez bien le remercier s'il est encore à Péking lorsque cette dep. vous parviendra. L'un est le journal de voyage du chef de la mission chinoise venue en Europe dans le courant de l'année dernière, l'autre est un mémoire présenté à l'Empereur de la Chine au sujet de la création du collège Européen à Péking, Celui-ci de beaucoup le plus important nous fait entrevoir un travail considérable opéré dans les esprits en Chine par les rapports des envoyés Chinois et il suggère la pensée qu'avec des peuples observateurs et réfléchis comme le sont ceux de l'extrême Orient, c'est moins par la force des armes ou par la propagande d'un commerce quelquefois peu recommandable que nous [_____] des chances de faire prévaloir nos idées et notre civilisation, que par le spectacle même de notre civilisation étudiée par eux sur place que nous devons nous préoccuper de les attirer chez nous encore plus que d'aller chez eux et que par conséquent il serait d'une bonne politique d'encourager le gouvt. Chinois à envoyer le plus souvent qu'il le pourra en France des gens chargés de le renseigner par eux mêmes sur nos écoles, nos établissements scientifiques et industriels, d'y apprendre notre langue, d'y suivre des cours et à qui nous financerions de nôtre côté toutes les facilités nécessaires pour ces études dont ils rapporteraient ensuite les fruits dans leur pays. Le Gouvt Japonais est entré dans cette voie et vous ne sauriez trop engager celui de Péking la chine à l'imiter.

Les Etats-Unis ayant à venger l'incendie d'un bâtiment de commerce le "*G*[al] *Sherman*" et le massacre de son équipage par les Coréens nous ont au mois de mars dernier proposé de nous joindre à eux pour exercer ensemble des représailles contre ces populations et les décider en même temps à accepter un traité conforme à ceux que nous avons imposés à la Chine et au Japon. Le Gouvt. de l'Empereur considérant pour le moment comme suffisante la leçon infligée par M. l'Amiral Roze aux Coréens qui avaient massacré nos missionaires n'a pas jugé opportun d'accueillir les ouvertures du cabinet de Washington et tout en appréciant une offre dont le résultat eut été d'étudier une fois de plus la solidarité des Puissances Chrétiennes en Orient Il n'a point voulu s'engager dans une expédition dont il n'eut peut-être pas été aisé de circonscrire la portée. J'ai répondu dans ce sens à M. Seward à Washington qui vient du faire savoir que le Gouvt. Américain défaut de notre concours actif va chercher à arriver au résultat qu'il se propose par l'entremise du Gouvt. Chinois.

Je compterais, ajoute M. Berthemy, sur l'appui du Gouvt. russe qui serait prêts à agir à Pékin concurrement avec lui et n'hésiterait même pas en dernière analyse à unir ses armes aux siennes contre la Corée. Je vous écris ceci pour votre information. A votre arrivée à Péking vous même serez sans doute à même de me transmettre q.q. détails sur les démarches des missions russe et américaine auprès du Gouvt. Impérial Chinois.

A. de Lallemand (1867. 7. 2) → Moustier (1867. 9. 9)

Bellonet와 總署의 마찰에 대한 보고

Péking, le 2 Juillet 1867

Monsieur le Marquis,

J'ai dû écarter de ma dépêche ostensible n° 9 ou, du moins, n'y indiquer que faiblement, le trait le plus essentiel, peut-être, de la situation qui m'est faite ici; mais comme il est nécessaire que Votre Excellence la connaisse tout entière et sans réserve, soit pour pouvoir s'expliquer ma conduite, soit pour pouvoir me donner des instructions en conséquence, je suis forcé de parler et je vais le faire.

M. de Bellonet, dans l'excès d'une imagination très concevable d'ailleurs, et que j'éprouve déjà moi-même, contre la conduite du Tsong-Ly-Yamoun, lui a adressé, non pas une fois ou deux, mais souvent, les menaces les moins déguisées. Surtout, le 16 Juillet 1866, il lui remit un mémorandum de quelques vingtaine de pages dans lequel les ressources du langage comminatoire étaient épuisées. Les plus dures extrémités de la guerre, par exemple la déposition et le détrônement de la dynastie mandchoue, s'y trouvaient suspendues sur l'Empire Chinois. Le lettré Chinois, chargé de remettre ces communications au Tsong-Ly-Yamoun et qui les lit préalablement dans la traduction chinoise qu'en fait M. Lemaire sur le texte français, est venu, dans la frayeur la plus comique et la face contre terre, conjurer M. de Bellonet de le dispenser de remettre aux ministres ce texte épouvantable. M. Lemaire lui-même crut devoir faire quelques observations.

Mr de Bellonet fut inflexible. La date du document en explique, d'ailleurs, la teneur. On avait appris les meurtres commis en Corée sur nos misisonnaires. Le chargé d'affaires de l'Empereur venait de prendre des résolutions dont il attendait un très grand effet. Il venait de dicter, ou il allait dicter, ces instructions à l'Amiral Roze que Votre Excellence connaît. Il disposait du trône de Corée et se préparait à afficher aux portes de l'hôtel de la Légation la déchéance de la dynastie coréenne pour l'édification des Coréens, nos voisins, qui habitent un caravansérail à peu de distance de nous.

Je suis loin de médire de la menace. Je la crois nécessaire ici de temps en temps, et même seule efficace, mais à la condition d'être suivie d'effet. Le seul reproche donc que je fasse aux menaces de M. de Bellonet — dont je n'ai pas d'ailleurs à juger la conduite — c'est de n'avoir été suivies d'aucun effet en Chine et d'avoir abouti à un échec en Corée.

Et, quiconque a eu recours à la menace, sans y donner suite, se trouve plus faible après qu'auparavant. Le crédit de la Légation était bien faible à l'époque où éclatèrent les événemetns de Corée à mon arrivée, il était entièrement ruiné et nul.

Pour le relever un peu, j'ai besoin de faire sentir l'aiguillon à ces messieurs du Tsong-Ly-Yamoun qui sont persuadés, non sans apparence, qu'on peut se moquer impunément de nous et qui le font. En attendant les grosses questions que je ne puis entamer qu'avec l'autorisation du Département ou d'accord avec mes collègues, je vais probablement arracher de vive force l'exécution d'un chinois qui, depuis plus d'un an, a tué avec guet-à-pens un agent de police fraçais à Chang-Haï, qui est condamné à mort depuis 9 ou 10 mois, mais dont on nous refuse l'exécution avec un luxe effronté de chicane et de fourberie. J'ai besoin de la corvette le "*Primauguet*" et de la canonnière qui la suit pour faire ce petit coup de main dont je me promets le plus entier succès. J'ai écrit à Chang-Haï pour m'assurer d'abord de la présence de ces deux bâtiments qui pourraient avoir pris la mer et manquer à mon appel.

Je suis avec respect,
Monsieur le Marquis,
De Votre Excellence
Le très humble et très obéissant serviteur,

A. de Lallemand

A. de Lallemand (1867. 7. 20) → Moustier (1867. 9. 30)

일본의 사절 파견에 대해 부정적 견해 표명

Péking, le 20 Juillet 1867

Monsieur le Marquis,

Le Ministre d'Angleterre au Japon a écrit à Sir Rutherford Alcock qu'une députation japonaise était partie ou allait partir pour la Corée avec mission de réconcilier, en quelque sorte, ce pays avec les nations civilisées. Je suppose que l'agent de l'Empereur au Japon n'est pas étranger à cette démarche et que même il en est peut-être l'instigateur principal. J'ignore dans quelles conditions de succès elle se présente, mais à moins que ces conditions ne soient particulièrement favorables grâce à des circonstances que je ne puis ni deviner ni apprécier, je me crois fondé à douter de l'heureuse issue de l'entreprise.

Le pays de Corée a été, il est vrai, pendant un temps, possédé ou dominé par le Japon, mais les rapports entre les deux peuples n'en sont pas meilleurs pour cela et je ne pense pas que les Coréens soient disposés à reconnaître aisément le bienfait de cette sorte de médiation que le Gouvernement Japonais tenterait d'exercer entre eux et les nations de l'Occident.

Cette œuvre, ainsi que je l'ai montré dans ma dépêche No. 5, est le partage naturel de la Cour de Péking qui a témoigné déjà, l'an dernier, quelque penchant à s'en charger et qui se trouve dans de bonnes conditions pour le faire. L'Empereur de la Chine, en effet, est le suzerain de la Corée et suzerain d'autant plus respecté et influent que son joug est à peine senti, tant il est léger. Les rapports entre la Chine et la Corée sont fréquents et réguliers, chaque année, au moment du nouvel an chinois, une ambassade coréenne apporte à Péking des hommages et des présents. Ce serait une occasion naturelle pour la Légation de l'Empereur de veiller au maintien des relations une fois établies entre nous et la Corée en pratiquant adroitement ces ambassadeurs.

Je me suis expliqué fort au long, d'ailleurs, par ma dépêche précitée du 27 Mai No. 5 sur les conditions qui devraient être réalisées pour obtenir que la médiation de l'Empereur de la Chine entre nous et la Corée fût offerte dans des termes acceptables pour le Gouvernement de l'Empereur et utilement. Je n'ai rien à y changer. Mais je prie instamment Votre Excellence de ne pas permettre que cette œuvre sorte de mes mains pour entrer dans d'autres, quelles qu'elles soient. La Corée étant dépendante de la Chine, il me paraît que le soin de nos relations avec elle doit rester confié à la Légation de l'Empereur à Péking.

Ouo-Yen, ce précepteur de l'Empereur qui avait été mis en disgrâce pour son opposition à l'institution de l'école des langues et sciences européennes et qui avait été nommé malgré lui membre du Tsong-Ly-Yamoun, vient d'être, par décrêt, dispensé de ces fonctions et réintégré dans les bonnes grâces de son maître. Cet acte implique contradiction avec l'autre décret, si récent, qui était joint à ma dépêche No. 11 et je me demande s'il n'y a pas dans cette comédie trop longue quelque intrigue dont les membres du Tsong-Ly-Yamoun seraient probablement les complices, s'ils n'en étaient pas un peu les victimes. J'essaierai de pénétrer, si je puis, ce mystère.

Je suis avec respect, Monsieur le Marquis,
De Votre Excellence
Le très humble et très obéissant serviteur,

A. de Lallemand

宗義達(1867. 7/慶應三年六月) ➜ 任冕鎬

조선 중재사절 파견계획 통보

遣禮曹參議 答異樣船情形書

日本國對馬州太守拾遺平 義達 奉復

朝鮮國禮曹參議大人 閤下

曩辱華翰就諦 啓居珍毖傾慰良深 所示戰鬪一款 臚列顚末 副以所見 旣已稟啓東武 則廷議以爲去秋法國之開釁也 實出于不虞(*Sic*)不啻唇齒相患 抑於鄰睦世敦之誼 憂恤那有措哉 欲使貴國永計綏安者 此東武盛意所在也 不佞在職曷任感戢 今番有使節至貴國之命 東武官員身親開陳時務 則在貴朝豈無宣當之處置耶 覼縷事實 要在使節陳述 何待多及 總惟照亮 肅此不備

慶應三年丁卯六月 日

對馬州太守拾遺平 義達

安俊卿, 玄德民(1867. 7/高宗四年六月) ➜ 寺田市郎兵衛

일본의 중재사절 파견 계획에 대한 조선측의 거절

覺

一頃因口陳 以東武耑使之由 另稟萊府 轉達朝廷矣 今兼回下 則以爲東武厚誼 實是感佩 然曾以年事之荐歉 有懇聘禮之緩期者 而且洋擾絶經凡務方劇 疫氣流行 薰染遍甚 此時接儐實屬難愼 故回答書契中 亦有懇摯矣 幸須以此諒悉 詳報貴州 轉告東武 無至耑使越溟 事歸順便之地 千萬是冀

訓導俊卿安僉知

別差德氏(*Sic*)玄主簿

講信大差使

都船主 尊公

208

Moustier (1867. 9. 10) ➞ A. de Lallemand

프랑스와 미국의 공동 조선원정에 대한 비개입을 당부하는 전보

Je ne vois pas la nécessité d'engager pour le moment l'affaire des lettres de créance. En ce qui regarde la Corée, renfermez-vous dans une attitude d'obstention complète. Quant à la protection de nos nationaux, évitez avec soin tout ce qui pourait créer des complications.

吉川主計(1867. 9. 30/慶應三年九月三日) ➞ 幕府

중재사절 파견 계획에 대한 조선 측과의 사전 교섭상황 보고

丁卯九月三日

宗對馬守家來より差出候書付

當四月朝鮮國之儀ニ付御達之御旨早速國許え相運彼國舊來之御交誼深被思召弥御信義之厚き所を以彼國差向候危難相免候道御取扱之爲此節爲御使節平山圖書頭樣古賀筑後守樣御國書御持渡被爲在候段(*Sic*)御達之御主意柄兼て差渡置候講信參判使より厚く相掛合候處彼國應接之役向より相答候は東武御信義之厚き所は深く奉感佩候へ共何分重大之事柄朝議一朝一夕に相決候譯に無之右御返答三ヶ月を相待吳候樣申出候趣に候へ共彼國禍亂旦夕に迫り御傍觀難相成所より我大君御深慮被爲在御使節をも被差渡候御主意柄今日にも御渡海可相成も難計猶篤と致熟考是非御信義之厚き所都表にも致貫徹御使節致疑待候樣速に返答可仕旨切迫相掛合候處彼國役人にも是迄御先例無之儀と申殊國内混雜之砌旁内實驚愕致上京候と相聞候得は今程は追々返答申出居候運にも至居候事と奉存候先是迄之御手續國許より申越候間此段奉添御内聽候以上

九月　　　　　　宗對馬守家來 吉川主計

210

板倉勝靜(1867. 10. 25/慶應三年九月二十八日) ➞ 對馬守家來

조선 중재사절단 출발 시기와 준비 간소화를 통보

丁卯九月廿八日

宗 對 馬 守

對州表爲御用平山圖書頭始役々出立之儀御用も有之追々延ニ相成居候處愈來る十一月中出帆之筈に候尤非常之儀に付前々之規則等に不拘雙方無益之手數相省可相成丈簡易に執行候御旨意に候條得其意朝鮮國掛合向精々果敢取使節對州著之頃には否挨拶有之候樣可被取計候

九月

右板倉伊賀守宅ニ於テ對馬守家來呼相渡之

平山敬忠(1867. 11/慶應三年十月)

平山敬忠이 작성한 德川慶喜의 친서 초안

朝鮮國御書翰

日本國源 奉書

朝鮮國王殿下比因貴國禮曹議投宗對馬守之書領承去年外國船擾貴國海口爲是警備尤嚴後聞貴國燒外國船一隻竊謂曩擾貴國海口則法蘭西國之船而其後所燒者北亞美理駕國之船也貴國有怨於法國而燒亞國之船則二國合從勢必併力報怨於 貴國舊好之義不忍座視玆遣若年寄並外國總奉行平山圖書頭目付古賀筑後守赴貴國京城面謁顓議事宜使解怨釋紛且欲益敦世好共承天休寸忱鑑諒惟冀不宜

慶應三年丁卯月 日

日本國源

【日譯文】

一書致拜呈候抑貴國昨年外國船其境え侵入騷亂及ひ候儀に付邊海警備之事情等禮曹參議より宗對馬守え申越候書翰同人より奏進致披見候其後異國船一艘焚燒被致候由元來貴國にては一様に外國船を以視られ候哉に候得共前に邊海騷擾に及ひしは法蘭西國にて謂も有之由に候得共後に焚燒せしは米利堅國の商船にて東西三万里を隔實に無辜のものに有之兩國とも世界の强國にて復仇之爲不容易企も有之由踪と之踪跡幷世界之公許も有之候儀にて貴國は舊來之隣誼何共不安儀に付今度爲使節若年寄並外國總奉行平山圖書頭目付古賀筑後守差遣候間被許面謁方今宇內之形勢萬國之事情篤と相悉し余か深意の立る處を諒せられ隣交之永遠唇齒之保固を祈る併貴國安寧景祉を禱る謹言

慶應三年卯十月　　　　　　御 諱 ○

別 牘 案

日本國特派使臣若年寄並外國總奉行平山圖書頭源敬目付古賀筑後守劉等謹奉書

朝鮮國執政閣下貴國構怨於米利堅法蘭西兩國將有事於貴國我大君厚隣之義不忍座視速告兩國緩其再擧之期且將命吾儕齎國書至貴國王城述大君深意所存今春使宗對馬守先報其旨以我更詳兩國事情今使吾儕航到馬島俟曩日之報旣久矣而未得回音雖復使島臣刻日促之杳然無消息大君厚隣之深意竟不能通吾儕誠辱使命今敢致國書謄本而去亦出乎不得已也抑我大君使吾儕遠涉海波以盡隣誼者全出於歷年舊好而情意之不達至玆實爲遺憾無量苟貴國他日悔悟以情來報我大君天地洪量豈不尋舊盟修信耶今將解纜東歸聊留一書以期國論一定之日請亮察焉拜具

【日譯文】

貴國歐羅巴米利堅各州と怨を結旦夕危難に迫り候儀報告も有之我か大君隣義不忍座視不取敢米佛兩國えも再擧緩期之儀掛合を遂拙者共爲使節被差渡國書於王城可相渡縷々被仰含之趣可及演述積を以當春來宗對馬守より其段相達置追々兩國之事情も得候上今度對州表迄渡海いたし候處未た春來之回音も無之今更君上隣誼之厚意も不相貫殆辱命の罪に陷候得共素より君上之厚義を推戴し猶亦王城往復之日程相量り寬かに期限を相立聢と返答可有之旨對馬守家來を以申進日々企望致居候處期限に至り杳として消息無之候上は如何なる國情に哉も難測猥りに文辭を通し候儀も不容易候へ共深く君上隣義を被重候厚意を奉推察候へは更に其情實も不相徹候は千載之遺憾に付別紙君上より貴國王え被贈候書翰寫し相示し候遠海態々使節被差遣斯迄隣誼を盡され候に對し餘り瞑頑不靈之所爲と存候得共追て必悔悟の秋も可有之其事情に依り我か君上天地之洪量を以舊交を尋き信義を伸られ候事も可有之余等不果使命對州解纜之期に臨み後日貴國國論一定之節拭目之金篦とも可相成哉と惆然一書を遺置候拜具謹言

慶應　　年　月　日

平 山 圖 書 頭
古 賀 筑 後 守

板倉勝靜, 牧野貞利(1867. 11. 11/慶應三年十月十六日) ➞ 幕府

중재사절 연기를 포함한 大政奉還 이후의 상황

丁卯十月十六日

以内狀啓上いたし候然は過便申進候通御國體之義に付思召之御趣意御奏聞相成候處明十五日御參内被爲在表狀を以申進候通於朝廷於聞屆相成候趣諸役人へ御達相成候ハヽ必定議論沸騰或は激動或ハ解体致し候者も可有之此度御心配被遊御直書をも被下候間右之御趣意篤と御了得被成過便にも申進候當今内願之形勢を御熟察之上皇國之御爲至誠之御赤心にて被仰立候義に付誠に以恐入候御趣意之程且又是迄之御體裁も有之候處一時之御大變革被遊候に付驚愕之處より當表時勢之切迫より被仰立候なと、輕易ニ相心得一己之私心を立候樣之者有之候ては御趣意ニ相悖り愈以恐入候義に付上樣にも夫是之義御心配被遊御供役々へ御直諭も被遊候程之義ニ御座候間呉々御誠意貫徹致し候樣役々へ御說諭可被成候尤上樣思召は前書之通只皇國之爲め御誠意を被爲盡候御義にて臣子之身ニ於ては實以恐入感泣之至人心有之者之必感激奮發勉勵愈以御實力相立候樣銘々可存込義ニ御座候得共當世之人情御趣意取違荷擔いたし候者無之共難申候間此上は御旗本御家人之面々實ニ御奉公可仕期と相心認十二分奮發可致樣是又御教諭可被成候委細者原弥十郎よりも御聞取可被成候

一前文之義御奏聞に相成候節佛公使より申出候ハヽ御伺中之趣を以先御答置可被成樣申進候處已ニ朝廷にて御聞濟相成候へは御決定之處を以佛翁え之御直書之御趣意ニ基き御答可被成候

本文之義に付御辨解猶此上御依賴被遊候爲佛翁え之御直書可被下之處今便は御廻しに相成不申候兩三日中御遣し之思召に御座候

御政權は御返上被遊候得共大將軍は空名なからも御返上ニ不相成候間外國引合之御稱號は矢張公方樣大君號にて御差支も有之間敷存候得とも猶御評議可被成候

一今般之御次第に付ては塚原但馬英行平山圖書朝鮮行之義共公論一定之處迄出船先ッ見合置候方と存候

一前書之御次第各國公使より必本國へも運ひる相成民部公子を初御陪從之

者幷栗本安藝等新聞紙のミにて承知相成候様にては御不都合故メール便早速公子初へ御運ひに相成候様御取計可被成候

一今般御軍役金半高上納被仰出候に付ては最前評決之趣にては右は全く海陸兩軍之御入用に御充ニ相成候事故別段倉庫取設不勤之者より年番相立出納取扱候積り之處先日半高上納被仰出候節右之義は不被仰越如何之模様ニ相成居候哉否可被仰越候

一水府筑波黨之内諸家へ御預ヶ相成居候者病死も多人數有之候得共猶六百人程存在致し居此儘ニ永々打過候ハヽ終ニ死盡可仕殊ニ愍然之至而已ならす何れも屈强之者之由ニ相聞候間歩兵隊之見合を以御手當御組立ニ相成候ハヽ一廉之御用相勤可申殊ニ右人種中組役ニ可相成程之者も有之候由旁相應之御手當被下御抱や御雇やニ相成當節之御場合早々兵隊ニ御取建に思召に被爲在候委細者弥十郎へ被仰含歸府致し候間急々御取計可被成候先は右申進度早々如斯御座候以上

十月十六日

伊賀守
越中守

江戶御同列中様

德川慶喜(1867. 11. 20/慶應三年十月二十五日) ➜ 日本朝廷

중재사절파견을 조정이 허락하도록 요청하는 건의서

丁卯十月廿五月

御所え相伺候書

昨年朝鮮國ニて佛蘭西教師を致殺害候ニ付佛國之水師提督軍艦數艘を以及戰鬪候所時寒氣ニ向ひ一先解兵今年春暖を待大兵再擧之企有之趣ニ相聞且佛戰爭之後亞國商船朝鮮國之海岸へ漂着候所佛國と誤認候哉韓人妄リニ船中之人を殺し其中ニ英人二名乘組居候所被殺候由ニ付三國申合軍艦差向候聞有之朝鮮國禮曹よりも戰爭之次第宗對馬守へ及報知候朝鮮國之儀從來之舊好唇齒之國柄彌三國合從之大兵を向ケ彼國滅亡ニ至り候ハヽ皇國之大患共可相成其上同國之儀ニ付去癸亥年對馬守ヨリ申立之趣建言仕朝廷御聞濟ニも相成居旁今度和議可取扱心得を以佛亞兩國公使へ申談猶朝鮮國へは爲使節若年寄竝平山圖書頭目付古賀筑後守差遣候積對馬守お(*Sic*)以先ニ彼國へ可及掛合候間內外多事之折柄とハ乍申兩人差遣方此上遲延候てハ隣交之信義難立候ニ付十一月中出帆之積猶又爲掛合置申候右之通之次第ニて兩人渡海期月差延居候ニ付是迄之手續ニて取計候儀ニ御座候ハヽ改て從朝廷其扱被仰出對馬守えも同樣御達被成候樣仕度奉存候以上

十　月　　　　　　　　　　　　　　　　　　　　　　　　　慶　喜

214

大島友之允(1867. 11. 20/慶應三年十月二十五日) → 三条實美

중재사절 파견계획의 경위

丁卯十月廿五日

表書

議奏正親町三條大納言殿え大島友之允持參差出候書面寫

乍恐口上書取

昨年朝鮮國佛蘭西と戰鬪之次第は兼て佛國之教師潛に韓國ニ入其邪教を廣め黨類日ニ繁く種々之奸邪國害を釀候より朝鮮國政府相議し其巨魁幷教師を致殺戮候ニ相起り佛國之水師提督復仇之爲軍艦數艘を以て韓國被及戰鬪候處時寒氣に向一と先ツ解兵今年春暖を待大兵再擧之企有之趣外國新聞誌中具ニ相見候間右戰爭之後亞國之商船朝鮮國之海岸え漂着之處佛國と誤認候哉韓人妄りニ舟中之人を殺し其中ニ英人二名乘組居同樣被害候由右暴擧に依三國憤怒問罪之師差向候聞も有之然内朝鮮國禮曹より佛國戰爭之次第表立及報知尚其顚末委曲幕府え轉達之儀をも申越隨て朝鮮國之儀は從來之御舊好殊ニ脣齒之國柄今日之危急御皇國御傍觀可被爲在樣無之弥三國合從兵を向候に至ては彼國亡滅旬月を不出擧國忽外異之有と相成神州之大患難勝數其上同國之儀に付去る癸亥年對馬守より幕府へ建言之主意朝廷御聞濟にも至居旁此度和議御取扱被下彼國危禍相免候ハヽ皇國之御仁恩深奉感戴往々御德化に服從仕候御遠國之御手始と奉存候處則於幕府和議御取扱方御決定に至り其趣佛亞兩國へ被及御說得尚朝鮮國へは爲御使節平山圖書頭殿古賀筑後守殿國書を以渡海之手筈前以て彼國へ掛合置候處當四月幕府之命に依不取敢其趣朝鮮表え掛合罷在候内淸國於上海我國之漂人八戶順叔と申者無稽之妄說を唱右流言朝鮮國へ傳播致し韓人甚た皇國を疑訝いたし候意味有之當六月禮曹より書翰を以右事件不審之趣申越候に付事實辨白之返答向幕府より内命之書面中國使旣に行李を戒め不日解纜渡海之赴相見候處其後に至御國使渡海方又々數月相後尤御邦内御用多之折柄格別無御余儀次第奉存候得共兼々切迫相掛合置候末其期限相扒候ては談判向之不都合者不申及外國へ對し御信義難相立殆苦心罷在候處本月初旬圖書頭渡海之期限來十一月中出帆可有之趣朝鮮表へ掛合置候樣兼て幕府之命有之右に付詰合家

來之内急々歸國方御差圖に相成今程は敏に彼國え申達居候事と奉存候然處今般御大政向不容易御變革被仰出隨ては右朝鮮國事件委曲幕府より御伺之上御取計に相成候儀と奉存候得共是迄之手續一と通奉達御内聽置候條可然御聞通被爲下度奉希候尚亦朝鮮國來翰寫其外書類御勘考之御爲別紙之通り差上之候以上

十月廿五日　　宗對馬守内　　大 島 友 之 允

佛國戰爭之儀ニ付卯四月朝鮮國より相達候書翰寫　一通
同四月七日老中稻葉美濃守殿より被相達候御書付寫　一通
六月朝鮮國より相達候書翰寫　一通
六月五日老中板倉伊賀守殿より被相渡候御書付寫　一通
右一條ニ付朝鮮國へ返答向之主意柄監察原一之進殿より被相渡候御書取　一通
九月廿八日板倉伊賀守殿より被相達候御書付　一通

215

日本朝廷(1867. 11. 29/慶應三年十一月四日)*➞幕府

조선 중재사절단 파견 허가 요청

兼て御聞濟にも相成候儀旁是迄之手續を以使者差遣和議之儀可然取扱候樣被仰出候對馬守へも右之段可相心得旨可被相達候

*본 문서에는 일자 및 수·발신자가 명기되지 않았으나, 문서출처인 『日本外交文書』에 의거하여 표기.

日本朝廷(1867. 11. 29/慶應三年十一月四日) ➜ 對馬藩京都留守居

조선 사절단 파견 허가

관련문서 (1) 본문서 對馬藩 도달(1867. 12. 25/慶應三年十一月三十日)

宗 對 馬 守

朝鮮國之儀ニ付幕府伺有之候右者兼テ御聞濟ニモ相成居候儀ユヘ是迄之手續ヲ以使節差遣和議可取扱御返答被仰出候條此段對馬守ニモ可心得旨被仰出候事

十一月

【관련문서 1】

十一月晦日雨天

當番 八木繁左衛門

日帳番 繁野政之助

嶋雄益城村岡近江小川丹下樋口鐵四郎出仕

在京吉川主計方より當月六日附之書狀昨夜相達候處一昨四日傳奏飛鳥井權大納言樣より御達之儀有之御留守居御呼出ニ付御周旋掛內罷出候處此度御國使朝鮮御渡海方之儀當時御大政御變革之折柄猶改て自幕府叡慮御伺之處兼て御聞濟ニも相成居候儀ニ付是迄之手續を以使節差遣和議可取扱旨大樹家え御返答被仰出右ニ付此方樣えも其旨被成御心得候樣左之通被蒙御達候段申來

朝鮮國之儀ニ付自幕府伺有之候右は兼て御聞濟ニも相成居候儀故是迄之手續を以使節差遣和議可取扱御返答被仰出候條此段對馬守ニも可相心得旨被仰出候事

十一月

平山敬忠，大島友之允(1868.1.6/慶應三年十二月十二日，1868.1.18/慶應三年十二月二十四日)

중재사절 철회 후 뒷처리에 관한 平山敬忠와 大島友之允의 대담

朝鮮國御用邊ニ付平山圖書頭様御下向之儀本月中旬兵庫表御開帆之御治定を以去ル九日十日兩日之際京師御發途御下坂之御運迄至ル處不圖九日以來不容易御形勢ニ至り前將軍ニ茂俄ニ御下坂御入城有之平山樣ニ茂御下坂ニ付去十二日御旅宿江罷出全體之御形勢且外國御取扱向朝鮮御用邊之廉々今日ニ至り如何之御評議向ニ可有之哉相伺候處

平山　何分官武之御際御混雜之砌萬般爲聢御目的も難相立其内外國向之儀者皇國之御大體ニ相關り候儀と申是迄幕府ニ於而取扱候手續も有之俄ニ手を引候樣ニ而者朝廷ニ於而茂差向御手を被爲束候譯ニ付德川家ニ於而可相成丈朝廷之御心配ニ不至樣盡力之心容ニ有之併朝議何レニ出可申哉難圖候得共迚茂是ニ而相濟可申樣無之朝鮮之事茂矢張其一節目ニ付大體之御評議相決候時者自ら相運候都合ニ可至何分紛擾之砌有無之決着茂難相成尤佛亞兩國江引合有之候行懸も有之朝鮮之方迚茂同樣之儀既ニ朝權御復古之後も是迄之手續を以相運候樣御沙汰も有之何レニ致此儘ニ而者不相濟次第ニ有之結局外國ニ對し皇國之御失體ニ不至樣不相成候而不協段勿論之儀ニ付兎ニ角今暫く相待候ハゝ何とか模樣も可有之との御口氣ニ在之

其後去ル廿四日又々參上過日御應答之續を以卽今之御樣子相伺候處

平山　萬端共ニ今日迄聢と見留難相立候得共大體此節之御變革ハ公明正大天下之公議を盡し天下と共ニ皇國を御維持被爲在候御主意柄ニ爲相起事ニ候處今日之姿ニ而者全其御主意ニ反し益人心之不居合を生し此儘ニ而者忽テ內亂を釀し候而已迚茂連續被相行候事ニ無之此邊ニ者大ニ次第も有之不遠何とか一定之見留も附可申第一外國御取扱向之儀者別而差向候事柄何ら迄も今日之振合ニ候得者果而破ヲ生し候儀必然ニ付外國之事萬端共何レ之道眞ニ天下之公議を被盡候事ニ不至候而難協との御內話有之

大嶋　尙申上候者朝鮮國事件ニ付而者初段佛亞兩國江御應接被置候御主意も候處今日御邦內之御混雜他ニ可被及之御暇無之問罪之師差向候者心任ニ可致抔被仰渡朝鮮江茂御同樣御隣誼之譯を以一旦國使御渡海方被仰渡候得

共云々之次第ニ依御手不行屆趣申達候時皇國之御失體申迄も無之脣亡齒寒之患目下相生折角之御鴻業一時御廢棄ニ至候段遺憾無限何分此場國惡を不顯侮を海外ニ不招樣御所置ニ至度趣申上候處

平山　此度之儀者所謂内モメニ而外邦江被相洩筋ニ無之然ル上朝鮮國事件者御邦内之政權何レニ歸し候時皇國ニ於而是非可被遂行之事柄ニ有之殊ニ外國江御引合被置候始末今更御變改難相成何レニ致せ結局之處夫々相運ヒ候ニ相違無之唯國使渡海方朝鮮江相達有之候期限此迄延引ニ至候儀不都合無限此邊者御藩ニ於而是迄之手續不取失樣御談判之道無之哉佛亞之處者兩國申合先ツ日本ニ相委居候姿ニ付此方ニ而取扱向不相整時者兩國合從兵を向候者勿論ニ候得共取扱向調否之決答不申渡間者妄ニ兵を加候儀者無之相心得昨今ニ至せして相促候勢も無之乍去今日之時機尚更暫之間妄擧無之樣談判之會ニ在之唯今兩國より事を不發時者假令國使渡海方暫及遲延候節何時も取扱者出來候譯ニ付差上者只朝鮮之談判向手繋を不失斗ニ有之隨而青木晟次郞朝鮮渡海後之模樣未相知候哉兼而内話之通彼國ニ者卽今迄も矢張國使相拒ニ候勢ニ可在之哉御尋ニ付

大嶋　及御答候者右者追々達御内聽置候通兩國間御隣誼之厚處より國難御見流難被下遙々御渡海被爲下候御使節表立可及御斷條理弁別茂無之筈ニ候得共元來頑固之國習宇内之大勢ニ疎く彼國危難旦夕ニ迫り偏ニ政府之御取扱を以暫兵機相弛居候情實を茂不相弁唯眼前之國費邦内之煩雜を厭或者上海浮客之妄說等を以皇國を相疑居候意も可在之哉第一深く内地ニ御入込被爲在候を諱嫌候意味十分可在之旁事を左右ニ寄せ何卒弊藩之周旋を以御渡海無之相濟度之底意ニ相見乍去す分彼之冗費不被爲懸合之御手賄ニ而御入國ニ相成殊更彼國燒肩之危急親敷御忠告之御談判ニ被爲出候ハゝ彼れ防ク ニ辭無キ筈ニ奉存候其上ニも陋習不可說ニ至候而者則亞國江御差渡之御書翰中彼仰示候通ニ而實ニ不被爲得止儀ニ候得共御隣誼之分を被盡然上承服不仕者曲レルコト彼レニ有之道理ニ而何國江被對候而も御國威を被損候儀者無之御事と奉存候此處ハ晟次郞克く相體し居候儀ニ付同人渡海之上者彼地役々申合多分其緖を得候時宜ニ至可申尤同人儀當月中旬對州江歸着仕候哉ニ承り候得共未タ爲聢便りも無之同人歸着之上者朝鮮國之模樣早速長崎表江御注進申上候手筈兼而申合置候付唯今程ハ彼地江御報知申上候運と奉存候然ルニ未御發艦之御運ニも不至處不都合之御事ニ有之第一昨今朝鮮國ニ於而御國使御引請方承服之機會ニ至候哉否哉難計候得共何レニいたし當

時御渡海方御猶豫ニ至其際是迄應接之手續を不取失繫を取り置可申迚者卽今朝鮮國之機會ニ依時宜之應接を以暫時日を延御使節御渡海迄之都合相合セ置不申候而難叶奉存候其子細此度晟次郞渡海之上茂朝鮮國之振合矢張是迄之勢ニ而何卒御國使御斷申上度之意ニ候ハゝ是迄之談判向御渡海之御期限少し茂御猶豫不相成と申處之振をもて此度可申出候者國使御渡海方決而御猶豫不相協等時宜ニ候得共貴國國情之趣弊州ニ於而無餘儀承り候付不容易儀ニ者候得共是迄之好を以孰レとの周旋暫之內御渡海御猶豫方相盡見可申尤今日ニ至國使御渡海御取止との儀者何分不相屆事ニ有之少敷其期限を弛メ候丈之儀者相働見可申との振ニいたし如何可有御座候哉將亦此節ニ至り東武之御實意貫徹御國使御引請可申趣內々ニても返答申出居候時宜ニ候得者尙更不都合之儀ニ付其節ニ可申達者兼々申向候通御國使敏ニも御渡海可有之筈之處貴國ニ於而內々彼是故障被申立其次第白地ニ東武江轉達候致候筋合ニ無之乍去貴國內輪之評議不相整內突然御渡海被下候而者貴國ニ於而狼狽當惑可被致と存知弊州限種々致盡力御渡海方少敷御差延被下候內追々事遲緩ニ至候付又々貴國一昨秋之擧ニ起り佛亞兩國より政府江申立候次第有之右御取繼之方御見留を不心得候而者御渡海難相成是全く貴國之爲不容易御苦配ニ出候儀故落着次第御渡海可有之抔申候而相懸合置如何可有御座候哉是等者頗ル事を設候筋ニ相當候得共皇國御內輪之御現實御顯し不被爲在彌縫修飾是迄之御手續を以時月相延し候處ニて者尤是等之邊を以應答可仕外有之間敷勿論右等之驅引者國許幷朝鮮居込役々ニ於而臨機之所置可仕儀なから大要御伺置不申して難叶是等宜敷御指揮被成下度申上候處

平山　心得尤之次第ニ承り候何卒右邊を以可然應接有之何分是迄談判之手續を不失繫を取置候樣縷々御沙汰有之

大嶋　尙又申上候者尊臺御下向方當時御猶豫被爲在候得者何分ニ茂御用邊目的難相立國許ニ於而定而心配可仕第一朝鮮國談判向之駈引も在之吉川主計儀者蒙御免御先ニ致歸國當時之形勢幷朝鮮御用筋之儀茂委細相伺歸國仕度內評罷在尤同人歸國仕候時國許ニ於而目的相立候丈之御指揮不相伺候而者州中方向茂不相立と申姿ニ而對馬守ニ茂嘸以苦心可罷在朝鮮御用邊之儀此儘不相濟者申迄も無之乍併又々當春以來之如く事遷延ニ及候而者彌御成切を害候而已ならす差向主計歸國之上國許役々始弁解說得も不相屆儀ニ付此先キ御手を被下候御順序御頃合等ニ至同人發程迄ニ者何とか御賢慮之御差圖を蒙り度同人儀早春之歸國と相立罷在候得共彼是十日頃ニ茂可及哉夫

迄ニ御目度被爲在被下度申上候處
平山　主計歸國之處者至極可宜來月中旬比迄ニ者必定何とか見留も付可申
其時分尚亦可爲示談との御返答ニ在之(하략)
　　　　卯 十二月　大嶋友之允

安俊卿, 玄德民(1868. 1/高宗五年十二月) ➜ 青本晟次郎

중재사절의 정사(停使)를 요청하는 훈도 · 별차의 서한

丁卯十二月

今夏以

東武使停寢事公幹 非止一再而至 有我禮曹書契中添句之擧 而況尊公職在幹事中 歸則幹旋之方 想不虛徐也 僕等跂俟回音 這間四五個月 意謂使事之已寢矣 今見書示 則滿紙臚列 惟始料之所未及 亦多究說不得之語 此或弊邦衷懇之未孚而然歟 貴州周旋之悠泛而然歟 第念東武遣使 爲出眷鄰盛意 則謝不容筆 感不以言 而項於書契中仰懇者 非但迎送煩弊之爲念 交鄰章程 係是兩國先世之述作 而三百年誠信愈篤 賴以後人之典守也 今此東武使 卽是舊約之所未有 則章程一毀 約條難守 可不慎哉 近因洋船之出沒遠近 貴國之長崎交易 弊邦之江都剿却 各有措處 亦相通報者也 今我深海諸防 設備益嚴 固無貽惱於鄰國 則自東武亦何須遠勞神思 遣使超溟乎 且交鄰庶務之專管於貴州 自是不易之舊約也 今若以機密之事 或恐泄漏 不使間攝於貴州 寧有是理乎 窃爲之萬々訝惑 而況今年則例使之外 漂差與大差使行相續出來 又有將來之大差兩使 裁判兩次 則弊邦館接之節 未有若此時稠疊也 其於惟隣省弊之誼 冀當爲加意幹旋 而如有商議事 則開春海官入去時務盡停當 未爲不可也 惟望尊公之參量事勢 終始力圖 期於停使之地 而多少事狀 備告于使道前 則答教如右 故玆以敷陳 洞諒是希

丁卯十二月 日

訓導俊卿安僉知

別差德氏(*Sic*)玄主簿

幹事官 尊公

F. F. Low (1873. 2. 1) ➞ H. Fish (1873. 4. 2)

1866년 조불(朝佛) 교전 경과에 관한 M. Geofroy와의 대화 보고

Legation of the United States
Peking, February 1, 1873

Subject,

French Expedition to Corea in 1866, and a proposition made by Mr. Seward to France in 1867 for an alliance between France and the United States with a view of sending a joint expedition to Corea.

Reports no substance of a conversation with the French Minister upon these subjects, and encloses copy of the draft of a dispatch from the French Government to M. Berthémy at Washington in reply to the proposition which has been made by Mr. Seward.

In a conversation recently with the French Minister, Corean affairs were mentioned and the policy of Western Nations respecting that Country briefly discussed.

In connection with this subject, M. de Geofroy gave me some interesting information concerning the French Expedition of 1866, which explains the action of the French Government which has hitherto seemed mysterious and contradictory. Hints and insinuations to the same effect has been thrown out by the late Charge d' Affairs, but as it was impossible to verify their accuracy. I did not deem it admirable to communicate the rumors to the Department.

It appears that the French Expedition of 1866 against Corea was undertaken by the Admiral in Command in these Seas, whom the advice of M. Bellonet then Charge d'Affairs in Peking, without consultation with, or orders from the home Government. When the report that such an Expedition was contemplated reached Paris instructions were dispatched to Admiral Roze directing that no movement be made without positive orders. These dispatches did not arrive in China until after the Expedition had started, and of course did not reach the Admiral until after his return from Corea.

When the report of the Admirals operations reached France, the Government disapproved of the whole affair and censured the principal actors in it. It is understood that the Admiral was relieved of his command and suspended, pending and enquiry which had been ordered, and M. Bellonet was recalled from Peking. This action of the Government coupled with the published reports of the Expedition caused the public to believe that French arms had suffered an ignominious defect, which the opposition in the Corps Legislatif were not slow to take advantage of; and as a natural consequence unpleasant and embarrassing questions were propounded to the Ministry touching the causes of the dispatch in Corea as well as Mexico; pointed inquiries were also made as to the course of the Government proposal to pursue to restore the prestige of France and vindicate her honor.

The Executive Government finding it difficult to answer these interrogatories chose a new line of action. It was suddenly discovered that the fresh reports about the defeat of the Corean Expedition were erroneous; that the Command of Admiral Roze, instead of suffering defeat had severely chastised the Coreans; that the outrages inflicted by that people whom the Missionaries had been effectually and amply redressed; and that the dignity and honor of the Government had been fully vindicated.

As a natural result of this change of position Admiral Roze was reinstated and promoted, and M Bellonet was assigned to a new and better post.

In the conversation referred to M. de Geofroy disclosed another interesting piece of information which though quite new to me is without doubt well known to you. I refer to a formal proposition made to the French Government for a joint Expedition to Corea. If I am correctly informed such a proposition was made by Mr. Seward, late Secretary of State, early in 1867, to the French Minister in Washington, with the request that he would submit it to his Government and get an answer. It was proposed to organize and send a joint Expedition (American and French) strong enough to conquer Corea. Details were not discussed. One proviso only was strongly insisted on by Mr. Seward: that England should not under any circumstances be permitted to join.

M Berthémy dispatch conveying Mr. Seward proposal reached Paris about the time that the events previously referred to were transpiring, and of course the Government determined at once that the proposition could not be entertained; and M. de Geofroy, who was at that time Under Secretary in the

Foreign Office, was directed to frame a dispatch in reply which would embody the views of the Government. The draft was submitted to the Cabinet, who, after making, some unimportant changes in the phraseology without altering the sense, directed it to be copied and sent M Geofroy has in his possession the original draft, which he showed me confidentially; he has also allowed me since to take a copy of it; and, as it may interest you to see the instructions such on that occasion I beg to enclose a copy.

I have the honor to be
Sir
Your obedient Servant
Frederick F. Low

【關係資料】

1. 燕行記

上使伴倘沈裕慶錄送

水洋之說膽掉難記而抵舘第三日各國捻理衙門遣通官問今春鞫獄事有無於首譯曰貴國緣此搆釁果有是事否云云三使會議而首譯主諱之吾力言不可諱也旣知之故有此語諱他不得一也適足以諱於捴衙後来不知有何様事端則將何以問議中朝二也自柵而遼自遼而瀋人皆聞之則中國之所知捴衙之不得瞞過三也雖諱之必通譯捴衙問其事由云云議論不一竟諱其獄而不通譯甚歎歎我是翫景来人不復與其議心切憂之往見南邊朝士董黃王張方汪孫諸人則張黃為人慷慨黃則尚氣而稍燥張則內而沉靜外而神明足可與論事亦係散班也朝中事無遺知而辨論明快天下形勢槩可指掌筆談随見便扯不教一字走漏王願齋黃雲鶴是義經上一套語也轉生憂慮乃裝作買賣之様觀於市得見雲南人李姓江蘓人劉姓湖南人吳姓三人俱是投筆成功現在知縣知府姑未赴任者也習於軍制延攬英雄面察邊情問無不知而至於三國俄那斯皆言〇悍甚於洋尚不相關未可料量云連三日往見卽六月十九日也劉姓人乃問我國山川道里人物風俗曰設有洋人之来將何以處之云我荅曰我國踈於兵制近者冲主明達每詢民情必憂形於色主事英邁盖世貪墨(歛跡)士曰時犹民曰樂犹衆心成城且有山川之險水而大舶淺陸而飛車阻碍而但恬嬉日久兵未精鍊云云其人皆舉手稱賀曰然則貴國其無憂乎大抵洋國必借糧於商人而一船載五百餘人一月糧費千五百已上每患糧少不能支久堅守勿戰則彼必自退每國先結奸細潛通虗實彼每得志痛禁奸細為上策若便交兵彼之機巧殊甚雖習於兵者每每見欺所謂機械不及於中國之射踈及遠故山川險阸之處火具無功彼不能入云俄而二客去劉乃言於我曰本月初八日自登州海上乘火輪船初十日至天津橋衢下来而見兵船一隻裝在海中故招廣東人自其船来者問之則曰彼今聚十數兵船將有事于朝鮮云問其聚来何處兵則曰聚来諸處駐察而安南兵聚多云我因發船未見其船之去就而大船日行千五百里則想已抵東國云自聞此說罔知所措以其意言於上副房使譯官雖費多小銀錢詳探前言以審其實蹟為言明日往見黃翔雲使之探知禮部禮部管外旺事務云故也黃乃許之而禮部有事黃亦未卽見禮部也而二十六日與副使書状往見黃則黃乃誦示某國致

書於捻理衙門要出公文東去行教故囬示以東國士民不願行教則不可強抑云云又以前言囬示而咨文于貴國以為萬全之計云云此筆談卽副使持来

2. 조선사신과 청국 관료 필담(筆談)

陳玉章 瀋陽城内居人其父年前殉節於南匪勅達忠義祠於瀋

朝鮮與倭隣講好夂矣何不問計於倭人倭人盡學洋之器械雖與洋約條通商倭人深恨洋可以求得其器械耳中國人亦能倣得其器械而精巧尚不如洋惟南邊人造成而只在巧匠之模得北方但知其糟粕耳俄夷之俗與洋大同而不與中國交兵故未能深知其長技然性悍甚於洋人耳

李日乾 雲南人以軍功上京候選

外各國俗尚不同皆人理上有同異而惟洋人身獸性只可以力服不可以恩化知人有財則必悉其巧盡取乃已知人有力則必盡其恭惟恐有事故只可力服而巧黠之極無恥之甚故臨陣交兵未易應機遣使通信亦難開導但無絶倫之力故陸戰本無斬將搴旗之徒

張丙炎 號午橋今翰林編修

法夷之行教云者要結奸細以知他國之情狀也苟無奸細之暗導不敢八他境其性如狂猘畏而避則趕來立以待則反走故禦洋之策莫如固守我境禁戢奸細勿與相戰則渠自退矣如不得已通商必以物換物勿以金銀貿易則渠亦無利而必自退金銀一八他手不復還故中國財竭矣

王軒 號顧齋現今兵部郎中

先禁我國奸細使彼不得探我虛實則其無憂矣已有奸細則為難然彼之大舶不能泊於水濱則禁他之道自有地形與人謀耳

吳懋林 湖南人亦以軍功候選

洋夷之欲不在土地欲化天下盡為商從中取利之計也所謂鴉片烟本不直一錢之物而欺人倍價弱人氣力促人壽命若通其貨而行其教則但其國之亡各有遲速而已陸戰○其長技然不可輕進交鋒矣海上大砲懸於船○之間巧無不中故不可水

戰大舶非不能懸於砲矣欲破高城則懸砲而放之然貴國聞是山城城不可破矣

劉培芬江蘇昆陵人以軍功今年九月當差福建通判之人

六月初八日自登州乘船時有洋兵船十数隻故招廣東人之在洋船者問之則曰方搆兵於高麗云問兵多少則一船五六百人問粮多少則可支一月餘云云未見其發船而來矣盖洋之長技火輪船日行千四五百里而兵船稍少而烟通短故望見可知水深一丈則浮二丈則行前此以擱淺敗故変其制可行二丈水深矣商船則依舊行六丈水深矣貴國之海濱石用潜隱故洋人本自畏若有鄉人導之則可行然逶迤屈曲火輪無用彼以小船行則貴國亦應以兵船禦之則洋之砲火藥甚烈故發丸速不可迫戰貴国山川險阨火輪車不得馳矣渠雖有馬船來故不多但據阨而防之使之持久則渠之粮少矣必不能支久而撤去矣渠之砲有飛天大砲丸之大如盆其中包小包千百箇放八陣中則落地然後大丸坼而小丸發散四傷人此可畏也望見其發砲預為避之則可免矣銃頭鎗但両用而長不過丈許故不能及遠不如中國之長鎗而貴國久不用兵必不習兵但守而勿戰見其必勝然後戰慎勿輕進彼夷見人之弱則必進見人之强必退勿示我之弱大抵借粮借兵之徒不可持久明若觀火不惟今時為然矣且数年前借得八百萬金於冨商矣大海臭載尚未償殖則是天不助洋之時也故今行只以十数隻船向東者的是粮少故也萬尚書之言曰移去住雲南兵云故問之則曰此洋之誰語也雲南之水路在南京為八千餘里而淺深無常洋人大畏之且中國人多八雲南尚無洋人之難則焉有駐雲南之兵也不過誇張其聲勢以慴中國之計也以請行教公文之理問之則曰他之興兵初不関於中國焉有請公文之理然知貴國服色大國故欲一藉其文也且洋俗興兵之時但書奏其國之主事成則受爵號之賞不成則受爵故今欲興無名之兵而欲告其主故以中國公文托作藉口之柄而已中國節制何関於法國耶其國甚貧不商不支故期欲行商也彼堇以十数隻船去則必驅海上漁與商之船助其威勢其實兵船十二而已中國二十年兵革流民多入于海或商或盜所謂中國人皆通洋人者貴國之禍根雖漁船必禁之則貴國之奸細安得飛渡海為洋人指路耶洋人自稱有信而一通商則漸次行巧期於竭人之財仍變吾人為禽獸矣問今年去洋人法夷耶英夷耶曰法也非英也然一相借兵豈無英人耶云云彼夷每患粮少故戰與和間欲其速成制洋之術在遲且緩也云云

萬青藜號○今禮部尚書

洋人所謂公帖不過渠自主管初非中國之所知也此次總理衙門之不許行文傳教可揣也洋人專以財利為尚英利主通商法夷主行教法人鷙悍凡舉事不勝不休衰

羅斯尤不可測貪狼無厭又所欲者土地

萬尚書抵右閤短札

承駕狂顧得遂瞻仰喜見半姿矍鑠足徵德足神全也副行人何號何年歲閤下官戢乃議政府右議政殆古之丞相也軍國大事當無不與議不比六卿各分一職也貴國事僕稍知之前日曾奏准由本部行知矣其中委曲不能以口舌相傳而尤不敢形諸筆墨惟強埸之事不比尋常當求其萬全庶不為人所乘耳法國現已調兵君等得知否現在僕嚴催本部明貢吻賞件早為催辦以便閤下早旼也於二十一日行文馬上飛遞去矣由禮部封交兵部沿途飛遞盛京兵部轉行貴國聞所調乃伊駐安南之兵此事審不便洩露也計此時伊之兵不日當抵貴境矣切不可冒昧與之争戰止宜固守與之講理若不得講切不可來中國請兵既遠不能濟事且亦無可調發徒托空言必至誤事欲於中國止求將道理與之講說排觧大意云中國地大物愽諸國可以相安朝鮮僻處一隅諸凡樸陋他国得之不足為益無之亦不足為損即以行教而論法國之教行於天下亦不以一隅之行否為重輕但立言不亢不卑或者彼自退阻耳國之所恃者戰守而已今貴國小弛急於講求恐有不逮愚意此事當先以理折之朝鮮之法向來如此不自今始今所殺者洋人少而本地之人多且知止為莠民不知其為隣國之教士也自今以後如有外人八我本鏡傳教者本國之法但加於本國之民隣國之人則以禮遣之截不殺害如此相約於理甚足而彼亦可可置辨然後以其暇日選將鍊兵為自固之策得数十年卽可自強矣以為何如此事不可私為當彼此約乞如有成約卽具表八奏以為乞章但知可言各國所習不同朝鮮民人願從者少不便相強切不可言彼教之不可行則立言得躰矣我等乃数百年相與之國政教○不相同而禮義皆知遵守不比他國之以勢力相傾者此事已成故愚甚為貴國憂然戢典禮曹不與軍事空切憂慮無可如何前因本部飛咨貴國者恐無一豫備為人所乘耳該國桀驁性成恃其兵力不勝不止中國受害屢屢現因中原不靖各處用兵力量寀有不及止得設法羈縻而其心固難乞也閤下禮成之後趕早旼家熟為籌劃切勿輕於一試是為最要再閤下屢次欲枉顧而不敢相請者亦有此心事不言不可明言又不可故遅遅至今惟彼此心照而已不能盡言也李君在此與之談及此事臨别之時相對愀然執手無言而别李興敏君當猶記之也若有辦法幸告我以釋鄙懷此言在此處切勿洩之於人本處禁談此事也聞貴國大院君當國甚厲精明能了此事否愚有一言不惟此處不可洩也卽在貴國亦不可洩文内切勿言我所云止言本國之意

부록

문서 목록

번호	발신일/수신일*(음력)	문서제목	발신	수신	문서출처	번역문 출처	관련문서 제목	관련문서 출처
1	1866.8.21(高宗三年七月十二日)/1866.8.24*(高宗三年七月十五日)	제너럴 셔먼호 문정(問情) 보고	朴承輝	議政府	『일록』 丙寅 7월 15일; 『황해계』 丙寅 7월 12일 戌時에 황해감사의 보고서 원문 수록			
2	1866.8.22(高宗三年七月十三日)	제너럴 셔먼호 문정(問情) 보고	朴珪壽	議政府	『평안계』 丙寅 7월 13일 巳時			
3	1866.8.23(高宗三年七月十四日)	서양 선박과의 접촉을 엄금하는 교서	高宗		『일기』 丙寅 7월 14일			
4	1866.8.24(高宗三年七月十五日)*	제너럴 셔먼호 문정(問情) 보고	李容象	議政府	『일록』 丙寅 7월 15일; 『실록』 丙寅 7월 15일에 같은 내용 수록			
5	1866.8.24(高宗三年七月十五日)	제너럴 셔먼호 문정(問情) 보고	朴珪壽	議政府	『평안계』 丙寅 7월 15일 巳時			
6	1866.8.24(高宗三年七月十五日)	제너럴 셔먼호 동태 보고	朴珪壽	議政府	『평안계』 丙寅 7월 15일 巳時			
7	1866.8.26(高宗三年七月十七日)	제너럴 셔먼호 동태 보고	朴珪壽	議政府	『평안계』 丙寅 7월 17일 酉時			
8	1866.8.27(高宗三年七月十八日)*	제너럴 셔먼호 문정(問情) 보고	李容象	議政府	『일록』 丙寅 7월 18일			
9	1866.8.28(高宗三年七月十九日)	중군(中軍) 이현익(李玄益) 구출 경위 보고	朴珪壽	議政府	『평안계』 丙寅 7월 19일 亥時; 『일록』, 『일기』, 『실록』 丙寅 7월 27일에 같은 내용 수록			
10	1866.8.30(高宗三年七月二十一日)	내응자 단속 및 경계 강화 보고	朴珪壽	議政府	『평안계』 丙寅 7월 21일			
11	1866.8.31(高宗三年七月二十二日)/1866.9.3*(高宗三年七月二十五日)	제너럴 셔먼호와의 교전 경과 보고	朴珪壽	議政府	『평안계』 丙寅 7월 22일 戌時; 『일록』, 『일기』, 『실록』 丙寅 7월 25일에 관련 내용 수록			
12	1866.9.1(高宗三年七月二十三日)	제너럴 셔먼호와의 교전 경과 보고	朴珪壽	議政府	『평안계』 丙寅 7월 23일 亥時			
13	1866.9.2(高宗三年七月二十四日)/1866.9.5*(高宗三年七月二十七日)	제너럴 셔먼호와의 교전 경과 보고	朴珪壽	議政府	『평안계』 丙寅 7월 24일 亥時; 『일록』, 『일기』, 『실록』 丙寅 7월 27일에 같은 내용 수록			
14	1866.9.3(高宗三年七月二十五日)	시원임대신 등을 불러 서양선박 출몰에 대해 논의	高宗, 時原任大臣		『일록』 丙寅 7월 25일; 『일기』, 『실록』 丙寅 7월 25일에 같은 내용 수록			
15	1866.9.11(高宗三年八月三日)	사교(邪敎) 척퇴(斥退)를 명하는 교서	高宗		『일기』 丙寅 8월 3일; 『일록』, 『실록』 丙寅 8월 3일에 같은 내용 수록			

번호	발신일/수신일*(음력)	문서제목	발신	수신	문서출처	번역문 출처	관련문서 제목	관련문서 출처
16	1866. 9. 21(高宗三年八月十三日)	서양국가와의 통상 불허 방침 전달	李興敏	萬青藜	『中朝』 pp. 356-8; 『夷務始末』 권 45. pp. 1084-6.		(1) 이홍민 사함(私函)의 도부(到付)를 알리는 萬青藜 상주문	『清代中朝關係檔案史料續編』, p. 355.
17	1866. 9. 30(高宗三年八月二十二日)	제너럴 셔먼호 사건 전말 통보	高宗	禮部	『동문』, 권 3. 「歷陳洋舶情形咨」, pp. 2468-70(혹은 pp. 3468-70); 『夷務始末』 6, 권 45. pp. 1074-7.			
18	1866. 10. 8	제너럴 셔먼호 사건 발생 보고	E. Sandford	G. F. Seward	ADPP, Vol. 9, p. 6-8.			
19	1866. 10. 12	제너럴 셔먼호 사건 경과 보고	E. Sandford	G. F. Seward	ADPP, Vol. 9, p. 9-11.			
20	1866. 10. 23	제너럴 셔먼호의 생존자 확인 및 구호 여부 문의	S. W. Williams	總署	FRUS, 1867, part, 1, China, pp. 414-7; ADPP, Vol. 9 , pp. 12-4;AADM, pp. 798-801. inclosure B	[漢譯] 『夷務始末』 6, 권 45. p. 1081.		
21	1866. 10. 24	서프라이즈호 선원 송환 및 제너럴 셔먼호 선원 피살 보고	S. W. Williams	W. H. Seward	FRUS, 1867, part 1, China, pp. 414-7; ADPP, Vol. 9, pp. 12-4; AADM, pp. 798-801			
22	1866. 10. 28 (同治五年九月二十日)	미국측 요청의 처리 결과 통보	總署	S. W. Williams	『동문』 洋舶情形, p. 2472.			
23	1866. 11. 30/ 1867. 2. 19*	제너럴 셔먼호 사건 경과 및 천주교도 탄압 사실 보고	H. H. Bell	G. Wells	ADPP, Vol. 9, pp. 19-28; NA I, M89 R257			
24	1866. 12. 11 (高宗三年十一月五日)	제너럴 셔먼호 생존자설 부정 및 프랑스 군사 행위의 부당성	議政府	禮部	『동문』, 권 3. 「覆陳洋舶事實仍請總理衙門相機酌辦咨」, pp. 2476-7. 『中日韓』, 권 2. 「總署收軍機處鈔交禮部摺附件二: 朝鮮國王咨文」. pp. 40-4 에도 동일문건 수록			
25	1866. 12. 12	제너럴 셔먼호 사건 경과 보고	H. H. Bell	G. Wells	ADPP, Vol. 9, pp. 32-8; NA I, M89 R251.			
26	1866. 12. 14	한양 점령 건의	H. H. Bell	G. Welles	ADPP, Vol. 9, pp. 42-5.			
27	1866. 12. 15	제너럴 셔먼호 사건 경과 보고	A. Burlingame	W. H. Seward	FRUS, 1867, Part I, China, pp. 425-8.			
28	1866. 12. 27	미국의 단독 조선 침공 건의 및 거문도의 지정학적 중요성 보고	H. H. Bell	G. Wells	ADPP, Vol. 9, pp. 47-51.			

번호	발신일/수신일*(음력)	문서제목	발신	수신	문서출처	번역문 출처	관련문서 제목	관련문서 출처
29	1866. 12. 27	제너럴 셔먼호 사건 경과 전달	H. H. Bell	R. W. Shufeldt	Shufeldt Papers, Division of Manuscript, the Library of Congress			
30	1866. 12. 31	제너럴 셔먼호 사건 경과 보고	E. Sandford	W. H. Seward	ADPP, Vol. 9, pp. 52-63; NA II, M102 R1			
31	1866. 12. 31	조선 해안 항해 시 유의사항 전달	H. H. Bell	R. W. Shufeldt	Shufeldt Papers, Division of Manuscript, the Library of Congress			
32	1867. 1. 8	제너럴 셔먼호 관련 정보 수집 보고	R. W. Shufeldt	H. H. Bell	Shufeldt Papers, Division of Manuscript, the Library of Congress			
33	1867. 1. 9	Shufeldt와 Ridel 신부의 대화 기록	R. W. Shufeldt, Ridel		Shufeldt Papers, Division of Manuscript, the Library of Congress			
34	1867. 1. 19	上海와 芝罘에서의 제너럴 셔먼호 사건 관련 정보 수집 보고	R. W. Shufeldt	H. H. Bell	Shufeldt Papers, Division of Manuscript, the Library of Congress			
35	1867. 1. 24	제너럴 셔먼호 생존자 송환 요구	R. W. Shufeldt	高宗	ADPP, Vol. 9, pp. 64-6.			
36	1867. 1. 25	제너럴 셔먼호 사후 처리 관련 Shufeldt의 견해	R. W. Shufeldt		ADPP, Vol. 9, pp. 67-70.			
37	1866. 1. 27(高宗三年十二月二十二日)/1866. 2. 1*(高宗三年十二月二十七日)	와츄세트호 출현 및 투서(投書) 보고	朴承輝	議政府	『황해계』 丙寅 12월 22일 卯時			
38	1867. 1. 28(高宗三年十二月二十三日)	와츄세트호의 동태 및 경계 상황 보고	朴承輝	議政府	『황해계』 丙寅 12월 23일 未時			
39	1867. 1. 29	조선 관리와의 대화 기록	R. W. Shufeldt		NA I, M89 R251			
40	1867. 1. 30	대동강변 탐사 결과 및 조선 관리와의 접촉 보고	R. W. Shufeldt	H. H. Bell	NA I, M89 R251			
41	1867. 2. 1(高宗三年十二月二十七日)	와츄세트호의 투서(投書)에 대한 조처	議政府	高宗	『일록』 丙寅 12월 27일			
42	1867. 2. 3	거문도 해역 탐사 결과 보고, 거문도 점령 건의	R. W. Shufeldt	H. H. Bell	NA I, M89 R252.	[英譯] NA I, M89 R251	(1) H. H. Bell이 G. Wells에게 보낸 Shufeldt의 거문도 해역 조사 내용	NA I, M89 R252

번호	발신일/수신일* (음력)	문서제목	발신	수신	문서출처	번역문 출처	관련문서 제목	관련문서 출처
43	1867. 2. 16/1867. 4. 19*	Shufeldt의 제너럴 셔먼호 관련 정보 수집 결과 보고	H. H. Bell	G. Wells	NA II, M112 R9			
44	1867. 2. 23	Gillie 신부에 대한 감사 및 제너럴 셔먼호 조사 촉구	W. H. Seward	A. Burlingame	FRUS, 1867, Part 1, China, p. 459.			
45	1867. 5. 10(慶應三年四月七日)	조미(朝美) 관계 중재 제안	板倉勝靜, 稲葉正邦, 小笠原長行	R. B. Van Valkenburgh	『全覽』, 「平山圖書頭古賀筑後守渡韓奉命一件」 3, pp. 216-7.	[英譯] FRUS, 1867, Part 2, Japan, pp. 36-7; AADM, pp. 814-5.		
46	1867. 5. 18	일본의 조미(朝美) 관계 중재 제안 보고	R. B. V. Valkenburgh	W. H. Seward	FRUS, Part 2, Japan, pp. 36-7; AADM, pp. 814-5.			
47	1867. 7. 23	일본의 조미(朝美) 관계 중재 제안에 대한 감사 표시	W. H. Seward	R. B. V. Valkenburgh	FRUS, 1867, Part 2, Japan, pp. 46-7.		(1) Seward의 답변 보고	『全覽』, 「平山圖書頭古賀筑後守渡韓奉命一件」 5, p. 268.
48	1867. 11. 20	조선에서 일본의 중재 제안을 거절한 사유 보고	R. B. V. Valkenburgh	W. H. Seward	FRUS, 1867, Part 2, Japan, pp. 75-6; ADPP, Vol. 10. pp. 3-8; AADM, pp. 815-6.			
49	1867. 12. 3	제너럴 셔먼호 사건 관련 정보 보고	E. Sanford	W. H. Seward	NA II, M102 R1; ADPP, Vol. 9. pp. 71-3.			
50	1868. 1. 27	일본의 중재 제안에 대한 미국무성 훈령	W. H. Seward	R. B. V. Valkenburgh	FRUS, 1868-9, Japan, pp. 634-5; AADM, p. 816.			
51	1868. 3. 3*(同治七年二月十日)	于文泰로부터 제너럴 셔먼호 생존자 정보 입수, 송환 협조 요청	S. W. Williams	總署	FRUS, 1868-9, Japan, p. 544-7. inclosure A	[漢譯] 『夷務始末』 6, 권 57, p. 1334; 『中日韓』 권 2, pp. 93-4. 문서번호 78	(1) 總署의 회신 영역문	FRUS, 1868-9, Japan, p. 544-7. inclosure C
52	1868. 3. 10(同治七年二月十七日)	제너럴 셔먼호 생존자 보호 요청에 대한 회신	總署	S. W. Williams	『夷務始末』 6, 권 57, pp. 1334-5; 『中日韓』 권 2, pp. 95-6. 문서번호 80	[英譯] FRUS, 1868~9, Japan, p. 544-7. inclosure B		
53	1868. 3. 12* (同治七年二月十九日)	미국과 영국의 생존자 확인 및 보호 요청에 따른 조처	禮部	總署	『中日韓』 권 2, pp. 98-9. 문서번호 83			
54	1868. 3. 17(同治七年二月二十四日)	미국과 영국의 생존자 확인 요청 사실 등을 알림	禮部	高宗	『동문』 洋舶情形, p. 2482.			

번호	발신일/수신일* (음력)	문서제목	발신	수신	문서출처	번역문 출처	관련문서 제목	관련문서 출처
55	1868. 4. 14(高宗五年三月二十二日)	셰난도어호 출현 보고	李敏宰	議政府	『일록』 戊辰 3월 22일; 『실록』 戊辰 3월 22일에 같은 내용 수록			
56	1868. 4. 15(高宗五年三月二十三日)	李基祖, Febiger 문답기	李基祖	議政府	『동진기』 戊辰 3월 27일 三月二十三日三和懸旗問情記			
57	1868. 4. 16(高宗五年三月二十四日)	셰난도어호 문정(問情) 보고	朴珪壽	議政府	『평안계』 戊辰 3월 24일 辰時			
58	1868. 4. 17(高宗五年三月二十五日)	제너럴 셔먼호 생존자설 부정	議政府	禮部	『동문』 洋船情形, pp. 2482-3.			
59	1868. 4. 17(高宗五年三月二十五日)	황해도 관찰사가 미국에 답하는 서신	議政府	禮部	『동문』 洋船情形, pp. 2483-4.	[英譯] NA I, M89 R253		
60	1868. 4. 17	제너럴 셔먼호 생존자 관련 정보 보고	G. Welles	S. C. Rowan	NA I, M89 R253			
61	1868. 4. 19(高宗五年三月二十七日)	셰난도어호 문정(問情) 보고	朴珪壽	議政府	『평안계』 戊辰 3월 27일 午時			
62	1868. 4. 19	셰난도어호 내항 이유 통지	J. C. Febiger	朴鼎和	NA I, M89 R253	[漢譯] 『양박등서』 縣當臺開坼, p. 20.		
63	1868. 4. 19	조선국왕에게 봉정한 Febiger의 조회문	J. C. Febiger	高宗	NA I, M89 R253	[漢譯] 『양박등서』 照會, pp. 19-20.		
64	1868. 4. 24/1868. 6. 24*	Jenkins로부터 입수한 정보 보고 및 조선과의 교섭 전권 부여 요청	G. F. Seward	W. H. Seward	FRUS, 1870, China, pp. 336-7; ADPP, Vol. 9, p. 74; AADM, pp. 817-8.			
65	1868. 4. 26(高宗五年四月四日)	이동을 중지하고 조정의 회답을 기다릴 것을 요청	俞初煥	Febiger	『양박등서』 龍岡送彼船照會草. p. 23. 『동진기』 戊辰 4월 5일 夜大寒初四日龍岡問情後報艸에서 관련 내용 참고	NA I, M89 R253		
66	1868. 4. 27(高宗五年四月五日)	조선 조정의 회답 대기, 증급 물품 목록	J. C. Febiger	李基祖	NA I, M89 R253	[漢譯] 『양박등서』 大美國欽命督理善安多火輪兵船水使副將官費爲照覆事, pp. 26-7.		
67	1868. 4. 29(高宗五年四月七日)	조선 조정의 회신을 기다린다는 답서	J. C. Febiger	李基祖	『양박등서』 大美國欽命督理善安多火輪兵船水使副將官費爲照覆事, p. 26.			
68	1868. 5. 2~4(高宗五年四月十日~十二日)	김자평(金子平)을 대동한 셰난도어호 문정(問情) 보고	朴承輝	議政府	『양박등서』 余初十日 및 問答記, pp. 27-9.			

번호	발신일/수신일* (음력)	문서제목	발신	수신	문서출처	번역문 출처	관련문서 제목	관련문서 출처
69	1868. 5. 16(高宗五年四月二十四日)/1868. 5. 17*(四月二十五日)	조회문에 대한 회신 촉구	J. C. Febiger	李基祖	『동진기』 戊辰 4월 27일			
70	1868. 5. 17(高宗五年四月二十五日)	Febiger의 서신 전달 요청 거부	李基祖	J. C. Febiger	『동진기』 戊辰 4월 27일 責諭文			
71	1868. 5. 19(高宗五年四月二十七日)	셰난도어호 철수 보고	朴珪壽	議政府	『평안계』 戊辰 4월 27일 辰時			
72	1868. 5. 19	셰난도어호 조사 결과 보고	J. C. Febiger	S. C. Rowan	ADPP, Vol. 9, pp. 75-9.			
73	1868. 5. 25/1868. 7. 13*	조선과의 교섭을 위해 무력 사용이 불가피함	G. F. Seward	W. H. Seward	FRUS, 1870, China, p. 337; ADPP, Vol. 9, p. 80; AADM, p. 818.			
74	1868. 7. 24	조선의 사과가 없을 시 무력 응징 방침 천명	S. C. Rowan	G. Welles	ADPP, Vol. 9, pp. 81-2.			
75	1868. 7. 31	청조의 조미 관계 주선 보고	S. W. Williams	W. H. Seward	FRUS, 1868-9, China, pp. 544-7.			
76	1871. 6. 15/1871. 8. 21*	조선내 천주교도로부터 입수한 제너럴 셔먼호 사건 관련 정보 보고	F. F. Low	H. Fish	FRUS, 1871, China, pp. 124-6; ADPP, Vol. 9, p. 142; AADM, pp. 849-51.			
관계자료	1866. 7. 18(高宗五年六月七日)~1866. 8. 31(高宗五年七月二十二日)	제너럴 셔먼호 승선기(乘船記)			『용호』 979. 平壤事實			

번호	발신일/수신일*(음력)	문서제목	발신	수신	문서출처	번역문 출처	관련문서 제목	관련문서 출처
77	1866. 6. 28	조선에서의 천주교도 박해 보고	E. Verrolles	G. Roze	Documents, pp. 267-8.			
78	1866. 7. 10	2명의 주교와 7명의 선교사 처형 보고 및 보복 건의	G. Roze	P. de Chasseloup-Laubat	Documents, pp. 255-7; Roze I, p. 40.			
79	1866. 7. 11	Saïgon 출동 보고	G. Roze	P. de Chasseloup-Laubat	Documents, p. 259-60; Roze I, p. 45.			
80	1866. 7. 13	조선에 대한 청조의 종주권 부정, 조선 국왕 폐위 및 조선 침공 선언	H. de Bellonet	恭親王	Documents, p. 271.	[漢譯] 『中日韓』 2, p. 27, 문서번호 18; 『夷務始末』 6, p. 1012. [英譯] FRUS, 1867, Part, 1, China, pp. 420; AADM, pp. 802-3.		
81	1866. 7. 13	Bellonet의 해군 병력 동원 지시	C. H. M. Bellonet	G. Roze	Archives Française [1976], pp. 73-4; Documents, pp. 272-3.			
82	1866. 7. 14	조선에 대한 자료 송부	G. Roze	P. de Chasseloup-Laubat	Documents, p. 263.		(1) 조선 정부의 선교사 처형에 관한 Ridel 신부의 보고문	Piacentini, l'Abbé Arthur (1890) Mgr. Ridel, évêque Philippopolis vicaire apostolique de Corée, d'après sa correspondance. Lyon 3ed. pp. 107-9.
83	1866. 7. 16(同治五年六月五日)	프랑스 함대의 조선 원정 계획 통보에 대한 회신	總署	H. de Bellonet	『夷務始末』 6, 권 42. pp. 1012-3; 『中日韓』 권 2. p. 28. 문서번호 19.	[佛譯] Deuxième annexe à la Dépêche Politique No. 21 de Pékin 28 Novembre 1866. Documents, pp. 210-3. [英譯(美國)] FRUS, 1867, part 1, China, pp. 421; ADPP, Vol. 9, pp. 29-30. [英譯(英國)] TNA, FO 881/1505		
84	1866. 7. 18(同治五年六月七日)	프랑스의 조선 원정에 대한 중국의 입장 보고	總署	同治帝	『中日韓』 권 2. p. 30. 문서번호 21			

번호	발신일/수신일* (음력)	문서제목	발신	수신	문서출처	번역문 출처	관련문서 제목	관련문서 출처
85	1866. 7. 19*(同治五年六月八日)	조선에서 탈출한 프랑스인의 입항 보고	崇厚	總署	『中日韓』 권 2. pp. 31-2. 문서번호 22			
86	1866. 7. 24(同治五年六月十三日)	프랑스 공사와의 교섭 경과 통보	總署	禮部	『中日韓』 권 2. p. 32. 문서번호 23			
87	1866. 7. 28(同治五年六月十七日)	프랑스 공사와의 교섭 경과 통보	總署	南洋大臣	『中日韓』 권 2. pp. 33-4. 문서번호 24			
88	1866. 7. 28/1866. 10. 11*	조선 원정의 승인 및 인력과 물자 지원 요청	G. Roze	P. de Chasseloup-Laubat	Roze I, pp. 49-55.			
89	1866. 8. 1(同治五年六月二十一日)	프랑스 함대의 원정 계획을 조선에 통지할 것을 상주	禮部	同治帝	『夷務始末』 6, 권 42. p. 1018.			
90	1866. 8. 8	프랑스 함대 및 조선 조정의 동정 보고	S. W. Williams	W. H. Seward	FRUS, 1866, Part. 1, China, pp. 536-7; ADPP, Vol. 9, p. 4; AADM, p. 797.			
91	1866. 8. 16* (1866. 8. 16/同治五年七月七日)	프랑스와의 교섭 과정 통보 및 방비 권고	禮部	高宗	『동문』, 洋舶情形, pp. 2467-8			
92	1866. 8. 20(高宗三年七月十一日)	천주교도 처형 배경 설명	高宗	禮部	『동문』, 洋舶情形, p. 2468.			
93	1866. 8. 28/1866. 10. 8*	원정을 위한 조선 해안 사전 탐사	G. Roze	P. de Chasseloup-Laubat	Documents, pp. 265-6.			
94	1866. 9. 7	7월 10일자 조선에서의 선교사 살해에 관한 로즈의 보고 전달	P. de Chasseloup-Laubat	Moustier	『한불』, p. 207; Documents, p. 120.			
95	1866. 9. 7	Roze와 Bellonet의 조선 원정 주도권에 관한 논쟁	G. Roze	H. de Bellonet	Documents, pp. 274-5.			
96	1866. 9. 7/1866. 11. 4*	Bellonet의 월권적 행위 인정 불가	G. Roze	P. de Chasseloup-Laubat	Documents, p. 269-70; Roze I, p. 56.			
97	1866. 9. 11	조선 공격을 위한 함대 사령부의 芝罘 회의 보고	G. Roze	P. de Chasseloup-Laubat	Roze I, p. 60.			
98	1866. 9. 16	*Guerrière*함 함장에게 보낸 Roze의 훈령	G. Roze	Lieutenant de Vaisseau de *la Guerrière*	Roze I, p. 5.			
99	1866. 9. 17	선교사 처형에 대한 Roze의 의견	G. Roze	E. Verrolles	Roze I, p. 6.			
100	1866. 9. 24(高宗三年八月十六日)	시무상소(時務上疏)	奇正鎭		『일기』 丙寅 8월 16일; 『일록』, 『실록』 丙寅 8월 16일에 같은 내용 수록			

번호	발신일/수신일* (음력)	문서제목	발신	수신	문서출처	번역문 출처	관련문서 제목	관련문서 출처
101	1866. 9. 26(高宗三年八月十八日)	프랑스 함대에 대한 대처 방안 논의	高宗, 時原任大臣 등		『일기』 丙寅 8월 18일; 『일록』, 『실록』 丙寅 8월 18일에 같은 내용 수록			
102	1866. 9. 28(高宗三年八月二十日)	동진(東津) 수비 강화책 건의	議政府	高宗	『일기』 丙寅 8월 20일; 『일록』, 『실록』 丙寅 8월 20일에 같은 내용 수록			
103	1866. 10. 1(同治五年八月二十三日)	프랑스 회신 미접수 사정을 조선에 통지할 것을 상주(上奏)	總署	同治帝	『夷務始末』 6, 권 44. p. 1052.			
104	1866. 10. 2(同治五年八月二十四日)/1866. 10. 18(高宗三年九月十日)*	조선 원정과 관련된 프랑스 회신의 미접수 통보	禮部	議政府	『동문』 洋船情形, p. 2471-2.			
105	1866. 10. 5	강화도부터 서울까지의 해안 탐사 고려	G. Roze	B. de Montmorand, H. de Bellonet 등	Roze I, p. 8.			
106	1866. 10. 5	한강 봉쇄 통고	G. Roze	상하이 주재 각국 공사 등	Roze I, p. 7.	[英譯] FRUS, 1867, part 1, China, pp. 417; ADPP, Vol. 9, pp. 12-4; AADM, pp. 798-801.		
107	1866. 10. 6	조선 해안 탐사에 대한 의견, 원정을 위한 군수물자 보급 요청	G. Roze	P. P. M. Grandière	Roze I, pp. 9-12.			
108	1866. 10. 6	조선 해안 탐사 보고	G. Roze	P. de Chasseloup-Laubat	Documents, pp. 276-318.			
109	1866. 10. 11*(同治五年九月三日)	조선에 대한 미국, 영국, 프랑스의 연합 공격 가능성 보고	崇厚	總署	『中日韓』 권 2. p. 37. 문서번호 29			
110	1866. 10. 16(高宗三年九月八日)	프랑스 함대에 대한 대처 방안 논의	高宗, 時原任大臣 등		『일기』 丙寅 9월 8일; 『일록』, 『실록』 丙寅 9월 8일에 같은 내용 수록			
111	1866. 10. 17(高宗三年九月九日)	척사윤음(斥邪綸音)	高宗		『일기』 丙寅 9월 9일; 『일록』, 『실록』 丙寅 9월 9일에 같은 내용 수록			
112	1866. 10. 18(高宗三年九月十日)	선교사 살해 책임자 처벌 및 전권대표 파견 요구	G. Roze	高宗	『실록』 丙寅 9월 11일			

번호	발신일/수신일* (음력)	문서제목	발신	수신	문서출처	번역문 출처	관련문서 제목	관련문서 출처
113	1866. 10. 19 (高宗三年九月十一日)	선교사 처형의 정당성 강조, 프랑스 군의 군사 행위 비난	巡撫營	G. Roze	『실록』 丙寅 9월 11일	[佛譯] Documents, pp. 328-30; Roze I, p. 87-91.		
114	1866. 10. 19(高宗三年九月十一日)	척화문(斥和文)	大院君		『실록』 丙寅 9월 11일			
115	1866. 10. 19 (高宗三年九月十一日)	프랑스 군과의 교전 상황 보고	鄭雲龜	議政府	『일기』 丙寅 9월 11일; 『일록』, 『실록』 丙寅 9월 11일에 같은 내용 수록			
116	1866. 10. 19	작약도(芍藥島) 탐사에 관한 Roze의 보고	G. Roze	H. de Bellonet	Roze II BB4 1511-4-1866, no. 388 bis			
117	1866. 10. 20* (高宗三年九月十二日)	프랑스 군 철수 보고	巡撫營	議政府	『일록』 丙寅 9월 12일; 『실록』 丙寅 9월 12일에 같은 내용 수록			
118	1866. 10. 20* (高宗三年九月十二日)	척사상소(斥邪上疏)	李恒老		『일기』 丙寅 9월 12일; 『일록』, 『실록』 丙寅 9월 12일에 같은 내용 수록			
119	1866. 10. 21	한강 봉쇄 통보	H. de Bellonet	恭親王	Documents, p. 214.	[漢譯] 『夷務始末』 6, 권 45, p. 1080. [英譯] FRUS, 1867, part 1, China, pp. 424; ADPP, Vol. 9, pp. 29-30.		
120	1866. 10. 22	강화도 도착 및 점령 보고	G. Roze	P. de Chasseloup-Laubat	Documents, pp. 319-24; Roze I, pp. 81-7.			
121	1866. 10. 22	강화도 획득 물품 보고서	G. Roze	P. de Chasseloup-Laubat	Documents, pp. 351-2.			
122	1866. 10. 22	강화도 점령, 조선 국왕의 서신 접수 및 회신 발송 보고	G. Roze	P. de Chasseloup-Laubat	Documents, pp. 325-30; Roze I, p. 87-91.			
123	1866. 10. 22	통역 파견 요청	G. Roze	B. de Montmorand	Roze I, p. 18.			
124	1866. 10. 22.	강화도 공격 결과 보고	G. Roze	H. de Bellonet 등	Roze I, pp. 18-20.			
125	1866. 10. 24* (高宗三年九月十六日)	척사윤음(斥邪綸音)	高宗		『일기』 丙寅 9월 16일; 『일록』, 『실록』 丙寅 9월 16일에 같은 내용 수록			
126	1866. 10. 27* (高宗三年九月十日)	척사상소(斥邪上疏)	李恒老		『일록』 丙寅 9월 19일; 『일기』 丙寅 9월 19일에 같은 내용 수록			

번호	발신일/수신일* (음력)	문서제목	발신	수신	문서출처	번역문 출처	관련문서 제목	관련문서 출처
127	1866.10.27* (高宗三年九月十九日)	문수산성 교전 경과 보고	巡撫營	議政府	『일기』丙寅 9월 19일; 『일록』, 『실록』丙寅 9월 19일에 같은 내용 수록			
128	1866.10.29* (高宗三年九月二十一日)	프랑스군과의 교전 후 피해 상황 보고	巡撫營	議政府	『일기』丙寅 9월 21일; 『일록』, 『실록』丙寅 9월 21일에 같은 내용 수록			
129	1866.10.31* (高宗三年九月二十三日)	프랑스 함대 정황 보고	巡撫營	議政府	『일기』丙寅 9월 22일; 『일록』, 『실록』丙寅 9월 22일에 같은 내용 수록			
130	1866.10.31(高宗三年九月二十三日)	군민(君民) 단결 및 내응자 엄벌을 지시하는 교서(敎書)	高宗		『일기』丙寅 9월 23일; 『일록』, 『실록』丙寅 9월 23일에 같은 내용 수록			
131	1866.11.1/1867.1.7*	조선 원정이 청국 정부에 미친 영향 보고	H. de Bellonet	Moustier	Document, pp. 134-7.			
132	1866.11.3*(高宗三年九月二十六日)	프랑스 함대의 내습(來襲) 보고	鄭雲翼	議政府	『일록』丙寅 9월 26일; 『일기』, 『실록』丙寅 9월 26일에 같은 내용 수록			
133	1866.11.4(同治五年九月二十七日)	무력 행위 자제 및 사전 진상 조사 제안	總署	H. de Bellonet	『夷務始末』6, 권 45. pp. 1080-1.	[佛譯] Documents, pp. 215-7. 4e annexe à la dép. pol. no. 21 de Pékin 28 Novembre 1866 [英譯(美國)] FRUS, 1867, part 1, China, pp. 421-2; ADPP, Vol. 9, pp. 29-30 [英譯(英國)] TNA, FO 881/1505		
134	1866.11.6	Bellonet의 월권적 행위 비판	P. de Chasseloup-Laubat	Moustier	Documents, pp. 143-64.			
135	1866.11.9* (高宗三年十月三日)	시무상소(時務上疏)	李恒老		『일록』丙寅 10월 4일; 『일기』丙寅 10월 4일에 같은 내용 수록			
136	1866.11.10* (高宗三年十月四日)	정족산(鼎足山) 전투 승전 보고	巡撫營	議政府	『일록』丙寅 10월 4일; 『실록』丙寅 10월 3일에 같은 내용 수록			

번호	발신일/수신일* (음력)	문서제목	발신	수신	문서출처	번역문 출처	관련문서 제목	관련문서 출처
137	1866. 11. 10	Bellonet가 취한 조치의 무효화 주장	Moustier	H. de Bellonet	Documents, pp. 165-8.		(1) Le Moniteur universel 1866년 12월 28일, 1867년 1월 8일자 보도문	Documents, pp. 433-5.
138	1866. 11. 10	전등사(傳燈寺) 전투 경과 보고	Olivier	G. Roze	Documents, pp. 342-5.			
139	1866. 11. 11* (高宗三年十月五日)	프랑스 함대 정황 보고	巡撫營	議政府	『일록』 丙寅 10월 5일; 『실록』 丙寅 10월 5일에 같은 내용 수록			
140	1866. 11. 11* (高宗三年十月五日)	정족산(鼎足山) 전투 후 양측 사상자 보고	巡撫營	議政府	『일록』 丙寅 10월 5일; 『실록』 丙寅 10월 5일에 같은 내용 수록			
141	1866. 11. 11*	總署의 사전조사 제안의 거절 사유 및 조선 침공의 정당성 주장	H. de Bellonet	恭親王	Documents, pp. 218-28; TNA, FO 881/1505	[漢譯] 『夷務始末』 6, 권 45. pp. 1086-8. [英譯] FRUS, 1867, part 1, China, pp. 422-3; ADPP, Vol. 9, pp. 29-30.		
142	1866. 11. 12* (高宗三年十月六日)	강화도 피해 상황 및 조곡(漕穀) 탈환 보고	巡撫營	議政府	『일록』 丙寅 10월 6일; 『실록』 丙寅 10월 6일에 같은 내용 수록			
143	1866. 11. 12* (高宗三年十月六日)	덕포(德浦) 매복 작전 성공 보고	巡撫營	議政府	『일록』 丙寅 10월 6일; 『실록』 丙寅 10월 13일에 같은 내용 수록			
144	1866. 11. 13	강화도에서 전사한 프랑스 해병 3인의 인적 사항 송부	G. Roze	P. de Chasseloup-Laubat	Roze I, p. 92.			
145	1866. 11. 15* (高宗三年十月九日)	프랑스 함대 정황 보고	巡撫營	議政府	『일록』 丙寅 10월 9일; 『일기』 丙寅 10월 9일에 같은 내용 수록.			
146	1866. 11. 15	프랑스 함대의 한강 봉쇄 보고	G. F. Seward	W. H. Seward	NA II, M92 R25			
147	1866. 11. 15	한강 봉쇄의 해제선언	G. Roze	북경 주재 각국 공사	Roze I, p. 20.			
148	1866. 11. 15	강화도 점령과 서울의 공격을 위한 추가병력 지원 요청	G. Roze	상하이 주재 총영사 외	Roze I, p. 20.			
149	1866. 11. 16	8월 8일자 Williams의 공문에 대한 회신	W. H. Seward	S. W. Williams	FRUS 1866. Part 1. China, p. 563.			
150	1866. 11. 16(同治五年十月十日)	조불(朝佛) 중재 시도에 대한 해명	總署	H. de Bellonet	『夷務始末』 6, 권 45. p. 1088.	[佛譯] Documents, pp. 229-34. [英譯] FRUS, 1867, part 1, China, pp. 423-4; ADPP, Vol. 9, pp. 29-30.		

번호	발신일/수신일* (음력)	문서제목	발신	수신	문서출처	번역문 출처	관련문서 제목	관련문서 출처
151	1866. 11. 16	강화도에서 탈취한 현금 상자 수송에 관한 지시	G. Roze	Primauguet 함장	Roze I, p. 21-2.		(1) Laplace 함장에게 보낸 Roze의 현금상자 수송 지시	Roze I, p. 22
152	1866. 11. 17	서울 공격이 불가능함을 보고	G. Roze	P. de Chasseloup-Laubat	Roze I, pp. 92-4.			
153	1866. 11. 17	강화도 점령을 위한 군사 활동 및 조선으로부터의 철수 보고	G. Roze	P. de Chasseloup-Laubat	Roze I, pp. 95-102.			
154	1866. 11. 17	강화도에서 획득한 서적, 은괴 등 물품 발송 보고	G. Roze	P. de Chasseloup-Laubat	Roze I, pp. 105-6.			
155	1866. 11. 17	은괴 발송 보고	G. Roze	P. de Chasseloup-Laubat	Roze I, p. 104, Documents, pp. 354-5.			
156	1866. 11. 19* (高宗三年十月十三日)	프랑스 함대 팔미도(八尾島) 철수 보고	巡撫營	議政府	『일록』丙寅 10월 13일; 『실록』丙寅 10월 13일에 같은 내용 수록			
157	1866. 11. 21* (高宗三年十月十五日)	서양 선박 관련 전말을 일본에 통지할 것을 지시	高宗	議政府	『일록』丙寅 10월 15일; 『일기』丙寅 10월 15일에 같은 내용 수록		(1) 대마도 주에게 서양 선박의 침입에 대비할 것을 권고하는 예조참의의 서신	『동문』邊禁, pp. 3901-2; 『日外』, 第1卷 第1册, pp. 72-4, 문서 번호 21번, 부속서 1에도 동일 내용 수록
158	1866. 11. 23 (同治五年十月十七日)	조불(朝佛) 문제의 국제 공론화 시도	總署	북경 주재 각국 공사	『夷務始末』6, 권 45. p. 1088.	[佛譯] Documents, pp. 235-8. [英譯(美國)] FRUS, 1867, part 1, China, pp. 424-5; ADPP, Vol. 9, pp. 29-30. [英譯(英國)] TNA, FO 881/1505		
159	1866. 11. 25/ 1866. 12. 20*	공문을 왜곡하여 각국대신에게 조회문을 발송한 것에 대한 항의	H. de Bellonet	總署	TNA, FO 881/1505	[漢譯] 『夷務始末』 6, 권 46. p. 1112. [英譯] FRUS, 1867, part 1, China, pp. 425; ADPP, Vol. 9, pp. 29-30.		
160	1866. 11. 26 (高宗三年十月二十日)	외양(外攘)과 관련한 선후책(善後策) 논의	高宗, 議政府堂上官, 巡撫使 등		『일록』丙寅 10월 20일; 『일기』丙寅 10월 20일에 같은 내용 수록			

번호	발신일/수신일* (음력)	문서제목	발신	수신	문서출처	번역문 출처	관련문서 제목	관련문서 출처
161	1866. 11. 27	프랑스 함대 원정 관련 기사 송부 및 조선과의 통상조약 필요성	G. F. Seward	W. H. Seward	NA II, M92 R33			
162	1866. 11. 28/ 1867. 2. 8*	조선 문제에 미온적인 청조의 태도 비난	H. de Bellonet	Moustier	Documents, pp. 191-238.		(1) Bellonet와 恭親王 간 왕래한 조선 문제에 관한 서신을 번역한 *Shanghai Evening Courrier*의 기사	Documents, pp. 172-90.
163	1866. 11. 30(高宗三年十月二十四日)	프랑스 함대와의 교전 경과 및 결과 보고	議政府	禮部	『동문』洋舶情形, pp. 2472-3.			
164	1866. 11. 30	원정에 참여한 선박의 귀항 보고	H. de Bellonet	P. de Chasseloup-Laubat	Roze I, p. 109.			
165	1866. 12. 3(同治五年十月二十七日)	Bellonet, Williams 등과 왕래한 조회문 전달	禮部	高宗	『동문』洋舶情形, pp. 2474-6.			
166	1866. 12. 8	로즈의 한강 봉쇄 해제에 대한 항의	H. de Bellonet	G. Roze	Documents, pp. 251-4.			
167	1866. 12. 11 (高宗三年十一月五日)	총서에 사의(謝意) 표시와 함께 서양선박 관계 사실 통보	高宗	議政府	『일록』丙寅 11월 5일; 『실록』丙寅 11월 5일에 같은 내용 수록			
168	1866. 12. 11/ 1866. 12. 12*	향후 조선 원정 계획에 대한 질문	P. de Chasseloup-Laubat	Moustier	Documents, pp. 246-7.			
169	1866. 12. 12	조선 문제 관련 恭親王과의 면담 결과 보고	A. Burlingame	W. H. Seward	FRUS, 1867, part 1, China, pp. 419-25; ADPP, Vol. 9, pp. 29-30.			
170	1866. 12. 13/ 1867. 3. 8*	조선 문제 관련 청불(淸佛) 관계 및 양국 교섭 과정 보고	R. Alcock	Stanley	TNA, FO 881/1505			
171	1866. 12. 14	12월 11일자 Chasseloup-Laubat의 서신에 대한 답신	Moustier	P. de Chasseloup-Laubat	Documents, pp. 248-9.			
172	1866. 12. 15 (高宗三年十一月九日)	프랑스 함대의 강화부 침입과 회격(回擊) 내용 통보	高宗	禮部	『夷務始末』6, 권 46. p. 1109.		(1) 조선 자문의 禮部 상주문	『夷務始末』6, 권 46. p. 1109.
173	1866. 12. 15	조불(朝佛) 교전 경과 보고	A. Burlingame	W. H. Seward	FRUS 1867. Part I, China. pp. 425-6.			
174	1866. 12. 16	프랑스 고시문(法國告示)	H. de Bellonet		『夷務始末』6, 권 46. pp. 1109-10.			

번호	발신일/수신일* (음력)	문서제목	발신	수신	문서출처	번역문 출처	관련문서 제목	관련문서 출처
175	1866. 12. 20(同治五年十一月十四日)	프랑스의 장정 체결 등 요구와 관련하여 조선에 철저한 대비를 촉구하도록 상주(上奏)	總署	同治帝	『夷務始末』 6, 권 46. pp. 1111-2.			
176	1866. 12. 20(同治五年十一月十四日)	조불(朝佛) 문제 조회문을 각국 공사관에 발송한 것에 대한 해명	總署	H. de Bellonet	『夷務始末』 6, 권 46. p. 1113.	[英譯(美國)] FRUS, 1867, part 1, China, pp. 419-25; ADPP, Vol. 9, pp. 29-30. [英譯(英國)] TNA, FO 881/1505		
177	1866. 12. 23(慶應二年十一月十七日)	병인양요 이후 서양 열강의 재침략 풍문	長崎奉行(?)	幕府	『全覽』, 「平山圖書頭古賀筑後守渡韓奉命一件」 1, pp. 171-2.			
178	1866. 12. 24(同治五年十一月十八日)	조선국왕의 자문접수 후 상주(上奏)처리했음을 알림	禮部	高宗	『동문』, 洋舶情形. p. 2477.			
179	1866. 12. 24(慶應二年十一月十八日)	병인양요 후 大島友之允의 화의사절 제안	大島友之允	平田主殿, 森川玉城, 相良丹藏, 早田作左衛門, 仁位格之介, 內野廣之允	「御內容綴」(국사편찬위원회 소장 對馬島宗家文書 기록류 4046)		(1) 大島友之允와 長崎奉行의 제1차 대담 (2) 大島友之允와 長崎奉行의 제2차 대담 (3) 大島友之允와 長崎奉行의 제3차 대담	(1) 「朝鮮國之儀ニ付長崎奉行御應答大意」, 『含書并半切內狀』(국사편찬위원회 소장 對馬島 宗家文書 기록류 6415) (2) 「朝鮮國之儀ニ付長崎奉行御應答大意」, 『含書并半切內狀』(국사편찬위원회 소장 對馬島 宗家文書 기록류 6415) (3) 「朝鮮國之儀ニ付長崎奉行御應答大意」, 『含書并半切內狀』(국사편찬위원회 소장 對馬島 宗家文書 기록류 6415)
180	1866. 12. 29(慶應二年十一月二十三日)	병인양요 대응 방안 건의	宗義達	幕府	『覆歷』, 第8冊, pp. 338-9.			
181	1867. 1. 15	Bellonet의 강화도 원정 실패 평가에 대한 반박	G. Roze	P. de Chasseloup-Laubat	Documents, pp. 365-72.			

번호	발신일/수신일* (음력)	문서제목	발신	수신	문서출처	번역문 출처	관련문서 제목	관련문서 출처
182	1867. 1. 18	Roze의 조선원정 결과 평가	P. de Chasseloup-Laubat	G. Roze	Documents, pp. 361-4.			
183	1867. 1. 31	조선원정 결과의 비난에 대한 반박	G. Roze	P. de Chasseloup-Laubat	Roze I, p. 108; Documents, pp. 373-5.			
184	1867. 1. 31	프랑스의 2차 조선 침공 가능성 및 각국 동태 보고	A. Burlingame	W. H. Seward	Burlingame Paper, the Library of Congress			
185	1867. 2. 1*(高宗三年十二月二十七日)	조불(朝佛) 교전 경과 통보	高宗	禮部	『中日韓』 권 2. pp. 39-40. 문서번호 32의 부건 1			
186	1867. 2. 1(慶應二年十二月二十七日)	제너럴 셔먼호 사건과 병인양요 직전의 조선 상황 탐문 보고	吉川主計	幕府	『全覽』, 「平山圖書頭古賀筑後守渡韓奉命一件」 1, p. 177.			
187	1867. 2. 27(同治六年正月二十三日)	조불(朝佛) 교전 경과 및 향후 대응 방안 정리	總署	同治帝	『中日韓』 권 2. pp. 48-9. 문서번호 34			
188	1867. 3. 9(同治六年二月四日)/1867. 3. 30*(同治六年二月二十五日)	프랑스조약(法國條約) 제 31관을 초록하여 발송	禮部	高宗	『동문』, 洋舶情形, p. 2478-9.			
189	1867. 3. 12	강화에서 입수한 군기의 발송	G. Roze	P. de Chasseloup-Laubat	Documents, p. 376.			
190	1867. 3. 12(慶應三年二月七日)	조불(朝佛) 분쟁 중재에 관한 제안	德川慶喜,	L. Roches.	『江戸』, 第3卷, pp. 488-9.			
191	1867. 3. 13(慶應三年二月八日)	조불(朝佛) 분쟁 중재에 관한 대화	板倉勝靜,	L. Roches	『江戸』, 第3卷, pp. 490-1.		(1) 막부의 중재제안에 대한 프랑스 공사의 견해	栗本鋤雲, 『遺稿』, 第1冊, pp. 187-8.
192	1867. 3. 16	강화에서 체류가 연장된 것에 대해 변명	G. Roze	P. de Chasseloup-Laubat	Documents, pp. 377-9.			
193	1867. 3. 29	미국의 공동 출병 제안에 대한 프랑스 외무성 훈령	Moustier	W. H. Seward	W. H. Seward Paper, University of Rochester			
194	1867. 3(慶應三年二月)	화의중재사절 正使 平山敬忠의 건의서	平山敬忠	幕府	『全覽』, 「平山圖書頭古賀筑後守渡韓奉命一件」 1, pp. 180-1.		(1) 건의서에 대한 幕府의 회신 (2) 위임장 요청 및 위임장안 (3) 사절 호위 병력 2대대 요청을 철회하는 平山敬忠의 건의서	(1) 『全覽』, 「平山圖書頭古賀筑後守渡韓奉命一件」 1, p. 182. (2) 『全覽』, 「平山圖書頭古賀筑後守渡韓奉命一件」 2, p. 203-4. (3) 『全覽』, 「平山圖書頭古賀筑後守渡韓奉命一件」 3, p. 215.

번호	발신일/수신일* (음력)	문서제목	발신	수신	문서출처	번역문 출처	관련문서 제목	관련문서 출처
195	1867. 4. 5(慶應三年三月一日)	화의중재사절 파견 통보	幕府	宗義達	『全覽』,「平山圖書頭古賀筑後守渡韓奉命一件」 2, p. 187.			
196	1867. 4. 7(高宗四年三月三日)	3월 9일자 禮部 자문에 대한 회신	高宗	禮部	『동문』洋舶情形, p. 2479.			
197	1867. 5. 6	1월 31일자 Burlingame 보고에 대한 회신	W. H. Seward	A. Burlingame	NA II, M77 R38			
198	1867. 5. 10(慶應三年四月七日)	조선 중재사절 파견계획 통보 지시	稲葉正邦	對馬藩京都留守居	『全覽』,「平山圖書頭古賀筑後守渡韓奉命一件」 3, p. 216.			
199	1867. 5. 15	미국의 조선원정 소문에 대해 부정적 견해 표명	G. Roze	P. de Chasseloup-Laubat	Documents, pp. 380-1.			
200	1867. 5. 27/1867. 8. 8*	조선 원정의 결과에 대한 평가 및 청조와의 교섭 훈령 요청	A. de Lallemand	Moustier	Documents, pp. 385-404.			
201	1867. 5. 27	미국의 공동 조선원정 제안에 대한 Roze의 거부 의사	G. Roze	P. de Chasseloup-Laubat	Documents, pp. 382-3.			
202	1867. 6. 15	미국의 공동 조선원정 제안에 대해 부정적 견해 표명	G. Roze	de Genouilly	Documents, p. 384; 한불, pp. 267-8.			
203	1867. 6. 28	Lallemand의 지역 순회 및 미국의 공동 원정 제안 등 보고	G. Roze	A. de Lallemand	Documents, pp. 413-8.			
204	1867. 7. 2/1867. 9. 9*	Bellonet와 總署의 마찰 보고	A. de Lallemand	Moustier	Documents, pp. 405-12.			
205	1867. 7. 20/1867. 9. 30*	일본의 사절 파견에 대해 부정적 견해 표명	A. de Lallemand	Moustier	Documents. pp. 419-25.			
206	1867. 7(慶應三年六月)	조선 중재사절 파견계획 통보	宗義達	任冕鎬	『日外』, 第1巻 第1冊, pp. 75-6, 문서번호 21번, 부속서 3.			
207	1867. 7(高宗四年六月)	일본의 중재사절 파견 계획에 대한 조선측의 거절	安俊卿, 玄德民	寺田市郎兵衛	『全覽』,「平山圖書頭古賀筑後守渡韓奉命一件」 4, p. 232.			
208	1867. 9. 10.	프랑스와 미국의 공동 조선원정에 대한 비개입을 당부하는 전보	Moustier	A. de Lallemand	Henri Cordier, Histoir des Relations de la Chine avec les puissances occidentales 1860~1900, vol. I. p. 273.			
209	1867. 9. 30(慶應三年九月三日)	중재사절 파견 계획에 대한 조선측과의 사전 교섭상황 보고	吉川主計	幕府	『全覽』,「平山圖書頭古賀筑後守渡韓奉命一件」 4, pp. 237-38.			

번호	발신일/수신일* (음력)	문서제목	발신	수신	문서출처	번역문 출처	관련문서 제목	관련문서 출처
210	1867. 10. 25(慶應三年九月二十八日)	조선 중재사절단 출발 시기와 준비 간소화를 통보	板倉勝靜	對馬守家來	『全覽』, 「平山圖書頭古賀筑後守渡韓奉命一件」 4, p. 243			
211	1867. 11(慶應三年十月)	平山敬忠이 작성한 德川慶喜의 친서 초안	平山敬忠		『全覽』, 「平山圖書頭古賀筑後守渡韓奉命一件」 5, pp. 273-5.			
212	1867. 11. 11(慶應三年十月十六日)	중재사절 연기를 포함한 大政奉還 이후의 상황	板倉勝靜, 牧野貞利	幕府	『全覽』, 「平山圖書頭古賀筑後守渡韓奉命一件」 5, pp. 251-3.			
213	1867. 11. 20(慶應三年十月二十五日)	중재사절파견을 조정이 허락하도록 요청하는 건의서	德川慶喜	日本朝廷	『日外』, 第1卷 第1册, pp. 67-8, 문서번호 20번			
214	1867. 11. 20(慶應三年十月二十五日)	중재사절 파견 계획의 경위	大島友之允	三条實美	『全覽』, 「平山圖書頭古賀筑後守渡韓奉命一件」 5, pp. 255-6.			
215	1867. 11. 29(慶應三年十一月四日)	조선 사절단 파견 허가 요청	日本朝廷	幕府	『日外』, 第1卷 第1册, p. 104, 문서번호 30번			
216	1867. 11. 29(慶應三年十一月四日)	조선 사절단 파견 허가	日本朝廷	對馬藩京都留守居	『日外』, 第1卷 第1册, pp. 104-5, 문서번호 31번.		(1) 본문서 對馬藩 도달	『綱要』 Reel No. 慶應−150, p. 44.
217	1868. 1. 6(慶應三年十二月十二日), 1868. 1. 18(慶應三年十二月二十四日)	중재사절 철회 후 뒷처리에 관한 平山敬忠와 大島友之允의 대담	平山敬忠, 大島友之允		「平山圖書頭様御應答大意書」국편 소장 對馬島宗家文書 기록류 6430			
218	1868. 1(高宗五年十二月)	중재사절의 정사(停使)를 요청하는 훈도·별차의 서한	安俊卿, 玄德民	青本晟次郎	『全覽』, 「平山圖書頭古賀筑後守渡韓奉命一件」 5, p. 272.			
219	1873. 2. 1/1873. 4. 2*	1866년 조불(朝佛) 교전 경과에 관한 M. Geofroy와의 대화 보고	F. F. Low	H. Fish	NA II, M92 R25			
관계자료 1.		연행기(燕行記)			『양요록』, pp. 38-44.			
관계자료 2.		조선사신과 청국 관료 필담(筆談)			『어양』, 上副使在北京時筆談, pp. 11-20; 『양요록』, pp. 1-10에도 같은 내용 수록			

동북아역사 자료총서 118

近代韓國外交文書 1

2009년 11월 10일 초판 1쇄 인쇄
2014년 11월 24일 초판 2쇄 발행

편 근대한국외교문서편찬위원회
펴낸이 김학준
펴낸곳 동북아역사재단

등록 제312-2004-050호(2004년 10월 18일)
주소 서울시 서대문구 통일로 81(미근동 267) 임광빌딩
전화 02-2012-6065
팩스 02-2012-6189
e-mail book@nahf. or. kr

ISBN 978-89-6187-445-8 94910
978-89-6187-444-1 세트